DEEPER INTO DIVING

Published by **J.L. Publications**, a Division of
Submariner Publications Pty Ltd ABN 39 059 509 474,
PO Box 387, Ashburton, Victoria 3147, Australia.
Tel/Fax: +61-3-9886 0200.
Email: jlpubs@bigpond.net.au
www.submarinerpublications.com

Design and desktop publishing by John Lippmann.

First Edition published July 1990.
Second Edition published October 2005.
Reprinted May 2007.

National Library of Australia Cataloguing-in-Publication Data.

Lippmann, John.
    Deeper into diving : an in-depth review of decompression
    procedures and of the physical and physiological aspects of
    deeper diving.

    2nd ed.
    Bibliography.
    Includes index.
    ISBN 0 9752290 1 X.

    1. Deep diving - Physiological aspects. 2. Decompression
    (Physiology). I. Mitchell, Simon, 1958- . II. Title.

    612.014415

Cover photograph: Chandelier Cave, Palau © David Doubilet, 2005.

DEEPER INTO DIVING

An in-depth review of decompression procedures, and of the physical and physiological aspects of deeper diving.

by

John Lippmann
and
Dr. Simon Mitchell

Second Edition

J.L. Publications   Melbourne

Foreword

John Lippmann and Dr. Simon Mitchell, both experts in diving, have revised and updated Lippmann's excellent earlier edition, and made it even better. *Deeper into Diving* provides comprehensive discussions of both technical/procedural and physiological/medical issues of diving.

Lippmann and Mitchell are both skilled writers, and in this book they have made many complicated subjects easily understood.

The book is comprehensive enough to appeal not only to advanced recreational divers and instructors, but also to those who want to learn about decompression tables and technical diving.

Specific chapters on nitrox diving, technical diving, decompression table development, dive computers, flying after diving and rebreathers are particularly topical.

As a complement to more specialized diving medical texts, *Deeper into Diving* will be very useful to both medics and physicians who take care of divers or perform diving fitness evaluations. Its state-of-the-art overview of specific diving-related medical issues is perfectly matched with divers' and medical providers' common concerns regarding decompression illness, women's health, pregnancy, bone necrosis, hypothermia and the interaction of drugs with the diving environment.

For the reader who wants more information, pertinent additional sources are listed. For anyone looking for a delightfully written overview of diving, this book is a must.

Richard E. Moon,
MD, FRCPC, FACP, FCCP
Professor of Anesthesiology
Associate Professor of Medicine
Medical Director, Center for Hyperbaric
Medicine & Environmental Physiology
Duke University Medical Center
Senior Medical Consultant,
Divers Alert Network
Durham, North Carolina, USA.

About the Authors

John Lippmann OAM began diving some 35 years ago and developed an avid interest in deeper diving. He has been involved in researching, teaching, writing and consulting on safe diving, decompression and accident management for the past 30 years. He has specialised in certain areas including resuscitation, first aid, oxygen administration, dive rescue and various aspects of decompression and deeper diving.

John has authored, or co-authored, many books which have been published and distributed worldwide. These include *The DAN Emergency Handbook*, *Deeper Into Diving (First Edn)*, *The Essentials of Deeper Sport Diving*, *Scuba Safety in Australia*, *Oxygen First Aid*, *First Aid & Emergency Care*, *Automated External Defibrillators*, *Advanced Oxygen First Aid*, *Basic Life Support*, *Cardiopulmonary Resuscitation*, the *Ambulance Service Victoria First Aid Training Manual*, and others. John's articles and papers on dive safety, decompression and accident management have been published in medical, technical and recreational diving journals throughout the world.

John is currently the Executive Director and Director of Training of the Divers Alert Network Asia-Pacific (DAN AP), which he founded in 1994 in an effort to improve the safety of scuba diving within the Asia-Pacific.

Dr Simon Mitchell (BHB, MB ChB, DipDHM, DipOccMed, PhD) began diving in his teenage years and what became a recreational passion subsequently drove his academic and professional career.

Simon now looks back on a 33 year diving history that has spanned sport, scientific, commercial, and military diving and more than 6000 dives.

Simon trained in medicine, completed a PhD in embolic brain injury, and received certification in diving and hyperbaric medicine from the Australian and New Zealand College of Anaesthetists.

He has published more than 30 research and review papers in the medical literature, and wrote two chapters for the latest edition of Bennett and Elliott's Physiology and Medicine of Diving.

He is an active technical diver, and in 2002 with Trevor Jackson completed a 178m dive to the wreck of the "Kyogle" off Brisbane. This was the world's deepest wreck dive. Simon is a dual New Zealand and Australian citizen and currently lives in Auckland with his wife Sian.

DISCLAIMER

The contents of this book represent the authors' view of current learning on this subject at the time of writing. However, the reader is warned that hyperbaric medicine and decompression theory are relatively new and dynamic fields. As our understanding and knowledge increases, certain currently held beliefs (some of which are subject to some conjecture) may be disproved or modified. The reader is strongly advised to read new literature as it is released and, if necessary, to reassess appropriate areas of the text of this work accordingly.

Neither the author nor publisher accept responsibility for the accuracy of any examples or interpretations of the workings of the decompression systems included in this work, nor for the accuracy of the comparative tables. Whilst all care and skill have been taken in the preparation of these technical aspects, the reader should be aware of these limitations.

Acknowledgements

We wish to acknowledge the contributions of the following people for their input into the original and / or this edition of **Deeper Into Diving**.

Dr. Cheryl Bass
Dr. Bruce Bassett *(dec.)*
Prof. Peter Bennett
Prof. Albert Bühlmann *(dec.)*
Trevor Davies
Dr. Carl Edmonds
Dr. Andrew Fock
Prof. Des Gorman
Dr. Max Hahn *(dec.)*
Dr. Tom Hennessey
Prof. Brian Hills
Karl Huggins
Dr. John Knight
Dr. George Lewbell
Prof. Richard Moon
Dr. Peter Mosse
Ron Nishi
Dr. John Parker
Dr. Drew Richardson
Dr. Peter Rogers
Dr. Peter Sullivan
Dr. Richard Vann
Capt. Paul Weathersby
Dr. Mark Wellard
Dr. Bruce Wienke
Dr. Peter Wilmshurst
Gain Wong

John would particularly like to thank his family, Angela, Michael and Adam for putting up with him when he again took on this project. Thanks also to Dr. Mark Wellard for his proof-reading and help with the graphs, and to Dr. John Knight for originally nuturing his interest in diving medicine.

Simon thanks his partner Sian for her unwavering support, his mentor Des Gorman for his teaching, and his inspirational mates Trevor Jackson and Bill Day for the best diving adventures you could ever have.

Many thanks also to the following magnificent photographers whose work is displayed throughout this book. The photographers retain the copyright for their photographs.

Barry Andrewartha
Michael Aw
Gary Bell
David Bryant
Keith Chesnut
David Doubilet
Mark Fyvie
Max Gleeson
Dr. Richard Harris
Euiook (Travis) Jung
Dr. Simon Mitchell
Maj. Marc Moody
Mary-Anne Stacey
Dr. David Taylor
Ingrid Visser
Dr. Jurg Wendling

This book is dedicated to the memory of Professor Albert A Bühlmann.

DEEPER INTO DIVING

Contents

SECTION 3:   Altitude considerations and diving

SECTION 4:   Technical & occupational diving

APPENDICES:

INDEX

Preface

In 1838, William Newton first filed a patent for a diaphragm-actuated, twin-hose demand valve for divers. The first self-contained underwater breathing apparatus (SCUBA) appears to have been developed and patented in 1918 by Ohgushi, from Japan. This system could either be operated with a surface supply of air or as a self-contained system with an air supply carried on the diver's back. The diver used his teeth to trigger air flow into his mask. In 1943, Cousteau and Gagnon developed the first SCUBA system incorporating a demand valve to release air as the diver inhaled.

Drawing from Newton's patent specifications.

These early milestones marked the beginnings of what has developed into an enormous industry - the recreational diving industry. Many millions of people throughout the world have now enjoyed the rich wonders of the underwater world with the aid of scuba.

The type of diving undertaken by recreational divers has changed dramatically over the years. The early divers mainly did relatively shallow, shore-based dives and used standard decompression tables to guide their decompression. However, the improvement of diving equipment, the increasing availability of dive computers, the ready access to a multitude of dive charter boats and liveaboards, and the discovery and lure of new wrecks and reefs in deeper water has encouraged many divers to venture deeper into the sea. In addition, the emergence and growing popularity of technical diving using heliox and trimix, and the increasing availability of rebreathers has extended the depth envelope considerably. At the time of writing, the deepest recorded open circuit dive is an astounding 330m. No doubt this limit will be extended in the future.

Although deeper dives may at times offer a certain challenge and excitement, the greater depth introduces new problems which make such dives potentially far more hazardous than dives conducted in shallower water. A diver, especially one who tends to dive in deeper water, must be aware of, and must have a clear understanding and appreciation of, the potential problems associated with depth, so that they can minimize the risks associated with this type of diving.

When I wrote the first edition of **Deeper into Diving** which was published in 1990, it was a time when technical diving was in its infancy. At that time, the book was aimed predominantly at dive educators, to provide them with further insight into diving physiology, decompression and some aspects of dive accident management - something that I felt that they lacked and, unfortunately, I still feel that this is so.

Since that time, there have been significant advances in knowledge and equipment and this new edition addresses these developments, while maintaining the historical perspective. With this edition, I have enlisted the assistance of Dr. Simon Mitchell, who has brought with him a wealth of knowledge of diving medicine and technical diving. We believe that this text should be suitable not only for recreational and commercial dive professionals, but also for technical divers and diving medical professionals.

The plethora of information available to divers on the internet is unfortunately poorly scrutinized, and much of the information is personal opinion and seldom referenced. While this book is not designed to be a fully referenced text, it has been carefully researched and at the end of most chapters we have included some of our sources so that readers can check these and further their knowledge if desired. We have also listed, separately, references which we believe are particularly suitable.

Deeper Into Diving is written at a level which should be understood by the recreational diving professional, and should help them to understand some of the more technical texts and reports that are available. It should be an invaluable aid to diving instructors and technical divers as it provides a lot of the background information and technical data that is not always easily obtainable.

Deeper Into Diving is designed to be a thorough and accurate reference, and we have enlisted the assistance of some of the world's authorities on decompression and diving medicine in an attempt to ensure its accuracy at the time of writing. However, the reader must realize that decompression theory and diving medicine are both dynamic areas, and some of the current theories and procedures may change with time. It is important to keep abreast of new developments and to modify our practices accordingly.

Simon and I sincerely hope that you will find this book to be a valuable addition to your diving library.

Safe, enjoyable diving,

The earliest oxygen rebreather, designed by Henry Fleuss.

Note about units used:

The units of measurement used in this book are primarily metric, with imperial equivalents usually provided. However, in chapters dealing with tables in which imperial units predominate, the primary units used are imperial, often with metric equivalents provided. The equivalent measures given are often not exact conversions, but are those commonly used (e.g. 30m (100ft)). Those expressed in the form 40m / 130ft are similar 'benchmarks' used in the various systems and, again, not direct conversions.

SECTION 1

Physical, Sensory, Physiological and Psychological Considerations

© Dr. Richard Harris

1

Physical, sensory, physiological and psychological changes due to immersion

Wrapped up in a wetsuit, wearing gloves and floating neutrally buoyant, the diver is not exposed to the multitude of stimuli received on the surface. Gravity is hardly felt. Sounds can be heard but cannot be localized. Touch is blunted by gloves. The diver's sensory window on the world is his eyes, and they are peering into the murk through a facemask which reduces the field of view to a few degrees. No wonder that divers in nil visibility become disorientated! Add to this the effects of cold, interfering with the sense of touch, muscular movement, and nerve transmission, and the effects of nitrogen narcosis interfering with logical thought. The deep diver is exposed to a hostile environment and at the same time is heavily handicapped.

The human has evolved as an animal adapted to living in an air environment and eating, drinking, walking, talking and reproducing on land. Our physiology and responses are geared to a warm air environment at an ambient pressure of one atmosphere.

When we choose to enter the sea, we must suddenly adapt to a foreign environment. Masks help us to see in this new environment, fins help to push us along, scuba allows us to breathe, wetsuits help maintain warmth, but the functioning of most of our senses is altered and/or reduced. We suffer from **a relative sensory deprivation.** To add to this, the effects of the increasing pressure cause disadvantageous physiological changes within our bodies, and the unfamiliar and sometimes threatening nature of the environment may induce adverse psychological changes.

Safe diving requires that we adapt to the physical, sensory, physiological and psychological changes imposed. Complete adaptation is restricted to fishes and beyond humans, and as divers we must learn to cope with our inadequacies. Most of the problems and changes are inherent to all dives but some problems are magnified, and some new problems arise, as the depth of diving increases. Unless adequately managed, these may become potentially hazardous.

This chapter introduces some of the physical changes that we must accommodate when we decide to gear up and slip into the "silent world". The physiological changes will be dealt with in depth in the following chapters.

Vision

To most of us vision is the most important sense both on land and underwater. Diving masks generally cut out the peripheral vision on which we are normally quite reliant and which is one of the most sensitive areas of our vision. Some masks also have blind spots in the plane of vision. For example, masks with two lenses introduce a central blind spot, while those with extra side lenses do increase peripheral vision but also introduce extra blind spots and, at times, double images. Therefore, our **field of vision is normally greatly reduced when we dive**. We cannot often see as far underwater as we can on land due to particles in the water, so the **depth of vision is usually greatly reduced** while diving.

The greater refraction (bending) of light in water **alters the size and perspective of what we see**. Objects appear to be closer (by about 25%) and thus larger (by about 30%) than they really are. This magnification or displacement effect can actually be an advantage to some short-sighted divers. The effect is shown in Figure 1.

FIGURE 1

Magnification underwater.

Light of longer wavelengths (the warmer colors) penetrate water less efficiently than the shorter wavelength colours such as blue. At deeper depths most of the red, orange and yellow light is absorbed. Since the colour of an object is determined by the wavelength of the light it reflects, and since only the blue wavelengths penetrate water

efficiently, the **colour of objects seen at depth is usually blue, which is often not the true colour of the objects.** A red object will still appear blue because there is no red light to reflect. To see the true colours of objects underwater the diver must provide white light (which contains all wavelengths) from a torch. Viewing the true colours of marine life is one of the great advantages of carrying a torch underwater.

Sound

Sound is greatly affected when transmitted through the water. **Sound originating from above the surface is greatly reduced** when transmitted into the water, as many sound waves are reflected at the surface. When we are underwater our **hearing is reduced** to some degree by the effect of water on the eardrum, and some frequencies are affected more than others, causing the **sound to be distorted.** The wearing of a hood further decreases the hearing. Sound travels much faster in water than in air (about four times normal speed). Since we localize the direction of a sound source by subconsciously processing the delay between its arrival at both ears, this makes it far more **difficult to detect the direction of the source of the sound**.

Smell and Taste

Smell and taste are usually important senses to us when we are land bound but they usually are not utilized underwater unless there is a detectable impurity in the breathing air.

Touch

Touch is an important sense both on land and underwater. Cooling of the skin reduces the sensitivity to touch, and sensitivity is further reduced when we wear gloves. Cooling and gloves also reduce our manual dexterity and can make normally simple tasks, such as readjusting a mask or fin strap, quite difficult.

Balance and sense of orientation

Balance and a perception of our orientation are essential senses on land. They enable us to walk, co-ordinate other movements and orientate our body correctly. Balance and orientation are partly achieved by vision, but even with our eyes closed a combination of other sensory mechanisms allows us to maintain balance and co-ordinate movements. Position-sensing nerves ("proprioceptors") in the muscles and joints tell us exactly what our body is doing. The vestibular apparatus (semi-circular canals) in our inner ears provide information about our orientation and movement. Skin pressure receptors, as their name implies, detect pressure on the skin. They detect the pressure on the soles of our feet when we stand, and pressure on our backsides when we are sitting. In other words these receptors let us know which way gravity is acting.

Many of these "systems" are affected in some way in the underwater environment. Vision may lose its effectiveness as a source of information about orientation if visibility is poor, or if there are no visual cues within the field of view. A classic example of the latter is when the diver is completely surrounded by blue water; an experience frequently described as "disorienting", and sometimes referred to as the "blue orb syndrome". It can be overcome by focusing on familiar objects or people; such as focusing on your gauges or on your buddy. The function of the vestibular organs in the ears can be disturbed if cold water suddenly enters one ear and not the other (such as can happen with a tight hood). The temperature imbalance causes an unequal stimulation of the vestibular organs that the brain misinterprets as movement. This can produce a very disturbing phenomenon known as vertigo. The diver feels as though they are "spinning" whereas they are not actually moving at all. This can also occur transiently during ascent if the pressure bleeds out of one middle ear faster than the other, a phenomenon referred to as "alternobaric vertigo".

When we are underwater, we are buoyed up by a force equal to the weight of water we displace. This means that when immersed we are essentially "weightless" and our perception of the effects of gravity are significantly diminished. This contributes to difficulty determining which way is down and, more importantly, which way is up. The result of the combination of these factors is that **underwater there is diminished sense of the vertical or of balance**. Without visual cues it is difficult tell if we are lying horizontally or vertically, or whether we are facing the surface or the seabed. Divers who operate in zero visibility can very easily become disorientated.

Weightlessness

A neutrally buoyant diver is essentially weightless. Weightlessness is one of the delights of diving in that it gives us the ability to move freely in three dimensions. However, **it can make normally simple tasks a little more difficult**. If we push on an object underwater we get forced back in the opposite direction, unless we are sufficiently anchored. This must be compensated for if certain tasks are to be done. Professional divers often overweight themselves in order to gain sufficient anchorage. For safety these divers are attached to a rope from the surface ("lifeline"). Free-swimming divers should never be over-weighted and must compensate for the weightlessness in other ways.

Heat Loss

Water conducts heat about twenty-five times faster than does air, so, unless we are adequately insulated, **we lose heat rapidly when underwater.** As we dive deeper the water gets cooler, our wetsuit compresses, the air we breathe becomes denser and these all combine to cause us to lose body heat more rapidly. Hypothermia becomes a greater potential threat as we begin to dive deeper. The **cold slows down our thinking and our reflexes, it makes manual tasks more difficult and depletes our energy**.

Effects on Ventilation

Being immersed means that we must **work harder to breathe**. Immersion forces extra blood into lung blood vessels, making the lungs stiffer and making breathing more of an effort. Breathing from a regulator increases this effort due to the breathing resistance within the regulator. Wearing a tight wetsuit and bulky equipment which envelope our chest further increases the effort of breathing. As we go deeper the air becomes denser and breathing requires more and more effort.

The net effect of these factors is that the maximum volume of air that we can move in and out of our lungs each minute ("maximum voluntary ventilation") is reduced, and it becomes progressively less as we go deeper. Indeed, at 30m (100ft) it is about one half that at the surface. This is important since the elimination of carbon dioxide from the body is entirely dependent on ventilation.

Even using the best high performance regulators, it is certainly possible for our ability to ventilate the lungs to lag behind that required to keep carbon dioxide levels stable, especially if we try to work (swim) hard at depth. Underwater work, combined with the increased work of breathing during diving causes greater carbon dioxide production and this, combined with a reduced maximum voluntary ventilation may lead to an **increase in carbon dioxide levels** in our blood ("hypercapnia"). The body's automatic response to hypercapnia is to increase the breathing rate further increasing the effort of breathing, and producing an uncomfortable feeling of being short of breath. Hypercapnia may potentiate other diving ailments and in extreme cases may of itself, cause us to become unconscious. The key to avoiding these problems is to avoid overexertion underwater.

Psychological Effects

Little is known about the psychological effects of diving, but there is evidence to suggest that psychological factors often contribute to diving accidents. Unless we are confident in our own diving ability and also confident in our equipment, when under stress our anxiety can turn to **panic**. Panic can, and does, cause serious incidents. Our training is designed to teach us strict procedures to adopt in the event of an emergency, so that we may avoid the tendency to panic.

Physiological abnormalities such as **nitrogen narcosis**, **hypoxia** and **carbon dioxide toxicity** can cause variable psychological reactions, depending on the personality of the diver, the environment and the severity of the physiological effect. **Nitrogen narcosis distorts our thinking, narrows our attention and may allow us to do stupid things.**

It becomes obvious that we must do a lot of adapting, whether we realize it or not, in order to safely progress deeper into the underwater world. Many of the potential problems mentioned here will be discussed more fully in the following chapters.

SUMMARY

- The human has evolved as a land animal and is not naturally equipped to cope with the underwater environment.

- The underwater environment introduces many potential problems to which a diver must adapt.

- Various physical, sensory, physiological and psychological changes occur when we dive.

Some of these changes are:
- reduced vision
- loss of colour
- sound distortion
- reduced input from smell and taste
- reduced sense of touch
- loss of balance and orientation cues
- weightlessness
- temperature loss
- impaired ventilation
- anxiety
- nitrogen narcosis
- high carbon dioxide levels

© Euiook (Travis) Jung

© Euiook Jung

2

Physiology

2.1 Respiration and Circulation

The functions of the respiratory and circulatory systems are intimately related; so much so that it is appropriate to consider them together. The respiratory system provides a mechanism to bring blood and air close together (without actually allowing physical mixing) so that gas exchange can occur. Gas exchange is the uptake of oxygen from the lungs and removal of carbon dioxide from the blood. The circulatory system then circulates the blood to all the tissues of the body where another round of gas exchange occurs: this time oxygen passes from the blood to the tissues and carbon dioxide from the tissues to the blood.

THE RESPIRATORY SYSTEM

The respiratory tract can be divided into two portions, the "conducting" and the "respiratory" portions. The "conducting portion" connects the external environment with the gas exchange area of the lung. It consists of the nose, nasal passages, pharynx, larynx, trachea, bronchi and bronchioles. It is responsible for warming or cooling of inspired air, humidifying inspired air and filtering particles from it. Speech is also made possible by the flow of air over the vocal cords which form part of the conducting portion. The "Respiratory portion" is the area where actual gas exchange occurs - the alveolar sacs. Other important components include the ribs,

intercostal muscles, and diaphragm which provide the mechanical drive to ventilate the lungs. These components are collectively illustrated in Figure 2.1.1.

The two lungs are roughly cone-shaped and are situated in the thorax. The thorax consists of the ribs, sternum and thoracic vertebrae and is separated from the abdomen by the diaphragm, a dome-shaped muscle attached to the vertebrae and lower ribs. All the ribs are attached to the vertebral column at the back, however, only the first seven ribs on each side are attached directly to the sternum ("breast bone") at the front. The next three are attached to the ribs just above, while the front ends of the last two ribs are free. Between the ribs lie the intercostal muscles, which help in the action of breathing. The diaphragm is composed of muscle and strong fibrous tissue.

The lungs themselves are composed of elastic tissue and each is surrounded by two very thin membranes, the so-called "pleural lining". One membrane is attached to the lung itself and the other to the chest wall. The space enclosed between the pleura is called the pleural cavity, although it is not really a "cavity" as such under normal circumstances. This "cavity" contains an extremely thin layer of fluid that acts as a lubricant to allow free movement of the lungs during breathing. It is notable that the lungs are not physically attached to the chest wall or diaphragm in any way. It is only the

FIGURE 2.1.1

The respiratory system

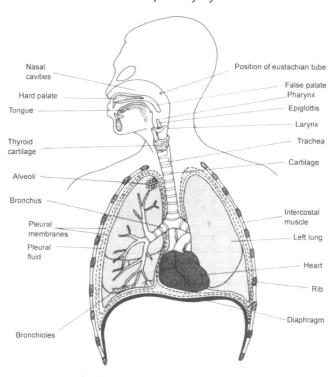

adhesion between the two pleural membranes, facilitated by the thin layer of fluid that keeps the lungs from collapsing down to a much smaller size. This is best conceptualized by thinking of two sheets of glass stuck against each other with a microfilm layer of fluid in between. The two sheets of glass (one representing the chest wall or diaphragm and the other representing the lung) can slide over each other, but they cannot be pulled apart. Of course, should air get between the two sheets of glass, they would come apart quite easily, and this is the situation that can arise in a so-called "pneumothorax": air gets introduced into the pleural cavity and the lung, being an elastic structure that is stretched in its normal inflated state, can collapse down.

Air is drawn into the mouth and nose and then passes into the pharynx, which is a short common pathway for air and food. The pharynx divides into two tubes - the trachea (windpipe) and the oesophagus. The oesophagus lies behind the trachea and takes food and fluids into the stomach. Air travels through the larynx ("voice box") and on into the trachea. Food is normally prevented from entering the larynx by the epiglottis, a flexible flap at the back of the tongue, which folds over the larynx during swallowing. The trachea is reinforced by a series of semi-circular cartilaginous rings and a layer of muscle. It passes down into the chest and divides into two tubes, the right and left bronchi which enter the right and left lungs respectively. Inside the lungs the bronchi progressively divide into smaller and smaller tubes, rather like the branches of a tree. The larger of the tubes, like the trachea, are supported by cartilage. The trachea and bronchi are lined by cells with tiny hairs (cilia) on their surface. These cilia, along with mucus secreted by glands, act to trap foreign particles and move them up into the pharynx where they are subsequently swallowed. It is these that are damaged in chronic smokers who need to resort to the "smoker's cough" to bring up the mucus and trapped particles. The smallest branches of the respiratory tree are called the bronchioles and it is from these that the alveoli or air sacs arise. Unlike the larger airways, the brochioles are not supported by cartilage and may collapse (eg. as occurs with asthma).

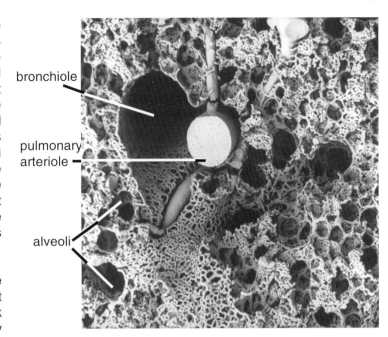

FIGURE 2.1.2 *Cast of a lung.*

The alveoli have extremely thin walls that are only one cell thick and are surrounded by many capillaries. Figure 2.1.2 shows a cast of the blood vessels making up the lungs magnified many hundreds of times under a scanning electron microscope. Note the small pocket-like structures (the alveoli) surrounded by a basket-like mesh of capillaries.

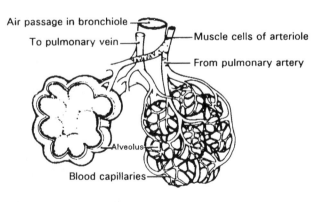

FIGURE 2.1.3

An alveolus surrounded by capillaries.
Reprinted with permission of P. Gadd and Macmillan Publishers Ltd.

The alveoli can be likened to tiny balloons with a basket of fine blood vessels wrapped around (Figure 2.1.3). The inner surfaces of the alveoli are coated with a soapy substance known as surfactant. Surfactant acts to decrease the surface tension of the thin fluid layer that lines the inside of the alveoli, thereby reducing their tendency to collapse. If this surfactant is washed off, as for example may occur during drowning, the alveoli may collapse. The walls of the alveoli and the capillaries are so thin that the distance separating the gas in the alveoli from the blood in the capillary is only 1μm (very roughly 1/20 of the thickness of this page). Molecules of gas can freely diffuse across this so-called alveolar-capillary membrane. If the alveolar-capillary membrane is torn and air enters the blood, an arterial gas (air) embolism may result (see Chapter 5).

There are approximately 300 million alveoli (in both lungs). If all the alveoli were opened out and laid flat they would cover an area of about 100m^2 (1090ft^2), which is roughly the area of a tennis court.

Mechanism of breathing

Inspiration and expiration are brought about by the up and down movement of the diaphragm and the elevation and depression of the ribs by the intercostal muscles. Upward movement of the chest wall and downward movement of the diaphragm causes the pressure in the thorax to fall, creating a pressure gradient between lungs and mouth, and so air begins to flow through the nose and/or mouth into the lungs. During expansion of the lungs, the pulmonary capillaries adjacent to the alveoli are "pulled open", resulting in an increase in blood flow during inspiration and producing ideal conditions for the transfer of gases between the alveoli and the blood in the capillaries. Expiration occurs when the diaphragm and intercostal muscles relax. The elastic recoil of the lung causes an increase in chest cavity pressure, and air flows outwards.

Thus, normal ventilation is achieved by *active* movement of the diaphragm and the intercostal muscles (for inhalation), followed by *passive* recoil of the lung, chest wall and diaphragm (for exhalation). In fact at rest, breathing is brought about solely by the action of the diaphragm. During exercise, the intercostal muscles also become involved, actively expanding the thorax during inhalation and squeezing the chest to force the air out of the lungs during exhalation.

Figure 2.1.4 shows the physiological volumes and capacities which make up the total lung volume.

The Tidal Volume (TV), approximately 500ml, is the volume breathed in each breath.

The Inspiratory Reserve Volume, (IRV), approximately 3000ml, is the volume which can still be inspired after a normal tidal volume inspiration.

The Expiratory Reserve Volume (ERV), approximately 1100ml, is the volume which can still be exhaled after a normal tidal volume expiration.

The Residual Volume (RV), approximately 1200ml, is the volume which remains in the lungs after a forced exhalation.

The Vital Capacity (VC) is the sum of the IRV, the TV and the ERV.

The Total Lung Capacity (TLC) is the sum of the VC and the RV.

At rest the tidal volume is around 500ml. The tidal volume increases with exercise intensity. Thus since the vital capacity is constant for an individual, a greater proportion of the IRV and ERV are used during exercise.

The Respiratory Minute Volume (RMV) is the amount of air moved into the respiratory system each minute. It is the product of the tidal volume and respiratory rate and is approximately 6 litres/minute at rest (i.e. 500ml/breath x 12 breaths/minute).

A related physiological volume of importance to divers is the FEV_1 (The Forced Expiratory Volume in the first second). This is the proportion of the vital capacity which can be exhaled forcefully in the first second. For divers it should normally be in excess of 75%. Values below this may indicate significant trapping of air in the lungs, which may predispose a diver to pulmonary barotrauma.

The volume of air not involved in gas exchange is known as "dead space". It is important to realize that most of the air in the respiratory tract is not available for exchange. Thus the air that fills the respiratory passages (approx. 150ml) makes up what is known as the "anatomical dead space".

FIGURE 2.1.4 *Respiratory volumes and capacities*

(Figures for a young adult male)

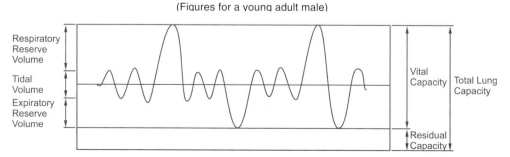

Gas Exchange

Oxygen is a colourless, odourless and tasteless gas that constitutes about 21% of the air we breathe. We need oxygen to effectively metabolize food and provide energy for cell function. The body consumes oxygen and produces heat and other forms of energy, as well as carbon dioxide.

The blood carries oxygen in two forms: dissolved in plasma (the liquid component of blood) and chemically combined with haemoglobin (which is found in the red blood cells). Oxygen is not very soluble in plasma at normal temperatures and pressures, so very little is normally dissolved in plasma. The vast majority of oxygen is chemically combined with haemoglobin. Quantitatively speaking, the average male carries approximately 200ml of oxygen per litre of blood bound to haemoglobin, whereas there is only about 3ml per litre dissolved in plasma.

When breathing air at normal atmospheric pressures the haemoglobin is approximately 98% saturated with oxygen. In other words, it is carrying about 98% of the total oxygen that it is possible for it to carry. As the oxygen-rich blood reaches the tissues, the haemoglobin releases some oxygen but still remains about 75% saturated in the venous blood. The oxygen is released from the haemoglobin because the partial pressure of oxygen in the tissues is lower than in the blood. The greater acidity of the blood in the tissues also promotes unloading of the oxygen from the haemoglobin.

Carbon dioxide is a waste product of our metabolism. It combines with water in the body to form carbonic acid, a weak acid which breaks down readily to form bicarbonate. Carbon dioxide is carried in our blood in three ways. A small amount (7%) is dissolved in the plasma, another small amount (23%) is bound to haemoglobin or plasma proteins, but most of the carbon dioxide (70%) in our blood is carried as bicarbonate. As the carbon dioxide diffuses from the tissues into the blood, the acidity of the blood increases by a very small amount.

Composition Of Alveolar Gas

Alveolar gas differs quite markedly from atmospheric air (Table 2.1.1) because:

(i)   Alveolar gas is only partially replaced by atmospheric air each breath, and

(ii) Air is humidified as it travels to the lungs, thereby changing the composition of the gas by adding water vapour.

TABLE 2.1.1

Pressure (mmHg) of gases in air, alveolar gas, and expired gas.

	Air	**Alveolar gas**	**Expired gas**
Nitrogen	597	569	566
Oxygen	159	104	120
Carbon dioxide	0.3	40	27
Water vapour	3.7	47	47

In the expired gas, the partial pressure of oxygen is increased and the partial pressure of carbon dioxide is decreased (compared to the alveolar gas) due to mixing with air in the conducting passages of the respiratory tree. After an inspiration this air (about 150ml in an adult) has not participated in any gas exchange, and apart from the addition of water vapour, differs little from atmospheric air. Note that the partial pressure of oxygen in expired gas is actually quite high. This is why expired air resuscitation is effective.

At all times the partial pressure of oxygen in the alveoli is higher than that of the venous blood entering the lung capillaries, while the partial pressure of carbon dioxide in the

FIGURE 2.1.5

The exchange of gases across the alveolar-capillary membrane.

Note: the shaded area in the pulmonary blood vessels represents oxygenated blood whereas the unshaded area represents deoxygenated blood.

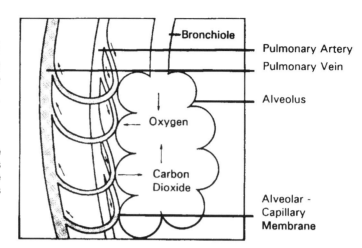

venous blood is higher than in the alveolar air. Thus, there is a gradient for the diffusion of oxygen from the alveoli into the blood and carbon dioxide out of the blood into the alveoli. *Diffusion is the movement of substances (including gases) from areas of high concentration to areas of lower concentration.* It is notable that this process of diffusion is so efficient, that in the fraction of a second it takes for blood to pass through the alveolar capillary, the oxygen and carbon dioxide pressures equilibrate between alveoli and blood. Similarly, in the tissues, after the oxygen unloads from the haemoglobin it diffuses along a concentration gradient into the tissues with carbon dioxide moving in the reverse direction.

Control of Respiration

The partial pressure of carbon dioxide in the arterial blood (normally about 40mmHg) and the acidity (pH) of this blood are the fundamental factors regulating breathing.

The respiratory centre, located in the medulla (in the brain stem), contains groups of nerve cells, called chemoreceptors, sensitive to the subtle changes in tissue fluid acidity which occurs as blood carbon dioxide levels rise. In addition, acidity levels, and to some degree, falling oxygen levels, may stimulate chemoreceptors in the major arteries.

When blood carbon dioxide levels rise even subtly, the acidity in the tissue fluids of the medulla increases and nerve impulses pass to the diaphragm and other respiratory muscles, making them contract, causing inspiration and the subsequent removal of carbon dioxide with expiration. The depth and frequency of breathing is adjusted so that carbon dioxide is discharged in the expired gas at the same rate as it is produced in the tissues (about 200ml/min at rest). This ensures that the carbon dioxide and acidity levels of the blood remain normal.

The rate of breathing set by the regulatory action of carbon dioxide ensures that ventilation is more than adequate to supply the oxygen needed by the body. The resting body needs around 250ml of oxygen per minute. Exercise can increase this to as much as 3000ml a minute. During exercise, production of carbon dioxide increases and the body responds as described above. The resultant increase in the rate and depth of respiration maintains constant carbon dioxide and oxygen levels. This fundamental reliance on CO_2 levels to stimulate breathing has important implications for breath-hold divers (see Chapter 7).

Lack of oxygen does not normally provide a primary stimulus to breathe unless the arterial oxygen levels fall significantly. There are chemoreceptors sensitive to low arterial oxygen in the walls of the aorta and the carotid arteries. These stimulate the breathing if oxygen levels fall significantly. .

An increase of only 0.3% in the carbon dioxide content of the blood will normally result in the doubling of the volume of air breathed in and out. In normal breathing, 85% of the stimulus is due to rising carbon dioxide and only 15% is due to falling oxygen levels.

Finally, stretch receptors located in the pleura transmit impulses to the respiratory centre. During inspiration these are stretched and send messages to the brain, leading to an inhibition of particular nerve cells which control inspiration (inspiratory neurons), and an activation of other nerve cells which cause expiration (expiratory neurons). The reverse occurs during expiration. These act to limit overinspiration but add additional impetus to swap from inspiration to expiration and vice versa.

BLOOD

Blood can be considered to be the middleman in the functioning of the respiratory and circulatory systems. The body contains 4 to 6 litres of blood, the actual amount depending on the body size and sex, with females having lower blood volume than males. Figure 2.1.6 shows the composition of blood and a brief description of what the constituents are.

Blood cells are formed in the bone marrow. Red blood cells, called erythrocytes, live for approximately 120 days and are then removed by the spleen. White blood cells, called leukocytes, live from six hours, to two weeks, to a year, depending on the type of cell. Red blood cell formation is controlled by a hormone erythropoietin which is produced by the kidneys. In the medium term (days to weeks) reduced oxygen levels stimulate the release of erythropoietin, thus producing more red blood cells.

FIGURE 2.1.6
Composition of blood.

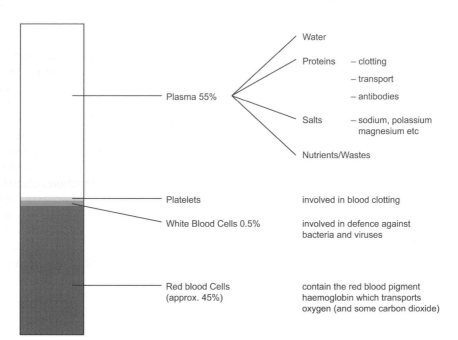

Plasma 55%

Water
Proteins — clotting
— transport
— antibodies
Salts — sodium, polassium magnesium etc
Nutrients/Wastes

Platelets — involved in blood clotting

White Blood Cells 0.5% — involved in defence against bacteria and viruses

Red blood Cells (approx. 45%) — contain the red blood pigment haemoglobin which transports oxygen (and some carbon dioxide)

THE CIRCULATORY SYSTEM

The circulatory system consists of the heart and blood vessels.

The Heart

The heart is situated in the mediastinum (the central part of the thoracic cavity), surrounded by a thin connective tissue sac, the pericardium that, in a manner similar to the pleural membranes of the lungs, allows the heart to beat independently and without friction. The heart is positioned obliquely in the chest, one third to the right and two thirds to the left of the sternum.

The heart is a strong muscular pump which, in the average adult, beats about 70 times per minute. Every minute about six litres of blood is pumped around the body. When we exercise this output may be vastly increased, depending on how hard we work. The heart actually consists of two separate pumps, one on the left side and one on the right side. The left heart receives oxygenated blood from the lungs and pumps it to the various tissues of the body (the "systemic circulation") while the right heart receives this blood when it returns from the body, and pumps it to the lungs to be oxygenated again (the "pulmonary circulation"). The general layout of the circulatory system is shown in Figure 2.1.7). Each side of the heart has two chambers

which pump blood through non-return valves by muscular contraction. The upper chamber, or atrium, receives the incoming blood and acts as a priming pump for the lower chamber (ventricle). The ventricle pumps the blood forward from the heart.

The systemic circuit is an extensive network of vessels that presents a relatively high resistance to flow, which means that the left ventricle has to work hard to circulate the blood. Like any muscle forced to work hard, it gets bigger. In contrast, the pulmonary circuit is less extensive and exerts lower resistance to flow. Thus, the right ventricle does not have to work as hard as the left ventricle and therefore has a thinner wall.

Special one-way valves, which work simply on pressure differences, prevent back flow from the ventricles to the atria during ventricular contraction (tricuspid and mitral valves), and prevent back flow from the pulmonary artery and aorta into the ventricles during relaxation of the ventricles (semilunar valves).

The heart goes through cycles of ventricular relaxation and filling (diastole) and ventricular contraction and emptying (systole).

FIGURE 2.1.7

The circulatory system.

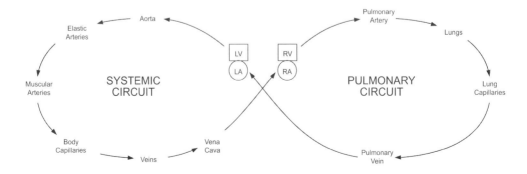

FIGURE 2.1.8

The heart - internal structure.

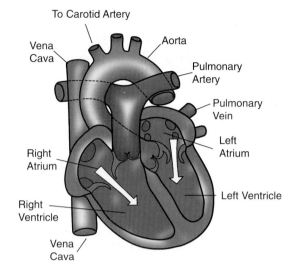

To Carotid Artery

Vena Cava

Aorta

Pulmonary Artery

Pulmonary Vein

Left Atrium

Right Atrium

Left Ventricle

Right Ventricle

Vena Cava

Foramen Ovale

The "foramen ovale" is an opening between the right and left atria of the heart. In the developing foetus the lungs are not functional so the blood bypasses the lungs, with some passing directly from the right atrium to the left atrium through the foramen ovale. When the baby is born and begins to breathe, the foramen ovale closes, allowing the blood to be pumped through the lungs for oxygenation.

Initially the foramen ovale is closed by means of a "flap" valve that seals against the wall of the left atrium. This remains closed under normal circumstances, as the pressure in the left atrium is slightly higher than that in the right atrium. In most people the valve eventually seals over and the foramen ovale disappears. However, in some individuals the valve fails to seal completely and they have what is known as a Patent Foramen Ovale (PFO). These lesions vary in their nature, size and significance. If the "flap valve" is malformed or absent the foramen ovale remains widely open and there is spontaneous "shunting" of blood (usually from left to right). Such lesions are often discovered and surgically

corrected early in life, though this is not always the case. Most PFOs are smaller, the flap valves are at least partially effective, and so spontaneous shunting does not occur constantly. Indeed, the "flap valve" may continue to function without healing shut in the long term. However the PFO provides a means by which blood may move from the right side to the left side should the pressure in the right atrium ever exceed that in the left

Echocardiography, a diagnostic test which provides accurate images of the beating heart, can be used to detect a patent foramen ovale. The technique utilizes the reflection of ultrasound waves in a similar manner to the Doppler monitors used to detect circulating bubbles in divers.

Differential reflection of the sound waves off solid tissues of varying consistencies and liquids allow an image of the area to be constructed. The best views of the heart are obtained when an echocardiographic probe is inserted into the oesophagus, and so images are obtained from behind the heart rather than through the chest wall from the front. This former technique is referred to as "transoesophageal echocardiography (TOE).

Bubbles are highly reflective of ultrasound, and can be clearly seen during echocardiography. To test for blood shunting between the atria, a saline solution containing minute air bubbles (microbubbles) may be injected into one of the subject's peripheral veins. These will arrive first in the right atrium and can be clearly seen because of their high reflectivity. The left atrium is then carefully observed during a series of manoeuvres designed to raise right atrial pressure. If the bubbles can be seen passing across the atrial wall, this indicates the presence of a PFO. (Figures 2.1.9 to 2.1.11).

Echocardiographic studies have indicated an incidence of patent foramen ovale of between 5% and 24% in the general population.[1,2] However, post mortem studies have indicated that a patent foramen ovale - sometimes only the size of a pin prick - may be present in up to 30% of the population.[3]

Individuals with a patent foramen ovale are usually unaware of it as it may cause no problems under normal circumstances. However, in divers, if large numbers of bubbles form in the veins returning to the right heart during or after decompression, these bubbles may cross a PFO, especially if it is spontaneously shunting in both directions. It is also possible that if bubbles become lodged in the capillaries of the lungs in sufficient numbers, this may generate back-pressure in the right atrium causing

blood (and bubbles) to shunt across the PFO to the left atrium. Once on the left side of the heart, these bubbles enter the arterial circulation and distribute off around the body where they are potentially more harmful than in the veins where they formed. A diver might inadvertently promote this process by performing a Valsalva manouvre or by lifting something heavy, both of which tend to increase right heart pressure. The significance of a PFO in decompression illness is further discussed in Chapter 5.

Some individuals have a defect in the wall between the ventricles (a "ventricular septal defect") which will also allow blood to follow an abnormal pathway through the heart. In theory, this may lead to a similar problem to that described above. However, most VSDs are discovered early in life, and flow across them is almost always from left to right.

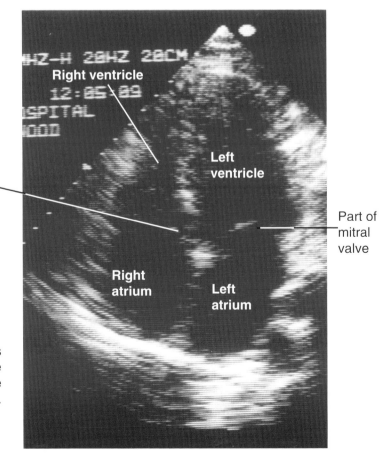

FIGURE 2.1.9
Echocardiogram before contrast injection.

The photograph shows the four chambers of the heart viewed from the apex of the heart at top.

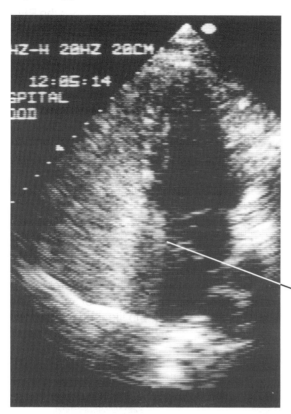

FIGURE 2.1.10
*Contrast bubbles
entering right side of heart.*

Taken immediately after the contrast
enters the heart and fills the right
atrium and ventricle (which appear
white and are now indistinguishable
due to the bubbles they contain).

Bubbles crossing interatrial
shunt

FIGURE 2.1.11
*Contrast bubbles passing
into left side of heart.*

Bubbles pass
through the mitral
valve and disperse
in the left ventricle
(lots of bright dots in
left ventricle).

Photographs courtesy
Dr. Peter Wilmshurst.

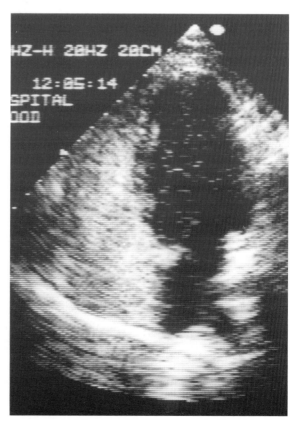

Control of the Beating Heart

The heart is capable of beating totally independently of any nerve supply (a fact readily attested to by any heart transplant patient). A small "pacemaker" area in the wall of the right atrium (the sino-atrial node) generates a pattern of regular electrical discharges that spread first over the atria, and then via a specialized conducting system, down over the ventricles. These impulses cause the orderly and coordinated contraction of the heart muscle. The atria contract first expelling the blood into the ventricles and then, following a brief pause to allow complete filling, the ventricles contract, ejecting blood. Clearly, if both the atria and ventricles contracted together, inefficient pumping would result. Thus, the atria contract first filling the ventricles, which contract shortly after.

Although the heart can contract in the absence of nerves, in the normal person nerves of the autonomic nervous system supply the pacemaker region in the wall of the right atrium. The Autonomic Nervous System is responsible for controlling involuntary activities. There are two parts, the sympathetic and parasympathetic divisions which generally have opposite effects. In the heart, sympathetic nerve activity increases both the rate and strength of contraction, while the parasympathetic nerve activity has the opposite effect.

Blood Vessels

When blood leaves the left ventricle it passes into the aorta, which is the largest artery in the body. It has thick elastic walls that recoil during ventricular relaxation to maintain arterial pressure whilst the ventricle refills. The aorta gives off branches to all parts of the body. Blood leaving the right ventricle passes into the pulmonary trunk which divides almost immediately into left and right pulmonary arteries. These supply the left and right lung respectively and in general run parallel to the airways of the respiratory tract.

In all tissues of the body, the large arteries give rise to a branching vascular "tree", with each branch giving rise to narrower vessels with progressively thinner walls. The smallest arteries are called arterioles and it is from these that the capillaries, the smallest blood vessels, arise. The arterioles have the job of controlling flow to the capillary beds. The capillaries are the business end of the entire cardiovascular system. It is through their thin walls that gas (and nutrient) exchange occurs. The heart and large blood vessels are really only a pump and distribution system for the capillaries. Figure 2.1.12 shows a cross section of a capillary running through a muscle tissue.

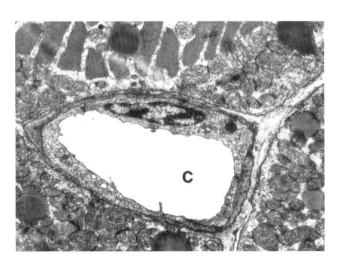

FIGURE 2.1.12

Cross section of capillary.

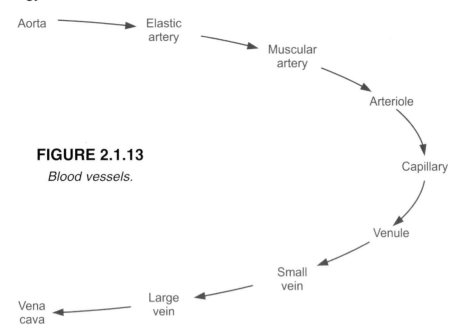

FIGURE 2.1.13

Blood vessels.

From capillaries, the blood is gathered into small thin-walled veins and finally returned to the right atrium (Figure 2.1.13). Most veins direct the blood flow by means of one-way valves, which prevent the blood traveling in the wrong direction.

Arteries are thick-walled vessels which, by definition, always carry blood **away** from the heart. Veins generally have thinner walls and may be somewhat flattened. Veins always carry blood **towards** the heart. A common source of confusion is that oxygenated blood is sometimes referred to as "arterial blood", but not all arteries carry oxygenated blood. The exceptions are the pulmonary arteries, which carry deoxygenated blood from the right heart to the lungs. They qualify to be called arteries because they are carrying blood away from the heart. Similarly, while most veins carry deoxygenated blood, the pulmonary veins carry oxygenated blood from the lungs to the left heart.

Heart muscle is very active and requires a constant supply of oxygenated blood. The coronary blood vessels arise from the base of the aorta. Figure 2.1.14 shows a cast of the coronary blood vessels magnified many hundreds of times by a scanning electron microscope, and the dense mass of capillaries surrounding the muscle cells. The tissue has been digested away with acid to show just the blood vessels.

FIGURE 2.1.14

Coronary blood vessels.

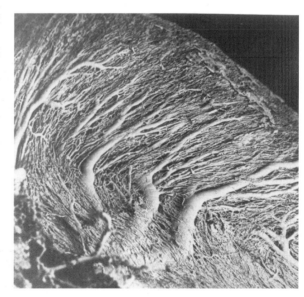

The function of the cardiovascular system is usually measured in terms of blood pressure and cardiac output (in litres per minute). Physiologically it is the flow to particular tissues which is important, not blood pressure. However, blood pressure is more easily measured than flow and, since flow is often proportional to pressure, the latter is the most commonly used index of cardiovascular function. Blood pressure is measured as systolic (maximum pressure during contraction of the left ventricle) over diastolic (minimum pressure during relaxation of the left ventricle) e.g. 130/80. The most common pressure units are mmHg (millimetres of mercury).

Small changes in the diameter of the arterioles and specially adapted "pre-capillary vessels" effectively control the flow through any particular tissue bed and, therefore, the distribution of blood. The arterioles can be thought of as "taps" controlling blood flow into the capillary beds. As arterioles constrict the resistance to blood flow increases and flow beyond the point of constriction is reduced. Dilation of arterioles reduces resistance thus increasing flow to the tissues beyond the point of dilation. Generalised constriction and dilation of arterioles ("vasoconstriction" and "vasodilation") mediates an increase or decrease in the overall resistance of the circulation respectively, which in turn would contribute to a corresponding rise or fall in blood pressure,

The diameter of arterioles and pre-capillary vessels is controlled by local and central controls.

Local controls serve the metabolic needs of the tissue in which they occur. For example, during increased muscular activity changes in the local levels of oxygen, carbon dioxide and acidity act on the muscle within the blood vessel walls, causing the vessels to dilate and therefore allowing increased blood flow.

The diameter of arterioles is also affected by the activities of the autonomic nervous system For example, if blood pressure is high, it is detected by baroreceptors in the major arteries and relayed to the brain. As a result of increased parasympathetic nerve activity and reduced sympathetic activity, the heart rate decreases and arterioles dilate causing a reduction in both heart output and the resistance to blood flow. This returns blood pressure toward normal. The opposite is also true. For example, the dizziness sometimes experienced upon standing up quickly after having been laying down is due to pooling of blood in the veins under the effect of gravity, thereby causing a drop in blood pressure. The body responds in the opposite way to that described above (that is, the rate and force of contraction of the heart increases, and blood vessels constrict), to restore blood pressure. The time it takes for the dizziness to pass is the time it takes blood pressure to be restored.

Circulatory Failure

Generalised circulatory failure is manifest as shock. Shock can be defined as a generalized loss of effective tissue blood supply. This may be due to an actual physical loss of blood or plasma, or a physiological state in which there is pump (heart) failure or excessive vasodilation leading to a similar loss of blood pressure and tissue blood flow. The net result of this *loss of adequate blood supply to the tissues is failure to meet the oxygen demands of the cells,* thereby depressing cellular metabolism.

Shock is usually classified according to the event which causes it. The resultant physiological changes, however, are often similar in each case.

Hypovolemic Shock
(Reduced blood volume)

Hypovolemic shock can be caused by:

haemorrhage - such as trauma (accidental or surgical), childbirth or internal (crushing) injuries. It is often very difficult to know how much blood is lost in crushing injuries. e.g. a thigh muscle can accommodate 1 litre of blood with only approximately 1cm) (^{5}/16inch) increase in diameter. Haemorrhage due to a traumatic injury (such as shark attack, or boat propellor injury) is the most likely cause of shock in divers. Only the most severe forms of decompression illness (DCI) result in shock, and disease of this severity is very rare.

plasma loss - from burns or DCI (though note the above comment)

dehydration - due to heat exhaustion, heat stroke, diarrhoea, diuresis (excess urinary output)

Neurogenic Shock
(Nervous system generated)

The cause in this case is a generalized vasodilation due to decreased tensions in the muscles that make up the walls of the blood vessels (decreased "vasomotor tone"). Blood volume is not changed but the capacity of the blood vessels is increased. The increased diameter of the small arteries reduces the resistance to blood flow and leads to a reduction in blood pressure. Because the veins have dilated and the blood pressure has dropped, blood pools in the veins. The result is a decreased return of blood from the veins to the heart leading to a decreased cardiac output.

Conditions such as spinal cord injury, damage to the brain stem, severe pain, action of tranquilizer, narcotic or sedative drugs, a bad fright or grief can all cause neurogenic shock.

Vasogenic Shock (Blood vessel generated)

Vasogenic Shock is quite rare. The commonest form is the so-called "anaphylactic shock" which results from a severe allergic reaction. This leads to the release of histamine and several other potent chemicals that cause vasodilation and increased capillary permeability (i.e. a widening of the gaps between the cells of the walls of the capillaries). The latter greatly increases the normal leakage of plasma from the capillaries into the tissues causing a loss of blood volume.

Cardiogenic Shock (Heart generated)

Any condition which reduces cardiac output can cause signs and symptoms of shock. Conditions such as a heart attack, heart surgery, prolonged arrhythmias and other heart diseases are included in this category.

Septic or Endotoxic Shock

This is caused by any widespread overwhelming infection which, usually because of toxin release by the bacteria, results in severe generalized vasodilation and loss of plasma from the circulation. Persons at risk include those with peritonitis, burns, post partum (post childbirth) infection, as well as those who have undergone gastrointestinal or urinary tract surgery, and those taking medication to suppress their immune system.

The Effects of Shock

Regardless of the cause of shock the effects are essentially the same. The reduction in blood pressure is detected by the arterial baroreceptors and the body tries to compensate in the following ways:

Compensatory Reactions

Activation of the sympathetic nervous system and an associated release of adrenaline from the adrenal gland mediates effects on both the heart and the blood vessels. There is an increase in heart rate and an increased force of contraction, which together act to increase cardiac output. There is constriction of blood vessels which increases both peripheral resistance and the return of blood to the heart. Vasoconstriction is most prominent in non-essential vascular beds such as the skin and gastrointestinal tract and, therefore, blood is directed to the essential vascular beds of the brain, heart and kidneys.

The decrease in blood pressure also activates mechanisms which act on the kidneys to reduce urine production, so retaining fluid. This assists in maintaining blood pressure, but frequently at the expense of kidney damage if the shock continues for too long.

The signs and symptoms at this stage are the familiar ones of:

- rapid, weak, thready pulse (due to the reduced blood volume) cold, pale and clammy skin dry mouth and throat (all due to generalized stimulation of sympathetic nerves. e.g. the pale, cold skin is due to blood being prevented from entering the skin by the shutting down of skin arterioles)

- nausea
  restlessness
  apprehension
     (all due to stimulation of the brain
     associated with the general
     sympathetic response)

- rapid respiration
  (due to increasing accumulation of lactic acid and other acidic metabolites. As described earlier, the acid load stimulates breathing)

If the underlying cause is not treated or corrected the compensatory mechanisms may no longer be able to maintain a stable state and the victim's condition may rapidly worsen. This is the so-called *decompensatory phase* and frequently leads to death.

Progressive Shock leading to Decompensated Shock

Sustained constriction of arterioles results in decreased blood flow to the capillary circulation (microcirculation) of most organs. This has a variety of effects which include:

- damage to tissues due to lack of oxygen (ischaemic hypoxia), and a continuing increase in lactic acid and other metabolites produced by anaerobic (without oxygen) metabolism, leading to changes in the acid-base balance of the blood

- local vasodilation of arterioles (and to a lesser degree venules) from the accumulation of lactic acid, carbon dioxide and other metabolites

- pooling of blood in the capillaries, due to the poor blood flow, causing a loss of fluid and plasma proteins from the circulating blood

Eventually, metabolism may cease and organ systems may fail.

In the brain, severe ischaemia (poor blood supply) and hypoxia lead to depressed function. When the regions of the brain responsible for control of heart and blood vessels (cardio-vascular centre) are affected, sympathetic stimulation of the heart and blood vessels is reduced resulting in a further decrease in blood flow to the brain.

In the heart, as the blood pressure drops, coronary blood flow is reduced despite vasodilation. The increased acidity of the blood (acidosis) further depresses cardiac function.

Thus in summary:

Compensated Shock
▼
Progressive Shock
▼
Decompensated (Irreversible) Shock
(Death)

First Aid for Shock

The aim of first aid in the case of shock is to ensure that compensated shock is not allowed to progress to decompensated shock. The first aid steps, which should be familiar to all divers are as follows:

- Act to prevent further shock. Look for *arterial bleeding* and, if present, stop it. Except for arterial blood loss, the particular cause of the shock is often of little importance to the first aider as the first aid is the same for all types of shock.
- Lay the victim down and raise their legs
- Provide supplemental oxygen
- Provide reassurance
- No oral fluids (as an operation and anaesthetic may be required)
- Protect from extremes of temperature (i.e. hot or cold). Overheating causes vasodilation which will worsen the condition
- No sedatives or alcohol
- Monitor the airway, breathing and pulse
- Medical advice

The rationale behind these strategies is as follows:

Since the primary problem is decreased delivery of oxygen to the tissues because of the reduced blood supply, breathing 100% oxygen may allow the remaining blood to carry more oxygen and so maximize tissue oxygenation. This will allow more aerobic (oxygen-using) metabolism and reduce the amount of acidification of the tissues (from anaerobic metabolism).

As mentioned earlier, in the upright position blood tends to pool in the legs. So by laying the victim down and raising their legs, the blood can run "downhill" in the leg veins and assist return of blood to the heart, thereby improving cardiac output and so blood pressure. It is notable that raising the legs is not recommended in the decompression illness victim who is not suffering from shock (see Chapter 5).

Alcohol and sedatives depress central nervous system function and, in addition, alcohol causes dilation of peripheral blood vessels, leading blood away from where it is needed most.

Similarly, overwarming causes opening up of peripheral blood vessels in much the same way as alcohol. A first aider should aim to keep the victim at a "comfortable" temperature, neither too hot nor too cold.

Reassurance is also extremely important in stopping the progression from compensated to decompensated shock. Indeed much of the progression in the degree of shock is probably mediated via the brain. If the first aider reassures the victim and exudes confidence (often contrary to reality), the victim may adopt a similar attitude, which may be important in their survival. The higher centres of the brain (the points we associate with being human) can greatly influence how the more primitive centres (such as the cardiac and respiratory control centres) work.

Finally, first responders should avoid moving a shock victim except to avoid immediate danger to life. Moving the victim may provoke a deterioration in their condition. In past years many victims of shark attack, who were in compensated shock on the beach after the bleeding had been stopped, died in the ambulance while being moved to medical care. The South Africans, in the 1960s, introduced the idea of restoring the blood volume to normal with intravenous fluids (blood or plasma) on the beach, before moving the victim. The results were spectacularly good and this routine was widely adopted. Nevertheless, there has been some controversy in the emergency medicine literature over how much delay should be imposed in pursuit of this goal, especially in shock from other causes such as multiple trauma in car accidents where the biggest problems may be internal ones that the first aid provider cannot see. No doubt this debate will continue. Notwithstanding any debate, transport of the unstable victim from a remote location may be unavoidable. In this situation, the victim should be transported laying down with their legs elevated if possible.

Fainting

The commonest form of circulatory failure is a faint (known to doctors as a vaso-vagal attack). Although the mechanism in many cases is the same as that outlined under neurogenic shock, it is most often transient and self-correcting. Most faints occur as a result of a sudden drop in blood pressure, with a concomitant and equally short-lived fall in blood flow to the brain below levels required to maintain consciousness. A variety of events can lead to fainting. For example, if one stands up too quickly from a hot bath, significant quantities of blood can pool in the vessels of the legs, which have been dilated by the heat. There may be a sudden drop in venous return to the heart and therefore a sudden fall in cardiac output, leading to the faint. Alternatively, someone might see something particularly distressing, and this can lead to a strong para-sympathetic nervous system stimulus to the heart which reduces the rate and strength of its contractions. At the same time, a reduction in sympathetic nervous system activity might cause blood vessels to dilate. These influences combine to cause a sudden fall in blood pressure. In a healthy person, these problems are quickly compensated for, but this may not be quick enough to prevent a transient faint. Frequently a faint will end as soon as the unconscious person falls over. This is because the heart no longer has to pump the blood against gravity and the blood pressure is then adequate to immediately ensure adequate blood flow for consciousness. There is, of course, a danger that the victim may injure themselves in the process of fainting.

THE LYMPHATIC SYSTEM

Closely associated with the functions of the circulatory system is the lymphatic system. The capillaries of the circulatory system are specialized for gas and nutrient exchange. As such their walls are thin and relatively "leaky". In fact the only things that almost never leak out of the blood are the blood cells. Some of the serum which leaks from the capillaries is later drawn back into the blood vessels by the osmotic pressure generated by the blood proteins. However, a total of about three litres every 24 hours is not. If this were not returned to the circulation the blood would effectively "run out" (and our tissues would become severely swollen with fluid). Clearly this does not happen. The role of the lymphatic system is to return the leaked fluid to the circulatory system.

The lymphatic system consists of a series of lymphatic vessels and lymph nodes. Lymphatic vessels originate as microscopic blind-ending capillary-like structures which progressively join one another to form larger vessels. The two largest lymph vessels then empty into the great veins of the chest, just near their entry into the right atrium. Along the way lymph vessels pass through lymph nodes - small bean-shaped structures packed with lymphocytes, specialized cells which are involved in filtering the lymph and attacking foreign bacteria. The lymph nodes tend to be aggregated in the groin, armpit, lower jaw, abdomen and mediastinum (Figure 2.1.15). These areas tend to become swollen and tender when you have an infection in the territory drained by that particular part of the lymphatic system. What is actually happening is that the lymphocytes are busily trying to destroy the foreign bacteria and the lymph nodes become larger and sensitive to pressure as a result of this.

FIGURE 2.1.15
The lymphatic system

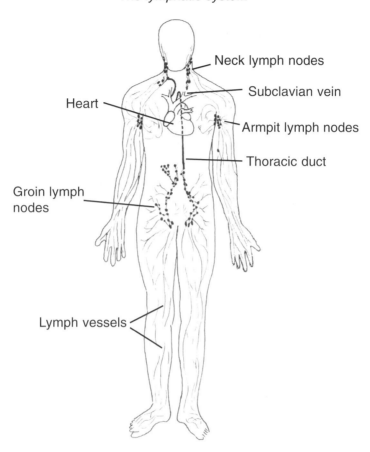

Neck lymph nodes

Subclavian vein

Heart

Armpit lymph nodes

Thoracic duct

Groin lymph nodes

Lymph vessels

Flow of fluid in the lymph vessels is largely determined by the action of skeletal muscles (muscles attached to bone) which, when they contract, put pressure on the lymph vessels and squeeze the fluid through them. Small one-way valves prevent back flow. Thus, in people who are sedentary for long periods, fluid builds up, particularly around the ankles. This is why your shoes feel tighter after long airplane flights.

Apart from its important accessory role to the cardiovascular system, the lymphatic system is important to divers for another reason. It has been shown that toxins delivered by many of our dangerous marine animals (and terrestrial animals for that matter) are transported through the lymphatics. Hence, the basis of the Pressure-Immobilization technique. The wide pressure bandage applied from the wound, and extending as far as possible beyond it, collapses the lymph capillaries and so reduces the flow of toxin towards the heart. Since muscular activity is needed to make the lymph flow, immobilizing the affected limb prevents that process.

Finally, although rare, occasional cases of DCS involving the lymphatic system have been seen. Usually this occurs along with other symptoms of DCS, and is manifest as surprisingly localized tissue swelling (presumably because bubbles block the lymph vessels).

SUMMARY

- Arteries have thick, elastic walls and carry blood away from the heart. Most arteries carry oxygenated blood.

- Veins have thinner walls and carry blood toward the heart. Blood flow is directed by means of one-way valves. Most veins carry de-oxygenated blood.

- Blood pressure in veins is much lower than in arteries.

- Blood is a fluid (plasma) containing various cells. There are red cells which contain the oxygen-binding protein, haemoglobin, white cells to fight infection and platelets to activate clotting. The average body contains about 6 litres of blood.

- We need oxygen to metabolize food effectively and provide energy. The body consumes oxygen and produces heat and other forms of energy, as well as carbon dioxide.

- Most of the oxygen carried around the body is bound to haemoglobin but a small amount is dissolved in the plasma.

- Carbon dioxide is a waste product of our metabolism. Most of the carbon dioxide in our blood is carried as bicarbonate.

- The partial pressure of carbon dioxide in the arterial blood and the acidity of this blood are the main factors regulating breathing. Chemoreceptors in the medulla (the respiratory centre in the brain) detect the level of carbon dioxide in the arterial blood and regulate the breathing to maintain normal carbon dioxide levels.

- Lack of oxygen does not normally stimulate breathing significantly unless the arterial oxygen levels fall substantially.

- *Shock can be defined as inadequate blood flow to the tissues resulting in an inadequate supply of oxygen.* This may be caused by an actual physical loss of blood, or a physiological loss where profound dilation of blood vessels or leaking of plasma into the tissues will also result in inadequate blood flow.

- The signs and symptoms of shock include rapid, weak, thready pulse, cold, pale, clammy skin, dry mouth and throat, weakness, nausea, restlessness, apprehension, and rapid respiration.

- The first aid for shock includes action to prevent further shock (e.g. stopping severe bleeding immediately), laying the victim down and raising their legs, giving elevated concentrations of oxygen, reassurance, protection from extremes of temperature, monitoring ABC, medical advice.

- The lymphatic system consists of a series of lymphatic vessels and lymph nodes. Its role is to return leaked fluid to the circulatory system and to fight any infecting organisms that find their way into the lymph vessels.

REFERENCES

1. Lynch J et al. Prevalence of right-to-left atrial shunting in a healthy population: detection by Valsalva maneuver contast echocardiography. *Am J Cardiol 1984*; 53:1478-80.

2. Wilmshurst P et al. Relation between interatrial shunting and decompression sickness in divers. *The Lancet 1989;* 8675:1302-6.

3. Hagen P. Incidence and size of patent foramen ovale during the first 10 decades of life: an autopsy study of 965 normal hearts. *Mayo Clin Proc 1984;* 59:17-20.

RECOMMENDED FURTHER READING

Guyton AC, Hall JE. Medical Physiology (10th ed). Philadelphia: WB Saunders Co.; 2000.

2.2 Effects of SCUBA diving on respiration and circulation

RESPIRATION

The Effort of Breathing Underwater

Normally, the majority of the work of breathing is performed to overcome the elastic forces resisting expansion of the lungs during inspiration. Work is also done to overcome the frictional resistance to air flowing through the air passages. At normal pressures and breathing rates, far less energy is required to overcome the frictional resistance than the elastic forces.

As the breathing rate increases the proportion of work done in overcoming the resistance to air flow increases because rapid flow causes turbulence, and turbulent flow causes more resistance. This resistance increases even more as the breathing gas becomes denser as it does when breathed under pressure. This increase in density is directly proportional to depth.

Not surprisingly, the resistance to air flow at 30m (100ft) in a chamber has been shown to be twice that at the surface. The maximum breathing capacity (the maximum volume of air which can be breathed in and out over a given time) was shown to be halved.[1] These tests were performed on subjects who were at rest and were using equipment that is far more efficient than scuba equipment.

While using scuba, the resistance to air flow through the narrow passages of the regulator makes breathing even more of an effort. In addition, since the regulator supplies air at ambient pressure at the level of the mouthpiece, and since the mouthpiece sits about 20cm (8in) above the lungs in the upright diver, the muscles driving inspiration must overcome a head of pressure equivalent to 20cm (8in) of water on each breath. Finally, wearing a tight wetsuit, buoyancy compensator and weight belt restricts chest and abdomen movement and further exacerbates the problem.

Impaired gas exchange

It follows from the above that a diver is not capable of increasing ventilation in response to the demands of work to the same extent as a person performing work at the surface. Since ventilation is increased during work to facilitate the necessary uptake of oxygen and excretion of CO_2, the danger in diving is that ventilation and therefore gas exchange may be insufficient for the amount of work performed. In particular, the levels of CO_2 are very sensitive to inadequate ventilation and can rise. This is made even more likely because of the increased dead space imposed by scuba equipment. Carbon dioxide build-up (hypercapnia) can and does occur during scuba diving and causes a number of problems which are discussed in Chapter 7. In contrast, hypoxia rarely develops as a result of reduced ventilation during scuba diving since the reduced ventilation is offset by the rise in the partial pressures of oxygen in the high pressure air.

Adaptation

A few studies have been done to determine whether or not scuba divers adapt to breathing underwater. Some studies have indicated that divers may develop a reduced responsiveness to carbon dioxide, meaning that they are less likely to increase their ventilation in response to increasing CO_2 and are therefore more likely to "retain" CO_2 during a dive. However, it is not entirely clear whether the reduced responsiveness seen in some divers is a pre-existing characteristic or an adaptive response to diving.[2] The main concern over insensitivity to CO_2 levels is that higher blood CO_2 levels may predispose to cerebral oxygen toxicity, and CO_2 tolerant individuals ("CO_2 retainers") may be at greater risk during use of gas mixtures with a high PO_2, such as when nitrox or rebreather diving. Unfortunately, it is very difficult to test for this characteristic.

CIRCULATION

Upon immersion with the body vertical, the veins of the legs and abdomen are squeezed by the higher hydrostatic pressure (relative to the upper body), causing the blood to be pushed to regions of lower pressure. In addition, the exposure to cold water usually causes a degree of constriction in peripheral blood vessels ("vasoconstriction") on immersion, which also serves to route blood away from the peripheries and toward the central circulation. As a result, immersion increases the amount of blood in the lungs, heart and great veins. Pressure receptors in the veins in the chest and the atria sense the increase in central blood volume and through a complicated signaling mechanism, the kidneys are prompted to remove water from the circulation in an attempt to return blood volume to normal. Thus, with immersion, there is an increase in urine output and an inconvenient urge to empty the bladder. This "immersion diuresis" may contribute to dehydration in divers.

Another potential (but relatively rare) adverse consequence of the vaso-constriction that occurs with immersion is a phenomenon known as "immersion induced pulmonary oedema". When the amount of blood in the central circulation is increased, there is a corresponding increase in the work the heart must do. First, it is receiving more blood, so its "preload" is greater. Second, the resistance against which it is pumping ("afterload") is greater because of the constricted peripheral blood vessels. In the normal individual the heart can cope with these increased demands, but in a person whose capacity to respond is impaired (for example, because of undiagnosed heart disease) then a degree of "back-pressure" in the pulmonary circulation may develop as the left ventricle fails to cope. This, in turn, may result in leakage of fluid out of the lung capillaries and into the alveoli, creating a situation not unlike drowning. Fluid in the alveoli impairs gas exchange and the victim can become dangerously hypoxic quite quickly. The victim usually feels short of breath and may cough pink-tinged frothy sputum. Removal from the water and oxygen administration are the appropriate treatments, and interestingly, the symptoms often settle quite quickly (minutes to hours) once the victim is no longer immersed. Divers with disease of the coronary arteries or heart valves are almost certainly at greater risk of such events. It also seems that divers with hypertension, and possibly those receiving so-called "beta-blocker" medication for their hypertension may be predisposed. However, it is notable that immersion pulmonary oedema has occurred in divers who do not appear to suffer any of these predispositions.

Diving Reflex

Cardiovascular changes occur with breath-hold diving. Diving animals such as seals and whales can perform breath hold dives of very long duration. Whales can "hold their breath" for up to two hours and seals for over 20 minutes.

These animals have a higher blood and tissue capacity for oxygen than humans. The muscles contain high concentrations of a molecule called myoglobin which binds oxygen in a similar fashion to haemoglobin in blood, and this myoglobin represents a vast pre-dive oxygen store. There is further oxygen storage capacity in large circulatory system reservoirs of red blood cells held in so-called "sinuses" in the liver and spleen. These can be released into the circulation during a dive. The diving animals also utilize oxygen more efficiently. On diving, the blood vessels supplying organs such as the skin, kidneys and intestines constrict, reducing blood supply to these organs and permitting a selective supply to the vital organs; especially the heart and brain. This vasoconstriction is accompanied by a dramatic reduction in the heart rate (bradycardia). This combination of effects reduces heat loss and conserves oxygen.

Although this "diving reflex" is not as well developed in humans, similar changes have been observed in some breath-hold divers. The pulse rate may decrease by up to 50%.[3] Diving bradycardia in humans appears to be stimulated by the combination of breath-holding and facial cooling (sudden facial immersion in cold water stimulates parasympathetic nervous system activity which slows the heart). Although the bradycardia and vasoconstriction reduce oxygen consumption in diving animals, some experiments have shown that cardiovascular changes due to breath-hold diving do not appear to significantly reduce oxygen consumption in man.[4]

It is notable that a number of sudden deaths have occurred in swimmers (usually elderly) on initial facial immersion in cold water. It seems likely that in predisposed individuals (especially those with previous heart disease or electrical instability) the profound parasympathetic activity brought on by facial immersion, can cause a cardiac arrest and subsequent death.

SUMMARY

- When we scuba dive the resistance to air flow through our airways and regulator increases the effort of breathing. The problem is magnified by the increased gas density at depth, a tight wetsuit, buoyancy compensator and/or weight-belt.

- The increased breathing effort at depth may reduce ventilation markedly and result in high carbon dioxide levels in the blood.

- Scuba divers may develop a reduced responsiveness to carbon dioxide, making the diver more subject to oxygen toxicity.

REFERENCES

1. Marshall R et al. Resistance to Breathing in Normal Subjects During Simulated Diving. *J Appl Physiol* 1956; 9:5-10.

2. Florio J et al. Breathing Pattern and Ventilatory Response to Carbon Dioxide in Divers. *J Appl Physiol 1979*; 46:1076-80.

3. Hong S and Rahn H. The Diving Women of Korea and Japan. *Scientific American* 1967; 216:34-43.

4. Craig A and Medd W. Man's Responses to Breath-Hold Exercise in Air and Water. *J Appl Physiol 1968*; 24: 773-7.

OTHER SOURCES

Camporesi EM, Bosco G. Ventilation, gas exchange and exercise under pressure. In Brubakk AO, Neuman TS (eds) Bennett and Elliott's Physiology and Medicine of Diving (5th ed). London: Saunders Publishers; 2003:77-114.

Ferrigno M, Lundgren CE. Breath-hold diving. In Brubakk AO, Neuman TS (eds) Bennett and Elliott's Physiology and Medicine of Diving (5th ed). London:Saunders Publishers; 2003:153-180.

© Michael Aw

3

Nitrogen uptake and elimination

REVISION OF SOME GAS LAWS

Dalton's Law

The partial pressure of a gas in a gas mixture is the part of the total pressure of the gases in the mixture that is contributed to by that gas.

For example, air is composed of a mixture of gases, being approximately 21% oxygen and 79% nitrogen. So, whatever the pressure acting on a given volume of air, the partial pressure of oxygen will be 21% of the total pressure, and the partial pressure of nitrogen will be 79% of the total pressure exerted by the air.

Dalton's Law puts it the other way round.

The total pressure exerted by a mixture of gases is the sum of the partial pressures that would be exerted by each of the gases if it alone occupied the total volume.

Henry's Law

At a constant temperature, the amount of gas that will dissolve into a liquid is proportional to the partial pressure of the gas over the liquid.

Doubling the partial pressure will double the amount (number of molecules) of gas that will dissolve into the liquid. Another influence on gases dissolving in liquids is temperature. Cold liquids hold more gas than do hot ones.

Inert Gases

An inert gas is defined as one that is chemically inactive and hence participates in no chemical reactions within the body. These include nitrogen, argon, helium, krypton, neon, radon and xenon.

Although the following discussion describes the behavior of nitrogen within the body, the other inert gases behave in a similar manner.

Nitrogen Absorption

After a long period at sea level, the average human body contains about one litre of dissolved nitrogen. All of the body tissues contain nitrogen dissolved at the same partial pressure ("**nitrogen tension**") as the nitrogen partial pressure in the alveoli of the lung - about 570mmHg (0.75ATA). We are said to be in a state of "**saturation**" or "**equilibrium**", and our body cannot absorb any more nitrogen unless the partial pressure of the nitrogen in the breathing gas is increased. If the partial pressure of inspired nitrogen should change because of a change in either the pressure (e.g. during a dive) or the composition of the breathing mixture, the pressure of the nitrogen dissolved in the body will eventually attain a matching level since nitrogen (or any gas for that matter) will move from areas of higher tension to lower tension. If the nitrogen tension in the alveoli increases relative to tissue nitrogen tension, then nitrogen will be absorbed into the blood and thence into the tissues. The reverse applies if nitrogen tension in the alveoli falls in relation to tissue tension. Nitrogen movement will continue until alveolar and tissue tensions are equal again.

If we dive to a depth of 10m (33ft) of seawater where the ambient pressure is 2ATA, our regulator will supply us with air at ambient pressure and the partial pressure of nitrogen in our lungs increases to approximately 1.6ATA. In accordance with Henry's Law, the amount of nitrogen which will be absorbed is almost directly proportional to the change in partial pressure. If one litre of nitrogen is absorbed at a pressure of one atmosphere, then two litres could be absorbed after sufficient time at two atmospheres (10m or 33ft depth), and three litres at three atmospheres (20m or 66ft depth). The additional nitrogen in the lungs is quickly dissolved into the blood and carried throughout the body. Wherever the blood passes tissues that are not saturated, that is, where the nitrogen tension of the tissue is lower than that presently in the blood, some of the gas will diffuse into those tissues. The partial pressure in the blood will therefore be somewhat reduced and, as it once again passes through the lungs, it will absorb more nitrogen which will then be carried on to the still-unsaturated tissues. This cycle will continue until all of the tissues of the body, and the blood as well, reach equilibrium with the partial pressure of the nitrogen in the lungs.

If the tissue offers little resistance to the diffusion of nitrogen (or other inert gas) from the blood, the nitrogen is absorbed in the tissue as rapidly as it is supplied by the circulation, and the nitrogen tensions of the tissue and blood quickly equalize. This is known as *perfusion (blood-flow) limited gas exchange*. In this case, the rate of nitrogen absorption is solely determined by blood flow. If, however, the tissue offers substantial resistance to the diffusion of nitrogen from the blood, then the circulation will supply nitrogen faster than it can be absorbed by the tissue. This is known as *diffusion-limited gas exchange*.

Some body tissues absorb nitrogen far more rapidly than others and, therefore, become saturated sooner. As mentioned, the differing rate of nitrogen absorption depends primarily on two factors: the solubility of nitrogen in the tissue and the amount of blood flow it receives.

Nitrogen is five times more soluble in fat than in water and, since body tissues contain various amounts of fat, they are capable of holding various amounts of nitrogen. All other factors being equal, a fatty tissue that can dissolve more nitrogen will take longer to become saturated than an aqueous (watery) tissue that can dissolve less nitrogen. However, the tissue blood flow is probably an even more important determinant of the rate of saturation since it is blood flow that brings nitrogen to the tissue in the first place. Some tissues such as muscle and the brain are well-perfused and thus receive a greater "delivery" of nitrogen. Other tissues such as fat or tendon have a poor blood flow so they will take longer to become saturated with nitrogen.

Thus, well-perfused tissues with a low fat content will saturate very quickly because the small amount of nitrogen they can hold is rapidly delivered by their luxurious blood flow. In contrast, those tissues with a high fat content and poor perfusion will saturate very slowly because they can hold a lot of nitrogen, but it is delivered only slowly. Obviously, there are many combinations of tissue nitrogen solubility and perfusion in the real organs of the body.

Tissues which become saturated rapidly are sometimes called "fast tissues" (e.g. brain, heart, kidney, muscle), and those which become saturated slowly are called "slow tissues" (e.g. cartilage, tendon and fat stores). The saturation of either fast or slow tissues with nitrogen invariably follows the so-called "first order" kinetic pattern described in Figure 3.1. The initial flux of nitrogen into a tissue is relatively quick, and then progress toward saturation (where the curve plateaus) slows.

FIGURE 3.1

The pattern of nitrogen uptake into tissues.

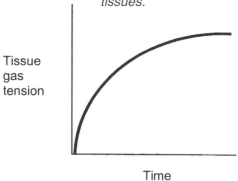

Although this *pattern* of gas influx does not differ between fast and slow tissues, the *time taken* for the plateau to be achieved obviously does. Traditionally, the speed at which tissues take up nitrogen has been expressed in terms of their "half-time" (T½), that is, the time it takes for the tissue to become 50% saturated (see Figure 3.2)

FIGURE 3.2

The concept of tissue half-times.

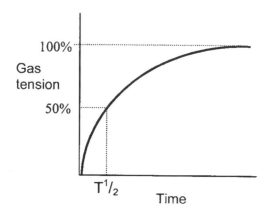

Fast tissues have a short half time and slow tissues have a longer half time. For example, a fast tissue might become 50% saturated in 5 minutes whereas a slower tissue might take 2 hours. This means that it will take about 30 minutes (6 half-times) for the fast tissue to approach full saturation and about 12 hours for the same to be true of slow tissue. It is fairly obvious that because of the short duration of recreational scuba dives, the slower tissues never become fully saturated with nitrogen, but it is certainly possible for some of the fast tissues to saturate.

A couple of further clarifying points regarding the half-time concept are important. First, the absorption half-time is independent of the quantity of nitrogen involved in the process. In other words, if a tissue takes 40 minutes to become half saturated at 2 atmospheres, it would also take 40 minutes to become half saturated at 4 atmospheres, even though the absolute quantity of nitrogen that must be absorbed will have more than doubled. The reader should also note that the notion of "tissues" with various half-times is a theoretical construct, and that we cannot attribute specific half-times to particular body organs. Early decompression modelers reasoned however, that by taking into account the behavior of a range of theoretical tissues (of various half-times) their calculations of nitrogen uptake would "by default" account for the gas uptake behavior over the range of real body tissues.

It is also important to understand that *factors such as temperature and exercise can alter the perfusion and nitrogen solubility (and therefore the half-time) of tissues.* The most important effect is on tissue perfusion. Exercise during a dive increases cardiac output and tissue perfusion (some tissues more so than others). This increase in blood flow delivers nitrogen to tissues more quickly, and for this reason hard work during diving is considered a risk factor for decompression sickness (DCS) (see Chapter 5). Exposure to cold reduces blood flow to peripheral tissues by inducing a vasoconstriction. If this occurs early in the dive it may reduce nitrogen loading into the affected tissues. However, if the diver is warm and well-perfused in the early part of the dive, but becomes cold and poorly-perfused towards the end (during decompression), then the elimination of nitrogen may be impaired and the risk of DCS increased. Exposure to cold (and heat) also affects the solubility of nitrogen (nitrogen is more soluble in cooler tissues). In theory, if a cold tissue is rewarmed too quickly (such as by jumping in a hot shower early after a dive) the solubility of nitrogen may be reduced rapidly and bubbles may form. There are case reports of DCS having been precipitated in this way. These issues are further discussed in Chapter 5.

Nitrogen elimination

("off-gassing" or "out-gassing")

When we ascend, the reverse of the in-gassing process occurs. As the ambient pressure is reduced, the partial pressure of the nitrogen in the lungs decreases. The blood now has a higher nitrogen tension than the air in the lungs, so nitrogen passes from the blood into the lungs, and leaves the body in the expired breath, leaving the blood with a lower nitrogen tension. When this blood again circulates through the tissues, nitrogen passes from the tissues into the blood and, so, the process continues. The elimination of nitrogen from the various tissues has traditionally been considered to follow a similar first order exponential pattern to nitrogen absorption (see Figure 3.3). Indeed, a particular tissue's half-time for nitrogen in-gassing has been assumed to apply to out-gassing also. In other words, nitrogen uptake and elimination have been assumed to be symmetrical processes. We now know that elimination may be a slower process than uptake under certain circumstances, such when bubbles form (see below). Notwithstanding these concerns, the fact remains that tissues that take up nitrogen quickly (fast tissues) will also eliminate it quickly and vice versa.

FIGURE 3.3

The pattern of nitrogen elimination from tissues.

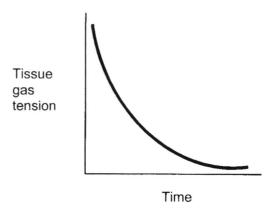

Tissue gas tension

Time

SUPERSATURATION AND BUBBLE FORMATION

After a period at depth, the body's various tissues will be in different states of nitrogen saturation. The very fast tissues may be fully saturated with nitrogen, whilst the slow tissues may contain very little. With the initiation of ascent, the ambient (surrounding) pressure falls quite rapidly (depending on the rate of ascent), and in accordance with the elimination process described above, the partial pressure of nitrogen in the tissues begins to fall as nitrogen is transported away. However, the transport of nitrogen out of tissues takes time, and except in the fastest tissues, which lose their nitrogen very quickly, the fall in tissue nitrogen pressure lags behind the fall in ambient pressure. At some point in the ascent the partial pressure of nitrogen in some tissues will exceed the ambient pressure. This situation in which tissue nitrogen pressure exceeds ambient pressure is called "**supersaturation**". Development of tissue nitrogen supersaturation during ascent is illustrated in Figure 3.4.

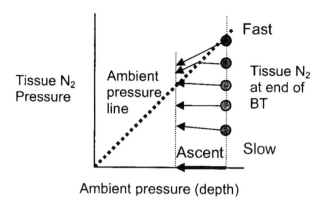

FIGURE 3.4

Tissue N₂ supersaturation on ascent.

The large dots represent tissue nitrogen pressure (vertical axis) after a period of time at depth (horizontal axis) just prior to beginning ascent. As expected, the faster tissues contain more nitrogen than the slower tissues. Indeed, the fastest tissue depicted has reached the ambient pressure line where tissue nitrogen pressure is "equal" to ambient pressure; in other words, the fastest tissue is saturated. An ascent toward the surface (thick arrow on horizontal axis) causes a rapid decrease in ambient pressure, but tissue nitrogen pressure does not fall as quickly (thin arrows). Indeed, the slower tissues will even continue to absorb nitrogen until the falling ambient pressure becomes less than the tissue nitrogen pressure, at which time tissues will begin to lose nitrogen. Note that early in the ascent the tissue nitrogen pressures in some of the faster tissues cross the ambient pressure line, that is, the tissue nitrogen pressure exceeds ambient pressure and the tissue is thus "supersaturated".

It is clear from Figure 3.4 that supersaturation of some tissues with nitrogen will occur during the ascent from virtually every dive. A state of supersaturation will encourage nitrogen to be eliminated from tissues, but it is also a potential problem. Under conditions of nitrogen supersaturation it is very likely that some of the nitrogen molecules may come together to form a bubble. It is possible that tiny bubbles or "micronuclei" are present in our blood and tissues all the time, and act as seeds for these larger nitrogen bubbles when supersaturation occurs. Indeed, just as tissue nitrogen supersaturation is inevitable after every dive, we now recognize that some nitrogen bubbles form, also after every dive. While we appear to tolerate some bubble formation without ill-effect, if the bubble formation is excessive, it may lead to DCS (see Chapter 5).

It follows from the above that prevention of DCS reduces to an exercise in controlling the degree of tissue nitrogen supersaturation and therefore the degree of bubble formation during ascent. This is essentially what the dive tables and computers that we use to control our time, depth and ascents set out to do. The process of bubble formation is further discussed in Chapter 4, along with some of the basic principles used by the designers of dive tables and computers to prevent excessive bubble formation. The adverse consequences of bubble formation are discussed in Chapter 5.

SUMMARY

- A diver is said to be "saturated" when the partial pressure of nitrogen in all of his body tissues is the same as the partial pressure of nitrogen in his lungs.

- Some body tissues absorb (and release) nitrogen more rapidly than others and thus become saturated sooner. The differing rate of nitrogen absorption depends on the fat content of the tissue and the tissue perfusion.

- Temperature, exercise and various other factors may affect the rate of nitrogen uptake and elimination.

- Complete saturation in very slow tissues can take up to 3-4 days.

- When the partial pressure of nitrogen in a tissue is greater than that in the lungs, the tissue is said to be "supersaturated".

- If the blood or tissues become super-saturated, bubbles will begin to form.

- Nitrogen elimination is slowed down when bubbles are present.

- Most current decompression tables and dive computers assume gas uptake and elimination occur at identical rates. However, gas elimination often appears to be slower than uptake.

RECOMMENDED READING

Tikuisis P, Gerth WA. Decompression Theory In: Brubakk AO, Neuman TS (eds). The Physiology and Medicine of Diving, 5th edition. London: Saunders; 2003:41-54.

Vann RD, Thalmann ED. Decompression Physiology and Practice. In: Bennett PB, Elliott D (eds). The Physiology and Medicine of Diving (4th ed). London: WB Saunders Co; 1993:376-432.

Vann RD. Inert gas exchange and bubbles. In Bove AA (ed) Bove and Davis' Diving Medicine. Philadelphia: Saunders Publishers; 2004:53-76.

© Gary Bell

4

Bubble formation

THE PHYSICS OF THE BUBBLE

For a bubble to exist the total gaseous pressure within the bubble (P_{bubble}) must be equal to or greater than the crushing pressures exerted on it. These crushing pressures are:

1. The ambient pressure (P_{amb})

2. The pressure that the tissue exerts in resistance to deformation by the bubble (P_{tissue}). Localized falls in this tissue pressure may result from areas of turbulence and from tissue movements.

3. The pressure due to the surface tension at the gas / fluid interface of the bubble ($P_{tension}$). This pressure due to surface tension increases as the radius of the bubble decreases. Hence, smaller bubbles have greater surface tensions and vice versa. Very small bubbles are subjected to extremely high crushing pressures and tend to collapse, whereas larger bubbles have negligible surface tensions and are more stable.

Hence, for a bubble to exist:

$$P_{bubble} > P_{amb} + P_{tissue} + P_{tension}$$
$$(\text{equal to or greater than})$$

FIGURE 4.1

The forces acting on a bubble.

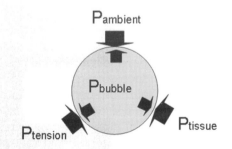

If P_{bubble} is greater than the crushing pressures, the bubble expands.

If P_{bubble} is equal to the crushing pressures, the bubble remains stable.

If P_{bubble} is less than the crushing pressures, the bubble is reduced in volume.

THEORIES OF BUBBLE
(GAS PHASE) FORMATION

Although it is inherently understood that supersaturation of tissues with inert gas is the key prerequisite to bubble formation after diving, the actual mechanism of bubble formation in this setting is something of a mystery. Physical theory predicts that the supersaturation required to spontaneously form bubbles in isolated fluids is far greater than can be generated following conventional scuba dives. This is because of the huge surface tension forces that a tiny bubble must overcome early in its growth (see above). However, as we know, bubbles do form after conventional scuba dives. Indeed, bubbles have been detected in divers after a saturation dive as shallow as 3.7m (12ft). There are a number of theories which attempt to explain this discrepancy between theory and reality. To date, no theory has been indisputably proven. The truth may lie in a combination of varies aspects of these theories.

One theory presumes that bubbles form afresh (de novo - i.e. where none existed before) due to localised and transient reductions in pressure induced by movement in tissues or by turbulent flow in blood. Such a mechanism is considered capable of producing gas in tissues even in the absence of gas supersaturation. For example, when you pull a finger and the knuckle pops, the pop is thought to be due to gas suddenly entering the vacuum created by the pulling.

Another theory suggests that tiny bubbles "micronuclei" (microscopic pockets of gas) are normally present within our bodies. These micronuclei avoid being crushed by surface tension forces by acquiring a layer of surfactant or detergent-like molecules from the surrounding tissue which reduce the surface tension at the gas fluid interface. When a nitrogen supersaturation arises after a dive, the excess gas diffuses into these nuclei, expanding them and creating

bubbles. Some theorists suggest that the nuclei are created by gas diffusing into low-pressure areas created by either the movement of surfaces over one another (tribonucleation), turbulence in the blood (Reynold's cavitation) or muscle activity. One intriguing aspect of this theory is that it might be possible to crush these micronuclei with an initial high pressure (deep) exposure. Experimental evidence in support of this theory first emerged when it was noted that the number of bubbles formed in water during decompression could be reduced by applying much greater pressures to the water before decompression. Pre-pressurizing the water was thought to crush the nuclei, forcing microbubble gas into solution and, hence, reducing the number of nuclei available to form bubbles. A similar procedure was tried on shrimps, which are transparent so bubbles are clearly seen, and on rats, and the pre-pressurization seemed to reduce the number of bubbles. Alternatively, it might be possible to consume bubble nuclei (faster than they can be replaced) by encouraging their growth and subsequent dissipation over a course of strategically spaced sequential dives. This latter mechanism is one potential explanation for the fall in the risk of decompression sickness (DCS) that is seen when dives are performed once daily over multiple days (sometimes referred to as "acclimatization").

A third theory relates to the existence of small defects in solid surfaces where bubbles can hide, and which avoids having their entire surface subject to the crushing pressure of fluid surface tension forces. Imagine that you are looking into a glass of beer, coca-cola or some other carbonated drink. The bubbles forming in the drink consist of carbon dioxide gas which comes out of solution when the top is removed. Looking closely at the bubbling drink, you might notice that bubbles only arise from the bottom or the sides of the glass. If a solid object is submerged into the drink, bubbles will also form on its surface. This is true as long as the drink is held still, but if the drink is shaken, new bubbles form from within the liquid itself, rather than only at points of contact with the glass.

Why do bubbles only form at tiny cracks or imperfections in the glass in the still drink?

It is argued that a small "nucleus" of gas is trapped in each of these cracks, and this nucleus resists being crushed. When the lid is removed and the excess dissolved gas begins to come out of solution, some gas diffuses into the bubble nucleus and expands its volume. Eventually, a bubble will form, break away, and leave the nucleus free to create another bubble. This process is shown in Figure 4.2.

FIGURE 4.2

Bubbles forming at a small crack in the wall of a container.

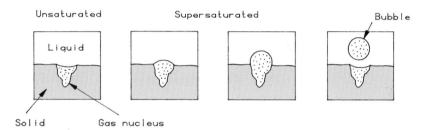

A fourth and related theory holds that bubbles might form more readily when at least some of their "skin" is in contact with a "non-wettable" or "hydrophobic" surface, many of which exist in the body. A non-wettable interface appears to facilitate the growth of bubbles, as it seems that less energy is required for bubbles to overcome surface tension forces at such an interface. Significantly, the walls of the cells that line capillaries have a hydrophobic layer of surfactant and one theory holds that the non-wettable nature of this surface may play an important part in allowing bubbles to form and grow.[1] A simple practical demonstration of this principle is seen when bubbles form readily around paraffin (a non-wettable surface) when it is submerged in soda water, no matter how well the paraffin has been cleaned (Figure 4.3). Bubbles also form at the interface between fat and certain solutions. Fat and paraffin are both non-wettable (hydrophobic) substances, as they repel water upon their surfaces.

FIGURE 4.3

Bubbles forming around a candle submerged in soda water.

Once a bubble exists, a reduction in the ambient pressure will cause further growth as the bubble will expand according to Boyle's law. In addition, any reduction in ambient pressure will further lower the solubility of inert gas in the surrounding tissue, thus increasing its tendency to diffuse into the bubble and expand it further.

One problem with bubble formation other than the production of DCS symptoms (discussed in Chapter 5) is that **the presence of bubbles slows down nitrogen elimination**. This is probably due to the different behaviour of nitrogen in its gas phase as opposed to its dissolved form. In other words, it takes longer to eliminate nitrogen once it has formed a bubble than it does if it remains dissolved. This complicates subsequent inert gas kinetic modeling. *There is evidence to suggest that bubbles can, at times, remain in a diver's body for days and even weeks after diving.*[2]

DETECTION OF BUBBLES

For obvious reasons, a means of detecting bubble formation is a potentially vital tool in developing accurate decompression strategies for use in diving. We can separate bubble detection technologies into those that aim to detect bubbles in tissue, and those that aim to detect bubbles in blood.

Electrical conductance studies have proved promising in detecting gas trapped in tissues. If gas bubbles form, or accumulate, in a tissue the electrical resistance through the tissue increases. X-ray studies can detect large pockets of tissue gas. Unfortunately, however, we still have no reliable and readily available means of detecting small bubbles forming in tissues.

In contrast, divers with an interest in medical issues and decompression science will frequently encounter the term "Doppler ultrasound" in relation to detection of bubbles in blood. We hear claims that "divers were monitored with Doppler", or that a particular dive table or computer has been "Doppler validated". Indeed, claims of such "Doppler validation" are often trundled out in debates over the relative merits of disparate decompression strategies. But what does it all mean?

The term "ultrasound" refers to very high frequency sound (usually 2 megahertz and above) which is well outside the range of normal human hearing. Such sound penetrates a fluid medium very readily and its main application in medicine is in organ imaging technologies. An ultrasound beam is applied at the body surface using a small wand held against the skin by the operator. The ultrasound penetrates inward, and as it passes through layers of tissue with differing composition and density, some of it is reflected and this is detected by a transducer back at the wand. The amount of sound reflected is related to the density of the tissue, and the delay in reflection is related to the depth at which it occurs. These two properties can be exploited to construct a two dimensional image of the tissues through which the sound is passing. It is both convenient and safe since minimal preparation is required, results are instantaneous, and no radiation is involved. However, ultrasound imaging has its limitations: ultrasound is poorly conducted in gas or air, so it cannot image within or through the lungs or other gas containing spaces. Similarly, it is not effective through thick bone.

Doppler ultrasound is a somewhat different technology. It utilises the "Doppler effect", named after the person who first discovered it. This is something most of us are familiar with. The classic description is of the train sounding its horn as it comes towards you, and the pitch of the horn suddenly changing as the train passes and heads away from you. The horn itself has not changed, but the sound you are hearing certainly does. This is because the wavelength of the sound emitted from a moving source is effectively shorter (thus the higher pitch) as the source moves towards you, and longer (thus the lower pitch) as it moves away. This is the Doppler effect.

Application of the Doppler effect in medicine is slightly different, because as you will see it is not the sound source that is moving, but the principle is similar. Most commonly, Doppler ultrasound is used to detect flow in blood vessels and the heart. Remember, blood is not like water - it has millions of microscopic particles in the form of red and white blood cells, and platelets. The presence of these cells works to our advantage because they reflect sound. If you aim an ultrasound beam at a segment of tissue with no blood flow through a major vessel, then some of the ultrasound is reflected back in a predictable and uniform manner. In contrast, if you aim an ultrasound beam at a large vessel in which there is flowing blood, then the ultrasound will be reflected by the moving blood cells, and the frequency of the reflected ultrasound beam will be influenced by that movement. If the cells are moving toward the ultrasound source, the reflected beam will be at a higher frequency, and if the cells are moving away from the ultrasound source, the reflected

beam will be at a lower frequency in accordance with the Doppler effect. Moreover, the speed of the blood cell movement will influence the difference in frequency between the initial and reflected ultrasound beams. So, for example, if blood is flowing very rapidly toward the ultrasound source, the reflected ultrasound beam will be at a significantly higher frequency. All of this can be summarised by saying that ultrasound is reflected by particles moving in a liquid at a shifted frequency proportional to the velocity of the particles. As you might imagine, this application of ultrasound and the Doppler effect to detect flow in blood vessels has a variety of uses in medicine. Most devices built for this purpose produce an audible flow output that in pulsatile flow (such as in a blood vessel) produces a "whooshing noise", and some provide a depiction of flow velocity versus time in graphical format (see Figure 4.4).

FIGURE 4.4

Screen from a Doppler device that provides a graphical flow display as well as an audible output.

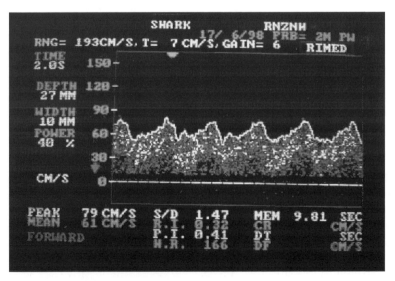

This screen was photographed during monitoring of a patient's right carotid artery during cardiac surgery. The horizontal axis represents time, and the vertical axis represents blood flow velocity through the vessel. The fact that the trace has peaks and troughs suggests the pulsatile nature of the flow. The sound obtained during recording would best be described as a "...whoosh, whoosh, whoosh..." corresponding with each of the peaks.

The link with diving medicine comes from the ability of Doppler ultrasound technology to detect bubbles moving in blood vessels. Bubbles have markedly different ultrasound reflective properties to blood cells. Thus, when a bubble enters the ultrasound beam it is not surprising that it causes a dramatic, instantaneous disturbance of the ultrasound signal. This is manifest as an audible harmonic "chirp" or "pop", and a perturbation of the flow velocity / time display (see Figure 4.5). Thus, the development of Doppler ultrasound technology has enabled us to monitor flow through blood vessels, and to detect the presence of bubbles in those vessels after diving.

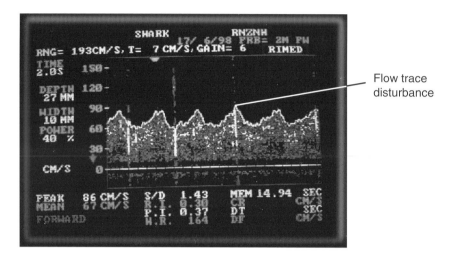

Flow trace disturbance

FIGURE 4.5

Same patient as Figure 1, showing three flow trace disturbances characteristic of the passage of a bubble. With the appearance of each of these disturbances there was a harmonic chirp-like sound, which is also characteristic of a bubble.

FIGURE 4.6

Diver being monitored for bubbles with a Precordial Doppler Monitor.

There have been numerous attempts to accurately count circulating bubbles using Doppler ultrasound. In non-diving applications, such as the detection of bubbles in the cerebral circulation during cardiac surgery, devices have been developed that automatically derive a count from the Doppler shifted signal. In diving applications the most common approach has been to monitor the central venous circulation (near the heart) after diving using small portable systems that produce an audible signal (see Figure 4.6), and to employ grading systems to quantify the bubbles detected.

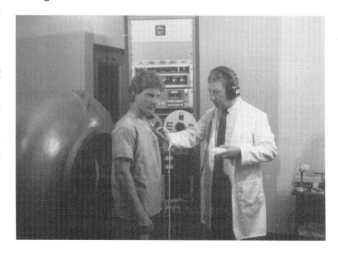

TABLE 4.1

The Spencer grading system for quantification of bubble activity.

0 = no gas bubbles detected in at least 10 heart cycles

1 = occasional gas bubbles detected in 10 heart cycles

2 = few bubbles detectable; some cycles may have 2 to 4 bubbles per cycle

3 = several gas bubbles detectable per cycle

4 = gas bubbles present continuously (systole and diastole), gas bubble amplitude louder than flow sounds.

As most will be aware, decompression from most dives causes a degree of bubble formation in the veins. It is generally accepted that the numbers of these bubbles are an indicator of both the decompression stress (more decompression stress is likely to produce more bubbles) and the probability of decompression sickness (DCS) developing (higher numbers of bubbles are more likely to result in DCS). This has resulted great significance being attached to the Doppler detection of these bubbles. In part, this is appropriate, but the significance of Doppler-detected venous bubbles is often over-called by commentators who do not have a thorough understanding of the confounding issues. These issues relate to the detection technology itself, and also to the significance of these venous bubbles.

With regard to the technology itself, it is important to understand that interpretation of the sounds obtained by portable Doppler devices, and the application of bubble grading systems is quite subjective. Accuracy is highly influenced by the experience and expertise of the operator, as well as their potential bias if they are involved in a project with a "point to prove". The timing of monitoring is important. If monitoring is conducted either very early or several hours after diving then the peak of venous bubbling may be missed. Indeed, a diver with obvious symptoms of DCS who presents late may have no venous bubbles detected at all. Other important influences on bubble detection include the duration of monitoring, and the nature of the monitoring device.

With regard to the significance of the bubbles themselves, there are a few problems. Bubbles are commonly detected in the veins following dives that do not produce DCS. While the risk of developing DCS does appear to be greater following those dives that produce high bubble grades, a significant proportion of such dives still do not result in obvious problems. It follows that Doppler bubble detection is certainly not a valid diagnostic test for DCS, and high bubble grades on Doppler in the absence of DCS symptoms would not be an indication for recompression treatment. The uncertain relationship between Doppler detected bubbles and DCS may relate to the fact that Doppler detects bubbles in veins, whereas many of the symptoms of DCS almost certainly have nothing to do with bubbles forming in the veins. For example, the typical musculoskeletal pain of DCS, and spinal manifestations are most likely to be related to bubbles forming within the tissues themselves, and there are currently no readily available technologies that easily detect such bubbles.

To summarise all of this, while Doppler bubble detection is and will continue to be a useful tool in comparing various decompression strategies, the significance of venous bubbles detected by Doppler is not as great as it might intuitively appear. Doppler will continue to be used by the developers of dive tables and computers as a barometer of decompression stress but any claims along the lines of "safety proven by Doppler" need to be interpreted with caution.

ATTEMPTS TO PREVENT OR CONTROL BUBBLE FORMATION

It has been known for a long time that decompression sickness is caused by bubbles formed from nitrogen (or another inert gas) dissolved in the blood and tissues during a dive. Early researchers believed that during ascent the partial pressure of inert gas dissolved in a tissue had to exceed the ambient pressure (i.e. the tissue is **supersaturated**) by some critical amount before bubble formation occurred. Some believed that this critical amount was best described as a ratio (for example, the tissue gas pressure could "safely" rise as high as twice the ambient pressure), while a subsequent approach was to estimate a critical degree of supersaturation (expressed as an absolute pressure) for each tissue at each depth that should not be exceeded (see below) if bubble formation was to be avoided. Decompression guidelines were therefore designed to avoid exceeding this degree of supersaturation. With the advent of Doppler technology capable of detecting bubbles in venous blood (see above), it became clear that bubbles actually formed with very small supersaturations, and that the critical degrees of supersaturation that

tables were designed to avoid probably defined a threshold amount of bubble formation likely to cause DCS symptoms, rather than determining the presence or absence of bubbles per se.

This revelation did little to dampen enthusiasm for using critical levels of supersaturation as a guide for developing decompression algorithms. It seemed to matter little whether the algorithm controlled bubble formation or development of DCS symptoms, so long as the latter remained a rare event if the algorithm was followed. The practical application of such theories can be illustrated by reference to the US Navy concept of "M-values" and how they are used to control an ascent. M-values are essentially the critical tissue nitrogen pressures mentioned above that should not be exceeded in each tissue at each depth during ascent. If we refer back to the type of depiction we used in Figure 3.4 in the previous chapter, but consider the events in only one tissue, it will help us understand this concept (see Figure 4.7 and its caption).

© Euiook Jung

FIGURE 4.7

i.

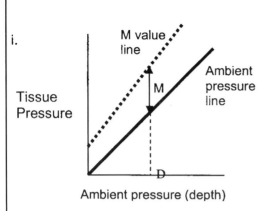

ii.

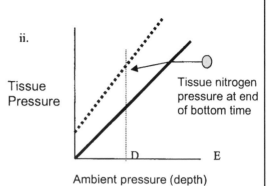

Remember that in all figures, the "ambient pressure line" represents the point at each depth (ambient pressure) where the tissue pressure of nitrogen equals the ambient pressure. You can revise this in Figure 3.4.

In *(i)* the M-value line (dotted) represents the tissue nitrogen pressures that should not be exceeded for this particular tissue during ascent through the range of depths. Thus, the decompression modeler knows that at depth D the maximum allowable tissue pressure of nitrogen is shown where the top of the double ended arrow "M" intersects the M-value line. You can see that the double ended arrow itself represents the amount of supersaturation permitted in that tissue at depth D. It is termed the "M-value gradient".

In *(ii)* we start at the grey dot which represents the tissue nitrogen pressure that has accumulated over a period at depth E. Now, watch what happens during our ascent (arrowed line). Obviously, the ambient pressure falls relatively quickly as we ascend but tissue nitrogen pressure does not. It crosses the ambient pressure line (which marks the point where tissue nitrogen pressure = ambient pressure) and the tissue is now supersaturated with nitrogen. As the ascent continues, although some nitrogen is being lost from the tissue, its nitrogen pressure quickly approaches the M-value line. If the tissue nitrogen pressure is allowed to exceed the M-value, then dangerous bubble formation might occur and so a stop is needed at depth D.

iii

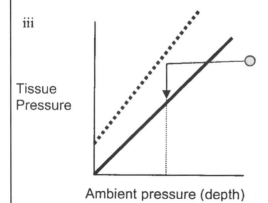

iv

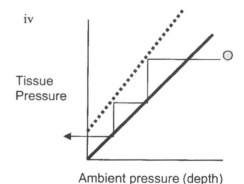

In *(iii)* we see the effect of imposing a stop in the ascent. Ambient pressure (depth) does not change, but there is now time for the tissue pressure of nitrogen to fall so that the ascent can be resumed safely.

In *(iv)* we see how the ascent is made with a series of decompression stops which prevent the tissue nitrogen pressure from exceeding the M-value at any point until the surface is reached.

FIGURE 4.7
(continued)

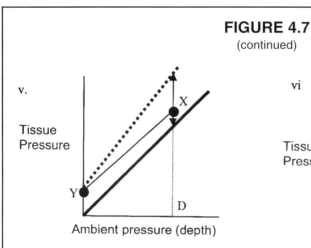

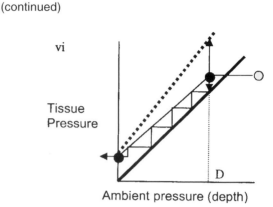

In (v) we see a depiction of a recent trend towards modifying decompression algorithms using "gradient factors". It is reasoned that normal inert gas kinetics can best be preserved and risk of DCS minimized by minimizing bubble formation. It has been deduced that allowing ascent to proceed until a tissue reaches its M-value supersaturation may allow too much bubble formation even though the risk of clinical DCS is still low. Thus, an empirical fashion for using "gradient factors" has evolved whereby a decompression modeler might elect to allow a tissue to only reach a supersaturation value of 0.25 x the M-value gradient (double ended arrow) early in the ascent. In this case, 0.25 is the "gradient factor" and this point is approximately

shown for depth D in the diagram at point X. The modeler might choose to allow a greater supersaturation on arrival at the surface, for example, a gradient factor of 0.8, and this is shown at point Y. The line between points X and Y represents a modified M-value line across which there will be a gradual change in gradient factors.

In (vi) we see an ascent controlled according to this modified gradient factor line. You can see that in practical terms, this approach imposes deeper decompression stops and smaller supersaturations than would occur if allowing ascent until a tissue reaches its classical M-value.

The above approach to the generation of decompression algorithms remains popular today, and those tables or computers incorporating this type of logic are loosely grouped into a subset of so-called "neo-Haldanian" decompression tools. The first set of M-values were published by Dr R.D. Workman of the US Navy in the 1960s, but the most widely utilized M-values in the modern context are those published by the Swiss physiologist Dr AA Bühlmann. See Section 2 for more information on decompression algorithms.

A process that helps to reduce bubble formation is that of the so-called **inherent unsaturation** (frequently referred to the as the "Oxygen Window"*).

As the blood is transported throughout the body, oxygen is unloaded into various tissues. The body uses more oxygen than it produces carbon dioxide and, because the carbon dioxide produced is more soluble than the oxygen, more of it remains

---

* A further description of the practical application of the Oxygen Window in the treatment is explained in Chapter 5.

dissolved. The result is that the total pressure (tension) of the gas in the tissues and in the venous blood is less than the ambient pressure. Therefore, the venous blood and tissues are said to be "unsaturated" and the amount of this unsaturation can be shown to be about 60mmHg (0.08Ats). This unsaturation provides an inherent safety margin during decompression. It appears that one can ascend a distance which is equivalent to a pressure reduction of 60mmHg (i.e. 0.8msw / 2.6fsw) before the inert gas tension in the tissue begins to exceed the ambient pressure, resulting in supersaturation of the tissue.

This unsaturation of the venous blood and tissues provides a carrying capacity for excess nitrogen during decompression. Also, since any bubbles formed are at ambient pressure (which is higher than the tissue or venous pressure), gas will tend to move from the bubbles into the venous blood, helping to resolve the bubbles.

REFERENCES

1. Hills B. Bubble Growth in Biological Systems. *SPUMS J* 1990; 20(1): 65-70.
2. Acott CJ, Gorman DF. Decompression illness and nitrous oxide anaesthesia in a sports diver. *Anaesth Intensive Care* 1992; 20: 249-50.

OTHER SOURCES

Vann RD, Thalmann ED. Decompression Physiology and Practice. In: *The Physiology and Medicine of Diving (4th ed)*. Bennett P, Elliott D (Eds), WB Saunders Co: London; 1993:376-432.

SUMMARY

- A tissue is said to be "supersaturated" when the pressure of inert gas in the tissue is greater than the ambient pressure.

- The developers of many of the early tables assumed that the partial pressure of inert gas in a tissue can exceed ambient pressure by some amount before bubbles form.

- Most experts now believe that bubbles will form whenever the partial pressure of inert gas in a tissue exceeds the ambient pressure by any amount and that decompression tables aim to prevent the formation of *symptomatic* bubbles rather than the formation of bubbles per se.

- For a bubble to exist the total gaseous pressure within the bubble must be equal to, or greater than, the crushing pressures exerted on it.

- There are a number of theories describing bubble formation in the body. However, no theory has as yet been indisputably proven.

- It is possible that bubbles may form readily at the interface of the blood and blood vessels.

- The presence of bubbles slows down nitrogen elimination.

- Doppler ultrasonic bubble detectors can only detect circulating bubbles and not those trapped in the tissues.

© Michael Aw

5

Decompression illness

5.1 TERMINOLOGY, HISTORY, MECHANISMS, MANIFESTATIONS AND MANAGEMENT

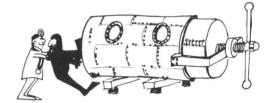

Cartoon Dr. Bart McKenzie

TERMINOLOGY

Unfortunately, it is necessary to begin this chapter by explaining confusing terminology issues that have arisen in relation to bubble-related diving diseases.

As will be explained in more detail later, there are two important mechanisms that may result in bubble formation during or after ascent from a compressed gas dive.

First, if air is trapped in the lungs during ascent it will expand and may cause damage to the lungs (pulmonary barotrauma), possibly introducing bubbles into the arterial blood.

Second, bubbles may form from dissolved nitrogen (or another inert gas in mixed gas diving) in the tissues themselves and in venous blood.

Both of these processes are discussed in much more detail later, but the salient point here is that there are two quite distinct mechanisms in diving that can give rise to bubble-induced problems. The symptoms that arise as a result of these two respective mechanisms have some potentially distinctive features, but not surprisingly they also have much in common.

This has given rise to confusing terminology. Prior to 1990, those problems caused by the formation of bubbles from dissolved nitrogen were referred to as **decompression sickness (DCS)**. Decompression sickness was further classified as either Type I (musculoskeletal pain only) or Type II (neurological manifestations). Those problems caused by introduction of bubbles to the arterial blood by pulmonary barotrauma were referred to as **cerebral arterial gas embolism (CAGE** or just **AGE)**.

Divers were diagnosed as suffering either "DCS" or "CAGE" based on the assumption that it was possible to distinguish between the symptoms of nitrogen bubble formation in tissues and veins (DCS), and of the introduction of air bubbles to the arterial circulation by pulmonary barotrauma (CAGE). This distinction was based on the essential truth that CAGE almost invariably arose within minutes (if not seconds) after ascent from a dive, and the symptom pattern strongly indicated arterial bubbles being carried to the brain.

However, the assumption that rapid onset brain problems were invariably related to pulmonary barotrauma was challenged in the late 1980s when it became clear that bubbles formed in the veins from dissolved nitrogen could reach the arterial circulation across a patent foramen ovale (PFO) in the heart (see Chapter 2). It is also possible, although currently unproven in humans, that the rapid delivery of bubbles to, and consequent overloading of, the pulmonary circulation may result in some bubbles passing directly into the arterial circulation. Such bubbles then (theoretically) behave like the arterial bubbles introduced by lung barotrauma. Thus, in this way the "DCS" process could, in theory, produce "CAGE" symptoms.

With this established, it was not surprising that several surveys demonstrated poor agreement between diving physicians in allocation of a 'diagnosis' (DCS or AGE) to ambiguous cases. Many diving physicians considered it nonsensical to have a classification system that separated DCS and CAGE when it was sometimes not clear in an actual patient which one was causing the problem. Hence the *collective* term **"decompression illness" (DCI)** was coined to <u>encompass both DCS and CAGE</u>.

"DCI" was proposed as more appropriate when discussing patients where it might not be possible to distinguish the underlying cause. Indeed, the diagnosis of DCI implies no assumption about the underlying source of bubbles. These interrelationships

FIGURE 5.1.1

Inter-relationships between DCI, DCS, and CAGE.

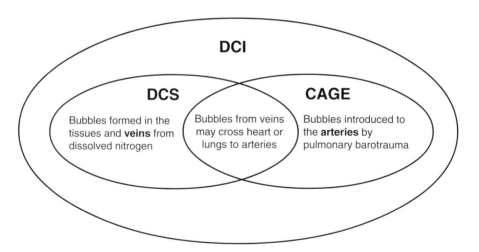

between bubble processes and terms are illustrated in Figure 5.1.1.

Notwithstanding its widespread use and the fact that it makes sense, the use of "DCI", has created as many problems as it has solved.

To begin with, the choice of the term "DCI" for the collective diagnosis was unfortunate because it is so similar to the old term DCS.

This has led many people (including physicians) who lack insight into this background to use the terms DCS and DCI interchangeably. Often this does not really matter, but sometimes it creates confusion. Secondly, although use of the system has gained considerable momentum in diving medicine circles, it remains controversial and terminology is a constant source of bickering among authorities in the field. Finally, a term that does not imply a mechanism is inadequate when discussing or inferring mechanisms of disease (as we frequently do in this Chapter and the rest of the book) or when referring to those cases where the underlying mechanism is reliably known.

Most of these problems could be solved if clinicians or commentators utilized the term DCS and CAGE when wishing to refer specifically to bubble formation from dissolved inert gas or pulmonary barotrauma respectively, and the term DCI to refer to the broad spectrum of bubble related symptoms that may arise from both DCS and CAGE. Thus, to summarize, the appropriate use of the various terms is as follows:

Decompression illness (DCI): Used in clinical discussion (i.e. discussion of patients) where no distinction between bubble formation from dissolved inert gas or bubble introduction by pulmonary barotrauma is possible or implied.

Decompression sickness (DCS): Used when there is a need to specifically refer to the process of bubble formation from dissolved inert gas.

Cerebral arterial gas embolism (CAGE): Used when there is a need to specifically refer to the process of bubble introduction to arterial blood by pulmonary barotrauma (i.e. air embolism).

We will try to use these conventions through this book.

HISTORICAL PERSPECTIVE

Perhaps the first of the great diving medicine innovators was Robert Boyle, the English physicist who gave us Boyle's law to agonize over as diving students.

In 1667, essentially before "diving" was even known, Boyle discovered DCS. He observed that a snake (a "viper" to be precise) became very distressed when the air was "exhausted" from the "receiver" in which it resided. This in itself is perhaps not so surprising. Most animals would become agitated if placed in a vacuum. But Boyle's additional observation of "a very apparent bubble moving from side to side in the aqueous humor of the eye" during this decompression was more intriguing. This was the first recorded observation of the bubble formation that leads to DCS.

Diving was only in its infancy at this time. Rebreathing from air-filled bags had been tried, but while this served to exercise the respiratory muscles it did little to sustain the diver underwater. The combined unpleasant effects of hypoxia and CO_2 accumulation soon forced the diver to the surface. As a child, one of the authors (SJM) became familiar with this problem (though with no true understanding), after many frustrating attempts to make prolonged observations of the bath plug using goggles while rebreathing from a hot water bottle.

One of the earliest serious attempts at "diving" was perpetrated in 1690 by the multitalented Edmund Halley (of comet fame), who constructed a diving bell that was lowered to the sea floor and resupplied with air from weighted barrels! It is reported that this apparatus was used to perform dives as deep as 18m (60ft) for up to 90 minutes. If DCI ever occurred as a result of these adventures, it was never recorded. Indeed, DCI was not described with any regularity in humans until some 150 years later.

During the 1700s diving technology continued to develop, with English and

I'VE GOT THE BENDS!!

French engineers independently developing diving apparatus that allowed diving with air supplied from the surface. However, the limited depth and duration achieved using these devices meant that DCI was rarely, if ever recorded. However, in the late 1700s, there were developments that finally extended man's underwater capabilities to such extent that he was able to get himself into trouble. An English engineer called Smeaton perfected a pump that was capable of pressurising a caisson system sufficiently to keep water out and allow meaningful work at depth. A caisson is essentially an upside down container that sits on the bottom and is pressurised to keep water out. Its occupants can perform work on the sea floor without actually wearing diving dress, although they are under pressure. This same improvement in air pump technology also paved the way for development of superior surface supplied diving helmets and suits.

Thus, in the early 1800s there was an explosion in underwater construction and salvage work, and problems began to be recorded. In the early 1840s divers involved in salvage operations on the British warship HMS Royal George reported suffering "cold and rheumatism", with the rheumatism at least almost certainly a symptom of DCS. Around this time Caisson workers involved in bridge construction projects in the USA were suffering more severe forms of the same affliction. Indeed, 30 of 352 workers employed in the Eade Bridge project at St Louis were seriously injured (paralysis) and 13 died. These problems in caisson workers gave rise to the terms "caisson disease" (rarely used today) and "the bends" (which is still commonly employed). Apparently the painful gait adopted by victims of mild DCS resembled the fashionable "Grecian Bend" style of walking adopted by the ladies of the period. Hence DCS became known as "the bends". In 1841, Frenchmen Pol and Wattelle observed that these unpleasant symptoms could be relieved by recompression. In their case, this initially took the form of returning to work; a unique way of minimizing absenteeism was to get your workers mildly bent!

Despite the magnitude of these problems, DCS was poorly understood. Indeed, it was not clearly linked to bubble formation until the 1870s when another Frenchman, Paul Bert, published a 1000 page work "La Pression Barometrique" describing a variety of experiments into the physiology of decompression. He showed that DCS was caused by formation of nitrogen bubbles, and thereby finally provided the link between Boyle's observation of bubble formation in the unfortunate snake's eye and this recently discovered disease. Bert also made several other important observations. First, he suggested that a gradual ascent was likely to prevent the problem; and second, he too noted that pain could be relieved with recompression. Caisson projects of the era began to use recompression in chambers while breathing air (rather than "on the job" recompression) to treat DCS.

But back to diving. In 1906, concerns over the incidence of DCS drove the British Government to commission John Scott Haldane, a Scottish physiologist, to investigate preventative strategies. Following up on Bert's observation that slower ascents prevented the problem, Haldane and his co-workers used goats to test various decompression protocols, resulting in the publication in 1908 (Journal of Hygiene) of the first set of true decompression tables for diving. The tables revolutionized diving safety, with the incidence of DCS dropping in whatever diving operation they were used for. These tables, and the physiological principals underpinning them, have formed the basis for many subsequent modifications and developments, right through to the present day. With regard to treatment of DCS, it is perhaps staggering to reflect on the fact that the only major step forward that has been taken since this time was the introduction of oxygen breathing during recompression; a strategy introduced in the mid 1930s.

In the modern context, few subjects are more central to diving medicine than decompression illness, the most important diving medical disorder. Diving physicians are frequently asked questions about this subject by curious divers. This is not surprising. We are all taught about the disorder and its potentially serious consequences during diver training courses, but the treatment given to the subject by the diver training organizations is relatively superficial. Recognizing its importance, many divers want to know more; those few extra details that might help them improve their diving practice, make things a little safer, or simply satisfy their curiosity. In this chapter, we will discuss the sources of the bubbles that are the central cause of this puzzling disorder, we will examine how these bubbles cause damage, and what symptoms result. We will discuss the various potential risk factors for decompression illness, and how the risk can be minimized. Finally, we will discuss the treatment of DCI.

THE MECHANISMS AND MANIFESTATIONS OF DECOMPRESSION ILLNESS

A simple definition

Decompression illness is a disorder caused by bubbles forming in blood or tissues, or being introduced into or in the blood. These bubbles cause damage by a variety of mechanisms which are described later.

There are two potential sources of bubbles, and, as mentioned earlier, even though these sources are quite distinct (see below), we refer to the adverse effects of bubbles from either source under the "umbrella" term "decompression illness" (DCI). As previously mentioned, this is because, of the frequent difficulty in distinguishing which source of bubbles has caused a victim's problem.

Bubbles can form in tissues and venous blood from dissolved gas

As mentioned in our discussion of terminology, the consequences of bubbles formed in this way are referred to as decompression sickness. The mechanisms underlying the formation of bubbles from dissolved nitrogen (or other dissolved inert gases) were discussed in detail in the previous chapter, but some key points relevant to an understanding of DCS are reiterated here. Take a few moments to study the very simplified human circulation diagram (Figure 5.1.2) and read the explanatory caption. During a dive, the nitrogen enters the blood in the lung capillary bed (top of diagram), and after passing through the left heart, is distributed to the tissues via the arteries. When blood reaches the capillary beds of the various body tissues, nitrogen leaves the blood and diffuses into these tissues. The deeper the dive, the faster the nitrogen is taken up from the air we breathe, and the longer the dive, the more time it has to accumulate in the tissues.

During the subsequent ascent, pressure falls and less nitrogen can remain dissolved in the tissues. Therefore, the nitrogen diffuses out of tissues and into the blood passing through the capillary beds of the various body tissues (see Fig 5.1.2). It is carried in the veins back to the lungs for elimination. Ideally, this elimination process occurs fast enough to dissipate the nitrogen molecules from tissues without bubble formation. However, in all but the very fast tissues, the pressure of dissolved nitrogen will exceed the ambient (surrounding) pressure at some point during the ascent ("supersaturation") and bubbles may form. As a rule, very fast tissues are quite resistant to bubble formation because although they take up nitrogen quickly, they usually get rid of it quickly enough to prevent bubble formation, so long as the ascent is made at the correct rate. *It's the medium – fast tissues, such as spinal cord white matter, that often cause the problem in typical short duration*

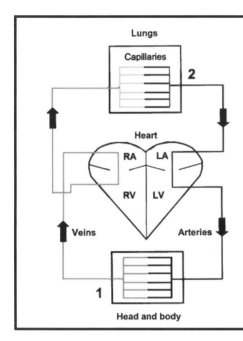

FIGURE 5.1.2

The human circulation.

RA = right atrium, LA = left atrium, RV = right ventricle, LV = left ventricle. Bubbles evolving from dissolved nitrogen during decompression are found in the in the veins since venous blood is carrying nitrogen from the tissues of the head and body back to the lungs to be expired. The first network of small blood vessels that may trap these bubbles is the capillary bed of the lungs. Pressure damage to the lungs (pulmonary barotrauma) introduces bubbles from the alveoli directly into the arterial side of the circulation. These bubbles may be distributed to almost anywhere around the head and body and may trap in the capillary bed of whichever tissue they enter. See text for explanation of numbers 1 and 2.

recreational dives. They can accumulate a large nitrogen load reasonably quickly, but might not lose it quickly enough during the ascent, especially if the bottom time was long and the ascent a little fast. *"Slower" tissues such as tendons are often not a problem after a short dive, even if it is deep, because they don't have enough time to accumulate significant quantities of nitrogen. However, they become more important during long dives, or repetitive dives, when nitrogen can build up over a long time.* Of course, these are the very considerations that our dive tables and computers are designed to take into account.

Bubble formation from dissolved gas can occur both within the tissues themselves and in the blood. Here's an important point: bubbles forming in the blood do so in the capillaries and veins leaving the head and body circulation (see point 1 in Figure 5.1.2). If we think about it carefully this is not surprising since, during ascent, the nitrogen molecules from the tissues will move in accordance with the concentration gradient between the tissues and the lungs to be eliminated as described earlier. They enter the blood in the capillary beds of the head

and body and the prevalent conditions of slow flow, low pressure and high nitrogen pressures appears to favour bubble formation there. These bubbles are then carried back to the right side of the heart in the veins (follow it on the diagram) and then to the capillary bed of the lungs.

The lung capillary bed is the first network of small blood vessels where bubbles in the veins are likely to be trapped. Indeed, *the lung appears to be a good filter for venous bubbles*, and seems able to tolerate a significant number of its capillaries being obstructed by bubbles without adverse effects. A diver usually will not experience any symptoms from the bubbles trapped in the lung circulation until they cause significant obstruction to flow. Once trapped, the gas gradually diffuses from the bubbles, across into the alveoli, and the bubbles eventually disappear. This is fortunate since without this "lung capillary filter" many of these bubbles might find their way into the arterial circulation where they can potentially do more harm (see later). The fact that blood bypasses the lungs in the circulation of a foetus (and is therefore not filtered in this way), is one of the concerns over diving during pregnancy.

Bubbles don't form from dissolved gas in the arteries since once the nitrogen-laden venous blood has passed through the lungs into the arterial circulation, the pressure of dissolved nitrogen has equilibrated with the nitrogen pressure in the alveoli and there is no supersaturation.

Bubbles can be introduced to the arterial blood by pressure damage to the lungs (pulmonary barotrauma)

As mentioned in our discussion of terminology, the consequences of bubbles formed in this way are often referred to as cerebral arterial gas embolism (CAGE). This has nothing to do with dissolved nitrogen, or time and depth for that matter. Indeed, this problem can arise during ascent from depths as shallow as 1 to 2 metres (3.3 to 6.6 feet) after very brief dives.

Open water trainees are always taught that the most important rule in scuba diving is "to breathe normally at all times; never hold your breath". This is because any air trapped in the lungs (by holding the breath for example) during an ascent will expand as pressure decreases. If there is sufficient over-expansion of the lung, it may rupture some of the delicate alveoli and the associated blood vessels. Such damage is referred to as *pulmonary barotrauma*. This, in turn, may result in the introduction of air to the lung capillary circulation (point 2 on in Figure 5.1.2). These bubbles are then carried back to the left side of the heart from whence they are pumped out into the arteries. You can see from the circulation diagram that the first network of small blood vessels where these bubbles are likely to trap is the capillary beds of various tissues in the head and body. Some of the organs potentially affected in this way, such as the brain, are much less tolerant of bubbles in blood vessels than are the lungs (which readily filter bubbles from the veins as we mentioned above). Indeed, bubbles arriving

in the circulation of the brain may cause stroke-like symptoms (see later). These arterial bubbles are therefore considered very dangerous.

Venous bubbles can become arterial bubbles

Considering that the lungs remove nitrogen bubbles formed in the veins, while arterial bubbles can block blood and/or damage vessels in vital structures such as the brain, it might seem fair to conclude that the bubbles forming from dissolved nitrogen in the veins are less dangerous than bubbles introduced to the arteries by lung barotrauma. However, as mentioned in Chapter 2, there is evidence that if the diver has a patent foramen ovale (PFO), it may allow venous nitrogen bubbles to cross into the arterial circulation, bypassing the lung capillary "filter" (see Figure 5.1.3). You may recall that a PFO is a communication between the two upper chambers of the heart which usually closes at birth. When venous nitrogen bubbles cross a PFO the "arterialized" bubbles can, in theory, cause the same problems as air bubbles introduced to the arteries by pulmonary barotrauma.

There is increasing evidence that this is a significant issue. In a study at Duke University, the hearts of 30 divers who suffered from DCI were examined by two-dimensional echocardiography. Eleven of these divers were found to have a patent foramen ovale. These 11 divers were among the 18 divers who had the more serious, neurological symptoms of decompression illness.[1] A British study detected shunts in 15 of 63 (24%) of control divers with no history of DCI, 41% of 61 divers who had suffered DCI, and 66% of 19 patients who had suffered early onset neurological DCI.[2] More recently, the same research group demonstrated a medium to large PFO in 52% of 100 divers with neurological DCI compared to 12.2% of diver controls who had not suffered DCI.[3] These data strongly suggest that a patent foramen ovale,

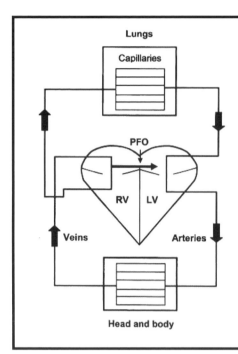

Lungs
Capillaries
PFO
RV   LV
Veins   Arteries
Head and body

FIGURE 5.1.3

The human circulation showing a persistent patent foramen ovale (PFO).

Compare this to Figure 5.1.2. In this situation a communication exists between the right and left atria of the heart, and blood may potentially move from the venous side of the circulation to the arterial side (see central arrow). This "shunting" blood may carry venous bubbles that would normally be filtered out by the capillary bed of the lungs into the arterial circulation where they are potentially more dangerous. In reality, most PFOs are small and may shunt very little, if at all. Small PFOs are of doubtful significance in diving, but there is a clear association between large shunting PFOs and DCI.

especially a large PFO, may impose a greater risk of serious neurological DCI.

The combined results of these studies and others published subsequently seem to indicate that *the presence of a large PFO, does predispose a diver to severe neurological DCI*. However, these observations must be balanced against the observation that the prevalence of PFO in the general diving population is probably somewhere between 20-30% (similar to that for the general population), and yet severe neurological DCI remains a relatively uncommon event. Not surprisingly, there is currently debate about the desirability and feasibility of testing for a PFO during the diving medical examination. The test is costly and there is a small associated risk since the test itself involves injecting microbubbles into the circulation. The current weight of opinion is that general screening of all prospective divers for a PFO is <u>not</u> justified, but divers with serious neurological DCI are frequently tested, especially if their DCI followed relatively unprovocative dives. Diving candidates with a known PFO are usually discouraged from diving.

Not all bubbles cause problems

As was discussed in Chapter 4, there is now a mass of evidence, mainly from Doppler studies of bubbles in the veins, suggesting that most dives result in bubble formation. Interestingly, in the vast majority of cases this does not produce symptoms or cause harm to the diver, and accordingly, this phenomenon is commonly referred to as *"silent bubbling"*. Even *in contemporary recreational diving using modern dive computers and techniques, a significant proportion of divers exhibit detectable venous bubbles after diving.*[4] The reason for bubble formation becoming symptomatic as opposed to "silent" is not clearly established, but problems are almost certainly more likely if there are more bubbles, they are larger, or they are forming in vital tissues. In addition, it seems likely that susceptibility to a given degree of bubbling may vary between individuals, or within individuals from day to day. The reason(s) for this is not clear either, but variation in the vigour of some of the harmful immune response processes initiated by bubbles (see below) may be important.

Problems caused by bubble formation in blood

Bubbles formed in blood, be it arterial or venous blood, are recognized as "foreign matter" and their presence turns on a variety of the body's inflammatory processes. These are designed to lead the way in attacking foreign invaders such as bacteria, but unfortunately, they serve little useful purpose in the presence of bubbles. Indeed, a vigorous inflammatory response may actually be harmful. For example, the release of certain chemicals by activated blood cells may cause leakiness in blood vessel walls, and loss of plasma from the blood into the surrounding tissues. This, in turn, may cause the blood to become thicker and to circulate less efficiently through the very small blood vessels. In addition, bubbles can initiate a clotting response, and if this gathers momentum and becomes widespread the victim can become very sick indeed.

Thankfully, these dangerous inflammatory and clotting processes appear only in the most serious of DCI cases. Indeed, although animal studies have produced a mass of evidence suggesting that these processes are important in DCS (in particular), most of the experiments have involved diving exposures that are much more provocative, and DCS that is much more severe than seen in the vast majority of human cases. The relevance to human disease is thus very uncertain (though see the next paragraph). *Perhaps the most common symptom of DCS that can be plausibly related to bubble-induced inflammation is fatigue and malaise similar to the early symptoms of flu-like illnesses which also activate inflammatory processes.*

There is one particular site in which the initiation of clotting may be very important in human DCS, and that is in the veins that drain the spinal cord. Flow through these vessels is particularly slow and because of a lack of one way valves, it can reverse direction. These veins may be abnormally vulnerable to both bubble formation and clotting as a result. Thus, one mechanism by which the spinal cord may be damaged in DCS is by the formation of bubbles and stimulation of clotting in its veins. This might cause the movement of blood through the spinal circulation to be impaired, and the spinal cord to be damaged as a result. This so-called "venous infarction" hypothesis for spinal cord DCS is one of several competing theories to explain this frequently devastating form of the disease. The symptoms of spinal cord DCS are discussed later.

Once introduced into blood, bubbles tend to move with the flow until they enter a blood vessel that is small enough to trap them. The fate of venous and arterial bubbles is somewhat different in this regard.

Venous bubbles

In the case of bubbles formed from dissolved nitrogen in the veins, trapping will occur in the capillary beds of the lungs. As mentioned earlier, it is fortunate that the lungs appear to be an efficient filter for venous bubbles since this prevents the majority of them getting through to the arterial side of the circulation. However, if there are sufficient bubbles entering the lung capillary bed over a short period, this can cause *cough, a feeling of chest discomfort and shortness of breath*; often referred to as "the chokes". If this is to happen, it usually does so within the first 30 minutes after a dive. Symptoms of pulmonary (lung) DCS are considered an ominous sign because if there are sufficient bubbles entering the lung circulation to cause this problem it usually means that there are many bubbles forming in other places, and that other symptoms are not far behind. In particular, pulmonary symptoms often precede the development of spinal DCS, and this would hardly be surprising since the presence of sufficient venous bubbles to cause pulmonary symptoms would likely indicate the presence of large numbers of bubbles in the veins of spinal cord. In this setting, the risk of a "venous infarction" event as described above would be high.

Arterial bubbles

As you can see from Figure 5.1.2, bubbles entering the arteries, either because of pulmonary barotrauma or because nitrogen bubbles formed in the veins cross to the arteries through a PFO, may end up in the small arterioles or capillaries of virtually any tissue in the body. The primary problem is that by blocking the vessel these bubbles may interrupt blood flow, denying tissues downstream of their oxygen supply. This may not merely be a function of the bubble's original size as it enters the arteriole or capillary. Although not yet proven beyond doubt, and depending on the tissue inert gas load accumulated on the dive, one theory holds that once these bubbles enter the arterioles and capillaries of the various tissues they may trap and grow because more dissolved inert gas from the tissue diffuses into them.

As with venous bubbles entering the lungs, many tissues are relatively tolerant of some bubbles entering their capillary circulation (depending, of course, on the size and number of bubbles). Two organs in particular, the brain and spinal cord, are not.

Unfortunately, because the **brain** receives a large proportion of blood flow, and because the buoyancy of bubbles will favour distribution to the brain in the upright diver, it also receives a significant proportion of any bubbles that enter the arteries. The nerve cells in the brain are very sensitive to any interruption of blood flow and oxygen supply. Thus, when bubbles become trapped in the blood vessels of the brain we usually see rapid onset of dramatic neurological symptoms such as *loss of consciousness, disorientation, loss of coordination of movement, visual changes, speech problems, cognitive difficulty, and weakness and sensory changes which may affect only one side of the body*. It is typical for this to occur immediately or within minutes of surfacing from the dive. For completeness, it must be mentioned that divers with DCI frequently complain of

headache, but the exact mechanism of such headaches is unknown. It is unlikely these are caused by arterial bubbles because headaches frequently occur in cases of DCI who experience none of the more serious neurological symptoms (listed above) which might be considered likely if arterial bubbles were interrupting blood flow in the brain.

Interestingly, depending on their size, bubbles may trap only very briefly in the brain circulation. They commonly dissipate through the blood vessels and flow is restored. The diver may appear to recover at this point, and this is frequently and inappropriately interpreted as a sign that nothing further needs to be done. Unfortunately, in their passing, the bubbles often damage the blood vessel walls, and the diver may slowly deteriorate again as white blood cells and platelets gather over the damaged area and gradually interrupt blood flow once more. In addition, there may be more arterial bubbles trapped in various places, which may also enter the brain circulation, especially if the diver is allowed to sit or stand from a recumbent position. It follows that **divers who have exhibited rapid onset neurological symptoms soon after a dive should, irrespective of any spontaneous recovery that occurs, be given high concentration oxygen, maintained in a horizontal posture, and urgently evacuated to a hyperbaric unit.** The first aid and definitive treatment for DCI is discussed in more detail later.

Finally, in respect of arterial bubbles entering the cerebral circulation, there is an ongoing debate as to whether or not this occurs relatively frequently without causing obvious clinical problems. If so, protagonists argue that this might cause long term, significant, and perhaps cumulative damage. Cumulative sub-clinical brain damage as a result of repeated arterial bubble exposure after "normal" diving cannot be completely ruled out, but it is safe to say that at this stage, no study has identified any good evidence of functional problems due to such injury in recreational divers.

It is possible that some arterial bubbles may distribute to the **spinal cord**. As has been mentioned previously, if a bubble lodges in an arteriole or capillary it may then grow as dissolved nitrogen from the surrounding tissue diffuses into it. This would deprive the spinal tissue downstream of blood, and therefore oxygen. The bubble may also damage nearby nerve cells by direct pressure. This mechanism for spinal DCI is referred to as the "arterial embolism hypothesis". Although long considered implausible because emboli seem to distribute to spinal arteries only rarely in other areas of clinical medicine, this mechanism appeals as the only obvious explanation for the proven association between PFO (which allows venous bubbles into the arteries) and serious spinal DCS.

Problems caused by bubble formation in tissues

As discussed above, bubbles may form from dissolved nitrogen within the tissues themselves rather than in blood. The mechanisms by which they cause damage and the symptoms they produce will vary from tissue to tissue.

One of the most serious forms of DCS is that involving the **spinal cord**. Although there is some controversy over the way in which bubbles injure the cord, (see mention of the "venous infarction" and "arterial embolism" hypotheses above) the formation of bubbles within the cord tissue itself is one of the most widely accepted mechanisms, and is referred to as the "autochthonous bubble hypothesis". It is not difficult to conceive that bubbles forming within this delicate tissue may cause damage by physically disrupting or distorting the fragile nerve fibres that run down its length. The bubbles may also disrupt small blood vessels lying nearby causing bleeding into the surrounding tissue. The injury resulting from these events may incite the same type of self-damaging inflammatory processes in the spinal tissue as was mentioned earlier in relation to bubble formation in the blood.

Whichever of the three mechanisms discussed above is responsible for bubble injury to the spinal cord, the symptoms will depend upon the degree of disruption and damage, and the level of the cord involved. If the lower part of the cord is affected, then *changes in power and sensation* in both legs can be expected. This may range from a little bit of *tingling to complete numbness*, or from a *vague sense of weakness or clumsiness to total paralysis*. It is common for *bladder function and bowel control to be impaired or lost* also. If the lesion is high in the cord, both the arms and legs may be involved. Very high lesions are life-threatening because the victim's ability to breathe may be compromised (although this seems extremely rare). The prognosis for successful treatment of this form of DCI probably depends in part on the degree to which swelling and distortion are responsible for the loss of function, since these processes are reversible once the bubbles resolve. Unfortunately, if irreversible disruption of tissue has occurred, then recovery is unlikely, even when bubbles are resolved by recompression.

Interestingly, bubble formation within the **brain** tissue itself (as distinct from bubbles arriving there in arteries) is of uncertain relevance. The brain receives a much higher blood flow per unit of tissue than the spinal cord, and this relatively luxurious perfusion is widely considered to protect from bubble formation by washing nitrogen out of the tissue quickly during ascent. The possibility of bubbles in the brain tissue itself cannot be completely ruled out, and this mechanism has been proposed to explain the relatively frequent complaints of *cognitive impairment* reported by DCS victims. However, animal experiments and pathological studies suggest that most brain injuries in DCI appear to be inflicted by arterial bubbles.

The typical symptoms of such injuries were described earlier.

The very common symptom of DCS, *musculoskeletal pain*, is also believed to arise from bubble formation from dissolved gas within tissue. Although divers often complain of "pain in the joints", the bubbles responsible for this pain do not form within joints. Rather, they almost certainly form in the pain-sensitive structures such as **tendons, ligaments, and the joint capsule** which are either part of, or in close proximity to the joints. Although this causes pain while the bubble is present, these structures usually (but not always) do not suffer any long term damage as a result of bubble formation within. Thus, musculoskeletal DCS can usually be successfully treated with minimal long-term effects. The most commonly affected joint is the shoulder, but the elbows, hips and knees may all be involved. Pain is frequently described as a *deep-seated dull ache*. It most often involves more than one site, and frequently appears to migrate between sites. The pain may wax and wane, but often builds over the initial hours following the dive, plateaus, and then persists for days to weeks if not treated.

Bubbles can form in the **skin**, though the exact anatomical location within the skin is not certain. There are several characteristic variants of cutaneous (skin) DCS and it seems likely that these are explained by bubble formation in different places. For example, there may be a *red itchy rash* which is caused by bubble formation (and damage to cells) within the skin tissue itself. Alternatively, we occasionally see a *blue or purple, mottled rash* which is often rapidly changing in appearance, and this may be due to formation of bubbles within the blood vessels of the skin. This latter appearance is sometimes associated with the onset of severe DCS.

Bubbles may form in the tissues of the **inner ear**. The exact mechanism by which these bubbles disturb function is uncertain, but symptoms such as *dizziness, nausea, vomiting, ringing* and *hearing loss* may occur. Recreational divers rarely complain of inner ear symptoms as the only manifestation of DCS. However, isolated inner ear DCS sometimes occurs in helium-oxygen diving, especially after changes to more nitrogen-rich mixes during decompression.

DIAGNOSIS: don't form preconceptions….

Decompression illness may present in many different ways, and very commonly follows dives that did not violate dive table or computer limits. Symptoms usually arise within minutes to hours after diving, but it is not uncommon for divers to report symptoms that they either did not notice, or intentionally tried to ignore until a day or two after diving. Most divers are only mildly affected; indeed, the *combination of pain, tingling in the skin and fatigue* arising several hours after diving sums up a large proportion of recreational diving cases. These are relatively "non-specific" symptoms; meaning that there are a number of other potential conditions that might produce them. Only about 50% of divers have any actual objective abnormalities to find when examined. Clearly, this is a long way from the widely perceived stereotype of a "bent diver" who within minutes becomes desperately ill and paralyzed after ascending too fast from a deep long dive. Not surprisingly, mildly sick divers often present other divers and doctors alike with a diagnostic quandary.

There is little room for preconception about what you expect to see in DCI, or for vacillation when faced with a sick diver no matter what the symptoms or the nature of the dive. *The most important rule is that a diver who becomes unwell on the same day as diving should be placed in a horizontal position, given 100% oxygen and urgently discussed with a diving physician* (see section on first aid).

Definitive treatment of DCI will be discussed further later. Leave it to someone with the appropriate training and experience to interpret the situation. Divers who present the following day or later with subtle symptoms can be assessed in a less dramatic fashion (that is, without throwing them on the floor and slapping an oxygen mask on!), but should still be discussed with a diving physician promptly.

While on the subject of diagnosis, we acknowledge the recent fashion for teaching a "field neurological examination" to divers learning more about diving medicine on special interest courses. We have no fundamental objection to the application of such techniques by divers at large, provided the performance of such examinations does not interfere with other important first aid measures or delay appropriate evacuation. However we are concerned that the failure to find abnormalities in such examinations has occasionally been cited as a reason for discounting the diagnosis of DCI. Divers must _never_ use these examinations as a tool to rule out the diagnosis of DCI because many sick divers have no abnormalities to find, and operators without formal medical experience frequently fail to detect abnormalities even when they are present. Dive medical advice must be sought.

TABLE 5.1

Signs and Symptoms of DCI.

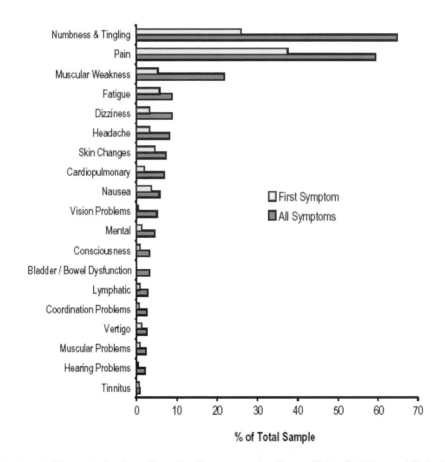

Reprinted with permission from *Report on Decompression Illness, Diving Fatalities and Project Dive Exploration.* Durham, North Carolina:Divers Alert Network; 2004.

RISK FACTORS FOR DCI

Every diver intuitively understands that the depth, duration and ascent protocol of a dive are perhaps the most important determinants of the risk of DCS in particular. In general, we assume that the longer and deeper the dive, the more nitrogen is absorbed, and the greater the risk; especially if the longer duration and deeper depth are not compensated for with a suitable ascent (decompression) protocol.

On top of this, there is a group of widely cited "factors" which are considered to increase risk, either by increasing the likelihood of nitrogen bubble formation, or by pre-disposing to the adverse effects of any bubbles that do form. It is fair to say that most of these risk factors are relevant mainly to the formation of bubbles from dissolved nitrogen and we will therefore use the term DCS in this discussion. The fact that such factors exist is suggested by studies which have used Doppler ultrasound to detect markedly variable numbers of venous bubbles after identical depth/time exposures, and studies which show that symptoms may occur even when relatively few bubbles are detected. Problem is, we really don't know for sure what these factors are. There are a number of ideas. For example, we all know that divers should lose weight, do the deepest dive first, and be more conservative if they are female in order to reduce risk. Right?? Well, maybe. Unfortunately, some of these "sacred cows" are rich in assumption and poor in supportive science.

Perhaps the biggest problem we face in assessing the significance of a "risk factor" is a lack of demographic data describing the diving habits of the recreational diving population. For example, we can look up treatment statistics that might tell us that 65% of all divers treated for DCS were repetitive diving. However, this figure of itself tells us nothing about the significance of repetitive diving as a risk factor for DCS. If 65% of all dives performed were repetitive dives, then, all other factors being equal, we would expect that 65% of DCS cases would come from repetitive dives. However, if only 40% of all dives were repetitive dives, but these dives produced 65% of our DCS cases, then we might begin to suspect that repetitive diving was a risk factor for DCS. Unfortunately, we usually do not have that critical denominator (the data that describe the activity of the general diving population) because there is no easy way of obtaining it. DAN's Project Dive Exploration / Safe Dive is a long term project that is trying to collect this important data.

With that in mind, in this following section we review many of the so-called risk factors for DCS and point out which are truly supported by sound science, those which are likely but are yet unproven, and those which should be treated with skepticism; and perhaps even ignored. The "risk factors" are most usefully divided into 3 categories: those relevant to the diver; those relevant to the dive; and those relevant to the post-dive period.

The Diver

Body fat

It has been suggested that since nitrogen is more soluble in fatty (lipid) than watery (aqueous) tissues, a greater percentage body fat results in

Bart McKenzie Cartoon

greater nitrogen loading, more bubble formation, and higher risk of DCS. This sounds plausible, and some old studies of compressed air workers are supportive of the notion.[5] But two more recent studies in have failed to show a relationship between body fat or body mass index and DCS.[6,7] It is probably fair to call this one "controversial" and conclude that divers are better off with a normal body mass index. But purging dive clubs or even the ranks of commercial divers of "fatties" on the basis of the available evidence is not justified.

Age

Advancing age may increase the risk of DCS, perhaps because of a general decline in physical fitness and ability to compensate for damage, or the presence of other possible risk factors such as previous

Bart McKenzie Cartoon

DCS and higher percentage body fat. Several studies appear to confirm increased risk in older subjects[8] and a recent study showed a positive correlation between advancing age and numbers of venous bubbles after decompression.[9] Although one study in the late 1980s found that increasing age of itself was not a significant risk, it must be concluded that the weight of evidence supports age as a risk factor.[5] Not surprisingly, no clear threshold age at which risk increases has been identified.

Previous DCS

Previous DCS may predispose to another episode by reducing the body's ability to compensate for any subsequent bubble formation, or some unknown mechanism. This theory is supported by caisson work data,[5] and there are limited supportive data from contemporary diving. Divers previously treated for DCS do appear over-represented in the Diver's Alert Network database of divers treated for DCS. However, these divers may just dive more than everyone else, or they may repeatedly indulge in risk-taking behaviour. In general, we consider the risk of another episode after *successful treatment of mild DCS* to be only trivially greater than baseline. However, if recovery from either mild or more serious DCS is incomplete, then the risk of another episode is considered to be unacceptably high and

cessation of diving is usually recommended (see section on return to diving after previous DCS).

Being female

For many years it has been proposed that women might be at higher risk of DCS than men. This notion has been based on a variety of hypotheses. Most popular has been the concept that a woman's higher mean body fat percentage might put them at risk (see above). It has also been suggested that hormonal changes during menstruation can result in fluid retention (oedema) and fluid shifts, and that some oral contraceptive pills can cause a microsludging or slowing of the circulation. All these factors theoretically suggest that women might be more prone to DCS than men. Results of surveys comparing the relative rates of DCS between men and women have been inconclusive, and the results of actual experiments comparing the risk of DCS between the sexes have often been contradictory. There has been some interesting recent work that supports the notion that the risk of DCS for women may change in different phases of the menstrual cycle. However, there is no conclusive answer on the question of how their risk compares to men. Most diving physicians agree that if there is a difference, it is likely to be small.

Dehydration

Pre-dive dehydration may exacerbate DCS because blood will tend to be "thicker" and flow less easily through any small blood vessels damaged by bubbles. Despite the conviction with which this theory is taught, there are no supportive data from actual diving, and the two best animal studies drew opposite conclusions.[10,11] Nevertheless, in view of the strong theoretical basis for this risk factor and the known potentiation of dehydration during immersion, it is probably appropriate to encourage divers to actively maintain good hydration. Since alcohol has a diuretic effect, concerns over dehydration constitute reason enough to advise against anything more than minimal consumption of alcohol on an evening prior to diving.

Physical fitness

It has always been believed but not proven that being physically fit would be protective from DCS. Recently, a line of research in Norway has produced an intriguing and growing body of evidence that a *single bout of heavy exercise at a specific time interval before diving* may be profoundly protective from DCS.[12,13] The mechanism responsible for this protection is not established, and nor (yet) is the relevance of these data to human divers. Nevertheless, it will be an interesting area of research to watch. In the meantime, remaining physically fit for diving makes sufficient intuitive sense to warrant it being a goal for all divers.

Fatty food

It has long been suggested that the high concentration of lipo-protein complexes in the blood after a fatty meal may be disadvantageous in diving because interactions between bubbles and these complexes might result in the release of insoluble fatty emboli. All that can be said is that this mechanism is of highly uncertain relevance in human DCS.

Patent foramen ovale

For completeness, it must be reiterated that there are compelling human data suggesting that a patent foramen ovale (PFO) is a risk factor for serious neurological DCS. This communication between the two upper chambers of the heart (the atria) was explained in Chapter 2, and earlier in this chapter.

© Dr. Richard Harris

The dive

Repetitive diving and multi-day diving

Repetitive recreational dives, multiple ascents to the surface within a single "dive", and multi-day diving are considered to increase risk of DCS. The suggested basis for increased risk in closely spaced sequential dives is bubble formation from dissolved inert gas after the first ascent to the surface. During any subsequent dive, these bubbles may affect inert gas kinetics (thus making the diver's tables or computers less accurate) and may act as seeds for larger bubbles. In addition, it has been demonstrated in animals that venous bubbles trapped in lung capillaries after diving will redistribute into the arterial circulation during another dive if the surface interval is short. This sounds disadvantageous, but it is of unknown relevance in human DCS.

These concerns warrant attention to conservatism during repetitive and multi-day programs of diving, but they do not mandate avoidance of repetitive or multi-day diving. Indeed, the issues are much more complex than portrayed here. For example, *once* daily dives on sequential days have repeatedly been shown to progressively *lower* the risk of DCI as the sequence proceeds; a phenomenon referred to as "acclimatization".[14] The mechanism is uncertain but it may relate to consumption of gaseous micronuclei by bubble formation on each single daily dive, but with sufficient time for most bubbles to decay and disappear before the next dive, thus leaving less nuclei available for bubble initiation. The protective effect seems to disappear after about 5 days without diving, and this is interpreted as the time it takes for micronuclei to be replaced. Interestingly, as implied above, this phenomenon has not been recorded in recreational divers. This may be because recreational multi-day diving frequently involves multiple dives on each day of the multi-day program. This may not allow sufficient time for bubbles to resolve prior to the next day's first dive. Just to complicate matters further, recent unpublished studies from the DCIEM in Canada and some earlier studies of the pearl divers in western Australia[15] suggest that *closely-spaced* repetitive dives may actually be a good thing because the subsequent dive resolves bubbling from the previous one before the process reaches a peak. Not surprisingly however, their work suggests that the final decompression the day is the one that needs to be particularly conservative (and, in the case of the pearl divers, includes underwater oxygen decompression) because that is when the day's "sins" will catch up with you.

Deep diving

There is some reasonable data from carefully controlled military operations that suggests deeper dives are associated with more risk. U.S. Navy experience, between 1968 and 1981 was that the accident rate for dives of 15m (50ft) or less was 0.06%. The accident rate for dives to between 15.5-30m (51-100ft) was 0.23%, nearly four times the rate for shallow fives. The accident rate for dives between 30-61m (101-200ft) was 0.54%, more than double the 15.5-30m (50-100ft) rate and nine times the rate for shallower dives.[16] This is probably also true for recreational diving.

Reverse profile diving

The performance of several dives in shallow to deep sequence, or performing a multi-level dive with increasing depth levels, is commonly referred to as "reverse profile" diving. This particular form of repetitive diving has been considered to increase the risk of DCS. The edict against reverse profile diving has become both enshrined in dive training dogma, and adhered to with almost religious fervour. Interestingly, a recent workshop hosted by the Smithsonian Institute concluded there was no need for such a rule, provided: the dives are conducted without the need for decompression stops, the dives are within the recreational diving depth range (0–40m/130ft); and the reverse profile gradient does not exceed 12m (40ft).[17]

This issue is not yet fully resolved, and is further complicated by definitions. For example, "reverse profile" could imply that two dives that are allowable in forward (deep then shallow) order, are merely reversed with no adjustment of the deeper dive to make it safer. The practical reality is that divers sometimes want to perform "reverse depth" dives; in other words, they would perform a deeper dive after a shallower one, but are quite prepared to adjust the deeper profile in accordance with the dictates of the tables or dive computer used. At this stage, these authors advise that those following the Smithsonian workshop rules for reverse depth diving should do so conservatively. Further research is being conducted in this area and the advice being given on the matter may alter accordingly. See Chapter 23 for further discussion on reverse dive profiles.

Heavy exercise

Exercise during diving accelerates absorption of inert gas in those tissues whose perfusion is increased during work. Not surprisingly, moderate to heavy exercise during a dive has been clearly shown to increase decompression requirements and the risk of DCS in both animals and humans.[18] This is one of the few unequivocal risk factors. Interestingly, blood flow to the legs and inert gas elimination is enhanced, and the risk of DCS reduced, if *mild* exercise is performed during decompression.[18]

Cold

Exposure to cold is often cited as a risk factor for DCS. There is human data to support this contention, and the explanation is not so much the cold per se, but the change in the diver's temperature during the dive. If uptake of nitrogen occurs while the diver is warm and blood flow to the peripheries is good, and elimination occurs while the diver is cool and peripheral blood flow has reduced, then nitrogen elimination will be slower than uptake and the risk of DCS increased. Thus, divers are best advised to keep their temperature as stable as possible through the dive. In cold water, this is best achieved by wearing a drysuit.

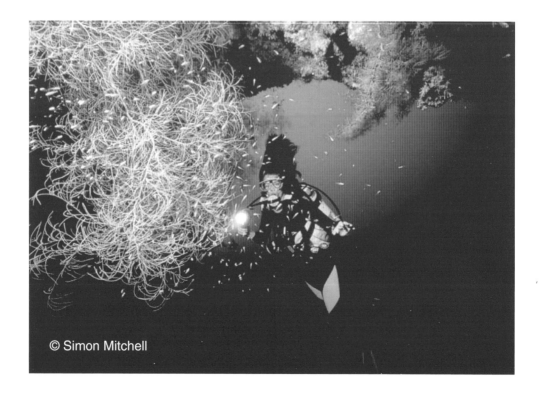

© Simon Mitchell

Post-dive

Exercise

Human data suggest that exercise after diving may hasten onset, and increase both severity and incidence of DCS.[19] The mechanism is not certain but may involve the generation of momentary areas of depressurization in working tissues, thus promoting bubble formation. Some forms of exercise, particularly lifting heavy weights have a tendency to raise right heart pressures and may promote the passage of venous blood (and any bubbles) across a PFO.[20]

Rewarming

As has been mentioned previously, the solubility of dissolved nitrogen falls as the temperature of a tissue rises. The main implication of this is that if rewarming of cold peripheral tissues is conducted too quickly (for example, by getting straight into a hot shower), then it may precipitate bubble formation and DCS. There are at least several published case reports of DCS arising under such circumstances.[21]

Altitude exposure

Ascent to altitude following diving favours nitrogen bubble formation and growth, and is an undisputed precipitant for DCS. Ascent to as little as 300m (1,000ft) soon after diving has precipitated DCS in sport divers leaving dive sites by road. However, the most troublesome altitude issue is the prescription of a safe interval between diving and flying in passenger aircraft, which are pressurised to a maximum of the equivalent of approximately 2,400m (8,000ft) altitude.

DAN's Flying After Diving trials suggest that a 12 hour delay is sufficient following a single no-decompression dive, and a minimum interval of 18 hours is required after multiple dives.[22] (see Chapter 25). Unfortunately, no pragmatic recommendation will prevent all cases. Unequivocal DCS has occurred in recreational divers with no pre-flight symptoms, who delayed flying more than 48 hours after diving.

We can see from the above that some of the so-called risk factors for DCS (such as heavy underwater work) are undisputed and should be carefully considered in our diving planning strategies. Others (such as dehydration) are less well established, but given the uncertainty we should probably assume they are significant and act accordingly. Finally, one or two (such as female gender) appear to be discredited as risk factors and can largely be ignored.

© Simon Mitchell

DEFINITIVE TREATMENT FOR DCI

Recompression

The definitive treatment for DCI is recompression in a chamber breathing 100% oxygen.

Recompression reduces the size of the bubbles, perhaps relieving the obstruction of blood vessels by bubbles in blood, and reducing any physical effects of bubbles on structures in their immediate vicinity. Reducing the size of the bubbles also increases their internal pressure due to surface tension and, therefore, favors spontaneous resolution of the bubbles. The higher oxygen pressure serves several purposes. First, it helps provide greater oxygen delivery to any hypoxic tissue. Second, it may also reduce the injurious activities of white blood cells that are activated by bubble-induced tissue injury. Third and perhaps most importantly, it accelerates nitrogen elimination by increasing the pressure difference (pressure gradient) between the nitrogen in the bubble and in surrounding tissues and the lung.

Let's briefly consider some approximate figures to illustrate this concept. If you think about it, a stable nitrogen bubble in the tissue or blood at the surface after a dive will contain nitrogen at the same pressure as ambient (close to 1ATA). If the diver is breathing air, the alveolar nitrogen will be about 0.75ATA (slightly less than the nitrogen pressure in surrounding air because there is also water vapour and carbon dioxide in the alveoli – not just nitrogen and oxygen). This means that there is a 0.25ATA pressure differential driving nitrogen elimination between the bubble and the lungs. Actually, it is even less than this because the bubble contains water vapour, carbon dioxide and a small amount of oxygen too; but we are using approximate figures here to illustrate a principle.

Now, if we give the diver 100% oxygen to breathe at the surface (such as is done in first aid for DCI), then the nitrogen in the alveoli falls to close to zero while the nitrogen pressure in the bubble remains close to 1ATA. This more than quadruples the gradient for nitrogen "outgassing" from the bubble, and it will shrink faster. The effect is even more dramatic if we now recompress the diver to 2.8ATA whilst continuing to breathe 100% oxygen. The nitrogen pressure in the bubble is now approximately 2.8ATA (same as ambient) whilst the nitrogen pressure in the alveoli remains close to zero. This even further enhances the gradient for outgassing. Under hyperbaric conditions, some oxygen may diffuse into the bubble, and this may even cause it to grow transiently. However, the net effect in the short term is accelerated shrinkage. We utilize this process to give us a profound outgassing advantage and this is what is meant when we refer to "opening the oxygen window".

A diver who is suspected of suffering from DCI is usually recompressed to 2.8ATA (18msw (60fsw)) breathing 100% oxygen. This pressure has been chosen as an acceptable compromise between pressure (to achieve a reduction in bubble size), and the continued ability to breathe 100% oxygen with an acceptably low incidence of cerebral oxygen toxicity. The most frequently utilized treatment table for mild to moderately affected divers is the US Navy Treatment Table 6 (RN62) shown is Figure 5.1.4. This involves a stepwise decompression to 1ATA from the initial treatment pressure of 2.8ATA over a period of 4.75 hours. The majority of the time is spent at 2.8ATA and 1.9ATA with the patient breathing 100% O_2. These periods at 2.8 and 1.9ATA may be extended, so that the table lasts longer than 4.75 hours if the patient is making slow progress.

FIGURE 5.1.4

US Navy Treatment Table 6.

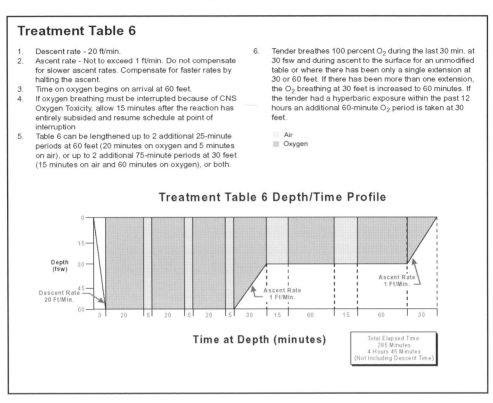

Treatment Table 6

1. Descent rate - 20 ft/min.
2. Ascent rate - Not to exceed 1 ft/min. Do not compensate for slower ascent rates. Compensate for faster rates by halting the ascent.
3. Time on oxygen begins on arrival at 60 feet.
4. If oxygen breathing must be interrupted because of CNS Oxygen Toxicity, allow 15 minutes after the reaction has entirely subsided and resume schedule at point of interruption
5. Table 6 can be lengthened up to 2 additional 25-minute periods at 60 feet (20 minutes on oxygen and 5 minutes on air), or up to 2 additional 75-minute periods at 30 feet (15 minutes on air and 60 minutes on oxygen), or both.

6. Tender breathes 100 percent O_2 during the last 30 min. at 30 fsw and during ascent to the surface for an unmodified table or where there has been only a single extension at 30 or 60 feet. If there has been more than one extension, the O_2 breathing at 30 feet is increased to 60 minutes. If the tender had a hyperbaric exposure within the past 12 hours an additional 60-minute O_2 period is taken at 30 feet.

☐ Air
☐ Oxygen

Treatment Table 6 Depth/Time Profile

Depth (fsw)

Descent Rate 20 Ft/Min.

Ascent Rate 1 Ft/Min.

Ascent Rate 1 Ft/Min.

Time at Depth (minutes)

Total Elapsed Time:
285 Minutes
4 Hours 45 Minutes
(Not Including Descent Time)

The USN Table 6 protocol is often successful in relieving symptoms of DCI and, in scuba (air) divers with mild manifestations, compression to greater pressures is rarely considered necessary, even where complete relief does not occur at 2.8ATA. The 2.8ATA regimens produce an acceptably low frequency of overt central nervous system oxygen toxicity, are relatively short, cheap, and can be administered in most recompression chambers. Medical attendants who accompany the patient during the treatment are not incapacitated by narcosis and rarely develop DCS themselves as a result of the exposure.

Where the diver has very serious disease and presents early, and especially where such a case fails to respond adequately with the initial compression to 2.8ATA,

consideration is often given to compression to 4 or even 6ATA, and having the patient breathe an appropriate oxygen-helium or nitrox mixture. The obvious advantage of this strategy is a small but significant additional reduction in bubble size beyond what is achieved at 2.8ATA. There may also be a nitrogen elimination advantage for helium breathing, though this remains controversial. These treatments are longer, more expensive, logistically difficult, and impose a small risk of DCS on the treatment attendant. Nevertheless, there is a reasonable amount of anecdotal evidence to support higher pressure treatments though they cannot be considered "a standard of care". Very little formal research has been performed in which different recompression algorithms have been compared.

Many divers will relapse, or deteriorate, even after an initial successful treatment. Experience has shown that repeated treatments with hyperbaric oxygen (HBO) often provoke further improvement in patients who are left with problems after the initial treatment. The repeated treatments are usually given 12-24 hours apart and are usually shorter than the initial treatment. These follow-up treatments are usually continued until the patient recovers or they fail to make any sustained improvement over two consecutive treatments.

Adjuvant therapies

Recompression does not always provide complete recovery. Moreover, diving is often conducted in locations where recompression facilities are remote. As previously discussed, the pathophysiology of DCI has been shown to involve events like white blood cell activation, clotting and other inflammatory processes that are potentially susceptible to control by drugs. It follows that there has been much interest in drugs that might be useful either as adjuncts to recompression or for administration in the field when recompression is not immediately available.

A number of drugs have been proposed as potentially useful, including: aspirin; steroids, non-steroidal anti-inflammatory agents, lignocaine (lidocaine), and perfluorocarbon emulsions. The current opinion on the use of these agents is outlined below.

Intravenous fluids

Although not a drug as such, it should be pointed out that since dehydration may well exacerbate DCI, and since divers are often mildly dehydrated, it is almost routine for intravenous fluids to be given during the initial recompression for DCI. There is no data that supports the use of intravenous fluids in typical cases, but the theoretical advantages and lack of obvious harm constitute reason enough to recommend them.

Aspirin

Aspirin inhibits platelet aggregation. The aggregation of platelets and clot formation have been shown to be stimulated by bubbles in blood, and as previously discussed, this may contribute to the venous infarction form of spinal DCS. Aspirin has therefore been recommended as treatment and even as a preventative for DCI, but this appears to have been based on the theoretical attractiveness of its anti-clotting activity rather than on any animal or clinical data describing true effectiveness. More recently, the potential role of bleeding from blood vessels damaged by bubbles in spinal cord DCS has been highlighted, and this could potentially be made worse by drugs that prevent normal clotting. Since there are both theoretical advantages and disadvantages for aspirin administration in DCI, and in the absence of definitive data describing benefit, the current view is that aspirin administration cannot be recommended.

Steroids

Steroids are potent inhibitors of many inflammatory reactions. Since DCI results in activation of white cells and several inflammatory processes it has been reasoned that administration of steroids may be beneficial. Moreover, a randomized trial of a powerful steroid in *traumatic* spinal cord injury showed gave some benefit provided the drug was given within 8 hours.[23] There has been some anecdotal support for the use of steroids in DCI. However, using animal models of spinal cord DCI and arterial gas embolism of the brain, a group in the U.S. found no benefit from therapeutic administration of steroids. Indeed in the spinal DCI model the steroid treated animals did worse. A worse outcome (greater death rate) was also noted when steroids were given prophylactically in a pig model of severe DCI.[24] Thus, there seems little justification for advocating the administration of steroids to humans with DCI at this time.

Non-steroidal anti-inflammatory agents (NSAIDS)

These agents are commonly used to treat sprains and strains. NSAIDS inhibit the release of certain inflammatory mediators after tissue injury. Among other things, these mediators enhance the discomfort emanating from areas of injury. Since the aches and pains of musculoskeletal DCI can be persistent and troublesome, it has been suggested that treatment with NSAIDS might be appropriate. A recent large Australian trial in divers confirmed that faster resolution of symptoms was achieved in those receiving NSAIDS and that they required fewer recompression treatments.[25] The long term outcome was neither better nor worse however.

Lignocaine (lidocaine)

Lignocaine is an agent commonly used in clinical medicine for stabilizing the heart rhythm and as a local anaesthetic agent. Almost by accident, it was discovered to help protect the brain from the effects of arterial bubbles in animals, and it was subsequently found to be of benefit in several other types of injury where blood flow to the brain is interrupted. The mechanisms by which lignocaine protects the brain are complex and beyond the scope of this book. There have been several case reports of apparent benefit when lignocaine was given to divers with severe neurological DCI,[26,27] and there have been two randomized trials that showed lignocaine reduced the incidence of post-operative thinking function problems in cardiac surgery patients (who are often exposed to many small arterial bubbles).[28] Lignocaine is presently considered useful in the early treatment of divers in who are suspected of suffering CAGE. It's role in DCS is much less clear.

FIGURE 5.1.5

Multiplace recompression chamber.

Perfluorocarbon (PFC) emulsions

PFCs are synthetic compounds with low surface tension and viscosity, and very high solubility for inert gases and oxygen. It is proposed that improved oxygen delivery by intravenous PFCs might ameliorate DCI by improving oxygenation in territories whose perfusion has been compromised by bubbles. In addition, since these compounds may dissolve 27 times more nitrogen than plasma, it is also likely that administration of a PFC will accelerate elimination of nitrogen from tissues. Other potential mechanisms of benefit include improved blood flow, restoration of blood volume (important in patients suffering shock) and suppression of white cell activation. PFC administration has been shown to reduce the death rate in rats,[29] and hamsters[30] subject to severe decompression stress. Similarly, survival was improved in a rabbit model of arterial gas embolism when a PFC was administered.[31] PFCs are perhaps the most exciting new strategy for the treatment of DCI, but at present there are no forms licensed for human administration.

FIGURE 5.1.6

Monoplace Chamber.

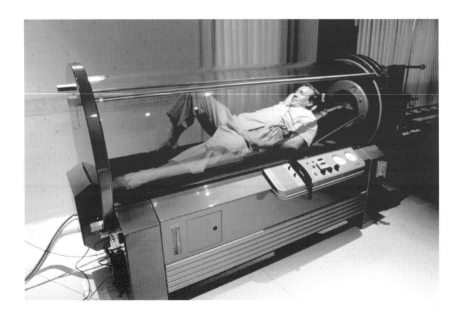

FIRST AID FOR DCI

The protocols discussed below are designed mainly for use with divers who notify first responders of their symptoms of DCI relatively soon after diving; as a rough guide, on the same day as the dive. Many divers with mild symptoms of DCI tolerate their symptoms for days before reporting them. When such divers are identified more than 24 hours after diving, the first responder can be fairly sure that the person is not in grave danger of serious injury and is not going to progressively worsen. It follows that while such divers must be brought to the attention of the relevant experts, it is not usually necessary to immediately impose aggressive first aid measures.

For divers with moderate to severe DCI, the longer the interval between the onset of symptoms of DCI and the commencement of hyperbaric oxygen treatment, the more likely is the possibility of incomplete symptom resolution. Therefore, it is essential to get such a diver to a recompression chamber as soon as possible, preferably breathing high concentration oxygen en route.

First aid is designed to minimize the damage to the diver during this interval. The first aid procedure and its rationale is as follows:

■ **Monitor consciousness, breathing and circulation and resuscitate if necessary**

Supporting life is the most urgent requirement and, if resuscitation is indicated, it takes precedence over other first aid measures.

■ **Lay the diver down**

A diver suffering from severe DCI may also be suffering from shock. Blood delivery to the vital organs will be increased if the diver lies down.

The diver should be laid flat without raising the legs. Raising the legs may encourage circulating venous bubbles to by-pass the lungs and enter the arterial circulation if a PFO is present. This is because raising the legs is known to increase the pressure in the right side of the heart. The advice is somewhat controversial since in most cases, leg-raising alters right and left atrial pressures similarly and this would produce no net change in the tendency for blood to flow from right to left. Indeed, one study in which the effect of leg-raising on blood shunting through a PFO was tested, found no consistent effect. Leg-raising increased the shunting in some individuals but reduced it in others. On balance, it seems best to avoid raising the legs, unless the diver is assessed as being severely shocked.

The choice of the horizontal position is somewhat controversial. The previously advised head-down position *does* help prevent the distribution of arterial bubbles to the brain, and this may be appropriate in a case of pulmonary barotrauma with CAGE. But if we are really dealing with a DCS case and the arterial bubbles are coming from the veins across a PFO, then the problem might be made worse by being head-down (by increasing both flow and the transfer of bubbles across the PFO). Unfortunately, it is frequently difficult for even an experienced diving physician to say with certainty whether a diver with DCI has been affected by arterial bubbles at all, let alone to determine whether those bubbles have arisen from pulmonary barotrauma or by crossing a PFO from the veins. Thus, once again, on balance it seems most appropriate just to recommend that the diver is placed flat.

Once horizontal, it is best if the diver stays that way, and this is especially so if there is any suspicion that arterial bubbles are part of the problem. This is because some bubbles may still be trapped in the heart chambers or other sites, and these might be released into the circulation with significant changes in posture. If this occurs and the diver is upright, it is most likely the bubble(s) will distribute to the brain. Unresponsive or nauseated victims should be placed in the recovery position to avoid aspiration of vomitus.

FIGURE 5.1.7

*Diver being administered
first aid for DCI.*

■ **Administer oxygen**

Oxygen breathing will increase the oxygenation of any hypoxic body tissues and also help to flush out any dissolved nitrogen and nitrogen present in bubbles as described earlier. The concentration of inhaled oxygen should be as near to 100% as can be reached in order to achieve the maximum benefit. (Oxygen administration is explained in detail in Chapter 8).

The periods of oxygen breathing should be recorded (i.e. time(s) put on oxygen and time(s) taken off oxygen) and the victim's response should also be recorded. The doctor who will recompress the diver will then know for how long the higher partial pressure of oxygen has been breathed, and will use this information to minimize the effects of pulmonary oxygen toxicity during the subsequent hyperbaric oxygen treatment. If a diver has had very long periods of breathing 100% oxygen prior to arrival at the chamber for recompression, the treatment regimen may need to be altered. Despite this, most hyperbaric units do not recommend "air breaks" during first aid oxygen administration, unless the evacuation is going to take many hours. First aid providers should not worry about giving air breaks in an evacuation that will take less than 3-4 hours, but if a longer duration is anticipated, they should take advice from the receiving doctors.

The breathing of oxygen is a first aid measure and in most circumstances is not a substitute for recompression, regardless of the response. Moreover, first aid oxygen administration to a diver with suspected DCI should never be used as a "diagnostic test". If the suspicion of DCI is strong enough to warrant oxygen administration, the injured diver should be discussed with a diving physician no matter what the response to oxygen.

■ **Treat for shock**

The first aid for shock includes laying the victim down and administering oxygen and, hopefully, these will have been initiated already. The diver should be kept thermally comfortable, reassured and still and quiet. This will maximize the blood supply to vital organs. Remaining still will discourage further bubble formation as a result of physical agitation. Luckily, shock is rare in DCI.

■ **Arrange recompression**

Contact the appropriate diving accident advisory service (e.g. DAN-supported dive emergency hotline) and/or the nearest recompression chamber.

They will give advice about any further first aid treatment that might be necessary, and may initiate the contacts necessary in order to transport the diver to a recompression facility.

■ **Seek medical aid**

The injured diver should be taken to the nearest competent medical facility as soon as possible so that proper medical treatment can be initiated. *Strongly encourage the attending medical person to contact a diving medical expert (e.g. DAN hotline) if this has not yet been done.* Occasionally, divers must be quite assertive in their dealings with medical practitioners who may have never seen a case of DCI previously. In some unfortunate cases, attending doctors in isolated peripheral hospital emergency departments have lost valuable time in the pursuit of alternative diagnoses even though a diver has presented with obvious symptoms of DCI. Doctors unfamiliar with the problem must be strongly encouraged to make contact with an appropriate diving emergency hotline as quickly as possible.

Intravenous fluids will probably be given and the diver will be stabilized before being transported to the recompression chamber. If the diver is unable to urinate a urinary catheter might be inserted.

■ **Encourage a responsive and stable victim to drink non-alcoholic fluids**

Drinking fluids will rehydrate the diver. The ideal oral fluids are electrolyte-type fluids such as one-half strength Gatorade, although virtually any non-alcoholic fluid will do the job. An easily obtainable and adequate fluid is water. Alcohol should never be given as it will further dehydrate the diver. Acidic drinks should be avoided. **Allow oral fluids at the rate of approximately 110ml (four fluid ounces) every 15 minutes, as comfortably tolerated by the diver, providing that the following conditions are met**:

- *Oral fluids should not be given to a diver who rapidly deteriorating or is not fully responsive.* If the diver were to drink a lot of fluid and later became unconscious and required ventilation, he would be far more likely to regurgitate his stomach contents.

- *Oral fluids should not be given if the diver is suffering from stomach pain, nausea, vomiting, urinary retention or paralysis* (unless a urinary catheter can be inserted).

- *The amount and type of fluid given should be recorded, as well as the urinary output* (i.e. number of times and volume of urine passed).

Note, intravenous fluids are appropriate in any diver with suspected DCI, though a urinary catheter must be inserted in unconscious victims or those with signs suggestive of or urinary retention.

■ **Record details of the dive profile, first aid given and divers's response to first aid**

This information will be useful in confirming the nature of the injury and possibly in its subsequent treatment.

RETURN TO DIVING AFTER DCI

There is uncertainty among doctors over the implications of an episode of DCI for a diver's future fitness for diving. Perhaps understandably, when faced with uncertainty many doctors reflexively resort to a conservative stance. Pronouncements of "never fit to dive again"

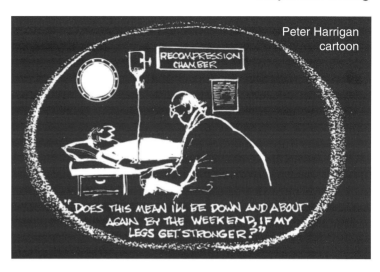

Peter Harrigan cartoon

"DOES THIS MEAN ILL BE DOWN AND ABOUT AGAIN BY THE WEEKEND, IF MY LEGS GET STRONGER?"

after cases of DCI are sometimes issued. Unfortunately, this is often unnecessary and may encourage unsafe behaviour by divers. For example, divers sometimes claim that their delay in reporting symptoms was predicated on fear that they might be "banned" from diving ever again if the diagnosis was confirmed.

There are a number of issues which must be addressed in consideration of the "safety" of diving after DCI, but perhaps the pivotal one is embraced by this simple question: does an episode of DCI makes another one more likely in future?

What clues do we have to help answer this question? Data published by DAN in 1997 (the data was actually from the 1995 year) showed that 36 out of 590 divers (6%) who suffered DCI that year (and who provided sufficient information) had previously had DCI.[32] At a superficial level, one might interpret these figures as follows: 6% of divers with DCI had previously been "bent"; we know that the proportion of divers out there who have previously suffered DCI is much lower than 6%; therefore divers with previous DCI were "over-represented" in the accident figures for 1995; and thus, previous DCI appears to be a risk for further episodes in the future.

It's not quite as simple as that however. What the DAN data also showed was that the 1995 DCI cases with a previous history of DCI were approximately 10 times as active in diving as the 1995 DCI cases without previous DCI. It may be that those 6% of recurrent DCI cases have suffered repeat episodes because they dive far more often. One might therefore draw the very reasonable conclusion that "diving is a risk factor for DCI". It is also possible that these previously injured divers repeatedly indulge in risky diving practices. It follows that there is no clear answer as to whether or not an episode of DCI per se makes another more likely in future.

A second issue that must be addressed in considering fitness for diving after DCI is whether there is any difference in risk implied by failure to fully recover from the previous episode. In other words, are divers who make a full recovery from DCI at less risk in subsequent diving than those who have on-going symptoms?

The answer to this is also not apparent from available data. However, it is a generally accepted principal of medicine that the central nervous system has an intrinsic functional "reserve". This essentially means that some degree of injury can be sustained without actual functional problems. A logical extension of this concept is the argument that patients with clinically obvious injury must have depleted their "neurological reserve" to a greater degree, and that any further injury will be inevitably reflected in more severe impairment. In diving, this would mean that a diver with permanent neurological symptoms after DCI can sustain no further injury without an "automatic" deterioration in condition. In contrast, a diver with previous DCI but no on-going symptoms might still have some "reserve" to cope with injury. While simplistic, this concept has wide acceptance and has to some degree, influenced fitness for diving decisions for some time (see below).

A third issue in considering fitness for diving after DCI, particularly those episodes thought to be due to DCS, is the nature of the diving that led to the illness. If DCS has arisen after very trivial depth - time exposures, with no identifiable risk factors such as rapid ascents or multiple ascents, then the episode can be interpreted as suggesting both a predisposition to DCS and an increased risk in diving for that diver. Unfortunately, such is the unpredictability of DCS that it is very difficult to accurately define a "trivial" exposure. Certainly, we do not consider a dive to be "trivial" just because it was inside the limits of the tables. Indeed, *it is very common for divers to suffer DCS when diving within the limits imposed by the dive tables or computers* and most of these will have no inherent predisposition. The consistency of the diving history with the development of DCS is a judgment that must be made by the individual diving physician based on their experience.

Finally, it is reasoned that if DCI is of the CAGE form and is thus suspected to have arisen because of lung barotrauma, the diver should be considered permanently unfit because the consequent lung scarring will predispose the diver to a future episode.

The synthesis of these considerations in most determinations of fitness after DCI can be summarised as follows:

A diver <u>can</u> return to diving after DCI if:

1. They have made a full recovery;

2. The diving they did is reasonably consistent with the occurrence of DCI; and

3. It is not suspected that lung barotrauma was part of the problem.

These criteria seem sensible, but it must be acknowledged that they are based to a large degree on good sense rather than good data. More than 80% of divers treated in Australasian hyperbaric units do "qualify" to be made "fit" again, usually after a rest period of at least one month for a *mild* case of DCI.

© Simon Mitchell

SUMMARY

- Decompression illness (DCI) results from the development of bubbles within the body.

- Decompression sickness (DCS) is a subset of DCI and this term refers specifically to the formation of bubbles from dissolved nitrogen or another inert gas.

- Cerebral arterial gas embolism (CAGE) is a subset of DCI and this term refers specifically to the introduction of bubbles to the arterial circulation by pulmonary barotrauma.

- The lungs act as a filter and trap most of the bubbles that form from dissolved nitrogen in the venous blood. Venous bubble formation can occur without producing symptoms.

- If there is a patent foramen ovale (PFO), bubbles in the venous blood can cross to the arterial circulation and avoid filtration in the lung. There is evidence that a PFO increases the risk of serious neurological DCS.

- Bubbles can cause harm by distorting and disrupting tissue and blocking and damaging blood vessels. Bubbles may also precipitate harmful inflammatory reactions.

- The location number and size of the bubbles determines the type of symptoms and the severity.

- Symptoms of DCI usually occur within minutes to hours of diving.

- The vast majority of divers suffering from DCI have mild disease characterized by combinations of fatigue, pain and tingling in the skin.

- Treatment for DCI includes:
  recompression, hyperbaric oxygen and intravenous fluids. The recompression reduces the size of the bubbles and restores circulation. The hyperbaric oxygen provides greater oxygenation to hypoxic tissue and encourages nitrogen elimination. The intravenous fluid rehydrates the diver and improves circulation.

- Most divers make a full recovery and are able to return to diving after and appropriate rest period (of at least a month in mild cases). However, some divers with serious DCI are left with problems.

- The possibility of unnoticed and perhaps cumulative neurological injury in divers who have never suffered DCI cannot be excluded, but there is currently no evidence that any functional problems arise from such damage in recreational divers.

- The following are some of the factors that may predispose a diver to DCI (particularly DCS):
  - Deep and/or long dives, rapid and multiple ascents, cold water, obesity, heavy exercise during or after the dive, dehydration, presence of a patent foramen ovale, older age, flying after diving ...

First aid for Decompression Illness

- Assess the airway, breathing and circulation and resuscitate if necessary.

- Lay the victim flat and maintain their airway. Do not raise their legs.

- Provide 100% oxygen.

- Treat for shock if appropriate.

- Immediately contact the emergency services if life is threatened.

- Contact a DAN-supported Dive Emergency Hotline for advice.

- Assist with transfer to a recompression chamber.

- Record details of dive profile, first aid given and response to first aid.

- Encourage a conscious and stable victim to drink non- alcoholic fluids (See Notes).

Note:

Record amount and type of fluid given. Record urinary output and check for bladder distension.

Fluids are only given if the victim is not suffering from stomach pain, urinary retention or paralysis unless a urinary catheter is used. If the bladder becomes distended give no more fluid until a urinary catheter is inserted.

WHY WORRY ABOUT GETTING DCI?

Most cases of decompression illness in recreational divers are mild, are successfully treated, and the diver makes a successful return to diving. However, recreational divers should make no mistake that this is not always the case. Serious neurological DCI does occur in recreational diving, and outcomes are not always good. Spinal DCS in particular is associated with a high incidence of persistent problems such as weakness, numbness, dyscoordination, and bowel and bladder difficulties. Some patients may even remain completely paralysed for life. Thankfully, such cases are rare, but their existence is something we should all have in the backs of our minds. We cannot allow ourselves a bit of reckless behaviour on the basis that any problems can be sorted out with a "quick trip to the chamber". We should use the misfortune of others to motivate ourselves to adhere as closely as possible to good diving practices.

Without wanting to sound unduly pessimistic, we must also remind the reader that good diving practice is not always sufficient to protect from DCI. Decompression illness, even the more serious forms, can and does arise in divers who have performed essentially faultless and conservative dive profiles.

An issue that frequently troubles divers is the possibility of long term adverse effects, even in the absence of having suffered obvious decompression illness. Much of the research done in this area has been of poor quality, and extreme care is needed in interpreting the results. Many anecdotal descriptions of long term effects and almost all of the relevant studies pertain to commercial rather than recreational divers. Furthermore, although various studies have identified phenomena (such as small brain lesions detected by advanced scanning techniques) that are suggestive of tissue injury due to some unnoticed event (probably bubble formation) during commercial and recreational diving, it remains true that no study in recreational divers has yet shown that diving actually produces any problems that might impair the diver's function in daily living. We do not dismiss this possibility however, and this is an area of research that will be watched with interest over the next decade.

REFERENCES

1. Moon RE, Camporesi EM, Kisslo JA. Patent foramen ovale and decompression sickness in divers. *Lancet* 1989; i: 513-4.

2. Wilmshurst PT, Byrne JC, Webb-Peploe MM. Relation between interatrial shunts and decompression sickness in divers. *Lancet* 1989; ii:1302-6.

3. Wilmshurst P, Bryson P. Relationship between the clinical features of neurological decompression illness and its causes. *Clin Sci (Colch)* 2000; 99:65-75.

4. Dunford RG, Vann RD, Gerth WA, Pieper CF, Huggins K, Wacholz C, Bennett PB. The incidence of venous gas emboli in recreational diving. *Undersea Hyper Med* 2000; 27 (supp):65.

5. Lam TH, Yau KP. Analysis of some individual risk factors for decompression sickness in Hong Kong. *Undersea Biomed Res* 1989; 16:283-92.

6. Conkin J, Gernhardt ML, Foster PP, Pilmanis AA, Butler BD, Beltran E, Fife CE, Vann RD, Gerth WA, Loftin KC, Acock K, Dervay JP, Waligora JM, Powell MR, Feiveson AH, Nishi RY, Sullivan PA, Schneider SM. Relationship of exercise, age, and gender on decompression sickness and venous gas emboli during 2-hour oxygen prebreathe prior to hypobaric exposure. *Undersea Hyper Med* 2000; 27(supp):12.

7. Curley MD, Robin GJ, Thalmann ED. Percent body fat and human decompression sickness. *Undersea Biomed Res* 1989; 16 (supp):29.

8. Hoiberg A . Consequences of US Navy diving mishaps: Decompression sickness. *Undersea Biomed Res* 1986; 13:383-94.

9. Carturan D, Boussuges A, Burnet H, Fondarai J, Vanuxem P, Gardette B. Circulating venous bubbles in recreational diving: relationships with age, weight, maximal oxygen uptake and body fat percentage. *Int J Sports Med* 1999; 20:410-4.

10. Broome JR, Kittel CL, Dick EJ. Failure of pre-dive hydration status to influence neurological DCI rate in pigs. *Undersea Hyper Med* 1995; 22(supp):52.

11. Dromsky D. Personal communication of unpublished data.

12. Wisloff U, Richardson RS, Brubakk AO. Exercise and nitric oxide prevent bubble formation: a novel approach to the prevention of decompression sickness? *J Physiol.* 2004 Mar 16; 555(Pt 3):825-9.

13. Dujic Z, Duplancic D, Marinovic-Terzic I, Bakovic D, Ivancev V, Valic Z, Eterovic D, Petri NM, Wisloff U, Brubakk AO. Aerobic exercise before diving reduces venous gas bubble formation in humans. *J Physiol.* 2004 Mar 16; 555(Pt 3):637-42.

14. Vann RD, Thalmann ED. Decompression physiology and practice. In: Bennett PB, Elliott DH (eds) *The Physiology and Medicine of Diving,* 4th edn. London: WB Saunders; 1993: 376-432.

15. Wong R. Western Australian pearl divers' mode of diving. *SPUMS J* 1995; 25(3):170-5.

16. Blood C, Hoiberg A. Analyses of variables underlying U.S. Navy diving Accidents. *Undersea Biomed Res* 1995; 12(3):351-60.

17. Lang MA, Lehner CE. Findings and Conclusion. In: Lang MA & Lehner CE (eds) *Proceedings of Reverse Dive Profiles Workshop.* Washington: Smithsonian Institution; 2000:290.

18. Vann RD. Decompression theory and applications. In: Bennett PB, Elliott DH (eds) *The Physiology and Medicine of Diving and Compressed Air Work,* 3rd edn. San Pedro CA: Best Publishing Co; 1982:352-82.

19. Pilmanis AA, Olson RM, Fischer MD, Wiegman JF, Webb JT. Exercise-induced altitude decompression sickness. *Aviat Space Environ Med* 1999; 70:22-9.

20. Balestra C, Germonpre P, Marroni A. Intrathoracic pressure changes after Valsalva strain and other maneuvers: implications for divers with patent foramen ovale. *Undersea Hyper Med* 1998; 25:171-4.

21. Mekjavic IB, Kakitsuba N. Effect of peripheral temperature on the formation of venous gas bubbles. *Undersea Biomed Res* 1989; 16:391-401.

22. Vann RD, Gerth WA, Denoble PJ, Pieper CF, Thalmann ED. Experimental trials to assess the risks of decompression sickness in flying after diving. *Undersea Hyperb Med* 2004; 31(4):431-44.

23. Bracken MB, Shepard MJ, Collins WF et al. A randomized controlled trial of methyl-prednisolone or naloxone in the treatment of acute spinal –cord injury. Results of the Second National Acute Spinal Cord Injury Study. *New Engl J Med* 1990;322:1405-11.

24. Dromsky DM, Toner CB, Fahlman A, Weathersby PK. Prophylactic treatment of severe decompression sickness with methylprednisolone. *Undersea Hyperb Med* 1999; 26(supp):15.

25. Bennett MH, Mitchell SJ, Dominguez A. Adjunctive treatment of decompression illness with a non-steroidal anti-inflammatory drug reduces compression requirement. *Undersea and Hyperb Med* 2003; 30:195-205.

26. Drewry A, Gorman DF. Lidocaine as an adjunct to hyperbaric therapy in decompression illness: a case report. *Undersea Biomed Res* 1992;19:187-90.

27. Cogar WB. Intravenous lidocaine as adjunctive therapy in the treatment of decompression illness. *Ann Emerg Med* 1997;29:284-6.

28. Mitchell SJ, Pellett O, Gorman DF. Cerebral protection by lidocaine during cardiac operations. *Ann Thorac Surg* 1999; 67:1117-24.

29. Spiess BD, McCarthy RJ, Tuman KJ, Woronowicz AW, Tool KA, Ivankovich AD. Treatment of decompression sickness with a perfluorocarbon emulsion (FC-43). *Undersea Biomed Res* 1988;15:31-7.

30. Lynch PR, Krasner LJ, Vinciquerra T, Shaffer TH. Effects of intravenous perfluorocarbone and oxygen breathing on acute decompression sickness in the hamster. *Undersea Biomed Res* 1989;16:275-81.

31. Spiess BD, Braverman B, Woronowicz AW, Ivankovich AD. Protection from cerebral air emboli with perfluorocarbons in rabbits. *Stroke* 1986;17:1146-9.

32. Report on decompression Illness and dive fatalities. Durham, North Carolina: Divers Alert Network; 1997.

RECOMMENDED FURTHER READING

Francis TJR, Mitchell SJ. The pathophysiology of decompression sickness. In: Brubakk AO, Neuman TS (eds). Bennett and Elliott's Physiology and Medicine of Diving, 5th edn. London: Harcourt Publishers; 2003:530-56.

Francis TJR, Mitchell SJ. Manifestations of decompression disorders. In: Brubakk AO, Neuman TS (eds). Bennett and Elliott's Physiology and Medicine of Diving, 5th edn. London: Harcourt Publishers; 2003: 578-599.

Moon RE, Gorman DF. The treatment of the decompression disorders. In: Brubakk AO, Neuman TS (eds). Bennett and Elliott's Physiology and Medicine of Diving, 5th edn. London: Harcourt Publishers; 2003: 600-50.

Neuman TS. Arterial gas embolism and pulmonary barotrauma. In: Brubakk AO, Neuman TS (eds). Bennett and Elliott's Physiology and Medicine of Diving, 5th edn. London: Harcourt Publishers; 2003: 557-77.

5.2 PREVENTION OF DECOMPRESSION ILLNESS

HOW CAN WE AVOID SUFFERING DCI?

Unfortunately, if we dive we cannot be guaranteed of avoiding DCI. Some unlucky divers will suffer problems after diving conservative and apparently safe profiles. For example, in Australia during 1985, four divers were treated for suspected DCS after single dive profiles of 18m (60ft) for 30 minutes (i.e. half of the U.S. Navy NDL).[1] An Australian Navy diver suffered DCI after a chamber dive for 10 minutes at 27m (90ft).[1] Two of these divers had severe symptoms. A review of DCS cases presenting to Australian Hyperbaric Units between 1996-97 included 38 divers who were treated from DCS (CAGE was excluded as a likely cause) after diving to 10m (33ft) or shallower. Ten of these cases resulted from single dives. Two of the divers had only dives to 5m (16.5ft) in training pools.[2] Over 83% of DCI cases treated in the USA in 1993-97 were divers who reported diving within the limits of their tables or dive computers.[3]

Paradoxically, divers sometimes flaunt the limits imposed by their computers or tables and show no signs of DCS. Thus, susceptibility to DCI (the DCS form in particular) varies substantially from diver to diver and perhaps from dive to dive for an individual diver. A diver can dive one day without any incident and do exactly the same dive profile at another time and end up suffering DCS, for no apparent reason. It seems that the only way we can guarantee that we will not suffer DCI is to give up diving and that seems a little too drastic for most of us. We can, however, modify the way in which we dive in order to minimize our risk. The following list of strategies are generally accepted within the diving and diving medicine communities as being both practical, and effective in reducing risk.

1. Avoid dives close to the limits prescribed by the table or computer used.

In the first edition of this book from 15 years ago, the advice was to "choose a table which prescribes conservative no decompression limits". Since that time, diving has evolved to the point where very few divers use tables to guide their time/depth and decompression. Most contemporary recreational divers use dive computers for this purpose, and it is somewhat difficult to easily assess the relative conservatism of the various devices on offer (See Chapter 24 for some indicative profiles). It thus seems most sensible to suggest that whatever computer is used, the diver uses them in accordance with the instructions, constructs sensible profiles, programs conservatism into the units where possible, and avoids diving close to the prescribed limits.

2. Shorten your allowable bottom time to cater for predisposing factors to DCS.

Factors such as exercise, cold, excess fat and older age may predispose to DCS. One long-time, arbitrary and unvalidated but reasonable suggestion is that *"the No-Decompression Limits be reduced by at least 10% for each predisposing factor present.*[4] Thus, it was suggested that you reduce the limit by 10% for every 10kg (22lbs) above normal weight. Reduce another 10% for every decade over the age of 40.[4] Take off another 10% if you are cold, at least another 10% if you are exerting yourself heavily during the dive, and so on. At times this will not leave much time to dive, but maybe these are just the times when we should not be diving at all!

Some supposed predisposing factors can be managed to eliminate or minimize their effect. For example, if the water is cold a drysuit can be worn. Similarly, the diver can ensure that he or she is well-hydrated before and after diving.

3. *Ascend slowly* and avoid multiple ascents.

The very early U.S. Navy Tables used an ascent rate of 8m (25ft) per minute. These tables were used for "hard hat" diving so a faster ascent rate was difficult to achieve. With the introduction of scuba it became possible to increase the ascent rate and, when these tables were superseded in 1957, the ascent rate was increased to 18m (60ft) per minute. The RNPL tables, published in 1972, suggest an ascent rate of 15m (50ft) per minute. The Bühlmann tables, first published in 1976, suggest an ascent rate of 10m (33ft) per minute. The current version of the U.S. Navy Tables now recommends a reduced ascent rate of 9m (30ft) per minute, so the pendulum appears to have swung back.

Several studies have compared the amount of doppler-detectable bubbles resulting from different ascent rates. Less bubbles were detected after ascent rates of 9-10m (30-33ft) per minute than at the slower rate (3m/10ft per minute), and faster rates (17-18m/56-60ft per minute) tested.[5,6]

Slower ascent rates have become popular over the past few years and most modern diving computers use rates of 9-10m (30-33ft) per minute, or slower. Some devices allow faster ascents through the deeper depths, and slower rates when the diver gets shallower, but there is some controversy over the merits of this. The ascent rate warning alarms on modern dive computers are one of their best and most important features. When these first became available it was remarkable the number of "long-term" divers (the authors included) who were astounded at how slow 10m (33ft) per minute actually was. Clearly, most ascents to this time had been faster. It is our opinion that an important reason for the gratifying failure of DCS case numbers to keep pace with the growth of the diving population over the last decade is simply that modern divers are glued to their computer displays during ascent in order to avoid violating their conservative ascent rates. It is an important issue since there is no doubt that the risk of DCS is greater if a rapid ascent rate is adopted. Slow ascents also reduce the likelihood of a lung overpressure injury and CAGE.

With regard to safe ascents, it is worth taking note of a few other practical issues. Whenever possible, divers should ascend up a line to maintain a point of reference. Hand over hand ascents up a straight shotline will often result in something like the recommended rate. It is also important to have immediate access to the buoyancy control device exhaust valve so that buoyancy can be controlled rapidly. Good buoyancy control skills are critical to safe ascents. Inexperienced divers may benefit from specialty courses that make buoyancy control a number one priority. If not using a device that automatically warns you of an excessive ascent rate, make sure that you carefully observe your timer and your depth gauge. Each 10m (33ft) of ascent should take one minute. If you are beyond where you should be, then *slow down!* It is essential that you train yourself in ascent technique so that you never ascend too rapidly. Finally, the frequently quoted notion that by following the smallest exhaust bubbles you will not exceed an ascent rate of 18m (60ft) per minute is a misconception. Firstly, it is extremely difficult to follow the bubbles, especially when there are a number of divers, or if there is poor visibility or a substantial current. Secondly, the rates of ascent of the bubbles increase dramatically as they expand. Thirdly, 18m (60ft) per minute may often be too fast anyway.

Multiple ascents may increase the risk of DCS by causing bubble formation during the early ascent(s) and thereby altering rate of nitrogen elimination in the latter stages of the dive and after leaving the water.

If bubbles form during an ascent and the diver re-descends, the subsequent behaviour of nitrogen is altered by the presence of those bubbles. In particular, it is likely that gas elimination is slower during the next ascent. Therefore, *if you have ascended prematurely during a dive and then re-descended, consideration should be given to conducting the rest of the dive more conservatively.*

FIGURE 5.2.1

Divers using the descent / ascent line to perform a safety stop.

4. Do safety stops.

It is now common practice for divers to do a precautionary stop at the end of all, or most, dives, even though the tables may not require it. Many experts believe that by spending some time off-gassing in shallower water before surfacing we will reduce bubble formation and the subsequent risk of DCS. There is some evidence to suggest that safety stops may be effective because they give the body time to eliminate nitrogen while it remains in its dissolved state, prior to the formation of significant numbers of bubbles on surfacing. Bubble formation is considered likely to significantly reduce the rate at which nitrogen is subsequently eliminated. Indeed, one older US Navy study that measured nitrogen eliminated from the body after an exposure of 40 minutes at 4ATA (30m (100ft)), indicated that at times nitrogen elimination at depths of 15m (50ft) or shallower may be equal to or greater than that at the surface.[7]

© David Bryant

There have been several studies using Doppler that have demonstrated the efficacy of saftety stops in reducing venous bubble formation. For example, one landmark study involved divers ascending at 18m (60ft) per minute after a dive to 30m (100ft) for 25 minutes (the US Navy NDL) and monitored after different safety stop protocols. Some subjects who made no stop produced a lot of intravascular bubbles. If the divers put in a stop of 2 minutes at 3m (10ft) it drastically reduced the degree of bubbling. If they put in a 1 minute stop at 6m (20ft) and another 4 minute stop at 3m (10ft) the bubbles were eliminated.[8] These results are shown graphically in Figure 5.2.2.

FIGURE 5.2.2

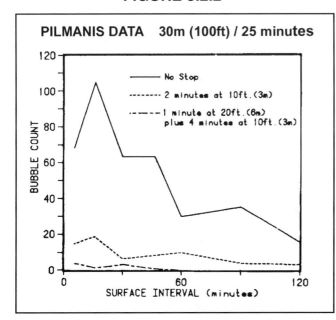

Note that the bubble count is highest in the first 30 minutes or so and then diminishes.

Although these stop depths / times were only tested for this specific exposure, subsequent studies have shown that the addition of similar stops may reduce bubbling after various other exposures.

Safety stops also have other benefits. A diver who is controlling their ascent in order to stop before surfacing will be less likely to ascend rapidly through those last few metres before the surface where the risk of pressure injury is at its highest. The stops also allow a diver to get organized, re-adjust gear and to look, and listen, for surface hazards.

Many different depth-time combinations have been suggested for safety stops. The most desirable sequence is largely a matter of conjecture. In some conditions it is difficult to do any stop at all and, if this is anticipated, the initial bottom time should be reduced accordingly.

A 1990 Workshop convened by the American Academy of Underwater Sciences (AAUS) to determine safe ascent criteria recommended that: "A stop in the range of 10-30ft (3-9m) zone for 3-5 minutes is recommended on every dive."[9]

A 2004 study has indicated that the addition of an additional deeper stop (at around half of the maximum depth of the dive) prior to a 6m (20ft) safety stop reduced, and in many cases eliminated Doppler detectable bubbles and so should reduce the likelihood of DCS.[5] This appears to be somewhat consistent with results of the U.S. Navy study mentioned earlier that indicated that, after the 30m (100ft) exposure nitrogen elimination was most effective at 15m (50ft).[7]

Notwithstanding the above recommendations, the exact depth of the safety stop(s) is not crucial as the stops are not mandatory. Reef dives often provide shallow sections of reef where a diver can spend time at the end of a dive. Otherwise, an anchor line, or other ascent line, can provide a point of reference and stability when doing a safety stop (Figures 5.2.1 and 5.2.3).

FIGURE 5.2.3

Diver doing a stop on a decompression bar.

© Barry Andrewartha

5. Avoid deep or very long dives.

There is no doubt that deeper diving is associated with more risk than shallow diving, and DCS following dives to depths greater than 24–30m (80-100ft) is more likely to result in neurological manifestations. *Excessively long dives also carry a greater risk of DCI.* Statistical analysis of a large number of dives has shown that the risk of DCI increases substantially for dives deeper than 30m (100ft) and/or longer than about 45 minutes.[10]

6. Avoid dives that require mandatory decompression stops.

By undertaking "decompression dives", a diver places themself at risk of being unable to satisfactorily complete the required decompression. If the air supply runs out, or if other problems arise and the stops are not completed, the risk of DCS is increased. Divers wishing to undertake decompression diving should undertake appropriate training on a "Decompression Procedures" course offered by a reputable technical diving training agency.

7. Ensure that your depth gauge or dive computer is accurate.

Depth gauges and the depth function in dive computers are occasionally found to be inaccurate, at times very much so.

If your gauge or computer tells you that you are at 24m (80ft) and you are actually at 26m (86ft), you will be one schedule out with your dive table calculations, or your computer will not be treating the dive with sufficient conservatism. Expensive and reputable depth gauges have been found to be inaccurate by up to 9m (30ft) or more at depth. Ideally, depth gauges and computers should be tested and calibrated at least once a year, but the reality is that this is rarely done. At a more practical level, a diver should regularly compare their depth to that given by their buddy's instruments. Any obvious discrepancy should be investigated.

8. Diving profiles

Although there is little hard data describing actual differences in risk, it is likely that some types of dive profile are more likely to result in DCS than others.

The safest dive profiles are probably those which have a short time at the maximum depth during the early portion of the dive, and then gradually get shallower throughout the remainder of the dive. This is shown in Figures 5.2.6 and 5.2.7 below.

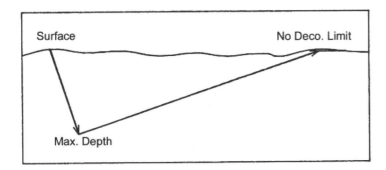

FIGURE 5.2.6

This profile is an ideal profile, especially for reef diving.

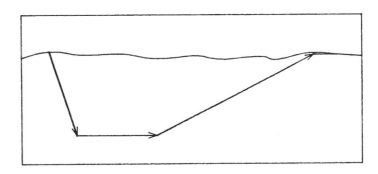

FIGURE 5.2.7

This, although (probably) not as safe as the previous profile, is a quite a good profile for gentle reduction in pressure.

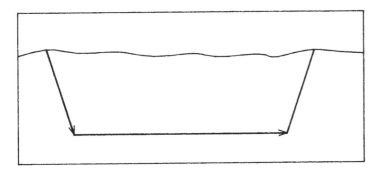

FIGURE 5.2.8

"Square wave" or "Rectangular" dive profile. This profile, often used in wreck diving, is conducive to maximizing nitrogen absorption.

Dive profiles that are more likely to produce DCS are those of a "square wave" or "rectangular" form as shown in Figure 5.2.8. Those in which a diver redescends or works deeper, rather than shallower, throughout the dive theoretically increase the risk of DCS. (See Chapter 23).

FIGURE 5.2.9

This type of profile, in which the diver descends to a deeper level, is likely to impose a greater risk of DCS.

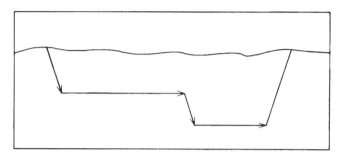

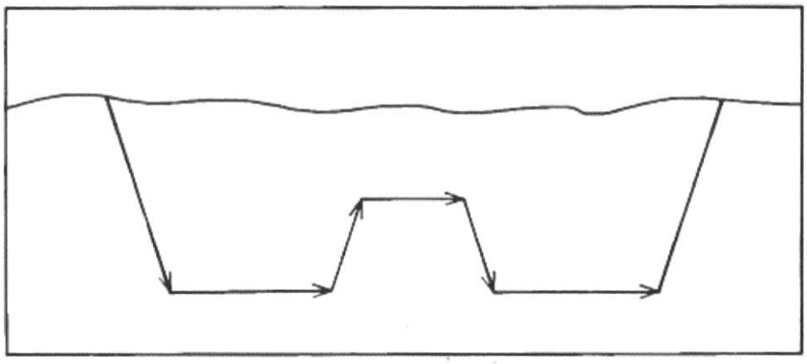

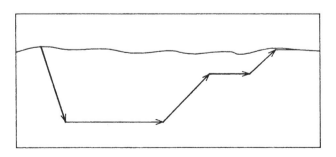

FIGURE 5.2.10

This profile, involving re-descent to depth, is also likely to be asociated with greater risk.

FIGURE 5.2.11

This type of profile may be more likely to cause DCS if the first big pressure change on ascent is too large.

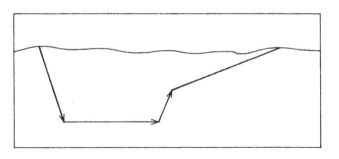

FIGURE 5.2.12

This type of profile can be used for wreck diving instead of the "square profile". It utilizes a slow ascent and a safety stop.

9. Frequent diving.

Some commentators have observed the phenomenon of acclimatization reported in commercial divers performing a single daily exposure, and have suggested that frequent diving might therefore be protective in recreational diving. This issue was discussed in some detail in the discussion of risk factors for DCS, and we reiterate that it is not a phenomenon that is associated with typical patterns of recreational diving. Repetitive diving and multi-day diving in the typical recreational pattern cannot be considered to be protective from DCS and seem more likely, in fact, to have the opposite effect.

10. Nitrox diving.

The use of appropriate nitrox mixes while treating the dive as an air dive is an increasingly popular way of building some conservatism into recreational dive plans. This issue is discussed in more detail in Chapter 28.

SUMMARY

- There will always be an incidence of DCI as long as people continue to dive.

- Some divers suffer DCS despite conservative dive profiles.

- The bottom time allowed by a table or computer should be shortened to cater for predisposing factors to DCS.

- An ascent rate of about 9-10m (30-33ft) per minute seems to be desirable from depths of about 30m (100ft) to the surface.

- It is often difficult to determine and control the rate of ascent. Using an ascent line and monitoring depth and time throughout the dive assists in this regard. Computers with ascent rate alarms are a huge advantage in this regard.

- Multiple ascents probably increase the risk of DCS.

- Safety stop(s) reduce the likelihood of bubble formation in venous blood and probably reduce the incidence of DCS.

- In general, deeper and / or long dives carry a higher risk of DCS.

- For recreational no-decompression diving, repetitive dives are probably more likely to cause DCS than single dives, and this is especially true for multi-day repetitive dives.

- Certain dive profiles are probably less likely to cause DCS. It may be desirable to go to the maximum depth early in the dive and then gradually work shallower throughout the rest of the dive.

- There is no evidence that frequent diving in a typical recreational diving pattern reduces the likelihood of DCS.

REFERENCES

1. Gorman, D. Guidelines for Safer Decompression for Sports and Scientific Divers. *Proceedings from "To Bend or Not to Bend" Symposium*, Adelaide; 1985.

2. Goble SJ. Shallow water bends - fact or fiction. Scuba Diver 1998; Jan-Feb:42-3.

3. Report on decompression illness and diving fatalities. Durham, North Carolina: Divers Alert Network; 1999.

4.. Edmonds C. Decompression Sickness - Its History and Physiology. *SCUBA Diver* 1987; June-July: 22-6.

5. Marroni A, Bennett PB, Cronjé FJ et al. A deep stop during decompression from 82fsw (25m) significantly reduces bubbles and fast tissue gas tensions. *Undersea Hyperb Med* 2004; 31(2):233-43.

6. Carturan D, Boussuges A, Vanuxem P et al. Ascent rate, age, maximal oxygen uptake, adiposity, and circulating venous bubbles after diving. *J Appl Physiol* 2002; 93(4):1349-56.

7. Kindwall EP, Baz A, Lightfoot EN, Lanphier EH, Seireg A. Nitrogen Elimination in Man During Decompresion. *Undersea Biomed Res 1975*; 2 (4):285-97.

8. Pilmanis AA. Decompression Tables and Dive Computers. *SPUMS J* 1987; 17 (2): 71-72.

9. Lang MA, Egstrom GH. Biomechanics of safe ascents workshop. American Academy of Underwater Sciences Diving Safety Publication AAUSDSP-BSA-01-90, California: American Academy of Underwater Sciences; 1990.

10. Weathersby PK et al. Statistically Based Decompression Tables III: Comparative Risk Using U.S. Navy, British and Canadian Standard Air Schedules. Naval Medical Research Institute Report NRMI 86-50; 1986.

© Gary Bell

6

Nitrogen narcosis

"I am personally quite receptive to nitrogen rapture. I like it and fear it like doom. It destroys the instincts of life. Tough individuals are not overcome as soon as neurasthenic persons like me, but they have difficulty extricating themselves. Intellectuals get drunk early and suffer acute attacks on all the senses, which demand hard fighting to overcome" ...

Jacques Cousteau

In 1835 it was first noted that individuals exposed to hyperbaric air behaved as if intoxicated. It is now widely accepted that divers breathing sufficiently raised pressures of air exhibit signs and symptoms of narcosis and intoxication.

Nitrogen narcosis will affect all divers breathing air at depths in excess of 30m (100ft). Some will notice the effects at shallower depths while others may not notice them until deeper. They appear on arrival at a particular depth and, generally, will not worsen as exposure continues at this depth. The effects increase progressively with increasing depth and are readily reversible on ascent to shallower depths.

As with the action of anaesthetic gases, the mechanism of nitrogen narcosis is uncertain. In recent years, there have been two major theories. One relates to the increased nitrogen partial pressure, while the other

relates to carbon dioxide retention. There has been a substantial amount of experimental evidence refuting carbon dioxide build-up (hypercapnia) as the cause of narcosis although, if present, hypercapnia does appear to increase the narcotic effects.[1]

It is generally believed that when breathing hyperbaric air, narcosis is due to the raised partial pressure of nitrogen. Nitrogen is considered an inert (non-reactive) gas as it is thought to participate in no chemical reaction in the human body. Therefore, it must exert its effects by physical means only.

Nitrogen is soluble in fat (lipid), and nerve cell (neuron) membranes contain a high amount of fat. This enables the nitrogen to dissolve into the nerve cell membranes causing a change in width or some other aspect of physical configuration which interferes with transmission of impulses along or between neurons. The greater the depth (and pressure), the greater amount of nitrogen that may dissolve into the membrane, thus establishing the relationship between depth and effect. This may be a similar process to that explaining the mechanism of gases like isoflurane and sevoflurane used in general anaesthesia, with the main difference being that these agents are so extraordinarily soluble in lipid that they exert a profound effect at 1ATA with no need for extra pressure.

The reticular centre of the brain receives messages (nerve impulses) from throughout the body and re-distributes them through the brain. The neurons in the reticular centre seem to be very sensitive to the effects of various narcotic agents, including nitrogen. If the reticular centre is not functioning properly, brain function becomes disrupted. This most commonly affects the neurons within the brain that are responsible for alertness and coordination.

If another narcotic agent such as alcohol, or some other sedative, is also dissolved in the membrane fat of the neurons or otherwise altering neural transmission, the effects will combine and the narcosis will become more severe.

Most other inert gases produce narcosis with similar signs and symptoms to nitrogen narcosis but they vary in regard to potency. With reference to the above discussion, it is not surprising that the narcotic potency of the gases appears to increase with increased solubility in fat and, with the exception of hydrogen and neon, with an increase in molecular weight. Various gases listed in order of increasing narcotic potency are shown in Table 6.1.

TABLE 6.1

Relative narcotic potency of various gases.

Gas	Relative narcotic potency*
helium (4)	4.26
neon (20)	3.58
hydrogen (2)	1.83
nitrogen (14)	1
argon (40)	0.43
krypton (84)	0.14
xenon (131)	0.039

* in order of increasing potency, where 1 = the potency of nitrogen (molecular size in brackets)

SIGNS AND SYMPTOMS

The manifestations of inert gas narcosis have been compared to the effects of alcohol, the early stages of general anaesthesia, hypoxia and hallucinogenic drugs. A list of the signs and symptoms and the depth at which they commonly occur is given in Table 6.2. *It is important to realize that the severity of symptoms and the exact depth of their onset varies greatly between individuals and at different times.*

At shallower depths, brain functions such as memory, concentration, reasoning and judgment are the first affected by narcosis. If a diver is feeling secure in their surroundings a sense of well-being (euphoria) may ensue. However, if the diver is not feeling comfortable, anxiety may result. As the diver goes deeper, movement becomes more difficult and coordination becomes poor. A simple task may be difficult to perform. The diver may make serious errors in judgment and may react slowly to directions or stimuli. At extreme depths hallucinations and eventual unconsciousness may occur.

TABLE 6.2

Signs and symptoms of nitrogen narcosis.

10-30m
(33-100ft)

Mild impairment of performance of unpracticed tasks. Mildly impaired reasoning.
Mild euphoria possible.

30-50m
(100-165ft)

Delayed response to visual and auditory stimuli.
Reasoning and immediate memory affected more than motor co-ordination.
Calculation errors and wrong choices.
Idea fixation.
Over-confidence and sense of well-being.
Laughter and loquacity (in chambers) which may be overcome by self control.
Anxiety (common in cold murky water).

50-70m
(165-230ft)

Sleepiness, impaired judgment, confusion.
Hallucinations.
Severe delay in response to signals, instructions and other stimuli.
Occasional dizziness.
Uncontrolled laughter, hysteria (in chamber).
Terror in some.

70-90m
(230-300ft)

Poor concentration and mental confusion.
Stupefaction with some decrease in dexterity and judgement.
Loss of memory, increased excitability.

90m+
(300ft+)

Hallucinations.
Increased intensity of vision and hearing.
Sense of impending blackout, euphoria, dizziness, manic or depressive states, a sense of levitation, disorganization of the sense of time, changes in facial appearance.
Unconsciousness. Death.

Note: Death may occur at much shallower depths due to errors caused by impaired judgment or over-confidence.

FEATURES OF NITROGEN NARCOSIS

The narcotic effect usually becomes apparent soon after reaching a particular depth. Divers often perceive some improvement in the effects followed by a relatively stable level of narcosis. However, it has been reported that improvement is primarily only subjective as objective tests indicate that there is no change in the narcotic effect. *Narcosis does not worsen as exposure continues at this depth unless the diver's blood carbon dioxide levels become elevated due to anxiety, exertion or some other cause.*

At depths of around 40m (132ft) the effects can usually be overcome by increased concentration and effort. If you read your gauge and do not understand what it says, concentrate on it until it does make sense. If you still cannot understand the reading, ascend immediately to a depth at which you begin to function adequately.

The effects of narcosis decrease immediately on ascent to shallower depths, although, at times, a diver will not remember events that happened during the dive.

Some divers are more susceptible to narcosis than others. The physical and mental state of the diver will affect his or her predisposition to it, so *an individual diver's susceptibility will vary from dive to dive.*

Certain factors increase the effects of nitrogen narcosis. Some of these are:

- Anxiety, apprehension or inexperience
- Recent intake of alcohol or of certain drugs or medications (e.g. sedatives, hallucinogens, some antihistamines)
- Fatigue, heavy physical work
- Cold water
- Rapid descent
- Poor visibility, reduced sensory input
- Excess carbon dioxide
- Changes in oxygen levels
- Task loading

Factors that reduce the effects of narcosis include:

- Strong motivation to perform a task.
- Concentration on the task at hand.
- Acclimatization - prolonged and frequent exposure may provide some degree of adaptation but tolerance can change from day to day. Very experienced deep divers routinely report an increased tolerance to the effects of narcosis, however, some of this at least may be subjective and performance may not always be improved.[2,3] If a deep dive is planned, it may be a good idea to build up to the dive by performing progressively deeper dives during the days prior to the deep dive. These "work-up" dives prior to deep dives help a diver to get more used to the effects of narcosis. However, the risk of decompression sickness must be carefully monitored and dive tables or dive computers must be followed very conservatively.
- Reducing the partial pressure of nitrogen in the breathing gas. The use of gas mixes other than air is discussed in Chapters 28 and 31.

Some divers claim that they have never been "narked", even on air dives at times far deeper than 30m (100ft). It is important to realize that we all suffer from nitrogen narcosis to some degree when we dive on air to 30m (100ft), or deeper. *When tests are performed on any air-breathing diver at 30m (100ft), or deeper, it is possible to demonstrate impairment of concentration and some slowing of thought.* Sometimes, because we are "narked" it is difficult to realize that we are in fact suffering from narcosis. This is similar to the drunk driver who feels perfectly capable of driving safely. Although tests would show that co-ordination is impaired and that senses are dulled, the driver might not be aware of this temporary debility.

It does not take much logical thought to swim around at depth and look around us, so we might not notice the effects of narcosis in this situation. However, if we read our gauges it might take a little longer than normal to absorb what they are telling us. If we must perform a task it might become more difficult than it really should be. Although reflexes and thought processes are slowed down, most problems can be sorted out provided that we remain calm, have sufficient time to do it safely, and do not get lost in our determination to solve one problem only. "Task fixation" often occurs when a narcosis-affected diver encounters a problem. In the effort to solve the immediate problem, the diver may forget to check the air supply or bottom time and, in so doing, might create new problems. The "fixated" diver might also, inadvertently, lose buoyancy and, as they sink, the narcosis will increase, further delaying the response time and, therefore, magnifying the problem.

If you are suffering from narcosis it is possible that your buddy is also "narked", all other factors being equal. Observe your buddy constantly during any dive, especially a deeper dive, regularly checking their gas supply as well as your own. If your buddy does not appear to be adequately alert, ascend with them to the relative safety of shallower water.

The best way to prevent nitrogen narcosis is to avoid diving on air to depths known to cause substantial narcotic effects. Some training agencies prescribe against diving which will result in narcotic effects greater than that experienced using air at 30m (100ft). This essentially implies that all dives deeper than this must be performed using mixtures containing helium (see Chapter 31). Other agencies are less prescriptive, leaving it to divers themselves to evaluate their own ability to operate with increased levels of narcosis. However, most would agree that dives deeper than 50m (165ft) using air are unwise.

Safe diving beyond 30m (100ft) requires adequate diving experience and an awareness of the ever-increasing risk of narcosis and its effect on a diver's judgment and performance. It also requires a diver to be in good physical condition, as well as mentally stable and alert.

It is impossible to state an exact depth limit that is acceptable for all recreational divers. It depends on the experience and condition of the divers, the task to be done (if any), the prevailing conditions and the diver support available.

The combination of narcosis and decompression and air consumption considerations makes deeper diving far more hazardous than diving in shallower water.

SUMMARY

- Nitrogen narcosis affects all divers breathing air at depths greater than 30m (100ft).
- The effects increase progressively with increasing depth, usually appearing on arrival at a depth.
- Narcosis is readily reversible on ascent.
- The exact process that produces narcosis is uncertain.
- The severity of symptoms and the exact depth of their onset vary between individuals and from dive to dive in the same individual.
- Initially brain functions such as memory, concentration, reasoning and judgment are affected. Eventually, movement and coordination may become affected.
- At depths of around 39m (130ft) narcosis can usually be overcome by increased concentration and effort.
- Factors which increase the effects of narcosis include but are not limited to: anxiety, apprehension, inexperience, alcohol/drug ingestion, fatigue, hard work, cold water, task loading and high carbon dioxide levels
- Factors that reduce narcosis include high motivation, concentration and acclimatization.
- Breathing mixtures with a lower percentage of nitrogen than air are often used to reduce narcosis at depth.

REFERENCES

1. Bennett PB, Rostain JC. Inert Gas Narcosis. In: Brubakk AO, Neuman TS (eds). Physiology and Medicine of Diving, 5th edition. Saunders; London; 2003:300-22.

2. Hamilton K, Laliberte MF, Heslegraver R. Subjective and behavioral effects associated with repeated exposure to narcosis. *Aviat Space Environ Med* 1992; 63:865-9.

3. Hamilton K, Laliberte MF, Fowler BI. Dissociation of the behavioral and subjective components of nitrogen narcosis and diver adaptation. *Undersea Hyper Med* 1995; 22(1):41-9.

OTHER SOURCES

Bennett PB. Inert Gas Narcosis and High-Pressure Nervous Syndrome. In: Bove AA (ed). Bove and Davis' Diving Medicine, 4th Edition. Saunders; Philadelphia; 2004:225-39.

Lowry C. Inert Gas Narcosis. In: Edmonds C, Lowry C, Pennefather J, Walker R. *Diving and Subaquatic Medicine*, 4th edition. Arnold; London, 2002:183-94

Gilliam B and Von Maier R. Deep Diving. Watersport Publishing Inc, San Diego; 1992.

RECOMMENDED FURTHER READING

Bennett PB, Rostain JC. Inert Gas Narcosis. In: Brubakk AO, Neuman TS (eds). Physiology and Medicine of Diving, 5th edition. Saunders; London; 2003:300-22.

Bennett PB. Inert Gas Narcosis and High-Pressure Nervous Syndrome. In: Bove AA (ed).Bove and Davis' Diving Medicine, 4th Edition. Saunders; Philadelphia; 2004 225-39.

Carbon dioxide and diving

Carbon dioxide is a waste product of normal metabolism. It is produced in the tissues and carried in blood back to the lungs for elimination in the exhaled breath.

Carriage in blood is in three forms. A small amount is dissolved in the plasma, another small proportion is bonded to haemoglobin or plasma proteins, but most of the carbon dioxide in our blood is carried in a soluble form as bicarbonate, the end product of a chemical combination of carbon dioxide with water. Carbon dioxide diffuses from the tissues into the red blood cells and combines with water to form carbonic acid. This in turn dissociates into bicarbonate and hydrogen ions. Although most of the hydrogen ions are buffered by haemoglobin and other proteins, this dissociation of carbonic acid causes the acidity of the blood to increase. Increased acidity (due to hydrogen ions) is detected by the chemoreceptors in the respiratory centre of the brain (medulla), and to a lesser extent by peripheral chemoreceptors in the carotid arteries and aorta, and the rate and depth of breathing is increased in order to eliminate carbon dioxide until the acidity is reduced to normal levels. In this regard, increasing carbon dioxide levels are recognized as the most important stimulus that drives us to increase ventilation of the lungs.

It is critical to understand, at this early stage of the discussion, that the elimination of carbon dioxide from the body is directly related to ventilation of the lungs. Indeed, the relationship between carbon dioxide levels and ventilation can be described by this very simple equation:

$$PaCO_2 = VCO_2 \div VA$$

Where:

$PaCO_2$ = Pressure of carbon dioxide in arterial blood

VCO_2 = carbon dioxide production by the tissues

VA = alveolar ventilation

In words, this equation tells us that arterial carbon dioxide will tend to increase if carbon dioxide production increases or if alveolar ventilation decreases. Obviously, the opposites apply.

Atmospheric air contains about 0.04% carbon dioxide at a partial pressure of 0.3mmHg (0.0004ATA). The partial pressure of carbon dioxide in our lungs is normally 40mmHg (0.05ATA), the extra being that produced by our body. The carbon dioxide levels in the lungs (alveolar) and the blood leaving the lungs in the pulmonary veins are identical. The carbon dioxide levels in the rest of the venous blood are around 45mmHg(0.06ATA). The body regulates breathing to maintain the arterial carbon dioxide levels at around 40mmHg(0.05ATA).

At rest, our bodies produce around 200ml of carbon dioxide each minute. When we exercise more carbon dioxide is produced, with levels rising as high as 3 litres per minute or more for a short period of time. However, under normal circumstances, the breathing rate increases and flushes out this excess carbon dioxide.

CARBON DIOXIDE BUILD UP DURING DIVING

An excess of carbon dioxide in the blood is called *"hypercapnia"*. It is associated with certain lung diseases, such as emphysema, where gradual respiratory failure results in the body adapting to and tolerating higher levels of carbon dioxide. It is also associated with diving, for a variety of reasons.

From the above equation, we can predict that carbon dioxide may accumulate if there is an increase in carbon dioxide production or a decrease in ventilation. Whilst this equation applies equally in non-diving and diving situations, there are some "unique" aspects of diving that are important, particularly with respect to ventilation.

If we consider carbon dioxide production first, we can immediately appreciate that any extra exercise associated with diving (just like exercise in any context) will result in increased carbon dioxide production. Perhaps the only unique thing about diving is that breathing itself becomes an increasingly important part of the exercise load at deeper depths. This is because of the increased density of the breathing gas, and the extra work the diver's respiratory muscles must perform in order to continue shifting the same volumes. Put into context, a diver swimming at 0.5 knots at 5m (16.5ft) depth will be performing less work and producing less CO_2 than the same diver swimming at exactly the same speed at 30m (100ft), because at 30m there is extra work associated with breathing.

Now, if we consider ventilation, we start encountering some very interesting problems. Because of the increased density of breathing gas at greater depths, our ability to ventilate the lungs is reduced; more or less because it is just too hard to move the same volumes as we can at the surface. Indeed, breathing air at 4ATA (30m (100ft)) our "maximum voluntary ventilation" (breathing as rapidly and deeply as we can to move as much air as possible) is only 50% that at the surface! Herein lies the big problem. Whilst it is easy to start working just as hard at depth as we can at the surface (swimming per se is no harder at 30m than it is at the surface), it is entirely possible that we fail to eliminate the increased amount of carbon dioxide produced because we can't breathe hard enough at this depth (whereas we could at the surface). Under these circumstances of increased production and decreased ventilation (and hence decreased CO_2 elimination), carbon dioxide will start to accumulate.

There are other unique circumstances of diving that can amplify this basic physiological problem:

First, even greater depth-dependent breathing resistance may be imposed by the regulator or other breathing equipment, especially if they are poorly tuned or incorrectly set up. Breathing resistance may also be imposed by a tight exposure suit, buoyancy compensator or harness.

Second, the increased respiratory dead space created by a regulator may allow some expired carbon dioxide to be rebreathed, although this only happens to a small extent with the masks and regulators normally used by recreational divers. It can also occur during helmet diving if the gas flow is insufficient to remove the diver's expired carbon dioxide.

Third, in rebreather diving, any failure of the scrubber to remove all carbon dioxide from the recycled gas will result in the diver inhaling carbon dioxide. This is not accounted for by the above equation, and potentially can cause very dramatic increases in arterial carbon dioxide levels. In a similar vein, if a diver's air supply has been contaminated with extra carbon dioxide the consequences may be disastrous. For example, if a cylinder contains 2% carbon dioxide relatively little effect might be noticed on the surface, but at 40m (132ft) the partial pressure of carbon dioxide in the lungs would be about 0.10ATA (75mmHg) and will cause severe mental impairment in the diver. However, in reality, air contamination with carbon dioxide is vanishingly rare.

Fourth, it has been argued that both nitrogen narcosis and breathing oxygen at higher partial pressures than we are accustomed to at 1ATA may blunt the usual increased drive to breathe that arises from increased carbon dioxide levels as described above.

Fifth, there is good evidence to suggest that an increased drive to breathe (from increasing carbon dioxide levels) coupled simultaneously with increased breathing resistance (such as we see in diving – especially deeper diving) will cause adoption of a disadvantageous pattern of rapid shallow breathing that does not move much "fresh gas" and is only likely to exacerbate the problem. Indeed, this may induce a catastrophic spiral of increasing carbon dioxide levels, and less and less efficient ventilation.

Sixth, some divers intentionally indulge in practices that are likely to promote retention of carbon dioxide. Fixation on reducing air supply consumption and indulging in intentional hypoventilation is the obvious example. So-called "skip breathing" where the diver intentionally holds their breath to reduce consumption is the ultimate expression of this dangerous practice.

Finally, although not unique to diving, certain individuals have a lower ventilatory response to increasing carbon dioxide levels than others and may therefore be at more risk of suffering problems in diving where there are many risk factors promoting hypercapnia as we have seen above. In addition, one study indicates that scuba divers may actually *develop* a reduced responsiveness to carbon dioxide and higher resting carbon dioxide levels than non-divers.[1] Once again, this was more pronounced in certain individuals. It was suggested that this increased tolerance may be a consequence of the higher carbon dioxide levels experienced with some equipment designs during dives.

We can see from the above that there are many circumstances of diving that favour carbon dioxide accumulation, and this is a problem that all divers should be very aware of.

CARBON DIOXIDE TOXICITY

Carbon dioxide acts as a respiratory stimulant, relaxes the smooth muscles of certain blood vessels, and when levels rise sufficiently, can increase the acidity levels in the blood (acidosis) and cause a variety of unwanted biochemical reactions. At sufficiently high levels, carbon dioxide will cause depression of the nervous system. The effect depends on the levels of carbon dioxide in the blood.

The rapid breathing caused by hypercapnia can warn a diver of increasing carbon dioxide levels but, if he is exercising, the symptom can be masked by the increased breathing due to the exercise (due, in part, to raised carbon dioxide levels). It has also been shown that a diver's ability to detect carbon dioxide build-up may be affected by water temperature, being more difficult in warm water than in cold water.[2]

If allowed to accumulate in the body, carbon dioxide will exert a noticeable toxic effect when a sufficient quantity is present.

SIGNS AND SYMPTOMS

The signs and symptoms of carbon dioxide toxicity depend on the rate of build-up of the carbon dioxide and the amount of carbon dioxide present.

A very rapid build-up may cause a diver to become unconscious with few prior warning signs or symptoms except for a desire to breathe deeper and faster.

A gradual build-up, which is more likely to occur with recreational open-circuit scuba diving, will normally cause various other symptoms before loss of consciousness would occur.

As the carbon dioxide level gradually increases, the first sign is often an increase in the depth and rate of breathing. *Shortness of breath with rapid, deep breathing occurs.*

As the level continues to increase, the blood vessels dilate and the pulse rate and blood pressure rise. *A throbbing headache*, usually at the front of the head, results from the dilation of blood vessels in the brain. The headache can be severe and can last for many hours after a dive.

The increased breathing rate and throbbing headache are the two symptoms of carbon dioxide excess commonly encountered by recreational divers.

If the level continues to rise, (as it may in a malfunctioning closed-circuit rebreather system) *dizziness, nausea, confusion, disorientation and restlessness can occur. The diver may become flushed and their face may feel warm. Lightheadedness, muscle twitches and jerks, reduced vision, unconsciousness, tremors and convulsions* may occur as the hypercapnia progresses. These symptoms are similar to those of acute oxygen toxicity.

A further increase produces depression of the nervous system which reduces the pulse rate, blood pressure and breathing rate.

Death can occur and is usually from respiratory or cardiac arrest.

Although death can occur in rare cases, recovery from carbon dioxide toxicity is the norm providing drowning does not supervene.

FIRST AID

At the surface:

- Remove the diver from any contaminated breathing supply.
- Assess the airway, breathing and circulation and resuscitate if necessary.
- Keep the diver still to minimize production of additional carbon dioxide.
- Provide high concentration oxygen.
- Seek medical aid.

Underwater:

If a diver develops symptoms of carbon dioxide toxicity they should immediately *stop moving, take deep, regular breaths and try to relax. The dive should be terminated and the diver should return to the surface with as little effort as possible.* The buoyancy compensator can be carefully adjusted to maintain neutral buoyancy. This will allow the diver to ascend with the minimum of finning and consequent exertion.

Once on the surface, the diver should be allowed to breathe fresh air, and any tight-fitting equipment and exposure suit should be loosened or removed.

Elevated concentrations oxygen can be given, if available. Divers have sometimes reported an improvement in symptoms after breathing elevated oxygen concentrations. This may be due in part to the oxygen narrowing the dilated blood vessels in the brain.

Ordinary analgesics may provide some relief from the headache but it is not uncommon for a "carbon dioxide headache" to persist for many hours after a dive despite the use of analgesic medication.

In the context of rebreather diving, symptoms of carbon dioxide toxicity can mean that the diver is simply exerting too much and ventilating insufficiently, just as in open circuit diving. However, as alluded to above, such symptoms may also indicate that there is a problem with the carbon dioxide scrubber. A detailed discussion this rebreather failure mode is beyond the scope of this chapter, however there are several potential responses in such a situation:

First, the diver could "bail-out" onto an emergency supply of open circuit gas carried for this purpose. Second, the diver could flush the rebreather loop with fresh gas to displace any gas contaminated with carbon dioxide. In a situation where there has been transient carbon dioxide breakthrough (through the scrubber) because of a short period of intense work, this strategy combined with rest and deep breathing is likely to bring the situation under control. Third, a closed circuit rebreather diver could adopt a "semi-closed circuit" mode of operation in which they exhale every third or fourth breath, resulting in the periodic drawing of fresh gas into the rebreather loop. The option that is taken will depend upon the rebreather type and the circumstances under which the carbon dioxide toxicity arises.

PREVENTION

A minor degree of hypercapnia is perhaps inevitable in divers, especially those who dive deeper. Some of the extra breathing effort is unavoidable as it is inherent to breathing denser gas through a regulator. The degree of hypercapnia can be minimized by:

- Always breathing normally. Never try to conserve air by "skip breathing".
- Using a regulator which provides the minimum resistance to breathing. Some regulators perform far better than others in this respect. Any regulator must be properly adjusted, maintained, and cleaned to minimize deposits of salt, sand and other foreign bodies which will affect its performance. Some unbalanced regulators are not suitable for deep diving as they become harder to breathe from as the cylinder pressure drops.
- Ensuring that the air supply is not contaminated.
- Minimizing exertion during a dive, especially a deep dive.
- Correctly maintaining, assembling and monitoring the carbon dioxide "scrubber" as appropriate if planning to use a rebreather
- The use of less dense helium-containing mixes for deep dives in order to reduce the work of breathing and improve the ability to ventilation efficiently

THE EFFECT OF HYPERCAPNIA ON OTHER DIVING DISORDERS

Hypercapnia has been known, or believed, to predispose various other diving ailments. Its influence on some of these conditions is discussed briefly in the following paragraphs.

Decompression sickness

High levels of carbon dioxide cause the blood vessels to dilate, increasing the blood flow to the body tissues. This vasodilatation, together with the increased breathing and heart rates, may cause more nitrogen to be delivered to various tissues during a dive and, so, increase the potential for bubble formation during ascent. In addition, any extra carbon dioxide present will diffuse into and enlarge existing bubbles.

Nitrogen narcosis

Hypercapnia does appear to increase the narcotic effects of nitrogen. The depressive effects of both carbon dioxide and nitrogen, as well as the increased delivery of nitrogen combine to increase the narcosis.

Oxygen toxicity

Hypercapnia has been shown to markedly increase the potential for cerebral oxygen toxicity. One explanation for this is that increased cerebral blood flow caused by hypercapnia increases the amount of oxygen delivered to the brain.

Hypothermia

Carbon dioxide accumulation may impair temperature regulation. When higher concentrations are reached, heat production is impaired, while heat loss is increased due to the increased perfusion of the skin and limbs (unless vasodilation due to excess carbon dioxide is overcome by vaso-constriction due to cold).

LOW CARBON DIOXIDE LEVELS - HYPOCAPNIA

"Hypocapnia", which means low carbon dioxide levels, usually occurs as a result of overbreathing (hyperventilation). Hyper-ventilation commonly occurs involuntarily in an anxiety or panic situation, but is at times done voluntarily by breath-hold divers in order to lengthen their breath-hold time.

Hyperventilation, whether voluntary or involuntary, reduces the carbon dioxide levels in the blood without significantly raising the blood oxygen levels. In a breath-hold situation the lower carbon dioxide level delays the breathing stimulus and can allow blood oxygen levels to fall dangerously low before breathing is triggered. The low carbon dioxide level can further complicate the situation by constricting cerebral blood vessels and reducing the oxygen supply to the brain. During a breath-hold dive after hyperventilation, carbon dioxide may not rise quickly enough to stimulate breathing before loss of consciousness results from the low oxygen levels. The swimmer often drowns. A scuba diver who is very anxious might begin to hyperventilate, but is unlikely to suffer significant hypocapnia, especially at depth. However, hyperventilation before breath-hold diving has been known to cause a substantial number of cases of drowning. The diver becomes unconscious due to hypoxia before, but more often during or immediately after the ascent, because the partial pressure of oxygen in the lungs falls with ascent.

© Euiook Jung

© Barry Andrewartha

SUMMARY

- High carbon dioxide levels can occur when diving due to:
  - increased work of breathing and increased carbon dioxide production
  - reduced ventilation
  - exertion
  - failure of rebreather carbon dioxide scrubbers
  - contamination of air supply

- The problem potentially increases as the depth of the dive increases.

- Some divers are more susceptible.

- The most common manifestations of carbon dioxide toxicity are rapid, deep breathing and a throbbing headache, but other more severe symptoms can occur if the problem is allowed to continue.

- Hypercapnia is a potentially serious problem for a diver exerting himself at depth. It can cause a diver to become unconscious underwater. It is also a potential problem for the diver using closed, or semi-closed breathing apparatus.

- First aid in severe cases involves removal from source of toxicity and supporting life. For mild cases, minimize exertion, breathe deeply and regularly and abort dive. Breathe fresh air or oxygen if available.

- Carbon dioxide toxicity can be minimized by breathing normally, using a good, well-maintained regulator, ensuring clean air, avoiding exertion at depth, and always maintaining the carbon dioxide scrubber in a rebreather.

- High carbon dioxide levels can predispose to decompression illness, nitrogen narcosis, oxygen toxicity and hypothermia.

- Low carbon dioxide levels (hypocapnia) delay the breathing response and may cause hypoxia and consequent loss of consciousness in breath hold diving.

REFERENCES

1. Florio J et al. Breathing pattern and ventilatory response to carbon dioxide in divers. *J of Appl Physiol 1979;* 46:1076-80.

2. Fothergill DM, Taylor WF, Hyde DE. Physiologic and perceptual responses to hypercarbia during warm- and cold-water immersion. *Undersea Hyperb Med* 1998; 25(1):1-12

OTHER SOURCES

Bayne C. Breath-hold Diving. In: Davis J (ed). Hyperbaric and Undersea Medicine. California: Medical Seminars Inc.; 1981.

Camporesi EM, Bosco G. Ventilation, Gas Exchange and Exercise Under Pressure. In: Brubakk AO, Neuman TS (eds). Physiology and Medicine of Diving, 5th edition. London: Saunders; 2003:77-114.

Clark JM and Thom SR. Toxicity of Oxygen, Carbon Dioxide and Carbon Monoxide. In: Bove AA (ed). Bove and Davis' Diving Medicine, 4th Edition. Philadelphia: Saunders; 2004:241-60.

Donald K. Carbon dioxide and hyperbaric oxygen. In: Oxygen and the Diver. Hanly: The SPA Ltd; 1992: Chapter 6.

Donald K. Are divers really different. In: Oxygen and the Diver. The SPA Ltd; 1992: Chapter 7.

Edmonds C. Carbon dioxide toxicity. In: Edmonds C, Lowry C, Pennefather J, Walker R. Diving and Subaquatic Medicine, 4th edition. London: Arnold; 2002:223-31.

Kerem D, Melamed Y, Moran A. Alveolar PCO2 during rest and exercise in divers and non-divers breathing O2 at 1 ATA. *Undersea Biomed Res* 1980; 7(1):17-26.

RECOMMENDED FURTHER READING

Edmonds C. Carbon dioxide toxicity. In: Edmonds C, Lowry C, Pennefather J, Walker R. Diving and Subaquatic Medicine, 4th edition. London: Arnold; 2002:223-31.

8

Oxygen

OXYGEN UTILIZATION & TRANSPORT

Oxygen is a colourless, odourless and tasteless gas that constitutes about 21% of the air we breathe. Oxygen is essential for life. It is principally utilized in the cell mitochondria, where oxygen facilitates production of adenosine triphosphate (ATP) which fuels biological processes within the body.

Oxygen diffuses into and throughout the body down a pressure gradient ("oxygen cascade") from the atmosphere (where the partial pressure (PO_2) of saturated room air is 150mmHg) to alveolar gas (PO_2=100-105mmHg), to arterial blood (PO_2=95-100mmHg) and finally to the mitochondria (PO_2=2-22mmHg).

Tissue oxygenation depends on oxygen delivery by the cardiorespiratory system and oxygen extraction by tissues.

Oxygen is carried in the blood by both attachment to haemoglobin and dissolved in plasma. A resting adult requires about 250ml of oxygen per minute, and this can increase to as high as 3 litres per minute (lpm) when exercising heavily.

Under normal conditions, around 15ml of dissolved oxygen is transported around the body by the plasma per minute, far less than required to meet metabolic needs. Obviously a more effective mechanism of oxygen carriage is needed.

Haemoglobin (Hb) is a far better oxygen carrier. The red blood cells contain around 150g of Hb per litre of blood, and each gram of Hb can carry approximately 1.34ml of oxygen. This means that each litre of blood can carry 150g x 1.34ml/g = 201ml of oxygen bound to Hb under normal circumstances. With a cardiac output at rest of 5lpm, this provides just over 1000ml of oxygen per minute - well in excess of the normal resting requirement of 250ml per minute

The Hb in arterial blood is normally almost fully saturated (approx. 97.5%) with oxygen. This means that 97.5% of its oxygen-binding sites are occupied by oxygen molecules. From the above paragraph you can see that the body extracts only 250ml from a possible 1000ml of oxygen each minute, and it should come as no surprise therefore that Hb in venous blood still remains around 75% saturated with oxygen.

EFFECTS OF TOO LITTLE OXYGEN

When body tissues receive too little oxygen they become hypoxic, and, if no oxygen is received, anoxia results. **Hypoxia** is a state of low oxygen levels, and **anoxia** is a complete lack of oxygen.

Hypoxia causes cells to change to non-oxygen (anaerobic) metabolism, which may create a shortage of cell energy and causes an increase in blood acidity. Body cells cannot survive for long without oxygen. Brain cells are particularly sensitive to oxygen starvation and may die within minutes because they cannot change to non-oxygen metabolism.

The amount of oxygen delivered to a tissue depends on the quantity of oxygen in the blood and the rate of blood flow (perfusion). There are many ways that delivery can be impaired, resulting in tissue hypoxia. Potential causes of hypoxia or anoxia include:

Reduction of oxygen in the inspired gas.
This can be an issue in technical diving where mixes with a low fraction of oxygen are employed safely at greater depth (and therefore greater pressure), but these same mixes contain too little oxygen to be safely used nearer to the surface. Symptoms of hypoxia can be expected if the inspired fraction of oxygen (FIO_2) falls below 16% at the surface, and unconsciousness will normally occur if the FIO_2 at the surface falls below 12%. This corresponds to an arterial PO_2 of approximately 36mmHg.

Failure of efficient ventilation of the lungs.
Air must be moved in and out of the lungs if oxygen levels in the lung's alveoli are to be maintained.

Lung diseases, including acute problems like drowning.
Interestingly, the most important problems are those that cause blood to pass through the lungs without coming into contact with well-ventilated alveoli. This means that venous blood gets directly across to the arterial circulation without being oxygenated, and the resulting mixture of poorly oxygenated venous blood with arterial blood can markedly lower the oxygen content of arterial blood. This phenomenon is known as "shunt". In drowning, some of the alveoli might contain water rather than air, and any blood passing through their associated capillaries will not become oxygenated. Pneumothorax is another potential diving-related situation which can result in the same problem. Blood passing through the circulation of a lung that is collapsed will not be oxygenated properly and will contribute to shunt.

Low levels of Hb in the blood.
This can reduce oxygen delivery to tissues by reducing the blood's oxygen carrying capacity. To some extent this can be compensated by increasing cardiac output and therefore the volume of blood circulating, but eventually, falling Hb levels will result in tissue hypoxia.

Inadequate circulation.
In this setting, there is inadequate blood flow to tissues, and even if the blood is well-oxygenated, not enough is reaching the tissues. This is the situation commonly referred to as shock, and it can arise in a variety of situations such as heart attack and haemorrhage. In diving, it can also occur in very severe decompression sickness, when the circulation of the lungs becomes significantly blocked by bubbles. Decompression sickness of this severity is extremely rare.

BENEFITS OF BREATHING HIGHER CONCENTRATIONS OF OXYGEN

Depending on the cause of hypoxia, breathing an increased inspired fraction of oxygen may help relieve the problem.

Obviously, if hypoxia is, or has been, caused by low inspired fraction of oxygen, then breathing an increased inspired fraction is likely to correct it very quickly.

If hypoxia is caused by reduced ventilation of the lungs, then increasing the inspired fraction of oxygen can markedly improve the oxygen levels in the alveoli and therefore in the blood, even if the ventilation of the lungs remains relatively reduced.

If hypoxia is caused by shunt in the lungs (see above), then unfortunately, oxygen administration is only partly effective. This is because the oxygen really only comes into contact with the blood that is flowing past well ventilated alveoli. This blood gets well oxygenated even during air breathing (remember, arterial Hb is usually 97.5% saturated under normal circumstances) and so exposing it to oxygen cannot improve things much. In contrast, the oxygen will not reach alveoli that are collapsed or that have water in them, so any blood flowing past these alveoli will not be any better oxygenated and will still mix with the arterial blood, lowering its oxygen content.

One other advantage of breathing increased fractions of oxygen deserves mention. Specifically, any increase in the fraction of oxygen in the alveoli by definition increases the PO_2 in both alveoli and the blood passing through its associated blood vessels. The resulting increase in the PO_2 of the arterial blood is important because it is the PO_2 that provides the driving force for diffusion of oxygen into the tissues. Thus, a greater PO_2 will tend to increase diffusion of oxygen into tissues, and this may be important in tissues whose circulation has been reduced.

If tissue oxygenation can be improved for any number of these reasons, then this is likely to be profoundly beneficial in any situation where hypoxia might prevail. In a victim of shock it might be life saving.

Overall, it is safe to say that *maximizing the inspired oxygen concentration to an ill or injured person will maximize the haemoglobin saturation and increase the amount of oxygen dissolved in plasma. This increases the chances of survival of hypoxic tissues with a poor blood supply.*

For injured divers there are other reasons to provide a very high inspired fraction of oxygen, probably close to 100%, especially where decompression illness is suspected. Breathing 100% oxygen provides very important benefits for a diver suffering from DCI. These are:

• By eliminating nitrogen from the inspired gas 100% oxygen breathing accelerates nitrogen elimination from the body, thus reducing bubble size more quickly.

A gas diffuses from an area of high concentration to areas of lower concentration. The greater the difference in concentrations of the gas, the faster this diffusion occurs. When breathing 100% oxygen, the injured diver is not inhaling the large amounts of nitrogen present in air. Washing out nitrogen from the lungs encourages the nitrogen in the blood to diffuse into the lungs, and lowers the partial pressure of nitrogen in the arterial blood. This arterial blood then passes through the tissues and since it now contains much less nitrogen than the tissues, nitrogen diffuses from the tissues and from the bubbles into the blood and is taken to the lungs and eliminated. This cycle continues until all the excess nitrogen is removed.

Interestingly, some experiments show that nitrogen washout may actually be reduced by increasing the concentration of oxygen too greatly, probably due to the cardiovascular changes such as the reduced perfusion, heart rate and cardiac output that may accompany increased inspired oxygen concentrations[1] Nevertheless, this should not deter the diving first aid provider administering 100% oxygen to a DCI victim.

Not surprisingly, it has been shown that breathing an increased oxygen concentration will reduce bubble size. An experiment in which bubbles were observed in various aqueous tissues of the rat demonstrated accelerated bubble resolution when either oxygen or heliox were breathed compared to air. Interestingly, it was noted that some bubbles grew for short periods prior to shrinking. This effect was most pronounced with oxygen,[2] and may provide a possible explanation for the transient worsening of DCI symptoms that has sometimes been noted during the early stages of oxygen administration.

- Any reduction in blood flow due to bubble formation may cause hypoxia in affected tissues. The higher oxygen partial pressures may help to oxygenate any hypoxic tissues by increasing diffusion of oxygen to those areas. It has been suggested, but not proven, that oxygen (especially hyperbaric oxygen) may also assist in reducing the swelling in hypoxic tissues by drawing fluid away from injured tissue.

Although pure oxygen is recommended for the first aid management of DCI, it is possible that helium-oxygen mixtures could sometimes prove even more advantageous for nitrogen elimination. However, the use of such mixtures would introduce many practical disadvantages and 100% oxygen currently remains the gas of choice for the first aid management of DCI.

EXPERIENCE WITH OXYGEN FIRST AID

Many divers who received oxygen first aid have reported reduction or resolution of symptoms prior to recompression.[3, 4, 5, 6,7,8]

One report examined 2,192 cases of DCI taken from the DAN America database for the years 1989-93.[3] It concluded that divers who received oxygen first aid were more likely to have complete or partial resolution of symptoms prior to recompression than those who did not receive surface oxygen. This report also found that those divers who received surface oxygen had a lower likelihood of residual symptoms after treatment. This trend was significant with mild DCI and approached significance with severe DCI.

A more recent report examined 2,231 DCI cases from 1998-2003, again from the DAN America database.[8,9] This study examined divers who received surface oxygen within 6 hours of symptoms (11.5%), those who received surface oxygen after delays longer than 6 hours (39.5%), and those who received no surface oxygen (49%). It indicated that oxygen first aid was most effective in reducing symptoms of DCI if given within 6 hours of the onset of symptoms. Divers who received surface oxygen within 6 hours appeared to have a faster resolution of symptoms with recompression and required fewer treatments. However, in this study, there was no significant difference in post treatment residual symptoms between the three groups.

Prompt provision of high concentrations of inspired oxygen may reduce symptoms of DCI and may minimize the damage that can occur while the diver is being transported to a recompression facility.

FIGURE 8.1

Diver receiving oxygen first aid.

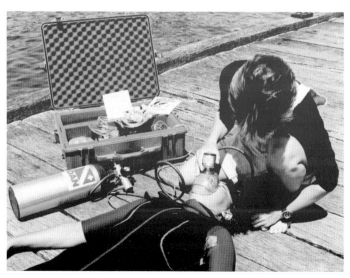

Oxygen breathing prior to recompression may reduce the amount of recompression required and, on rare occasions, make recompression unnecessary. It is likely that fewer treatments will be necessary if the delay to oxygen first aid and/or recompression is minimized.

However, oxygen provision is often delayed. It is not uncommon for divers to fail to recognize or accept that symptoms they are experiencing after diving could be DCI, or to ignore these symptoms. In some cases oxygen equipment is not readily available, or if available, it may not provide high concentration oxygen effectively. As a result, *oxygen provision is often delayed, not continuous and frequently at a far lower concentration than desired.*

Supplemental oxygen is also beneficial in the management of hypoxia resulting from a broad range of diving-related and non-diving-related injuries and illnesses. These include pulmonary barotrauma, drowning, salt-water aspiration, toxic gas and smoke inhalation, stroke, heart attack, trauma, envenomation, and many others.

In summary, 100% oxygen provides the following benefits to the diver:

- adds no more inert gas
- washes out dissolved nitrogen
- washes out the nitrogen in bubbles thus reducing bubble size
- Improves blood and tissue oxygenation
- may reduce respiratory distress
- may reduce shock and cerebral oedema

Oxygen breathing should not be considered a final treatment for diving emergencies. It is a supplement to normal diving first aid procedures and should increase the effect of those procedures and give the injured diver the greatest chance of a full, and speedy, recovery. *Even though an injured diver may appear to have improved greatly, or even completely since breathing oxygen, they must usually still receive prompt specialist attention as symptoms may return and /or worsen if not adequately managed. Such a diver must refrain from further diving until cleared to do so by a diving physician.*

The breathing of oxygen is a first aid measure and should not under most circumstances substitute for the appropriate medical assessment and recompression required for decompression illness, regardless of the response.

An occasional exception to this rule may occur when a diver has mild, equivocal symptoms or is injured in a remote location and access to a recompression chamber is difficult and will be greatly delayed (probably by more than about 24 hours. In such circumstances, divers are advised to breathe high concentration oxygen for 4–5 hours continuously and to seek advice from a diving physician. Further periods of oxygen breathing may well be advised, as well as hydration management. The physician will ultimately decide whether an evacuation is required, based on their assessment of the severity of the DCI, the diver's response to oxygen breathing, the availability of oxygen supplies, the availability of local medical care, and various other factors.

ADVERSE REACTIONS TO OXYGEN BREATHING

OXYGEN TOXICITY

Oxygen breathed at sufficient partial pressures and for sufficient duration will impair the function of, and eventually damage, any living cell. The level of toxicity depends on the partial pressure of oxygen, the length of exposure and the susceptibility of the individual.

Cell metabolism normally produces as one of its by-products an entity (superoxide anion) that can become harmful to cells in sufficient quantity. This entity, and others, known as an oxygen "free radical", carries an electrical charge that can influence and disrupt the normal function of nearby cells. The production of free radicals is sometimes increased to toxic levels when elevated oxygen concentrations are breathed.

The dose of oxygen to which a body tissue is exposed depends on a variety of factors that include the oxygen tension in the arterial blood, the blood flow and supply (perfusion) to the tissue and the metabolic rate of the tissue.

Breathing oxygen partial pressures above 0.5bar affects a variety of body organs, predominantly the lungs. Higher partial pressures can affect the central nervous system.

PULMONARY OXYGEN TOXICITY

The lung is exposed to higher oxygen tensions than other body organs. When oxygen is breathed at partial pressures greater than 0.5bar for extended periods it gradually causes damage to the lungs. Prolonged oxygen poisoning will permanently damage lungs, and can cause death.

High concentrations of oxygen damages airways and lungs by initially causing irritation and swelling of cells in the walls of the airways, capillaries and alveoli, so increasing the distance oxygen has to diffuse to enter the blood. This swelling stiffens the lungs and makes breathing more difficult. Early in the exposure, the damage is reversible when the oxygen concentration returns to normal. However, if oxygen breathing continues, there may be irreversible inflammatory damage to the lung tissue. Death from hypoxia can occur in spite of high oxygen partial pressures.

Continual breathing of 100% oxygen at the surface will cause irritation of the respiratory tract and lungs, usually within 12-16 hours of exposure, although symptoms have occasionally been known to appear far sooner. Symptoms such as

coughing, wheezing, shortness of breath and a constant feeling of burning and pain along the trachea and bronchi may occur. Other general symptoms including *malaise, headache, nausea, numbness and tingling (paraesthesias)* may appear after several days of breathing oxygen. Lower partial pressures can be breathed for longer before causing ill-effects.

Although pulmonary oxygen toxicity is a major consideration in diving habitats, it does not generally threaten most recreational divers unless they require recompression for decompression illness. In these circumstances, the periods of oxygen breathing are carefully monitored and "air breaks" (periods of breathing air) are given, if required.

Divers who breathe oxygen-enriched gas mixes for multiple, sequential, prolonged dives monitor their exposure to oxygen in an attempt to minimize the likelihood of lung toxicity. This is usually done by calculating "Oxygen Tolerance Units" (OTUs) or Units of Pulmonary Toxicity Dose (UPTD).

A method of calculating OTUs is by:

$$OTU = t((PO_2 - 0.5)/0.5)^{0.83}$$

where

t   = exposure time in minutes;
PO_2 = the inspired oxygen partial
       pressure in bars; and
0.5 = the exposure threshold in bar.

The OTU is then maintained at what is calculated to be a "safe" level.

Air breaks

If a diver is receiving oxygen first aid for suspected decompression illness, the periods of oxygen breathing should be recorded (i.e. time(s) put on and time(s) taken off oxygen). *The injured diver's response to oxygen should also be recorded, noting any improvement or deterioration.*

The doctor who will recompress the diver will then know how long the higher partial pressure of oxygen has been breathed for, and has the potential to use this information to minimize the effects of pulmonary oxygen toxicity during the subsequent hyperbaric oxygen treatment if it is thought necessary.

If a diver has had very long periods of 100% oxygen breathing without breaks, treatment options may have been diminished. For this reason, it was sometimes recommended that the injured diver breathe air for 5 minutes after each 25 minutes on oxygen, while en route to the chamber. The air breaks minimize the toxic effects of the oxygen on the lungs.

However, in reality, most divers do not receive true 100% oxygen due to inadequacies in the equipment and/or air being entrained due to poor mask seals or other leaks. In addition, irregular air breaks are introduced when the victim eats, drinks, goes to the toilet and speaks.

Valuable oxygen first aid is often missed by oxygen providers mistakenly believing that it is always necessary to stop oxygen provision and give air breaks. For this reason the procedure has been de-emphasized over the past few years. However, air breaks may be considered if true 100% oxygen is being provided continuously for longer than 5-6 hours. In this case, advice should be sought from a dive physician.

CENTRAL NERVOUS SYSTEM OXYGEN TOXICITY

When oxygen is breathed at partial pressures usually greater than about 1.5ATA it may cause toxic effects in the brain. This is known as Central Nervous System (CNS) Oxygen Toxicity. Unlike pulmonary oxygen toxicity which appears gradually and is relatively predictable, CNS oxygen toxicity can occur rapidly and is comparatively unpredictable.

The partial pressure at which this acute oxygen toxicity occurs varies. A variety of factors seem to lower an individual's tolerance to CNS oxygen toxicity. High levels of carbon dioxide and high temperatures increase susceptibility, as well as doing heavy work and being underwater, rather than in a dry chamber. Susceptibility varies between individuals and with the same individual from day to day.

Certain drugs can also reduce one's tolerance while others may increase it. Although it has been suggested that pseudoephedrine, a decongestant commonly used by divers, may increase susceptibility to CNS oxygen toxicity, it has not to date been proven.[10]

The most dramatic direct result of acute oxygen toxicity is an epileptic-like convulsion that may occur with, or without, warning. Commonly, minor symptoms such as *nausea, muscle twitching (particularly lips), vertigo, light-headedness, visual abnormalities, irritability and numbness* precede the convulsion. However, these symptoms may not be noticed underwater and a convulsion can occur without apparent warning.

The convulsions usually last for about two minutes. Initially, the body becomes rigid and the victim loses consciousness. Breathing stops and the airway can become obstructed. If decompression (e.g. ascent) occurs at this stage a lung injury could result. After about 30 seconds the convulsion begins and breathing resumes. If a convulsion occurred in a diver using a normal scuba regulator, the regulator would probably be dislodged and the diver may drown. For this reason, commercial and military divers usually wear full-face masks when diving with elevated concentrations of oxygen.

Recompression therapy for decompression illness routinely involves breathing 100% oxygen at an equivalent depth of 18msw (60fsw), with a PO_2 of 2.8ATA. The incidence of convulsion during hyperbaric therapy is reported to be 0.01% when predisposing factors are controlled. When convulsions occur they are relatively easily managed by trained staff in a dry chamber.

It is important to realize that convulsions are far more likely to occur, and at a lower PO_2, to a diver underwater. Possible symptoms of CNS toxicity have been reported in a resting diver breathing 100% oxygen at 7.5m (25ft). Convulsions have been documented in resting divers breathing 100% oxygen at 9m (30ft), a PO_2 of 1.9ATA.[11]

To minimize the likelihood of having an oxygen convulsion, divers should ensure that the partial pressure of oxygen (PO_2) in their breathing gas remains below about 1.4ATA, but convulsions have occurred after prolonged exposures even at this PO_2.

For those diving on air, this equates to staying shallower than 57m (188ft) which is well advised, not only for potential oxygen toxicity, but for the very significant effects of nitrogen narcosis.

Those breathing oxygen-enriched gas mixtures need to carefully monitor their mix and depth control to ensure the PO_2 doesn't exceed 1.4ATA. Those breathing 100% oxygen need to remain shallower than 4m (13ft) if the PO_2 of 1.4 is not to be exceeded.

Oxygen has increasingly been used during decompression to accelerate the removal of nitrogen and to either shorten decompression times or add a margin of safety. Divers in certain navies routinely decompress breathing pure oxygen at 9m (30ft). However, as mentioned earlier, a full-face mask is usually worn to prevent the diver from drowning if they become unconscious. The pearl divers of Western Australia routinely decompress at 9m

(30ft) breathing 100% oxygen for periods of 5 to 30 minutes without apparent problems.[12] An increasing number of other professional and technical divers decompress at 6m (20ft) breathing 100% oxygen without apparent incident.

Transient worsening of symptoms

Occasionally, the symptoms of a diver suffering from DCI may worsen transiently shortly after oxygen is provided. This is generally believed to result from oxygen rapidly diffusing into and temporarily increasing the size of existing bubbles before substantial nitrogen has diffused from the bubble.[2]

If, when receiving a higher concentration of oxygen, a diver's symptoms worsen, oxygen provision should be continued. The transient deterioration should not last for more than a few minutes unless it is caused by something other than oxygen breathing. The equipment should be checked to ensure it is functioning correctly. Things to check include the oxygen supply, flowrate if appropriate, and if using a demand valve, that the oronasal mask is sealed and the demand valve is triggering properly.

WHEN SHOULD OXYGEN BE ADMINISTERED?

Oxygen should be provided to all divers who are thought to be suffering from a diving-related condition, who have respiratory distress, whose illness or injury suggests the possibility of hypoxia, and to all unresponsive victims.

The ultimate goal is to deliver 100% oxygen to the victim from the time the accident is recognized until a knowledgeable medical specialist orders it discontinued.

Oxygen breathing should be commenced as soon as possible to gain the maximum benefit. If only a limited supply of oxygen is available it should usually be given at the highest possible concentration from the time the accident is recognized, until the supply of oxygen is exhausted. Exceptions to this include the management of a drowning event, and/or where the diver is not breathing and is being ventilated using supplemental oxygen via a constant flow device, such as a resuscitation mask (see below). In such cases the oxygen should be "budgeted" so as to give as high a concentration possible in the early stages, and then reducing the flowrate if necessary to try to ensure that the supply lasts until more oxygen can be obtained.

All divers should have fast access to oxygen should it be needed after a dive. To achieve this, equipment capable of delivering high concentrations of oxygen to both responsive and unresponsive, breathing and non-breathing divers, as well as and an oxygen provider trained in its use, should be available wherever diving activities are taking place.

OXYGEN EQUIPMENT

For the diving industry, it has now become the "Standard of Care" to provide suitable oxygen equipment and a person trained in its use where diving is conducted. In some countries, failure to do so has led to litigation in the event of injury. Although many dive operators now carry oxygen equipment, some of it is not very suitable.

Despite the significant advances in the availability of oxygen equipment and training, DAN America data indicates that still only around 30-50% of divers suffering from DCI receive oxygen prior to recompression.[4,5,6] Possible explanations for this low figure include the delayed onset, recognition, and/or delayed reporting of symptoms. Many of these divers would have left the dive site where oxygen may have been available by the time symptoms became apparent. Sadly, this figure would be significantly lower in many parts of the world where equipment is less readily available and where the knowledge of the importance of oxygen provision and training in the use of the equipment are less prevalent.

One must also consider the likelihood that inspired oxygen concentrations well below 100% would often have been delivered due to unsuitable equipment or other limitations.

There are now many different types of oxygen equipment in the marketplace and it is important to choose the most suitable gear. When looking for oxygen equipment some of the points that should be considered are:

- What type of victims can be provided with oxygen using the particular equipment?
- The amount of training and practice that is required to become and remain competent in the use of the equipment.
- Affordability of the equipment.
- Durability of the equipment in the aquatic environment.

Appropriate equipment should be capable of easily and effectively providing high inspired oxygen concentrations to the responsive victim; the unresponsive, breathing victim; and the non-breathing victim.

Many people mistakenly believe that because an oxygen cylinder contains almost pure oxygen, and this gas flows out from the regulator and down the tubing, a person breathing from an oxygen set will be breathing 100% oxygen, no matter what mask or other delivery device is used. This is generally not true because, when the person inhales, a substantial amount of air is normally entrained, thereby diluting the concentration of oxygen.

To supply 100% oxygen, an oxygen delivery system must be able to provide for all of the person's respiratory requirements. In addition, air entrainment must be prevented and expired breath must be vented effectively to prevent hypercapnia.

Consider a person with a tidal volume of 0.5 litres with a breathing cycle of four seconds - one second being for inhalation and 3 seconds for exhalation. With such a cycle, a person's respiratory requirement is 0.5

litres per second, or 30lpm. In other words, unless there is a reservoir in which oxygen can collect during the exhalation phase, an oxygen delivery system needs to provide an oxygen flowrate of 30lpm in order to provide 100% oxygen. If a lower flowrate is supplied, as it is with most oxygen regulators, air will be entrained and the oxygen concentration will be reduced accordingly.

The addition of an oxygen reservoir enables a reduction in flowrate. However, such a reservoir should generally have a minimum volume of the wearer's tidal volume.

Demand valves

The easiest and usually the most effective way to provide an oxygen concentration approaching 100% to a breathing injured diver is via an oxygen demand valve.

Most current model medical oxygen demand valves are capable of providing oxygen flowrates in excess of 100lpm and so are capable of supplying all of a person's respiratory requirements.

Demand valves are often designed to entrain some air so that the user doesn't asphyxiate if the oxygen supply runs out. If the breathing resistance is too high, air will be entrained when the user inhales and the inspired oxygen concentration will fall. This problem may be increased if the victim is sitting with their head down or laying on the side, as gravity will make it harder for the valve to open.[13]

Injured divers who are breathing only weakly may be unable to trigger the demand valve and should not be administered oxygen by demand valve. A person who is breathing rapidly (hyperventilating) may have difficulty breathing from a demand valve and so may need to be provided with oxygen via a constant flow device.

Apart from the above-mentioned limitations, well-designed and maintained demand valves provide a very simple and effective method of administering near 100% oxygen. They are the delivery system of choice in the first aid management of scuba diving injuries for which near 100% oxygen is required, as well as for other conditions for which the inspired oxygen concentration needs to be maximized. They can be relatively economical with oxygen usage as long as the user's breathing rate and volume are not too high.

Instead of using a specially designed medical oxygen demand valve and the associated medical oxygen regulator, some divers use a diver demand valve and regulator to provide oxygen (or EANx) from a scuba cylinder. This mode of delivery has some potential problems.

First, unless the equipment is oxygen cleaned and dedicated, there is a greater risk of fire. Second, as with any demand valve, the breathing resistance must be low in order to minimize the effort required to deliver oxygen to an injured diver. Third, since diving demand valves are fitted with a mouthpiece, they cannot readily be used to provide oxygen to unresponsive victims. Finally, **if a regulator with mouthpiece is used, the victim's nostrils must be closed** with a noseclip, fingers or some other effective method. *Unless this is done, a lot of air will be entrained through their nose and the oxygn concentration will fall and be well below the desired 100%.*

FIGURE 8.2

DAN demand valve.

Constant flow delivery devices

The most commonly available oxygen delivery systems are those that deliver a constant flow of oxygen at either a fixed or variable flowrate.

Constant flow delivery devices may not be as economical with oxygen usage as demand valves. In addition, most such devices cannot provide such high oxygen concentrations. Despite these potential limitations, certain constant flow devices are very useful in the management of a non-breathing victim, or one who cannot use a demand valve effectively.

The oxygen concentration delivered by a constant flow system depends on a variety of factors and, in most cases, will be well below 100%. It varies from about 25-35% with a loose-fitting mask or nasal cannula, to up to 98% with a tight-sealing mask-valve-bag system with an additional oxygen reservoir bag attached, and a flowrate of about 15lpm.

There are a number of different constant flow delivery masks available and the concentration of oxygen delivered by these masks depends on how well the mask seals, the flowrate, the breathing rate, the inspiratory volume and rate of the user, and whether or not a reservoir bag is used in conjunction with the mask. A tight-sealing mask will minimize air dilution. If the flowrate is too low, excess carbon dioxide can remain in some masks between breaths. High flowrates will minimize this but will also use up the oxygen supply more rapidly. The oxygen concentration will fall if the user's breathing rate increases.

There is a plethora of constant flow delivery devices and only three commonly used devices will be briefly discussed here.

The **non-rebreather mask** is now probably the most commonly used oxygen delivery device for injured divers.[7] This mask is fitted with both a reservoir bag and a set of three one-way valves. It is designed to reduce the amount of air and carbon dioxide inhaled, thereby increasing the concentration of oxygen. The reservoir bag fills with oxygen and, when the wearer inhales, a one-way valve ensures that primarily oxygen is breathed from the reservoir. When the wearer exhales, the one-way valve system prevents exhaled gas from entering the reservoir. Other one-way exhaust valves cover either one or both sets of holes in the mask to prevent or minimize air entry. If valves cover both sets of holes the wearer cannot breathe easily unless there is an adequate flow of oxygen. This potential problem is overcome in those masks with a one-way valve fitted to only one set of holes or by ensuring the wearer is constantly monitored.

For proper use, the reservoir bag must be primed and should always contain enough oxygen so that it does not deflate fully (ideally no more than one third) when the wearer takes the deepest inhalation. In addition, all three one-way valves should be fitted and seated properly. A good seal also needs to be achieved. Under these ideal circumstances, a non-rebreather mask is reputedly capable of supplying an oxygen concentration of up to 95% with flowrates of 10 to 15lpm. However, in practice such a high concentration is difficult to achieve and the mask will generally deliver a substantially lower oxygen concentration, probably closer to 75%. A flowrate of around 25lpm may be required to achieve an oxygen concentration near 90%.

FIGURE 8.3

Non-rebreather mask.

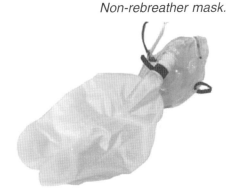

In general, the simplest way to provide supplemental oxygen to a non-breathing victim is via a **resuscitation mask** with oxygen inlet.

Such masks are capable of providing a good seal on the victim's face and enable a rescuer to perform mouth-to-mask ventilations, supplementing their expired breaths with additional oxygen.

Using this technique, it is possible to provide an oxygen concentration of up to about 55% to the non-breathing victim, at a flowrate of 15lpm.

Although this potential oxygen concentration falls considerably short of the desired 100 percent, because this technique is so simple to perform, it is recommended by many resuscitation and oxygen provider training bodies worldwide, including DAN.

A rescuer can use both hands to open the victim's airway and seal the mask. There is plenty of air available in their lungs to ventilate the victim adequately and compensate for any leaks.

The skills required to perform mouth-to-mask ventilations are easily acquired and retained far longer than more complicated ventilation techniques.

FIGURE 8.4

Resuscitation mask.

Bag-valve-mask (BVM) devices fitted with a reservoir are capable of providing near 100% oxygen. However, as with most oxygen delivery systems, the oxygen concentration delivered to the lungs depends on a variety of factors, including oxygen flowrate, seal, depth, rate of ventilation and others.

A major problem with bag-valve devices lies is the level of skill required to ventilate a non-breathing victim. Several studies[14,15] have shown clearly that the one operator technique generally produces very poor ventilations, even when performed by well trained and regular users. Experience has shown that such devices generally require two trained operators to use effectively with the non-breathing victim; one to open the airway and hold the mask, and the other to gently squeeze the bag. Hence, although a bag-valve-mask is capable of providing higher concentrations of oxygen to the non-breathing victim than a resuscitation mask with oxygen, it will provide little benefit if the ventilations are inadequate.

FIGURE 8.5

Bag-valve mask.

Other oxygen delivery devices

Manually triggered resuscitators utilize a button which, when depressed, will initiate a flow of oxygen to ventilate the lungs of a non-breathing victim. Such devices are capable of providing 100 percent oxygen for resuscitation.

Previously, very high flowrates (often 160lpm) were recommended to ventilate a victim. However, the stomach often became distended and regurgitation was not uncommon. Current devices, such as the Allied Healthcare Inc. EMT-Resuscitator (previously MTV-100) have been modified to deliver a maximum of 40lpm for resuscitation but up to 100lpm on demand.

However, as with BVM devices, experience has shown that manually-triggered resuscitators often require two trained operators to use effectively with the non-breathing victim; one to open the airway and hold the mask, and the other to press the button to ventilate.

FIGURE 8.6

EMT-Resuscitator.

Closed circuit portable oxygen resuscitation systems (e.g. the DAN REMO$_2$) are based on systems commonly used in anaesthesia. The main benefit of such a system is the potential to increase the duration of the oxygen supply. Such units provide advantages to divers who dive in very remote areas and cannot carry a large oxygen supply. A 450l oxygen cylinder which would last around 30 minutes with a constant flow device set at 15lpm, could potentially provide oxygen for up to 4 hours using a closed circuit device, depending largely on the size of the carbon dioxide absorbent canister and the flowrate utilized.

Other than the additional maintenance requirements, the major drawback with closed circuit devices is again the extra training and skill required to use them effectively, especially with the non-breathing

victim in the closed circuit mode. As with BVM devices, it usually requires two people to adequately ventilate a non-breathing victim.

Another area of some contention has been the potential for nitrogen to be trapped in the closed system, and the consequent reduction of the oxygen concentration. Due to retained nitrogen and entrained nitrogen, normobaric oxygen rebreathers typically maintain a mean oxygen concentration in the order of 80-95%. When using such devices to provide first aid for DCI (and toxic gas inhalation) it is important to flush the circuit periodically and to use an adequate oxygen flowrate.

FIGURE 8.7

DAN REMO$_2$.

Chemical reaction systems utilize a chemical reaction to produce oxygen. One such system that has been marketed to divers in some parts of the world consists of a plastic flask in which the chemical reaction takes place, with delivery tubing connecting the closure cap to a mask. Pre-packed quantities of the powders are placed in the flask and a measured amount of water added. The chemical reaction commences immediately and the flask is then closed to direct the oxygen produced via the delivery hose to the facemask.

Although the system has some advantages in certain very limited situations, it is not suitable for use in the treatment of divers with decompression illness. The most important reason for this is the inability of this system to provide anything near to 100% oxygen to the injured diver. The advertised mean flowrate of 6.4 litres per minute (lpm) is often incapable of producing inspired oxygen concentrations higher than about 30-40% using the supplied delivery system.[16]

DAN Oxygen Units The Divers Alert Network has configured and assembled a series of oxygen units, designed specifically to cater to divers' requirements. DAN oxygen units are not only effective, but also easy to use and so require minimal training.

FIGURE 8.8

A variety of DAN Oxygen Units.

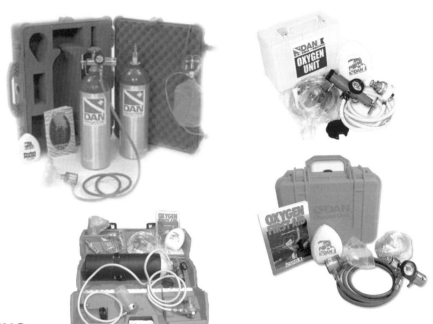

TRAINING

It should be obvious from the discussion above, that some types of equipment are easier to use than others.

As mentioned, a demand valve is usually the simplest system to use with a breathing injured diver. A resuscitation mask with oxygen inlet is the easiest method for ventilating a non-breathing victim. *These techniques require far less initial training and continued practice than other methods, and can be done effectively by one trained person.*

BVMs, manually-triggered ventilators and closed circuit devices all require considerably more initial training and continued practice to achieve and maintain proficiency. In addition, it often requires two trained operators to effectively ventilate a non-breathing victim with these devices in the field. So, even though such devices are capable of delivering higher oxygen concentrations for artificial ventilation, in practice they may often be less effective because of the greater skill and manpower required.

All divers are strongly advised to undergo training in oxygen provision, and should be thoroughly familiar with any oxygen equipment that they might use. Skills must be regularly updated as they deteriorate relatively quickly.

SUMMARY

- Oxygen is a colourless, odourless and tasteless gas that constitutes about 21% of the air we breathe.

- Oxygen is carried in the blood attached to haemoglobin and dissolved in plasma.

- The amount of oxygen delivered to a tissue depends on the quantity of oxygen in the blood and the rate of blood flow.

- Hypoxia is a state of low oxygen levels. In the event of hypoxia, increasing the concentration of oxygen in the inspired gas may help to increase haemoglobin saturation. Increasing the oxygen concentration will also cause more of it to dissolve in the plasma.

- For injured divers, it is important to provide an oxygen concentration close to 100%, especially where decompression illness is suspected.

- Many divers who received oxygen first aid have reported reduction or resolution of symptoms prior to recompression.

- Prompt provision of high concentrations of inspired oxygen may reduce or eliminate symptoms of DCI.

- The breathing of oxygen is a first aid measure and should not under most circumstances substitute for the appropriate medical assessment and recompression required for decompression illness, regardless of the response.

- Oxygen breathed at sufficient partial pressures and for sufficient duration will become toxic and the level of toxicity depends on the partial pressure of oxygen, the length of exposure and the susceptibility of the individual.

- When oxygen is breathed at partial pressures greater than 0.5bar for extended periods it gradually causes damage to the lungs. However, pulmonary oxygen toxicity does not generally threaten most recreational divers unless they require recompression for decompression illness, or breathe oxygen-enriched gas mixes for very extended periods.

- When oxygen is breathed at partial pressures usually greater than about 1.5bar it can cause CNS Oxygen Toxicity. The most dramatic direct result of CNS Oxygen is an epileptic-like convulsion that may occur with, or without, warning.

- Susceptibility to CNS toxicity varies between individuals and is affected by factors such as oxygen concentration, hypercapnia, temperature and exercise.

- Oxygen should be provided to all divers who are thought to be suffering from a diving-related condition, who have respiratory distress, whose illness or injury suggests the possibility of hypoxia, and to all unresponsive victims.

- Oxygen breathing should be commenced as soon as possible to gain the maximum benefit.

- If only a limited supply of oxygen is available it should usually be given at the highest possible concentration from the time the accident is recognized, until the supply of oxygen is exhausted.

- For the diving industry, it has now become the "Standard of Care" to provide suitable oxygen equipment and a person trained in its use where diving is conducted.

- There are now many different types of oxygen equipment in the marketplace and it is important to choose the most suitable gear.

- The easiest and usually the most effective way to provide an oxygen concentration approaching 100% to a breathing injured diver is via an oxygen demand valve.

- Injured divers who are breathing very rapidly or only weakly may be unable to trigger the demand valve and should not be administered oxygen by demand valve.

- The concentration of oxygen delivered by a constant flow oxygen delivery device depends on how well the mask seals, the flowrate, the breathing rate and depth and size of the wearer, and whether or not a reservoir bag is used in conjunction with the mask.

- A resuscitation mask with oxygen inlet is the easiest method for ventilating a non-breathing victim. This technique requires far less initial training and continued practice than other methods, and can be done effectively by one trained person.

REFERENCES

1. Anderson D, Nagasawa G, Norfleet W, Olszowka, Lundgren C. O_2 pressures between 0.12 and 2.5 atm abs, circulatory function, and N_2 elimination. Undersea Biomed Res 1991; 18(4):279-92.

2. Hyldegaad O, Madsen J. Effect of air, heliox, and oxygen breathing on air bubbles in aqueous tissues in the rat. Undersea Hyperb Med 1994; 21(4):431-44.

3. Moon RE, Uguccioni D, Dovenbarger JA et al. Surface oxygen for decompression illness. Undersea Hyperb Med 1995; 22(supp):37-8.

4. Report on decompression illness and diving fatalities. Durham, North Carolina: Divers Alert Network; 1999.

5. Report on decompression illness and diving fatalities. Durham, North Carolina: Divers Alert Network; 2000.

6. Report on decompression illness diving fatalities and Project Dive Exploration. Durham, North Carolina: Divers Alert Network; 2003.

7. Report on decompression illness diving fatalities and Project Dive Exploration. Durham, North Carolina: Divers Alert Network; 2004.

8. Longphre JM, Freiberger JJ, Denoble PJ, Vann RD. Utility of first aid oxygen prior to recompression treatment for diving injuries. Undersea Hyperb Med 2005; 32(4):229.

9. Longphre JP. First Aid Surface Oxygen. Alert Diver 2005; Jul/Aug:44-7.

10. Thalmann ED. To mix or not to mix. Alert Diver 1999;Nov-Dec:18-21.

11. Donald K. Oxygen and the Diver. Worcs: The SPA Ltd; 1992.

12. Wong R. Western Australian pearl divers' mode of diving. SPUMS J 1995; 25 (3):170-5.

13. Hobbs GW, Natoli MJ, Pollock NW. Divers Alert Network (DAN) Emergency Oxygen Demand Regulator Validation Trials. Center for Environmental Physiology & Environmental Medicine. Duke University Medical Center, Durham NC 27710.

14. Lawrence PJ, Sivaneswaran N. Ventilation during cardiopulmonary resuscitation: which method? The Medical Journal of Australia 1985; 143:443-6.

15. Elling R and Politis J. An evaluation of emergency medical technician's ability to use manual ventilation devices. Annals of Emergency Medicine 1983; 12:765-8.

16. Lippmann J, Mitchell SJ. Oxygen administration for divers. Alert Diver SEAP 2000; Jul-Sept:14,17.

OTHER SOURCES

Clark JM, Thom SR. Toxicity of Oxygen, Carbon Dioxide and Carbon Monoxide. In: Bove AA (ed). Bove and Davis' Diving Medicine, 4th Edition. Philadelphia: Saunders; 2004: 241-60.

Clark JM, Thom SR. Oxygen Under Pressure. In: Brubakk AO and Neuman TS (eds). Physiology and Medicine of Diving, 5th edition. London: Saunders; 2003:358-418.

Edmonds C. Oxygen therapy. In: Edmonds C, Lowry C, Pennefather J, Walker R. Diving and Subaquatic Medicine, 4th edition. London: Arnold; 2002: 503-9.

Lippmann J. Oxygen First Aid – Second Asia-Pacific Edn. Melbourne: J.L. Publications; 2002.

RECOMMENDED FURTHER READING

Edmonds C. Oxygen therapy. In: Edmonds C, Lowry C, Pennefather J, Walker R. Diving and Subaquatic Medicine, 4th edition. London: Arnold; 2002: 503-9.

Lippmann J. Oxygen First Aid – Second Asia-Pacific Edn. Melbourne: J.L. Publications; 2002.

9

Heat loss

THE IMPORTANCE OF TEMPERATURE REGULATION

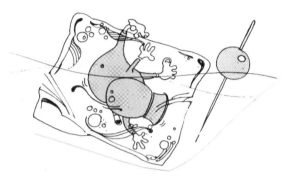

So called "homeotherms" such as man maintain a relatively constant body temperature despite fluctuations in environmental temperature. "Poikilotherms" such as reptiles, allow temperature to vary in closer equilibrium with that of the environment.

Homeotherms in particular have an ideal internal temperature where they function most effectively. Below that temperature muscles are sluggish, nerve impulses travel slowly and thought processes are slowed. If it gets cold enough the animal is unable to continue activities, becomes increasingly unresponsive, and eventually dies. This is particularly true of mammals such as man. Not surprisingly, homeotherms have acquired vital physiological and behavioural adaptations to allow maintenance of constant temperature in a changing environment.

HEAT BALANCE: GAIN vs LOSS

In man, the normal body "core temperature", which is the temperature of the vital organs, is around 37°C (98.6°F).

This internal temperature depends on the balance between heat production and heat loss. The body has a basal heat output due to the metabolic activity of the internal organs such as the heart, liver, respiratory muscles, kidneys and gut in the torso (the **core**), and from the brain.

Extra heat production and therefore **heat gain** in adults is most efficiently generated by muscular activity. If necessary, involuntary muscle activity can be initiated, and this is called shivering. Shivering can increase the basal heat output more than fivefold, but shivering stops after a few hours of exposure due to exhaustion and depletion of muscle energy supplies. So this system is not adequate to preserve body temperature for long periods.

Heat loss is by one of three processes: radiation, conduction, and convection.

Radiation is the flow of heat from one place to another by means of electromagnetic waves, mainly in the infra-red spectrum. For the physics purists, radiation is interesting because it is the only form for heat transmission that does not require the presence of matter. In other words, it can take place in a vacuum. Radiation is how heat reaches earth from the sun. The rate at which a body will cool due to radiation depends to a significant degree on the surface area from which it is radiating compared to its volume. The higher the surface area to volume ratio, the faster a body will cool.

Conduction is the flow of heat **through matter** from places of higher temperature to places of lower temperature. The lower the temperature of the conducting matter, the faster heat will be lost from the warmer body. In addition, the thermal conductivity of the conducting matter is also important. Still air is a poor conductor of heat, and the creation of areas of still air is one of the benefits of wearing clothes, or a drysuit in divers (see below). Water is actually quite a poor conductor of heat compared to many metals, but it is still more than 20x better than air, which is why water at 30°C (86°F) still feels cool when air at the same temperature feels warm. Heat loss via conduction is the critically important process when immersed in water.

Convection is the flow of heat through air or a fluid, from places of higher temperature to places of lower temperature, by movement of the air or fluid itself. This movement can be induced by heat conducted to the surrounding air or fluid, which upon heating becomes less dense and so "rises", drawing more air or fluid in underneath, thus creating a "convection current".

In "real life", these heat loss processes are influenced by several important factors.

1. Constriction ("vasoconstriction") or dilation ("vasodilation") of blood vessels in the skin. Vasodilation (widening of blood vessels) brings more blood into close proximity with the surrounding air that is at environmental temperature. Assuming that the environment is cooler than 37°C (98.6°F), this will potentially result in greater heat loss by all three processes described above. In contrast, vasoconstriction (narrowing of blood vessels) reduces blood flow through the superficial blood vessels and reduces heat loss. The areas of the body where heat loss is greatest are the head, the base of the neck, the armpits and the groin. These are all places where large arteries pass close to the skin and processes of vasoconstriction or dilation will not make much difference to heat loss. In addition, the superficial blood vessels in the face and scalp do not efficiently constrict in response to cold and, although studies vary, it has been estimated that, in a fully vasconstricted adult, 40% or more of the total heat lost in a cold environment can occur from the scalp, face and neck.[*]

2. The evaporation of sweat from the skin. Conduction of heat to a layer of water on the skin is enhanced if there is simultaneous evaporation of that same water layer. This is because evaporation involves the escape of faster moving molecules of water from the water surface. This lowers the average speed and kinetic energy of the molecules left behind which, in practical terms, lowers the water temperature and enhances conduction. The body can produce more sweat at times when heat loss needs to be enhanced.

3. The nature of any insulation in the form of clothing or exposure suits in divers. Clothes act by holding layers of still air over the skin thus preventing convection. Still air is also a relatively poor conductor of heat thus enhancing the effect of clothes. However, heat loss from conduction is potentially markedly increased in wet clothing (and evaporation from wet clothes caused by wind makes this worse).

---

[*] When the skin temperature falls below about 10°C (50°F), blood vessels to the extremities may dilate for a while before constricting again. It has been suggested that this cold vasodilation (which may help to prevent frostbite) increases heat loss from areas where it occurs.

FIGURE 9.1

Major regions of heat loss from the body.

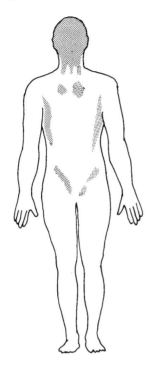

Human heat regulation is controlled by a part of the brain (the *hypothalamus,* and the *raphé nucleus* in the brain stem) in response to blood temperature variations and messages from the skin and a variety of deep body sites. It is achieved by stimulation of 'effectors', which are smooth muscle cells in the blood vessels, sweat glands and shivering or exercising muscles.

HEAT LOSS IN WATER

As implied above, heat loss is greatly increased during immersion in water. Water conducts heat approximately 23 times faster than air, and it needs approximately 1,000 times more heat to warm a given volume of water than to warm the same volume of air by the same amount.

When we first enter the water there is a high rate of heat loss which decreases as vasoconstriction occurs. *The rate of heat loss is influenced by water temperature, insulation, movement / exercise, heat production and, for divers, gas composition and gas density (which depends on depth).*

In the naked human immersed in water, movement of the surrounding water that has been warmed by contact with the skin, increases heat loss. Swimming may actually speed up heat loss in spite of the extra heat generated by the muscular effort. It is often better for an immersed person to avoid moving and huddle into a ball, the *Heat Exchange Lessening Posture (HELP)*, than to try to swim. By tucking the upper arms tightly against the sides of the chest, the forearms over the front, the thighs tucked to protect the groin and keeping the head out of the water, heat is conserved in those areas of greatest heat loss. For a diver, the buoyancy compensator should be inflated to keep the head out of the water, and the mask left in place to keep spray off the face (Figure 9.2). It has been reported that a person can increase cold water survival time by up to 50% or more by adopting this position.[1]

FIGURE 9.2

The H.E.L.P. position.

A diver's air supply is close to sea temperature and has to be warmed to body temperature in the lungs. Each molecule has to be warmed and, as you go deeper, the gas becomes denser and so there are more molecules to be warmed. Therefore, *a diver loses more heat from his lungs at depth.*

Exposure suits

Wetsuit

By increasing insulation, a wetsuit retains heat. A wetsuit works by trapping a layer of water between the suit and the body. That layer of water warms up to close to skin temperature. Thus, after a short period, the wetsuit reduces conduction by reducing the gradient for heat transfer from skin to the surrounding water layer. It also prevents convection by preventing movement of water over the skin. The gas in the foam fabric of the wetsuit, which is a mass of bubbles of nitrogen or air in rubber, acts as an efficient insulator because still gas in the bubbles is a relatively poor conductor of heat. This reduces conduction of heat from the skin and the warmed water layer to the sea.

It is notable that the wetsuit becomes a less efficient insulator the deeper a diver goes because the foam bubbles compress with depth. (Figure 9.3). This is particularly disadvantageous because as depth increases the water temperature often decreases and the temperature drop can be dramatic if a "thermocline" is present. Some waters, especially still waters, may have levels of vastly different temperatures and the boundaries between such layers are called "thermoclines". Wetsuits are also less efficient if wet out of the water because they *can cool the diver by evaporation from the wetsuit surface.* The wind-chill effect magnifies this problem. In cold weather it is a good idea to wear a waterproof and windproof jacket to, and from, the dive site.

Someone in a well-fitting wetsuit, that does not allow water to move in and out with

movement, can stay quite warm for some time, even in very cool water. It is often advisable to have a wetsuit custom-made if a well-fitting one is not readily available. However, even a well-fitting wetsuit does not stop heat loss, it only reduces it. In addition, *a diver must wear a hood in cold water.* The head is about ten percent of the body's surface area, and more than half of the head is scalp. *Since the blood vessels in the scalp do not constrict with cold, and because so much blood passes through the head, a lot of heat will be lost if a hood is not worn.* Gloves or mitts should be worn in cold water. If the hands get too cold, grip strength and dexterity are reduced and simple tasks such as adjusting a mask or fin strap become difficult to perform and the diver's safety may be compromised.

There are a number of different thicknesses of neoprene available ranging from about 1-9mm (1/16-3/8in). The appropriate thickness depends mainly on the temperature of the water. One should be aware that some neoprenes are denser than others, compress less at depth, and provide better insulation than a less dense neoprene does, even though it has the same thickness on the surface.

Semi-drysuits are really wetsuits, but incorporate neck, ankle and wrist seals and/ or straps, zipper covers and an attached or detachable hood. The better seals in these suits reduce water entry and exit and so enable thinner neoprene to be used to achieve insulation similar to a thicker wetsuit.

Drysuit

For very cold water, and / or for dives of extended duration, a drysuit is advisable. A drysuit works by trapping a layer of warm air, rather than water, around the diver's body. Air conducts heat away from the body far more slowly than water does, so as long as the drysuit is functioning properly it is warmer than a wetsuit.

FIGURE 9.3

Compression of a wetsuit under pressure

The above photos show a piece of 7mm (1/4inch) neoprene, initially at 1ATA
and then at 4ATA (30m/100ft). Note how much the neoprene has compressed.

There are several types of drysuit available. Some are made from thick neoprene, which provides a good portion of the insulation. Another type is the "shell suit", which is a thin layer of rubber, compressed neoprene or other fabric. Insulation in the form of heavy "woolly" undergarments or thermal jackets and pants such as those used by skiers, is worn under the shell. The advantage of the shell suit is that the amount of insulation is more variable, so the suit can be worn in a wider range of temperatures.

All drysuits require more weight than a wetsuit, and some divers wear ankle weights to help them keep in trim. To compensate for buoyancy changes and prevent suit squeeze, air is added to the suit from a low pressure inflator hose attached to the regulator. A dump valve is usually located in the shoulder area in order to release expanding air on ascent. Although the air can be regulated in a drysuit, it is strongly recommended that a standard buoyancy compensator still be worn as the primary buoyancy control device.

Seals of either neoprene or latex prevent water from entering the suit at the wrists and neck. Either attached or separate hoods are available for drysuits. Wet neoprene gloves or mitts as well as dry mitts can be worn with a drysuit.

Drysuits are more bulky than wetsuits and require more exertion when swimming. They are also more expensive than wetsuits, and the valves, seals and zipper require regular maintenance in order to function properly.

In spite of added problems associated with drysuits, in colder water and especially at depth they are well worth the extra cost and maintenance. Using a drysuit, however, is considerably more complicated than using a wetsuit. Drysuit diving requires special training in buoyancy adjustment, maintenance and emergency procedures. *Do not use a drysuit without obtaining this additional training.*

Much has been made of the practice of using argon as a drysuit inflation gas, particularly by technical divers. This is based on the lower thermal conductivity (approximately 65%) of argon when compared to air. However, the only formal blinded evaluation of this practice[2], found no objective or subjective benefit from suit inflation with argon compared to air in cold water diving. It is therefore doubtful whether it is worthwhile to carry an extra cylinder of non-respirable gas for the sole purpose of drysuit inflation.

WATER CONTACT REFLEXES

There are a number of reflexes that occur when cold water touches the skin. If the face is put into cold water there may be slowing of the heart rate (bradycardia) and breath holding (apnea). This is a component of the diving reflex, and is found to some extent in many mammals and birds. In the *true* diving reflex (not necessarily in we humans), this bradycardia is accompanied by vasoconstriction of most vascular beds except the vessels supplying the brain, heart and lungs. This restricts the supply of oxygenated blood to vital organs and increases the survival time without breathing. Occasional reports of cardiac arrest immediately on immersion in very cold water are probably related to an exaggerated bradycardic response. In other words, the heart does not just slow, it stops! Unfortunately, although normal rhythm would probably be restored in a short period under normal circumstances, during immersion the victim will often drown during the inevitable period of unconsciousness.

In addition to the above, some people suffer from a very dangerous reflex, the Cold-Shock Response, usually within the first one to four minutes of submersion into very cold water (cooler than about 15°C / 60°F), dependant on the extent and rate of skin cooling. Such victims may exhibit very rapid and deep breathing that is quite beyond their control. This is sometimes combined with a decreased ability to move. This situation could very likely prove fatal to a diver unless they had a regulator in their mouth and a buddy nearby and/or an inflated buoyancy compensator.

ACCLIMATIZATION TO COLD

Although it appears that humans do not develop strong adaptive responses to cold, some acclimatization to cold has been observed in a number of groups of individuals exposed to cold environmental conditions for extended periods of time. The relatively minor adaptation to cold appears to result from combinations of a variety of different physiological responses which may include increased peripheral vaso-constriction, increased shivering, increased metabolic rate and increased subcutaneous (under the skin) insulation.

Early studies of the Ama divers of Korea, women who for many years wore cotton bathing suits and dived in waters as cold as 10°C (50°F) during winter, showed that they developed a greater body tissue insulation and did not begin to shiver until reaching lower water and skin temperatures than a non-diving control group. It appeared that the divers had learned to restrict their cutaneous circulation better than the non-divers. Although these responses suggested an insulative acclimatization, the Ama also increased their basal metabolic rate by 30% during winter. Interestingly, since the Ama began wearing wetsuits, they appear to have lost their adaptation and their responses to cold are now comparable to those of non-diving Korean women. It took five years to lose all the cold adaptation changes they had acquired when diving without wetsuits.[3]

Other studies found that scuba divers, exposed to either cold[4] or relatively warm[5] water for extended periods maintained their core temperatures without increasing their metabolic rates substantially, and did not begin to shiver until reaching lower water and skin temperatures than control subjects. However, as mentioned earlier, despite some indications of minor adaptive changes to cold, there is no clear evidence that humans can develop a significantly increased resistance to core cooling when immersed in cold water.

Cartoon by the late Peter Harrigan

HYPOTHERMIA

Hypothermia occurs when the body's core temperature drops to a level that causes unwanted changes. Medically it means a drop in body temperature from 37 to 35°C (98.6 to 95°F) or lower. It can result from a variety of situations that include cold water immersion and exposure to cold conditions whether wet or dry. Some recreational drugs (including alcohol), medications and medical conditions can predispose to hypothermia.

Hypothermia is often categorized as mild (34-35°C/93-95°F), moderate (30-33°C/86-91.4°F) and severe (below 30°C/86°F), although there is not universal agreement on these categories.

SIGNS AND SYMPTOMS

The first symptom of heat loss is *feeling cold, especially in the extremities.* Normal skin temperature in cool weather is 32-34°C (90-93°F), which can drop to 21-23°C (70-73°F) before core cooling begins. *Numbness, blueness, pallor or blotching of the skin, especially of the hands, feet and earlobes* occur as the blood vessels to these areas begin to constrict.[*]

Pain is sometimes felt in the extremities. The cold affects the transmission of nerve impulses and also affects the rate of contraction of muscles. This combination results in muscle malfunction and *difficulty in fine movements* and, as one grows colder, the grosser movements get affected as well. As one's fingers go numb the sensation of touch is reduced, and fine movements are soon impaired. A simple task such as adjusting a mask strap may become more difficult. At the time these peripheral changes are predominant the core temperature may still be normal. However, by the time shivering begins, significant body cooling has already occurred. Other responses to cold include *shivering, increased heart rate,* and increased release of adrenal hormones. The initial shivering can be suppressed if the diver makes a conscious effort. A diver who is exerting himself might not shiver at this stage because of the muscular activity of exertion. As cooling continues, shivering increases.

If the diver does not stop the heat loss, **mild hypothermia** will develop. Symptoms may include *maximum / uncontrollable shivering,* increasingly *poor coordination, slurred speech* and *slowed mental processes.*

---

[*] The cheeks may remain quite red due to less marked vasoconstriction of blood vessels in the face.

Uncontrollable shivering severely reduces coordination and can make it difficult to hold the regulator mouthpiece in place. W*eakness* or *fatigue* may set in and make swimming far more difficult.

As the brain cools, mental changes begin to occur. *Slowness of thought, confusion, slurred speech, poor co-ordination, impairment of rational thought and memory, and apathy may occur.* **Cold induced mental changes are probably the greatest danger to the diver because once the brain does not work properly wrong decisions can easily be made. The diver may ignore threats to his safety and finally, realizing the danger, may be unable to rectify the situation because of the loss of power and dexterity in his hands.** A diver should get out of the water long before manifestations of this type occur.

A diver who *does not shiver in spite of being very cold* is, or will soon be, *suffering from* **moderate hypothermia** as the body is not replacing the lost heat. A person under the influence of alcohol may have decreased shivering. Consciousness will become increasingly clouded and the victim may become unresponsive.

If cooling continues and the core temperature drops below about 30°C (86°F) **severe hypothermia** will develop. *Muscles become increasingly rigid and reflexes are lost.* The *pulse and breathing slow down,* the victim's pupils become fixed and dilated and they appear to be dead. In prolonged cases, the blood volume is reduced, causing the blood to thicken and become sticky, and various chemical changes occur in the blood, which, together with the cold, will affect the function of the heart and other major organs. (This is usually not apparent in divers unless they have become progressively cooled over a period of days.) The *heartbeat may become irregular and ventricular fibrillation can occur if the heart is irritated.* Further cooling will cause spontaneous ventricular fibrillation and subsequent *death*.

The above sequence of events describes the development of hypothermia when the heat loss is relatively rapid. However a "silent" or "undetected" hypothermia sometimes results from the long, slow body cooling that may follow several days of diving in water temperatures as high as 27°C (81°F), or higher. It is not uncommon for recreational divers to complain about getting colder towards the end of several days of tropical diving.

This slow cooling may result in reduced performance, fatigue, loss of motivation and impairment of thinking. Some authorities believe that long, slow cooling of the body is less likely to stimulate shivering and the subsequent heat re-generation. As a result the diver might not notice the heat drain from their body until significant hypothermia has developed and shivering finally occurs. Some consider this "silent" hypothermia to be the major hazard to the diver in cold water, as it will make the diver more accident-prone without them being aware of it. In commercial diving, investigators have implicated cold as a major cause of diving accidents, particularly the silent, progressive onset of hypothermia of which the diver is not aware.

FIRST AID

First aid for hypothermia must be rapid in order to prevent further heat loss. Mild hypothermia can progress quickly if heat loss is allowed to continue.

General steps in the management of accidental hypothermia include:

- Assessment of the ABCs
- Diagnosis
- Gentle handling of the victim
- Preventing further heat loss
- Consideration of providing additional heat to the victim
- Evacuation as required.

TABLE 9.1

Signs and symptoms of different levels of hypothermia.

Level	Core temperature		Signs & symptoms
	(°C)	*(°F)*	
Normal	37.6	99.6±1	"Normal" rectal temperature
	37.0	98.6±1	"Normal" oral temperature
Cold	36.0	96.8	Subjectively cold
	35.0	95.0	Shivering
Mild hypothermia	34.0	93.2	Slurred speech
			Slowed thinking & movement
Moderate	33.0	91.4	Hallucinations & amnesia
Hypothermia	32.0	89.6	Shivering ceases
	31.0	87.8	Decreasing consciousness
	30.0	86.0	Unconsciousness
Severe	29.0	85.2	Slow pulse & respiration
Hypothermia	28.0	82.4	Heart arrhythmias develop
	27.0	80.6	Reflexes lost
	26.0	78.8	Appears dead
	25.0	77.0	Spontaneous ventricular fibrillation may develop

These are typical signs and symptoms at different core temperatures – individuals may vary considerably. (Reprinted from Sullivan P, 1996[6]).

Note: Standard mercury thermometers are designed to read high rather than low temperatures. Low-reading thermometers are available. However, infrared tympanic thermometers appear to give a reasonably accurate indication of core temperature when used correctly.

The above steps are continually monitored, reassessed and acted upon as necessary during the management of the victim.

Despite agreement with the above general principles, there remains some controversy about certain aspects of the field management of hypothermia. Experts disagree about whether or not to actively rewarm a hypothermic victim in the field and, if so, how this can best be done. The debate is primarily about the treatment of a person with severe hypothermia. Some experts feel that because of the potential dangers of re-warming a severely hypothermic victim in the field, it is best to put the victim in a warm environment, insulate them and allow them to warm up on their own *(passive rewarming)*.

Others argue that extra heat should be added, and debate various ways this can best be done. All agree that *the first aid must minimize further cooling* and some argue that, with the severely hypothermic victim, the only effective way to do this is by adding heat *(active rewarming)*. In any event, it is agreed that the victim requires urgent transport to hospital.

Some of the arguments are presented (see box overleaf) for the sole purpose of providing some insights into the debate for those who are interested. *However, the non-medical reader should avoid getting bogged down in this discussion and should focus on basic first aid principles highlighted below.*

Some of the controversy about management of hypothermia.

It has been observed that once a drop in core temperature occurs, it continues to fall for some time after rewarming begins. Studies have been conflicting and the extent of this so-called "after-drop" can vary from almost nothing to several degrees. It appears to depend on how the temperature is measured, the condition of the victim and the method of rewarming. After-drop results from a combination of two mechanisms operating simultaneously. First, the core region of the body is surrounded by a shell of progressively colder tissues. Heat is drawn away from the core in order to warm the cooler adjacent tissues. Second, when the constricted vessels supplying the skin and limbs dilate as the skin is warmed, the cold blood that has been trapped in these vessels returns to and cools the core.

In the past, after-drop has been blamed for the sudden collapse, and in some cases subsequent death of certain victims while being rewarmed. However, it is likely that death associated with early rewarming results from a different mechanism. When the constricted blood vessels reopen during rewarming, blood pressure is reduced and, since the blood volume is already low from the effects of immersion, the heart must work hard to restore blood pressure. The cooled heart may not be capable of this increased effort and may fibrillate.

The rapid vasodilation and subsequent drop in blood pressure is one of the arguments used against actively rewarming a moderate to severely hypothermic victim in the field, for example, by placing them in a hot bath. There are also a number of other problems associated with placing an unresponsive, or unstable, victim in a bath.

GENERAL FIRST AID GUIDELINES FOR HYPOTHERMIA

Probably the safest action for a first aid provider assisting any hypothermic victim in the field is to:

- *Carefully remove the victim from the water (horizontally if submersion has been for an extended period)*
- *Arrange medical advice / assistance as soon as possible*
- *Handle the victim gently*
- *Minimize further heat loss by ensuring that the victim is dry, adequately insulated, placed in a warm environment*
- *Allow slow, passive warming.*

Provision of warmed, humidified oxygen if available may help to reduce heat loss from respiration.[7] There are oxygen units specially designed for this purpose. However, closed circuit oxygen therapy units such as the DAN REMO$_2$ may be helpful as they warm and humidify the gas in the circuit.

Active rewarming may be considered if the victim is no longer shivering or has a core body temperature below 32°C (89.6°F) (if able to measure this – which is highly unlikely in most circumstances) and medical advice / aid is unavailable or delayed. This can be attempted following the basic care, by applying heat packs or warm hot-water bottles to the groin, armpits, trunk and the side of the neck[8]. Unfortunately, even this is controversial.*

Following are more detailed first aid suggestions, expanding on the general first aid principles listed above.

---

* There is some evidence that this may hinder the rewarming process by inhibiting the shivering response by reducing the activity of skin temperature receptors. A slight increase in surface temperature may make a victim feel warmer, so inhibiting shivering and allowing the core temperature to fall further.[9]

Cold

When a diver feels cold and their extremities are beginning to go blue and numb, and/or they are beginning to shiver, they should get out of the water, shelter from the wind and, if possible, replace the wetsuit with warm, dry clothing. A warm, sweetened, non-alcoholic drink will help rewarm them, and a warm (not hot) shower may provide relief, but care needs to be taken to avoid fainting or falling. Alcohol should never be taken as it may dilate peripheral blood vessels, and increase the blood flow to the skin and extremities and may, therefore, increase heat loss after the victim has been removed from the cold. As previously mentioned, alcohol can also suppress shivering.

If no dry clothing is available then leave the diver in their wetsuit, wipe excess water off the surface of the wetsuit, shelter from the wind and cover them with a windproof layer to prevent evaporation from the wetsuit. A windproof jacket, a large sheet of plastic, or very large plastic bag(s) are suitable.

If correct action is taken at this stage, heat loss should be stopped and the diver should not become hypothermic.

Mild Hypothermia

Many of the signs and symptoms of mild hypothermia are similar to those of cold, the difference being the degree. *When a cold diver begins to shiver uncontrollably and/or the diver becomes uncoordinated they may be assumed to be suffering from mild hypothermia.*

The diver must be removed from the water and protected from the cold, wind and/or rain. If conditions allow and suitable dry clothes or other coverings are available, the wetsuit should be carefully removed and the diver dried and covered warmly. Warm blankets are ideal. A space blanket is less effective but can be used. Insulation should be placed both above and below the victim.

If used, a space blanket should be made to fit as snugly as possible to minimize escape of warmed air.

The victim must be handled gently. This is more important with more severe hypothermia as the heart becomes increasingly unstable with cold. Rough handling may precipitate ventricular fibrillation. If it is necessary to remove the victim's exposure suit it should be done gently, avoiding unnecessary manipulation of the throat and limbs. The best way to remove the suit is to carefully cut it off, especially the hood and/or neck section.

Ensure that the head and neck are protected. The diver can then be placed in an exposure bag, a large plastic bag(s), or wrapped in a space blanket or other plastic sheet if available. Blankets can then be wrapped around to further insulate the diver and another plastic covering can be used to keep the blankets dry if necessary. If no other insulation is available, a number of people dressed in warm, dry clothing, can huddle around the victim.[*] As the blood vessels to the limbs and skin begin to dilate, the blood pressure may drop, so the hypothermic victim should be kept lying down with the legs slightly raised and movement should be minimized to avoid shock.

Warm, sweet, non-alcoholic drinks should be given as long as the victim is not shivering uncontrollably, is alert and responsive and has the ability to swallow. It is often recommended that coffee, or other high-caffeine drinks, should not be given as they may stimulate a potentially unstable heart. However, there is little evidence of this.

If no dry coverings are available or if it is impractical to remove the wetsuit (as may

---

[*] It has often been suggested that bare torso skin to skin contact is desirable. However, while skin warmth may feel good, it may sometimes reduce shivering and so reduce net heat gain despite temporary improvement in comfort.

sometimes be the case on a small boat) the wetsuit should be left in place, excess water wiped off its surface and the diver covered and protected from the elements. Plastic bags / sheets and blankets can be used. The wetsuit will provide reasonable insulation as long as it is covered with a windproof layer to prevent evaporation. It also provides pressure to help counteract the blood pooling effect of vasodilatation when the diver rewarms.

In general, the victim should be placed in a comfortable, warm environment, kept dry, well-insulated and lying down, monitored carefully and allowed to rewarm spontaneously. If their condition worsens in any way, medical aid should be sought immediately.

The victim should not be placed near a fire or similar heat source and should not be massaged. A warm shower or bath should usually be avoided. However, it may sometimes be appropriate to consider placing the victim in a warm bath. This will depend largely on the degree of isolation from medical facilities when a long delay to proper treatment is likely, the condition of the victim, and the ability of the rescuers to manage the situation. If a warm bath is used, the victim's arms and legs should also be placed in the bath, contrary to previous belief. Great care must be taken to monitor and support the victim.

Moderate to Severe Hypothermia

A diver (or anyone else) who has been immersed for an extended period and is likely to be suffering form moderate or severe hypothermia should be carefully removed from the water in a <u>horizontal</u> position. There have been numerous reports of victims who had survived for long periods at sea, only to rapidly collapse and die when plucked from the water in a vertical position. The pressure from the water (hydrostatic pressure) helped to maintain adequate blood pressure in the dehydrated and hypothermic victims until it was suddenly removed. A horizontal posture minimizes the rapid drop in blood pressure that occurs when the person taken from the water.

If the victim is very cold and has a slow, weak pulse, low blood pressure, reduced responsiveness including slurred speech, poor coordination decreased mental skills and/or no shivering in spite of being very cold, moderate to severe hypothermia should be suspected.

Handle the diver very gently and carefully remove them and protect them from the cold environment. ***Send for medical assistance immediately.***

Carefully assess the breathing and pulse for 30 to 45 seconds. Both may be hard to detect as they can be very weak and slow. At times, despite the presence of minimal breathing and circulation, they are undetectable without the aid of an appropriate monitor.*

Listen closely to the nose and mouth, feel for the breath and look for chest and/or abdomen movement. Feel for the carotid (neck) and/or femoral pulse (groin). It is unlikely that a radial (wrist) pulse will be detectable due to the reduced blood flow to the limbs. As mentioned earlier, the victim must be handled gently as the heart will be unstable and rough handling, especially pressure on the neck, armpits or groin, may precipitate ventricular fibrillation.

There are two schools of thought on whether or not a severely hypothermic victim without vital signs (i.e. "apparently dead") should be resuscitated before being rewarmed. Some believe that although the vital signs may be undetectable adequate respiration and circulation may still be present and, if resuscitation is begun, ventricular fibrillation may be precipitated.

---

*There have been documented cases of victims of hypothermia being certified dead and later regaining consciousness, sometimes in the morgue!

They argue that in the absence of vital signs resuscitation should be delayed until the victim has been rewarmed to at least 32°C (90°F). If no vital signs are apparent after rewarming, resuscitation should begin.

The other school of thought, that is probably more relevant to the diving situation, suggests that a rescuer should spend up to about 45 seconds looking for vital signs before commencing CPR if indicated. There is little controversy about this advice in the case of a witnessed submersion. **However, if resuscitation is commenced it should be continued until the body core temperature has returned to at least 32°C (90°F).** If CPR is applied it should be applied at the normal rates and ratios. If the submersion was not witnessed, the victim is apparently dead upon discovery and medical assistance is many hours away, it may sometimes be better not to begin CPR but instead to insulate the victim, maintain a patent airway and get them to medical aid as soon as possible. In this case, possibly the victim's best chance lies in the existence of undetectable life.

If a defibrillator is available, defibrillation may be attempted if indicated. However, despite some successful outcomes in severely hypothermic victims, defibrillation appears to be less effective if the core temperature is below about 30°C (86°F).

If resuscitation is not required, the diver should be dried off and insulated as described previously. Give warm, sweet, non-alcoholic drinks as, and when, described previously. The provision of heat packs and warmed, humidified oxygen can be considered as described previously. The victim must be monitored continually. *Ensure medical assistance is accessed urgently.*

Once the victim is in hospital there are a number of ways that heat can be added. These include warming the gases (air or oxygen) the victim breathes, forced air rewarming using an inflated convective "blanket", putting the trunk in a warm bath and gradually raising the temperature, hot compresses to the chest, giving warmed intravenous fluid, passing heated water through the stomach and even being placed on a heart-lung machine. The heart function and blood chemistry are carefully monitored throughout.

When treating a person with hypothermia **do not:**

- exercise or massage them
- give alcohol (or possibly coffee or other high-caffeine drinks)
- put victim in front of a fire or heater

Note:

Victims have at times made dramatic and successful recoveries after resuscitation following long periods (up to 60 minutes or more) of immersion without breathing in very cold water. The lower oxygen usage resulting from the reduced blood flow to the non-vital organs and slowed metabolic rate from hypothermia, together with the higher oxygen partial pressures associated with depth, have been used to explain this phenomenon.

To date, the lowest core temperature recorded for an adult victim who survived from accidental hypothermia with circulatory arrest was an amazing 13.7°C (57°F). The 29 year-old woman was trapped between ice and rocks and constantly drenched with icy water for 70 minutes before being rescued. Once extricated, CPR was immediately commenced and followed by prompt advanced life support. She eventually had a near full recovery.

In one series of 50 cases of individuals who had been submerged without breathing in cold water for periods of between six to sixty minutes, 45 had suffered no detectable neurological impairment after being resuscitated and rewarmed.[100]

On balance, *there appear to be strong indications that resuscitation attempts should be made on immersion victims, especially in very cold water and / or with young victims after extended periods of immersion.*

PREVENTION

Hypothermia can be prevented by:

- Wearing an adequate exposure suit. A hood is essential in cold water and gloves and boots are also necessary to maintain dexterity in the hands and prevent cramping in the feet.

- Eat a meal before diving to ensure energy levels are optimized.

- In most cases, reducing exercise in water to reduce heat loss through convection.

- Reducing dive time if getting cold. If possible leave the water when, or before, the hands or feet begin to get numb and/or blue.

- Leave the water if noticing difficulty in performing routine tasks, confusion, or a tendency to repeat tasks or procedures.

- Leave the water if noticing feelings of being chilled followed by intermittent shivering, even though routine tasks can still be done.

- Adopting the H.E.L.P. position if stranded in the water.

- Refraining from further dives until adequately rewarmed. Divers often disregard the cumulative effects of repetitive diving. After the initial dive a diver might experience superficial skin rewarming and thus feel warmer. However, their core temperature may still be reduced. *Feeling warm is no guarantee that your heat losses have been replaced. The best way to show that your heat losses have been replaced is to start sweating.* This shows that the body needs to lose heat.

- Never drink alcohol before diving. Alcohol can cause errors in judgment, reduced coordination, and increased body cooling.

It is easy to recognize that hands and feet are cold by the familiar sensations of discomfort, numbness, pain and diminished usefulness. However, a loss of body heat is difficult to recognize and individuals are usually poor judges of their own thermal state. The ability to think clearly and rationally is affected seriously by cold.

The risks of hypothermia to a diver are not normally those of death through heart irregularities brought on by cold. They are much more the risks of cold-induced errors due to clumsiness and weakness in muscles, clumsiness in thinking with resultant increased risk of mistakes, and, if the person does become unconscious from cold, drowning through loss of protective reflexes.

SUMMARY

- The human body copes with cold by vasoconstriction and increased heat output.

- The areas of greatest heat loss are the head, neck, chest and groin.

- The normal core temperature is around 37°C (98.6°F).

- As water conducts heat far better than air, heat is rapidly lost from a submerged body.

- The rate of heat loss from a diver depends on water temperature, movement, heat production, insulation and depth.

- A well-fitting wetsuit reduces heat loss. A hood is essential in cold water. An appropriate drysuit will provide better insulation.

- A wetsuit compresses at depth and thus does not insulate as well as in the shallows.

- A wet wetsuit out of the water cools the diver by evaporation.

- Although it appears as though humans do not develop strong adaptive responses to cold, some acclimatization to cold has been observed after extended periods of time.

- Hypothermia is when the body core temperature drops below about 35°C (95°F).

- Signs and symptoms of mild hypothermia include feeling cold, numbness and blueness of extremities, profuse shivering and mild mental changes.

- If heat loss is not stopped, mild hypothermia can rapidly develop into moderate or severe hypothermia. The transition is a continuum and it is therefore difficult to differentiate between levels of hypothermia.

- Symptoms of a moderate to severe hypothermia include increasing mental changes, muscle rigidity, no shivering despite being very cold, unconsciousness, heart irregularities and death.

- Mental impairment is probably the greatest threat to the diver as it leads to inappropriate decisions and actions.

- First aid for hypothermia is aimed at stopping further heat loss and, in severe cases, preserving life until proper medical assistance is available. General first aid guidelines include:
  - *Carefully remove the victim from the water (horizontally if submersion has been for an extended period)*
  - *Arrange medical advice / assistance as soon as possible*
  - *Handle the victim gently*
  - *Minimize further heat loss by ensuring that the victim is dry, adequately insulated, placed in a warm environment*
  - *Allow slow, passive warming.*

- Hypothermia can usually be prevented by wearing adequate insulation, and leaving the water and drying off before shivering begins.

REFERENCES

1. Hayward JS, Eckerson JD, Collis ML. Effect of behavioral variables on cooling rate in man in cold water, *J Appl Physiol* 1975; 38:1073.

2. Risberg J, Hope A. Thermal insulation properties of argon used as a drysuit inflation gas. *Undersea Hyperbaric Med* 2001;28:137-43.

3. Hong S. Cold Adaptation in Humans - A Lesson from Korean Women Divers. *SPUMS J* 1984; 14(2): 6-8.

4. Skreslet S, Arefjord F. Acclimatization to cold in man induced by frequent SCUBA diving in cold water. *J of Appl Physiol* 1968; 24(2):177-81.

5. Hanna J, Hong S. Critical water temperature and effective insulation in SCUBA divers in Hawaii. *J of Appl Physiol* 1972; 33(6):770-3.

6. Sullivan P. Cold injuries – hypothermia and frostbite, In: The Science of First Aid, Pearn J, et al (eds). Canberra: St John Ambulance Australia; ; 1996:201-16.

7. Weinberg AD. The role of inhalation rewarming in the early management of hypothermia. *Resuscitation* 1998; 36(2):101-4.

8. Australian Resuscitation Council. Hypothermia: First Aid Management. *Policy Statement 8.8.* Melbourne: Australian Resuscitation Council; 2000.

9. Giesbrecht GG, Goheen MS, Johnson CE et al. Inhibition of shivering increases core temperature afterdrop and attenuates rewarming in hypothermic humans. *J Appl Physiol.* 1997; 83(5):1630-4.

10. Millar, I. Cold and the Diver". *SPUMS J* 1990; 20(1):33-9.

OTHER SOURCES

Advanced challenges in resuscitation: Special challenges in ECC: Hypothermia. *Resuscitation* 2000; 46:267-71.

Crawshaw LI et al. Thermoregulation. In: Auerbach PS (ed). Wilderness Medicine, 4th edition. St Louis: Mosby; 2001:112-28.

Danzl DF. Accidental Hypothermia. In: Auerbach PS (ed). Wilderness Medicine, 4th edition. St Louis: Mosby; 2001:135-77.

Froese G, Burton A. Heat loss from the human head. *J of Appl Physiol* 1957; 10: 235-41.

Hamlet MP. Nonfreezing cold injuries. In: Auerbach PS (ed). Wilderness Medicine, 4th edition. St Louis: Mosby; 2001:129-34.

Harnett R et al. A Review of the Literature Concerning Resuscitation from Hypothermia: Part 1 - The Problem and General Approaches. *Aviat Space and Environ. Med* 1983; 54(5):425-34.

Harnett R et al. A Review of the Literature Concerning Resuscitation from Hypothermia: Part 11 - Selected Rewarming Protocols". *Aviat Space and Environ. Med* 1983; 54(6):487-95.

Haymes E, Wells C. Environment and Human Performance. Illinois: Human Kinetics; 1986.

Keatinge W. Survival in Cold Water. Oxford: Blackwell Scientific Publications; 1969.

Pennefather J. Cold and hypothermia. In: Edmonds C, Lowry C, Pennefather J, Walker R. *Diving and Subaquatic Medicine*, 4th edition. London: Arnold; 2002:293-304.

Pozos R and Wittmers L (eds). The Nature and Treatment of Hypothermia", Vol. 2. Minneapolis: University of Minnesota Press; 1983.

Samuelson T et al. Hypothermia and Cold Water Near Drowning: Treatment Guidelines". *Alaska Medicine* 1982; 24(6):106-111.

Tipton MJ, Mekjavic IB, Golden F StG. Hypothermia. In: Bove AA (ed). Bove and Davis' Diving Medicine, 4th Edition. Philadelphia: Saunders; 2004:261-74.

Steinman AM. Cardiopulmonary resuscitation and hypothermia. *Circulation* 1986; 74:2932.

Steinman AM and Giesbrecht GG. Immersion Into Cold Water. In: Auerbach PS (ed). Wilderness Medicine, 4th edition. St Louis: Mosby; 2001:1197-225.

Sullivan P. Hypothermia, cold water immersion and cold injuries. In: *Cruise Medicine*, 2nd edition. Maryland: Maritime Health Systems Ltd; 1999:111-161.

Vanggaard L et al. Immersion of distal arms and legs in warm water (AVA rewarming) effectively rewarms mildly hypothermic humans. *Aviat Space Environ Med* 1999; 70(11):1081-8.

RECOMMENDED FURTHER READING

Advanced challenges in resuscitation: Special challenges in ECC: Hypothermia. *Resuscitation* 2000; 46:267-71.

Sullivan P. Cold injuries – hypothermia and frostbite, In: The Science of First Aid, Pearn J, et al (eds). Canberra: St John Ambulance Australia; 1996:201-16.

Tipton MJ, Mekjavic IB, Golden F StG. Hypothermia. In: Bove AA (ed). Bove and Davis' Diving Medicine, 4th Edition. Philadelphia: Saunders; 2004:261-74.

Auerbach PS (ed). Wilderness Medicine, 4th edition. St Louis: Mosby; 200.

The authors wish to thank Dr. Peter Sullivan for his editorial comments on this chapter.

© Dr. David Taylor

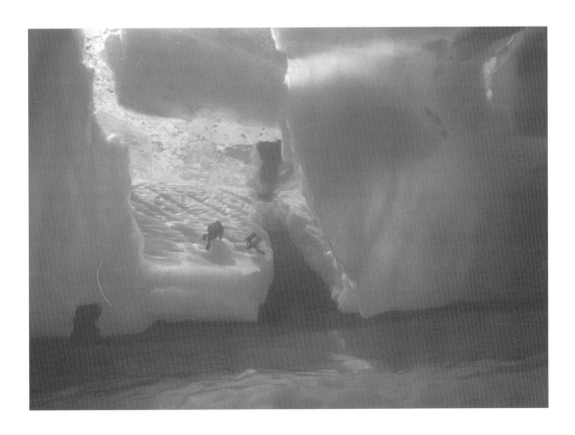

© Michael Aw

10

Dysbaric osteonecrosis

Compressed gas diving may be associated with patchy necrosis (death) of bone tissue in the long bones of the arms and legs. The death of bone tissue is known as **osteonecrosis**. Osteonecrosis can occur as a result of many medical conditions such as diabetes, alcoholism, rheumatoid arthritis, and conditions in which high dose steroids are administered for prolonged periods. The bone death associated with diving is known as **Dysbaric Osteonecrosis (DON)**. Many of the lesions on the shafts of bones do not produce problems, but this is a significant disorder because articular (joint) lesions can produce a disabling osteoarthritis-like condition.

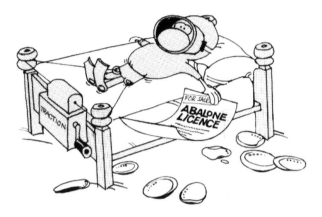

EPIDEMIOLOGY

The prevalence of bone necrosis varies greatly among different groups of divers.

The first reports of DON were published in 1911 when the disease was noted in caisson workers. Surveys among caisson workers (who spend very prolonged periods working under pressure) have consistently shown that 50 – 60% of subjects have bone lesions.

The incidence of this bone necrosis in divers varies greatly. However, the types of diving with a high rate of decompression illness are also associated with an increased incidence of bone necrosis. This is prevalent among

some groups of indigenous diving fishermen.

Over the years, there have been a variety of studies to determine the incidence of dysbaric osteonecrosis in fishermen divers in places such as Hawaii, Japan, Korea, Honduras, Mexico, Turkey and the Philippines. There have also been reports on the abalone and pearl divers in parts of Australia. Some of these divers use scuba, while many use surface supplied compressed air. The dives are typically approaching, or in excess of, 30m (100ft), and often involve long bottom times, relatively short surface intervals and multiple repetitive dives on a daily basis. Decompression stops are generally minimal, or non-existent.

Both the incidence of decompression illness, and of bone necrosis, were observed to be relatively high in most of these diving groups. The incidence of bone necrosis ranged from about 35% of the 134 Filipino divers who were examined by X-ray[1], to 100% of 23 Japanese fishermen divers who were examined using MRI scans.[2]

A 1986 survey of Australian abalone divers indicated either suspected or confirmed bone necrosis in 32% of the 108 divers tested.[3]

Other occupational groups of divers with a more disciplined approach to decompression had a lower incidence. DON was detected in 4% of naval divers in the UK[4] and 2.5% of their USN counterparts.[5] A report of the prevalence of bone necrosis in 4,980 North Sea divers (another disciplined group) which was published in 1979, showed no lesions in divers who dived on compressed air at depths shallower than 30m (100ft). Dives between 31-30m (103-165ft) carried an incidence of 0.8%.[6]

It is rare for recreational divers with DON to come to the attention of diving physicians, and there is a paucity of data from good surveys in this group. In Australia in 1976, a group of 19 sport divers volunteered to be X-rayed for signs of DON. Three of the divers (15.8%) were found to have bone lesions, however, this is far higher than expected for sport divers,[7] and the volunteer nature of the population unquestionably creates the potential for bias.

Some interesting facts that emerge from studies of the various diving populations:

Dysbaric osteonecrosis is rare in recreational divers who breathe air at depths shallower than 50m (165ft), and who follow the customary decompression tables.

Not all divers with bone lesions have suffered DCS. Although it has often been suggested that DON is a delayed manifestation of DCS, it is clear that DON can occur in the absence of any clear history of clinical DCS.

Many divers who have suffered DCS never develop bone necrosis. Although the risk of DON does seem higher in divers who have suffered DCS (particularly the musculoskeletal form), DON most certainly does not automatically follow an episode of DCS.

Overall, the incidence of DON appears to be greater in divers who:

- are indigenous sea harvesters who utilize their own empirical decompression strategies (or no decompression strategies at all!)
- spend long times underwater
- have been diving for many years
- dive deeper than 30m (100ft)
- undertake experimental diving
- have suffered from DCS
- are fatter or heavier

Notwithstanding the obvious emphasis on a long career of diving in these risk factors, DON has occurred in people subjected to only one dive in their entire careers, albeit a dive that resulted in DCS. The best documented of such cases have arisen in escapees from sunken submarines.

CAUSE

The exact cause of DON is unknown but numerous mechanisms have been suggested.

One theory suggests that the necrosis is a result of arterial emboli blocking the supply of oxygen and nutrients to the bone. The most obvious source of emboli would be venous bubbles arising from dissolved gas (that subsequently cross a PFO) or arterial bubbles arising from pulmonary barotrauma. Other possible diving-related emboli have also been proposed. For example, it is possible that bubbles may incite platelets to form "microaggregates" (stick together). Alternatively, bubbles may cause molecules of fat to separate from the proteins that keep them water soluble in blood, thus allowing them to coalesce (join) into small fat globules. The fact that DON lesions frequently occur in the heads of the bones where end arteries are found supports this theory. However, the large areas of necrosis sometimes found are unlikely to result from the blockage of single arteries.

Another theory focuses on the possibility that inert gas bubbles are formed within the bones themselves. The long bones are rich in the fatty white bone marrow, and nitrogen is very soluble in this fatty marrow. The large quantities of nitrogen released from this marrow on decompression could cause bubbles, which might expand and press on blood vessels from the outside. The end result is then the same as if an embolus was causing blockage on the inside; if the circulation is obstructed, bone death might occur.

A third theory focuses on an adverse effect of high oxygen partial pressures. For example, it has been suggested that a high PO_2 might cause small blood vessels to constrict sufficiently to reduce bone blood flow to critical levels. The main shortcoming of this theory is that an oxygen effect could be expected to be generalized, and it therefore fails to account for the patchy and isolated nature of many lesions.

Finally, a fourth theory proposes that an osmotic process may damage bone. Osmosis refers to a process in which water will move from a region of low solute concentration to one of high solute concentration. It is suggested that during a dive the dissolved gas molecules themselves may act as a solute. Since they do not penetrate into the very hard cortical areas of bone as fast as they do into the surrounding softer tissues, this may set up a process of osmosis that "drags" water out of the bone resulting in dehydration and tissue damage. Once again, this theory does not cope so well with the patchy nature of the typical DON lesion.

SIGNS AND SYMPTOMS

The earlier stages of dysbaric osteonecrosis are generally asymptomatic and are detected by bone scan or X-ray. It may take three to twelve months before the lesions are detectable by X-ray examination, but technetium bone scans can detect the lesion a week or two after the injury. Magnetic resonance imaging (MRI) scans, can probably detect the lesion within hours of it occurring, but such scans are seldom performed in the clinical treatment of recreational divers because of the high cost, the low number of positive results, and the likelihood that the result will not alter the management of the patient.

Most lesions occur on the shafts of long bones which, generally, do not cause symptoms, nor do they seem to significantly weaken the shaft. If the lesions occur near the joint surfaces of the femur and humerus, the weakened underlying bone that supports the joint cartilage may ultimately collapse with weight bearing and activity, causing the joint surface to break down and become irregular. This will cause *pain and restriction of movement that gradually becomes worse over time.*

FIGURE 10.1

Regions of the femur.

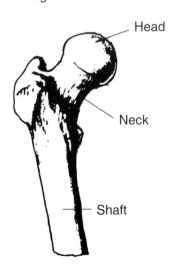

Head

Neck

Shaft

The most common sites for these juxta-articular lesions are the hips and shoulders. It has rarely been reported in other joints such as ankles, elbows, knees or wrists. The lesions at times occur symmetrically about the body, such as in both shoulders or both hips. Since it takes time for the bone to break down, it take be months or even years after the damage is done for the problem to become clinically obvious.

FIGURE 10.2

Sites of dysbaric osteonecrosis.
(shaded areas)

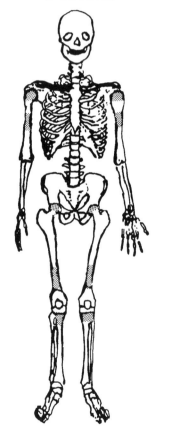

TREATMENT

Once bone lesions are discovered, there appears to be no treatment that will prevent progression and the later manifestations of the disease. Bone necrosis not involving the

bone surface near a joint requires no treatment as it causes no disability. Even some juxta-articular lesions do not progress to cause symptoms or disability. It has been suggested that if such a lesion is found early and the joint immobilized for six months or longer, the necrosis might cease. This is highly controversial, of uncertain efficacy, and is usually impractical. Where juxta-articular DON progresses to a disabling degree, the joint may need replacement.

PREVENTION

Since the exact cause of these bone lesions is unknown, it is difficult to know what measures need to be taken to prevent DON.

Conservative diving (avoidance of long, deep, decompression dives) will certainly minimize the chances of developing this type of bone necrosis. Other conservative strategies such as strict adherence to no-decompression limits, ascending slowly and doing safety stops also seem advisable.

It seems plausible that prompt recompression in cases of DCS might help prevent development of DON. A 1998 study, on the development of bone necrosis following DCS in sheep demonstrated that early recompression (4 to 8 hours post dive) substantially reduced the subsequent incidence of DON.[8] Recompression after 24 hours made no difference. However, it remains unclear to what degree the timely treatment of DCS by recompression helps to prevent this problem in humans. The relevance of the sheep data to recreational diving in humans is uncertain. The sheep model involved a saturation dive which produced DCS and DON in virtually every sheep exposed. The mechanism of disease in this saturation model may be quite different to most cases of human DCS.

Early recognition of the problem is desirable in order to weigh up the potential risk of further damage from continued diving. Cessation of diving should prevent further lesions from developing although, at present, there is no evidence to demonstrate that a diver who already has lesions is any more likely to suffer further lesions if he continues diving. Indeed, this is another very controversial issue, and it is far from clear that discovery of a mid-shaft lesion in a diver without symptoms should prompt a recommendation not to dive. This might be quite unjustified in someone who earns their living from diving or who derives a great deal of pleasure from the sport.

Nevertheless, there is reasonable agreement that it is better to know one's "DON status", and to make an informed decision about further diving from this position of awareness. It follows that long bone X-rays are often performed in the following situations:

- 3-4 months after a case of DCS
- periodically in divers exposed to frequent and prolonged repetitive hyperbaric conditions (e.g. professional divers).

If bone necrosis is detected diving activity may be modified or ceased, depending on the severity and location of the lesion.

SUMMARY

- The exact cause of dysbaric osteo-necrosis is unknown.

- Various causes have been suggested. These include intravascular and extravascular bubbles, an effect of high PO_2, and osmotic changes.

- The early stages of bone necrosis are usually asymptomatic and detectable only by various scans.

- Lesions of the long bone shaft are usually asymptomatic but lesions on the articular surface can be painful and may cause the eventual collapse of a joint.

- There appears to be no treatment which will prevent progression of the process.

- Bone necrosis is rare in recreational divers who breathe air at depths shallower than 50m (165ft), and who follow the customary decompression tables or computers.

- If lesions are found, cessation of diving is an option that should prevent further lesions developing.

REFERENCES

1. Dawson RA, Bourke A, Cross MR. A survey to quantify the prevalence of aseptic bone necrosis in two populations of diving fishermen in the Philippines. *Undersea Hyperb Med* 1998; 25(suppl):37.

2. Shinoda S, Hasegawa Y, Kawasaki S, et al. Magnetic resonance imaging of osteonecrosis in divers: Comparison with plain radiographs. *Skeletal Radiol* 1997; 26:354-9.

3. Edmonds CE. The Abalone Diver. Melbourne: National Safety Council of Australia; 1986.

4. Elliott D, Harrison, T. Aseptic Bone Necrosis in Royal Navy Divers. Proceedings of Fourth Symposium of Underwater Physiol. New York: Academic Press; 1971:251-62.

5. Harvey C, Sphar,R. Dysbaric Osteonecrosis in Divers. A survey of 611 selected Navy divers. *U.S. Navy Submar Med. Res. Lab 1976;* NSMRL 832:55.

6. Knight RJ. How Common is Dysbaric Osteonecrosis. *SPUMS J 1982; 16*:12-6.

7. Williams B, Unsworth I. Skeletal Changes in Divers. *Aust Radiol 1976*; 20:83-94.

8. Lehner CE, Wilson MA, Dueland RT, et al. Early recompression treatment of limb bends can prevent dysbaric osteonecrosis. In: Smith NE (ed). Proceedings of the 14th Meeting US-Japan Cooperative Program in Natural Resources (UJNR), Panel on Diving Physiology. Silver Spring, MD: National Oceanic Atmosphere Adm; 1998:117-37.

RECOMMENDED FURTHER READING

Jones JP, Neumann TS. Dysbaric osteonecrosis. In: Brubakk AO, Neuman TS (Eds). Bennett and Elliott's Physiology and Medicine of Diving (5th ed). London: Saunders; 2003: 659-79.

Lowry C. Dysbaric Osteonecrosis. In: Edmonds C, Lowry C, Pennefather J,,Walker R. *Diving and Subaquatic Medicine* (4th ed). London: Arnold; 2002:167-82.

Walder DN, Elliott DH. Aseptic Necrosis of Bone. In: Bove AA, (ed). Diving Medicine (4th ed). Philadelphia: WB Saunders Co; 2004:421-30.

© Dr. Richard Harris

11

Women in diving

The study of Man underwater has been just that. Dive tables were originally designed for fit, healthy, young males, and most of the studies of the effects of the underwater environment on humans have been based on male subjects. The number of women scuba divers has grown enormously over the past few years and many questions have been raised about various physiological issues of specific relevance to women divers.

The two areas of greatest concern are:

(i) the effects of diving in relation to pregnancy, and

(ii) whether or not women are more susceptible to DCS than men.

These and other aspects of women and diving will be discussed in this chapter.

DIVING IN RELATION TO PREGNANCY

Early pregnancy (first three months)

During the early stages of pregnancy, often before the mother knows she is pregnant, the developing embryo is no more than a clump of cells within the uterus. Damage to these cells during the early stages of pregnancy may have serious consequences, often leading to spontaneous abortion and possibly major birth abnormalities.

The effects of increased pressure (including increased partial pressures of nitrogen, oxygen and carbon dioxide) on the developing embryo are not known. It has been argued that these cells are sensitive to hypoxia, and that there are several potential causes of hypoxia in the pregnant woman who dives. It has also been argued that the elevated oxygen partial pressures (hyperoxia) associated with diving and especially with any treatment for DCI might be hazardous, though this is unsubstantiated. Indeed, many women have dived during early pregnancy, prior to realizing that they were pregnant, seemingly without any problems. In one relevant study, pregnant sheep were exposed to pressures of 4.6ATA (breathing air) during peak development of the embryo. Towards the end of pregnancy the foetuses were examined and no structural deformities were found.[1] There is little evidence for an adverse effect of uneventful diving on an early stage embryo. This is not to say that we advocate diving during the early stages of pregnancy (see later). However, nor do we think that women who discover they are several months pregnant should be concerned by the fact they have performed several scuba dives during that period.

Later pregnancy

Later in pregnancy the developing child develops its own discreet organ systems, but still depends upon the mother not only for its oxygen and food supply, but also for the removal of waste products and carbon dioxide. The transfer of these materials occurs across the placenta. This is an area of the uterus that specially develops during pregnancy, where the maternal and foetal blood come into very close contact. Materials are transferred from one system to the other without the blood of the mother ever mixing with that of the child. If for any reason the mother's blood supply to the placenta is dramatically reduced or stopped, the child is deprived of oxygen and brain damage can occur within minutes. If the blood supply is more subtly reduced over a longer period, gradual changes in the developing foetus such as reduced size and impaired development may occur.

The key question is - *Does diving disturb the placenta, disrupt normal foetal development, or cause premature labour or other pregnancy problems? The answer is not completely clear.*

SUGGESTED REASONS WHY DIVING COULD CAUSE PROBLEMS IN PREGNANCY

1. Oxygen toxicity

When compressed air is breathed, the partial pressure of oxygen rises progressively with depth. Moreover, if treatment for DCI is necessary, the mother and foetus will be exposed to very high partial pressures of oxygen.

It has been suggested that a foetus exposed to very high oxygen pressures late in pregnancy could develop damage to the retina of the eye (retrolental fibroplasia), possibly leading to blindness. This problem can develop in newborn babies exposed to 100% oxygen for extended periods.

Oxygen partial pressures of 3ATA or more may also cause some circulatory changes in the foetus. In the fetus, blood bypasses the lungs via the foramen ovale and special blood vessels; the latter only closing when the oxygen level in the foetal blood is raised at birth. Premature closing of these vessels, due to the higher oxygen levels from recompression treatment or perhaps diving, may cause problems in the foetus. However, we are not aware of a single case report in which such problems have been described and the highly speculative nature of these concerns is emphasized. For obvious reasons, no experiments have ever been conducted in humans to confirm or refute them.

2. Decompression sickness

Most of the concern about diving during pregnancy is over the possibility of decompression sickness in the foetus.

It is known that bubbles can form in, or enter, the blood even when decompression tables and computers are adhered to. Bubbles formed within the mother's circulation will not reach the foetus across the placenta. However, it has been suggested that bubbles trapped in the placenta might reduce the supply of oxygen and nutrients to the foetus sufficiently to cause damage. This is generally thought to be unlikely as the placental vessels are large and highly interconnected, making them very hard to obstruct.

It is also possible that bubbles could form within the foetal blood or tissues. Since the lungs of a foetus are not functioning and do not receive significant blood flow, most venous bubbles formed within the foetus will not be filtered out by the lungs as they are in the adult, and will pass directly into the arterial system through the foramen ovale and ductus arteriosis. Once in the arterial system the bubbles may cause damage. In other words, the foetus does not enjoy the protective effect of the pulmonary bubble filter as do adult divers.

Animal experiments have been conducted in an attempt to determine whether or not bubbles do form in the foetus after decompression. The results have been inconsistent.[2] In dogs and rats, the mother appears to be substantially more vulnerable to forming bubbles than the foetus. These results could be interpreted as suggesting that provided the dives are conducted conservatively to minimize bubble formation

© Ingrid N. Visser

in a human mother, then the foetus would be very unlikely to suffer problems. However, several experiments in sheep demonstrated the opposite distribution of vulnerability in this larger animal model. In other words, the foetus was <u>more</u> likely to form bubbles after decompression than the mother. Moreover, at least one study has demonstrated that untreated DCS in pregnant sheep frequently results in stillborn lambs.

Drawing conclusions about humans from these animal data is impossible, though some have argued that bubble behaviour in sheep may well be the more accurate indicator of human traits. Thus, we are left with the fact that in (perhaps) the most applicable animal model yet tested there is some evidence for selective vulnerability to bubble formation in the foetus.

Ethical problems prevent similar studies to those carried out on animals being done on humans. The only relevant data come from surveys of volunteer respondents, which are notoriously unreliable at producing accurate data on relative risks of specific activities such as diving.

In 1977, 72 women who dived while pregnant were questioned and it was found that more than one third stopped during the first trimester (when they found out they were pregnant), more than one third stopped in the second trimester (mainly due to increased size), and the remainder continued to dive. Most were very experienced divers. The deepest dive was 54.5m (180ft) and there were five decompression stop dives performed. All live-birth babies were normal, however, there were some complications, e.g. there was one premature birth, one septic abortion, two miscarriages and two non-elective caesarian sections.[3] These results did not represent a significant increase over the general pregnant population.

In 1980, a survey was performed in America, when 208 female divers replied to questionnaires placed in diving magazines.[4] 136 of these had dived during pregnancy. It was found that women who had dived during pregnancy had children with more birth defects than those who did not dive. Defects included skeletal deformation, heart deformities and other minor defects. The risk of a birth defect due to diving during pregnancy was put at 5.5% (6/109) from this study. However, it must be said that this is a very small sample group and that, statistically, this figure of 5.5% is not significantly different from the average for minor abnormalities in the normal population, although it is higher.

In the above survey, 18 out of the 20 women who dived deeper than 30m (100ft) during the first three months of pregnancy reported no foetal or neonatal complications. Two women who dived deeper than 30m (100ft) reported that their babies had been born with deformities. One child's vertibrae had not completely fused, and the other was born with one hand missing. Of the 20 women who made more than 10 dives deeper than 10m (33ft) during the first three months of pregnancy, four reported abnormal vaginal bleeding during pregnancy. Two of these four had abortions, one delivered nine weeks prematurely and one (previously mentioned) delivered a baby without a hand. In addition, more than 6% of the babies in the diving group had low birth weights compared to 1.4% in the control group.

Another survey, which included 76 pregnancies reported in 54 women, included 10 women who dived deeper than 30m (100ft) during the early stages of pregnancy.[5] Three of the women reported having babies with congenital abnormalities. One of the children suffered spina bifida (in which the vertebral arch and the skin failed to cover the spinal cord, leaving it exposed), another suffered from a hole in the heart, and the third baby's penis failed to close properly around the urethra. All three demonstrated a specific sort of abnormality; the "mid-line fusion defect". That is, things down the middle of the body had failed to come together properly. The survey concluded that there was no increase in premature labour or foetal abnormality when diving to less than 20m (66ft), but an increase in foetal abnormality when diving deeper than 20m.

A report from a Sydney hospital tells of numerous birth defects in a child born to a mother who undertook about 20 dives during pregnancy to depths up to 33m (110ft), and including one emergency ascent from 18m (60ft). The mother had not noticed any symptoms of DCI and had not been recompressed.[6]

It is frequently mentioned that the pregnant woman may herself be more prone to DCS for various hypothetical reasons such as increased fluid retention, and the increase in blood clotting sensitivity. However, there is no data to support these claims, many of which are based on dubious premises.

3. Hypoxia and hypercapnia from breath-hold diving

Breath-holding is associated with low oxygen levels and high carbon dioxide levels. It has been shown that women who consistently breath-hold dive and exert themselves during pregnancy have a greater chance of having low birth weight babies. The Ama divers of Korea, women who do many deep breath-hold dives for pearls, dive until a few days before giving birth. They have an incidence of 44.6% of prematurity with an infant of less than 2.5kg, (5.5lbs) compared to a 15.8% incidence in non-diving women from the same area.[7] Of course, it is possible that other aspects of their environment and lifestyle (rather than diving) may be responsible for this finding.

Salt water aspiration from snorkeling (or scuba) can cause hypoxia which may affect the foetus.

Overall, there is no evidence that breath-holding in moderation has any undesirable effect on the foetus. Recreational snorkeling should be fine as long as exertion, thermal stress and substantial water aspiration is avoided.

4. Medications often used during diving activities

Many drugs and medications are potentially harmful to the developing foetus. These include some of the decongestants and anti-seasick medications often used by divers. A pregnant women should consult her doctor before using any medications.

5. Physical exertion

Physical exertion will not cause a foetal abnormality as such, but extreme exertion, perhaps made necessary by an unforeseen emergency situation, may make a spontaneous abortion or premature labour more likely. There are no data to support these concerns in diving, but it is widely believed that all pregnant women should refrain from extremes of exertion at all stages of their pregnancy.

6. Miscellaneous potential problems for the pregnant mother

There are a number of potential problems of specific relevance to the pregnant mother. These include nausea, vomiting, fatigue and the inability to fit into the wetsuit or to fit a weight-belt in the position where the waist once was. Many expectant mothers have sore breasts, making both a wetsuit and buoyancy compensator uncomfortable to wear, even in the early stages of pregnancy. Practical problems such as getting in and out of a dive boat may create difficulty.

© Mary-Anne Stacey

From the fourth month onwards it may become more difficult to equalize the ears and sinuses due to fluid retention and mucosal swelling.

During pregnancy, respiratory function becomes progressively impaired. These changes may make it more difficult for the woman to cope with strenuous activity and may increase the possibility of pulmonary barotrauma, though this is highly speculative.

7. Potential post-natal problems

Many obstetricians are quite happy for women to go back into the water soon after the birth of their baby, although some recommend a wait of about six weeks. There will definitely be a stand down period after birth involving a caesarian section for proper healing of the surgical wound. (The same applies to diving after a hysterectomy.) It is important to check with the doctor before recommencing diving activities after childbirth.

Enlarged breasts often will not fit into the wetsuit. Nipples can be extremely sensitive to cold water and this can be a problem if the baby wants a feed immediately after the dive. There are no physiological problems with breast feeding and diving.

The pelvic ligaments, which stretch to facilitate delivery, can stay lax for up to six months, so it is probably not advisable to be carrying heavy weights for long distances. Lack of fitness may present a problem. In addition, it may be difficult to obtain life-jackets for small babies, which can be a problem if a woman wishes to take the baby with her in a boat. However, most of these problems can be overcome.

8. Effect of diving on the gender of the baby

A related matter though not a "problem" as such, and by definition not to diving *during* pregnancy, is the question of whether diving can influence the gender of a baby conceived by an actively diving mother and / or father. Since gender is determined by chromosomes from the father, this issue is less likely to be relevant to diving by women. Some years ago it was observed that a small group of Royal Navy divers had more female offspring than male offspring. A retrospective survey of the gender of the children of all Royal Australian Navy (RAN) compressed air divers was undertaken to determine whether or not any differences were apparent. The survey included 240 children. The results indicated that there was no significant difference in the sex of the children of these RAN divers.[8]

There is no evidence that recreational diving in either parent makes it more likely that a baby of a particular gender will be born.

Conclusions

It is impossible to make definitive statements about the safety of diving during pregnancy. There are some data, essentially anecdotal, that suggest that even "uneventful" diving,

especially deeper diving, may be hazardous to the foetus. However, it is far from certain that the reported cases of foetal abnormality in diving mothers occur at a greater rate than in non-diving women. It must be remembered that many women who dive uneventfully while pregnant have no problems with their pregnancies or with their babies. Things might be quite different if a pregnant woman were to suffer DCS. It makes sense that DCS in the mother may also be associated with at least an equivalent risk of DCS in the foetus. Indeed, because of the lack of a pulmonary filter, the foetus may be more at risk, though this is not proven.

Given that to most people diving is a discretionary pleasure activity, and the consequences of diving injury to either the mother or the foetus are potentially disastrous, we are obligated to take the conservative view that the foetus might be prone to harm if diving is continued throughout pregnancy. **Thus, erring on the side of caution, most authorities, including these authors, recommend that pregnant women should refrain from scuba diving.** Excessive breath-hold diving should also be avoided, but snorkeling on the surface should be fine, as long as the diver stays thermally comfortable, does not exert herself, and avoids water aspiration.

Practically speaking it can be very difficult for a woman to know what to do when trying to get pregnant - which could take some time. Some women are happy to give up diving at this time. Otherwise, it is probably wise to dive conservatively, and to perform a pregnancy test expeditiously if menstruation is delayed. Urine testing kits are readily available and are quite inexpensive.

Many women continue to dive before realizing they are pregnant. If this occurs the expectant mother should not spend the rest of the pregnancy worrying about the possible repercussions. The vast majority of women who reported diving in early pregnancy pregnant gave birth to healthy babies. As with any other concern during pregnancy, a discussion with the obstetrician should help to allay any fears. Many major birth defects can be detected relatively early using ultrasound, and such a procedure (which is routine in most places in the modern context) might be reassuring for a woman who has dived through the first weeks of her pregnancy.

ARE WOMEN MORE SUSCEPTIBLE TO DECOMPRESSION SICKNESS?

There has been considerable speculation about the relative risk of DCS in women and men. Most of the speculation has focused on the possibility that women might be at higher risk, based on a number of fairly weak concerns. For example, women have a greater percentage of fatty tissue than men. Fatty tissue absorbs a lot of nitrogen and releases it slowly. Hormonal changes during menstruation can result in fluid retention (oedema) and fluid shifts. Also, some oral contraceptive pills can cause a micro-sludging or slowing of the circulation. While there has been much speculation on the relevance of these issues, there is little in the way of hard data.

Dr. Bruce Bassett collected and analyzed data on female flight nurses exposed to high altitudes in the U.S. Air Force.[9] Between 1968 and 1977 the incidence of altitude decompression sickness in male students was 0.09%, while in the female nurses it was 0.36%. DCS in the women appeared more rapidly and recurred more frequently. The nurses had four times the DCS incidence of the male students, and many have quoted these figures to support the notion that women are more susceptible to DCS than are men.

In contrast, there have been a number of survey-type studies that have failed to demonstrate any difference in DCS susceptibility between men and women.

Diving log data from the Naval Diving and salvage Training Centre (NDSTC) demonstrated that there is no increased risk of DCS among Navy female divers compared to their male counterparts under similar dive exposures.[10] This data relates to relatively short duration dives and the authors of the report suggested that it may be applied to the recreational scuba diver as well. They concluded that "if any increased susceptibility to decompression sickness does exist for female sport divers it will be minimal and should not be a deterrent to women diving on the same decompression schedules as men." However, they add that the women's greater proportion of adipose (fatty) tissue may make them more susceptible to DCS after saturation, experimental and multiple repetitive dives, during which the fatty tissues absorb large quantities of gas.

The Men and Women in Diving Study[11] based on more than 450,000 dives initially found that women had a significantly higher rate of DCI per 1000 dives than men. However, when controlled for confounding variables such as experience, the result was essentially reversed, with women appearing to be less vulnerable to DCI than men. The authors also noted a potentially important reporting bias, with men being more reluctant to report adverse events than women.

The two most recent reports describing risk of hypobaric (altitude) DCS found no evidence for gender related risk.[12,13]

DAN's database of diving accidents in the USA in 2002 shows that 28% of the injured divers were women. This proportion has gradually risen since the 1980s, and probably reflects the proportion of diving performed by men and women. For example, DAN's Project Dive Exploration data for that year indicated that women represented 29% of the participants.[14]

Virtually no experimental work has been performed to examine this issue. Several small studies have compared numbers of Doppler detected bubbles in male and female subjects after carefully controlled dives or altitude exposures. If anything, it appears that men may form venous bubbles more readily than women after equivalent altitude exposures.[13]

This is an issue whose resolution is blighted by poor or inadequate data. The only conclusion that can be drawn at present is that while the definitive answer is not known, women are probably not at greater risk than men, and if there is any gender-based difference in risk of DCS it is likely to very small.

Effect of the menstrual cycle

A separate question to the issue of differences between men and women, is whether women are more vulnerable to DCS at different phases of the menstrual cycle. Once again, there has been much speculation on this issue, based on issues like "fluid retention" and its potential influence on inert gas kinetics. Though such discussion has been largely speculative, there is now some data that suggests that risk may indeed be greatest during the first week of the cycle (menstruation) and lowest during the third week.[15] The basis for this uneven distribution of risk has not been determined.

Apart from the risk of DCS, there are other diving issues pertinent to the menstrual cycle. A common fear is that of shark attack, however, there is no evidence to support this anxiety. Perusal of the statistics of shark attacks indicates that female divers have a lower incidence of shark attack than males (Is this because sharks are "man eaters"!). Some women suffer from pre-menstrual tension (PMT), or period cramps, which may make them less capable at both a physical and emotional level and may impair their judgment. Those who experience only mild symptoms may find that PMT has little or no effect on their diving. However, those suffering from more severe symptoms such as depression, anxiety or poor concentration may be unfit to dive and probably will not wish to do so anyway.

Effect of oral contraceptives

Because of the association between the use of oral contraceptives (OCs) and the formation of blood clots (thrombosis), and the observed sludging of platelet cells around bubbles, it has been thought that OCs might aggravate DCS. However, blood clotting is an extremely complex mechanism involving many substances and mechanisms, and its importance in the majority of cases of clinical DCS is tenuous.

Once again, there are few relevant data, and conclusions are impossible. It is possible that the use of an OC reduces the variation in risk of DCS across the phases of the menstrual cycle,[15] but any OC-related change in the absolute risk of DCS averaged across the cycle (if any) is likely to be very small. However, it may be prudent for women to dive more conservatively during menstruation, especially if also taking OC.

Effect of breast implants

As a result of questions about mammary implants and decompression safety, some experiments were conducted to determine the degree of bubbling within these implants after exposure to various pressures.[16] Bubble formation did occur in the implants causing them to increase in volume. However, it was concluded that the degree of bubble formation in an implant following typical sport dives should not cause damage to the surrounding tissues, and can be tolerated safely. Deep saturation diving should be avoided as inert gas exchange will be very slow and the implant will require a lot of time to get rid of its large gas load. In the worst case, the resulting bubble formation might increase the implant volume enough to cause trauma to the surrounding tissue.

Once sufficient time has passed after surgery, when the diver has resumed normal activities and there is no danger of infection, she may begin scuba diving. It may be advisable to avoid buoyancy compensators with constrictive chest straps, which can put pressure on the seams and contribute to risk of rupture

CONCLUSION

The anatomical and physiological differences between men and women may affect various aspects of diving, although the extent of some of these effects is not known. Overall, there are no convincing data that suggest any significant gender-based differences in diving safety.

SUMMARY

- Because women are anatomically and physiologically different to men, there may be differences in how the sexes are affected by diving.

- If a pregnant mother suffers severe hypoxia, the foetus may be endangered.

- At this stage the effects of increased pressure on the developing foetus are not adequately known.

- High partial pressures of oxygen due to very deep scuba diving or hyperbaric oxygen treatment may damage the foetus.

- Since the lungs of a foetus are not functioning, circulating venous bubbles will not be filtered out and may enter the arterial system. Once in the arterial system these bubbles may cause damage. However, there is no conclusive evidence from animal or human studies that confirms the foetus is at higher risk of DCS than the mother.

- If a pregnant mother suffers from DCI, the foetus may be damaged.

- There is some weak data from retrospective surveys which indicates that diving during pregnancy (especially to deeper depths) may increase the chances of spontaneous abortion, low birth weight, and congenital deformities. These data are subject to considerable potential bias and must be treated with extreme caution. Nevertheless, for safety, pregnant women are usually counseled not to dive.

- Women who extensively breath-hold dive and exert themselves during pregnancy appear to have a greater incidence of premature and low birth weight babies.

- Problems for the pregnant diver can include, nausea, vomiting, wetsuit and weight-belt fit, fatigue and getting in and out of boats.

- There is no evidence that diving affects the gender of a baby.

- Although certain physiological factors would theoretically make women more susceptible to DCS, it appears that women may have a comparable risk to that of men.

- It has not been shown that women taking the oral contraceptives are more at risk from DCS.

- Women who feel well enough to dive during menstruation can usually do so safely, although it is wise to dive more conservatively at that time.

REFERENCES

1. Bolton-Klug ME, Lehner CE, Lamphier EH, Rankin JH. Lack of harmful effects from simulated dives in pregnant sheep. *Am J Obstet Gynecol* 1993; 146(1):48-51.

2. Fife W. Effects of diving on pregnancy. Proceedings of the 19th Workshop of the Undersea Medical Society. Bethesda MD: Undersea Medical Society; 1978,.

3. Bangasser S. Medical Profile of the Woman SCUBA Diver. Proceedings of the 10th International Conference on Underwater Education. California: NAUI; 1978:31-40.

4. Bolton M. Scuba diving and foetal well-being: a survey of 208 women". *Undersea Biomed Res* 1980; 7(3):183-9.

5. Betts J. Diving and the Unborn Child. *Diver* 1985; 30(1):14-5.

6. Turner G, Unsworth I. Intrauterine Bends?. *SPUMS J* 1982; January-March:24-5.

7. Edmonds C. The female diver. *Skindiving* 1984; 14(4):119-27.

8. Edmonds C. The Diver. Royal Australian Navy School of Underwater Medicine Report, Project Report 4-74; 1974.

9. Bassett B. Decompression Sickness in Female Students Exposed to Altitude During Physiological Training. Ann. Scient. Meet. Aerospace Med. Assoc., 44th Meeting; 1973.

10. Zwingelberg KM, Knight MA, Biles JB. Decompression sickness in women divers. *Undersea Biomed Res* 1987; 14(4):311-7.

11. St Leger Dowse M, Bryson P, Gunby A, Fife W. Men and Women in Diving. Plymouth: Diving Diseases Research Centre; 1994.

12. Conkin J, et al. Relationship of exercise, age, and gender on decompression sickness and venous gas emboli during 2-hour oxygen prebreathe prior to hypobaric exposure. *Undersea Hyper Med* 2000; 27(supp):12.

13. Webb JT, Kannan N, Pilmanis AA. Gender not a factor for altitude decompression sickness risk. *Aviat Space Environ Med* 2003;74(1):2-10.

14. Report on Decompression Illness, Diving Fatalities and Project Dive Exploration. Durham NC: Divers Alert Network; 2004.

15. Lee V, St Leger Dowse M, Edge C, Gunby A, Bryson P. Decompression sickness in women: a possible relationship with the menstrual cycle. *Aviat Space Environ Med* 2003;74(11):1177-82.

16. Vann RD, Georgiade GS, Riefkohl RE. Mammary Implants in Divers. *SPUMS J* 1985;15(3):32-3.

OTHER SOURCES

Fife WP, Simmang C, Kitzman JV. Susceptibility of fetal sheep to acute decompression sickness. *Undersea Biomed Res* 1978; 5(3):287-92.

Fife CE, Fife WP. Should Pregnant Women Scuba Dive? *J Travel Med* 1994; 1(3):160-7.

Lehner C et al, Fetal health during decompression studies in sheep. *Undersea Biomed Res* 1982; 9(1-Suppl):A 71.

McIver R. Bends resistance in the fetus. In Reprints of Scientific Program. 1968 annual scientific meeting, Aerospace medical Association. Washington: Aerospace Medical Association; 1968.

Nemiroff M, Willson JR, Kirshbaum TH. Multiple hyperbaric exposures during pregnancy in sheep, *Am J Obstet Gynecol* 1981; 140:651-5.

Powell M, Smith M. Fetal and maternal bubbles detected non-invasively in sheep and goats following hyperbaric decompression". *Undersea Biomed Res* 1985; 12:59-66.

Stock M et al. Response of Fetal Sheep to Simulated No-Decompression Dives. *Journal of Applied Physiology* 1980; 48:776-80.

RECOMMENDED FURTHER READING

Fife CE, Fife WP. Should Pregnant Women Scuba Dive? *J Travel Med* 1994; 1(3):160-7.

Taylor L. Women in Diving Part 2 –The menstrual cycle and contraceptive pill. *Alert Diver SEAP*; 2004; Apr-Jun: 11-2.

Taylor L. Women in Diving Part 3 –Diving during pregnancy. *Alert Diver SEAP*; 2004; Jul-Sep:11-2.

Uguccioni DM, Moon RE, Taylor MB. DAN Explores Fitness and Diving Issues for Women. *Alert Diver* 1999. Jan-Feb:41-8.

Many thanks to Dr. Chery Bass and Dr. Peter Rogers for their input into this chapter in the first edition.

12

Drug use and the diver

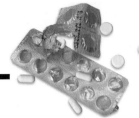

Drugs are most frequently used to treat disease, and **more often than not it is the disease process being treated rather than the drugs being used that is of most significance for diving**. In this regard, and notwithstanding any information provided in this account, divers should **always discuss their medication and the illness that necessitates it with a diving physician** in order to receive proper counseling about the implied risks.

Drugs are agents that produce biological effect in living organisms. They include medicines, recreational drugs and drugs of abuse. Most drugs have side-effects, that is they produce changes in the body in addition to the change or effect that is desired. For example, antihistamines, which are often used to combat nasal congestion, often cause drowsiness, which can be dangerous for the driver or diver.

The effects of drugs are not always consistent from one environment to another, from one person to another and within an individual from one time to another. The effect of a drug may be altered by pressure, changes in nitrogen, carbon dioxide and oxygen levels, cold, fatigue, mental state, exercise, altered sensory input and various other factors. Thus, in diving, even medications that may normally be considered useful and safe can have unpredictable effects on body physiology and mood state. Whenever a drug is used by a diver, consideration must be given to any potential interaction between the drug and diving.

Very few controlled studies have been undertaken to determine the suitability of various drugs for use underwater, and some of the studies done may not be applicable to recreational scuba diving to the depths normally encountered. Not surprisingly, it is often very difficult to assess the relative safety of drug use by a diver, and most divers are not in a position to make such determinations without expert advice. *Even diving medicine experts will frequently have difficulty drawing firm conclusions, and divers who use medications whilst diving must accept that the information provided by such experts and in this book are informed opinions at best. No guarantees of safety can be given.*

A useful framework within which to consider the potential effects of a drug in diving is to ask the following questions:

1. Will the drug make a diving illness more likely?
2. Will diving enhance any unwanted effects of the drug?
3. Does the drug adversely affect exercise tolerance or mentation?

It is clearly impossible to review the broad spectrum of drugs and their interaction with diving in a short summary such as this. However, we will briefly consider some of the more common or important agents below.

RECREATIONAL DRUGS

Alcohol

Alcohol generally depresses the brain, interfering with a wide range of cognitive and motor functions. Its use is implicated in a frightening proportion of drownings, and a significant proportion of fatal motor accidents.

Will alcohol use make a diving illness more likely?

Alcohol is a diuretic (promotes water loss in urine). Although the status of dehydration as a risk factor for DCI is unproven, it is possible that alcohol may predispose to DCS by causing dehydration. The dehydrated state may persist well after the early phase of intoxication, and is thought to be one of the contributing factors to the feeling of "hangover". The probability of DCI is also increased by the mental impairment caused by alcohol which will make errors of calculation and judgment (and therefore accidents) more likely.

A study designed to assess the performance of scuba divers after alcohol ingestion found that performance was significantly degraded at a blood alcohol count (BAC) of 0.04 percent or higher. It demonstrated a clear increase in the risk of injury at this level, and also that the divers failed to appreciate the degradation in their performance and the increased risk of injury.[1]

Alcohol is known to cause peripheral vasodilation which will enhance heat loss. It has therefore been suggested that hypothermia might be more likely in a diver or swimmer following recent alcohol consumption.

Will diving enhance any unwanted effects of alcohol?

It is almost certain that the effects of nitrogen narcosis and alcohol intoxication will be additive and perhaps even synergistic. As mentioned above, this is likely to raise the possibility of the diver making a crucial mistake.

Does alcohol adversely affect exercise tolerance or mentation?

As previously discussed alcohol most definitely impairs mentation in direct relation to its concentration in the blood, and will therefore make errors of judgment more likely. Any direct effect on exercise tolerance is likely to be less prominent, though at severe levels of intoxication, the performance of exercise would be impaired through an effect on coordination and dexterity.

In summary, it is clear that there are a number of potential and important adverse interactions between diving and alcohol use. It is recommended that alcohol is never drunk to excess within 24 hours of beginning a dive. There is probably no harm in having "a drink with a meal" on the night before diving.

There is no convincing data addressing the significance of alcohol consumption after diving in relation to risk of DCS. There seems little reason to discourage "a beer" or a glass of wine with dinner at the end of a day's diving, but it is probably best to avoid becoming drunk, if only because the diver may fail to recognize symptoms of DCS that may develop.

Tobacco

Despite the well-proven health disadvantages of smoking, it is still a prevalent habit in many societies. Diving physicians are frequently asked about the implications of a smoking habit for diving.

Will smoking make a diving illness more likely?

There is essentially no evidence that smoking prior to a dive raises the risk of DCI. There has been some suggestion that increased mucus production in response to irritation by cigarette smoke may cause "plugging" of small airways, and in doing so might increase the risk of pulmonary barotrauma and CAGE. This is speculative rather than proven. However, an analysis of DAN America accident data for 1989-97 indicated that when DCI does occur in recreational divers, smoking is a risk factor for increased severity of symptoms.[2]

Will diving enhance any unwanted effects of smoking?

There is no known interaction of this nature.

Does smoking adversely affect exercise tolerance or mentation?

The answer must really be given in two parts. In the short term, it is difficult to make a case for impairment of exercise tolerance by smoking just prior to diving. After all, there are occasional smokers even among the ranks of Olympic athletes and other elite sports people. However, in the longer term smoking is highly likely to accelerate disease processes such as heart disease, which will impair exercise capacity and prematurely limit a diving career.

In summary, the major argument for a diver not to smoke is the long-term preservation of their health and maintenance of their diving careers, rather than any acute effect of smoking on diving.

Hallucinogens and Narcotics

The predictable effects of drugs such as marijuana, cocaine, and opiates such as heroin determine that their combination with diving might be very dangerous indeed. It seems a matter of common sense, but nevertheless, some of the key issues are outlined below.

Will these drugs make a diving illness more likely?

Some of these agents exhibit vasodilatory activity, and this will result in more rapid heat loss and a greater risk of hypothermia when immersed. Such a phenomenon has been reported for marijuana.[3] There is probably no direct physiological effect of these drugs which will predispose to DCI. However, their effect on mentation is likely to make errors of judgment and accidents much more likely.

Will diving enhance any unwanted effects of these drugs?

It is highly likely that the effect of nitrogen narcosis will be additive or synergistic with the effect of any narcotic drugs. For example, marijuana has been reported to cause a variety of undesirable effects underwater. One such report described unpleasant effects such as extreme anxiety and idea fixation.[3] Another unconfirmed report describes a group of divers who experimented with marijuana in warm water. The drug caused the divers to become ultra-relaxed, sleepy, unaware and unable to think or work. Upon reaching a depth of 15-18m (50-60ft) each diver became unconscious at some stage.[3]

Does the use of these agents adversely affect exercise tolerance or mentation?

The narcotic effect of these recreational drugs is the chief concern in their combination with diving. A diver who is mentally impaired by a drug-induced narcosis is much more likely to make errors of judgment and crucial underwater mistakes.

In summary, it is obvious that the use of recreational or prescription narcotic agents (such as opiate-based pain killers) should not be combined with diving. The same is almost certainly true for non-narcotic sedatives and tranquillizers such as diazepam (valium) which is often prescribed to stressed or anxious patients.

Separate mention should probably be made of methamphetamine based drugs such as "P" and "Ecstasy". Unlike marijuana and opiates which tend to have a "depressant" effect (albeit resulting in euphoria), methamphetamines are stimulating, leaving the user feeling energized as well as euphoric, hence their popularity among members of the so-called "party culture". Emergency physicians and anaesthetists will attest to the unpredictable and sometimes dramatic effects these drugs can have on normal physiology. Their interaction with diving is unknown, but there are some potentially lethal possibilities, and it is recommended that such agents are never used in relation to diving. Indeed, a regular user is advised against diving even in periods when they consider they are not affected by the drug.

It is important to realize that, like alcohol, these other drugs may still be active in the human body for quite a while after their last use.

DRUGS USED TO FACILITATE DIVING

Decongestants

Decongestants are used to counter vasodilation and oedema (swelling) of the tissues lining the nasal passages. They are commonly used by divers to prevent or treat ear or sinus barotrauma. They act by causing vasoconstriction, which gives a temporary improvement in patency of the nasal airway. They may also improve the ability to equalize pressure in the middle ear by reducing congestion in the Eustachian tube. There is a reasonable amount of anecdote that supports this claim. There are two forms of these agents: those that are applied topically (usually as a nasal spray) and those that are taken systemically (as a pill).

Will decongestants make a diving illness more likely?
Although most commentators agree that decongestants may facilitate ear and sinus equalization in a congested patient, it is notable that these agents may, somewhat paradoxically, contribute to middle ear barotrauma in several ways. First, although they are usually fairly long-acting agents, it is possible that the effect might "wear off" or decline at depth thus allowing the airways to become congested during the dive. This will predispose the diver to a reverse

squeeze during the ascent. In addition, if they are used for a prolonged period (usually quoted at more than 5 days) decongestants can induce a "rebound effect" in which congestion actually becomes worse. Thus, a diver using them for several weeks might actually find it more difficult to equalize the ears in the latter stages of the trip. This does not apply to steroid type nasal decongestants such as *flixonase* and *beconase* which do not have a rebound effect and are commonly used for months at a time. However, these sprays do little to unblock an acutely congested nose, and are only effective if used over a long period.

Another frequently expressed concern in relation to these agents, especially the systemic forms (taken as pills such as pseudoephedrine) is that they might increase the risk of oxygen toxicity. Although there is very little evidence that this is so, the possibility must be borne in mind.

Will diving enhance any unwanted effects of decongestants?
There is no well-established interaction of this nature.

Does the use of decongestants adversely affect exercise tolerance or mentation?
These agents are not considered likely to affect exercise tolerance or mentation. Indeed, the use of the most common systemic agent (pseudoephedrine) is banned in athletes because of a possible performance enhancing effect. Pseudoephedrine has had some testing of its effect on cognitive and cardiovascular function in the hyperbaric environment (3ATA), and no significant effects were recorded.[4]

In summary, the use of nasal decongestants is generally discouraged, although it is undeniable that they have safely facilitated diving for many divers with slight upper airway congestion from time to time. It is frequently argued that divers with significant and chronic difficulty "equalizing the ears" should probably not be diving, and most would agree that the chronic use of decongestants to facilitate a diving hobby is not recommended. An exception to this is the longer term use of steroid-type decongestant sprays which do not have a "rebound" effect and appear safe in diving.

This is a controversial area and there are no clear cut right or wrong answers. The concern about decongestants (particularly the oral form) and risk of cerebral oxygen toxicity is unresolved, and technical or nitrox divers are probably best to avoid using these agents if possible.

Antihistamines

Antihistamines act by blocking the release of histamine, which is a mediator for allergic inflammation. They may be particularly useful in those divers who have nasal congestion due to hay fever.

Will antihistamines make a diving illness more likely?

It is speculated but not clearly demonstrated that the drowsiness caused by some of the older anti-histamines (see below) might be enhanced by nitrogen narcosis, or that nitrogen narcosis might be worse in the diver taking anti-histamines. There is probably no direct physiological effect of these drugs that would predispose to DCI. However, their effect on mentation (see below) may make errors of judgment and accidents more likely.

Will diving enhance any unwanted effects of antihistamines?

There is no well-established interaction of this nature, although it has been suggested that the effects of nitrogen narcosis may be additive to the sedating effects of certain antihistamine agents.

Does the use of antihistamines adversely affect exercise tolerance or mentation?

Some of the older antihistamines (some of which are still in common use) have a prominent sedating effect and were not considered safe for use when driving or operating dangerous machinery. It would seem logical that such agents would also be unsuitable for use in diving. Over the last 10 years there has been development of a generation of non-sedating antihistamine agents that seem more suitable. One of these agents (*terfenadine*) has undergone limited testing in the hyperbaric environment and found to cause no untoward effects.[5]

In summary, antihistamine agents may be useful in reduction of upper airway congestion secondary to hayfever. The new generation non-sedating agents are probably suitable for use in conjunction with diving, but the older agents which might produce sedation are best avoided.

Anti-motion sickness drugs

There are few more troublesome and controversial "drugs and diving" topics than the issue of anti-motion sickness medication. This is mainly because sea sickness is common and the use of these agents is consequently prevalent. There is a wealth of anecdote describing the "safe" use of anti-motion sickness drugs by divers notwithstanding a number of theoretical concerns about their use. Many drugs are used in attempts to prevent motion sickness. There are various classes of agents that act at different points in the various central nervous system connections that mediate nausea and vomiting, and there appears to be quite a degree variation in response to different agents between individuals.

Will anti-motionsickness drugs make a diving illness more likely?

A number of anti-motion sickness drugs belong to the anti-histamine family. As mentioned above, it is possible that nitrogen narcosis might be worse in the diver taking anti-histamines. There is probably no direct physiological effect of any of these drugs which will predispose to DCI. However, the effect on mentation exhibited by these

Cartoon by the late Peter Harrigan

agents (see below) may make errors of judgment and accidents more likely. It is also relevant to mention that the side effect of some agents may mimic DCI. For example the use of *scopoderm (scopolamine) patches* may cause visual changes that might be mistaken for DCI.

Will diving enhance any unwanted effects of anti-motion sickness drugs?

There is no well-established interaction of this nature, although it has been suggested that the effects of nitrogen narcosis may be additive to the sedating effects (see below) of certain antihistamine agents.

Does the use of anti-motion sickness drugs adversely affect exercise tolerance or mentation?

As mentioned above, some of the older antihistamines have a prominent sedating effect and these are the ones that are frequently used in anti-motion sickness medication. Preparations containing these older antihistamines often carried warnings to the effect that they were not considered safe for use when driving or operating dangerous machinery. It would seem logical that such agents would also be unsuitable

for use in diving. Unfortunately, while the non-sedating agents are effective in allergy, they do not seem so effective in preventing motion sickness, although limited data suggest that terfenadine might be useful.[5] *Terfenadine* is unlikely to cause problems in the hyperbaric environment because it does not readily enter the central nervous system.

In summary, there are several theoretical concerns about the use of motion sickness medications, especially those containing sedating antihistamines. Only transdermal *scopolamine* (which is not an antihistamine) has undergone limited testing in the hyperbaric environment,[6] and does not appear to have any prominent adverse effects. In addition, the non-sedating antihistamine *terfenadine* (or derivatives such as *fexofenadine*) might possess useful anti-motion sickness properties, and is unlikely to have any adverse effects. Notwithstanding the theoretical concerns, the use of anti-motion sickness medication is prevalent in the diving community, and there are few, if any, reports of related adverse events. It is probably advisable to use such medication for the first time in a non-diving situation so that an individual's response to the drug can be assessed. If, for example, a particular preparation made a diver feel drowsy, it would probably be unwise to use that agent in association with diving.

MISCELLANEOUS MEDICATIONS

There are a vast number of drugs that may be prescribed in various illnesses, and it is clearly beyond the scope of this book to review any significant number of them. However, we have selected a number for special mention, either because of their particular significance in diving, their frequency of use in the community, or the fact that we are often asked questions about them.

Aspirin

Aspirin has achieved the status of something of a "wonder drug" in recent years, having been shown to have a variety of beneficial effects. In particular, it is frequently prescribed to patients who appear vulnerable to heart attack. Aspirin inhibits platelet aggregation and platelets are early players in the formation of clots in the coronary vessels. Many patients take low dose aspirin chronically from middle age onwards.

Will aspirin make a diving illness more likely?

As has been mentioned elsewhere, a potential role of bleeding from blood vessels damaged by bubbles in spinal cord DCS has been identified, and this could potentially be made worse by drugs which prevent normal clotting. This is a theoretical concern and there is no proof that it is a significant risk.

Will diving enhance any unwanted effects of aspirin?

There is no well-established interaction of this nature.

Does the use of aspirin adversely affect exercise tolerance or mentation?

There is no well-established interaction of this nature.

In summary, the use of aspirin is discouraged in association with diving. However, given its proven benefit in prevention of certain cardiovascular diseases, and the theoretical nature of its disadvantages in diving, it is not recommended that aspirin be ceased to facilitate a diving hobby. A diver taking aspirin for sound medical reasons (that do not contraindicate diving) must choose between continuing with both the aspirin and diving (and thus accepting a degree of theoretically increased risk) or giving up diving. Based on current knowledge, and given our passion for diving, both authors would choose the former. The same concerns are even more relevant to the use of more potent anticoagulants such as **warfarin**, and most diving physicians would recommend that a patient on warfarin should not dive.

There is no evidence that taking aspirin prophylactically before or after diving will reduce the likelihood of DCI.

Oral Contraceptives

Oral contraceptives are widely used by younger women.

Will oral contraceptives make a diving illness more likely?

There has been an association between some oral contraceptives (especially those containing high doses of oestrogen) and the formation of blood clots (thrombosis). Since bubbles may induce clotting as part of the pathophysiological process of DCS, it has been speculated that oral contraceptives might increase the risk of DCS. The limited data available do not convincingly support this notion however.

Will diving enhance any unwanted effects of oral contraceptives?

There is no well-established interaction of this nature.

Does the use of oral contraceptives adversely affect exercise tolerance or mentation?

There is no well-established interaction of this nature.

In summary, the jury is still out on this issue. There is no good evidence that women taking oral contraceptives are at higher risk of DCIS and if there is an increased risk it is almost certainly very small. It would probably not prove reason enough for a woman on a well-tolerated oral contraceptive regimen to change in order to facilitate diving.

Beta blockers

Beta blocking drugs are common agents used to treat hypertension (high blood pressure). They act by blocking the heart's response to stimulation by nerves and hormones that usually act to make the heart beat faster and harder.

Will beta blockers make a diving illness more likely?

Anecdotal links have been made between the use of beta blockers and the risk of a condition called immersion induced pulmonary oedema. This was explained in Chapter 2. To recap, it may arise if the heart cannot cope with the extra workload that arises when blood is forced into the central circulation during immersion. There is back pressure in the circulation of the lungs, and this causes leakage of fluid from the blood vessels into the alveoli. Beta blockers may increase the risk of such an event by blunting the heart's response to the increased demands during diving.

Will diving enhance any unwanted effects of beta blockers?

There is no well-established interaction of this nature.

Does the use of beta blockers adversely affect exercise tolerance or mentation?

As implied above, beta blockers may blunt the heart's ability to respond to the extra demands of exercise. This is an obvious disadvantage if the diver finds him or herself in a situation demanding extra work, such as being caught in a current.

In summary, the use of beta blockers by divers is discouraged. There are several families of hypertensive agents, and an appropriate alternative to a beta blocker can usually be found. In particular, the use of agents known as angiotensin converting enzyme (ACE) inhibitors is generally considered preferable for diving.

Zyban

Zyban is an agent that was originally developed as an antidepressant, but was later discovered to markedly reduce nicotine cravings during withdrawal from smoking. It is now quite widely used in the latter context, and we are frequently asked about its use in diving.

Will zyban make a diving illness more likely?

Zyban may predispose to some manifestations of oxygen toxicity (see below).

Will diving enhance any unwanted effects of zyban?

Zyban is known to markedly lower the threshold for epileptic-like seizures. Indeed, about 1:1000 "normal" patients using zyban will suffer a seizure during a typical 6 month program. This, of itself, would probably constitute reason enough to avoid the use of zyban when diving. Moreover it is likely, though not proven, that the epileptogenic (i.e. increases the likelihood of a seizure) stimuli inherent in diving (such as elevated partial pressures of oxygen) would make a seizure more likely whilst underwater. Seizures underwater are frequently fatal.

Does the use of zyban adversely affect exercise tolerance or mentation?

There is no well-established interaction of this nature.

In summary, giving up smoking is probably the single most important step that can be taken by a young person to improve their long-term health. It follows that if zyban facilitates this, it is well worth using the drug, but taking 6 months off diving during the course.

Bleomycin

Bleomycin is a chemotherapeutic drug that is sometimes used in the treatment of testicular cancer and other tumours.

Will bleomycin make a diving illness more likely?

There is no well-established interaction of this nature.

Will diving enhance any unwanted effects of bleomycin?

Some patients receiving *bleomycin* develop an irreversible process of fibrosis in their lungs which can prove fatal. Interestingly, exposure to slightly elevated partial pressures of oxygen during or after *bleomycin* administration can precipitate or accelerate this process. Cases of oxygen-induced *bleomycin* lung toxicity have been recorded when oxygen has been given at least a year after discontinuation of the drug. Nobody knows for sure how long this sensitization lasts. The higher partial pressures of oxygen encountered in diving or during treatment for DCI could, in theory, precipitate a serious lung problem.

Does the use of bleomycin adversely affect exercise tolerance or mentation?

It is almost certain that no-one actually receiving *bleomycin* would be well enough to go diving, so this question is rather academic. In the longer term (after bleomycin is discontinued) there is no affect on mentation, and exercise tolerance might need to be assessed in view of the possibility of lung damage by this drug. Most patients previously treated with *bleomycin* would have no impairment of exercise tolerance.

For the above reasons any history of *bleomycin* use, no matter how long ago, is considered a contraindication to diving. This is probably too conservative since the sensitization of the lungs to oxygen probably diminishes over time. One of the authors (SJM) has treated a patient with *bleomycin* exposure some 19 years previously with 40 hyperbaric oxygen treatments because the benefit of the treatment was considered to outweigh the risk. There were no lung problems and the patient had an excellent response to treatment. Other similar cases arise in Australia from time to time. Unfortunately, no trials have been done (or are likely to be done) to establish a threshold time lapse beyond which oxygen exposure is likely to be safe in humans, hence, a blanket ban on all *bleomycin* recipients is the only possible response.

Antidepressants

Until relatively recently we would not have discussed the use of antidepressants in diving because we generally consider anyone with a major depressive illness (or a recent history of one) to be completely unfit for diving. However, in recent times some antidepressants (especially those known as selective serotonin reuptake inhibitors (SSRIs) of which the best known example is *prozac*) have been prescribed to treat relatively mild lowering of mood. Many dives have been performed by divers using SSRIs. Unfortunately there have been no systematic attempts to establish the safety of these agents in diving, and this is a very controversial area.

Will antidepressants make a diving illness more likely?

Like *zyban*, some antidepressants (including the SSRIs) appear to lower the seizure threshold, though not to nearly the same degree. However, when combined with some of the more potent epileptogenic stimuli that may be encountered in diving (such as a high PO_2), this effect may predispose to cerebral oxygen toxicity.

Will diving enhance any unwanted effects of antidepressants?

Almost paradoxically, some antidepressants (particularly the older types) may cause a degree of sedation. It makes sense that this effect might be enhanced by nitrogen narcosis, and if so, this is potentially hazardous.

Does the use of antidepressants adversely affect exercise tolerance or mentation?

Antidepressants are unlikely to affect exercise tolerance, but they are powerful psychotropic agents and are known to produce occasional cognitive function disturbances and even delerium.

For the above reasons, most diving physicians still counsel against the use of antidepressants of any sort whilst diving. Some divers who are stable on their medication and have no obvious side effects may consider this too conservative a stance, and may choose to go diving anyway. This is, perhaps, a reasonable stance for an informed risk acceptor. However, such divers should bear in mind that we really do not have any accurate idea of the true risk involved. We would also suggest that technical divers breathing very elevated PO_2s do not do so whilst using anti-depressant medication.

Viagra

Viagra (*sildenafil*) works by inhibiting the enzyme phosphodiesterase 5 (PDE5) that acts against sustaining erections.

In addition to its wide medical usage, in certain places, such as some backpackers' sea havens where diving is common, viagra has become a reasonably popular 'party drug'.

Will viagra make a diving illness more likely?

Several studies have shown that PDE5 inhibitors are also potent vasodilators of the pulmonary circulation, and viagra is becoming a new and promising treatment of pulmonary hypertension. It reduces the pulmonary resistance making it easier for blood to flow through the pulmonary circulation.

In diving, the pulmonary circulation acts as a bubble filter, trapping venous bubbles and allowing them to diffuse into the lungs and so resolve. A decrease in pulmonary resistance means that bubbles that should be captured by the lungs may get through into the systemic circulation and access the brain and spine, so causing DCS. However, this is only speculative and there is currently no evidence to support it.

Viagra has a short half-life of only 4 hours, so if used in the evening its effect on the lungs should have worn off by the following morning. However, some other PDE5 inhibitors have a longer half-life. *Cialis* (tadalafil) for example, has a half-life of 17.5 hours and would still be effective the next day.

Will diving enhance any unwanted effects of Viagra?

There is currently no data to indicate whether or not there is such an interaction.

Does the use of viagra adversely affect exercise tolerance or mentation?

There is currently no evidence to indicate that viagra reduces exercise tolerance (in fact there is some evidence to the contrary), or mentation.

In brief:

Drugs used to treat **epilepsy, active asthma**, and **diabetes** are not discussed here because the importance of the relevant drugs pales into insignificance next to the importance of the disease processes themselves. Patients using medications for these problems are unlikely to be diving, and if they are, they are strongly advised to discuss the situation with a diving physician so that they can be counseled about the risks involved. Most **antibiotics** are OK in diving though **mefloquine** (larium), used in the prevention of malaria, can cause side effects that may be mistaken for DCI and is best avoided when on diving trips. **Non-steroidal anti-inflammatory drugs (NSAIDS)** are commonly taken to help relieve the pain of strains, sprains, and arthritis, and are considered compatible with diving. There are no known problems associated with taking the simple pain-killer **paracetamol** in association with diving.

SUMMARY

- Drugs affect mental and / or physical function.

- Most drugs have side-effects in addition to their therapeutic effects.

- The effects of drugs may vary between individuals and from time to time with an individual.

- The effect of a drug may be altered by pressure, changes in nitrogen, carbon dioxide and oxygen levels, cold, fatigue, mental state and various other factors.

- Alcohol interferes with mental and physical function and can combine with nitrogen narcosis to cause a severe state of temporary mental incompetence. Its use is associated with many drownings and its diuretic effects may predispose to DCS.

- Cigarette smoking is associated with cancer of the lungs and mouth, other respiratory disease and damage to blood vessels; the coronary arteries in particular. It reduces cardiopulmonary fitness in the long term. The stimulation of excess mucus production may increase the risk of pulmonary barotrauma.

- Narcotics and hallucinogens may have unpredictable effects underwater. It is suspected that these effects include unpleasant psychological phenomena, circulatory changes, rapid heat loss, unconsciousness and perhaps sudden death.

- Decongestants counter vasodilation and oedema of the tissue lining the nasal passages. They act by temporary vasoconstriction and can have a rebound effect if used for more than about 5 days.

- Topical decongestants are usually safe if used for short periods.

- Oral decongestants (e.g. pseudo-ephedrine) have been used extensively, but their effect on susceptibility to oxygen toxicity is unknown.

- If a decongestant wears off during a dive an ear or sinus barotrauma may occur on ascent.

- Steroid-containing nasal sprays appear to be safe for diving.

- Antihistamines often produce drowsiness and are potentially disadvantageous in diving. Many anti-motion sickness preparations contain potent antihistamines. Although widely used, divers should be aware of the theoretical concerns over impairment of cognition at depth.

- There has been no evidence to indicate that current oral contraceptives predispose to DCS.

- **Divers should always consult a diving physician to determine or confirm the appropriateness of diving while taking a particular medication.**

REFERENCES

1. Perrine MW, Mundt JC, Weiner RI. When alcohol and water don't mix: diving under the influence. *J Stud Alcohol* 1994; 55(5):517-24.

2. Buch DA, El Moalem H, Dovenbarger JA, Uguccioni DM, Moon RE. Cigarette smoking and decompression illness severity: a retrospective sudy in recreational divers. *Aviat Space Environ Med* 2003; 74(12):1271-4.

3. Tzimoulis P. The Dangers of Underwater Drug Trips. *Skin Diver* 37(4):8.

4. Taylor DM, O'Toole KS, Auble TE et al. The psychometric and cardiac effects of pseudoephedrine in the hyperbaric environment. *Pharmacotherapy* 2000; 20(9):1045-50.

5. Kohl RL et al. Control of nausea and autonomic dysfunction with terfenadine, peripherally acting antihistamine. Aviat Space Environ Med 991;62:392-6

6. Williams, T. et al. Effects of Transcutaneous Scopolamine and Depth on Diver Performance. Undersea Biomedical Research 1988;15(2):89-98.

OTHER SOURCES

Lee AJ, Chiao TB, Tsang MP. Sildenafil for pulmonary hypertension. Ann Pharmacother 2005; 39(5):869-84.

ParkerJ. The Sports Diving Medical, 2nd Edn. Melbourne; J.L. Publications, 2002.

Ricart A, Maristany J, Fort N et al. Effects of sildenafil on the human response to acute hypoxia and exercise. High Alt Med Biol 2005; 6(1):43-9.

Thamann ED. To mix or not to mix? Alert Diver 1999; Nov-Dec:19-21.

RECOMMENDED READING

Campbell E. Psychological Issues in Diving III – Schizophrenia, Substance Abuse. *Alert Diver 2001; March:10-7.*

Nord D. DAN takes a look at over-the-counter medications. *Alert Diver* 1996; May-Jun:39-42.

ParkerJ. The Sports Diving Medical, 2nd Edn. Melbourne; J.L. Publications, 2002.

Thamann ED. To mix or not to mix? *Alert Diver* 1999; Nov-Dec:19-21.

Many thanks to Dr. John Parker for reviewing this chapter.

© Gary Bell

SECTION 2

Decompression Systems

© Max Gleeson

13

History of decompression tables

HALDANIAN THEORY

Prior to this century decompression profiles were generally slow, linear decompressions (i.e. continual slow ascent) following slow, linear compressions. Much diving time was wasted in getting to depth and returning from depth and, despite these precautions, many divers were getting decompression sickness (DCS). At the beginning of this century **J.S. Haldane**, a renowned physiologist, was appointed by the British Admiralty to develop safer decompression tables for use by Royal Navy divers, in order to reduce the high incidence of DCS in those divers.

Haldane experimented with goats in a recompression chamber. He kept the goats at a particular pressure for periods of time from 1½ to 2 hours, after which he believed them to be saturated. He then noticed that they could be decompressed to an ambient pressure half that of (what he believed was) saturation before displaying obvious signs of DCS. He believed that they could be decompressed from 2ATA to 1ATA, from 4ATA to 2ATA, and so on, without apparent problems. He also assumed (incorrectly) that because no signs of DCS were evident, no bubbles had formed within the goats.

By calculating the nitrogen pressure in the tissues and comparing it to the ambient pressure to which the goats could be decompressed without showing signs of DCS, Haldane observed that, in all cases, the tissue nitrogen tension was 1.58 times the ambient pressure. He concluded that as long as the ratio of tissue nitrogen tension to ambient pressure did not exceed 1.58 to 1, bubbles would not form and decompression sickness would be avoided. This became known as the "Critical (Supersaturation) Ratio Hypothesis".

Haldane also proposed that, when a diver first descends to depth, the rate of nitrogen uptake is rapid due to the large difference between the nitrogen tensions in the lungs and in the tissues. As the dive progresses and the pressures become more even , the rate of nitrogen uptake slows down. He suggested that the uptake of nitrogen follows a type of exponential curve. Gas elimination was believed to be the reverse of this process. These processes are shown in Figure 13.1.

Realizing that different tissues absorb and release nitrogen at different rates, Haldane suggested that the continuous spectrum of tissues within the body could be represented by five tissue groups. He assumed that a specific tissue group absorbed and released nitrogen at the same rate. Haldane then assigned theoretical "**half-times**" of 5, 10, 20, 40 and 75 minutes to his specific tissue groups. These theoretical tissue types became known as the T_5, T_{10}, T_{20}, T_{40} and T_{75} tissues, respectively. *They did not represent specific body tissues, but, instead, they represented tissue characteristics.*

FIGURE 13.1

Exponential nitrogen uptake and elimination curves.

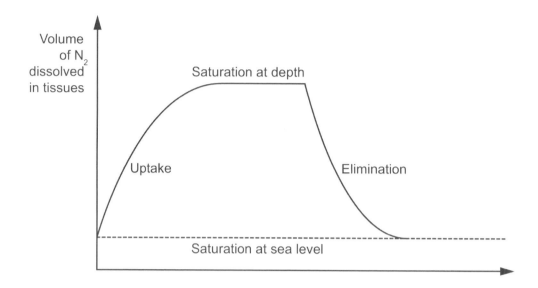

Tissue Half-Times can be explained as follows:

The "tissue half-time" is the time taken before a tissue has absorbed half of the volume of gas that it still needs to absorb in order to become saturated at that ambient pressure.

For example, the T_5 tissue will take five minutes to absorb half of the total volume of gas required for it to become saturated. During the next five minutes it will absorb half of the remaining amount of gas required for it to achieve saturation. This is shown in Table 13.1 and Figure 13.2.

TABLE 13.1

Nitrogen uptake in the T_5 tissue.

If V = the total amount of N_2 needed to be absorbed in order to achieve saturation:

Interval	Volume of N_2 absorbed during interval	Total volume of N_2 absorbed	% saturation
1st 5 min	$^1/_2$ V	$^1/_2$ V	50
2nd 5 min	$^1/_4$ V	$^3/_4$ V	75
3rd 5 min	$^1/_8$ V	$^7/_8$ V	87.5
4th 5 min	$^1/_{16}$ V	$^5/_{16}$ V	93.8
5th 5 min	$^1/_{32}$ V	$^{31}/_{32}$ V	96.9
6th 5 min	$^1/_{64}$ V	$^{63}/_{64}$ V	98.4

Table 13.1 can also be shown diagrammatically as in Figure 13.2.

FIGURE 13.2

The loading of the T5 tissue.

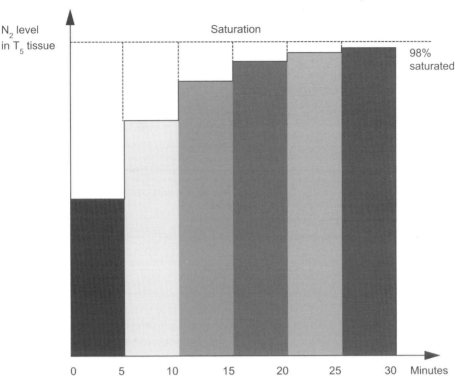

Similarly, the T_{20} tissue takes 20 minutes to absorb half of the nitrogen it requires to become saturated, and so on.

Thus, after 20 minutes, the T_5 tissue will have absorbed $^5/_{16}$ of the nitrogen that it can hold whereas the T_{20} would only be half-saturated. *A tissue is considered to be completely saturated (98.4%) after six units of half time.* Therefore, after 30 minutes (i.e. 6 x 5 min.) the T_5 tissue is considered fully saturated and, after 60 minutes (i.e. 6 x 10 min.) the T_{10} tissue is fully saturated.

Haldane believed desaturation to be the exact opposite to this saturation process. For example, after 5 minutes the T_5 tissue will have released half of the nitrogen required in order for it to return to saturation at sea level.

Using this totally theoretical mathematical model and an empirical observation that animals appeared to tolerate an overpressure (supersaturation) of nitrogen, expressed as a ratio of up to 1.58 to 1 (to ambient pressure), Haldane began to build a decompression schedule. He derived equations which were designed to calculate the amount of nitrogen absorbed after a given time at pressure, and could thus estimate the nitrogen tension in the tissue. Haldane could now calculate the depth to which a diver could ascend before the ratio of tissue nitrogen tension to ambient pressure exceeded the "critical ratio" of 1.58 to 1. He constructed decompression schedules which did not allow this critical ratio to be exceeded in any of the five tissue types.

The deepest stop on Haldane's decompression schedules is very short because it is determined by the tissue with the highest pressure of nitrogen, which is always the fast tissue which releases its gas load quickly. The diver must remain at the stop until the nitrogen pressure in this tissue drops enough to allow a further ascent, which ceases when the critical value is reached for any of the tissue types. The shallower stops become progressively longer as they are governed by the slower tissue types. This process is discussed in detail in Chapter 4. It can also be illustrated as shown in Figure 13.3.

Haldane tabulated his schedules and issued three separate air diving tables:

- Schedule 1 for all dives requiring less than 30 minutes of decompression time.
- Schedule 2 for all dives requiring more than 30 minutes of decompression time.
- Schedule 3 for deep air diving to 330ft (100m) using oxygen decompression.

All of his decompression procedures were characterized by a rapid ascent from depth to the first one or two stages, followed by a slow ascent to the surface.

The Royal Navy (RN) adopted the Haldane schedules in 1908 and used them for the next 50 years. However, Schedule 1 proved to be too conservative in practical use, and Schedule 2 proved to be not conservative enough.

Haldane's tables had a number of shortcomings, some of which are:

- The assumption that bubbles did not form until the supersaturation ratio exceeded 1.58 to 1 has repeatedly been shown to be incorrect. For example, Doppler ultrasound studies have repeatedly indicated that bubbles, often asymptomatic, form much sooner.

- His assumption that gas elimination takes the same time as gas uptake is often not valid, especially once bubbles have formed, as appears to often be the case with these schedules. Gas elimination can be much slower, especially if bubbles are present.

- Haldane believed that his goats were essentially saturated after 1½ to 2 hours at a particular pressure. Subsequent experiments indicated that 4 to 6 hours is required before the goats could be considered saturated. So Haldane's goats were not in fact saturated when he decompressed them and, therefore, had a lower nitrogen load than his calculations assumed.

Haldane assumed that humans became saturated after 5 hours when, in reality, it takes 24 hours or longer. Therefore, his longest tissue half time of 75 minutes is far too short to represent many long and/or multiple exposures to pressure. (e.g. The Bühlmann Tables use 635 minutes as the slowest tissue compartment).

POST HALDANE

In 1912, Sir Leonard **Hill** produced both experimental and theoretical evidence which questioned the use of staged decompression (i.e. decompression requiring stops at particular depths) as suggested by Haldane, over continuous uniform decompression. Hill believed that bubbles form whenever the tissue gas tension exceeds the ambient pressure by a particular amount. In other words bubble formation depends on upon a pressure difference rather than a pressure ratio (Critical Pressure Hypothesis).

In 1954, **Rashbass**, using the observation that a diver seemed able to remain indefinitely at 30ft (9m) and then ascend directly to the surface, assumed that a diver could tolerate "30 foot's worth" of excess gas in his tissues at any level - that is, that

FIGURE 13.3

Haldane Decompression Procedure.

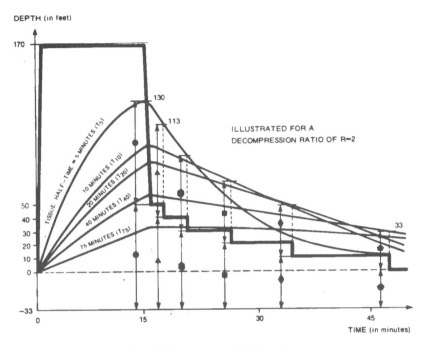

Reprinted from Edmonds, et al (1981), with permission.

Figure 13.3 represents an exposure to 168fsw for 15 minutes and illustrates the procedure Haldane used to calculate a decompression schedule. The procedure involves the following steps:

The tension in each of the five tissue compartments is computed for the exposure of 168fsw for 15 minutes.

The highest tension occurs in the T_5 tissue group and its tension can be calculated to be equivalent to the tissue being saturated at 130fsw. Since the T_5 compartment contains more gas than the "slower" compartments, it is the "controlling" tissue for the decompression.

The absolute pressure in the T_5 tissue is therefore 130 (from dive) + 33 (from atmosphere) = 163fsw.

Limiting the diver's ascent by allowing only a 2:1[*] pressure drop, the diver may ascend to 163/2 = 81.5 "footsworth" of gas, which corresponds to a depth of 81.5 - 33 = 48.5fsw. Since the decompression stops are in increments of 10fsw, the first stop occurs at 50fsw.

The diver must remain at 50fsw until the tissue tensions fall enough to allow ascent to 40fsw. Saturation at 40fsw corresponds to a tension of 40 + 33 = 73fsw. Since a pressure drop of 2:1 is allowed, the pressure on leaving 50fsw must not exceed 73 x 2 = 146fsw. This corresponds to a tissue tension of 146 - 33 = 113fsw.

Therefore, the diver must remain at 50fsw until the tension in the T_5 tissue compartment falls to 113fsw, at which time he may ascend to 40fsw.

The tensions are computed for all five tissue compartments at each 10fsw stop. Their tensions must not exceed the 2:1 ratio dictated by the model.

The T_5 tissue compartment limits the ascents from the first three stops. The T_{10} tissue compartment limits the fourth stop, and the T_{20} tissue compartment the fifth. The duration of the fifth stop is controlled by the T_{40} tissue compartment. When the T_{40} tissue is reduced to 66 "footsworth" of gas, the diver can ascend to the surface (1ATA or 33 "footsworth" of gas), thereby maintaining a 2:1 ratio and avoiding "bubbling".

---

[*] For simplicity, it is assumed that the breathing gas is pure nitrogen. Thus, a ratio of nitrogen tensions of 1.58:1 for air equates to 2:1 with this mix.

decompression is safe as long as a constant difference of 30 feet of sea water (fsw) is not exceeded.

In 1955, the **U.S. Navy** introduced some schedules based on the Haldanian model but used tissue half-times of 5, 10, 20, 40, 80 and 120 minutes. Instead of using a single critical ratio for all tissues for all depths, the U.S. Navy used ratios (expressed as pressures) that varied from tissue to tissue and from depth to depth. These are the commonly known U.S. Navy schedules, published in 1957.

In 1958, **Hempleman**, a British physiologist, introduced a different decompression concept. He had observed that over a particular depth range the first symptom of decompression sickness to appear was usually pain at or near a joint. He assumed that the tissue involved (e.g. tendon) was, therefore, the tissue with the greatest overpressure of nitrogen for that depth range, and that gas elimination from that tissue must control the decompression. He pictured the body as a single tissue and believed that the quantity of gas absorbed in the body could be calculated by a simple formula which related depth and time. Unlike Haldane, who believed that gas uptake and elimination took identical times, Hempleman assumed that gas elimination was one and a half times slower than uptake. Utilizing the theory that the tissues could tolerate an overpressure of 30fsw, Hempleman constructed a new set of decompression schedules. These schedules, metricated in 1972, are the Royal Navy schedules.

These schedules have theoretical limitations which have been confirmed in practice. Firstly, the concept that a single tissue (i.e. the slowest tissue) controls decompression only applies over a certain depth range. If deeper dives are performed vestibular symptoms, rather than niggling pain, may become the first overt sign of decompression sickness. Secondly, the concept of an allowable overpressure of 30fsw at all depths is often too conservative.

Hempleman realized these limitations and, in 1968, new schedules were introduced after extensive trialing. These schedules, known as the 1968 Air Diving Tables, still used the concept of a single tissue but used a variable ratio of tissue nitrogen tension to ambient pressure in order to calculate safe decompression. The RN rejected these tables claiming them to be too conservative. They were slightly modified, metricated and re-appeared as the RNPL 1972 tables.

Since the 1960s Professor Albert **Bühlmann** of the University of Zurich presented various decompression schedules using either nitrogen or helium as the inert gas. The Bühlmann decompression model (ZHL-16), based on 16 tissue compartments, assumes that gas uptake and elimination occur exponentially and at identical rates. The published tables are based on 12 tissue compartments and allow a certain degree of tolerated supersaturation within each compartment. Bühlmann Tables have been widely used in parts of Europe for the next 40 years. Derivations of the ZHL model have been used as the basis of many subsequent dive computer algorithms.

In 1966, Brian **Hills** introduced his "thermodynamic" approach to decompression. All of the previous theories assumed that the partial pressure of inert gas in the tissue must exceed the ambient pressure plus the "inherent saturation" by some critical amount before bubbles will form. Hills demonstrated that bubbles (gas phase) are present before these critical levels are reached, and argued that the presence of bubbles reduced the driving force for gas elimination. He proposed that bubbling could be avoided if decompression was performed so that the pressure of inert gas in the tissues remained essentially no higher than the ambient pressure. Hills introduced schedules based on this concept but difficulties were experienced with initial schedule trials. The problems were possibly due to excessively slow diffusion rates being chosen to account for gas uptake.

In 1983, the Defense and Civil Institute of Environmental Medicine (**DCIEM**) of Canada published some schedules based on a decompression model that utilized tissue compartments connected *in series*, rather than in parallel. The model utilizes the concept of allowable surfacing supersaturation ratios. In the early 1970s, a dive and decompression databank was established at DCIEM with a complete record of all research dives done using this model since 1964. This databank has been maintained and is now considered to be the most comprehensive diving database in the world.

During the 1980's some researchers led by Dr. David Yount at the University of Hawaii developed a decompression model based on the physical properties of bubble nucleation. Their model, the **Varying Permeability Model (VPM)**, assumed the presence of bubble nuclei in the water and watery tissues within our bodies. The nuclei are stabilized by elastic skins but will grow if gas enters them during decompression. Any nuclei with volumes larger than a "critical size" (related to the maximum dive depth) will grow during decompression. In this model, decompression is controlled to ensure that the total volume of gas in the bubbles is less than some critical volume, thought to be safe. The maximum allowable tensions in each tissue compartment can be calculated, and critical gradients (i.e. differences between calculated tissue tension and ambient pressure) can be determined. Tables based on this model were produced but never tested. They yielded NDLs that were more conservative than those of the U.S. Navy for depths shallower than 140ft (42m). The VPM Model was further developed by Dr. Bruce Wienke, who introduced reduced critical gradients to account for bubble formation over repetitive dive exposures. This became known as the **Reduced Gradient Bubble Model (RGBM)** which is now incorporated in part in several dive computer algorithms. Such "bubble models" yield shorter no decompression limits and repetitive dive times, deeper decompression stops and slower ascent rates than Haldanian models,

The **U.S. Navy** developed some new decompression models based purely on the mathematical chance (probability) of decompression sickness occurring. The models presume no specific knowledge regarding bubble formation or growth. In 1985, the Navy published two sets of air decompression schedules with an equal chance of DCS throughout. One schedule carried a 1% DCS risk and the other carried a risk of 5%. The schedules were modified and tested but were never adopted.

In 1988, **PADI** released the Recreational Dive Planner which is based on a Haldanian model similar to that used for the 1957 U.S. Navy Tables. The model, designed by Raymond Rogers, assumes that gas uptake and elimination occurs exponentially and at identical rates. The longest tissue half-time used is 60 minutes and it is on this tissue compartment that the repetitive system is based. The table has been designed so that it can be used for multi-level diving and is purely a no-decompression stop table.

1988 also saw the release of the **BS-AC '88** Tables. These sets of tables were designed by Dr. Tom Hennessy, who had worked alongside Hempleman. They are based on Hempleman's earlier model with various modifications to cater for current diving practices, particularly repetitive diving.

Dr. Valerie **Flook** has created a relatively simple decompression model that utilizes some traditional physiological and physical equations commonly used to describe the uptake and distribution of anaesthetic gases. Rather than using theoretical tissue compartments, this model uses 'time constants' for each tissue type. A time constant is defined in terms of the capacity which the tissue has for inert gas and the rate at which blood delivers or removes inert gas from the tissue. The total volume of gas in a tissue depends on the solubility of the gas, the volume of the tissue and the partial pressure of the inert gas. Gas elimination (which is linear) is almost always slower than uptake (which is exponential), even in the absence of bubbles. When tested in some human and animal trials using bubbles, rather than DCS symptoms as the endpoint, this model appears to perform reasonably well in predicting the 'average' decompression requirement.

Since the early 1990s, various individuals and companies have developed and marketed a range of decompression software incorporating a wide variety of decompression algorithms, mainly catering to the technical diving community. Some of these are based on more traditional concepts and equations that can be tailored to suit different breathing mixtures and dive requirements. Others include new ideas or developments. Some appear to be relatively sound, while others have questionable merit and may at times be hazardous.

Many of the above decompression systems are discussed in details in this book so that a reader may better understand the strengths and weaknesses and so better judge the appropriate application of various systems.

In any event, the use of any decompression tables by recreational divers is diminishing, rapidly being replaced by dive computers. Divers Alert Network (DAN) Project Dive Exploration data for 1998 to 2002 indicated that from a sample of 6,611 divers, 77% reported using dive computers and only used 2% tables.[1]

REFERENCES

1. Report on decompression Illness, dive fatalities and Project Dive Exploration. Durham, North Carolina: Divers Alert Network, 2004.

OTHER SOURCES

Bassett B. The Theoretical Basis of the U.S. Navy Air Decompression Tables. *SPUMS J* 1985; July-Sept:18-23.

Flook V. The Physics and Physiology of Decompression. *European Journal of Underwater and Hyperbaric Medicine* 2000; 1(1):8-13.

Hamilton RW, Rogers RE, Powell MR, Vann RD. Development and validation of no-stop decompression procedures for recreational diving: The DSAT Recreational Dive Planner. California: Diving Science and Technology Corp, 1994.

Hempleman HV. History of Evolution of Decompression Procedures. In: Bennett PB, Elliott DH (eds). Physiology and Medicine of Diving, 3rd edn. California: Best Publishing Co.; 1982.

Vann RD. Decompression Theory and Applications. In: In: Bennett PB, Elliott DH (eds). Physiology and Medicine of Diving, 3rd edn. California: Best Publishing Co.; 1982.

Vann RD. Mechanisms and Risks of Decompression. In: Bove AA (ed). Diving Medicine, 3rd edn. Philiadelphia: W.B. Saunders Co.; 1997.

Walker R. Decompression sickness: history and physiology. In: Edmonds C, Lowry C, Pennefather J, Walker R. Diving and Subaquatic Medicine, 4th edn. London: Arnold, 2002:111-130.

Wienke BR. Basic Decompression Theory and Application. Flagstaff: Best Publishing Co., 1991.

RECOMMENDED FURTHER READING

Hempleman HV. History of Evolution of Decompression Procedures. In: In: Bennett PB, Elliott DH (eds). Physiology and Medicine of Diving, 3rd edn. California: Best Publishing Co.; 1982.

14

U.S. Navy tables

14.1   History & design

HISTORICAL BACKGROUND

The first tables developed for the U.S. Navy were the Bureau of Construction and Repair Tables which emerged in 1915. They were based on the Haldanian concept of a decompression ratio, and also used oxygen decompression to achieve depths between 200-300ft (60-90m).

In the 1930s, some U.S. Navy researchers undertook a set of decompression experiments using human volunteers. The volunteers were exposed to increased air pressures in a chamber and then decompressed, without stops, back to surface pressure. When the results of these experiments were analyzed it became apparent that Haldane's view that the ambient pressure could be halved without ill effect was wrong. The researchers (Hawkins et al) concluded that each tissue half-time had its own allowable decompression ratio.

In 1937, it was decided that the T_5 and T_{10} tissue groups could tolerate so much overpressure that they could, in fact, be ignored. Schedules which involved only the T_{20}, T_{40} and T_{75} tissue groups were issued (Yarbrough). The allowable pressure ratios for these tissue types were increased to accommodate exercise at depth. These U.S. Navy Tables gained worldwide acceptance but were eventually found to offer too little protection from DCS after long dives. The tables had no real acceptable provision for performing repetitive dives since most dives were done in the surface supply mode with an unlimited air supply. If a repetitive dive was performed, the bottom times of the two dives were just added together, no matter how long the surface interval was. No allowance was made for off-gassing during a surface interval.

Later it was decided that the supersaturation ratio must be depth-dependent and deeper stops were introduced (Dwyer, 1956). The T_5 and T_{10} tissues were re-introduced and a new tissue group with a half-time of 120 minutes was added. What had now evolved were various tissue groups or compartments, each with a characteristic supersaturation ratio which varies with the amount of gas dissolved in it. The maximum supersaturation ratios were expressed as maximum permitted excess pressures ("M-values"). Tables based on these concepts were introduced by the U.S. Navy by Dwyer in 1955, and tested by des Granges in 1956. The tests involved some 564 man-dives resulting in 26 cases of decompression illness.[1]

The problem of repetitive diving was addressed in 1957. The resulting repetitive dive procedure was tested on 61 repetitive dive combinations. During testing, only 122 man-dives were undertaken resulting in 3 cases of DCS[1]. The resulting tables were published in the U.S. Navy Manual in 1957 and are the commonly known U.S. Navy Tables.

The tables are based on the Haldanian idea that gas uptake and elimination occur exponentially <u>and at the same rate</u>, and they utilize tissue compartments of 5, 10, 20, 40, 80 and 120 minutes. These compartments are not supposed to represent specific body tissues.

There are also separate schedules for exceptional exposures and these utilize additional half-times of 160 and 240 minutes, with allowable supersaturation pressures lower than those for the T_{120} tissue.

FEATURES OF THE U.S. NAVY SYSTEM

The nitrogen tension in each tissue compartment can be calculated and is expressed in feet of sea water (fsw). For example, when saturated at the surface the total gas tension in each tissue type is 33fsw. Since only 79% of this tension is due to nitrogen, the nitrogen tension is $0.79 \times 33 = 26.1$fsw. In general, when a diver is saturated at a depth of **D**fsw, the nitrogen tension in all tissue types is **0.79(D + 33)**fsw.

After being at depth for a certain time (less than saturation) the different tissue types will each have a particular gas tension. The nitrogen tension can be estimated using the equation:

$$P_t = P_o + (P_a - P_o)(1 - 2^{-t/T})\text{fsw}$$

where:
P_t is the nitrogen tension if the tissue group after **t** minutes;
P_o is the initial nitrogen tension;
P_a is the nitrogen pressure in the lungs;
T is the tissue half-time in minutes; and
t is the exposure time in minutes.

M-VALUES

All of the previous methods of calculation used the concept of a maximum permitted supersaturation ratio. It is possible to regard this permitted ratio as a permitted pressure. These permitted pressures became known as **"M-values"** (Workman), previously discussed in Chapter 4.

An "M-value" is the calculated partial pressure of nitrogen in a half-time tissue which is allowed when you reach a given decompression stop.

M-values are expressed in feet of sea water absolute. Dividing M-values by the barometric pressure at sea level (33fsw) will give the critical ratio. The limiting M-values and supersaturation ratios for surfacing (M_o) are given in Table 14.1.1.

The No-Decompression Limits can be determined by calculating which tissue type will reach its surfacing M-value first for a particular depth. For example, when saturated at 60fsw, the nitrogen tension in all tissue types is $0.79 \times 93 = 73.5$fsw. Therefore the T_5 and T_{10} tissues can never reach their surfacing M-values which are higher than 73.5fsw (from Table 14.1.1). The first tissue type to reach its maximum is the T_{40} tissue which reaches its maximum after about 60 minutes. Hence, the T_{40} tissue determines the NDL at 60fsw and is said to "control" the dive at this depth.

Decompression requirements are determined by defining maximum values for tissue nitrogen tensions in increments of 10fsw and requiring a diver to stop at a given depth until all tissues have desaturated to these M-values. In other words, if the tension in one or more of the tissue types is higher than its allowable value at that depth, the diver must stop and wait until the tension(s) has dropped sufficiently to allow further ascent. The M-value for a particular depth (**D**) is found using the formula:
M = M$_o$ + a x D, where **a** is a constant that represents the change in M-value for every fsw.

TABLE 14.1.1

Limiting surfacing values of U.S. Navy Tables.

Half time	M_O value	Ratio
5	104	3.15
10	88	2.67
20	72	2.18
40	58	1.76
80	52	1.58
120	51	1.55

REPETITIVE GROUP DESIGNATORS

The slower tissue compartments are generally the most important for predicting long-term saturation effects. It is therefore the slower compartments that are primarily used to predict the level of saturation at the beginning of a surface interval, as well as desaturation during the surface interval.

The letters A to O, and Z, are Repetitive Group Designators and are, in fact, a measure of the gas tension in the T_{120} tissue. At saturation on the surface, the gas tension in the T_{120} tissue is 33fsw. If, after a dive, the tension in the T_{120} tissue is between 33 and 35fsw, the diver will be in Repetitive Group A. If the tension is between 35 and 37fsw, the diver will be in Group B. Each ascending Repetitive Group represents an increase of 2fsw in the gas tension of the T_{120} tissue.

Surfacing tissue tensions after all dives in the Standard Air Table were computed and the appropriate Repetitive Group assigned.

THE SURFACE INTERVAL CREDIT TABLE

At the beginning of a surface interval a few of the tissue groups may be at, or near, their critical nitrogen level. After a surface interval of just under 10 minutes, the faster tissue compartments have (*theoretically*) off-gassed enough nitrogen to leave the 120-minute tissue group as the group nearest to its critical nitrogen level. Hence, it will control the decompression for a repetitive dive. For this reason the Surface Interval Credit Table cannot be entered unless the surface interval is greater than 10 minutes. Any repetitive dive done within 10 minutes of surfacing is considered to be part of the initial dive.

The Surface Interval Credit Table is based on the off-gassing (by exponential decay) of the T_{120} tissue. It gives the amount of time required for the 120-minute tissue to decrease its tissue tension by 2fsw while at an ambient pressure of 1ATA.

For example, if you are in Group B when you surface from a dive, the tension in the T_{120} tissue will be between 35 and 37fsw. The Surface Interval Credit Table indicates that after 2 hours and 11 minutes you will be in Group A. This means that it takes 2:11 hr for the T_{120} tissue to lose the 2fsw of excess gas to reduce its gas tension to 35fsw.

RESIDUAL NITROGEN TIME

This is the amount of time it would take the 120-minute tissue to saturate from a tension of 33fsw to the tension of the various repetitive groups. For example, if you are in Group B you will have a calculated tension of 35-37fsw in the T_{120} tissue. The time it takes for the tissue tension to rise from 33 to 37fsw is the **Residual Nitrogen Time (RNT)**. The RNT can be taken to be equivalent to the time already spent at a particular pressure.

THE TABLES

There are five different tables which are used for different purposes. Three of these tables are shown as Tables 14.1.2, 14.1.3 and 14.1.4. The Tables shown here are taken from the 1999 U.S. Navy Manual (updated 2001). These tables included several changes from the previous version, which include:

- A reduced recommended ascent rate, which is now 30ft (9m)/minute, rather than the previous 60ft (18m)/minute.
- No-decompression limits for dives between 25-30ft.
- More Repetitive Group Designators for depths shallower than 35ft.
- Residual Nitrogen Times for depths shallower than 40ft.

STANDARD AIR TABLE

A portion of this table is shown as Table 14.1.2, the entire table being in Appendix A.

The decompression schedules of the tables are given in 10ft (3m) depth increments and, usually, 10-minute bottom time increments. However, depth and bottom time combinations from actual dives rarely exactly match one of the decompression schedules listed in the table being used. As assurance that the selected decompression schedule is always conservative:

(a)   always select the schedule depth to be equal to, or the next depth greater than, the actual depth to which the dive was conducted, and
(b)   always select the schedule bottom time to be equal to, or the next longer bottom time than the actual bottom time of the dive.

If the Standard Air Decompression Tables, for example, were being used to select the correct schedule for a dive to 96ft (29m) for 31 minutes, decompression would be carried out in accordance with the 100ft (30m) for 40 minutes schedule.

Never attempt to interpolate between decompression schedules

Ascend at the rate of 30ft (9m) per minute when using the tables. Any variations with the rate of ascent must be corrected in accordance with the procedures described in Chapter 14.2.

The diver's chest should be located as close as possible to the stop depth.

The decompression stop times, as specified in each decompression schedule, begin as soon as the diver reaches the stop depth. Upon completion of the specified stop time the diver ascends to the next stop, or to the surface, at the proper ascent rate. **Do not include ascent time as part of stop time.**

Activity and the environment can alter gas uptake and elimination rates. If the diver was exceptionally cold during the dive, or if his work load was relatively strenuous, the next longer decompression schedule than the one he would normally follow should be selected. For example, the normal schedule for a dive to 90ft (27m) for 34 minutes would be the 90ft/40 (27m/40) schedule. If the diver were exceptionally cold or fatigued, he should decompress according to the 90ft/50 (27m/50) schedule. (See comment about this on Page 206).

NO-DECOMPRESSION LIMITS AND REPETITIVE GROUP DESIGNATION TABLE FOR NO-DECOMPRESSION AIR DIVES (Table 14.1.3)

The No-Decompression Table serves two purposes. First it summarizes all the depth and bottom time combinations for which no decompression is required. Secondly, it provides the Repetitive Group Designation for each no-decompression dive. Even though decompression is not required, an amount of nitrogen remains in the diver's tissues after every dive. If diving again within a 12-hour period, the diver must consider

TABLE 14.1.2

*Portion of U.S. Navy Standard Air
Decompression Tables.*

Table 9-8. U.S. Navy Standard Air Decompression Table (Continued).

Depth feet/meters	Bottom time (min)	Time first stop (min:sec)	50 15.2	40 12.1	30 9.1	20 6.0	10 3.0	Total decompression time (min:sec)	Repetitive group
80	40						0	2:40	*
	50	2:20					10	12:40	K
	60	2:20					17	19:40	L
	70	2:20					23	25:40	M
24.3	80	2:00				2	31	35:40	N
	90	2:00				7	39	48:40	N
	100	2:00				11	46	59:40	O
	110	2:00				13	53	68:40	O
	120	2:00				17	56	75:40	Z
	130	2:00				19	63	83:40	Z
	140	2:00				26	69	97:40	Z
	150	2:00				32	77	111:40	Z
	Exceptional Exposure								
	180	2:00				35	85	122:40	**
	240	1:40			6	52	120	180:40	**
	360	1:40			29	90	160	281:40	**
	480	1:40			59	107	187	355:40	**
	720	1:20		17	108	142	187	456:40	**
90	30						0	3:00	*
	40	2:40					7	10:00	J
	50	2:40					18	21:00	L
28.7	60	2:40					25	28:00	M
	70	2:20				7	30	40:00	N
	80	2:20				13	40	56:00	N
	90	2:20				18	48	69:00	O
	100	2:20				21	54	78:00	Z
	110	2:20				24	61	88:00	Z
	120	2:20				32	68	103:00	Z
	130	2:00			5	36	74	118:00	Z
100	25						0	3:20	*
	30	3:00					3	6:20	I
	40	3:00					15	18:20	K
30.4	50	2:40				2	24	29:20	L
	60	2:40				9	28	40:20	N
	70	2:40				17	39	59:20	O
	80	2:40				23	48	74:20	O
	90	2:20			3	23	57	86:20	Z
	100	2:20			7	23	66	99:20	Z
	110	2:20			10	34	72	119:20	Z
	120	2:20			12	41	78	134:20	Z
	Exceptional Exposure								
	180	2:00		1	29	53	118	204:20	**
	240	2:00		14	42	84	142	285:20	**
	360	1:40	2	42	73	111	187	418:20	**
	480	1:40	21	61	91	142	187	505:20	**
	720	1:40	55	106	122	142	187	615:20	**

* See No Decompression Table for repetitive groups
** Repetitive dives may not follow exceptional exposure dives

this residual nitrogen when calculating his decompression.

Each depth listed in the No-Decompression Table has a corresponding No-Decompression Limit (NDL) given in minutes. This limit is the maximum bottom time that a diver may spend at that depth without requiring decompression. The columns to the right of the No-Decompression Limits column are used to determine the Repetitive Group Designation which must be assigned to a diver subsequent to every dive. To find the Repetitive Group Designation, enter the table at the depth equal to, or next greater than, the actual depth of the dive. Follow that row to the right until you reach the bottom time equal to, or next greater than, the actual bottom time of the dive. Follow that column to the Repetitive Group Designation.

Depths shallower than 35ft (10.5m) do not have a specific No-Decompression Limit. They are, however, restricted in that they only provide Repetitive Group Designations for bottom times up to five to six hours.* These bottom times are considered the limitations of the No-Decompression Table and no field requirement for diving should extend beyond them.

Any dive below 35ft (10.5m) which has a bottom time greater than the No-Decompression Limit given in this table is a decompression dive and should be conducted in accordance with the Standard Air Table.

---

* However, Repetitive Groups for longer times can be found in Thalmann E, Butler F. A procedure for doing multiple level dives on air using repetitive groups. Navy Experimental Diving Unit, Report No. 13-83, Dept of the Navy, 1983.

TABLE 14.1.3

Table 9-6. Unlimited/No-Decompression Limits and Repetitive Group Designation Table for Unlimited/No-Decompression Air Dives.

Depth (feet/meters)		No-Decompression Limits (min)	A	B	C	D	E	F	G	H	I	J	K	L	M	N	O
10	3.0	unlimited	60	120	210	300	797	*									
15	4.6	unlimited	35	70	110	160	225	350	452	*							
20	6.1	unlimited	25	50	75	100	135	180	240	325	390	917	*				
25	7.6	595	20	35	55	75	100	125	160	195	245	315	361	540	595		
30	9.1	405	15	30	45	60	75	95	120	145	170	205	250	310	344	405	
35	10.7	310	5	15	25	40	50	60	80	100	120	140	160	190	220	270	310
40	12.2	200	5	15	25	30	40	50	70	80	100	110	130	150	170	200	
50	15.2	100		10	15	25	30	40	50	60	70	80	90	100			
60	18.2	60		10	15	20	25	30	40	50	55	60					
70	21.3	50			5	10	15	20	30	35	40	45	50				
80	24.4	40			5	10	15	20	25	30	35	40					
90	27.4	30			5	10	12	15	20	25	30						
100	30.5	25			5	7	10	15	20	22	25						
110	33.5	20				5	10	13	15	20							
120	36.6	15				5	10	12	15								
130	39.6	10				5	8	10									
140	42.7	10				5	7	10									
150	45.7	5				5											
160	48.8	5					5										
170	51.8	5					5										
180	54.8	5					5										
190	59.9	5					5										

* Highest repetitive group that can be achieved at this depth regardless of bottom time.

RESIDUAL NITROGEN TIMETABLE FOR REPETITIVE AIR DIVES (Table 14.1.4)

The quantity of residual nitrogen in a diver's body immediately after a dive is expressed by the Repetitive Group Designation assigned to them by either the Standard Air Table or the No-Decompression Table. The upper portion of the Residual Nitrogen Table is composed of various intervals between 10 minutes and 12 hours, expressed in hours : minutes (2:21 = 2 hours 21 minutes). Each interval has two limits; a minimum time (top limit) and a maximum time (bottom limit).

TABLE 14.1.4

Table 9-7. *Residual Nitrogen Timetable for Repetitive Air Dives.*

Locate the diver's repetitive group designation from his previous dive along the diagonal line above the table. Read horizontally to the interval in which the diver's surface interval lies.

Next, read vertically downward to the new repetitive group designation. Continue downward in this same column to the row that represents the depth of the repetitive dive. The time given at the intersection is residual nitrogen time, in minutes, to be applied to the repetitive dive.

* Dives following surface intervals of more than 12 hours are not repetitive dives. Use actual bottom times in the Standard Air Decompression Tables to compute decompression for such dives.

** If no Residual Nitrogen Time is given, then the repetitive group does not change.

Repetitive group at the beginning of the surface interval

Repetitive group at the beginning of the surface interval	Z	O	N	M	L	K	J	I	H	G	F	E	D	C	B	A
A																0:10–12:00*
B															0:10–3:20	3:21–12:00*
C														0:10–1:39	1:40–4:49	4:50–12:00*
D													0:10–1:09	1:10–2:38	2:39–5:48	5:49–12:00*
E												0:10–0:54	0:55–1:57	1:58–3:24	3:25–6:34	6:35–12:00*
F											0:10–0:45	0:46–1:29	1:30–2:28	2:29–3:57	3:58–7:05	7:06–12:00*
G										0:10–0:40	0:41–1:15	1:16–1:59	2:00–2:58	2:59–4:25	4:26–7:35	7:36–12:00*
H									0:10–0:36	0:37–1:06	1:07–1:41	1:42–2:23	2:24–3:20	3:21–4:49	4:50–7:59	8:00–12:00*
I								0:10–0:33	0:34–0:59	1:00–1:29	1:30–2:02	2:03–2:44	2:45–3:43	3:44–5:12	5:13–8:21	8:22–12:00*
J							0:10–0:31	0:32–0:54	0:55–1:19	1:20–1:47	1:48–2:20	2:21–3:04	3:05–4:02	4:03–5:40	5:41–8:50	8:51–12:00*
K						0:10–0:28	0:29–0:49	0:50–1:11	1:12–1:35	1:36–2:03	2:04–2:38	2:39–3:21	3:22–4:19	4:20–5:48	5:49–8:58	8:59–12:00*
L					0:10–0:26	0:27–0:45	0:46–1:04	1:05–1:25	1:26–1:49	1:50–2:19	2:20–2:53	2:54–3:36	3:37–4:35	4:36–6:02	6:03–9:12	9:13–12:00*
M				0:10–0:25	0:26–0:42	0:43–0:59	1:00–1:18	1:19–1:35	1:36–2:05	2:06–2:34	2:35–3:08	3:09–3:52	3:53–4:49	4:50–6:18	6:19–9:28	9:29–12:00*
N			0:10–0:24	0:25–0:39	0:40–0:54	0:55–1:11	1:12–1:30	1:31–1:53	1:54–2:18	2:19–2:47	2:48–3:22	3:23–4:04	4:05–5:03	5:04–6:32	6:33–9:43	9:44–12:00*
O		0:10–0:23	0:24–0:36	0:37–0:51	0:52–1:07	1:08–1:24	1:25–1:43	1:44–2:04	2:05–2:29	2:30–2:59	3:00–3:33	3:34–4:17	4:18–5:16	5:17–6:44	6:45–9:54	9:55–12:00*
Z	0:10–0:22	0:23–0:34	0:35–0:48	0:49–1:02	1:03–1:18	1:19–1:36	1:37–1:55	1:56–2:17	2:18–2:42	2:43–3:10	3:11–3:45	3:46–4:29	4:30–5:27	5:28–6:56	6:57–10:05	10:06–12:00*

New Repetitive Group Designation

Repetitive Dive Depth (feet)	(meters)	Z	O	N	M	L	K	J	I	H	G	F	E	D	C	B	A
10	3.0	**	**	**	**	**	**	**	**	**	**	**	797	279	159	88	39
20	6.1	**	**	**	**	**	**	917	399	279	208	159	120	88	62	39	18
30	9.1	†	†	†	349	279	229	190	159	132	109	88	70	54	39	25	12
40	12.2	257	241	213	187	161	138	116	101	87	73	61	49	37	25	17	7
50	15.2	169	160	142	124	111	99	87	76	66	56	47	38	29	21	13	6
60	16.2	122	117	107	97	88	79	70	61	52	44	36	30	24	17	11	5
70	21.3	100	96	87	80	72	64	57	50	43	37	31	26	20	15	9	4
80	24.4	84	80	73	68	61	54	48	43	38	32	28	23	18	13	8	4
90	27.4	73	70	64	58	53	47	43	38	33	29	24	20	16	11	7	3
100	30.5	64	62	57	52	48	43	38	34	30	26	22	18	14	10	7	3
110	33.5	57	55	51	47	42	38	34	31	27	24	20	16	13	10	6	3
120	36.6	52	50	46	43	39	35	32	28	25	21	18	15	12	9	6	3
130	39.6	46	44	40	38	35	31	28	25	22	19	16	13	11	8	6	3
140	42.7	42	40	38	35	32	29	26	23	20	18	15	12	10	7	5	2
150	45.7	40	38	35	32	30	27	24	22	19	17	14	12	9	7	5	2
160	48.8	37	36	33	31	28	26	23	20	18	16	13	11	9	6	4	2
170	51.8	35	34	31	29	26	24	22	19	17	15	12	10	8	6	4	2
180	54.8	32	31	29	27	25	22	20	18	16	14	11	10	8	6	4	2
190	59.9	31	30	28	26	24	21	19	17	15	13	10	10	8	6	4	2

Residual Nitrogen Times (MInutes)

† Read vertically downward to the 40/12.2 (feet/meter) repetitive dive depth. Use the corresponding residual nitrogen times (minutes) to compute the equivalent single dive time. Decompress using the 40/12.2 (feet/meter) standard air decompression table.

Residual Nitrogen Times corresponding to the depth of the repetitive dive are given in the body of the lower portion of the table. To determine the Residual Nitrogen Time for a repetitive dive, locate the diver's Repetitive Group Designation from his previous dive along the diagonal line above the table. Read horizontally to the interval in which the diver's surface interval lies. The time spent of the surface must be between, or equal to, the limits of the selected interval.

Next, read vertically downwards to the new Repetitive Group Designation. This designation corresponds to the present quantity of residual nitrogen in the diver's body. Continue downwards in this same column to the row which represents the depth of the repetitive dive. The time given at the intersection is the Residual Nitrogen Time, in minutes, to be applied to the repetitive dive.

If the surface interval is less than 10 minutes, the Residual Nitrogen Time is the bottom time of the previous dive. All of the residual nitrogen will be passed out of the diver's body after 12 hours, so a dive conducted after a 12 hour surface interval is not a repetitive dive.*

DEFINITION OF TERMS

Those terms which are frequently used in discussions of the decompression tables are defined as follows:

Depth - when used to indicate the depth of a dive, means the maximum depth attained during the dive, measured in feet of sea-water or metres of sea-water.

Bottom Time - the total elapsed time from when the diver leaves the surface in descent to the time (next whole minute) that they begin the ascent, measured in minutes.

Decompression Stop - specified depth at which a diver must remain for a specified length of time to eliminate inert gases from their body.

Decompression Schedule - specific decompression procedure for a given combination of depth and bottom time as listed in a decompression table; it is normally indicated as feet/minutes or metres/minutes.

Single Dive - any dive conducted after 12 hours of a previous dive.

Residual Nitrogen - nitrogen gas that is still dissolved in a diver's tissues after they have surfaced.

Surface Interval - the time that a diver has spent on the surface following a dive; beginning as soon as the diver surfaces and ending as soon as they start the next descent.

Repetitive Dive - any dive conducted within a 12-hour period of a previous dive.

Repetitive Group Designation - a letter that relates directly to the amount of residual nitrogen in a diver's body for a 12-hour period following a dive.

Residual Nitrogen Time - an amount of time, in minutes, which must be added to the bottom time of a repetitive dive to compensate for the nitrogen still in solution in a diver's tissues from a previous dive.

(Single) Repetitive Dive - a dive for which the bottom time used to select the decompression schedule is the sum of the Residual Nitrogen Time and the actual bottom time of the dive. This dive may follow on from multiple dives.

---

* However, for many years now it has been well known that it sometimes takes much longer than 12 hours before excess nitrogen is eliminated from a diver's body. This is clearly evidenced by divers getting DCS as a result of flying or otherwise ascending to altitude after surface intervals well in excess of 12 hours.

REFERENCES

1. Thalmann ED, Butler FD. A Procedure for doing Multiple Level Dives on Air using Repetitive Groups. Navy Experimental Diving Unit, Report No. 13-83. Dept. of the Navy; 1983.

OTHER SOURCES

Bassett B. The Theoretical Basis of the U.S. Navy Air Decompression Tables. *SPUMS J* 1982; July-Sept:18-23.

Bassett B. Theory of Air Decompression for SCUBA Instructors. In: *Decompression In Depth.* California: PADI; 1979:3-9.

Bell RL, Thompson AC, Borowari RE. The Theoretical Structure and Testing of High Altitude Diving Tables. In: *Decompression In Depth.* California: PADI; 1979:49-79.

Hempleman HV. History of Evolution of Decompression Procedures. In: Bennett PB, Elliott DH (eds). The Physiology and Medicine of Diving, 3rd Edn. California: Best Publishing Co.; 1982:319-351.

Joiner JT (ed). NOAA Diving Manual, 4th Edn. Flagstaff: Best Publishing Company; 2001.

Miller JW. (ed). NOAA Diving Manual, 2nd Edn. Washington DC: United States Department of Commerce; 1979.

U.S. Navy Diving Manual, Vol. 1, Air Diving. U.S. Government Printing Office; 1985. .

U.S. Navy Diving Manual. SS521-AG-PRO-010; 0910-LP-100-3199 Revision 4. Naval Sea Systems Command; 1999.

RECOMMENDED FURTHER READING

Bassett B. The Theoretical Basis of the U.S. Navy Air Decompression Tables. *SPUMS J* 1982; July-Sept:18-23.

Hempleman HV. History of Evolution of Decompression Procedures. In: Bennett PB, Elliott DH (eds). The Physiology and Medicine of Diving, 3rd Edn. California: Best Publishing Co.; 1982:319-351.

U.S. Navy Diving Manual. SS521-AG-PRO-010; 0910-LP-100-3199 Revision 4. Naval Sea Systems Command; 1999.

© Max Gleeson

14.2 Using the U.S. Navy Tables

The tables shown as Tables 14.1.3 and 14.1.4 are taken directly from the U.S. Navy Diving Manual.[1]

A. Planning no-decompression (stop) dives

1. SINGLE, OR FIRST NO-DECOMPRESSION DIVES

Table 14.1.3 was designed for planning single dives or the first of a group of dives.

Example 1.

You are planning to dive to a maximum depth of 80ft (24m). What is the No-Decompression Limit (NDL)?

Enter Table 14.1.3 from the left (in either the *ft* or *m* row) and move right until finding the exact, or next greater tabled, maximum depth of the dive. In this case, move across to the 80ft (24m) column and move across the row to the next column, labeled No-Decompression Limits. The NDL for 80ft (24m) is, therefore, *40 minutes.*

This 40 minutes is the actual allowable bottom time for the dive. (The NDL is also shown as the last (rightmost) number on each of the depth rows.)

Similarly, the NDL for 100ft (30m) is *25 minutes*, the NDL for 60ft (18m) is 60 minutes and the NDL for 50ft (15m) is *100 minutes.*

Example 2.

What is the NDL for a single/first dive to a maximum depth of 54ft (16m)?

Enter Table 14.1.3 from the left and look down the feet or metres column to find the depth of 54ft (16m). There is no row corresponding to 54ft (16m) so take the next greater tabled depth, which is 60ft (18m). Moving right along the 60ft row, the NDL is found to be *60 minutes.*

Similarly, the NDL for 66ft (20m) is *50 minutes*, the NDL for 37ft (11m) is *200 minutes*, and for 103ft (31m) is *20 minutes.*

FINDING THE REPETITIVE GROUP AFTER SINGLE/FIRST NO-DECOMPRESSION DIVES

Example 3.

Find the Repetitive Group (RG) after the previous single dive to 80ft (24m) for 40 minutes.

As before, enter Table 14.1.3 from the left at 80ft (24m). Move across to the right to the 40 (minutes). It is the last figure in the column. Moving up this column you will find the letter I. Thus, the Repetitive Group after a dive to 80ft (24m) for 40 minutes is Group *I.*

Similarly, the RG after a dive to 100ft (30m) for 25 minutes is Group *H.*

Example 4.

What is the Repetitive Group (RG) after a dive to 63ft (19m) for 30 minutes?

Enter Table 14.1.3 from the left at the 70ft (21m) row, which is the next greater depth increment as 63ft is not listed. Move across this row to the right until finding the exact, or next longer tabled, bottom time. In this case you will find the 30 minute bottom time. Move up this column to find the RG after the dive. It is Group *F.*

Example 5.

What is the RG after a dive to 113ft (34m) for a bottom time of 11 minutes?

Enter Table 14.1.3 from the left at the 120ft (36m) row and then move across to the right until you find 11 minutes or the next tabled time longer than 11 minutes. Take 12 minutes. Moving up this column the RG is found to be *E.*

2. REPETITIVE NO-DECOMPRESSION DIVES

During a surface interval nitrogen is off-gassed. After various intervals the Repetitive Groups, which represent the nitrogen levels in the 120-minute tissue, will be reduced. The top section of Table 14.1.4, the "Surface Interval Credit Table", enables us to calculate new Repetitive Groups after surface intervals which are greater than 10 minutes and less than 12 hours.

FINDING THE NEW REPETITIVE GROUP AFTER A SURFACE INTERVAL

Example 6.

If the RG immediately after a dive is H, what is the new group after a surface interval of 2 hours?

Enter Table 14.1.4 from the left at H, and move across to the right until you find an interval that includes the 2 hours. You will find it between the interval of 1:42 and 2:23, which is in the fourth column across. Move down this column to find the new RG. It is Group *E*.

Example 7.

If the RG immediately after a dive is F, find the new group after a surface interval of 2½ hours.

Enter Table 14.1.4 from the left at F, and move right along the row until you find an interval including the time of 2½ hours. It is between 2:29 and 3:57, so move down that column to find the new RG; which is *C*.

CALCULATING THE MAXIMUM ALLOWABLE NO-DECOMPRESSION BOTTOM TIME FOR A REPETITIVE DIVE

With these tables, a repetitive dive is defined to be any dive within 12 hours of a previous dive(s). When planning a repetitive dive(s), the excess nitrogen still remaining after the surface interval must be taken into account. This is done by adding a "Residual Nitrogen Time" (RNT). The Residual Nitrogen Time is the amount of time that must be considered already spent at the maximum depth of the repetitive dive before this dive is commenced. It is subtracted from the single dive NDL for that depth, and the result is the no-decompression bottom time still remaining at that depth.

The bottom section of Table 14.1.4 gives the Residual Nitrogen Times for the various depths of repetitive dives.

Example 8.

If you are in Group C immediately before a dive to 80ft (24m), find:

(i) the Residual Nitrogen Time (RNT) at 80ft (24m)

(ii) the maximum allowable no-decompression bottom time at 80ft (24m)

Enter the lower portion of Table 14.1.4 from the left at the row labeled 'Repetitive Dive Depth' and move across to the right to the column for Group C. Then move down this column until intersecting the row corresponding to the exact, or next greater tabled, maximum depth of the repetitive dive. In this case, move down to the row for 80ft (24m), as labeled on the left side. The number shown is the Residual Nitrogen Time, which, in this case, is 13 minutes. This means that before doing the dive you must consider that you have already spent 13 minutes at 80ft (24m). This 13 minutes is to account for nitrogen left over from the previous dive(s). To calculate the allowable no-decompression bottom time you must subtract the RNT of 13 minutes from the NDL for 80ft (24m) given in Table 14.1.3.

i.e. Allowable no-deco bottom time
      = 40 (NDL) - 13 (RNT)
      = 27 minutes.

Example 9.

At the end of a surface interval after a dive you are in group B. Find:

(i) the Residual Nitrogen Time

(ii) the maximum allowable bottom time for a no-decompression dive to 96ft (29m).

Enter the lower section of 14.1.4 from the left and move along the row of letters until reaching the Repetitive Group of B. Move down this column until intersecting the 100ft (30m) column. The RNT is, therefore, *7 minutes.*

To calculate the allowable no-decompression bottom time you must subtract the RNT of 7 minutes from the NDL for 100ft (30m) given in Table 14.1.3.

i.e. Allowable no-deco bottom time
      = 25 (NDL) - 7 (RNT)
      = 18 minutes.

PLANNING A PAIR OF NO-DECOMPRESSION DIVES

Example 10.

You are planning two no-decompression stop dives. The first dive is to 100ft (30m) followed 3 hours later by a dive to 73ft (22m). Find the maximum allowable bottom time for each dive.

Enter Table 14.1.3 from the left and move across to 100ft (30m). Moving across to the NDL column, the NDL is found to be 25 minutes, which is the maximum allowable no-decompression stop bottom time for the first dive. Move to the right to the final number in this 100ft (30m) row, which is the proposed bottom time of 25 minutes, and then up the column to find the RG after the dive. It is Group H.

Enter the top section of Table 14.1.4 from the left at the H row and move across the row to find an interval which includes the surface interval of 3 hours. It lies between 2:24 and 3:20. Move down this column to find the RG after the surface interval. It is D.

Enter the lower section of Table 14.1.4 at the letter D and move down the column until intersecting the row corresponding to 80ft (24m). The RNT is, therefore, 18 minutes.

Enter Table 14.1.3 from the left at 80ft (24m) and move across to find the NDL, which is 40. Therefore, the maximum allowable bottom time for the dive is:

      40 - 18 = *22 minutes.*

Example 11.

You are planning two no-decompression stop dives. The first is to 120ft (36m), followed 4 hours later by a dive to 110ft (33m). Find the maximum allowable bottom time for each dive.

Enter Table 14.1.3 from the left at 120ft (36m). Moving across to the NDL column, the NDL is found to be 15 minutes, which is the maximum allowable bottom time for the first dive. Move to the end of this 120ft (36m) row to the proposed bottom time of 15 minutes, and then up the column to find the RG after the dive. It is Group F.

Enter the top section of Table 14.1.4 at F, and move across this row to find an interval that includes the surface interval of 4 hours. It lies between 3:58 and 7:05. Move down the column to find the RG after the surface interval. It is B.

Enter the lower section of Table 14.1.4 at the column marked B and move down the column until intersecting the row corresponding to 110ft (33m). The RNT is, therefore, 6 minutes.

Enter Table 14.1.3 from the left at 110ft (33m) and move across to find the NDL, which is 20 minutes. Therefore, the maximum allowable bottom time for the dive is
    20 - 6 = *14 minutes.*

FINDING THE REPETITIVE GROUP AFTER A REPETITIVE DIVE

Example 12.

Before a repetitive dive to 100ft (30m) you are in group B. If you now dived to 100ft for a bottom time of 10 minutes, what would be your new Repetitive Group?

From the lower section of Table 14.1.4, the RNT at 100ft (30m) is 7 minutes. Subtracting this 7 minutes from the NDL for 100ft (30m) from Table 14.1.3, we get:
    25 - 7 = 18,
so the maximum no-decompression bottom time is 18 minutes.

To calculate the RG after this 10-minute dive you must first find the Equivalent Single Dive Bottom Time of the dive.

The Equivalent Single Dive Bottom Time is found by adding the Residual Nitrogen Time to the Actual Bottom Time of the dive.

In this case the Equivalent Single Dive Bottom Time is:
 10 (BT) + 7 (RNT) = 17 minutes.

To find the RG after this (repetitive) dive, go back to Table 14.1.3. Enter at the depth of the repetitive dive, 100ft (30m), and move across the row until you find the equivalent single dive bottom time of the repetitive dive. In this case take 20 minutes. Move up the column find the RG after the dive. It is *F.*

Example 13.

Before a repetitive dive you are in group C. If you now dived to 76ft (23m) for a bottom time of 20 minutes, what would be your new Repetitive Group?

From the bottom section of Table 14.1.4, the RNT at 80ft (24m) is 13 minutes. Adding this 13 minutes to the actual bottom time of 20

minutes gives an Equivalent Single Dive Bottom Time of 33 minutes.

Enter Table 14.1.3 at 80ft (24m) and move across until finding the equivalent bottom time (or next greater tabled) of 33 minutes. In this case, take 35 minutes. Move up the column to get the RG, which is *H.*

PLANNING A GROUP OF THREE NO-DECOMPRESSION DIVES

Example 14.

You are planning to do three no-decompression dives, two of which are repetitive. The first dive, which is to 80ft (24m), is followed 2 hours later by a dive to 66ft (20m), which is followed 3 hours later by a final dive to 50ft (15m). Find the maximum allowable no-decompression stop bottom times for each of the dives.

Enter Table 14.1.3 from the left at the row for 80ft (24m). Move across to the next column to find the NDL. It is *40 minutes*, which is the maximum allowable bottom time for the first dive.

Move to the rightmost number in this row (which is again the NDL of 40) and then up the column to get the RG at the end of the first dive. It is *I.*

Enter the top section of Table 14.1.4 from the left at and move across to find the 2-hour surface interval, which lies between 1:30 and 2:02. Move down the column to find the RG after the surface interval - Group F.

Continue down this column until intersecting the 70ft (21m) row. The RNT is 31 minutes and, subtracting this 31 minutes from the NDL for 70ft (21m) in Table 14.1.3, we get 50 - 31 = 19. So the maximum no-decompression stop bottom time for the second dive is 19 minutes. The equivalent bottom time of this second dive is, therefore:

19 (BT) + 31 (RNT) = 50 minutes, which is the NDL for a single dive to this depth.

To find the RG after this dive, enter Table 14.1.3 at 70ft (21m) and move across until finding the equivalent bottom time of 50 minutes. Moving up the column, the RG is J.

Enter the top section of Table 14.1.4 at J and move across to find the surface interval of 3 hours. It lies between 2:21 and 3:04, so move down column to get the RG, which is E. Continue to move down until intersecting the 50ft (15m) row. The RNT at 50ft (15m) is 38 minutes and, from Table 14.1.3, the maximum allowable bottom time is:
100 - 38 = 62 minutes.

Planning a pair of no-decompression dives
SUMMARY OF STEPS

1. Look up the NDL for the first dive (Table 14.1.3).
2. Find the RG after the first dive (Table 14.1.3).
3. Find the new RG after the surface interval (Table 14.1.4).
4. Find the RNT at the depth of the repetitive dive (Table 14.1.4).
5. Find the allowable no-decompression bottom time for the second dive by subtracting the RNT from the NDL for the depth of the repetitive dive (Table 14.1.3).
6. Calculate the RG at the end of the repetitive dive (Table 14.1.3) (Equivalent single dive BT = actual BT + RNT).

Example 15.

You are planning two no-decompression stop dives. The first is to 66ft (20m), followed 5 hours later by a dive to 60ft (18m). Find the maximum allowable bottom time for each dive.

Following the steps above, the calculations can be recorded as follows:

1. NDL for 66ft (20m) = 50
2. RG after first dive = J
3. RG after surface interval of 5 hr = C
4. RNT at 60ft (18m) = 17
5. Max. bottom time for 60ft (18m) = 60 -17= 43
6. RG after repetitive dive = J

FIGURE 14.2.1

Drawing a dive profile for Example 15.

Some divers prefer to draw the profiles and fill in the gaps as they work through the table. This may be done as in Figure 14.2.1.

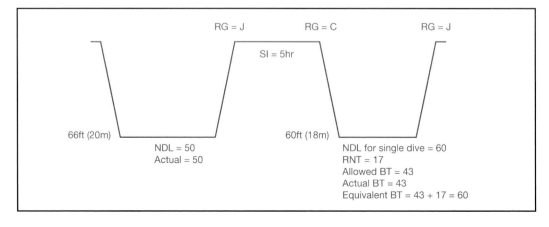

RG = J   RG = C   RG = J

SI = 5hr

66ft (20m)   60ft (18m)

NDL = 50   NDL for single dive = 60
Actual = 50   RNT = 17
                  Allowed BT = 43
                  Actual BT = 43
                  Equivalent BT = 43 + 17 = 60

B. Planning decompression (stop) dives

Table 14.2.1 is a shortened version of the U.S. Navy Air Decompression Tables that has been available commercially and is used here for ease of reference for the examples of dives involving decompression stops. This particular version of the table has been shortened. It does not include dives that require decompression stops at depths greater than 20ft (6m). The full U.S. Navy Air Decompression Tables are shown in Appendix A.

1. SINGLE, OR FIRST DECOMPRESSION DIVES

Example 16.

Calculate the decompression necessary for a first/single dive to 90ft (27m) for 40 minutes.

Enter Table 14.2.1 from the left at the box corresponding to the exact, or next greater tabled, maximum depth of the dive.

In this case enter the 90ft (27m) box. Move right to find the exact, or next longer tabled, bottom time of the dive, which is written in the third column. In this case 40 minutes is tabled so move into the row for 40 minutes (in the 90ft box), and move right to read off any required decompression stop(s). There is a 7 in the 10ft (3m) column so the required decompression is *7 minutes at 10ft (3m)*. This means that you must actually spend 7 full minutes at the 10ft (3m) stop. The time taken to ascend to the stop is not included in the stop time - it is extra.

Continue to move right along the row to find the RG after the dive. It is *J*.

Example 17.

Calculate the decompression required for a first/single dive to 103ft (31m) for 32 minutes.

Enter the 110ft (33m) box and look in column 3 for the exact, or next longer, tabled bottom time of 32 minutes. Take 40 minutes. Move across the 40-minute row to the right to find the required decompression. It is *2 minutes at 20ft (6m) followed by 21 minutes at 10ft (3m)*.

You must ascend to 20ft (6m) and spend a full 2 minutes at 20ft before ascending to 10ft (3m). You must then spend a full 21 minutes at 10ft before surfacing.

Moving right, the RG after the dive is *L*.

Notes:
  1. The first bottom time in column 3 of each box is the NDL for that depth.
  2. A (*) in the final column means that the RG can be found from Table 14.1.4.

2. REPETITIVE DECOMPRESSION DIVES

Example 18.

You are planning two dives. The first is to a maximum depth of 73ft (22m) for a bottom time of 46 minutes. After a surface interval of 3½ hours you wish to dive to 18m (60ft) for 50 minutes. Calculate the decompression required.

As 46 minutes is beyond the NDL for 80ft (24m), a stop(s) is required and can be found in Table 14.2.1.

Enter Table 14.2.1 from the left at the 80ft (24m) box. Move right to the bottom time column to find 46 minutes. Take 50 minutes. Move right to find the decompression. *It is 10 minutes at 10ft (3m)*. The RG after the dive is K.

Enter Table 14.1.4 from the left at K. Move across to find the surface interval of 3½ hour. It lies between 3:22 and 4:19 so move down this column to get the new RG, which is group

TABLE 14.2.1

Reprinted with permission of S. Harold Reuter M.D

TABLE 1-10 (1-5)   U.S. NAVY
Standard Air Decompression Table
(Simplified for the Sport Diver)

DEPTH (metres)	Depth (feet)	Bottom Time (min)	Decompression stops(min) 20(ft)10(ft)		Repetitive Group
12	40	200	0		(*)
		210	2		N
		230	7		N
15	50	100	0		(*)
		110	3		L
		120	5		M
		140	10		M
		160	21		N
18	60	60	0		(*)
		70	2		K
		80	7		L
		100	14		M
		120	26		N
		140	39		O
21	70	50	0		(*)
		60	8		K
		70	14		L
		80	18		M
		90	23		N
		100	33		N
		110	2	41	O
		120	4	47	O
		130	6	52	O
24	80	40	0		(*)
		50	10		K
		60	17		L
		70	23		M
		80	2	31	N
		90	7	39	N
		100	11	46	O
		110	13	53	O
27	90	30	0		(*)
		40	7		J
		50	18		L
		60	25		M
		70	7	30	N
		80	13	40	N
		90	18	48	O
30	100	25	0		(*)
		30	3		I
		40	15		K
		50	2	24	L
		60	9	28	N
		70	17	39	O
33	110	20	0		(*)
		25	3		H
		30	7		J
		40	2	21	L
		50	8	26	M
		60	18	36	N
36	120	15	0		(*)
		20	2		H
		25	6		I
		30	14		J
		40	5	25	L
		50	15	31	N
39	130	10	0		(*)
		15	1		F
		20	4		H
		25	10		J
		30	3	18	M
		40	10	25	N
42	140	10	0		(*)
		15	2		G
		20	6		I
		25	2	14	J
		30	5	21	K
45	150	5	0		C
		10	1		E
		15	3		G
		20	2	7	H
		25	4	17	K
		30	8	24	L
49	160	5	0		D
		10	1		F
		15	1	4	H
		20	3	11	J
		25	7	20	K
52	170	5	0		D
		10	2		F
		15	2	5	H
		20	4	15	J
55	180	5	0		D
		10	3		F
		15	3	6	I
58	190	5	0		D
		10	1	3	G
		15	4	7	I

*See table 1-11 (1-6) for Repetitive
Groups in "No Decompression Dives"

Moray Industries Ltd.
P.O. Box 32-064 Devonport.
Auckland New Zealand.

DACOR CORP.
Northfield, Ill., 60093 U.S.A.

"NO CALCULATION" DIVE TABLES
INSTRUCTIONS FOR USE

For a "no decompression" dive
1 Find the depth you have dived along the top of Table 1-11
2 Drop down to the figure which denotes your Bottom Time
3 Go across to the right to Table 1-12
4 Follow the arrow upward until you find the time spent out of the water since the last dive (Surface Interval)
5 Go across to the right to find the allowable Bottom Time (white numbers) for the next dive. These are listed under the appropriate depths at the top of each column
   The Black Numbers are "Residual Nitrogen Times" and are only important for figuring "Decompression" Dives
6 If the "no decompression" limits are exceeded, go to Table 1-10 for Decompression stops and times
7 If diver's surface interval is less than 10 minutes, add the Bottom Times of the preceeding and following dives, use the maximum depth attained and consider the two dives as one
8 SHORTENED OR OMITTED DECOMPRESSION. If a diver surfaces after a dive and finds he has not adequately decompressed but has no symptoms of decompression sickness, he has a maximum surface interval of 5 minutes to determine what his decompression for the dive should have been, get back in the water and begin the following decompression procedure

a Make a stop at 40ft. (12m)for 1/4 the 10ft. (3m)stop time
b Make a stop at 30ft. (9m)for 1/3 the 10ft. (3m)stop time
c Make a stop at 20ft. (6m)for 1/2 the 10ft. (3m)stop time
d Make a stop at 10ft. (3m)for 1 1/2 times the 10ft (3m)stop time, then surface.

Use of Table 1-10

a) All decompression steps are timed in minutes
b) Ascent rate is 60 feet per minute
c) The chest level of the diver should be maintained as close as possible to each decompression depth for the number of minutes listed
d) The time at each stop is the exact time that is spent at that decompression depth.

DEFINITIONS:

1 Bottom time (in minutes) starts when the diver leaves the surface and ends only when the diver starts a direct ascent back to the surface
   Always select the exact or next greater bottom time exposure
2 Depth (in feet) The deepest depth of descent Always enter the tables on the exact or next greater depth reached
3 Residual Nitrogen Time—Time in minutes that a diver is to consider he has already spent on the bottom when he starts a repetitive dive
4 Surface Interval—Time in hours and minutes actually spent on the surface between dives
5 Repetitive Dive—A dive begun within 12 hours of surfacing from a previous dive

PLAN YOUR DIVE—DIVE YOUR PLAN
Always carry the Dive Tables on a dive—they may save your life

4th	3rd	2nd	1st	DIVE
				DEPTH
				BOTTOM TIME
				ARRIVAL TIME AT SURFACE
				DEPARTURE TIME NEXT DIVE

MODEL PSNT

D. Continue down the column until intersecting the 60ft (18m) row. The RNT is, therefore, 24 minutes. The equivalent single dive bottom time of the second dive is thus:

24 (RNT) + 50 (BT) = 74 minutes.

This dive is equivalent to a single dive of 60ft (18m) for 74 minutes, which means that a decompression stop(s) is required and can be found in Table 14.2.1.

Enter Table 14.2.1 from the left at the 60ft (18m) box and look for 74 minutes in the bottom time column. Take 80 minutes. The required decompression is *7 minutes at 10ft (3m)* and the RG after the dive is *L*.

Planning a pair of decompression stop dives

SUMMARY OF STEPS

1. Find any decompression stop required for the first dive (Table 14.2.1).
2. Find the RG at the end of the first dive (Table 14.2.1).
3. Find the RG after the surface interval (Table 14.2.2).
4. Find the RNT at the depth of the second dive (Table 14.1.42).
5. Find the equivalent single dive bottom time of the repetitive dive (actual BT + RNT).
6. Find the decompression required for the repetitive dive (Table 14.2.1).
   (Look up max. depth and equivalent single dive bottom time of repetitive dive).
7. Find the RG at the end of the repetitive dive (Table 14.2.1).

Example 19.

You are planning two dives that will possibly require a decompression stop(s). The first dive is to 90ft (27m) for 35 minutes. The second dive, three hours after the first, is to 63ft (19m) for 35 minutes. Calculate any decompression stop(s) required.

Following the steps above, the calculations can be recorded as follows:

1. Decompression required first dive of 90ft (27m) for 35 minutes
   = 7 minutes at 10ft (3m)
2. RG after first dive = J
3. RG after surface interval of 3 hr = E
4. RNT at 63ft (19 m) = 26
5. Equivalent single dive bottom time of repetitive dive = 35 + 26 = 61

6. Decompression required for single dive to 63ft (19m) for 61 minutes
   = 14 minutes at 10ft (3m)
7. RG after repetitive dive = L

This may be represented in diagramatic form as shown in Figure 14.2.2.

FIGURE 14.2.2

Drawing a profile for Example 19.

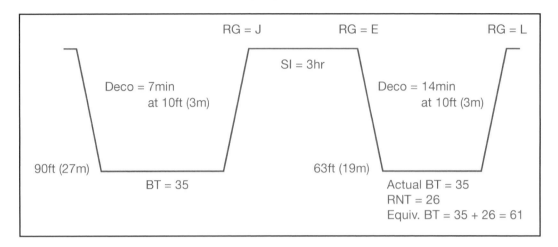

SOME SPECIAL RULES FOR USING THE U.S. NAVY TABLES

The following section is taken from the U.S. Navy Diving Manual[1] and highlights some situations where the U.S. Navy advises that decompression may be calculated in a slightly different manner to normal. What is shown here is only part of what is included in the Manual.

CAUTION: Never attempt to interpolate between decompression schedules.

If the divers are exceptionally cold during the dive or if the work load is relatively strenuous, select the next longer decompression schedule than the one that would normally be selected.

For example, the normal schedule for a dive to 90fsw for 34 minutes would be the 90/40 schedule. If the divers are exceptionally cold or fatigued, they should decompress according to the 90/50 schedule. This procedure is used because the divers are generating heat and on-gassing at a normal rate while working at depth. Once decompression starts, however, the divers are at rest and begin to chill. Vasoconstriction

of the blood vessels takes place and they do not off-gas at the normal rate. The additional decompression time increases the likelihood that the divers receive adequate decompression.

NOTE: Take into consideration the physical condition of the diver when determining what is strenuous.

If the diver's depth cannot be maintained at a decompression stop, the Diving Supervisor may select the next deeper decompression table.

ASCENT PROCEDURES

Rules During Ascent. After selecting the applicable decompression schedule, it is imperative that it be followed as closely as possible. Unless a Diving Medical Officer recommends a deviation and the Commanding Officer concurs, decompression must be completed according to the schedule selected.

Ascent Rate. Always ascend at a rate of 30fpm (20 seconds per 10fsw). Minor variations in the rate of travel between 20 and 40fsw/minute are acceptable. Any variation in the rate of ascent must be corrected in accordance with the procedures below. However, a delay of up to one minute in reaching the first decompression stop can be ignored.

Decompression Stop Time.

Decompression stop times, as specified in the decompression schedule, begin as soon as the divers reach the stop depth. Upon completion of the specified stop time, the divers ascend to the next stop or to the surface at the proper ascent rate. Ascent time is not included as part of stop time.

Variations in Rate of Ascent. The following rules for correcting variations in the rate of ascent apply to Standard Air Decompression dives.

Delays in Arriving at the First Stop.

Delay greater than 1 minute, deeper than 50fsw. Add the total delay time (rounded up to the next whole minute) to the bottom time, re-compute a new decompression schedule, and decompress accordingly.

Example: A dive was made to 113fsw with a bottom time of 60 minutes.

According to the 120/60 decompression schedule of the Standard Air Decompression Table, the first decompression stop is 30fsw. During ascent, the divers were delayed at 100fsw for: 03:27 and it actually took 6 minutes 13 seconds to reach the 30-foot decompression stop. Determine the new decompression schedule.

Solution: If the divers had maintained an ascent rate of 30fpm, it would have taken the divers 2 minutes 46 seconds to ascend from 113fsw to 30fsw. The difference between what it should have taken and what it actually took is 3 minutes 27 seconds. Increase the bottom time from 60 minutes to 64 minutes (3 minutes 27 seconds rounded up), re-compute the decompression schedule using a 70-minute

bottom time and continue decompression according to the new decompression schedule, 120/70.

Delay greater than 1 minute, shallower than 50fsw. If the rate of ascent is less than 30fpm, add the delay time to the diver's first decompression stop. If the delay is between stops, disregard the delay. The delay time is rounded up to the next whole minute.

Example: A dive was made to 113fsw with a bottom time of 60 minutes.

According to the Standard Air Decompression Table, the first decompression stop is at 30fsw. During ascent, the divers were delayed at 40fsw and it actually took 6 minutes 20 seconds to reach the 30-foot stop. Determine the new decompression schedule.

Solution: If the divers had maintained an ascent rate of 30fpm, the correct ascent time should have been 2 minutes 46 seconds. Because it took 6 minutes 20 seconds to reach the 30-foot stop, there was a delay of 3 minutes 34 seconds (6 minutes 20 seconds minus 2 minutes 46 seconds). Therefore, increase the length of the 30-foot decompression stop by 3 minutes 34 seconds, rounded up to 4 minutes. Instead of 2 minutes, the divers must spend 6 minutes at 30fsw.

Travel Rate Exceeded. On a Standard Air Dive, if the rate of ascent is greater than 30fpm, STOP THE ASCENT, allow the watches to catch up, and then continue ascent. If the stop is arrived at early, start the stop time after the watches catch up.

NOAA No-Decompression Dive Chart

Over the years there have been many formats of the U.S. Navy Tables available to divers. The National Oceanic and Atmospheric Administration (NOAA) has published an easy-to-use abbreviated format of the U.S. Navy 1999 No-Decompression Tables, shown as Table 14.2.2.

The following example describes how the NOAA USN Table can be used.

Example 20.

You are planning two no-decompression stop dives. The first is to 66ft (20m), followed 5 hours later by a dive to 60ft (18m). Find the maximum allowable bottom time for each dive.

Enter Chart 1 from the left at 70ft (21m) and move across to the right to the circled number, which is the NDL and in this case is 50 minutes. Move down the column to get the RG at the end of the dive, which is J. Continue to move down to find the surface interval of 5 hours, which lies between 5:40 and 4:03. Move left from this interval to get the RG at the end of the surface interval, which is C. Continue along this row until intersecting the column for the depth of the repetitive dive, 60ft (18m). The top number is the residual nitrogen time of 17 minutes. The lower number is the maximum dive time remaining for this dive, and is:

60 (NDL) - 17 (RNT) = *43 minutes.*

REFERENCES

1. U.S. Navy Diving Manual. SS521-AG-PRO-010; 0910-LP-100-3199 Revision 4. Naval Sea Systems Command; 1999.

2. Joiner JT (ed). NOAA Diving Manual, 4th Edn. Flagstaff: Best Publishing Company; 2001

RECOMMENDED FURTHER READING

U.S. Navy Diving Manual. SS521-AG-PRO-010; 0910-LP-100-3199 Revision 4. Naval Sea Systems Command, 1999.

Joiner JT (ed). NOAA Diving Manual, 4th Edn. Flagstaff: Best Publishing Company; 2001.

TABLE 14.2.2

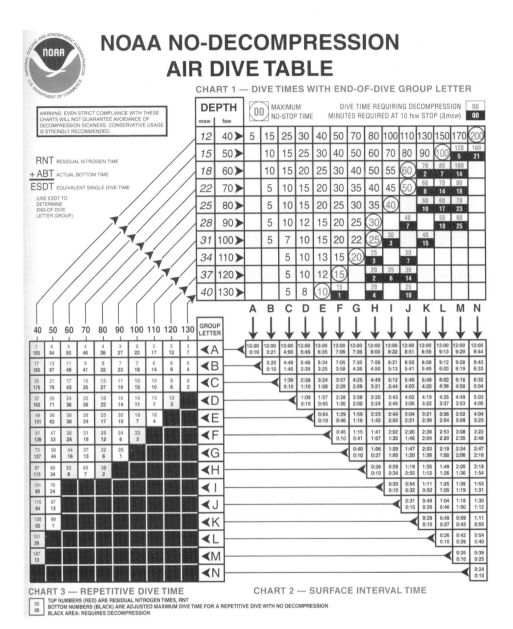

Reprinted with permission of Best Publications Inc.

EXERCISES ON THE U.S NAVY TABLES

1. Find the No-Decompression Limits for single dives to the following depths:

    a) 100ft (30m)

    b) 30ft (9m)

    c) 76ft (23m)

    d) 116ft (35m)

    e) 101ft (30.5m)

2. Find the decompression times required for the following single or first dives (the times given are bottom times):

    a) 60ft (18m) for 60 min

    b) 50ft (15m) for 75 min

    c) 63ft (19m) for 45 min

    d) 83ft (25m) for 40 min

    e) 92ft (28m) for 30 min

    f) 120ft (36m) for 38 min

3. Find the maximum allowable no-decompression stop bottom times for the following second dives:

    a) A dive to 66ft (20m), 2 ½ hours after a dive to 92ft (28m) for 26 minutes.

    b) A dive to 50ft (15m), 3 hours after a dive to 80ft (24m) for 25 minutes.

    c) A dive to 100ft (30m), 5 hours after a dive to 120ft (36m) for 12 minutes.

4. Find the decompression required for the following second dives (the times given are bottom times)

    a) A dive to 110ft (33 m) for 10 minutes, 1 hour after a dive to 100ft (30m) for 20 minutes.

    b) A dive to 80ft (24m) for 30 minutes, 4½ hours after a dive to 86ft (26m) for 20 minutes.

    c) A dive to 106ft (32m) for 18 minutes, 10 hours after a dive to 140ft (42m) for 16 minutes.

    d) A dive to 26ft (8 m) for 40 minutes, 1½ hours after a dive to 90ft (27m) for 20 minutes.

5. Find the maximum allowable no-decompression stop bottom times for each dive in the following pairs of dives:

    a) A dive to 92ft (28m) followed 2 hours later by a dive to 66ft (20m).

    b) A dive to 120ft (36m) followed 4½ hours later by a dive to 102ft (31m)

    c) A dive to 56ft (17m) followed 2½ hours later by another dive to 56ft (17m).

    d) A dive to 53ft (16m) followed 3 hours later by a dive to 66ft (20m).

    e) A dive to 135ft (41m) followed 6½ hours later by a dive to 40ft (12m).

ANSWERS

1. a) 25   b) no limit   c) 40
   d)15   e) 20

2.a) No deco   b) No deco   c) No deco
   d) 7 min at 10ft (3m)   e) 3 min at 10ft (3m)
   f) 5 min at 20ft (6m) and 25 min at 8.5ft (3m)

3. a) 24   b) 79   c) 18

4. a) 7 min at 10ft (3m)   b) No deco
   c) 3 min at 10ft (3m)   d) No deco

5. a) 25, 24   b) 15, 14   c) 60, 30
   d) 60, 24   e) 10, 183

14.3 Suitability of the U.S. Navy Tables for recreational diving?

U.S. Navy Tables were widely used by recreational divers until the introduction of the PADI Recreational Dive Planner and the growth in dive computer usage during the 1990s. DAN statistics for 1988 indicate that about 72% of the recreational divers treated for DCI in the U.S.A that year had dived within the U.S. Navy Tables.[1]

Although in the 21st century, there are relatively few recreational divers still using the U.S. Navy Tables, these tables were such a benchmark for so long and so widely used in recreational diving, that it is worthwhile having the opportunity to gain an historical perspective of some of the safety issues.

The U.S. Navy Tables were created to prevent decompression sickness (not bubbles) in Navy divers. At their acceptance trials in 1956, the schedules produced an overall DCI rate of 4.6% (26 cases in 564 dives) for single dives.[2,3] The schedules on which the DCI occurred were then re-calculated and tested again (involving very few tests) until no cases of DCI occurred. All schedules were then re-calculated in accordance to these modifications. The repetitive schedules were tested on 61 repetitive profiles involving 122 dives. Three cases of DCI occurred, an overall incidence of 4.9% (3 cases in 61).[2,4] There is no mention in the report whether or not the repetitive schedules were re-calculated and re-tested to produce no DCI - it appears that they were not. Although it is stated that the divers involved in the testing varied in experience, ability and condition, no older divers and women participated.

The U.S. Navy has since done an enormous number of dives and has had a very low overall incidence of decompression illness.

For example, in 1981, thirty five U.S. Navy divers developed DCI out of 92,484 dives; an incidence of about 0.04%.[5] In 1987, the Navy recorded 106,965 dives with only 77 cases of DCI (0.07%).[6]

The low rate of decompression illness in the U.S. Navy may give a distorted view of the actual safety of the tables. It has been reported that the vast majority of U.S. Navy dives are very shallow no-decompression stop dives, most of which do not even approach the limits of the tables.[7]

The U.S. Navy published a report in 1980 which covered all dives done *to the schedules* between the years 1971-78.[8] It included dives close to the No-Decompression Limits but did not include dives far shorter than the limits. This gave an incidence of 1.4% (13 cases out of 930 dives) for no-decompression dives made by U.S. Navy divers to depths between 40-140ft (12-42m).

These figures came from the U.S. Navy dive books. It has been claimed that the times that are logged in the dive books are rarely the same as the actual dives done.[9] The depths and times recorded may often be in excess of the actual depth and time of the dive. The procedures for recording dives may alter the statistics, and give the effect of a lower incidence of DCI for a particular profile than is warranted by the tables.

When some controlled dives were made in laboratory chambers, or in open water, to the No-Decompression Limits, the incidence of DCI was four or more times greater than that reported by the Navy. Merrill Spencer and Bruce Bassett independently subjected divers to pressure in recompression chambers.[10,11] They took the divers right to some of the NDLs of the U.S. Navy Tables. e.g. 60ft (18m) for 60 minutes, 70ft (21m) for 50 minutes and 80ft (24m) for 40 minutes. The results suggested that if no-decompression dives are performed to the full limits of the U.S. Navy Tables, the

incidence of DCI is about 5%. Using Doppler bubble detectors they both detected venous bubbles in about 30% of the divers. Some of the results of these studies are shown in Table 14.3.1.

TABLE 14.3.1

Comparison of USN, Spencer and Bassett schedules,
decompression illness (DCI) and venous gas emboli (VGE).

Source	Depth/Time (ft/min)	DCS/Dives	DCS	VGE
USN	60/60	2/183	1.1%	No record
USN	60/70	3/62	4.8%	No record
Spencer	60/60	1/13	7.6%	31%
Bassett	60/60(E)	1/18	5.6%	27.8%
USN	80/40	0/40	0.0%	No record
USN	80/50	2/34	5.9%	No record
Bassett	80/40(E)	1/16	6.3%	37.5%
(E) Equivalent Flying after Diving Schedule				

Note:

A dive recorded by the U.S. Navy as 60/70 may in reality be closer to 60/60. Similarly with 80/50, the true dive may be closer to 80/40. With this in mind, the DCI figures of the USN more closely match those of Bassett and Spencer.

A 1986 U.S. Navy report describes some dives conducted to test the algorithm for the U.S. Navy's Air-N_2O_2 decompression computer.[12] The Navy conducted 107 single air dives testing NDLs which ranged from 10-100% longer than the NDLs of the Standard Air Table. The limits tested were: 60ft (18m)/ 66, 100ft (30m)/30, 120ft (36m)/ 24, 150ft (45m)/14 and 190ft (58m)/10. No cases of DCI occurred during this initial testing and some have argued that this indicates that the standard NDLs are safe. However, when the 100ft/30 schedule was later re-tested a number of cases of DCI did occur. No doppler bubble monitors were used to determine the level of bubbling in the asymptomatic divers. In addition, these dives involved substantially slower ascent

rates at shallow depths. The ascent rates used were: 60ft (18m)/minute to 20ft (6m), 40ft (12m)/minute from 20ft to 10ft (3m) and 30ft (9m)/minute from 10ft to the surface. Short stops, of an unspecified length, were done at 10ft and it appears that some of the divers may have breathed 100% oxygen during the final part of the ascent. In addition, the NDLs at 40ft (12m) and 50ft (15m), which are potentially problematic, were not tested.

In summary, it appears that although the U.S. Navy have a low overall incidence of decompression illness, if the figures are carefully analyzed significant problems might arise if the tables are dived at, or close to, the limits. Although the U.S. Navy generally uses its tables safely, this does not mean that the tables are safe in themselves. When recreational divers use these tables problems can be expected to occur unless their diving practices, dive fitness and table calculations match U.S. Navy practices.

When comparing the U.S. Navy diver to the recreational diver there are a number of differences which may relate to the risk of DCI. Most of the Navy divers were between 17 to 40 years old and none of the divers were obese. In addition, they were all healthy enough to have passed the U.S. Navy physical.

The type of diving that the Navy divers perform is usually quite different to what recreational divers do. It has been reported that the vast majority of U.S. Navy dives are very shallow no-decompression dives, which carry the lowest risk of DCI.[7] Repetitive dives are not common in the U.S. Navy practice but are commonly carried out by recreational divers. It has been reported that the U.S. Navy dive supervisors also add safety factors to their decompression table schedules.[8] For instance, if a diver is within 2 minutes or 2 feet of a schedule they go to the next schedule. At 58ft you go to the 70ft schedule and at 58 minutes you go to the 70-minute bottom time (At times 5ft and 5 minutes are used instead).

To minimize the risk of DCS when using the U.S. Navy Tables, the recreational diver must use the tables at least as safely as the U.S. Navy divers. The diver who uses the tables in the same manner as the Navy does may still be at a greater risk of DCS than the Navy diver, due to differences in condition and training. It becomes obvious that a sensible recreational diver must add significant safety factors ("fudge factors") to the U.S. Navy Tables in order to lower the risk of decompression illness.

Various methods to add "fudge factors" (safety factors) to the U.S. Navy Tables emerged over the years.

These included:

- *Choosing the NDL for the next greater tabled depth than would normally be used*

  (e.g. For a dive to 66ft (20m), using the NDL for 80ft (24m), rather than 70ft (21m) as the initial NDL.)

- *Reducing this initial NDL further to cater for any possible predisposing factor(s) to DCS that are present.*

- *On a decompression stop dive, choosing a more conservative decompression schedule by adding one depth increment and one bottom time increment to the schedule that would normally be used.*

  (e.g. For a dive to 57ft (17m) for a bottom time of 65 minutes using the schedule for 70ft (21m) for 80 minutes.)

- *Ascending more slowly than the 60ft (18m)/minute then specified by the Navy.**

- *Doing a safety stop before surfacing on no-decompression dives.*

- *Using the total dive time to find the Repetitive Group after the dive.*

Although these procedures were not validated, they yield more conservative decompression and may therefore provide additional safety.

In addition, other tables, such as the Huggins and Bassett Tables were developed to offer more conservative alternatives, based on the U.S. Navy system.

---

* The ascent rate now recommended by the U.S. Navy is 30ft (9m) per minute.

REFERENCES

1. Report on 1988 Diving Accidents. Durham, North Carolina: Divers Alert Network; 1990.

2. Thalmann ED, Butler F. A Procedure for doing Multiple Level Dives on Air Using Repetitive Groups. U.S. Navy Experimental Diving Unit, Report No. 13-83; 1983.

3. Des Granges M. Standard Air Decompression Table. U.S. Navy Experimental Diving Unit Report No. 5-57; 1956.

4. Des Granges M. Repetitive Diving Decompression Tables. U.S. Navy Experimental Diving Unit Report No. 6-57; 1957.

5. Dembert M et al. Health risk factors for the development of decompression sickness among U.S. Navy divers. *Undersea Biomed Res* 1984; 11(4):395-406.

6. Garrahan R. Personal communication.

7. Blood C, Hoiberg A. Analyses of variables underlying U.S. Navy diving accidents. *Undersea Biomed Res* 1985; 12 (3):351-60.

8. Berhage T, Durman D. U.S. Navy Air Decompression Risk Analysis. Naval Medical Research Institute, Report No. NMRI 80-1, Naval Medical Research and Development Command; 1980.

9. Bassett B. The Safety of the United States Navy Decompression Tables and Recommendations for Sports Divers. *SPUMS J* 1982; Oct-Dec:16-25.

10. Spencer M. Decompression limits for compressed air determined by ultrasonically detected blood bubbles. *J Appl Physiol 1976*; 40 (2):229-35.

11. Bassett B. Decompression procedures for flying after diving, and diving at altitudes above sea level. Report No. SAM-TR-82-47, Brooks Air Force Base: United States Air Force School of Aerospace Medicine; 1982.

12. Thalmann E. Air-N_2O_2 Decompression Computer Algorithm Development. U.S. Navy Experimental Diving Unit Report No. 8-85; 1986.

RECOMMENDED FURTHER READING

Bassett B. The Safety of the United States Navy Decompression Tables and Recommendations for Sports Divers. *SPUMS J* 1982; Oct-Dec:16-25.

© Dr. Richard Harris

15

More conservative alternatives based on the U.S. Navy tables

15.1 Huggins Tables

In 1976, Dr. Merril Spencer published a report in which he stated that he had found that divers who were exposed to some of the U.S. Navy limits demonstrated large counts of "silent bubbles" (venous gas emboli) during and after ascent from depth.[1] He believed that the bubbles resulted from the release of excess nitrogen within the divers' bodies. The bubbles were detected using a Doppler Ultrasonic Bubble Detector. On the basis of this work, Spencer recommended new No-Decompression Limits (NDLs), which were calculated in an attempt to minimize bubble formation after a dive.[1] These limits are shown in Table 15.1.1 Subsequent studies carried out by Dr. Andrew Pilmanis[2] and Dr. Bruce Bassett[3] supported Spencer's findings.

These findings confirmed a growing concern in the sport diving community that the U.S. Navy No-Decompression Limits were not as safe for the recreational diver as was commonly thought at that time. As a result, in 1981, Karl Huggins, generated a new set of no-decompression tables that were based on Spencer's recommendations. These became known as the "Huggins Tables". They were designed in an attempt to minimize the formation of bubbles, asymptomatic or otherwise.

The Huggins Tables were based on the same concept and format as the U.S. Navy Tables. Using the same six theoretical tissue groups as the Navy tables, with half-times of 5, 10, 20, 40, 80 and 120 minutes,

TABLE 15.1.1

No-Decompresion Limits (min)

Depth ft m	U.S.Navy	Spencer	Depth ft m	U.S.Navy	Spencer
30 9	none	225	80 24	40	30
35 10.5	310	165	90 27	30	25
40 12	200	135	100 30	25	20
50 15	100	75	110 33	20	15
60 18	60	50	120 36	15	10
70 21	50	40	130 39	10	5

Huggins determined new, lower, critical nitrogen levels (M-values) corresponding to the shortened NDLs recommended by Spencer. Huggins also determined new Repetitive Group Designators which represented the nitrogen levels in all six tissue groups rather than just in the 120-minute tissue compartment as in the Navy tables. This made the Huggins Tables far more suitable for multi-level diving.

The Huggins tables were never validated but were more conservative than the U.S. Navy Tables when used to find the limits for single and repetitive no-decompression stop dives.

They consisted of a Repetitive Group Table, a Surface Interval Table and a Residual Nitrogen Table. The tables are shown as Table 15.1.2. The only difference in reading the table comes with the arrows " → " in the first table. These arrows indicated that the diver must move to the next higher Repetitive Group to the right.

REFERENCES

1. Spencer MP. Decompression limits for compressed air determined by ultrasonically detected blood bubbles. *J Appl Physiol* 1976; 40 (2):229-35.

2. Pilmanis AA. Intravenous gas emboli in man after selected open ocean air SCUBA dives. Abstract 5.1. Undersea Medical Society, Annual Scientific Meeting; 1974.

3. Bassett B. Decompression procedures for flying after diving, and diving at altitudes above sea level. Report No. SAM-TR-82-47, Brooks Air Force Base: United States Air Force School of Aerospace Medicine; 1982.

OTHER SOURCES

Huggins K. New No-Decompression Tables Based on No-Decompression Limits Determined by Doppler Ultrasonic Bubble detection. University of Michigan Sea Grant College Program, Report No. MICHU-SG-81-205, Michigan Sea Grant Publications; 1981.

Huggins K. Tables, Tables, What's with all these Tables? In: Bangasser S (ed). I.Q. '85 Proceedings. California: NAUI,1985:189-201.

Huggins K. Personal communications.

© Dr. Richard Harris

TABLE 15.1.2

Huggins No-Decompression Table.

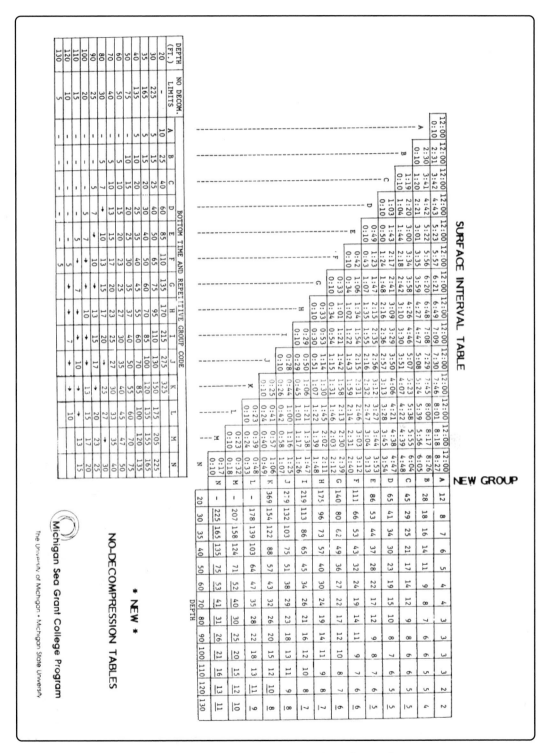

Reprinted courtesy of Michigan Sea Grant College Program

15.2 Bassett Tables

Dr. Bruce Bassett, a physiologist, was commissioned by the U.S. Air Force to validate some schedules for flying after diving. He had to construct a set of tables which would allow a diver to be flown to an altitude of 10,000 feet (3,000 metres) immediately after surfacing from a dive.

Using the mathematics of the U.S. Navy Tables, Bassett calculated a set of equivalent no-decompression stop dives after which a diver would not reach the critical nitrogen levels (maximum supersaturation ratios) of the U.S. Navy Tables until reaching 10,000ft. Bassett placed "divers" in a chamber for various periods of time before "surfacing" them and, then, reducing the pressure to its equivalent at 10,000ft. For example, the divers did not do a 60ft (18m) for 60 minutes dive. Instead, they spent 20 minutes at 60ft and then ascended to 10,000ft. Bassett believed that the calculated nitrogen pressures in the theoretical half-time tissue compartments on reaching 10,000ft were identical to that of surfacing after a 60ft for 60 minutes dive.

If the U.S. Navy Tables were safe, these shorter dives followed by decompression to altitude should have been safe. They were not, as Bassett's divers had a DCI incidence of about 6% and bubbles were detected in about 30% of the divers.[1] This was unacceptable. Bassett's results were similar to those of Dr. Merril Spencer, who had tested the U.S. Navy NDLs in a chamber and found a comparable DCI incidence and bubble counts.[2]

These two sets of dry chamber data and the knowledge that the U.S. Navy divers added depth and time increments before calculating decompression led Dr. Bassett to re-calculate his dive schedule using lesser maximum nitrogen values (M-values). That is, he reduced the allowable supersaturation in the various half-time tissue compartments.

When Bassett tested his revised decompression procedures in the chamber there were no cases of DCI.[1]

Bassett issued a new set of No-Decompression Limits which are more conservative and, he believed, far more appropriate for recreational diving than the U.S. Navy NDLs. These limits are shown in Table 15.2.1.

Bassett also recommended that "all dives greater than 30ft (9m) end with 3 to 5 minutes at 10-15ft (3-4.5m)". He also suggested that total time underwater be used (rather than just bottom time) to determine the Repetitive Group after a dive.[3]

The Bassett limits and recommendations were incorporated into a set of U.S. Navy-based Tables produced in Australia by Dr. John Knight and John Lippmann.[4] However, they were never widely used.

REFERENCES

1. Bassett B. Decompression procedures for flying after diving, and diving at altitudes above sea level. Report No. SAM-TR-82-47, Brooks Air Force Base: United States Air Force School of Aerospace Medicine; 1982.

2. Spencer MP. Decompression limits for compressed air determined by ultrasonically detected blood bubbles. *J Applied Physiology* 1976; 40 (2): 229-35.

3. Bassett B. The Safety of the U.S. Navy Decompression Tables and Recommendations for Sports Divers. *SPUMS J* 1982; Oct-Dec:16.

4. Knight J. Towards Safer Diving: Bruce Bassett's Revised No-Decompression Tables. *SPUMS J* 1985; 15(2):8-15.

OTHER SOURCES

Bassett B. Flying After Diving. In: I.D.C. Candidate Workshop. California: PADI; 1984.

Bassett B. Decompression Safety. In: IDC Candidate Workshop. California PADI; 1984.

Bassett B. Personal communication.

TABLE 15.2.1

No-decompression limits (min).

Depth ft m	U.S.Navy	Bassett	Depth ft m	U.S.Navy	Bassett
30 9	none	220	80 24	40	30
35 10.5	310	180	90 27	30	25
40 12	200	120	100 30	25	20
50 15	100	70	110 33	20	15
60 18	60	50	120 36	15	12
70 21	50	40	130 39	10	10
			140 42	10	5

15.3 NAUI Dive Tables

The 1990 NAUI Dive Tables are modified U.S. Navy Tables. Instead of the U.S. Navy NDLs, the NAUI Tables utilize Maximum Dive Times (MDTs) which are, in fact, the U.S. Navy NDLs reduced by one letter group for dives between 60ft and 130ft (18-39m), by two groups for 50ft (15m) dives and three groups for 40ft (12m) dives. The maximum ascent rate was originally published as 60ft (18m)/minute but has since been reduced to 30ft (9m)/minute. A precautionary decompression stop of 3 minutes at 15ft (5m) has been recommended after every dive, and *more recently an additional safety stop of one minute at one-half of the deepest point of the dive has been recommended to further reduce the likelihood of significant bubbling.* The time spent at the safety stops does not have to be counted as "Actual Dive Time" (NAUI's term for "Actual Bottom Time") which is used to find the Repetitive Group after the dive. Actual Dive Time is therefore taken as the total time underwater and may, or may not, include the time at the safety stops.

The Repetitive Groups are based on the off-gassing of the 120-minute tissue compartment, similarly to those of the U.S. Navy, and the Surface Interval Table is, essentially, the U.S. Navy Surface Interval Table. However, with these tables off-gassing is considered to take 24 hours rather than the 12 hours on which the U.S. Navy Tables are based, and the Group A times have been altered accordingly. This means that a repetitive dive is now considered to be any dive within 24 hours of a previous dive(s). A minimum surface interval of one hour between dives is recommended. Repetitive dives deeper than 100ft (30m) are discouraged, as are "bounce" repetitive dives and doing more than three dives in any one day.

Although these tables have not been empirically tested, they are more conservative than the U.S. Navy Tables and should, therefore, be more appropriate for the recreational diver.

TABLE 15.2.2

No-decompression limits (min).

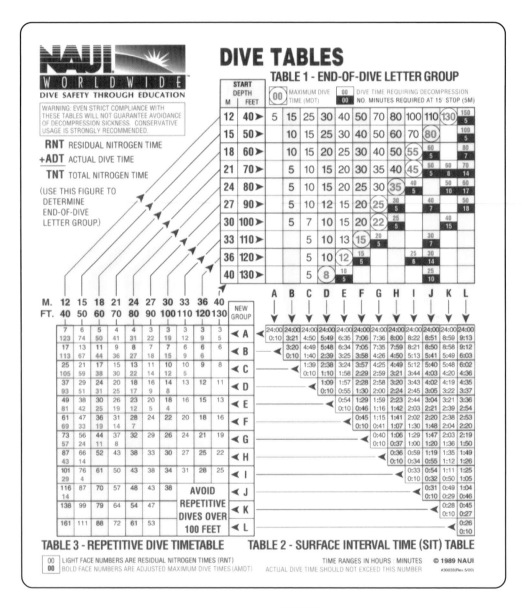

Reprinted with permission of NAUI Worldwide Inc.

16

Probabilistic tables

The traditional ("Deterministic") approach to decompression is based on a model to represent gas exchange that uses the depth, time and breathing gas to calculate the predicted gas loading for the particular dive or point in the dive. In addition, there must be some criteria (e.g. M-Values) to determine when it is safe to ascend. Decompression profiles and tables can be generated from this model and must then be tested and adjusted as required.

The testing requirements can be quite onerous. For example, 400 decompression sickness (DCS)-free tests on a particular profile are required to achieve 95% confidence that the true incidence of DCS would be lower than 1%. However, as a compromise, 20 dives without DCS are generally considered to be an acceptable compromise.[1]

So, although the traditional concept of DCS is that it will occur whenever a certain critical nitrogen level in the tissues is exceeded, in reality, whether or not a particular dive profile will cause DCS varies enormously between individuals, and in a particular individual on different days. None of the traditional decompression models account for this variability in the occurrence of DCS.

Statistical Approach to Decompression Risk

With the availability of modern biophysical, mathematical and statistical evaluation tools, it has become possible to evaluate the risk of DCS in a completely different way.

BACKGROUND

The "probability" of an event occurring is a measure of the chance or likelihood that it will occur. Probability is measured between 0 and 1. If an event has a probability of 0 it cannot occur, and a probability of 1 means that it is certain to occur. The nearer a probability is to 1, the more likely the event will occur. The nearer the probability is to 0, the less likely the event will occur.

When we stay on the surface, our probability of getting decompression sickness, PDCS, is 0. When we dive, our chances of getting DCS increase. If we dive very deeply for a very long time our PDCS increases even more and, if the decompression procedure is very inadequate, our PDCS may get close to 1.

Our chance of getting DCS is influenced by the dive profile. A mathematical equation, known as a *risk function*, can be constructed to predict the PDCS for a particular dive. This can be a simple equation which only depends on depth, a slightly more complex equation depending on gas, depth and time, or a variety of more complex equations that account for other variables such as gas uptake and elimination and/or bubble dynamics, in some ways not unlike those used in the deterministic approach.

Such a risk function will be of the form:

> PDCS = *some mathematical function of the dive (which includes some constants)*.

After experimenting with variety of models, the U.S. Navy eventually developed several decompression models that contained single or multiple compartments, and that employed either purely exponential functions to describe gas kinetics (behavior), or a combination of exponential and linear functions to provide a slower tissue washout than previous models.[2]

The next step is to use available data from actual dives to find values for any constants (parameters) used in the risk function, so that the equation closely matches the data. If a number of exposures to a particular dive profile and whether or not they resulted in DCS is known, the PDCS for that profile can be estimated. For example, if a particular profile was dived 100 times with 4 resultant cases of DCS, the PDCS is approximately [4]/100 or 0.04.* Inserting the PDCS in the left side of the equation will allow any constants to be evaluated. The equations must then be adjusted so that the predicted probabilities match the actual probabilities sufficiently accurately. The resulting equation can then be used to predict the chance of getting DCS after doing various dive profiles.

The method adopted by the U.S. Naval Medical Research Institute (NMRI) researchers is known as the Maximum Likelihood Method. Maximum Likelihood applies a theory, or model, to data, and adjusts the constants within the model (equation) until theoretical predictions and the actual experimental data are in closest possible agreement.

The data used to fit the latest models were compiled from U.S. Navy, Canadian and British chamber dive trials. For the final (USN93) model there were 1038 different dive profiles, representing 3322 man-dives, with a DCS incidence of 6.1% (190 DCS cases, 110 marginal cases).[3] One of the linear-exponential models provided the best fit to the data.[2]

EQUAL RISK TABLES

It is then possible to work backwards and calculate what profiles would be necessary to reduce the PDCS to a pre-defined level. For example, if we wanted to know what time at 18m (60ft) would give a DCS risk of 5%, we put PDCS equal to 0.05 in the equation for 18m (60ft) and find the associated time. In this way, entire decompression schedules can be constructed with each entry carrying the same theoretical DCS risk. A decompression table with a 1% DCS risk for each schedule can be computed or, if preferred, a schedule with 2% risk throughout.

Since at least the early 1980s, the NMRI has been carrying out such an exercise to produce sets of decompression schedules with various associated DCS risks.

In 1985, the NMRI published two new sets of air decompression tables with an equal chance of DCS throughout.[4] These included 1% risk schedules and 5% risk schedules. However, there was no capability for repetitive dives.

The early models were only designed to predict *whether or not* DCS will occur, New and improved models that included the ability to incorporate *when* DCS will occur were later calibrated, tested and used to generate a set of tables with a uniform DCS risk of 2.3% These became known as the USN93 Tables.[3] The same level of 2.3% risk was maintained for decompression dives requiring a stop of up to 20 minutes or less. Some of the USN93 NDLs are shown in Figure 16.1 in the 2.3% column.

---

* This profile does not have a precise PDCS = 0.04. It would be possible to observe four cases of DCS out of a sample of 100 dives of a particular profile, even if the true underlying PDCS was different to 0.04. A statistical analysis as a result of observing four out of 100 reveals that one can be 95% confident that the true PDCS is between 0.011 and 0.099.

The model itself utilizes three compartments with the shortest time constant being just 1.8 minutes. It can be readily extended to cater for repetitive diving by using the concept of 'conditional probability' (i.e. the probability that event A will occur given that event B has already occurred).

Interestingly, when the USN93 model is applied to the 1957 USN Tables, the 1957 NDLs yield a risk higher than 3% for 35 and 40ft (10.5 and 12m), 2-2.5% for 50-100ft (15-30m) and safer than 2% for deeper depths.[3]

Potential problems can arise with probabilistic models if the dives on which they are used are not compatible with the data used to calibrate the model. Although the USN93 model gave results consistent with its own calibration data, it overestimated the risks of more common dives such as no decompression exposures to 60ft (18m) for less than 50minutes.[5] Because the calibration data included few relatively low-risk dives, the risk estimates yielded by the

model had to be extrapolated from dives with a higher risk, and this can lead to inaccuracies

It has been reported that the U.S. Navy has not adopted the USN93 as a replacement for its Standard Air Tables (see Chapter 13) as it was decided that such a change was not necessary or desirable.[5] However, the ascent rate of the Standard Air Tables was reduced to 30ft (9m) per minute.

Other researchers have been designing and refining various probability models and risk estimation tools. Data collected from recreational divers through projects such as the Divers Alert Network (DAN) Project Dive Exploration (or DAN Europe Safe Dive) may be an invaluable source of low-risk data than can be used to refine current and future decompression models and the authors encourage divers to support these valuable projects.

FIGURE 15.1

Equal risk no-decompression limits[4]

Depth	No-D Limit (min)			Depth	No-D Limit (min)		
(msw/fsw)	1%	2.3%	5%	(msw/fsw)	1%	2.3%	5%
9/30	146	245	387	33/110	8	24	43
12/40	63	144	232	36/120	7	21	38
15/50	40	93	156	39/130	5	18	34
18/60	29	64	113	42/140	4	16	31
21/70	21	48	87	45/150	5	16	29
24/80	16	38	70	48/160	4	14	26
27/90	14	32	59	51/170	4	13	24
30/100	11	27	50	54/180	0	12	22

REFERENCES

1. Nishi RY and Tikuisis. Development of decompression tables and models: Statistics and data analysis. *J Human-Environ System* 1999; 2(1):19-31.

2. Parker EC, Survanshi SS, Thalmann ED, Weathersby PK. Statistically Based Decompression Tables VIII: Linear-Exponential Kinetics. Naval Medical Research Institute Report NMRI 92-73, Bethesda,MD; 1992.

3. Survanshi SS, Parker EC, Thalmann ED, Weathersby PK. Statistically Based Decompression Tables XII: Vol 1. Repetiitve decompression tables for air and constant 0.7 ATA PO2 in N2 using a probabilistic model. Naval Medical Research Institute Report NMRI 97-36 (Vol 1), Bethesda,MD; 1997.

4. Weathersby PK, Hays JR, Survanshi SS et al, Statistically Based Decompression Tables II. Equal Risk Air Diving Decompression Schedules". Naval Medical Research Institute Report NMRI 85-17; 1985.

5. Vann RD. Mechanisms and Risks of Decompression. In: Bove AA (ed). Bove and Davis' Diving Medicine, 4th Edn. Philadelphia: Saunders; 2004:127-64.

OTHER SOURCES

Homer BL and Weathersby PK. Statistical aspects of the design and testing of decompression tables. *Undersea Biomed Res* 1985; 12(3):239-49.

Thalmann ED et al, Testing of Decompression Algorithms for use in the U.S. Navy Underwater Decompression Computer. U.S. Navy Experimental Diving Unit Report 11-80; 1980.

Thalmann ED. Phase II Testing of Decompression Algorithms for use in the U.S. Navy Underwater Decompression Computer. U.S. Navy Experimental Diving Unit Report 1-84; 1984.

Thalmann ED. Air-N_2O_2 Decompression Computer Algorithm Development. U.S. Navy Experimental Diving Unit Report 8-85; 1986.

Tikuisis P and Gerth WA. Decompression Theory. In: Brubakk AO, Neuman TS (eds). Physiology and Medicine of Diving, 5th edn. London: Saunders, 2003:419-54.

Weathersby PK et al, On the Likelihood of Decompression Sickness. *J Appl Physiol* 1984; 57(3):815-25.

Weathersby PK, Survanshi SS, Homer BL et al. Statistically Based Decompression Tables 1. Analysis of Standard Air Dives: 1950-1970. Naval Medical Research Institute Report NMRI 85-16; 1986.

Weathersby PK et al. Statistically Based Decompression Tables III: Comparative Risk Using U.S. Navy, British and Canadian Standard Air Schedules. Naval Medical Research Institute Report NRMI 86-50; 1986.

Weathersby PK, Hart BL, Flynn ET, Walker WF. Human Decompression Trial in Nitrogen - Oxygen Diving. Naval Medical Research Institute Report NMRI 86-97; 1986.

RECOMMENDED FURTHER READING

Nishi RY and Tikuisis. Development of decompression tables and models: Statistics and data analysis. *J Human-Environ System* 1999; 2(1):19-31.

Vann RD. Mechanisms and Risks of Decompression. In: Bove AA (ed). Bove and Davis' Diving Medicine, 4th Edn. Philadelphia: Saunders; 2004:127-64.

The authors wish to thank Capt. Paul Weathersby and Dr. Richard Vann for their editorial comments on this chapter.

17

Bühlmann tables

The ZH-L Decompression System

HISTORICAL BACKGROUND

The laboratory of Hyperbaric Physiology of the Medical Clinic of the University of Zurich was established in 1960. The theme of the research, conducted under the guidance of the late Professor Dr. Albert Bühlmann, was that of assessing the well-being and functional ability of the human being in atmospheres of abnormal pressure and composition. The Swiss, up to then lacking a history of decompression research, were free from the shackles of traditional approaches and could begin to introduce new ideas in this area.

The effects of both nitrogen and helium were considered throughout their decompression research and the tolerance to nitrogen in decreased ambient pressure was also investigated due to the local interest in diving in mountain lakes.

FIGURE 17.1

Professor Bühlmann (rear) and Hannes Keller prepare for the first simulated dive to 300m (1000ft) on 25 April 1961.

Reprinted courtesy of the late Prof. Dr. A.A. Bühlmann.

The "Swiss Decompression Theory" evolved from the basic Haldanian approach *with gas uptake and elimination considered to occur exponentially and at the same rate.* The empirical factors utilized in this method were determined experimentally in Zurich and were modified continuously over the years as more data became available.

For decades, 240 minutes was considered to be the longest half-time for nitrogen in man, suggesting that saturation could be assumed to occur within 24 hours. However, in the mid 1960s, experimental evidence indicated that complete saturation with nitrogen may take 3-4 days or longer (and for helium 1 to 1.5 days), and, therefore, the longest half-time for nitrogen was calculated to be 8-10 hours.[1] Eventually, after various trials and experiments, sixteen tissue compartments with half-times for nitrogen of 2.65 to 635 minutes and for helium of 1 to 240 minutes were considered for calculating the equalization of the pressure of the inert gas.[2] Some of these half-times were subsequently modified to accommodate later experimental and practical experience and the half-times utilized in the 1986 Bühlmann Tables range from 4 to 635 minutes.[3] Although the ZH-L (Zurich Limits) system encompasses 16 tissue compartments (ZH-L16), 12 compartments were considered sufficient to generate the decompression tables (ZH-L12). This was later further reduced to 6, and subsequently, 8 compartments for use in certain dive computer algorithms.

The sixteen nitrogen (N_2) half-times are shown in Table 17.1. The helium half-times were largely derived from those of nitrogen, based on the results of some experiments that indicated that the rate of diffusion of helium is 2.65 that of nitrogen. However, this assumption has subsequently been shown to be somewhat unreliable. The postulated half-times used to represent various body organs are shown in Table 17.2.[4]

TABLE 17.1

Sixteen half-time values for N_2 saturation corresponding to various tissue compartments described by the ZH-L$_{16}$ system

(including coefficient values, a and b, for the ZH-86 Tables (see Equation 2 below))

Compt.	Halftime	a	b	Compt.	Halftime	a	b
1	4	1.2594	0.5050	9	109	0.4187	0.9092
2	8	1.0000	0.6514	10	146	0.3798	0.9222
3	12.5	0.8617	0.7222	11	187	0.3498	0.9319
4	18.5	0.7561	0.7825	12	239	0.3223	0.9403
5	27	0.6667	0.8126	13	305	0.2971	0.9477
6	38.3	0.5933	0.8434	14	390	0.2737	0.9544
7	54.3	0.5281	0.8693	15	498	0.2523	0.9602
8	77	0.4701	0.8910	16	635	0.2327	0.9653

TABLE 17.2

N_2 half-times associated with various body organs

Organ	N_2 Half-time (min)
Blood, brain, spinal cord	4 - 18.5
Skin and muscles	27 - 239
Joints and bones	239 - 635

THE ZH-L SYSTEM

As mentioned earlier, Bühlmann used a traditional Haldanian approach to calculate tissue gas uptake and elimination, with both processes presumed to occur exponentially. The equation used to describe this is:

$$pN_2 = pN_2^0 + (pN_2 insp - pN_2^0) \times (1 - 2^{-\Delta t/T})$$ *Equation 1*

where

pN_2 = tissue partial pressure of nitrogen
pN_2^0 = initial partial pressure of nitrogen
$pN_2 insp$ = partial pressure of inspired nitrogen
T = tissue compartment half-time
t = time of exposure

To see how this works, let's look at a tissue compartment with a half-time of 12.5 minutes on a dive to 30m (100ft) for a bottom time of 15 minutes. For simplicity we will assume that the descent was instantaneous.

Let's assume that the diver is at sea-level and has not been diving in the past days. In this case, for simplicity, we will take the partial pressure of nitrogen in the tissue compartment before the dive (pN_2^0) as 0.79bar. (In reality, it is a little lower if we consider the pressure of water vapour in the lungs).

At 30m, the partial pressure of nitrogen in the breathing gas ($pN_2 insp$) is about:

4 x 0.79 = 3.16bar

Substituting the values into *Equation 1*, we get:

pN_2 = 0.79 + (3.16 − 0.79) x (1 − 2$^{-15/12.5}$)
= 0.79 + (2.37) x (1-2$^{-1.2}$)
= 2.128bar

Therefore, the partial pressure of nitrogen in this tissue compartment after 15 minutes at 30m is 2.128bar. This calculation is done for each tissue compartment.

There is a maximum nitrogen pressure that can be tolerated in each tissue compartment at a particular ambient pressure before symptoms of decompression illness occur. The Swiss observed that the difference between the pressure of the inert gas in the tissue and the ambient pressure which could be tolerated without producing symptoms of DCS, the "overpressure" of nitrogen or helium, increases approximately linearly with increasing ambient pressure.

Tissue compartments with shorter half-times are presumed to be able to tolerate higher nitrogen pressures at a given depth (ambient pressure) than the "slower" tissue compartments because they quickly lose their excess nitrogen. Bühlmann believed that the amount of pressure reduction that could be tolerated by a tissue compartment is related to its half-time, and derived two constants *a* and *b* that he used to calculate the safe ascent depth.

The following formulae were used to calculate these constants:

$$a = 2 \times T^{-1/3} \quad \text{and} \quad b = 1.005 - T^{-1/2}$$

Equation 2 below is used to calculate the minimum ambient pressure that can be tolerated by each tissue compartment on ascent, equating to the depth to which the diver can safely ascend.

$$\boxed{Pamb_{tol} = (pN_2 - a) \times b}$$

Equation 2

where
$Pamb_{tol}$ = minimum ambient pressure to which ascent can be made.

So, after the 15 minutes at 30m, we can now calculate the depth we can safely ascend to according to this model.

From Table 17.1, we get a = 0.8618 and b = 0.7222; so

$$Pamb_{tol} = (2.128 - 0.8618) \times 0.7222$$
$$= 0.914\text{bar}$$

0.914bar equates to an ambient pressure less than sea-level so we can (theoretically) safely ascend directly to the surface without

creating an overpressure in this tissue compartment.

However, let's re-visit the calculation with a longer bottom time of 40 minutes of 30m. In this case, we get:

$$pN_2 = 0.79 + (3.16 - 0.79) \times (1 - 2^{-40/12.5})$$
$$= 0.79 + (2.37) \times (1 - 2^{-3.2})$$
$$= 2.902\text{bar}$$
and
$$Pamb_{tol} = (2.902 - 0.8618) \times 0.7222$$
$$= 1.473\text{bar}$$

1.473bar equates to about 4.7m, which is the maximum depth for safe ascent according to this tissue compartment. This would normally create at stop at 6m (20ft), using the 3m (10ft) stop increments of these tables for dives at or near sea-level.

This calculation needs to be done for each compartment to determine the "controlling tissue" (i.e. the tissue that has the deepest safe ascent depth) and the "ceiling" for decompression. Faster tissue compartments usually "control" the ascent on short, relatively shallow dives, whereas slower compartments come into play as dive time and depth increases. The controlling tissue can change at different stages of the dive. Faster compartments reduce their gas loads more rapidly and control will often shift to slower compartments which take longer to lose excess gas. In addition, during ascent some (slower) compartments may still be on-gassing while others (faster) are off-gassing.

Using the ZH-L system, both staged and continuous decompression can be calculated quite easily and computers can easily be programmed to carry out the decompression calculations, which is one reason why so many dive computers programmers and decompression software designers have utilized modified versions of this system.

Bühlmann conducted a variety of experiments including numerous chamber trials with human volunteers to confirm and, where necessary, adjust the coefficients for his system. During these trials, most of which were to depths shallower than 40m, certain mild symptoms of decompression illness were deemed acceptable and adjustments were not always done to try to eliminate these.[5] Test subjects were not monitored for asymptomatic venous bubbles, so this system was created and assessed using overt symptoms of DCS, rather than detectable Doppler bubbles as an endpoint.

With this model, alterations to the No-Decompression Limits and decompression requirements are easily made by adjusting the values of the constants a and / or b. Modified coefficients were used by Bühlmann for his tables to account for the reduced number of half-time compartments used to generate the tables. He also further modified these for use in dive computers (ZHL-16C) in an attempt to try to compensate for the loss of some conservatism gained by 'rounding-off' the depth when using tables rather than computers.

Various dive computer programmers and decompression table and software designers have also further modified the coefficients, often based largely on their own ideas, rather than controlled experimentation and hard scientific data. However, the model itself, with its assumption of exponential desaturation, has inherent limitations in predicting and compensating for bubble formation. This can become more of a problem when the model is applied to situations well beyond the envelope for which it was designed and tested, such as for very deep dives, multiple repetitive dives over multiple days and possibly certain types of multi-level dives. A study, assessing the health outcomes after some deep technical diving guided by the ZHL-16 model, indicated an increased risk of decompression illness with dives deeper than 90m.[6] Various modifications have been made with some derivative dive computer and other decompression software to try to deal with this potential problem.

FEATURES OF THE ZH-L SYSTEM

The difference between the maximum depth of the dive and the depth of the first decompression stop increases as dive depth increases, and the rate of ascent to the first stop is governed by both the maximum depth and the controlling half-time tissue. In practice, for scuba divers, the maximum ascent rate recommended for most dives is 10 m (33ft)/minute, as Swiss experience showed that this appeared to be a safe continuous decompression for saturated tissues in order to reduce bubble formation. Bühlmann believed that this ascent rate enhances gas elimination for dives to depths up to about 30m (100ft). However, he also believed that for depths greater than about 30m (100ft), a faster ascent rate can be beneficial in order to avoid allowing the "slower tissues" to absorb extra gas during the ascent.

Decompression stops are calculated at 0.3bar (3 msw/10fsw) intervals.

For short air dives the Bühlmann 1988 Tables give decompression times which are generally more conservative than the U.S. Navy Tables but less conservative with total decompression time than the DCIEM Tables. Both the ZH-L and DCIEM systems tend to utilize deeper stops than the U.S. Navy.

A typical comparison of a decompression profile given by the Bühlmann 1986, U.S. Navy and DCIEM tables for a decompression dive is shown in Figure 16.1. The ascent procedures recommended by both the Bühlmann (1986) Tables and DCIEM tables often lead to a more gentle reduction in pressure, which in turn may minimize bubble formation in the body tissues.

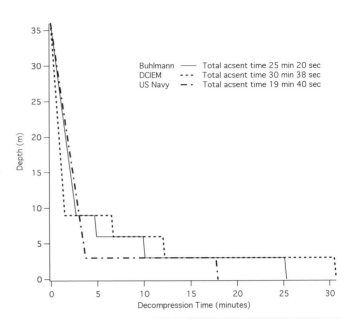

FIGURE 17.2

Comparison of decompression schedules for a dive to 36m (120ft) for a bottom time of 30 minutes

DIVING AT ALTITUDE

As previously mentioned, many Swiss have an avid interest in diving in mountain lakes and consequently, in 1973, decompression tables for diving at sub-atmospheric pressure were developed. They enabled the calculation of decompression after dives at altitudes of up to 3,200m (10,500ft) above sea-level. These tables were then thoroughly tested by Swiss Army divers and published in 1976.[7] Between 1973 and 1983, no cases of decompression illness were reported although well over 1000 real dives were performed, many of these being repetitive dives.[2]

The later ZH-L$_{16}$ system suggests somewhat different decompressions to those prescribed in the earlier tables, but allows a similar nitrogen excess on surfacing. The Bühlmann (1986) Tables were tested quite extensively before being released. A total of 544 real dives were carried out at altitude with no cases of decompression sickness resulting. 254 of the dives were carried out in Switzerland at altitudes between 1,000-2,600m (3,300-8,500ft), and 290 dives were done in Lake Titicaca, 3,800m (12,500ft) above sea-level. Most of the dives in Lake Titicaca were no-

stop dives using an ascent rate of 10m (33ft)/minute, many of which were repetitive.[8,9,10]

For dives above sea-level it is important to consider whether the divers will reach the mountain lake quickly and then dive immediately, or whether they will be at altitude for some time prior to the dive, thus commencing diving with a sub-normal nitrogen pressure (PN$_2$) in their tissues. To allow greater safety these tables assume that the diver had travelled to altitude very quickly and, consequently, has not yet adapted to the decreased atmospheric pressure. Adapting to altitude decreases the PN$_2$ in the tissues and thus provides additional safety. Furthermore, the supersaturation factor on surfacing was chosen to allow for a further reduction in pressure, which may occur as a result of travelling by plane or car to a higher place after the dive.

FLYING AFTER DIVING

Additional experiments were conducted to determine the surface intervals required before a diver may be subjected to further decreases in atmospheric pressure. On the basis of these experiments, reduced coefficients were calculated and have been incorporated in the tables to determine the period of time required before flying after diving ("waiting times"). The waiting times were calculated to allow a reduction in ambient pressure to 0.6bar (i.e. approx 4,100m/13,500ft), as this is the lowest cabin pressure not regarded as a technical failure.

REPETITIVE DIVING

Joints and bones have the least tolerance to an excess of inert gas and release any excess gas only very slowly. The 120-minute tissue half-time, which is the longest utilized in the U.S. Navy Tables (or the 240 minute tissue in the Exceptional Exposure Tables), may sometimes be inadequate in situations when repetitive dives are undertaken for a number of days in succession, such as on diving holidays. Bühlmann believed that, in these situations, the longer half-times of

nitrogen, with the lower tolerance towards nitrogen shown by the slower tissues, must be taken into consideration.

In the Swiss system, the inert gas pressure in the tissues with nitrogen half-times between 305-635 minutes play a leading role during a surface interval and, consequently, with repetitive dives. The Surface Interval Table and Residual Nitrogen Table are both based on all nitrogen half-times up to 635 minutes. This allows a better representation of the body's (theoretical) gas loading during, and after, a surface interval, than can be gained with the single tissue repetitive system such as that used in the U.S. Navy Tables. However, this also means that, despite the longer half-times used, the Bühlmann Tables may give less conservative No-Decompression Limits than the U.S. Navy Tables for some repetitive dive situations.

FIGURE 17.3
The hypo/hyperbaric facilities at the University of Zurich.
The water chamber is below the spherical chamber in the front.

Photo courtesy of the late Prof. Dr. A.A. Bühlmann.

The Bühlmann (1986) Tables

The Bühlmann 1986 Tables, derived using the ZH-L$_{12}$ system, were published in order to provide recreational divers with No-Decompression Limits and decompression stops for both single and repetitive dives.

The following definitions and rules apply to the tables:

DEFINITIONS

Depths listed are the maximum depths reached during a dive.

Bottom Time is the time from leaving the surface until commencing the final ascent to the surface or to any decompression stop(s).

Decompression Stop Time is the time actually spent at that stop. It does not include the time taken to ascend to it.

Repetitive Group is a measure of excess nitrogen remaining in the body after a dive.

Surface Interval is the time from surfacing from a dive to commencing the next descent.

Residual Nitrogen Time is a measure of the amount of excess nitrogen still in the body at the end of the surface interval. It is the time that the diver must consider that he has already spent at the planned depth of the repetitive dive when commencing a repetitive dive.

RULES

- The ascent rate must not exceed 10m (33ft)/minute.*
- For interim depths use the next greater depth on the table.
- For interim times use the next longer time on the table.
  e.g. For a dive to 17m (56ft) for 73 minutes look up the decompression for 18m (60ft) for 80 minutes.
- For "strenous" dives use the decompression prescribed for the next longer time increment.
  e.g. For a strenous dive to 17m (56ft) for 73 minutes look up the decompression for 18m (60ft) for 90 minutes.
- Repetitive dives require additional time to be added. This time is determined by using the repetitive dive table and is called the Residual Nitrogen Time (RNT). The RNT is a measure of any excess nitrogen already in a diver's body before a repetitive dive.
- If the depth of the repetitive dive is in between two increments then take the **shallower** figure when calculating the residual nitrogen time (This gives a greater RNT and is thus safer).
- A safety stop of 1 minute at 3m (10ft) is required after every no-decompression stop dive at altitudes up to 700m (2,300ft), and a stop of 1 minute at 2m (7ft) is required after dives at higher altitudes. Professor Bühlmann has stated that this stop is not necessary for actual decompression purposes but it suggested in order to control the ascent rate and ensure an orderly and safe arrival at the surface.#

---

* This is rounded-off to 30ft/minute on the imperial version of the tables.
# The authors recommend that, in light of current knowledge, the safety of stop should be modified to 3-5 minutes at 5-6m (15-20ft) with an additional stop of one minute at half the maximum depth of the dive for dives deeper than about 24m (80ft).

THE BÜHLMANN (1986) TABLES

TABLE 17.3
0 - 700m table

NO-DECOMPRESSION LIMITS — AIR DIVING DECOMPRESSION TABLE

Depth m	BT min	Stops 6	Stops 3	RG
12	125		1	G
15	75		1	G
15	90		7	G
18	51		1	F
18	70		11	G
21	35		1	E
21	50		8	F
21	60		16	G
24	25		1	E
24	35		4	F
24	40		8	F
24	50		17	G
24	60	4	24	G
27	20		1	E
27	30		5	F
27	35		10	F
27	40	2	13	G
27	45	3	18	G
27	50	6	22	G
30	17		1	D
30	25		5	E
30	30	2	7	F
30	35	3	14	G
30	40	5	17	G
30	45	9	23	G

m	min	9	6	3	RG
33	14			1	D
	20			4	E
	25		2	7	F
	30		4	11	G
	35		6	17	G
	40	2	8	23	G
36	12			1	D
	20		2	5	E
	25		4	9	F
	30	2	5	15	G
	35	2	8	23	G
39	10			1	D
	15			4	E
	20		3	7	F
	25	2	4	12	G
	30	3	7	18	G
	35	5	9	28	G
42	9			1	D
	12			4	D
	15		1	5	E
	18		4	6	F
	21	2	4	10	F
	24	3	6	16	G
	27	4	7	19	G

m	min	12	9	6	3	RG
45	12				5	E
	15			3	5	E
	18		2	4	9	F
	21		3	5	13	G
	24		4	6	18	G
48	9				3	E
	12			2	5	E
	15			4	6	F
	18		3	4	10	F
	21		4	6	16	G
51	9				4	E
	12			3	6	E
	15		2	4	8	F
	18		4	5	13	G
	21	3	4	7	18	G
54	9				5	E
	12		1	4	6	E
	15		3	4	10	F
	18	1	3	6	17	G
57	9			2	5	E
	12		2	4	6	E
	15	1	2	4	11	F
	18	3	4	7	18	G

Safety stop: 1 min at 3 m → Ascent rate: 10 m/min

Altitude 0–700 m above sea level

TABLE 17.4
Repetitive dive table (metric)

BUEHLMANN TABLE

REPETITIVE DIVE TIME-TABLE 0–2500 m above sea level

Surface Interval Times   "0" ✈

RG at start of surface interval:

							"0"	✈
						A	2	2
					B	20	2	2
				C	10	25	3	3
			D	10	15	30	3	3
		E	10	15	25	45	4	3
	F	20	30	45	75	90	8	4
G	25	45	60	75	100	130	12	5
G	**F**	**E**	**D**	**C**	**B**	**A**	hrs	hrs

RG at end of surface interval

Example:
Previous dive: 24 m, 35 min = Repetitive Group **(RG) = F**
- after 45 min at surface: **RG = C**
- after 90 min at surface: **RG = A**
  (intermediate time: use next **shorter** interval time)
- after 4 hrs: flying is permitted
- after 8 hrs: **RG = "0"**, no more Residual Nitrogen Time **(RNT)**

RG for No-Decompression Dives and RNT for Repetitive Dives

Repetitive dive depth m (intermediate depths: use next **shallower** depth)

RG	9	12	15	18	21	24	27	30	33	36	39	42	45	48	51	54	57
A	25	19	16	14	12	11	10	9	8	7	7	6	6	6	5	5	5
B	37	25	20	17	15	13	12	11	10	9	8	7	7	6	5	5	5
C	55	37	29	25	22	20	18	16	14	12	11	10	9	8	7	7	6
D	81	57	41	33	28	24	21	19	17	15	14	13	11	10	9	9	8
E	105	82	59	44	37	30	26	23	21	19	17	16	14	13	12	11	10
F	130	111	88	68	53	42	35	30	27	24	21	19	17	16	15	14	13

Example: RG = C at end of surface interval. Planned depth of repetitive dive = 27 m. **RNT = 18 min**, to be added to Bottom Time (BT) of repetitive dive.

TABLE 17.5
0 - 2,300ft table

NO-DECOMPRESSION LIMITS — AIR DIVING DECOMPRESSION TABLE

Depth ft	BT min	Stops 20	Stops 10	RG
40	125		1	G
50	75		1	G
	90		7	G
60	51		1	F
	70		11	G
70	35		1	E
	50		8	F
	60		16	G
80	25		1	E
	35		4	F
	40		8	F
	50		17	G
	60	4	24	G
90	20		1	E
	30		5	F
	35		10	F
	40	2	13	G
	45	3	18	G
	50	6	22	G
100	17		1	D
	25		5	E
	30	2	7	F
	35	3	14	G
	40	5	17	G
	45	9	23	G

ft	min	30	20	10	RG
110	14			1	D
	20			4	E
	25		2	7	F
	30		4	11	G
	35		6	17	G
	40	2	8	23	G
120	12			1	D
	20			5	E
	25		2	9	F
	30	2	5	15	G
	35	2	8	23	G
130	10			1	D
	15			4	E
	20		3	7	F
	25		4	12	G
	30	3	7	18	G
	35	5	9	28	G
140	9			1	D
	12			4	D
	15		1	6	E
	18		4	6	E
	21	2	4	10	F
	24	3	6	16	F
	27	4	7	19	G

ft	min	40	30	20	10	RG
150	12				5	E
	15			3	5	E
	18		2	4	9	F
	21		3	5	13	G
	24		4	6	18	G
160	9				3	E
	12				5	E
	15		3	4	6	F
	18		3	4	10	F
	21		4	6	16	G
170	9				4	E
	12			3	6	E
	15		2	4	8	F
	18		4	5	13	F
	21	3	4	7	18	G
180	9			1	4	E
	12		1	4	6	E
	15		3	4	6	F
	18	1	3	6	17	F
190	9			2	5	E
	12		2	4	8	E
	15	1	3	5	11	F
	18	3	4	7	18	F

Altitude **0-2300 ft** above sea level

Ascent rate: 30 ft/min — Safety stop: 1 min at 10 ft

TABLE 17.6
Repetitive dive table (imperial)

BUEHLMANN TABLE

REPETITIVE DIVE TIME-TABLE 0-8200 ft above sea level

Surface Interval Times — "0" ✈

RG at start of surface interval:

							"0"	✈
A						2	2	
B					20	2	2	
C				10	25	3	3	
D			10	15	30	3	3	
E		10	15	25	45	4	3	
F	20	30	45	75	90	8	4	
G	25	45	60	75	100	130	12	5
G	F	E	D	C	B	A	hrs	hrs

RG at end of surface interval

Example:
Previous dive: 80 ft, 35 min = Repetitive Group (RG) = F
– after 45 min at surface: **RG = C**
– after 90 min at surface: **RG = A**
   (intermediate time: use next **shorter** interval time)
– after 4 hrs: flying is permitted
– after 8 hrs: **RG = "0"**, no more Residual Nitrogen Time (**RNT**)

RG for No-Decompression Dives and RNT for Repetitive Dives
Repetitive dive depth ft (intermediate depths use next **shallower** depth)

RG	30	40	50	60	70	80	90	100	110	120	130	140	150	160	170	180	190
A	25	19	16	14	12	11	10	9	8	7	7	6	6	6	5	5	5
B	37	25	20	17	15	13	12	11	10	9	8	7	7	6	5	5	5
C	55	37	29	25	22	20	18	16	14	12	11	10	9	8	7	7	5
D	81	57	41	33	28	24	21	19	17	15	14	13	11	10	9	9	8
E	105	82	59	44	37	30	26	23	21	19	17	16	14	13	12	11	10
F	130	111	88	68	53	42	35	30	27	24	21	19	17	16	15	14	13

Example: RG = C at end of surface interval. Planned depth of repetitive dive = 90 ft **RNT = 18 min**, to be added to Bottom Time (BT) of repetitive dive.

TABLE 17.7
701 - 2,500m table

NO-DECOMPRESSION LIMITS / AIR DECOMPRESSION TABLE

Depth m	BT min	6	4	2	RG
9	238			1	G
12	99			1	G
	110			4	G
15	62			1	F
	70			4	G
18	44			1	F
	50			4	F
	60			11	G
21	30			1	E
	35			2	F
	40			5	F
	45			9	G
	50		1	13	G
	55		3	17	G
24	22			1	F
	30			3	F
	35			7	F
	40		2	11	G
	45		4	16	G
27	18			1	D
	20			2	E
	25			4	F
	30		2	7	F
	35		4	11	G
	40	1	6	16	G

m	min	9	6	4	2	RG
30	15				1	D
	20				3	E
	25			2	6	F
	30		1	4	11	G
	35		2	7	15	G
	40	1	5	10	20	G
33	12				1	D
	15				2	E
	20			2	4	F
	25		2	3	9	G
	30	1	3	6	14	G
	35	2	4	9	20	G
36	10				1	D
	15			1	3	E
	20		1	3	6	F
	25		3	5	12	G
	30	3	3	8	19	G
39	9				1	D
	12				3	E
	15			2	4	F
	18		2	3	7	F
	21		3	4	10	G
	24	2	3	6	15	G
	27	4	4	8	18	G

m	min	9	6	4	2	RG
42	8				1	D
	12			1	4	E
	15		1	3	5	F
	18		3	4	8	F
	21	3	3	5	13	G
	24	4	4	7	18	G
45	9				3	D
	12			3	3	E
	15		3	3	6	F
	18	2	3	4	11	F
	21	4	4	7	16	G
48	9			1	4	E
	12		1	3	4	F
	15	2	2	4	9	G
	18	4	5	5	14	G
51	6			1	2	E
	9		1	1	3	F
	12	1	2	3	5	F
	15	3	3	4	11	G
54	6			1	2	D
	9		1	3	3	F
	12	2	3	3	7	F
	15	4	4	6	13	G

Safety stop: 1 min at 2 m — *Ascent rate: 10 m/min*

Altitude **701–2500 m** above sea level

Tables 16.3-16.7 are protected by copyright and are reprinted courtesy of the late Prof. Dr. A.A. Bühlmann

USING THE BUHLMANN (1986) TABLES

A. PLANNING SINGLE DIVES

Enter Table 17.3 (or 17.5) at the exact, or next greater, depth box. The top, bold figure in the "Bottom Time" column (column 2) is the No-Decompression Limit (NDL) for that depth. If the planned dive exceeds this time, move down column 2, to the exact, or next longer, time then move right to read off the stops and, if required, the Repetitive Group at the end of the dive.

Example 1.

You are planning a single, no-decompression stop dive to 22m (73ft) and wish to know the NDL.

Enter the 24m (80ft) box. The NDL is written in bold at the top of the Bottom Time column (column 2). It is *25* minutes. Remember that a safety stop of at least 1 minute at 3m (10ft) is required.

Example 2.

What decompression is required for a dive to 36m (120ft) for 18 minutes?

Enter the 36m (120ft) box and read down the second column until the exact, or next longer, time is found, in this case 20 minutes. Moving right the decompression is found to be *2 minutes at 6m (20ft) followed by 5 minutes at 3m (10ft)*. Remember that the maximum ascent rate must be 10m/minute (33ft/minute).

The Repetitive Group after the dive, given in the last column, is *E*.

Note:

1. The time taken to ascend from 36m (120ft) to the 6m (20ft) stop is *not* included in the 6m (20ft) stop time of 2 minutes. It should take 3 minutes to ascend to this first stop.

2. The time taken to ascend from 6m (20ft) to 3m (10ft) (i.e. 20s) and from 3m (10ft) to the surface (20s) is not included in the 3m (10ft) stop time. The diver must spend the entire 5 minutes at 3m (10ft).

Example 3.

Calculate the decompression required for a dive to 31m (10 ft) for 36 minutes.

Enter the 33m (110ft) box and move down column 2 until 40 minutes is selected. Moving right, the decompression is found to be *2 minutes at 9m (30ft), 8 minutes at 6m (20ft) and 23 minutes at 3m (10ft)*. The Repetitive Group after the dive is *G*.

B. PLANNING REPETITIVE DIVES

Example 4.

Calculate the decompression required for the following pair of dives: 25m (83ft) for 20 minutes followed 2½ hours later by a dive to 18m (60ft) for 50 minutes.

Upon entering the 27m (90ft) box the NDL for 25m (83ft) is found to be 20 minutes. Hence, no decompression stop is required for the first dive. The Repetitive Group immediately after the dive is *E*.

Enter the upper portion of Table 17.4 (or 17.6), from the left, at *E* (the Repetitive Group), and move right until the 2½ hour surface interval is found. It is between 45 minutes and 4 hours, so, moving down, the Repetitive Group at the end of the interval is found to be *A*.

Enter the lower portion of Table 17.4, from the left, at *A*, and move right until intersecting

the column corresponding to the depth of the repetitive dive, in this case, 18m (60ft). The figure *14* which appears, represents the time to be considered already spent at 18m (60ft) before the repetitive dive. These 14 minutes must be added to the proposed bottom time in order to compute the correct decompression. Therefore, this repetitive dive has an equivalent bottom time of 50 + 14 = *64* minutes. From Table 17.3 the decompression required is found to be *11 minutes at 3m (10ft)*. After the dive the Repetitive Group is *G*.

Example 5.

You wish to carry out two no-decompression stop dives; the first to 20m (66ft) followed 3 hours later by a dive to 32m (106ft). Calculate the maximum allowable bottom time for each dive.

Enter the 21m (70ft) box. The NDL for 21m (70ft) is *35* minutes which is the maximum allowable time for the first dive. After this 20m (66ft) for 35 minutes dive, the Repetitive Group is *E*. (Remember the safety stop).

Entering the upper portion of Table 17.4 at *E*, move across to find the surface interval of 3 hours. It lies between 45 minutes and 4 hours, so the Repetitive Group after the surface interval is *A*.

Enter the lower portion of Table 17.4, from the left, at *A*, and move right until the 30m (100ft) row *(i.e. shallower in this case)* is intersected. The Residual Nitrogen Time is *9* minutes. Thus, your body still has an excess amount of nitrogen as if you had already spent 9 minutes at 32m (106ft) before the dive.

Returning to Table 17.3 and entering the 33m (110ft) box, the NDL is found to be 14 minutes. You have already used 9 minutes of this (i.e. your RNT), so you may still dive for 5 minutes. Hence, the maximum allowable bottom time for the second dive is *5* minutes. Again, do not forget to do the safety stop en route to the surface.

Example 6.

You are planning to do two dives. The first is to 34m (112ft) for 18 minutes and the second, five hours later, is to be a no-decompression stop dive to 27m (90ft). Calculate the decompression required for the first dive and the maximum allowable no-decompression stop bottom time for the second dive.

Enter the 36m (120ft) box, and move down column 2, to 20 minutes. Moving across, the required decompression is *2 minutes at 6m (20ft) and 5 minutes at 3m (10ft)*. The Repetitive Group is *E*.

Entering the upper part of Table 17.4 at *E*, move across to find the surface interval of 5 hours. This row ends at 4.00 hours, which means that, for group *E*, after 4.00 hours, no residual nitrogen needs to be added. In other words, the previous dive can be ignored. This is what RG "0" means. This situation occurs after a surface interval of 2.00 hr for group B, 3.00 hr for group C and up to 12.00 hr for group G. Therefore, to find the allowable bottom time for the second dive, return to Table 17.3, enter the 27m (90ft) box, and the maximum bottom time is found to be *20* minutes.

Determining the Repetitive Group after dives with Bottom Times less than the No-Decompression Limit

This is done by referring to the lower part of Table 17.4, the RG for No-Decompression Dives.

Example 7.

Find the Repetitive Group after a dive to 9m (30ft) for 30 minutes.

Enter the lower half of Table 17.4 at the 9m (30ft) column, and move downwards to find the 30 minutes (or next greater) Bottom Time. In this case we get 37 minutes and, by moving across to the left, the Repetitive Group is found to be Group *B*.

Similarly, after a dive to 30m (100ft) for 7 minutes we are in Group *A* (limit is 9 minutes) and, after a dive to 18m (60ft) for 38 minutes we are in Group *E* (limit is 44 minutes).

If the Bottom Time is exactly (or more than) the No-Decompression Limit the RG must be taken from Table 17.3. (The RG's in Table 17.3 do not always coincide with those in Table 17.4).

C. FLYING AFTER DIVING

The surface interval required before flying (or otherwise ascending) to normal commercial cabin altitude (2,400m/8,000ft) is found in the following manner:

Use the Repetitive Group after the last dive to enter the upper part of Table 17.4. Move across until entering the rightmost column, with the picture of the airplane. This gives the time required before flying. Theoretically, after this interval it should be safe to fly. (See comments about this in Chapter 25).

Note:

For calculating the waiting times Bühlmann used 0.6bar (i.e. approx 4100m/13,500ft) was this is the lowest cabin pressure which is not regarded as a technical failure.

Example 8.

What surface interval is required before flying after a dive to 27m (90ft) for 20 minutes?

After a dive to 27m (90ft) for 20 minutes, you are in Repetitive Group E. Entering Table 17.4 at E, and moving across, you will find that after 3 hours it should be safe to fly. If, after the dive, you were in group F, you would have to wait at least 4 hours before flying.*

---

* Current evidence with flying after diving indicates that such a short surface interval may be clearly inadequate.

D. DIVING AT ALTITUDE

Table 17.3 can be used for diving at altitudes between 0-700 metres. Table 17.7 is for use for dives at altitudes 701-2500 metres above sea level. This table is governed by the same rules as the 0-700 meter table and utilizes the same repetitive dive timetable (Table 17.4).

The equivalent 701-2500 meter table is not available in feet.

The Bühlmann Tables used for the first diving expedition to Lale Titicaca are shown in Appendix C. These were calculated for altitudes between 2,501 - 4,500m (8,200-14,800ft).

This author owes a debt of gratitude to the late Professor Dr. Bühlmann for providing various reports and for editing the text and examples in this chapter in the original edition. Sadly Dr. Bühlmann died on 16 March 1994.

Note: Dr. Max Hahn, a German physical scientist and enthusiastic and highly experienced technical diver and instructor, used the ZH-L system to derive the Bühlmann / Hahn Tables that were widely used in Germany for many years and were described in the previous edition of this book. Dr. Hahn also created a ZH-L-based algorithm that was incorporated in an early dive computer (Dacor Microbrain). Max Hahn tragically died in a rebreather accident on 11 June 2002, still doing what he loved at the age of 70.

REFERENCES

1. Bühlmann AA, Frey P, Keller H, Saturation and desaturation with N_2 and He at 4 ATA. *J Appl Physiol* 1967; 23:458-62.

2. Bühlmann AA. Decompression-Decompression Sickness. Heidelberg: Springer-Verlag; 1984.

3. Bühlmann AA. Computation of low risk compression. Computation model and results of experimental decompression research. *Schweiz Med Wochenschr,* 1988; 118(6):185-97.

4. Uwatec. Aladin Pro Manual. Hallwil; 1989.

5. Bühlmann AA. Personal communications.

6. Doolette DJ. Decompression practice and health outcome during a technical diving project. *SPUMS J* 2004; 34(4):189-93.

7. Boni M, Schibli RA, Nussberger P, Bühlmann AA. Diving at diminished atmospheric pressure: air decompression tables for different altitudes. *Undersea Biomed Res* 1976; 3 (3):189-204.

8. Bühlmann AA. Diving at Altitude and Flying After Diving, UHMS Symposium, *The Physiological Basis of Decompression*, Duke University Medical Centre; 1987.

9. Moody M. Exercise Paddington Diamond. Report on Exercise Paddington Diamond, Lake Titicaca, Bolivia, May 1987. Viersen; Ordinance Services; 1988.

10. Moody M. Personal communications.

OTHER SOURCES

Bühlmann AA. The Validity of a Multi-Tissue Model in Sport Diving Decompression. *Proceedings of the Diving Officers' Conference*, BS-AC, London; 1986.

Bühlmann AA. Decompression After Repeated Dives. *Undersea Biomed Res* 1987; 14(1):59-66.

Bühlmann AA. Personal communications.

RECOMMENDED FURTHER READING

Bühlmann AA. Decompression-Decompression Sickness. Heidelberg: Springer-Verlag; 1984

© Gary Bell

EXERCISES ON THE BÜHLMANN (1986) TABLES

1. Determine the No-Decompression Limits (NDLs) and associated Repetitive Groups for dives to the following depths:

   (a) 16m (53ft)   (b)   22m (73ft)

   (c) 40m (132ft) (d)   26m (86ft)

2. Calculate the decompression required and associated Repetitive Groups after the following single dives:

   (a) 17m (56ft) for 67 minutes
   (b) 24m (80ft) for 51 minutes
   (c) 35m (116ft) for 15 minutes.

3. Determine the Residual Nitrogen Times after the following dives and Surface Intervals:

   (a) 1st dive: 20m (66ft) for 35 minutes
       Surface Interval: $2^1/2$hr

       2nd dive: 16m.

   (b) 1st dive: 33m (110ft) for 20 minutes
       Surface Interval: 30 minutes
       2nd dive: 27m (90ft).

4. Calculate the maximum allowable No-Decompression Stop Bottom Time for the following repetitive dives:

   (a) 1st dive: 21m (70ft) for 50 minutes
       Surface Interval: 6hr
       2nd dive: 18m (60ft).

   (b) 1st dive: 36m (120ft) for 12 minutes
       Surface Interval: 4hr
       2nd dive: 30m (100ft).

5. Calculate the decompression required for the following group of dives:

       1st dive: 17m (56ft) for 60 minutes
       Surface Interval: 4hr
       2nd dive: 47m (155 ft) for 6 minutes
       Surface Interval: $4^1/2$hr
       3rd dive: 24m (80ft) for 25 minutes.

6. Determine the Surface Intervals required before flying after the following dives:

   (a) 15m (50ft) for 45 minutes
   (b) 9m (30ft) for 70 minutes
   (c) 36m (120ft) for 19 minutes.

ANSWERS

1. (a) 51,F (b) 25,E (c) 9,D (d) 20,E
2. (a) 11 min at 3m (10ft), G
   (b) 4 min at 6m (20ft) and 24 min at 3m(10ft), G
   (c) 2 min at 6m (20ft) and 5 min at 3m (10ft), E
3. (a) 16 (b) 12
4. (a) 37 (b) 17
5. 11 min at 3m (10ft), 2 min at 6m (20ft) and 5 min at 3m (10ft),
   safety stop of 1 min at 3m (10ft).
6. (a) 3hr (b) 3hr (c) 3hr.

17

The DCIEM sport diving tables

HISTORICAL BACKGROUND

Canadian decompression research began in 1962 at a military research facility that became known as the Defense and Civil Institute of Environmental Medicine (DCIEM), recently renamed Defense Research Development Canada (DRDC, Toronto). In the 1960s, Kidd and Stubbs set out to develop an instrument that could monitor a diver's depth-time profile, and provide instantaneous decompression information whenever complicated dive profiles were undertaken, or where wide variations of gas mixtures were used. In these situations, the traditional tabular approach to determine decompression was inadequate.

Initially, their decompression computer was based on the traditional Haldanian model in order to duplicate the U.S. Navy 1958 Standard Air Tables. However, parameters were changed and the model was modified until a very low incidence of decompression sickness (DCS) was achieved.

A variety of dives were tested, ranging from fixed depth dives, random depth dives and repetitive dives. Within five years they had developed a successful computer, based on 5,000 man-dives.

The final configuration of the KS (Kidd-Stubbs) computer algorithm utilized a bulk diffusion "serial model", in which the tissue compartments were connected in series instead of the separate parallel arrangement used by Haldane. In 1970, the KS model was adjusted in order to increase its safety in the 200-300fsw (60-90msw) range.[1] The result became known as the Kidd-Stubbs 1971 Model.

DCIEM decompression computer research eventually led to the release of an early microprocessor-based dive computer marketed to sport divers in the late 1970s. The computer, known as the "Cyberdiver", although very expensive and bulky by current standards, was a pioneer of micro-processor dive computers.[2]

The KS 1971 Decompression Model was used for some time at DCIEM but a few deficiencies became apparent. One of the problems was that the No-Decompression Limits were too conservative in some cases (especially at shallow depths), some limits being about half that of the Royal Navy and U.S. Navy Tables. In a few other areas, the model lacked sufficient conservatism. Consequently, more research and modifications were deemed necessary.[3]

THE DCIEM MODEL

In the early 1970s, a dive and decompression databank was established at DCIEM with a complete record of all research dives since 1964. This databank has been maintained and is now considered to be the most comprehensive diving database in the world.

In order to utilize the experience recorded on the database, the KS Model was chosen as the basis for a new set of air decompression tables. Doppler monitoring of dive profiles was introduced at DCIEM and, since 1979, has been used extensively during the development and testing of the tables as described below. The necessary modifications were made to the KS 1971 Model, and the earlier problems and anomalies that existed were overcome. The new decompression model became known as the DCIEM 1983 Decompression Model.

The DCIEM serial model assumes that the tissue compartments are connected in a series. Only the first compartment is exposed to ambient pressure and, as gas builds up in this compartment it bleeds into the next compartment, and so on. In the Haldanian model, each compartment is exposed to ambient pressure and loads up simultaneously. Each of the four tissue compartments in the DCIEM model has the same half-time, which is approximately 21 minutes. The model utilizes the concept of allowable surfacing supersaturation ratios. Critical ratios of 1.92 and 1.73 are used in the initial two compartments, while the pressure levels in the other compartments are not used to calculate the depth from which a diver can safely ascend. [4]

FIGURE 18.1

DCIEM Serial Decompression Model

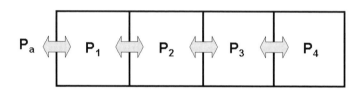

Features of the DCIEM 1983 model

The DCIEM 1983 Model produces decompression times that are more conservative than the U.S. Navy Tables, and the decompression profiles have deeper first stops. **The DCIEM tables were rigorously tested during test dives with working divers in cold water**. For strenuous dives in cold water, the U.S. Navy procedure is to decompress according to the next longer bottom time. The resulting times are somewhat comparable to the DCIEM 1983 times.

The DCIEM model was used to generate a complete set of diving tables, including standard air and helium-oxygen decompression, repetitive dive procedures, corrections for diving at altitude, in-water oxygen decompression and surface decompression with oxygen.[5,6] The modifications for helium-oxygen diving were accomplished by adding another set of four serial compartments in parallel to the set for air diving.[7]

Testing

The DCIEM tables have been extensively tested using specially designed Doppler ultrasonic bubble detectors. More than 900 man-dives were performed during the validation dive series over a two year period.[1] Because the model was continuous, and because of the large database of test dives done on the original K-S model, it seemed unnecessary to retest a large number of depth and bottom time combinations.

During the tests, the dive subjects were monitored for bubbles at both the precordial site (right ventricle and/or pulmonary artery) and the subclavian sites (left and right shoulders). At the precordial site, a reading was first taken when the diver stood at rest, and another reading was taken when the diver performed a deep knee-bend. At the subclavian site, the diver was initially monitored while at rest and then again after clenching the fist on the side being monitored. The Doppler signals were recorded on audio magnetic tape while being assessed aurally by experienced technicians.

The bubble signals were classified according to the Kisman-Masurel (KM) code which utilizes three criteria, each on a scale from 0 to 4. (Other systems only use 2 criteria to establish bubble grades). The criteria used were the number of bubbles per cardiac cycle, the percentage of cardiac cycles with bubble signals and the amplitude of the bubble signals relative to the background sounds. The resulting 3-digit code is converted to bubble grades from 0 to 4, resulting in a similar bubble grade to that developed by Spencer (and used to assess the PADI Recreational Dive Planner).

The divers were monitored before the dive(s) and at half-hour intervals for at least two hours after diving. When repetitive dives were undertaken, the divers were monitored between the dives as well as after the second dive.

The test dives were conducted in DCIEM's main hyperbaric facility which can accommodate simultaneous test dives with wet-working divers in cold water at 41-50°F (5-10°C), as well as dry-resting divers in the large dry chamber. All dives were done using a real-time on-line decompression computer, following the exact decompression profile specified by the DCIEM 1983 Decompression Model. The Standard Air Table was tested by 267 man-dives. Fifty-five dives had decompression times shorter than 30 minutes, and 90% of these subjects showed no, or few, detectable bubbles. Eighty-four no-decompression stop dives were tested with no detectable bubbles resulting. No cases of DCS were observed. The remaining 128 dives (66 single dives and 62 repetitive dive pairs) were near, or at, the normal air diving limit with decompression times between 48 and 88 minutes. Eight cases of DCS occurred after single dives, and 4 cases occurred after the second dive of a repetitive dive pair. However, some of these incidents are believed to have other contributing causes not attributable to the dive profiles alone.[1]

No diving tables can be expected to totally eliminate the occurrence of decompression sickness, but the DCIEM Tables are considered by many experts to be far safer than most other published tables. In many places they have been used as a benchmark for assessing decompression risk. *The DCIEM tables were not designed to be bubble-free, and low bubble grades were deemed acceptable during the assessment and finalization of some of the limits.*

There are little available data on the use of the DCIEM Sport Diving Tables by recreational divers in the field. However, they appear to be sound, well-tested tables (i.e. on rectangular dives) that should generally be suitable for the recreational diver. However, as with any table, an individual diver's susceptibility to DCS must still be factored in when planning the dive profile and bottom time for a dive.

DCIEM Sport Diving Tables

The DCIEM Sport Diving Tables used for the following exercises is the version published in 1995.[8]

DEFINITIONS, DESCRIPTION AND RULES

DEFINITION OF TERMS

Depth - the maximum depth of a dive conducted at sea level.

Bottom Time - the total time from beginning of Descent to beginning of direct Ascent to the surface.

No-D Dive - a dive that does not exceed the No-D Limit for a given depth.

No-D Limit - the maximum Bottom Time that a diver may spend at a given depth without having to conduct a scheduled Decompression Stop before surfacing.

Decompression Stop - a scheduled interruption of the Ascent at a specified depth for a specified time to allow for the elimination of excess nitrogen.

Decompression Dive - a dive that exceeds the No-D Limit and that requires a Decompression Stop.

Repetitive Group (RG) - a dive exposure guide given by letter according to the depth and Bottom Time. *(The DCIEM RGs are not compatible with Repetitive Groups given in other published tables.)*

Surface interval (SI) - time elapsed between reaching the surface after a dive and beginning the actual Descent on the following dive.

Repetitive Factor (RF) - a residual nitrogen indicator relating to the amount of nitrogen remaining in a diver's body after a Surface Interval.

Repetitive Dive - any dive conducted while the Repetitive Factor is greater than 1.0.

Effective Bottom Time (EBT) - the combined total of actual Bottom Time plus time included to account for residual nitrogen from a previous dive exposure. EBT is applied to Repetitive Dives and to Multi-Level Dives.

Altitude Dive - a dive conducted at an elevation greater than 999ft (300m) above sea-level.

Effective Depth - the equivalent sea level depth for an Altitude Dive.

Descent Rate - the proper Descent Rate is 60ft (18m) per minute, or slower.

Ascent rate - the ascent rate is 50ft (15m) plus or minus 10ft (3m) per minute.

The variable rate allows you to gradually reduce your rate of ascent as you reach shallower depths. *"For example, the proper ascent rate at depths below 90ft (27m) is 50-60ft (15-18m) per minute. Above 90ft, the ascent rate should be reduced to 40-50ft (12-15m) per minute. For dives deeper than 40ft (12m), a 3 minute Safety Stop at 15ft (4.5m) is recommended."*

Multi-Level Dive - a dive during which bottom time is accumulated at two or more depths. (See Chapter 23 for DCIEM Multi-Level Dive Procedures).

Decompression Time includes ascent time to the decompression stop at the rate of 50 + 10ft/min (15 + 3m/min).

Of interest to the recreational diver are four tables:

Table A. Air Decompression (Table 18.1)

Table B. Surface Interval Table (Table 18.2)

Table C. Repetitive Diving Table (Table 18.2)

Table D. Depth Correction Table for Altitude Diving (Table 18.2)

TABLE 18.1
The Air Decompression Table (Table A)

DCIEM SPORT DIVING TABLES

A: AIR DECOMPRESSION

Depth		No-Decompression Bottom Times (minutes)				Decompression Required Bottom Times			
20'	6m	30 A / 60 B / 90 C / 120 D	150 E / 180 F / 240 G / 300 H	360 I / 420 J / 480 K / 600 L	720 M / ∞				
30'	9m	30 A / 45 B / 60 C / 90 D	100 E / 120 F / 150 G / 180 H	190 I / 210 J / 240 K / 270 L	300 M	360	400		
40'	12m	22 A / 30 B / 40 C	60 D / 70 E / 80 F	90 G / 120 H / 130 I	150 J	160 K / 170 L	180 M / 190	200	215
50'	15m	18 A / 25 B	30 C / 40 D	50 E / 60 F	75 G	85 H / 95 I	105 J / 115 K	124 L	132 M
60'	18m	14 A / 20 B	25 C / 30 D	40 E	50 F	60 G	70 H / 80 I	85 J	92 K
Decompression Stops in minutes					at 10' 3m	**5**	**10**	**15**	**20**
70'	21m	12 A / 15 B	20 C	25 D	35 E	40 F	50 G	60 H / 63 I	66 J
80'	24m	10 A / 13 B	15 C	20 D	25 E	29 F	35 G	48 H	52 I
90'	27m	9 A	12 B	15 C	20 D	23 E	27 F	35 G	40 H / 43 I
100'	30m	7 A	10 B	12 C	15 D	18 D	21 E	25 F / 29 G	36 H
110'	33m		6 A	10 B	12 C	15 D	18 E	22 F	26 G / 30 H
120'	36m		6 A	8 B	10 C	12 D	15 E	19 F	25 G
130'	39m			5 A	8 B	10 C	13 D	16 F	21 G
140'	42m			5 A	7 B	9 C	11 D	14 F	18 G
150'	45m			4 A	6 B	8 C	10 D	12 E	15 F
Decompression Stops in minutes			at 20' 6m			-	-	5	10
			at 10' 3m			5	10	10	10

- **ASCENT RATE** is 50' (15m) plus or minus 10' (3m) per minute
- **NO-DECOMPRESSION LIMITS** are given for first dives
- **DECOMPRESSION STOPS** are taken at mid-chest level

→ Table B for **Minimum Surface Intervals**
→ Table C for **Repetitive Dive No-Decompression Limits**
→ Table D for **Depth Corrections** required at Altitudes above 1000' (300m)

TABLE 18.2
Surface Interval, Repetitive Diving and Depth Corrections Tables

B: SURFACE INTERVALS

Rep. Group	0:15 → 0:29	0:30 → 0:59	1:00 → 1:29	1:30 → 1:59	2:00 → 2:59	3:00 → 3:59	4:00 → 5:59	6:00 → 8:59	9:00 → 11:59	12:00 → 14:59	15:00 → 18:00
A	1.4	1.2	1.1	1.1	1.1	1.1	1.1	1.1	1.0	1.0	1.0
B	1.5	1.3	1.2	1.2	1.2	1.1	1.1	1.1	1.1	1.0	1.0
C	1.6	1.4	1.3	1.2	1.2	1.2	1.1	1.1	1.1	1.0	1.0
D	1.8	1.5	1.4	1.3	1.3	1.2	1.2	1.1	1.1	1.0	1.0
E	1.9	1.6	1.5	1.4	1.3	1.3	1.2	1.2	1.1	1.1	1.0
F	2.0	1.7	1.6	1.5	1.4	1.3	1.3	1.2	1.1	1.1	1.0
G	-	1.9	1.7	1.6	1.5	1.4	1.3	1.2	1.1	1.1	1.0
H	-	-	1.9	1.7	1.6	1.5	1.4	1.3	1.1	1.1	1.1
I	-	-	2.0	1.8	1.7	1.5	1.4	1.3	1.1	1.1	1.1
J	-	-	-	1.9	1.8	1.6	1.5	1.3	1.2	1.1	1.1
K	-	-	-	2.0	1.9	1.7	1.5	1.3	1.2	1.1	1.1
L	-	-	-	-	2.0	1.7	1.6	1.4	1.2	1.1	1.1
M	-	-	-	-	-	1.8	1.6	1.4	1.2	1.1	1.1

Repetitive Factors (RF) given for Surface Intervals (hr:min)

C: REPETITIVE DIVING

Depth		1.1	1.2	1.3	1.4	1.5	1.6	1.7	1.8	1.9	2.0
30'	9m	272	250	230	214	200	187	176	166	157	150
40'	12m	136	125	115	107	100	93	88	83	78	75
50'	15m	60	55	50	45	41	38	36	34	32	31
60'	18m	40	35	31	29	27	26	24	23	22	21
70'	21m	30	25	21	19	18	17	16	15	14	13
80'	24m	20	18	16	15	14	13	12	12	11	11
90'	27m	16	14	12	11	11	10	9	9	8	8
100'	30m	13	11	10	9	9	8	8	7	7	7
110'	33m	10	9	8	8	7	7	6	6	6	6
120'	36m	8	7	7	6	6	6	5	5	5	5
130'	39m	7	6	6	5	5	5	4	4	4	4
140'	42m	6	5	5	5	4	4	4	3	3	3
150'	45m	5	5	4	4	4	3	3	3	3	3

Repetitive Dive No-D Limits given in minutes according to Depth and RF

D: DEPTH CORRECTIONS

Actual Depth		1000' → 1999 / 300m → 599		2000' → 2999 / 600m → 899		3000' → 3999 / 900m → 1199		4000' → 4999 / 1200m → 1499		5000' → 5999 / 1500m → 1799		6000' → 6999 / 1800m → 2099		7000' → 7999 / 2100m → 2399		8000' → 10000 / 2400m → 3000	
30'	9m	10	3	10	3	10	3	10	3	10	3	10	3	20	6	20	6
40'	12m	10	3	10	3	10	3	10	3	10	3	20	6	20	6	20	6
50'	15m	10	3	10	3	10	3	10	3	20	6	20	6	20	6	20	6
60'	18m	10	3	10	3	10	3	20	6	20	6	20	6	20	6	30	9
70'	21m	10	3	10	3	10	3	20	6	20	6	20	6	30	9	30	9
80'	24m	10	3	10	3	20	6	20	6	20	6	30	9	30	9	40	12
90'	27m	10	3	10	3	20	6	20	6	20	6	30	9	30	9	40	12
100'	30m	10	3	10	3	20	6	20	6	30	9	30	9	30	9	40	12
110'	33m	10	3	20	6	20	6	20	6	30	9	30	9	40	12		
120'	36m	10	3	20	6	20	6	30	9	30	9	30	9				
130'	39m	10	3	20	6	20	6										
140'	42m	10	3														

Add Depth Correction to Actual Depth of Altitude Dive

10'	3m	10	3.0	10	3.0	9	3.0	9	3.0	9	3.0	8	2.5	8	2.5	8	2.5
20'	6m	20	6.0	19	6.0	18	5.5	18	5.5	17	5.0	16	5.0	16	5.0	15	4.5

Actual Decompression Stop Depths (feet/*metres*) at Altitude

Published in Canada by Universal Dive Techtronics (UDT), Toronto & Vancouver

AIR DECOMPRESSION TABLE: A

Table A provides No Decompression (No-D) Limits for first dives, Repetitive Group letters and Decompression Stop Times for dives which exceed the No-D Limits.

The **No-D Limits** are the maximum Bottom Times, expressed in minutes, that you may spend at given depths without having to conduct Decompression Stops before surfacing. To determine the No-D Limit for a given depth, enter Table A horizontally from the Depth column. Follow the row across to the bold double vertical lines. The largest number to the left of the double lines is the No-D Limit for first dives at that depth.

The letter immediately to the right of each bottom time is the **Repetitive Group (RG)** for that depth/time profile. *(RG letters are not interchangeable with RGs appearing in other tables).* Determine your RG according to the actual or next greater Bottom Time. If no RG letter appears beside your Bottom Time, allow at least **18 hours** to elapse before conducting another dive.

The DECOMPRESSION REQUIRED section is to the right of the bold, double vertical lines. **Decompression Stop** requirements are given at the bottom of each column.

Example: FIRST DIVE: 100ft (30m)
for 20 minutes
(1st Dive No-D Limit is 15 min)
Decompression Stop is
10 min at 10ft (3m)
(First Dive Repetitive Group = E)

Note:

Decompression stops for dives to 60ft (18m) are taken at 10ft (3m). Deeper dives may require decompression stops at both 20ft (6m) and 10ft (3m). Decompression stops are taken at mid-chest level for the times indicated at the specified depths.

SURFACE INTERVAL TABLE: B

The **Surface Interval (SI)** is the time elapsed between surfacing from a dive and beginning the actual descent on the following dive. The Surface Interval times across the top of Table B are expressed in hours and minutes. The maximum Surface Interval in the tables is 18 hours.

Use the Repetitive Group from your last dive to enter Table B. Match your Repetitive Group row with the column that corresponds with your Surface Interval.

Table B indicates your residual nitrogen level in the form of a **Repetitive Factor (RF)** or Residual Nitrogen Factor. As your Surface Interval increases, your Repetitive Factor decreases from a maximum of 2.0 to a minimum of 1.0 - the point at which you are considered free of residual nitrogen. *Any dive conducted while the Repetitive Factor is greater than 1.0 is a REPETITIVE DIVE.*

If your RF has diminished to 1.0, use the first dive No-D Limits in Table A to plan your dive.

If your RF is greater than 1.0, use the Table C No-D Limits to plan your Repetitive Dive.

If an emergency forces you to dive before a RF appears in Table B, apply the short Surface Interval guidelines that follow:

a. For dives to the SAME DEPTH: add the bottom times together and use the total time to determine your RG letter and decompression status.

b. For dives to DIFFERENT DEPTHS: take the RG letter from the first dive and find the same group letter at the second depth to determine the equivalent time that corresponds to the same RG at the second depth. Begin the second dive as if you had already spent the bottom time listed beside that Group letter.

Example: RG F, 2nd dive to 50ft (15m). Bottom time given for F at 50ft is 60 minutes.

REPETITIVE DIVING TABLE: C

The No-D Limits (NDLs) for repetitive dives are given in Table C. The maximum depth of a repetitive dive must not exceed that of the preceding dive. *"A maximum depth of 90ft (27m) is recommended for a second dive. For a third dive, a maximum depth of 50ft (15m) is recommended."*

1. To find the No-D Limit, match your RF with the depth of the repetitive dive.

2. On a repetitive dive, actual bottom time is added to Residual Nitrogen Time (RNT). Find the RNT by subtracting the repetitive dive NDL from the first dive NDL for the same depth.

Example: A dive to 50ft (15m) with an RF of 1.4
First Dive NDL = 75 min.
Rep. Dive NDL = 45 min.
RNT = 75 − 45 = 30 min.

3. Add the actual bottom time to the RNT. The total of actual bottom time plus RNT is the Effective Bottom Time (EBT). In this example, adding 40 minutes of actual bottom time to the RNT results in an EBT of 70 minutes at 50ft (15m) and an RG of G.

Example (continued):
RNT = 30 min.
+ Actual BT = 40 min
= EBT
= 70 min.

4. If the <u>actual</u> bottom time exceeds the No-D Limit given in Table C, a Decompression Stop will be required. Stop times are given in Table A according to depth and EBT.

Note:
On earlier versions of the DCIEM Sport Diving Tables the Equivalent Bottom Time of a repetitive dive was calculated by multiplying the Actual Bottom Time by the Repetitive Factor.

Example: Dive 1: 60ft (18m) for 50 min.
RG = F
SI = 1hr 45min
RF = 1.5
Dive 2: 60ft (18m) for 30 min.
EBT = 1.5 x 30 = 45 min.

This is the method covered in the DCIEM Diving Manual[5] and it is still acceptable. However, it is slightly less conservative than the RNT method introduced by the co-authors of the Sport Diving Tables and Procedures. (e.g. Using the RNT method for the above example would yield and EBT of 53 min).

MINIMUM SURFACE INTERVALS

Table C is used in conjunction with Table B to determine the Minimum Surface Interval required prior to conducting a No-D Repetitive Dive for a given Bottom Time.

1. In Table C, select the depth and find a NDL that meets or exceeds the actual bottom time. The RF required to conduct the dive is given at the top of the column.

2. In Table B, match this RF with the RG letter from the preceding dive. The minimum Surface Interval is given at the top of the column.

Example: 1st Dive was 80ft (24m)
for 25 min
RG = E
Repetitive dive will be 50ft (15m)
for 40 minutes
RF 1.5 allows an NDL of
41 minutes (Table C).
Group E becomes RF 1.5 after
Surface Interval of 1 hour
Table B).

Note:
For dive exposures exceeding the bottom times in the Sport Diving Tables, refer to the complete Standard Air Tables appearing in the publication "DCIEM Air Decompression Tables and Procedures"[5]. (These tables are shown in Appendix B).

REPETITIVE DIVES AND MULTI-DAY DIVING

1. The RG letter for each repetitive dive must be greater than that of the preceding dive. Otherwise, add one letter to the RG taken from the preceding dive and use the higher letter.

   Example: 1st Dive C, 2nd Dive D, 3rd Dive D, 3rd Dive RG is increased to E.

2. After three days of repetitive diving, a day off from using scuba is recommended.

USING THE DCIEM SPORT DIVING TABLES

A. SINGLE DIVES

Example 1.

To find the maximum allowable bottom time for a no-stop dive to 60ft (18m).

Enter Table A horizontally at 60ft (18m) and move across the row. The No-Decompression Limit (NDL) is the number immediately to the left of the bold double vertical lines. The NDL is thus *50* minutes and the Repetitive Group (RG) is *F*.

Example 2.

To find the decompression required after a dive to 95ft (29m) for 20 minutes.

Enter Table A horizontally at 100ft (30m) (which is the next greater depth for interim depths) and move across the row to 21 minutes (the next longer time for interim times). Moving down, the decompression is found to be *10 minutes at 10ft (3m)*. The RG is *E*.

Example 3.

To find the decompression required after a dive to 90ft (27m) for 30 minutes.

Enter Table A at 90ft (27m) and move across the row to 35 minutes. Moving down, the

decompression is found to be *5 minutes at 20ft (6m) and 10 minutes at 10ft (3m)*. The RG is *G*.

B.   REPETITIVE DIVES

Example 4.

Three hours after a dive to 80ft (24m) for 27 minutes, you wish to carry out another no-stop dive to 60ft (18m). What is the maximum allowable bottom time for the repetitive dive?

After the initial dive the RG is *F*. Enter Table B from the left at F, and move right, until intersecting the column corresponding to the surface interval. In this case 3 hours lies between 3:00-3:59, so the RF is *1.3*.

Enter Table C horizontally at the depth of the repetitive dive, in this case 60ft (18m). Move across the row until intersecting the column for an RF of 1.3. The number *31* results. This means that the No-D Limit for the repetitive dive is *31* minutes.

Example 5.

If the repetitive dive in the previous example was undertaken for a bottom time of 30 minutes, find the RG after the dive.

To find the appropriate RG, first you must find the Residual Nitrogen Time (RNT) and the Equivalent Bottom Time (EBT) of the repetitive dive.

A dive to 60ft (18m) with an RF of 1.3
First Dive NDL = 50 min.
Rep. Dive NDL = 31 min.
RNT = 50 - 31 = 19 min.
Equivalent Bottom Time (EBT) =
RNT + Actual BT = 19 + 30
= 49 min.

Looking up 60ft (18m) for 49 minutes in Table A, the RG after the dive would be *F*.

Example 6.

After a dive to 80ft (24m) for 25 minutes you wish to dive again, after an appropriate surface interval. What minimum surface interval is required so that you may dive to 60ft (18m) for 30 minutes without the need to make a decompression stop?

Enter Table A at 80ft (24m) and move across the row to 25 minutes. The first dive does not require a decompression stop, and the RG is *E*.

Enter Table C at 60ft (18m) (i.e. the depth of the proposed repetitive dive), and more across to find an allowable bottom time of 30 minutes. Taking 31 minutes, this occurs within the column for RF = 1.3, which means that after the surface interval you must have an RF of *1.3*.

Before the surface interval your RG was *E*, so enter Table B at *E*, and move right to find *1.3*. This occurs within the column corresponding to a surface interval of 2:00-2:59, which means that your minimum surface interval must be *2 hours*.

REPETITIVE DIVES REQUIRING DECOMPRESSION STOPS

Example 7.

Four and one half hours after a dive to 95ft (29m) for 20 minutes, you wish to dive to 55ft (17m) for 50 minutes. What decompression is required?

After the initial dive a stop of 10 minutes at 10ft (3m) was required and the RG is *E*.

Enter Table B at E, and move right until intersecting the column including 4½ hour (i.e. the column corresponding to 4:00-5:59). The RF is *1.2*.

Enter Table C at 60ft (18m) and move right to the column for RF 1.2 to get the NDL for the 55ft, which is 35 minutes.

Calculate the RNT:
First Dive NDL = 50 min.

Rep. Dive NDL =35 min.
RNT = First Dive NDL – Rep. Dive NDL
= 50 - 35
= 15 min.
EBT = RNT + Actual BT
= 15 + 50 = 65 min.

Entering Table A at 60ft (18m) and moving across to 70min, the appropriate decompression is found to be *10 minutes at 10ft (3m)*.

Example 8.

After a dive to 60ft (18m) for 50 minutes you wish to dive again, after a surface interval of 1 hour 45 minutes, to 60ft (18m) for 30 minutes. Calculate the required decompression.

From Table A, the first dive does not require a stop and the RG after the dive is *F*.

Entering Table B at F and moving across to the column corresponding to a surface interval of 1 hour 45 minutes gives an RF of *1.5*.

The RNT before the second dive
= 50 – 27 = 23 min.
EBT = 23 + 30 = 53 min.

From Table A, the decompression required is *5 minutes at 10ft (3m)*.

Example 9.

Thirteen minutes after a first dive to 60ft (18m) for 30 minutes you wish to dive again to 60ft (18m) for 25 minutes. Find the required decompression.

From Table A, the first dive requires no stop and the RG is *D*. *Since the surface interval is shorter than 15 minutes and the dives are to the same maximum depth*, you must add the bottom times of both dives and use the total time, in this case 30 + 25 = 55 minutes, to determine the decompression and RG. The decompression required is *5 minutes at 10ft (3m)* and the RG is *G*.

Example 10.

Ten minutes after a first dive to 120ft (36m) for 10 minutes you wish to dive again to 70ft (21m) for 20 minutes. Find the required decompression.

From Table A, the first dive requires no stop and the RG is *C. Since the surface interval is shorter than 15 minutes and the dives are to different depths*, you must use the RG from the first dive (C) to find the equivalent time for the same RG at the second depth.

Entering Table A at 70ft (21m), you find that a RG of *C* corresponds to a bottom time of 20 minutes. Adding this 20 minutes to the proposed bottom time of the second dive gives a total time of 20 + 20 = 40 minutes. Looking up 70ft (21m) for 40 minutes in Table A gives a required decompression of *5 minutes at 10ft (3m)* and a RG of *F*.

Example 11.

Find any decompression stops required in the following sequence of three dives:

Dive 1: 120ft (36m) for 12 minutes
S.I. = 3 hr
Dive 2: 120ft (36m) for 9 minutes
S.I. = 65 minutes
Dive 3: 80ft (24m) for 20 minutes

The decompression required at the end of the first dive is *5 minutes at 10ft* (3m) and the RG after the dive is *D*. The RF after the surface interval is 1.2.

The RNT before the second dive = 10 − 7 = 3 min. So the EBT for Dive 2 = 3 + 9 = 12min. From Table A, Dive 2 requires a stop of *5 minutes at 10ft* (3m) and the RG after Dive 2 is *D*. Since this RG is the same as the RG after the first dive you must add one letter to the RG after Dive 2. Thus, the RG after Dive 2 becomes *E* and the RF before Dive 3 is *1.5*.

The RNT before the third dive = 25 − 14 = 11 min. So the EBT for Dive 3 = 11 + 20 = 31min. From Table A, Dive 3 requires a stop of *10 minutes at 10ft (3m)* and the RG after Dive 2 is *G*.

Example 12.

Find any decompression stops required after the first two dives and the maximum allowable No-D bottom time for the third dive in the following sequence of three dives:

Dive 1: 90ft (27m) for 15 minutes
S.I. = 2½ hours
Dive 2: 70ft (21m) for 10 minutes
S.I. = 3 hours
Dive 3: 50ft (15m)

No decompression stop is required at the end of the first dive and the RG after the dive is *C*. The RF after the surface interval is 1.2.

The RNT before the second dive = 35 − 25 = 10 min. So the EBT for Dive 2 = 10 + 10 = 20 minutes and, from Table A, no stop is required and the RG is *C*. Because the RG after Dive 2 is the same as that of the preceding dive, you must add one letter to the RG of the preceding dive and use this new RG as the RG after Dive 2. So you must use a RG of *D* as the RG after Dive 2 (instead of a RG of C). Therefore, the RF before Dive 3 is *1.2* and the maximum allowable no-decompression stop bottom time is 55 minutes. If this maximum bottom time was used, the RG after the final dive would be *G*.

Note:

The Short Form No-Decompression Table, a derivative of the DCIEM Sport Diving Tables, was introduced in 1994 by one of the co-authors of the DCIEM Sport Diving Tables and Procedures. The Short Form Table has been widely used for training in Australia, Canada and Latin America (in a Spanish edition). The Short Form Table requires no calculation and is designed for no-stop dives only. In 1997, the Short Form Table was amended for disabled diving applications.

DEPTH CORRECTIONS FOR ALTITUDE DIVES: TABLE D

Any dive conducted at an altitude greater than 1000 feet (300 meters) above sea level is an Altitude Dive.

Depth Corrections are necessary when diving at altitude because the reduced atmospheric pressure at the surface of the dive site makes the altitude dive equivalent to a much deeper dive at sea level. Table D is used to convert the actual depth at altitude to an Effective Depth which corresponds with the depth figures intended for use at sea level.

When you arrive from a lower altitude, your body already has some residual nitrogen as a result of the decrease in atmospheric pressure. Use the following Depth Correction Procedure if you have acclimatized at the altitude of the dive site for at least 12 hours:

1. a. Establish the altitude of the dive site and the actual depth of the Altitude Dive;

    b. Find the depth correction by matching the actual depth with the altitude.

    c. Add the depth correction to the actual depth to determine the Effective Depth – the equivalent sea level depth for an Altitude Dive. Apply the Effective Depth to Table A (or Table C for repetitive dives);

    d. If the dive exceeds the NDL. Decompress at the Actual Decompression Stop Depth given in Table D.

    Example:
      Altitude = 6,000 feet (1,800 metres)

      Depth = 60ft (18m)
      Bottom Time = 35 minutes

      DEPTH CORRECTION = +20ft (6m)
      EFFECTIVE DEPTH = 80ft (24m)

Deco. Stop = 10 min at 10ft (3m) (from Table A)
Actual Stop Depth = 8ft (2.5m) (from Table D)

2. If you must dive before 12 hours have elapsed at the altitude of the dive site, begin the Depth Correction procedure by using the NEXT GREATER DEPTH than the actual depth. Following the example given above, begin the Depth Correction Procedure as if the actual depth were 70ft (21m). The EFFECTIVE DEPTH would be 70ft (21m) + 20ft (6m) = 90ft (27m).

    The decompression required and Actual Stop Depths would be 5 minutes at 16ft (5m), and 10 minutes at 8ft (2.5m).*

Chapter 26 includes a number of worked examples using the DCIEM Procedure for Altitude Diving.

FLYING AFTER DIVING

1. 12 hours is the minimum time required before flying after a No-D first dive. However, your RF must be 1.0 before you fly. *Example: Group E requires 15 hours (Table B).*

2. Allow at least 24 hours to elapse before flying after any other than a No-D first dive.

MULTI-LEVEL DIVING

The DCIEM Sport Diving Tables can also be used to plan Multi-Level dives. The procedure is described in Chapter 23.

---

* The imperial and metric figures given for the Actual Stop Depth are not direct conversions. The metric table for Depth Correction was calculated separately. Because of the effect of rounding the numbers on the imperial table, the imperial table equivalents may differ slightly from those in the metric table.

The authors wishes to thank Mr. Ron Nishi of DCIEM/DRDC, Toronto and Mr. Gain Wong of UDT/ASA (Adapted Scuba Association) for their co-operation and assistance with the preparation of this chapter, and for permission to reprint the DCIEM Sport Diving Tables and Procedures and the DCIEM 1984 Standard Air Decompression Tables[5] (Appendix B).

The Department of National Defence, Defense Research Development Canada and UDT Inc. disclaim any and all responsibilities for the use of the DCIEM tables and procedures.

The DCIEM tables are copyrighted by the Department of National Defence (Canada) and may not be produced in any form without permission from the DND and DRDC (Toronto).

Note:

Since their initial release, some changes have been made to the procedures for using the DCIEM Sport Diving Tables, as well as to the tables themselves, in an effort to make them more user-friendly. The latest update to the DCIEM Sport Diving Tables was in 1995.

The DCIEM Sport Diving Tables are available from www.bonicadiving.com.

REFERENCES

1. Nishi RY. The DCIEM Decompression Tables and Procedures for Air Diving. In: *Decompression in Surface-Based Diving*, Nashimoto I and Lanphier, E. (eds), UHMS Publication No. 73 (Dec) 6/15/87; 1987.

2. Wong G. Development of the DCIEM Diving Tables. *Sources* 1995; Jan-Feb:41-4.

3. Nishi RY, Hobson BA. The DCIEM/Canadian Forces Air Decompression Tables. DCIEM No. 86-P-23, for publication in the Proceedings of the Canadian Association of Underwater Science: Diving for Science, Assessing the Environment; 1986.

4. Huggins K. Microprocessor Applications to Multi-Level Diving. Michigan Sea Grant College Program, Report No. MICHU-56-87-201; 1987.

5. DCIEM Diving Manual. Part 1 Air Diving Tables and Procedures. Richmond BC: Universal Dive Techtronics; 1992.

6. DCIEM Diving Manual. Part 2 Helium-Oxygen Diving Tables and Procedures. Richmond BC: Universal Dive Techtronics; 1992.

7. Nishi RY. How the Kidd-Stubbs Model was used for the new DCIEM Heliox Tables. In: Workshop on Inert Gases in Decompression. Great Lakes Chapter UHMS; 1993.

8. Nishi RY, Wong G. Instructions for using the DCIEM Sport Diving Tables. UDT Inc., Toronto; 1996.

OTHER SOURCES

Lauckner G, Nishi RY. Decompression Tables and Procedures for Compressed Air Diving Based on the DCIEM 1983 Decompression Model, DCIEM No. 84-R-74, Defense and Civil Institute of Environmental Medicine; 1984.

Nishi RY. New Canadian Air Decompression Tables. DCIEM No. 86-P-06, *Canadian Diving J* 1986; Summer:22-7.

Nishi RY, Eatock BC. The Role of Ultrasonic Bubble Detection in Table Validation. *Proceedings of the UHMS Workshop on "Validation of Decompression Schedules"*. 13-14 Feb, Bethesda, MD; 1987.

Wong G. Guide to the DCIEM Sport Diving Tables (1987). UDT Inc, Toronto; 1987.

Wong G. Guide to the DCIEM Sport Diving Tables (Addendum). UDT Inc, Toronto; 1988.

Nishi RY and Wong G. Instructions for using the DCIEM Sport Diving Tables - 1990. UDT Inc, Toronto; 1990.

Wong G. Short Form No-Decompression Table. G Wong, Toronto; 1997.

Wong G. Doppler Research at DCIEM. *Sources* 1993; Jan-Feb:81-2.

RECOMMENDED FURTHER READING

DCIEM Diving Manual. Part 1 Air Diving Tables and Procedures. UDT Inc, Richmond BC, 1992.

EXERCISES ON THE DCIEM TABLES

1. Find the No-D Limits, (NDL) and corresponding Repetitive Groups (RG) for single dives to the following depths:

   (a) 82ft (25m)　(b) 145ft (44m)
   (c) 52ft (16m)

2. Determine the RG after each of the following dives:

   (a) 50ft (15m) for 46 minutes
   (b) 120ft (36m) for 17 minutes

3. Find the Repetitive Factor (RF) after each of the following Surface Intervals (SI):

   (a) Group C after SI of 3½ hours
   (b) Group B after SI of 1 hour
   (c) Group H after SI of 5 hours

4. Determine the No-D Limit for each of the following repetitive dives:

   (a) 90ft (27m) with RF of 1.4
   (b) 48ft (15m) with RF of 1.1
   (c) 115ft (35m) with RF of 1.8

5. The following questions relate to a dive to 80ft (24m) for 20 minutes, followed 3 hours later by a dive to 61 ft (19 m):

   (a) What is the RG after the first dive?
   (b) What is the RF after the SI?
   (c) What is the No-D Limit for the second dive?
   (d) If the actual bottom time of the second dive was 20 minutes, find the RG after the dive.

6. Repeat question 5 for a dive to 108ft (33m) for 10 minutes followed 4 hours later by a dive to 60ft (18m).

7. Complete the calculations for the following decompression stop dives:

   The first dive to 115ft (35m) for 15 minutes, SI of 1½ hours, second dive to 75ft (23m) for 30 minutes.

   (a) What decompression stop(s) is (are) required after the first dive?
   (b) What is the RF after the SI?
   (c) What is the decompression requirement and RG after the repetitive dive?

8. Repeat question 7 for the following dives:

   The first dive to 80ft (24m) for 28 minutes, followed 2½ hours later by 51ft (16m) for 40 minutes.

9. Determine the minimum SI necesary to stay within the NDL for the following dives:

   (a) First dive to 70ft (21m) for 30 minutes. Second dive to 50ft (15m) for 50 minutes.
   (b) First dive to 60ft (18m) for 50 minutes. Second dive to 60ft (18m) for 30 minutes.

10. Find the decompression requirements and RG after a single dive to 60ft (18m) for 35 minutes at an altitude of 8,500ft (2,575m) (Assume 12-hour acclimatization).

11. Find the No-D Limits for the following dives to be carried out at an altitude of 4,500ft (1363m) (Assume 12-hour acclimatization):

   The first dive to 80ft (24m) to No-D Limit, SI of 4 hours, second dive to 60ft (18m).

12. Find the No-D Limits for the following repetitive dives at sea level:

   (a) 70ft (21m) for 25 minutes followed 12 minutes later by a dive to 70ft (21m).
   (b) 80ft (24m) for 20 minutes followed 14 minutes later by a dive to 55ft (17m).

13. Determine the No-D Limits for the final dive in each of the following dive sequences:

(a) Dive 1: 110ft (33m) for 12 minutes
S.I. = 1¹/₂ hours
Dive 2: 100ft (30m) for 10 minutes
S.I. = 3¹/₂ hours
Dive 3: 70ft (21m)

(b) Dive 1: 80ft (24m) for 24 minutes
S.I. = 3¹/₂ hours
Dive 2: 70ft (21m) for 20 minutes
S.I. = 4¹/₂ hours
Dive 3: 60ft (18m)

(c) Dive 1: 80ft (24m) for 20 minutes
S.I. = 2 hours
Dive 2: 80ft (24m) for 10 minutes
S.I. = 3 hours
Dive 3: 60ft (18m) for 20 minutes
S.I. = 3 hours
Dive 4: 60ft (18m)

ANSWERS

1. (a) 20, D   (b) 6, B   (c) 50, F
2. (a) E   (b) F
3. (a) 1.2   (b) 1.2   (c) 1.4
4. (a) 11   (b) 60   (c) 5
5. (a) D   (b) 1.2   (c) 25
   (d) 30 min. (EBT), RG = E.
6. (a) B   (b) 1.1   (c) 40
   (d) 30 min. (EBT), RG = D.
7. (a) 10 min at 10ft (3m)
   (b) 1.4 (c) 5 min. at 20ft (6m) and 10 min. at 10ft (3m), H.
8. (a) 10 min at 10ft (3m),
   (b) 1.4 (c) 5 min at 10ft (3m), H.
9. (a) 2.00   (b) 3.00
10. 5 min at 15ft (4.5m) and 10min. at 8ft (2.5m), G.
11. 15, 18
12. (a) 10   (b) 20
13. (a) 25   (b) 31   (c) 31

19

The BS-AC tables

HISTORICAL PERSPECTIVE

In 1958, Hempleman, a British physiologist, introduced a completely different decompression concept to those that were currently in use, and devised some decompression schedules which were based on a completely different model to that of Haldane.

Hempleman had observed that, over a particular depth range, the first symptom of decompression sickness to appear was usually pain at or near a joint. He assumed that the tissue involved (e.g. tendon) was, therefore, the tissue with the greatest overpressure of nitrogen for that depth range, and that gas elimination from that tissue must control the decompression. Hempleman pictured the body as a single tissue (Figure 19.1) and believed that the quantity of gas absorbed in the body could be calculated by a simple formula relating depth and time.*

Unlike Haldane, who believed that gas uptake and elimination took identical times, Hempleman assumed that gas elimination was one and one half times slower than uptake. He also utilized the theory that decompression is safe if a constant difference, between the gas tension in the tissues and the environment, of 30 feet (9m) of sea water (fsw) is not exceeded.

The model represents the body as a single "slab" of tissue. One end of the slab is exposed to ambient pressure. As the pressure of inert gas increases, it diffuses through the "slab" as shown in Figure 19.1. As long as the pressure of the inert gas remains less than some specified amount (initially 30fsw) above ambient pressure, DCS should be avoided.

FIGURE 19.1

Hempleman's single tissue model

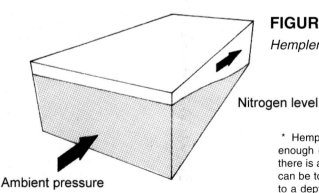

Nitrogen level

Ambient pressure

---

* Hempleman proposed that: "If this model is near enough correct for most practical purposes and if there is a fixed critical excess quantity of gas which can be tolerated on decompression, then for a dive to a depth P for a time t there will be some critical fixed quantity Q of dissolved gas such that:
$$Q = P\sqrt{t}$$

These initial schedules, metricated in 1972, became the current Royal Navy Tables. They had theoretical limitations that have been confirmed in practice:

First, the concept that a single tissue (i.e. the slowest tissue) controls decompression only applies over a certain depth range. Second, the concept of an allowable overpressure of 30fsw at all depths is often too conservative.

Hempleman realized these limitations and, in 1966, developed a new set of caisson workers' tables for a tunneling job in Blackpool. This job involved very long exposures of 4-8 hours, and the decompression model was designed to increase the decompression times in this range since existing times were known to be too short. These new tables became known as the "Blackpool Tables".

In 1968, Hempleman used the same caisson decompression model to generate a new set of tables for industry. These tables, known as the 1968 Air Diving Tables, still used the concept of a single tissue but used a variable ratio of tissue nitrogen tension to ambient pressure in order to calculate safe decompression.

Both the Royal Navy and industry rejected these tables claiming that the no-stop times were too conservative, and that the no-stop times given by the current RN Tables provided adequate safety. The 1968 Air Diving Tables were slightly modified (which apparently included replacing the no-stop times with the RN no-stop times), metricated and reappeared as the 1972 Metric Air Diving Tables, released by The Royal Naval Physiological Laboratory (RNPL) through the Underwater Engineering Group (UEG) of the Construction Industry Research and Information Association (CIRIA). A portion of these tables is shown as Table 19.1. Little has been published about these tables.

The metricated version also proved to be commercially unpopular because it was presented in 5m depth increments, which required substantial extra (and costly) decompression time if the diver slightly exceeded a depth entry.

Initially, with the RN Tables, repetitive dives were handled by adding the bottom times and decompressing for the depth of the deeper dive. Hempleman introduced "concession" rules for use with the 1968 Tables. The halving, quartering and eighthing of times of initial dives depending on the surface intervals offered much greater flexibility with repetitive diving, and it seemed reasonable to allow this freedom with these more conservative tables. Unfortunately, in 1972, when RNPL was preparing to release the metric version of the 1968 Tables, the RN released its own repeat dive rule - the 6-hour rule, where, if the first dive is shallower than 42m and above the Limiting Line it can be repeated after 6 hours. This forced Hempleman to alter his repeat dive system and, eventually, gave rise to the confusing set of repeat dive rules governing the RNPL/BS-AC Table.

A portion of the RNPL 1972 Tables is shown in Table 19.1 You will notice that there is a "Limiting Line" drawn across each depth schedule, and that the depth schedules increase in 5m increments. Below the Limiting Line equated to requiring more than 30 minutes of decompression time.

The meaning of the "Limiting Line" was as follows:

The Limiting Line represented a section of the tables in which there was a significantly increased risk of DCS and that this risk increased with an increase in duration below the line. Intentional diving below the Limiting Line was to be undertaken only when a compression chamber was available on the site and, even then, only when circumstances justified the risk. It was stated that the use of oxygen for decompression in no way reduced this risk. In addition, a

TABLE 19.1

Portion of the RNPL 1972 Tables.

Depth not Exceeding (metres)	Bottom Time Not Exceeding (min)	Stoppages at Different Depths (metres)					Total Time for Decompression (min)
		25 m	20 m	15 m	10 m	5 m	
20	45	—	—	—	—	—	1½
	50	—	—	—	—	5	5
	55	—	—	—	—	10	10
	60	—	—	—	—	15	15
	65	—	—	—	—	25	25
	Limiting 70	—	—	—	—	30	30
	Line 75	—	—	—	—	40	40
	90	—	—	—	—	60	60
	120	—	—	—	—	90	90
	150	—	—	—	—	110	110
	180	—	—	—	10	110	120
	240	—	—	—	10	120	130
25	25	—	—	—	—	—	2
	30	—	—	—	5	5	10
	35	—	—	—	5	10	15
	40	—	—	—	5	15	20
	Limiting 45	—	—	—	5	20	25
	Line 50	—	—	—	10	30	40
	55	—	—	—	10	40	50
	60	—	—	—	10	60	70
	75	—	—	5	—	80	85
	90	—	—	5	10	100	115
	105	—	—	5	10	120	135
	120	—	—	5	20	120	145
	150	—	—	5	30	120	155
	180	—	5	—	40	125	170

Crown Copyright/MOD Table.

diver who had dived below the Limiting Line was not to carry out a further dive within 12 hours and was to remain in the vicinity of a compression chamber and under surveillance for four hours.

The British Sub-Aqua Club (BS-AC), searching for a suitable table for its recreational diving members, adapted the RNPL 1972 Table, creating the RNPL/BS-AC Table. In its "short" form the RNPL/BS-AC Table (Table 19.2) covered depths to 50m in 2m increments (rather than the original 5m increments), and dive times leading to a total decompression time of 30 minutes (i.e. the tables end at the Limiting Line for each schedule). "No-stop" Times (i.e. No-Decompression Limits) were specified for each depth increment. Where stops were required, all dives to depths not exceeding 20m required a single stop at 5m, whilst dives from 20-50m required a first stop at 10m, followed by a second at 5m. The "full" table included two further depth increments of 5m (i.e. 55m and 60m), again with times leading to a maximum decompression requirement of 30 minutes.

TABLE 19.2

The RNPL/BS-AC Table.

Maximum Depth metres	No Stop Time minutes	BOTTOM TIME IN MINUTES					
10	232	431	–	–	–	–	270
12	137	140	159	179	201	229	270
14	96	98	106	118	125	134	144
16	72	73	81	88	94	99	105
18	57	59	66	71	76	80	84
20	46	49	55	60	63	67	70
Stops at 5 metres MINUTES		**5**	**10**	**15**	**20**	**25**	**30**
22	38	42	47	51	55	58	
24	32	37	41	45	48	51	
26	27	32	37	40	43	45	
28	23	29	33	36	39	41	
30	20	25	30	33	35	37	
32	18	23	27	30	32	34	
34	16	21	25	28	30	31	
36	14	20	23	26	27	29	
38	12	18	21	24	26	27	
40	11	17	20	22	24	25	
42	10	16	19	21	22	24	
44	9	15	18	20	21		
46	8	14	17	18	20		
48	8	13	16	17			
50	7	12	15	17			
Stops at 10 metres		**5**	**5**	**5**	**5**	**5**	
Stops at 5 metres MINUTES		**5**	**10**	**15**	**20**	**25**	

Promoters of the 1972 RNPL Tables claimed an "incidence factor" of less than 0.05%, but a substantial number of divers suffered decompression sickness while diving within the RNPL/BS-AC Table. For example, in 1987, 36% (25/69) of the DCI cases reported in Britain were divers who had apparently dived within the RNPL/BS-AC Table.[1]

Some of the major drawbacks of the RNPL/BS-AC Tables were:

- Some of the initial No-Stop Limits were too long.

- If you had dived to 40m or less and wished to dive again to 40m or less just over 6 hours later, you could do so without considering the previous dive. This often allows a bottom time in excess of many other systems and, although it may often be realistic (e.g. after a short dive), at times it may prove quite unsafe, especially after deep, long initial dives, and/or after a fast ascent.

- The recommended ascent rate of 15m/minute was often too fast.
- The RNPL/BS-AC Table was not really designed to cater for multiple dives. As a result many of the "rules" that evolved for use with the table were just the interpretation of the day and may not have been appropriate.

In 1988, the British Sub-Aqua Club released a new, and vastly different, set of tables that aimed to improve ease of use, flexibility and safety.

BS-AC '88 Tables

Note:

The BS-AC '88 Tables are only available in a metric version so the following discussion and examples will generally be confined to metric measurement.

BACKGROUND

A number of factors influenced the BS-AC's decision to replace the RNPL/BS-AC Table. Some of these were:

1. The high level of misunderstanding of decompression procedures amongst users and potential users of the RNPL/BS-AC Table, and

2. The inherent inflexibility of the RNPL/BS-AC Table itself. The BS-AC recognized that with the advent of the dive computer, the RNPL/BS-AC Table became even more unattractive to the user. The Club wished to have a set of tables that approached the versatility of a computer and that could comfortably co-exist alongside dive computers.

The table designer, Dr. Tom Hennessy, had worked alongside Hempleman, the designer of the original RNPL model, for many years. Hennessy initially decided to base the new tables on the same decompression model as the RNPL/BS-AC Table as the model on which that table is based had been tried and tested over a number of years. However, because the RNPL/BS-AC Table didn't have the facility to be used and, hence, tested over series of three or four dives per day, Hennessy had to first ensure that the model could be safely extended to cover these multiple diving situations. He believed that very long dives could produce a similar gas load in the tissues to that produced by multiple repetitive dives and, after receiving some data indicating that the model might be marginal when used for very long, deep dives, Hennessy decided to modify the model slightly.

The RNPL/BS-AC Table assumed that it is safe to ascend directly to the surface from saturation at 9m (30ft), but this is no longer believed to be true. *It now appears that the depth a safe direct ascent from which saturation can occur is around 7m (23ft), rather than 9m.** This ascent criterion is included in the BS-AC '88 Tables.

Hennessy believed that bubbles form after every decompression and that these bubbles affect the gas uptake and release for each subsequent dive. For example, if a diver who has nitrogen bubbles in his blood/ tissues descends on a repetitive dive, the nitrogen in the bubbles is exposed to the entire ambient pressure. So at 10m (33ft), the partial pressure of nitrogen in the bubble is 2ATA, which is higher than the 1.6ATA partial pressure of nitrogen at 10m on an initial dive. This means that a diver may saturate more rapidly during the repetitive dive than during an initial dive of the same depth and duration. The total amount of nitrogen will be a combination of this re-dissolved nitrogen and the nitrogen already dissolved, as well as the normal uptake of nitrogen delivered by the blood during the new dive. The gas in the bubbles does not re-dissolve as soon as it is recompressed. It takes a certain depth and time before the gas will completely re-dissolve, and, only then will the tissue revert to its normal state where uptake and elimination can be described by the model used for the first dive. Hence, the rates of gas uptake and elimination will alter from dive to dive and it becomes necessary to treat the second and subsequent dives quite differently to the first when trying to predict safe decompression.

Most traditional decompression models assumed that gas uptake and elimination occurred at the same rate during any dive and the models assumed that this rate is the same on a repetitive dive as it is on a single dive. This may be acceptable if

significant bubbling has not occurred within the blood and tissues, but, if bubbles are present they will slow down off-gassing and the rates may differ. The original RNPL model assumed that off-gassing is at 2/3 the rate of uptake, and *these BS-AC 88 tables also assume an asymmetry in the rate of gas uptake and elimination.* Hennessy set out to design a set of tables that become progressively more conservative as the number of dives, depth and duration increases.

The U.S. Navy Tables depict the theoretical amount of residual nitrogen in a diver by a single letter code, the Repetitive Group Designator, which is supposed to represent the nitrogen level in the 120-minute theoretical tissue compartment. The system assumes that, after a surface interval of ten minutes, this tissue compartment has the highest nitrogen load and, therefore, controls the decompression. The code is then used to determine the amount of residual nitrogen still remaining in this theoretical tissue (and, therefore, in our entire body) before a repetitive dive, and the original single dive model is used to predict the decompression for the repetitive dive. In reality, it has been shown that on a typical "deepish" dive, seven or eight different absorption rates may play a part in controlling the decompression. The U.S. Navy's approach also assumes that dives which give the same code can be treated identically, whether a short, deep dive or a long, shallow one. It assumes that because the amount of nitrogen that is theoretically dissolved in this one tissue compartment is the same, the dives can be treated equivalently. Unfortunately, our bodies do not work quite so simply. What is not accounted for is that the distribution of the gas load between the various tissues may be quite different in each of the cases, so simply adding some residual nitrogen to the level in one theoretical tissue is often not sufficient.

---

* However, there have been reports of divers suffering from suspected DCS after single dives to 5-6m.

To avoid using a single dive model to predict repetitive dives, Hennessy created an initial series of seven different tables to be used for an initial and subsequent repetitive dives, each corresponding to the appropriate *Surfacing Code* (i.e. Repetitive Group) before or after a dive. There is also a *Surface Interval Table* for determining the change in Surfacing Code after a surface interval. These tables are produced for each of four different Altitude/Atmospheric Pressure Ranges. In addition there is a *Transfer Table* to determine the *Tissue Code* when transferring between Altitude/Atmospheric Pressure Levels and an *Altitude/Atmospheric Pressure Chart* to determine the correct Table Level to use. In all, the current BS-AC '88 Tables consist of a set of a total of 32 separate tables.

The first table for each Level, *Table A*, is usually used for the initial dive. After the dive the diver surfaces with a letter code (the Surfacing Code) which relates to the depth and time of the dive. Following a surface interval, the diver selects a new code (the Current Tissue Code) which relates to the nitrogen load in the tissues after the surface interval, and enters a new table (rather than the original table) which bears the same letter code. The minimum surface interval required to gain credit for off-gassing is 15 minutes.

The tables utilize depth increments of 3m, and, instead of giving bottom times, give the time from leaving the surface until arriving at 6m during the ascent, or at 9m on dives requiring a 9m stop. The tables use initial No-Stop Times that are more conservative than those on the previous RNPL/BS-AC Tables.

The BS-AC '88 Tables require that the ascent to 6m is at a maximum rate of 15m/minute (which means that it may (and in these authors' view usually should) be slower than 15m/minute), and the ascent from 6m to the surface must take one minute (which means a rate of 6m/minute – not easy for most divers unless an appropriate ascent line is used).

Decompression stops are done at 9m, 6m *and at the surface.* It is stressed that a surface interval should in essence be treated as a decompression stop and a diver's activities should be modified accordingly. No 3m stops are given as they are too difficult to do successfully when there is wave action. Decompression times increase in increments of one minute and the maximum decompression given is 22 minutes.

The BS-AC '88 Tables are presented in a compact, easy-to-read format *and do not require any calculations at all.* The entire table set is bound in a water resistant booklet, and Tables A, B and C are also printed, in an abbreviated form, on a submersible card which should be carried by the diver and used in the event of a memory lapse or a change of dive plan.

COMPARING THE BS-AC '88 TABLES TO SOME OTHER TABLES

When the BS-AC '88 Tables are compared to tables such as the U.S. Navy Tables, the Bühlmann (1986) Tables and the DCIEM Tables some trends appear to emerge. These are:

- *The tables appear to be conservative for both single and multiple no-stop dives,* with the initial No-Stop Limits comparable with those of the Bühlmann (1986) and DCIEM Tables.
- For single/initial dives requiring stops, the decompression given is often, but not always, more conservative than that given by the U.S. Navy Tables, *but is often less conservative than that suggested by the Bühlmann (1986) and DCIEM Tables.*
- For repetitive dives requiring stops, the decompression given by the BS-AC '88 Tables is more conservative than that given by the U.S. Navy Tables, and often comparable to that given by the Bühlmann (1986) and DCIEM Tables.

These trends are demonstrated in Tables 19.3 to 19.6 and Figure 19.2.

Promoters of the BS-AC '88 Tables argue that even though the Total Decompression Time (TDT) given by these tables is sometimes shorter than that given by some other tables, the risk of decompression sickness is not only dependent on TDT. A longer decompression profile is not necessarily a safer one as other factors (procedural parameters) also affect the risk of DCS. Some of these parameters are the ascent rate, the depth and duration of the initial stop, the ease of maintaining the depth of the required stops, the surface interval required before diving again (or flying) and the activities during the surface interval.

If one compares the ascent procedure suggested by the BS-AC '88 Tables to that given by the U.S. Navy Tables, there are a few of differences which include:- a longer stay at 6m (although a slower ascent rate deeper than 6m), a slower ascent rate from 6m to the surface (although sometimes a shorter ascent time) and a longer stay at the surface before diving again. Although these comparisons may be valid for the U.S. Navy Tables, they do not necessarily apply to other tables. When the BS-AC '88 Tables are compared to the Bühlmann (1986) and DCIEM Tables, especially for first/single dives, the BS-AC Tables often appear less conservative, not only with TDT but also with respect to some of the procedural parameters previously mentioned. Careful examination of Figure 19.2 will indicate this trend. Hennessy has argued that the Bühlmann and DCIEM Tables are often overly conservative, but this is debatable. Although commercial divers may need to minimize decompression time for the sake of efficiency, a recreational diver who decides to conduct a dive involving mandatory stops should usually have no reason not to use a conservative table to gain any extra security that it may provide.

The U.S. Navy Tables, Bühlmann (1986) Tables and DCIEM Tables have been used for comparison with the BS-AC '88 Tables as they have all had a considerable amount of testing and/or usage. Although the basic model on which the BS-AC '88 Tables are based was tested and was used extensively, *the BS-AC '88 Tables in their current form were not validated prior to, or since, their release.*

The BS-AC considered mounting a series of trials using recreational divers but decided that, since the DCS incidence was expected to be low, unless a very large number of trials were conducted the results would not be statistically conclusive. The practical and financial constraints of a large test series proved prohibitive, so instead, a 4-month period of informal open-sea dives were conducted by a number of BS-AC members before the tables were released. No details of the profiles conducted and the number of dives has been released, but no cases of DCS were reported during the period.

A 1990 BS-AC report states that, in 1989 after the first full season of usage, there were 41 divers who developed DCS after diving according to the BS-AC '88 Tables. Eleven of the divers had misused the tables, 22 had dived within the tables and in the other eight cases there was insufficient information to determine whether the tables had been used correctly. The BS-AC estimate that possibly a million dives could have been conducted using the tables, which would yield an incident rate better than 1 in 10,000.[1] No information is available about how many of the DCS cases occurred on dives involving mandatory stops and the number that occurred after no-stop dives.[2]

Surprisingly, BS-AC appears to have published little or no subsequent data on the comparative rate of DCS with divers using the BS-AC '88 Tables and other decompression modalities.

Although essentially untested, the BS-AC '88 Tables appear to be quite conservative for no-stop dives and should generally (but obviously not always) be reasonably safe for such dives. *However, divers who plan to use the BS-AC '88 Tables for dives requiring mandatory decompression stops are urged to do so cautiously and conservatively as the tables are sometimes less conservative in this area than some well-tested tables.*

Table 19.3

Comparision of various schedules.

DIVE 1: Max. Depth = **27m** (90ft) Bottom Time = **20** min				
Table	**BS-AC '88**	**U.S. Navy**	**Bühlmann**	**DCIEM**
No Stop Limit (Bottom time)	22.5	30	20	20
Stops required	-	-	-	-

Surface Interval = 2 hr

DIVE 2: Max. Depth = **24m** (80ft) Bottom Time = **15** min				
Table	**BS-AC '88**	**U.S. Navy**	**Bühlmann**	**DCIEM**
No Stop Limit (Bottom time)	6.5	22	14	16
Stops required	3 / 6m	-	4 / 3m	-

Surface Interval = 4 hr

DIVE 3: Max. Depth = **18m** (60ft) Bottom Time = **40** min				
Table	**BS-AC '88**	**U.S. Navy**	**Bühlmann**	**DCIEM**
No Stop Limit (Bottom time)	31	43	37	35
Stops required	1 / 6m	-	11 / 3m	-

Notes applicable toTables 19.3 - 19.6:

- All dives calculated at sea-level
- Times are in minutes unless otherwise specified
- DCIEM times taken from Sport Diving Tables
- No-stop bottom time limits for the BS-AC '88 Tables are approximate
- Ascent rate used by the U.S. Navy Tables is 9m (30ft)/minute
- Ascent rate used by the Bühlmann Tables is 10m (33ft)/minute
- Ascent rate used by the DCIEM Tables is 15m (50ft)/minute

Table 19.4

Comparision of various schedules.

DIVE 1: Max. Depth = **36m** (100ft)   Bottom Time = **12** min

Table	BS-AC '88	U.S. Navy	Bühlmann	DCIEM
No Stop Limit (Bottom time)	12	15	12	20
Stops required	-	-	-	5 / 3m

Surface Interval = 1.5 hr

DIVE 2: Max. Depth = **30m** (100ft)   Bottom Time = **14** min

Table	BS-AC '88	U.S. Navy	Bühlmann	DCIEM
No Stop Limit (Bottom time)	0	11	8	10
Stops required	3 / 6m	3 / 3m	5 / 3m	10 / 3m

Surface Interval = 8 hr

DIVE 3: Max. Depth = **27m** (90ft)   Bottom Time = **20** min

Table	BS-AC '88	U.S. Navy	Bühlmann	DCIEM
No Stop Limit (Bottom time)	13.5	23	20	14
Stops required	1 / 6m	-	-	10 / 3m

Table 19.5

Comparision of various schedules

DIVE 1: Max. Depth = **33m** (110ft)   Bottom Time = **25** min

Table	BS-AC '88	U.S. Navy	Bühlmann	DCIEM
No Stop Limit (Bottom time)	15	20	14	12
Stops required	3 / 6m	3 / 3m	2 /6m 7 /3m	10 /6m 10 /3m

Surface Interval = 2 hr

DIVE 2: Max. Depth = **21m** (70ft)   Bottom Time = **18** min

Table	BS-AC '88	U.S. Navy	Bühlmann	DCIEM
No Stop Limit (Bottom time)	9	24	23	18
Stops required	1 / 6m	-	-	-

Table 19.6

Comparison of No-Stop Limits.
(Bottom Time)

Depth m ft		BS-AC 88	Buhlmann	DCIEM	U.S. Navy
9	30	242	400	300	405
12	40	121	125	150	200
15	50	73	75	75	100
18	60	50	51	50	60
21	70	36	35	35	50
24	80	28	25	25	40
27	90	22	20	20	30
30	100	18	17	15	25
33	110	15	14	12	20
36	120	12	12	10	15
39	130	10	10	8	10
42	140	9	9	7	10

Figure 19.2

A comparison of the decompression profiles given by various
tables for a dive to 36m (120ft) for a bottom time of 30 minutes.

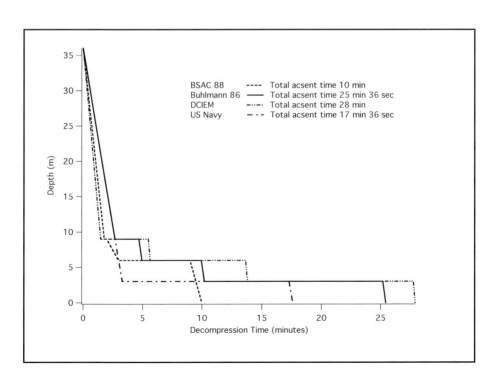

THE TABLES

Tables 19.7 to 19.14 are reprinted with permission from the British Sub-Aqua Club and Dr. Tom Hennessy. The BS-AC '88 Tables are protected by Copyright and the unauthorized copying and reproducing of any part of these tables is expressly forbidden.

Table 19.7 (TABLE A/1)

LEVEL 1 (greater than 984 millibar) — TABLE A

DEPTH (metres)	ASCENT (mins)		B	C	D	E	F	G	G	G	G	G	G	G	G
			No-Stop Dives					Decompression Stop Dives							
3	(1)	—	166	∞											
6	(1)	—	36	166	593	∞									
9	1	—	17	67	167	203	243	311	328	336	348	356	363	370	376
12	1	—	10	37	87	104	122	156	169	177	183	188	192	197	201
15	1	—	6	24	54	64	74	98	109	116	121	125	129	133	136
18	1	—		17	37	44	51	68	78	84	88	92	95	98	101
DECOMPRESSION STOPS (mins) at 6 metres								1	3	6	9	12	15	18	21
SURFACING CODE			B	C	D	E	F	G	G	G	G	G	G	G	G

DEPTH (metres)	ASCENT (mins)		B	C	D	E	F	G	G	G	G	G	G	G
21	1	—		13	28	32	37	51	59	65	68	72	75	77
24	2	—		11	22	26	30	41	49	53	56	59	62	64
27	2	—		8	18	21	24	34	41	45	47	50	52	55
30	2	—		7	15	17	20	29	35	39	41	43	45	47
33	2	—			13	15	17	25	30	34	36	38	40	42
36	2	—			11	12	14	22	27	30	32	34	36	37
39	3	—			10	12	13	20	25	29	30	32	33	35
DECOMPRESSION STOPS (mins) at 9 metres									1	1	1	1	2	
at 6 metres								1	3	6	9	12	15	18
SURFACING CODE			B	C	D	E	F	G	G	G	G	G	G	G

DEPTH (metres)	ASCENT (mins)		B	C	D	E	F	G	G	G	G	G	G	G
42	3	—			9	10	12	21	23	26	28	29	31	32
45	3	—			8	9	10	19	22	24	26	27	28	30
48	3	—				8	9	18	21	23	24	25	26	28
51	3	—					8	17	19	21	22	24	25	26
DECOMPRESSION STOPS (mins) at 9 metres									1	1	1	2	2	3
at 6 metres								2	3	6	9	12	15	18
SURFACING CODE			B	C	D	E	F	G	G	G	G	G	G	G

ASCENT RATE — 15 metres per minute. Take 1 minute from 6m to surface.

DIVE TIME — time from leaving surface to arriving at 6m on return to surface, or arrival at 9m on 2 Stop dives.

The infinity symbol ∞ in the Dive Time column indicates that there is no time limit for a dive at that depth which produces the Surfacing Code for that column.

If the Surfacing Code is in *italic* then there is no dive possible producing this code.

The symbol ● indicates that you must move to the next column on the right which includes a valid Dive Time. Small increases in Dive Time in such areas of the Table produce large changes in decompression requirements and extra caution is needed.

These Tables are designed for Sports Diving and assume an appropriate activity level. More demanding dives, involving heavy work or particularly cold conditions or divers whose physical condition/habits are a concern require extra caution.

Table 19.8
(TABLE B/1)

LEVEL 1 (greater than 984 millibar)
TABLE B

DEPTH (metres)	ASCENT (mins)	No-Stop Dives				Decompression Stop Dives							
3	(1)	—	∞										
6	(1)	—	80	504	∞								
9	1	—	27	113	148	188	255	272	284	292	300	307	314	321
12	1	—	14	52	67	84	116	129	137	143	148	152	156	160
15	1	—	8	31	40	48	69	79	86	90	94	98	101	105
18	1		—	21	27	32	47	55	61	64	68	71	74	76
DECOMPRESSION STOPS (mins) at 6 metres							1	3	6	9	12	15	18	21
SURFACING CODE		B	C	D	E	F	G	G	G	G	G	G	G	G

DEPTH (metres)	ASCENT (mins)	No-Stop Dives				Decompression Stop Dives						
21	1		—	15	19	23	35	42	47	50	52	55	57
24	2		—	12	15	19	28	35	39	41	43	45	47
27	2		—	10	12	15	23	29	33	35	36	38	40
30	2		—	8	10	12	20	25	28	30	32	33	35
33	2		—	8	10		17	22	25	26	28	29	31
36	2		—	7	8		15	20	22	24	25	26	28
39	3		—	8			14	19	21	23	24	25	26
DECOMPRESSION STOPS (mins) at 9 metres								1	1	1	1	2
at 6 metres							1	3	6	9	12	15	18
SURFACING CODE		B	C	D	E	F	G	G	G	G	G	G	G

DEPTH (metres)	ASCENT (mins)	No-Stop Dives				Decompression Stop Dives						
42	3					—	15	17	20	21	22	23	24
45	3					—	14	17	18	19	20	21	22
48	3					—	13	16	17	18	19	20	21
51	3					—	12	15	16	17	18	19	
DECOMPRESSION STOPS (mins) at 9 metres								1	1	1	2	2	3
at 6 metres							2	3	6	9	12	15	18
SURFACING CODE		B	C	D	E	F	G	G	G	G	G	G	G

Table 19.9 (TABLE C/1)

LEVEL 1 (greater than 984 millibar) — TABLE C

DEPTH (metres)	ASCENT (mins)	No-Stop Dives					Decompression Stop Dives							
3	(1)		—	∞										
6	(1)		—	359	∞										
9	1		—	49	79	116	182	199	211	220	227	234	241	248
12	1		—	20	31	44	71	83	90	95	100	104	108	112
15	1		—	11	17	24	40	48	54	57	61	64	67	70
18	1		—	7	11	15	27	34	38	40	43	45	47	50
DECOMPRESSION STOPS (mins) at 6 metres							1	3	6	9	12	15	18	21
SURFACING CODE		*B*	*C*	*D*	E	F	G	G	G	G	G	G	G	G

DEPTH (metres)	ASCENT (mins)	No-Stop Dives					Decompression Stop Dives						
21	1			—	7	10	20	26	29	31	33	35	37
24	2				—	8	16	22	25	26	28	29	31
27	2					—	13	18	21	22	24	25	26
30	2					—	11	16	18	19	20	22	23
33	2					—	10	14	16	17	18	19	20
36	2					—	8	12	14	15	16	17	18
39	3					—	8	12	14	15	16	17	18
DECOMPRESSION STOPS (mins) at 9 metres									1	1	1	1	2
at 6 metres							1	3	6	9	12	15	18
SURFACING CODE		*B*	*C*	*D*	E	F	G	G	G	G	G	G	G

DEPTH (metres)	ASCENT (mins)	No-Stop Dives					Decompression Stop Dives						
42	3					—	10	●	13	14	15	16	
45	3					—	9	●	12	●	14	●	15
48	3					—	8	●	12	●	13	14	
51	3					—	8	10	11	12	●	13	
DECOMPRESSION STOPS (mins) at 9 metres								1	1	1	2	2	3
at 6 metres							2	3	6	9	12	15	18
SURFACING CODE		*B*	*C*	*D*	*E*	*F*	G	G	G	G	G	G	G

ASCENT RATE — 15 metres per minute. Take 1 minute from 6m to surface.

DIVE TIME — time from leaving surface to arriving at 6m on return to surface, or arrival at 9m on 2 Stop dives.

The infinity symbol ∞ in the Dive Time column indicates that there is no time limit for a dive at that depth which produces the Surfacing Code for that column.

If the Surfacing Code is in *italic* then there is no dive possible producing this code.

The symbol ● indicates that you must move to the next column on the right which includes a valid Dive Time. Small increases in Dive Time in such areas of the Table produce large changes in decompression requirements and extra caution is needed.

These Tables are designed for Sports Diving and assume an appropriate activity level. More demanding dives, involving heavy work or particularly cold conditions or divers whose physical condition/habits are a concern require extra caution.

Table 19.10 (TABLE D/1)

LEVEL 1 (greater than 984 millibar)
TABLE D

DEPTH (metres)	ASCENT (mins)	DIVE TIME (mins) — No-Stop Dives					Decompression Stop Dives							
3	(1)		∞	231	—									
6	(1)			—	∞									
9	1			—	8	29	81	96	107	115	122	129	136	143
12	1				—	8	26	33	38	42	45	48	51	54
15	1					—	14	19	23	25	27	28	30	32
18	1					—	9	14	16	18	19	20	22	23
21	1					—	6	10	13	14	15	16	17	18
24	2						—	9	11	12	13	14	15	16
27	2						—	8	10	11	●	12	13	
30	2						—	7	9	●	10	11	●	12
33	2						—	8	●	9	●	10		
36	2						—	7	8	●	9			
39	3						—	8	●	9				
DECOMPRESSION STOPS (mins) at **6 metres**							1	3	6	9	12	15	18	21
SURFACING CODE		*B*	*C*	*D*	*E*	*F*	G	G	G	G	G	G	G	G
42	3									—	8	●	●	9
45	3									—	8	●	●	9
48	3									—	8			
DECOMPRESSION STOPS (mins) at **9 metres**										1	1	1	1	1
at **6 metres**										9	12	15	18	21
SURFACING CODE		*B*	*C*	*D*	*E*	*F*	G	G	G	G	G	G	G	G

ASCENT RATE — 15 metres per minute. Take 1 minute from 6m to surface.
DIVE TIME — time from leaving surface to arriving at 6m on return to surface, or arrival at 9m on 2 Stop dives.

The infinity symbol ∞ in the Dive Time column indicates that there is no time limit for a dive at that depth which produces the Surfacing Code for that column.

If the Surfacing Code is in *italic* then there is no dive possible producing this code.

The symbol ● indicates that you must move to the next column on the right which includes a valid Dive Time. Small increases in Dive Time in such areas of the Table produce large changes in decompression requirements and extra caution is needed.

These Tables are designed for Sports Diving and assume an appropriate activity level. More demanding dives, involving heavy work or particularly cold conditions or divers whose physical condition/habits are a concern require extra caution.

Table 19.11
(TABLES E/1 and F/1)

© Copyright 1988, British Sub-Aqua Club.

LEVEL 1 (greater than 984 millibar) — TABLE E

DEPTH (metres)	ASCENT (mins)	No-Stop Dives					Decompression Stop Dives							
3	(1)	∞	271	8	—									
6	(1)			—	∞									
9	1				—	9	50	63	73	81	88	94	101	107
12	1					—	14	22	26	28	31	33	36	38
15	1					—	8	13	16	17	19	20	21	23
18	1						—	9	11	12	13	14	15	16
21	1						—	7	9	10	●	11	12	13
24	2						—	7	8	9	10	●	11	12
27	2							—	7	8	●	9	●	10
30	2								—	7	●	8	●	9
33	2										—	7	●	8
36	2												—	7
DECOMPRESSION STOPS (mins) at **6 metres**							1	3	6	9	12	15	18	21
SURFACING CODE		B	C	D	E	F	G	G	G	G	G	G	G	G

LEVEL 1 (greater than 984 millibar) — TABLE F

DEPTH (metres)	ASCENT (mins)	No-Stop Dives					Decompression Stop Dives							
3	(1)	∞	303	25	5		—							
6	(1)		∞	339			—							
9	1					—	23	33	40	46	52	57	63	69
12	1					—	6	11	14	16	18	20	22	24
15	1						—	7	9	10	11	12	13	14
18	1								—	6	7	8	9	10
21	1									—	6	●	7	8
24	2										—	7	●	8
27	2												—	7
DECOMPRESSION STOPS (mins) at **6 metres**							1	3	6	9	12	15	18	21
SURFACING CODE		B	C	D	E	F	G	G	G	G	G	G	G	G

Table 19.12
(TABLE G/1 &
SURFACE INTERVAL TABLE L1)

© Copyright 1988, British Sub-Aqua Club.

LEVEL 1 (greater than 984 millibar)
TABLE G

DEPTH (metres)	ASCENT (mins)	DIVE TIME (mins) No-Stop Dives				Decompression Stop Dives						
3	(1)	∞	332	45	19	7	—					
6	(1)			∞	484	81	—					
9	1					—	9	12	16	19	23	27
12	1						—	6	7	8	10	
15	1								—	6		
DECOMPRESSION STOPS (mins) at **6 metres**						—	6	9	12	15	18	21
SURFACING CODE		*B*	*C*	*D*	*E*	*F*	*G*	*G*	*G*	*G*	*G*	*G*

Note *there are some dives possible on Table* **G** *that produce a SURFACING CODE of* **G** *but require no decompression stop.*

This SURFACE INTERVAL TABLE shows how your body tissues gradually release excess gas over periods of time, whilst you remain at LEVEL 1. Enter the left hand column with the SURFACING CODE from your last dive and move right along that row for your SURFACE INTERVAL and your CURRENT TISSUE CODE is indicated.

SURFACE INTERVAL TABLE LEVEL 1

Last Dive SURFACING CODE	Minutes 15	30	60	90	Hours 2	3	4	10	12	14	15	16
G	G	F	E	D	C			B				A
F	F	E	D		C			B			A	
E	E		D	C				B			A	
D		D		C				B			A	
C			C					B			A	
B				B					A			
A				A								

TABLE 19.13 (TRANSFER TABLE)

© Copyright 1988, British Sub-Aqua Club.

LAST LEVEL CURRENT TISSUE CODE	LAST LEVEL	NEW LEVEL CURRENT TISSUE CODE			
		LEVEL 1	LEVEL 2	LEVEL 3	LEVEL 4
A	1	A	B	B	C
	2	A	A	B	C
	3	A	A	A	B
	4	A	A	A	A
B	1	B	C	D	D
	2	B	B	C	D
	3	B	B	B	C
	4	A	A	B	B
C	1	C	D	F	X
	2	C	C	D	G
	3	B	C	C	D
	4	B	B	C	C
D	1	D	G	X	X
	2	D	D	X	X
	3	C	D	D	X
	4	C	C	D	D
E	1	E	X	X	X
	2	D	E	X	X
	3	C	D	E	X
	4	C	C	D	E
F	1	F	X	X	X
	2	D	F	X	X
	3	D	D	F	X
	4	C	C	D	F
G	1	G	X	X	X
	2	E	G	X	X
	3	D	D	G	X
	4	C	D	D	G

Enter the table by finding your CURRENT TISSUE CODE in the left hand column. Move to your right along your current LEVEL row. In the column corresponding to your intended LEVEL your new CURRENT TISSUE CODE is shown. If an **X** is shown then it is unsafe to change to that LEVEL until further de-saturation has taken place at your current LEVEL. Remain at your current LEVEL until you achieve a CURRENT TISSUE CODE that produces a valid code (A to G).

TABLE 19.14
(ALTITUDE/ATMOSPHERIC PRESSURE CHART)

© Copyright 1988, British Sub-Aqua Club.

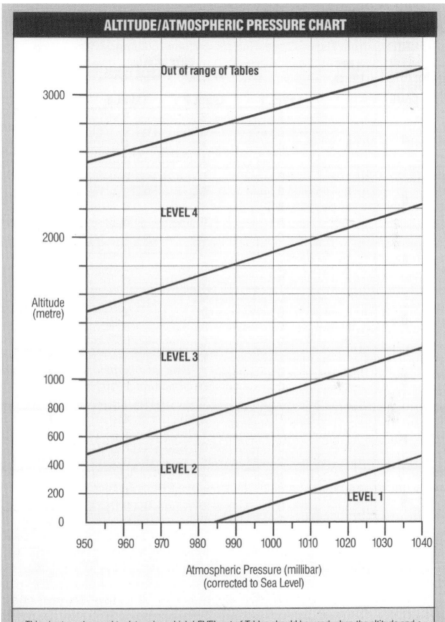

This chart can be used to determine which LEVEL set of Tables should be used when the altitude and a prevailing sea level atmospheric pressure are known. Weather forecasts usually provide atmospheric pressures corrected to sea level. By following the sea level atmospheric pressure vertically, and the known altitude horizontally, where these values meet the correct Level is shown. In borderline cases always choose the more punitive solution.

Pressurised aircraft are assumed to maintain a cabin pressure equivalent to LEVEL 4 which should be used to cover such flights.

USING THE BS-AC '88 TABLES

STARTING A SERIES OF DIVES

Before planning the first dive, it is important to determine the Current Tissue Code which is dictated by any recent exposure to pressure change. If no dives or changes in atmospheric pressure have occurred within the past 16 hours (10 hours for Levels 2,3 and 4), the Current Tissue Code is assumed to be A, and, therefore, Table A is used for the appropriate Level. However, if diving or changes of pressure have occurred, the procedures for planning repetitive dive or altitude changes should be followed.

Example 1.

What is the maximum No-Stop Dive Time for a single/first dive to 24m at an atmospheric pressure of 995 millibar (mb)?

Enter Table A/1, from the left, at 24m. Move to the right along the row until reaching the last (rightmost) number in the No-Stop Dives column (column 3). The number is 30, which means that the diver has a maximum of *30* minutes from the beginning of his descent until reaching 6 m during his ascent towards the surface. The ascent rate from the bottom to 6m must not exceed 15m/minute, and it must take one minute to ascend from 6m to the surface (an ascent rate of 6m/minute).

To find the Surfacing Code at the end of the dive, move down the column containing 30 minutes until intersecting the Surfacing Code row. The Surfacing Code after this dive would be *F*.

Example 2.

What is the maximum No-Stop Dive Time for a single/first dive to 36m (120ft) (atmospheric pressure 820mb)?

Enter Table A/3, from the left, at 36m. Move to the right along the row until reaching the last (rightmost) number in the No-Stop Dives column (column 3). The number is 8 which means that the diver has a maximum of *8* minutes from the beginning of his descent until reaching 6m during his ascent towards the surface. The ascent rate from the bottom to 6m must not exceed 15m/minute so the ascent must commence when no more than 6 minutes of bottom time has elapsed. It must take one minute to ascend from 6m to the surface.

To find the Surfacing Code at the end of the dive, move down the column containing 8 minutes until intersecting the Surfacing Code row. The Surfacing Code after this dive would be *F*.

Example 3.

What decompression is required after a single/first dive to 18m (60ft) for a dive time of 60 minutes at an atmospheric pressure of 1020mb? (Note that dive time is defined as the time from beginning the descent to arriving at 6m on return to the surface, or arrival at 9m on two-stop dives)

Enter Table A/1, from the left, at 18m, and move to the right across this row until finding the exact, or next longer, tabled bottom time. In this case 60 minutes is not tabled so select 68 minutes. As this time is beyond the maximum No-Stop Time of 51 minutes, at least one stop is required and can be found by moving down the column containing 68 minutes until intersecting the Decompression Stop row (deep yellow row). The number "1" in the 6m row means that a stop of *1 minute at 6m* is required before ascending to the surface at a rate of 6m/minute.

Notes:

- The dive time of 60 minutes begins when the diver leaves the surface at the start of the dive, and ends when he reaches 6m to begin the stop.

- The ascent from the bottom to 6m must be at a rate no faster than 15m/minute.

- The entire one minute of decompression stop time is spent at 6m.

- The diver must take one minute to ascend to the surface from the 6m stop.

- If a decompression stop is required after a dive to 18m or shallower, it will be a single stop at 6m. Dives deeper than 18m may require an additional stop at 9m.

Example 4.

What decompression is required after a single/first dive to 39m for a dive time of 30 minutes (atmospheric pressure 1010mb)?

Enter Table A/1 at 39m, and move along the 39m row until finding the exact, or next longer, tabled dive time. 30 minutes is tabled, so move across to the 30-minute column (which is in the pale yellow section for Decompression Stop Dives), and then move down the column until intersecting the Decompression Stop rows (bright yellow). The required stops are *1 minute at 9m* followed by *9 minutes at 6m*. The Surfacing Code at the end of the dive is *G*.

Notes:

- The maximum bottom time of the dive is 30 - 2 = 28 minutes (i.e. ascent to 9m stop must take at least 2 minutes).

- The 9m stop begins on reaching 9m, and ends on leaving 9m.

- Ascent from 9m to 6m must take at least 12 seconds (i.e. at 15m/minute maximum).

- The 6m stop begins on reaching 6m, and ends on leaving 6m.

- Ascent from 6m to the surface must take 1 minute (i.e. at a rate of 6m/minute).

- The diver should rest on the surface and should remain thermally comfortable and well-hydrated (with non-alcoholic fluids).

SECOND OR SUBSEQUENT DIVES

Any dive planned when the Current Tissue Code is higher than A (e.g. B, C etc.) is treated as a second or subsequent dive. This may result from a previous dive or from flying, or otherwise ascending to altitude, prior to diving. The higher code is designed to account for excess nitrogen still remaining in a diver's tissues as a result of a previous dive(s).

Finding the Current Tissue Code after a surface interval

Example 5.

If the Surfacing Code immediately after a dive is C/1, what is the Current Tissue Code after a surface interval of 2 hours?

Enter the Surface Interval Table Level 1 from the left at C, and move across to the right until directly below the 2-hour mark, shown in the top (white) row. After a surface interval of 2 hours the Current Tissue Code becomes B* so Table B can be used to plan the next dive.

Example 6.

If the Surfacing Code immediately after a dive is D/2, what surface interval is required before the Current Tissue Code is once again A/2?

Enter the Surface Interval Table Levels 2, 3 or 4, from the left at D. Move along the row to the right, until reaching the section for A. Looking directly above to the top (white) row, you will find that the line corresponds to a surface interval of *9 hours*.

---

* B begins at and includes 2 hours and ends at but does not include 12 hours.

Example 7.

You are planning two no-stop dives. The first dive is to 30m, followed, 3 hours later, by a dive to 22m. (Atmospheric pressure is 990mb) Find the maximum allowable dive time for each dive?

Enter Table A/1, from the left, at the maximum depth of the initial dive, in this case 30m. Move to the right along the 30m row until reaching the last (rightmost) time in the section for No-Stop Dives. Hence, the maximum dive time for a no-stop dive is *20* minutes, which means that the diver must begin to ascend after approximately 18 minutes in order to arrive at 6m on schedule. Move down the column containing the 20 minutes until intersecting the Surfacing Code row. The Surfacing Code is *F*.

To plan the second dive, turn to the Surface Interval Table Level 1. Enter from the left at F and move to the right to find 3 hours, and select the new Tissue Code, which is *C*. Enter Table C/1 at the maximum depth of the repetitive dive. In this case, 22m is not tabled so enter at the 24m row and move across to the right to determine the No-Stop Dive Time. It is *8* minutes, and the Surfacing Code after the dive would be *F*.

Example 8.

You are planning two no-stop dives at an atmospheric pressure of 910mb. The first is to 36m followed 4 hours later by a dive to 27m. Find the maximum allowable dive time for each dive.

Enter Table A/2 at 36m and move along this row to the last figure in the section for No-Stop Dives. Hence, the maximum dive time for a no-stop dive is *10* minutes (i.e. 8 minutes of bottom time and 2 minutes of ascent to 6m). Move down the column to find the Surfacing Code, which is *F*.

Enter the Surface Interval Table Levels 2, 3 or 4 at F and move right to the 4-hour line to find the Current Tissue Code after the interval. It has just become *B*. Enter Table

B/2 at 27m and move right to the last time in the No-Stop Dives section, which is *11* minutes. The Surfacing Code after the dive is *F*. Note that a dive any deeper would require a decompression stop.

Example 9.

Fifteen hours after arriving at a highland village, with atmospheric pressure 920mb, you board a commercial aircraft for a four-hour flight to a dive destination at the seaside (atmospheric pressure 1010mb). Eight hours later you plan to do a no-stop dive to 27m, What is the maximum allowable no-stop time at 27m?

An atmospheric pressure of 920mb puts you in Level 2. From the Transfer Table, your Code of A/1 when departing for the highland village becomes B on arrival at the village. From the Surface Interval Tables for Levels 2,3 or 4, after 5 hours your arrival Code of B/2 reduces to A/2. Therefore, when you leave the highland village you have a Tissue Code of A/2. The cabin pressure of the aircraft is Level 4. To find the Tissue Code during the flight, enter the Transfer Table from the left at A, move along the row marked 2 (i.e. A/2) and across to the Level 4 column to find the new Tissue Code. It is *C/4*.

To find your Current Tissue Code on arrival at the seaside (L1), enter the Transfer Table at C/4 and move to the right to intersect the Level 1 column. The Code is *B/1*.

To find the Tissue Code after 8 hours at this pressure, enter the Surface Interval Table Level 1 at B and move to the right until level with 8 hours. This indicates that the Tissue Code is still B/1 just prior to the dive.

Enter Table B1 at 27m and move right to find the no-stop time of *15* minutes.

Planning multiple dives involving decompression stops

Example 10.

You are planning two dives that may require decompression stops. The first dive is to 27m for a dive time of 35 minutes. The second dive, 3 hours later, is to 19m for a dive time of 35 minutes. Calculate the required decompression. (Atmospheric pressure is 1000mb).

Enter Table A/1 at 27m and move right along the row to 41 minutes (the next longer tabled dive time since 35 minutes is not tabled). Move down the column to the Decompression Stops row to determine the required stop(s). A stop of *3 minutes at 6m* is required, and the Surfacing Code is *G*.

Enter the Surface Interval Table Level 1 from the left, move across to 3 hours and determine the Current Tissue Code, which is *C*. Enter Table C/1 at 21m (next deeper tabled depth) and move to the right to find 35 minutes. It is tabled, so move down the column to find the required stop(s). They are *1 minute at 9 m followed by 15 minutes at 6m*. The Surfacing Code is *G*.

Example 11.

You are planning two dives. The first is to a maximum depth of 22m for a dive time of 50 minutes. After a surface interval of 2½ hours, you wish to dive to 18m for 50 minutes dive time. Calculate the required decompression. (Atmospheric pressure is 990mb)

Enter Table A/1 at 24m and look up the dive time of 50 minutes. Selecting 53 minutes, the stops required are *1 minute at 9 m followed by 6 minutes at 6 m*. The Surfacing Code is *G*.

From the Surface Interval Table for Level 1, after 2^1/2 *hours* the Current Tissue Code is *C*. Enter Table C/1 at 18 m, move across to 50 minutes and down to find the required stop of *21 minutes at 6 m*. The Surfacing Code is *G*.

FLYING AFTER DIVING

Flying in a pressurized aircraft (Level 4) following a sea-level dive is not permissible until the diver has reached CURRENT TISSUE CODE of A or B. In other circumstances, the Transfer Table is used to determine an appropriate Tissue Code to achieve before ascending to altitude is considered to be relatively safe. (See discussion in Chapter 25).

MULTI-LEVEL DIVING

The BS-AC has previously suggested a Multi-level dive procedure based on the BS-AC '88 Tables. This procedure is described in the first edition of this text.[4]

REFERENCES

1. Shaw D. BS-AC Incidents Report 1987. *SPUMS J* 1988; 18 (1):35-7.

2. Allen C, Ellerby D. Decompression Update. *NDC Bulletin* 1990; 16:1-2.

3. Allen C. Personal communication.

4. Lippmann J. Deeper Into Diving, 1st Edn. Melbourne: J.L. Publications, 1990:432-4.

OTHER SOURCES

British Sub-Aqua Club. Decompression Talkback. *NDC Bulletin* 1986:7.

British Sub-Aqua Club. A Paper Computer for Everyone. *NDC Bulletin* 1986:6.

British Sub-Aqua Club. Diver Training Material - Supplement to Sports Diver and Dive Leader Training Handbook (Lessons ST 6: ST 7: LT 6 using BS-AC '88 Decompression Tables with Theory Questions and Answers). London: BS-AC; 1988.

Busuttili M. The BS-AC '88 Sports Diving Decompression Tables. Proceedings from Diving Officers' Conference. London: BS-AC; 1987.

Busuttili M. The BSAC '88 Decompression Tables. *NDC Bulletin* 1988:13.

Busuttili M. The BS-AC '88 Decompression Tables - first review. *NDC Bulletin* 1989; 14:3-5.

Davies T. Personal communications.

Hennessy T. The New BS-AC Tables Project. Proceedings from Diving Officers Conference. London: BS-AC; 1986.

Hennessy T. Diving Deeper into the BS-AC '88 Tables. *Diver* 1988; 33(11):19.

Hennessy T. Personal communications.

The authors wish to thank Dr. Tom Hennessy for perusing the initial draft of this chapter and for the material and assistance he provided. Many thanks to Trevor Davies for his constructive editorial comments and to the BS-AC for its co-operation and for permission to re-print part of the tables.

EXERCISES ON THE BS-AC '88 TABLES

Use Level 1 for all of the following exercises.

1. Find the maximum No-Stop Dive Times for single/first dives to the following depths:

   (a) 30m   (b) 9m   (c) 23m
   (d) 35m   (e) 30.5 m

2. Find the decompression required for the following single or first dives (the times given are dive times):

   (a) 18m for 60 min. (b) 15m for 75 min.
   (c) 19m for 45 min. (d) 25m for 40 min.
   (e) 28m for 30 min. (f) 36m for 15 min.

3. Find the maximum allowable No-Stop Dive Time for the following second dives:

   (a) A dive to 20m, 2½ hours after a dive to 28m for 26 minutes.
   (b) A dive to 15m, 3 hours after a dive to 24m for 25 minutes.
   (c) A dive to 30m, 5 hours after a dive to 36m for 12 minutes.

4. Find the decompression required for the following second dives (the times given are dive times):

   (a) A dive to 33m for 10 min., 1 hour after a dive to 30m for 20 min.
   (b) A dive to 24m for 30 min., 4½ hours after a dive to 26m for 20 min.
   (c) A dive to 32m for 18 minutes, 10 hours after a dive to 42m for 16 min.
   (d) A dive to 8m for 40 minutes, 1½ hours after a dive to 27m for 20 min.

5. Find any decompression stops required for each of the following dives (the times given are dive times):

   (a) Dive 1: 30m for 15 minutes
       Surface interval = 3 hr
       Dive 2: 26m for 20 minutes
       Surface interval = 4 hr
       Dive 3: 20m for 10 minutes

(b) Dive 1: 36 m for 15 minutes

Surface interval = 4 hr

Dive 2: 27m for 10 minutes
Surface interval = 5 hr

Dive 3: 17m for 32 minutes

(c) Dive 1: 41m for 5 minutes
Surface interval = 7 hr

Dive 2: 30m for 10 minutes
Surface interval = 5 hr

Dive 3: 10m for 10 minutes

(d) Dive 1: 33m for 22 minutes
Surface interval = 3 hr

Dive 2: 25m for 21 minutes
Surface interval = 7 hr

Dive 3: 22m for 32 minutes
Surface interval = 5 hr

Dive 4: 16m for 32 minutes

(e) Dive 1: 18m for 40 minutes
Surface interval = 3 hr

Dive 2: 42m for 8 minutes
Surface interval = 10 hr

Dive 3: 30m for 5 minutes

6. Find the maximum allowable No-Stop Dive times for each dive in the following pairs of dives:

(a) A dive to 28m followed 2 hours later by a dive to 20m.

(b) A dive to 34m followed 4½ hours later by a dive to 31m.

(c) A dive to 17m followed 2½ hours later by another dive to 17m.

(d) A dive to 16m followed 3 hours later by a dive to 20m.

(e) A dive to 41m followed 6½ hours later by a dive to 12m.

7. Find any decompression stops required for the first and second dives and the maximum No-Stop Dive Time for the third dive in the following dive sequences:

(a) Dive 1: 24m for 20 minutes
Surface interval = 5 hr

Dive 2: 20m for 10 minutes
Surface interval = 3 hr

Dive 3: 18m

(b) Dive 1: 20m for 25 minutes
Surface interval = 3 hr

Dive 2: 21m for 25 minutes
Surface interval = 3 hr

Dive 3: 9m.

ANSWERS

1. (a) 20 (b) 243   (c) 30   (d) 14 (e) 17

2. (a) 1 min at 6m   (b) 1 min at 6m
   (c) 1 min at 6m   (d) 3 min at 6m
   (e) 3 min at 6m   (f) 1 min at 6m

3. (a) 10 (b)   24   (c)   12

4. (a) 18 min at 6m   (b) 3 min at 6m
   (c) 3 min at 6m   (d) No stops

5. (a) Dive 1: No stops
        Dive 2: 1 min at 6m
        Dive 3: No stops

   (b) Dive 1: 1 min at 6m
        Dive 2: No stops
        Dive 3: No stops

   (c) Dive 1: No stops
        Dive 2: No stops
        Dive 3: No stops

   (d) Dive 1: 1 min at 6m
        Dive 2: 1 min at 9m and 6 min at 6m
        Dive 3: 3 min at 6m
        Dive 4: No stops

   (e) Dive 1: No stops
        Dive 2: 2 min at 6m
        Dive 3: No stops

6. (a) 20, 10 (b) 14, 10 (c) 51, 15
   (d) 51, 10 (e) 12, 84

7. (a) Dive 1: No stops
        Dive 2: No stops
        Dive 3: 32

    (b) Dive 1: No stops
        Dive 2: 1 min at 6m
        Dive 3: 116

© John McLennan

© Barry Andrewartha Photo

20

The DSAT Recreational Dive Planner
(distributed by PADI)

BACKGROUND

The Standard U.S. Navy Tables were primarily designed as decompression tables suited to military divers with an unlimited air supply, usually working at a single depth on a single task. With the advent of scuba, the tables were adapted to cater for repetitive diving.

Recreational divers dive differently from military divers, often spending portions of dives at different levels rather than a single depth, and commonly doing shorter repetitive dives, often over multiple days.[1] Most also avoid dives requiring mandatory decompression stops.

Although recreational diving patterns differ from those of navy divers, until the 1990s, most recreational divers used navy tables, commonly the U.S. Navy Tables. This introduced a number of problems; some of which were (and still are for those still using such tables):

- The NDLs of the U.S. Navy Tables appear to be too long for recreational diving purposes as significant bubble formation has been shown to occur in divers who have dived right to these limits. Indeed there is a tangible risk of decompression sickness (DCS) that exceeds 1% for many schedules when dives are made to the limits.

- Although the U.S. Navy divemasters developed ways to add safety to their table calculations, many recreational divers could not, or would not, do this effectively.

- Recreational divers often exceeded the ascent rate recommended on the tables, which was until relatively recently 60ft (18m) per minute. In addition, in some situations this ascent rate was too fast.

- The Navy tables require that a schedule be selected according to the maximum depth and total bottom time of a dive. A diver who has spent very little time at the maximum depth is, therefore, penalized.

- Similarly, because of certain features of the underlying model (see below) there may be undue penalty when performing typical short repetitive recreational dives.

Such issues have resulted in years of debate over whether the U.S. Navy schedules are appropriate for safe recreational diving.

In the mid 1980s, PADI responded to the demand for an appropriate set of tables for the recreational diver by commissioning a team to design and test a table specifically for recreational diving that addressed some of the problems described. The table development was headed by Dr. Raymond Rogers, a dentist with a keen interest in diving and decompression theory, and a background in biochemistry. Dr. Rogers sourced the documents that described the development of the U.S. Navy Tables and systematically began to assess and re-work some of the underlying concepts and calculations.[2] The introduction of the table by Diving Science and Technology Corporation (DSAT), a corporate affiliate of PADI, followed more than three years of research, testing and development.

THE THEORY BEHIND THE TABLES

The RDP is based on Haldanian decompression theory and utilizes tissue compartments with half-times for nitrogen absorption of 5, 10, 20, 30, 40, 60, 80 and 120 minutes, (although additional half-times of 100, 160, 200, 240, 360 and 480 were also utilized in the development).[3,4] In theory, optimal dive schedules are found by tracking the gas partial pressures in each tissue compartment as it on-gasses during a dive and off-gasses during the ascent and surface interval after the dive. Tracking partial pressures in this way allows the table designer to ensure that no tissue exceeds its M-value (see Chapter 14.1) during the ascent or on arrival at the surface

Planning of an appropriate surface interval is based on the gas loading of a theoretical "controlling tissue" whose kinetics suggest it is likely to be most important in determining the length of subsequent dives, given the type of diving being performed. For example, if a diver only performed very long relatively shallow dives, then a tissue with a long half-time for nitrogen absorption would be used to control the surface interval. This is because such a tissue would become significantly loaded during the dive, and lose its nitrogen only slowly (necessitating a longer surface interval). In contrast, if a diver performed only short dives, then the longer half time tissues could largely be ignored because they would load little nitrogen during the dive, and a shorter half-time tissue could be assumed to "control" the surface interval.

With these issues in mind, we find that the RDP differs from the US Navy table in two important ways.

First, the maximum allowable nitrogen levels in the tissue compartments on arrival at the surface (M_0 values) have been reduced below those used by the U.S. Navy. It will be fairly obvious to the reader that this will result in either shorter no decompression limits, or slower ascents, or both.

Second, the RDP utilises a faster "controlling tissue" for determining outgassing during any surface interval. The U.S. Navy Surface Interval Credit Table is calculated on the basis of a controlling tissue with a 120-minute half-time. This was used to cover all diving situations, including those longer dives requiring long decompressions. For the recreational diver, who usually avoids decompression stop dives and who generally dives shallower than 130ft / 40m for relatively short periods, a repetitive system based on the 120-minute tissue compartment may often (but certainly not always) prove to be unnecessarily conservative.* Dr Rogers argued that the controlling tissue for repetitive diving in typical short recreational dives will be one with a half-time shorter than 120 minutes.

Rogers sought a controlling tissue compartment which, in his view, was more appropriate to recreational diving than the 120-minute tissue compartment used by the U.S. Navy. He analyzed various typical recreational diving profiles and decided that a tissue compartment with a half-time of 40

---

* However, in reality, if sufficient bubbles have formed after the initial dive to slow down off-gassing and possibly increase on-gassing during repetitive dives, a tissue compartment with a half-time slower than 120-minutes may be required. In addition, in these circumstances, relatively simplistic Haldanian models such as the one utilized by Rogers, become increasingly inaccurate. However, by restricting the RDP to no-stop diving with reduced limits, Rogers aimed to keep the diver within bounds where his assumptions were valid.

minutes was adequate to cover most recreational dives. He discovered, however, that a small percentage of profiles, primarily involving a series of long, shallow dives, required a slower tissue than 40 minutes. Consequently, he chose a tissue compartment with a half-time of 60 minutes on which to base the repetitive system of the RDP. Rogers' analyses indicated that a tissue half-time of 60 minutes came closer to the theoretical needs of the recreational diver than any other half-time. However, the question that needed to be answered was whether this theory would hold up in practice - whether or not it would be safe to perform repetitive dives with the 60-minute tissue as the controlling tissue.

TESTING THE RDP

The testing of the RDP involved dry hyperbaric-chamber as well as openwater studies. It was conducted in two phases. Phase 1 concentrated on single day diving whereas Phase 2 involved multi-day repetitive dives to reflect the practice on dive trips and liveaboard dive vessels.

The study used a group of 234 volunteer divers. In the initial phase of the testing, a total of 25 dive schedules were tested; three of them in the open water. The profiles were either repetitive, multi-level or various combinations of these. In the chamber tests, subjects were exercised on rowing machines and the chamber was kept warm to increase blood flow. A Doppler ultrasonic flowmeter was used in evaluating the test profiles by monitoring the level of detectable circulating bubbles.[4]

In all, 911 dives were included in Phase 1, 683 were in the chamber and 228 in openwater. It has been claimed that almost every dive was tested beyond the No-D limit of the RDP.[5] An analysis of the profiles by one of these authors found that this was correct for the majority of test dives, though just over 20% of the dives did not stress the limit, either because the dive was not long enough, or the preceding surface interval was longer than required to achieve the pre-dive pressure group.[6]

After the dives the divers were monitored for bubbles, initially while at rest, and then after doing two deep knee-bends. In all, bubbles were detected in 7.7% of the dives. Grade 1 bubbles (Table 20.1) were detected in 6.4% of dives, grades 2 or 3 in 1.4% and no bubbles of grade 4 were detected. There were no cases of decompression sickness (DCS) in Phase 1.[4]

Phase 2 of the testing involved two stages – Phase 2a and Phase 2b. Phase 2a was aborted after one diver developed mild DCS. Phase 2b testing involved 4 no-stop dives per day for 6 consecutive days; a total of 24 dives for each subject. Twenty divers were selected to yield a planned total of 480 dives. The dives were a mixture of single level and multilevel dives, and were, once again, conducted by volunteer subjects.

In all, 475 dives were successfully completed. There were no openwater dives tested in this phase of testing - all of the dives were done in the chamber, and all with limited exercise. The test profiles were purportedly chosen to test the model as near to the limits as practicable to provide a wide spectrum of depth-time exposures.

Table 20.1

Grading of Doppler-detected bubbles

0 = no gas bubbles detected in at least 10 heart cycles

1 = occasional gas bubbles detected in 10 heart cycles

2 = few bubbles detectable; some cycles may have 2 to 4 bubbles per cycle

3 = several gas bubbles detectable per cycle

4 = gas bubbles present continuously (systole and diastole), gas bubble amplitude louder than flow sounds.

Once again, Mitchell's 1990 analysis showed that this was not always so. Indeed, it should be pointed out that the final dive on every day of the multiday program was to 40ft (12m), and that on 3 of the 6 days (including days 5 and 6), the bottom time was only about 70% of the no decompression limit. Safety stops at 15ft (4.5m) for 3 minutes were included at the end of each dive in Phase 2 (no stops were included in Phase 1). Bubbles were detected on about 10% of dives and were within grades 1 to 3. There were no grade 4 bubbles and no cases of DCS.[4,5] The researchers concluded that it is safe to make repetitive dives controlled by the 60-minute tissue and that minimal bubbling follows such dives.

However, there has been some criticism and debate about these conclusions. It has been pointed out, correctly, that the results of dive profile testing in a dry hyperbaric chamber are of uncertain relevance to actual risk of DCS in true open water dives. The counter argument is that achieving large numbers of formal test dives in open water is logistically very difficult, and that the RDP is better validated than some tables that have had little or no formal testing at all. Another point that has been raised in relation to Haldanian models in general is that the repetitive dive calculations assume that very few bubbles have formed in the body after a single dive and, therefore, that the same mathematics can be used to describe gas uptake and elimination on subsequent repetitive dives. There is wide agreement that this is problematic because if sufficient bubbling does occur inert gas kinetics on subsequent dives may be altered and the mathematics may not be valid. Hence, it is probably fair to say that the more repetitive dives performed in a series, the less

FIGURE 20.1

Diver being monitored for bubbles - post dive

Photo courtesy Dr. Michael Powell

confident we can be in the safety of the predicted no decompression limits.

Not surprisingly, in an attempt to cater for the higher gas loads that may result after multiple repetitive dives, and, so that the 60-minute half-time does not solely determine repetitive dive times, DSAT included special rules to be applied when three or more dives are planned in one day. This avoids pushing the model to its limits and accounts for theoretical tissues with halftimes as long as 480 minutes.

EXPERIENCE WITH THE RDP

As well as being tested under well-controlled conditions, a dive table (or dive computer) should be proven in the field where conditions may not be as well-controlled as during the tests.

Since its introduction, the RDP has been used very extensively with students on PADI Openwater courses without significant problems, although most of these exposures would not have come close to the limits of the RDP. Most of the published data revealing the DCS rates in table-users do not specify which dive table the divers were using.

FIGURE 20.2

% of divers with DCS who reported diving within their table limits 1987-97.

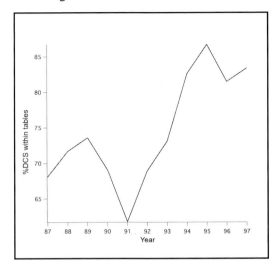

Figure 20.2, taken from DAN America data[7,8,9,10] presents the percentage of dive table-users treated for DCS between 1987 and 1997 who reported diving within the limits of their tables. There appears to have been a generally increasing trend, from 68.1% in 1987 to 83.4% in 1997.

Although the tables used were not specified, it may not be unreasonable to assume that an increasing proportion of these divers would have been using the RDP, rather than the previously predominant U.S. Navy Tables. Although there appears to have been a rise in DCS within the table limits, and although it is likely that many of these divers were using the RDP, this does not mean that the RDP limits are less safe than those of the U.S. Navy. It is important to remember that there was an enormous increase in multi-day repetitive diving during this period coinciding with the introduction of the RDP and the growing popularity of dive computers. The risk of DCS is increased with repetitive and multi-day diving activity, no matter what table or computer is used.

However, the reality is that millions of dives have now been done using the RDP with relatively few DCS incidents, and multi-day, multi-level, repetitive diving has become very common.

COMPARISON WITH OTHER TABLES

Table 20.2 compares the No-Decompression Limits of the RDP with those of some other tables and a comparision of times allowed by the RDP for a series of repetitive dives is shown in Tables 20.3 and 20.4.

TABLE 20.2

Comparison of No-Decompression Limits

| Depth | | U.S.Navy | RDP | | DCIEM | Bühlmann | BS-AC 88 |
ft	m		imperial	metric			
30	9	405	360	219*	300	400	242
40	12	200	140	147	150	125	121
50	15	100	80	72*	75	75	73
60	18	60	55	56	50	51	50
70	21	50	40	37*	35	35	36
80	24	40	30	29*	25	25	28
90	27	30	25	20*	20	20	22
100	30	25	20	20	15	17	18
110	33	20	16	14*	12	14	15
120	36	15	13	9*	10	12	12
130	39	10	10	9*	8	10	10

* These depths were not tabled on the metric RDP, so these times were taken from the next higher tabled depth

TABLE 20.3

Comparison of allowable times for some repetitive dives.

	Bottom time limits (minutes)			
	RDP	*US Navy*	*DCIEM*	*Bühlmann*
DIVE 1 **80ft** (24m) Actual bottom time (ABT) = 25 minutes. *Surface interval = 30 min.*	30 *(29)*	40	25	25
DIVE 2 **60ft** (18m) ABT = 15 minutes	30 *(30)*	24	26	37
Surface interval = 30 min. **DIVE 3** **60ft** (18m)	26 *(28)*	0	24	37
Note: Times in *(italics)* are those for the metric RDP.				

TABLE 20.4

Comparison of allowable times for some repetitive dives.

	Bottom time limits (minutes)			
	RDP	*US Navy*	*DCIEM*	*Bühlmann*
DIVE 1 **120ft** (36m) Actual bottom time (ABT) = 10 minutes. *Surface interval = 2hr*	13 *(9)*	15	10	12
DIVE 2 **100ft** (30m) ABT = 10 minutes	17 *(17)*	15	11	8 (stop of 5min at 10ft/3m)
Surface interval = 1hr **DIVE 3** **60ft** (18m)	44 *(45)*	30	29	37
Note: Times in *(italics)* are those for the metric RDP.				

Using the RDP

The RDP comes in three versions. There is a table version for those who prefer the conventional tabular layout. *It cannot be used for multi-level diving.* A second version of the RDP is called "The Wheel." By utilizing depth curves, rather than tables, The Wheel minimizes the time restrictions caused by rounding-off conventional tables. No calculations are required when using The Wheel, and it can be used to plan multi-level dives. The Wheel is shown in Figure 20.3 The third version is the eRDP, an electronic dive table. It is not a dive computer, but an electronic replication of the table. The eRDP uses a calculator-style device to yield the same information as the table version. The eRDP simplifies table use by prompting the user to enter dive profile information.

.

FIGURE 20.3
The Wheel version of the RDP

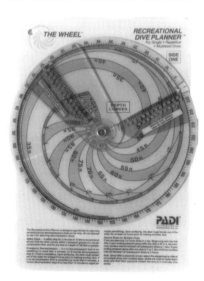

Since the imperial and metric versions of the RDP have a number of different depth increments, they will be dealt with separately.

TABLE VERSION

A.   IMPERIAL

This section relates only to the *imperial version* of the RDP.

GENERAL RULES OF USE[11]

Strictly adhere to the following rules when using The Recreational Dive Planner:

1. Any dive planned to 35ft or *less* should be calculated as a dive to 35ft.

2. Use the exact or next-greater depth shown for the depths of all dives.

3. Use the exact or next-greater time shown for the times of all dives.

4. Ascend from all dives no faster than 60ft/minute.*

5. As with any dive tables, be conservative and avoid using the maximum limits provided.

6. When planning a dive in cold water or under conditions that might be strenuous, plan the dive assuming the depth is 10ft deeper than actual.

7. Plan repetitive dives so each successive dive is to a shallower depth.

8. Limit your maximum depths to your training and experience level (Open Water Divers - 60ft; divers with greater training and experience - 100ft, with no dive in excess of 130ft).

---

* As with any table or computer it is important to control the rate of ascent. The RDP was tested using an ascent rate of 60ft/minute. If a diver ascends more rapidly more bubbling could occur. This might precipitate DCS, or might delay off-gassing during the subsequent surface interval and make the repetitive times allowed by the tables potentially less safe. PADI launched its Safe Ascent From Every Dive (S.A.F.E.) campaign to encourage divers to slow down their ascent rates to a maximum of 60ft/minute and to preferably ascend more slowly. A safety stop at the end of every dive was (and still is) also highly recommended. A diver may ascend slower than 60ft/minute without violating the RDP model; PADI encourages divers to see 60ft/minute as the *maximum* ascent rate, not the *desired* ascent rate with the RDP.

9. Always make a safety stop for 3 minutes at 15ft after any dive to 100ft (or greater) and any time you surface within three Pressure Groups of a No-Decompression Limit (NDL). Checking to see whether you are within three pressure groups of your NDL should always be your last step when planning a dive.

10. If you are planning 3 or more dives in a day: Beginning with the first dive, if your ending Pressure Group after any dive is W or X, the minimum surface interval between all subsequent dives is 1 hour. If your ending Pressure Group after any dive is Y or Z, the minimum surface interval between all subsequent dives is 3 hours.

11. Do not dive below 130 feet. As an emergency procedure, If you discover you have accidentally descended below 130 feet, immediately ascend (at a rate not to exceed 60 feet per minute) to 15 feet and make an emergency decompression stop for 8 minutes. Any dive below 130 feet must be followed by a surface interval of at least 6 hours.

12. An emergency decompression stop for 8 minutes at 15 feet must be made if a no-decompression limit is exceeded by 5 minutes or less. Upon surfacing, the diver must remain out of the water for at least 6 hours prior to making another dive. If a no-decompression limit is exceeded by more than 5 minutes, a 15-foot decompression stop of no less than 15 minutes is urged (air supply permitting). Upon surfacing, the diver must remain out of the water for at least 24 hours prior to making another dive. The Recreational Dive Planner is not meant for decompression diving – provisions for an emergency decompression stop are included only as a safety factor if you make a mistake. Proper planning and monitoring of your dives will avoid the need for emergency decompression.

Note: *Since little is presently known about the physiological effects of multiple dives over multiple days, divers are wise to make fewer dives and limit their exposure toward the end of a multi-day dive series.*

Planning no-decompression stop dives

1. SINGLE OR FIRST NO-DECOMPRESSION STOP DIVES

Table 1 (within Table 20.5) was designed for planning single dives or the first of a group of dives. Table 1 is the left-most table in Table 20.5.

Example 1.

You are planning to dive to a maximum depth of 80ft. What is the No-Decompression Limit (NDL)?

Enter Table 1 of the RDP, from the top, at 80ft and move down the column until coming to the *white* number in the *black* box. This is the NDL which, in this case, is *30* minutes. This 30 minutes is the maximum allowable *bottom time* for the dive.

Note:
If you dive to this NDL, you must then make a safety stop of 3 minutes at 15ft since you have dived to within 3 Pressure Groups (PG) of the NDL. Safety stops need not be added to bottom time with these tables (although the author advises it for the extra safety sometimes gained in any following repetitive dives).

Similarly, the NDL for 100ft is *20* minutes, the NDL for 60ft is *55* minutes, and the NDL for 50ft is *80* minutes.

Example 2.

What is the NDL for a single/first dive to a maximum depth of 54ft?

Enter Table 1 from the top at 60ft (i.e. the next greater tabled depth, since 54ft is not tabled). Move down the column until reaching the *white* number in the *black* box. The NDL is, thus, *55* minutes.

Note:
If this dive is carried out a safety stop would be mandatory (within 3 PGs of the NDL).

Similarly, the NDL for 66ft is *40* minutes, the NDL for 37ft is *140* minutes, and for 103ft is *16* minutes.

Table 20.5

Side 1 of the RDP (Imperial version).

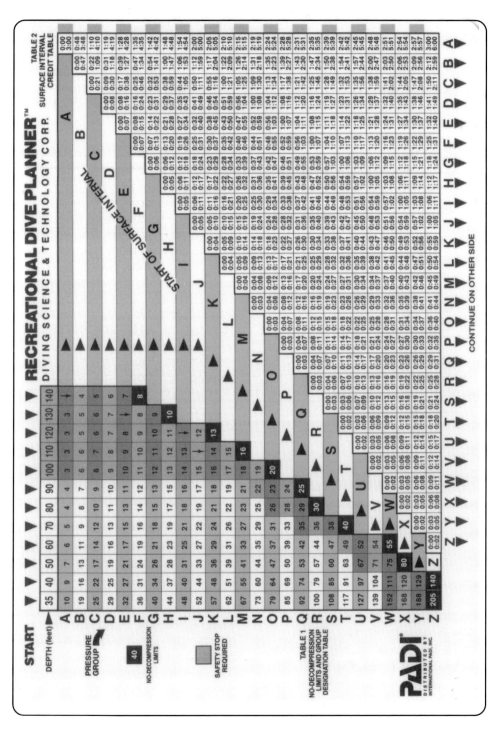

Reprinted courtesy PADI International and DSAT.

Finding the Pressure Group (PG) after single/first no-decompression stop dives

Example 3.

Find the PG after the previous single dive to 80ft for 30 minutes.

Enter Table 1, from the top, at 80ft. Move down the column until coming to the exact, or next longer, tabled bottom time. In this case 30 minutes is tabled so move down to 30 minutes, and then right to find the PG after the dive. It is *R*.

Note:
A safety stop would be required at the end of this dive.

Example 4.

Find the PG after a single dive to 50ft for 60 minutes.

Enter Table 1, from the top, at 50ft and move down until finding the bottom time of 60 minutes. Moving right, the PG is *S*.

Note:
Since 60 minutes is more than 3 PGs from the NDL of 80 minutes, a safety stop is not mandatory although it is highly recommended after any dive.

Example 5.

What is the Pressure Group (PG) after a dive to 63ft for 34 minutes?

Enter Table 1, from the top, at 70ft (i.e. the next greater tabled depth, since the exact depth is not tabled). Move down the column until finding the exact, or next longer tabled, bottom time. 34 minutes is not tabled so take 35 minutes, and then move right to find the PG. It is *Q*.

Example 6.

What is the PG after a dive to 113ft for a bottom time of 12 minutes?

Enter Table 1 at 120ft and move down to find the bottom time of 12 minutes (simply pass through the arrow at 11 minutes). Moving right, the PG is *J*.

2. REPETITIVE NO-DECOMPRESSION STOP DIVES

During a surface interval nitrogen is off-gassed. After various intervals the Pressure Groups, which represent the nitrogen levels in the 60-minute tissue, will be reduced. Table 2, the "Surface Interval Credit Table", enables us to calculate new Pressure Groups after surface intervals which are greater than 2 minutes and less than 6 hours.

Finding the new Pressure Group after a surface interval

Example 7.

If the PG immediately after a dive is H, what is the new group after a surface interval of 2 hours?

Enter Table 2, from the left, at *H* and move right until finding an interval that includes the surface interval of 2 hours. It is between 1:48 and 4:48, so move right to this box and then down the column to the bottom to get the new PG. It is *A*.

Example 8.

If the PG immediately after a dive is F, find the new group after a surface interval of 50 minutes.

Enter Table 2, from the left, at *F* and move right to find a box containing 50 minutes. It is included in 0:47 to 1:34, so move to this box and then down the column to find the PG, which is *B*.

Calculating the maximum allowable no-decompression stop bottom time for a repetitive dive

A repetitive dive is defined to be any dive within 6 hours of a previous dive(s). When planning a repetitive dive, the excess nitrogen still remaining after the surface interval must be taken into account. This is done by adding a "Residual Nitrogen Time" (RNT).

Table 20.6

Side 2 of the RDP (Imperial version).

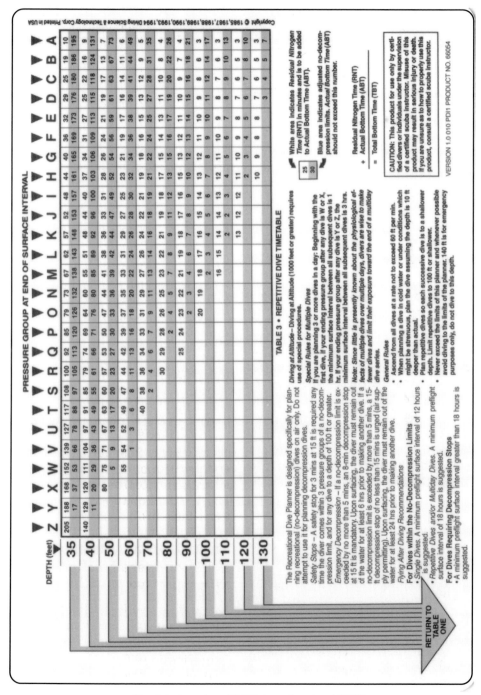

Reprinted courtesy PADI International and DSAT.

The Residual Nitrogen Time is the amount of time which must be considered already spent at the maximum depth of the repetitive dive before this dive is commenced. It is subtracted from the single dive NDL for that depth and the result is the no-decompression stop bottom time still remaining at that depth.

Table 3 (Table 20.7) gives the Residual Nitrogen Times and the maximum no-decompression stop bottom times still available for the various depths of repetitive dives.

Example 9.

If you are in group C immediately before a dive to 80ft, find:

(i) the Residual Nitrogen Time (RNT) at 80ft

(ii) the maximum allowable no-decompression bottom time at 80ft

Enter Table 3, from the top, at C and move down the column until intersecting the row for 80ft. You will find two numbers in the box. The top number, printed *on white*, is the Residual Nitrogen Time which, in this case, is *10* minutes. This means that before doing the dive you must consider that you have already spent 10 minutes at 80ft. This 10 minutes is to account for excess nitrogen left over from the previous dive(s). The remaining allowable no-decompression stop time (i.e. adjusted maximum no-decompression bottom time) is the number printed *on blue*. In this case it is *20* minutes. **The Actual Bottom Time (ABT) of a repetitive dive should never exceed the adjusted maximum no-decompression bottom time.**

Note:
If you planned to do this dive, you must end it with a safety stop of 3 minutes at 15ft, since you will be within 3 PGs of the NDL.

Example 10.

At the end of a surface interval after a dive you are in group B. Find:

(i) the Residual Nitrogen Time

(ii) the maximum allowable bottom time for a no-decompression stop dive to 96ft.

Enter Table 3, from the top, at B and move down the column until intersecting the row for 100ft. The RNT is *6* minutes, and the maximum no-decompression stop bottom time is *14* minutes. A safety stop would be required at the end of the dive.

Planning a pair of no-decompression stop dives

Example 11.

You are planning two no-decompression stop dives. The first dive is to 100ft, followed, 3 hours later, by a dive to 75ft. Find the maximum allowable bottom time for each dive.

Enter Table 1 at 100ft and move down the column to the black box which contains the NDL, which is *20* minutes.

Move right to find the PG, which is *O*. Continue across to the right until finding a box containing the surface interval of 3 hours. It is the 2:24-5:24 box, so move to it and then down the column to get the PG after the surface interval. It is *A*.

Enter Table 3, from the top, at A, and move down the column until intersecting the row for 80ft. The NDL for the dive is the number printed on blue, and is *26* minutes.

Note:
A safety stop would be mandatory at the end of each dive, but it is not necessary to include the time of the safety stop when determining the PG after the dive. However, by using the total dive time (i.e. bottom time + ascent time + time at safety stop), rather than just the bottom time to determine the PG, extra safety may be achieved.

Example 12.

You are planning two no-decompression stop dives. The first is to 120ft, followed, 4 hours later, by a dive to 110ft. Find the maximum allowable bottom time for each dive.

Enter Table 1 at 120ft and move down to find the NDL in the black box. It is *13* minutes, and is the maximum allowable bottom time for the first dive.

Move right to get the PG after the dive, which is *K*. Continue moving right to find the box which includes the 4-hour surface interval. It is the 2:05-5:05 box. Move across to this box and then down the column to get the new PG, which is *A*.

Enter Table 3 at A and move down to intersect the 110ft row. The adjusted maximum no-decompression bottom time is *13* minutes.

A safety stop would be mandatory at the end of each dive.

Finding the Pressure Group after a repetitive dive

Example 13.

Before a repetitive dive to 100ft, you are in group B. If you now dived to 100ft for a bottom time of 10 minutes, what would be your new PG?

From Table 3, the RNT before the dive is 6 minutes and the maximum no-decompression stop bottom time is 14 minutes.

To find the PG after this 10-minute dive, you must first find the Total Bottom Time (TBT) of the repetitive dive. The TBT is the sum of the Residual Nitrogen Time (RNT) and the Actual Bottom Time (ABT) of the dive. In this case, the TBT = $6_{(RNT)}$ + $10_{(ABT)}$ = 16 minutes. To find the PG after the dive, return to Table 1. Enter Table 1 at the depth of the repetitive dive, 100ft, and move down this column to find the TBT of 16 minutes (if the exact time is not tabled select the next greater tabled time). Move right to find the new PG, which is *K*.

Example 14.

Before a repetitive dive you are in group C. If you now dived to 75ft for a bottom time of 15 minutes, what would be your new Pressure Group?

From Table 3, the RNT at 80ft before the dive is 10 minutes (and the maximum no-decompression stop bottom time is 20 minutes).

To find the PG after this 15-minute dive, first find the TBT. The TBT = 10 + 15 = 25 minutes.

Turn to Table 1, and look up 80ft for 25 minutes. You will get a PG of *N*.

Planning a Group of Three No-decompression Stop Dives

Example 15.

You are planning to do three no-decompression stop dives, two of which are repetitive. The first dive, which is to 80ft, is followed, 2 hours later, by a dive to 65ft, which is followed, 3 hours later, by a final dive to 50ft. Find the maximum allowable no-decompression stop bottom times for each of the dives.

Enter Table 1 at 80ft and move down to find the NDL of *30* minutes, which is the maximum allowable bottom time for the first dive. A safety stop is mandatory.

Move right to find the PG, which is R, and continue across to find the surface interval. It lies in the 1:47-2:34 box, so move across to this box and then down the column to get the new PG, group B.

Enter Table 3 at B and move down to intersect the row for 70ft. The maximum no-decompression stop bottom time is 31 minutes, and the TBT = 9 + 31 = *40* minutes. A safety stop is mandatory.

Enter Table 1 at 70ft, move down to find the TBT of 40 minutes and right to find the PG. It is T. Continue right to find the 3-hour surface interval and down to get the new PG, which is A.

Enter Table 3 at A and move down to intersect the 50ft row. The maximum no-decompression stop bottom time is 73 minutes. A safety stop is mandatory.

Note:
Example 15 can be compared directly to the equivalent problem using U.S. Navy Tables shown on Page 201.

SPECIAL CASES

1. Cold and Strenuous Dives

When planning a dive in cold water, or under conditions that might be strenuous, plan the dive assuming the depth is 10ft deeper than actual.

For example, if you are planning to dive to 60ft and you expect to be cold, take the limit for 70ft as your maximum no-decompression stop bottom time.

If you get cold, or if you work hard during a dive to 85ft, ensure that you begin your ascent before the NDL for 100ft expires.

2. Special Rules for Multiple Dives

If you are planning 3 or more dives: Beginning with the first dive, if your ending Pressure Group after any dive is W or X, the minimum surface interval between all subsequent dives is 1 hour. If your ending Pressure Group after any dive is Y or Z, the minimum surface interval between all subsequent dives is 3 hours.

Example 16.

After a dive to 60ft for 55 minutes your PG will be W. If you are planning a second dive, you must remain at the surface for at least 1 hour. If, after an hour of surface interval you wish to dive to 50ft, the maximum no-decompression stop bottom time is 49 minutes. If you actually dive to 50ft for 30 minutes, you will surface with a PG of T. You must still wait at least an hour before diving again, since the previous dive brought you into group W.

Example 17.

After a dive to 60ft for 54 minutes you are in group V. After a 20-minute surface interval your PG is Q. You then dive to 40ft for 60 minutes, which puts you into group Z. You must not dive again for at least 3 hours and must have a minimum surface interval of 3 hours between any further dives, until there has been a 6-hour break from diving.

B. METRIC VERSION

This section relates only to the *metric version* of the RDP.

GENERAL RULES OF USE[12]

Strictly adhere to the following rules when using The Recreational Dive Planner:

1. Any dive planned to 10 metres or *less* should be calculated as a dive to 10 metres.

2. Use the exact or next-greater depth shown for the depths of all dives.

3. Use the exact or next-greater time shown for the times of all dives.

4. Ascend from all dives no faster than 18 metres per minute.

5. As with any dive table, be conservative and avoid using the maximum limits provided.

6. When planning a dive in cold water or under conditions that might be strenuous, plan the dive assuming the depth is 4 metres deeper than actual.

7. Plan repetitive dives so each successive dive is to a shallower depth.

8. Limit your maximum depths to your training and experience level (Open Water Divers - 18 metres; divers with greater training and experience - 30m, with no dive in excess of 40m).

---

* **As with any table or computer it is important to control the rate of ascent.** The RDP was tested using an ascent rate of 18m/minute. If a diver ascends more rapidly more bubbling could occur. This might precipitate DCS, or might delay off-gassing during the subsequent surface interval and make the repetitive times allowed by the tables potentially less safe. PADI launched its Safe Ascent From Every Dive (S.A.F.E.) campaign to encourage divers to slow down their ascent rates to a maximum of 18m/minute and to preferably ascend more slowly. A safety stop at the end of every dive was (and still is) also highly recommended. A diver may ascend slower than 18m/minute without violating the RDP model; PADI encourages divers to see 18m/minute as the *maximum* ascent rate, not the *desired* ascent rate with the RDP.

9. Always make a safety stop for 3 minutes at 5 metres after any dive to 30 metres (or greater) and any time you surface within 3 pressure groups of a No-Decompression Limit (NDL). Checking to see whether you are within 3 pressure groups of your NDL should always be your last step when planning a dive.

10. If you are planning 3 or more dives in a day: Beginning with the first dive, if your ending Pressure Group after any dive is W or X, the minimum surface interval between all subsequent dives is 1 hour. If your ending Pressure Group after any dive is Y or Z, the minimum surface interval between all subsequent dives is 3 hours.

11. Do not dive below 40 metres. As an emergency procedure, if you discover you have accidentally descended below 40m, immediately ascend (at a rate not to exceed 18m per minute) to 5m and make an emergency decompression stop for 8 minutes. Any dive below 40m exceeds the limits of the RDP and must be followed by a surface interval of at least 6 hours.

12. An emergency decompression stop for 8 minutes at 5m must be made if a no-decompression limit is exceeded by 5 minutes or less. Upon surfacing, the diver must remain out of the water for at least 6 hours prior to making another dive. If a No-Decompression Limit is exceeded by more than 5 minutes, a 5m decompression stop of no less than 15 minutes is urged (air supply permitting). Upon surfacing, the diver must remain out of the water for at least 24 hours prior to making another dive. The Recreational Dive Planner is not meant for decompression diving – provisions for an emergency decompression stop are included only as a safety factor if you make a mistake. Proper planning and monitoring of your dives will avoid the need for emergency decompression.

Note: *Since little is presently known about the physiological effects of multiple dives over multiple days, divers are wise to make fewer dives and limit their exposure toward the end of a multi-day dive series.*

Table 20.7

Side 1 of the RDP (Metric version).

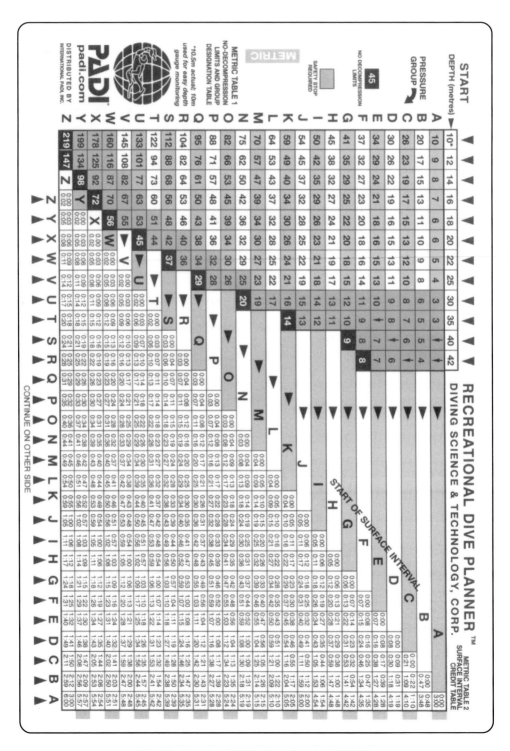

Reprinted courtesy PADI International and DSAT.

Planning no-decompression stop dives

1. SINGLE OR FIRST NO-DECOMPRESSION STOP DIVES

Table 1 (within Table 20.7) was designed for planning single dives, or the first of a group of dives. Table 1 is the left-most table in Table 20.7.

Example 1.

You are planning to dive to a maximum depth of 25m. What is the No-Decompression Limit (NDL)?

Enter Table 1 of the RDP, from the top at 25m, and move down the column until coming to the *white* number in the *black* box. This is the NDL which, in this case, is *29* minutes. This *29* minutes is the maximum allowable *bottom time* for the dive.

Note:
If you dive to this NDL, you must then make a safety stop of 3 minutes at 5m, since you have dived to within 3 Pressure Groups (PG) of the NDL. Safety stops need not be added to bottom time with these tables (although the author advises it for the extra safety sometimes gained in any following repetitive dives).

Similarly, the NDL for 30m is *20* minutes, the NDL for 18m is *56* minutes, and the NDL for 16m is *72* minutes.

Example 2.

What is the NDL for a single/first dive to a maximum depth of 15m?

Enter Table 1 from the top at 16m (i.e. the next greater tabled depth, since 15m is not tabled). Move down the column until reaching the *white* number in the *black* box. The NDL is thus 72 minutes.

Note:
If this dive is carried out, a safety stop would be mandatory (within 3 PGs of the NDL).

Similarly, the NDL for 19m is *45* minutes, the NDL for 11m is *147* minutes and for 31m is *14* minutes.

Finding the Pressure Group (PG) after single/first no-decompression stop dives

Example 3.

Find the PG after a single dive to 25m for 29 minutes.

Enter Table 1, from the top, at 25m. Move down the column until coming to the exact, or next longer, tabled bottom time. In this case 29 minutes is tabled so move down to 29 minutes and then right to find the PG after the dive. It is *Q*.

Note:
A safety stop would be required at the end of this dive.

Example 4.

Find the PG after a single dive to 15m for 60 minutes.

Enter Table 1, from the top, at 16m and move down until finding the bottom time of 60 minutes. Moving right, the PG is *T*.

Note:
Since 60 minutes is more than 3 PGs from the NDL of 72 minutes, a safety stop is not mandatory, although it is highly recommended after any dive.

Example 5.

What is the Pressure Group (PG) after a dive to 19m for 33 minutes?

Enter Table 1, from the top, at 20m (i.e. the next greater tabled depth, since the exact depth is not tabled). Move down the column until finding the exact, or next longer tabled, bottom time. 33 minutes is not tabled so take 34 minutes and then move right to find the PG. It is *O*.

Example 6.

What is the PG after a dive to 34m for a bottom time of 9 minutes?

Enter Table 1 at 35m and move down to find the bottom time of 9 minutes (simply pass through the arrow below 8 minutes). Moving right, the PG is *F*.

2. REPETITIVE NO-DECOMPRESSION STOP DIVES

During a surface interval nitrogen is off-gassed. After various intervals the Pressure Groups, which represent the nitrogen levels in the 60-minute tissue, will be reduced. Table 2, the "Surface Interval Credit Table", enables us to calculate new Pressure Groups after surface intervals greater than 2 minutes and less than 6 hours.

Finding the new Pressure Group after a surface interval

Example 7.

If the PG immediately after a dive is H, what is the new group after a surface interval of 2 hours?

Enter Table 2, from the left, at H and move right until finding an interval that includes the surface interval of 2 hours. It is between 1:48 and 4:48, so move right to this box and then down the column to the bottom to get the new PG. It is *A*.

Example 8.

If the PG immediately after a dive is F, find the new group after a surface interval of 50 minutes.

Enter Table 2, from the left, at F and move right to find a box containing 50 minutes. It is included in 0:47 to 1:34, so move to this box and then down the column to find the PG, which is *B*.

Calculating the maximum allowable no-decompression stop bottom time for a repetitive dive

A repetitive dive is defined to be any dive within 6 hours of a previous dive(s). When planning a repetitive dive, the predicted excess nitrogen still remaining after the surface interval must be taken into account. This is done by adding a "Residual Nitrogen Time" (RNT).

The Residual Nitrogen Time is the amount of time that must be considered already spent at the maximum depth of the repetitive dive before this dive is commenced. It is subtracted from the single dive NDL for that depth, and the result is the no-decompression stop bottom time still remaining at that depth.

Table 3 (Table 20.8) gives the Residual Nitrogen Times and the maximum no-decompression stop bottom times still available for the various depths of repetitive dives.

Example 9.

If you are in group C immediately before a dive to 24m, find:

(i) the Residual Nitrogen Time (RNT) at 24m

(ii) the maximum allowable no-decompression stop bottom time at 24m

Enter Table 3, from the top, at C and move down the column until intersecting the row for 25m (i.e. take the next greater tabled depth, since 24m is not tabled). You will find two numbers in the box. The top number, printed *on white*, is the Residual Nitrogen Time which, in this case, is *10* minutes. This means that before doing the dive you must consider that you have already spent 10 minutes at 24m. This 10 minutes is to account for excess nitrogen left over from the previous dive(s). The remaining allowable no-decompression stop time (i.e. adjusted maximum no-decompression bottom time) is the number printed *on blue*. In this case it is *19* minutes. **The Actual Bottom Time (ABT) of a repetitive dive should never exceed the adjusted maximum no-decompression bottom time.**

Note:
If you planned to do this dive, you must end it with a safety stop of 3 minutes at 5m, since you will be within 3 PGs of the NDL.

Table 20.8

Side 2 of the RDP (Metric version).

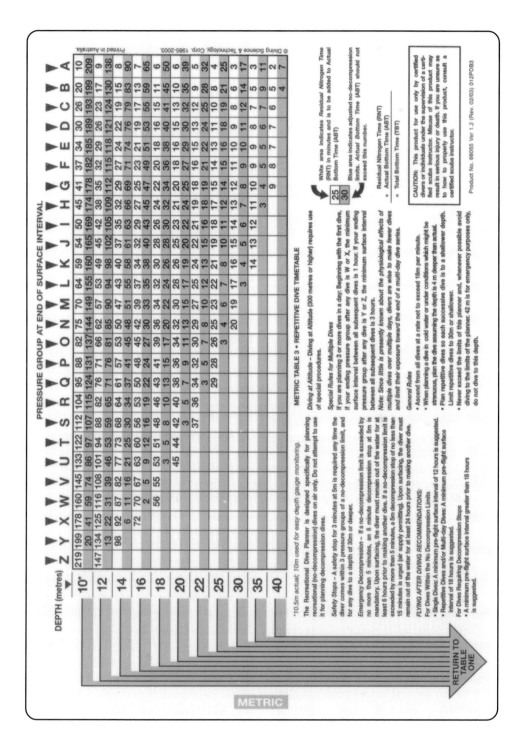

Reprinted courtesy PADI International and DSAT.

Example 10.

At the end of a surface interval after a dive you are in group B. Find:

(i) the Residual Nitrogen Time

(ii) the maximum allowable bottom time for a no-decompression stop dive to 29m.

Enter Table 3, from the top, at B and move down the column until intersecting the row for 30m. The RNT is *6* minutes and the maximum no-decompression stop bottom time is *14* minutes. A safety stop would be required at the end of the dive.

Planning a pair of no-decompression stop dives

Example 11.

You are planning two no-stop dives. The first dive is to 30m, followed, 3 hours later, by a dive to 23m. Find the maximum allowable bottom time for each dive.

Enter Table 1 at 30m and move down the column to the black box that contains the NDL, which is *20* minutes.

Move right to find the PG, which is *N*. Continue across to the right until finding a box containing the surface interval of 3 hours. It is the 2:19-5:19 box, so move to it and then down the column to get the PG after the surface interval. It is *A*.

Enter Table 3, from the top, at A and move down the column until intersecting the row for 25m. The NDL for the dive is the number printed on blue, and is *25* minutes.

Note:

A safety stop would be mandatory at the end of each dive, but it is not necessary to include the time of the safety stop when determining the PG after the dive. However, by using the total dive time (i.e. bottom time + ascent time + time at safety stop), rather than just the bottom time to determine the PG, extra safety may be achieved.

Example 12.

You are planning two no- stop dives. The first is to 36m, followed, 4 hours later, by a dive to 33m. Find the maximum allowable bottom time for each dive.

Enter Table 1 at 40m and move down to find the NDL in the black box. It is *9* minutes and is the maximum allowable bottom time for the first dive.

Move right to get the PG after the dive, which is *G*. Continue moving right to find the box which includes the 4-hour surface interval. It is the 1:42-4:42 box. Move across to this box and then down the column to get the new PG, which is *A*.

Enter Table 3 at A and move down to intersect the 35m row. The adjusted maximum no-decompression bottom time is *11* minutes.

A safety stop would be mandatory at the end of each dive.

Finding the Pressure Group after a repetitive dive

Example 13.

Before a repetitive dive to 30m, you are in group B. If you now dived to 30m for a bottom time of 10 minutes, what would be your new PG?

From Table 3, the RNT before the dive is 6 minutes, and the maximum no-decompression stop bottom time is 14 minutes.

To find the PG after this 10-minute dive you must first find the Total Bottom Time (TBT) of the repetitive dive. The TBT is the sum of the Residual Nitrogen Time (RNT) and the Actual Bottom Time (ABT) of the dive. In this case, the TBT $= 6_{(RNT)} + 10_{(ABT)} = 16$ minutes. To find the PG after the dive, return to Table 1. Enter Table 1 at the depth of the repetitive dive, 30m, and move down this column to find the TBT of 16 minutes (if the exact time is not tabled select the next greater tabled time). Move right to find the new PG, which is *K*.

Example 14.

Before a repetitive dive you are in group C. If you now dived to 23m for a bottom time of 15 minutes, what would be your new Pressure Group?

From Table 3, the RNT at 25m before the dive is 10 minutes (and the maximum no-stop bottom time is 20 minutes).

To find the PG after this 15-minute dive, first find the TBT. The TBT = 10 + 15 = 25 minutes.

Turn to Table 1 and look up 25m for 25 minutes. You get a PG of *N*.

Planning a group of three no-decompression stop dives

Example 15.

You are planning to do three no-stop dives, two of which are repetitive. The first dive, which is to 24m, is followed, 2 hours later, by a dive to 20m, which is followed, 3 hours later, by a final dive to 15m. Find the maximum allowable no-stop bottom times for each of the dives.

Enter Table 1 at 25m and move down to find the NDL of *29* minutes, which is the maximum allowable bottom time for the first dive. A safety stop is mandatory.

Move right to find the PG, which is Q, and continue across to find the surface interval. It lies in the 1:43-2:30 box, so move across to this box and then down the column to get the new PG, group B.

Enter Table 3 at B and move down to intersect the row for 20m. The maximum no-decompression stop bottom time is 35 minutes, and the TBT = 10 + 35 = *45* minutes. A safety stop is mandatory.

Enter Table 1 at 20m, move down to find the TBT of 45 minutes and right to find the PG. It is U. Continue right to find the 3-hour surface interval, and down to get the new PG, which is A.

Enter Table 3 at A and move down to intersect the 16m row. The maximum no-decompression stop bottom time is *65* minutes. A safety stop is mandatory.

Note:
Example 15 can be compared directly to the equivalent problem using U.S. Navy Tables shown on Page 201.

SPECIAL CASES

1. Cold and Strenuous Dives

When planning a dive in cold water, or under conditions that might be strenuous, plan the dive assuming the depth is 4 m deeper than actual.[13]

For example, if you are planning to dive to 18m and you expect to be cold, take the limit for 22m as your maximum no-decompression stop bottom time.

If you get cold, or if you work hard during a dive to 27m, ensure that you begin your ascent before the NDL for 35m expires (i.e. it is treated as a dive to 31m).

2. Special Rules For Multiple Dives

If you are planning 3 or more dives: Beginning with the first dive, if your ending Pressure Group after any dive is W or X, the minimum surface interval between <u>all</u> subsequent dives is 1 hour. If your ending Pressure Group after any dive is Y or Z, the minimum surface interval between <u>all</u> subsequent dives is 3 hours.

Example 16.

After a dive to 18m for 56 minutes your PG will be W. If you are planning a second dive, you must remain at the surface for at least 1 hour. If, after an hour of surface interval, you wish to dive to 15m, the maximum no-decompression stop bottom time is 43 minutes. If you actually dive to 15m for 30 minutes, you will surface with a PG of T. You must still wait at least an hour before diving again, since the previous dive brought you into group W.

Example 17.

After a dive to 18m for 54 minutes you are in group V. After a 20 minute surface interval, your PG is Q. You then dive to 12m for 60 minutes, which puts you into group Z. You must not dive again for at least 3 hours, and must have a minimum surface interval of 3 hours between any further dives, until there has been a 6-hour break from diving.

FLYING AFTER DIVING RECOMMENDATIONS

For Dives within the No-Decompression Limits

- Single dives: A minimum pre-flight surface interval of 12 hours is suggested.
- Repetitive Dives and/or Multi-day Dives: A minimum pre-flight surface interval of 18 hours is suggested.

For Dives Requiring Decompression Stops

- A minimum pre-flight surface interval greater than 18 hours is suggested

DIVING AT ALTITUDE

This planner is not designed for use at altitudes greater than 1000 feet (300 metres) above sea-level. However, adjustment procedures for using the RDP at altitude are discussed in Chapter 26.

Note:

Since originally released, various changes have been made to the rules for using these tables. More changes could still occur so the reader is advised to be vigilant.

REFERENCES

1. Richardson D, Shreeves K. 1991 survey of 27 recreational multi-day diving operations. *SPUMS J* 1992; 22(2):103-8.

2. Rogers RE. The development of the Recreational Dive Planner. *SPUMS J* 1991; 21(2):98-106.

3. Powell MR, Spencer MP, Rogers RE, Doppler Ultrasound Monitoring of Gas Phase Formation Following Decompression in Repetitive Dives. Santa Ana: Diving Science and Technology; 1988.

4. Hamilton RW, Rogers RE, Powell MR, Vann RD. The DSAT Recreational Dive Planner, Development and validation of no-stop decompression procedures for recreational diving. California: Diving Science and Technology Inc; 1994.

5. Rogers RE. Testing the Recreational Dive Planner. *SPUMS J* 1991; 21(3):164-71.

6. Mitchell SJ. Review of DSAT Document: Recreational Dive Planner Testing Program. Royal New Zealand Navy Hospital Internal Report, 1990.

7. 1990 Report on Diving Accidents and Fatalities. Durham: Divers Alert Network; 1992.

8. 1991 Report on Diving Accidents and Fatalities. Durham: Divers Alert Network; 1993.

9. 1992 Report on Diving Accidents and Fatalities. Durham: Divers Alert Network; 1994.

10. Report on Diving Accidents and Fatalities. Durham: Divers Alert Network; 1999.

11. Recreational Dive Planner (Imperial)_– General Rules of Use. Product No. 01113 (Rev 7/93) Version 1,1. California: Diving Science and Technology Corp.; 2003.

12. Recreational Dive Planner (Metric)_– General Rules of Use. Product No. 01117 (Rev 7/93) Version 1,1. California: Diving Science and Technology Corp.; 2003.

12. The Wheel. Instructions for use and study guide. California: Diving Science and Technology Corp.; 2003.

OTHER SOURCES

Richardson D. The Evolution of the Recreational Dive Planner. *Undersea J* 1988; First Quarter.

Richardson D. Editorial- A Word About Decompression DSAT Research and Doppler. *Undersea J* 1988; Third Quarter.

Richardson D. Slower Ascent Rates: The PADI S.A.F.E. Diver Campaign. *Undersea J* 1988; Third Quarter.

Richardson D. Multiple Dives over Multiple Days: An Area of Growing Interest and Concern. *Undersea J* 1988; Third Quarter.

Richardson D. Questions and Answers: On the Recreational Dive Planner, DSAT and the Table Research. *Undersea J* 1988; Third Quarter.

Rogers RE. Renovating Haldane. *Undersea J* 1988; Third Quarter.

RECOMMENDED FURTHER READING

Rogers RE. The development of the Recreational Dive Planner. *SPUMS J* 1991; 21(2):98-106.

Powell MR, Spencer MP and Rogers RE, Doppler Ultrasound Monitoring of Gas Phase Formation Following Decompression in Repetitive Dives. Santa Ana: Diving Science and Technology; 1988.

Rogers RE. Testing the Recreational Dive Planner. *SPUMS J* 1991; 21(3):164-71.

The authors are very grateful to Dr. Drew Richardson for reviewing this chapter.

EXERCISES ON THE RDP (Imperial version)

1. Find the No-Decompression Limits for single dives to the following depths:

   (a) 100ft   (b) 30ft   (c) 75ft
   (d) 115ft   (e) 102ft

2. Find the maximum allowable no-decompression stop bottom time for the following second dives:

   (a) A dive to 65ft, 2½ hours after a dive to 96ft for 20 minutes.

   (b) A dive to 50ft, 2 hours after a dive to 80ft for 25 minutes.

   (c) A dive to 100ft, 4 hours after a dive to 120ft for 12 minutes.

3. Find the maximum allowable no-decompression stop bottom times for each dive in the following pairs of dives:

   (a) A dive to 95ft, followed, 2 hours later, by a dive to 66ft.

   (b) A dive to 120ft, followed, 2½ hours later, by a dive to 105ft.

   (c) A dive to 56ft, followed, 2½ hours later, by another dive to 56ft.

   (d) A dive to 52ft, followed, 3 hours later, by a dive to 65ft.

   (e) A dive to 130ft, followed, 6½ hours later, by a dive to 40ft.

ANSWERS (Times in minutes)

1. (a) 20   (b) 205   (c) 30   (d) 13
   (e) 16
2. (a) 35   (b) 67   (c) 17
3. (a) 20, 31 (b) 13, 13 (c) 55, 44
   (d) 55, 35 (e) 10, 140.

EXERCISES ON THE RDP
(Metric version)

1. Find the No-Decompression Limits for single dives to the following depths:

   (a) 30m   (b)   9m   (c)   22m
   (d) 34m   (e)   33m

2. Find the maximum allowable no-decompression stop bottom time for the following second dives:

   (a) A dive to 19m, 2$\frac{1}{2}$ hours after a dive to 29m for 20 minutes.

   (b) A dive to 15m, 2 hours after a dive to 24m for 25 minutes.

   (c) A dive to 30m, 4 hours after a dive to 35m for 12 minutes.

3. Find the maximum allowable no-decompression stop bottom times for each dive in the following pairs of dives:

   (a) A dive to 28m, followed, 2 hours later, by a dive to 20m.

   (b) A dive to 35m, followed, 2$\frac{1}{2}$ hours later, by a dive to 32m.

   (c) A dive to 17m, followed, 2$\frac{1}{2}$ hours later, by another dive to 17m.

   (d) A dive to 16m, followed, 3 hours later, by a dive to 20m.

   (e) A dive to 40m, followed, 6$\frac{1}{2}$ hours later, by a dive to 12m.

ANSWERS (Times in minutes)

1. (a) 20   (b) 219   (c) 37   (d) 14
   (e) 14

2. (a) 39   (b) 59   (c) 17.

3. (a) 20, 35 (b) 14, 11 (c) 56, 45
   (d) 72, 39 (e) 9, 138.

21

Bubble models and tables

As discussed in Chapter 4, there are several theories that have been developed to describe the formation and growth of bubbles within the body. Currently, the predominant of these theories are based on the existence of small seeds, known as 'bubble nuclei', within our body tissues.

During the 1980s some researchers, led by Dr. David Yount at the University of Hawaii, developed a decompression model based on the physical properties of bubble nucleation. This model, known as the **Varying Permeability Model**, assumes the presence of bubble nuclei in the water and aqueous (watery) tissues within our bodies.[1] It is unclear where the nuclei arise but possible sources are thought to include radiation, blood turbulence, carbonated drinks, lymph drainage, the endothelial lining in the lungs, among others.

The nuclei are thought to have elastic, organic skins that stabilize them. The 'skin' is composed of 'surfactant' (i.e. surface active molecules like in soaps and detergents) that reduces surface tension and so prevents the nuclei from collapsing.[2,3] These nuclei are small enough to pass through the small blood vessels in the lungs (pulmonary filters) and to remain in solution via Brownian motion (movement of the molecules of the surrounding liquid). They are also strong enough to resist being crushed by the surface tension.

It is suggested that gas can diffuse across the skins at pressures normally encountered by divers, but they become far less permeable when subjected to very high pressures of about 10 ATA or more. It has also been suggested that they can be crushed by high pressures and reformed within about a week. There has been some experimental and clinical evidence that appears to support this theory.[4,5,6]

As mentioned, the skins are permeable to gas and the nuclei may grow if gas enters them during decompression. Any nuclei with volumes larger than a "critical size" (which is related to the maximum dive depth) will grow during decompression.

Given the common belief that decompression sickness (DCS) is dependent on the size and number of bubbles present, in this model it is proposed that the body can tolerate up to a certain total volume of 'free-phase' gas (i.e. gas in bubbles - as distinct from dissolved gas) before symptoms of DCS occur. Estimates are made of the total volume of free-phase gas within the body, and decompression is controlled to ensure that the total volume of gas in the bubbles is less than the critical volume thought to be safe.

With short exposures, nuclei have little time to grow so the maximum allowable volume will arise from a large number of small bubbles. On the other hand, with long exposures, bubbles grow much larger, so fewer are permitted by the model.

Any set of no-decompression limits can be selected and substituted into the model equations. The corresponding maximum allowable tensions in each tissue compartment can be calculated, and critical gradients (i.e. differences between calculated tissue tension and ambient pressure) can be determined. (See page 58) These maximum tensions and critical gradients can then be substituted and used to compute decompression for various exposures.[7]

Tables based on this model were produced but never validated. They yielded NDLs that were more conservative than those of the U.S. Navy for depths shallower than 42m (140ft).

The Varying Permeability Model has been superseded by Dr. Bruce Wienke. Wienke utilized more conservative no-decompression limits (from Spencer - see Chapter 15) arising from doppler studies and consistent with gas phase volume constraints. Generically the model is known as the **Reduced Gradient Bubble Model (RGBM)**. Wienke adapted the model for technical and then recreational and technical diving. The two versions are different in approach although not in physical dynamics.

Wienke introduced reduced critical gradients to account for bubble formation over repetitive dive exposures, reverse profiles, multi-day and altitude recreational diving, using the full RGBM model.[8]

The reduced gradient, $Gr = \xi G$, where G is the gradient for the initial dive and ξ represents a set of multi-diving fractions between 0 and 1.

$\xi = 1$ for bounce dives and $\xi < 1$ for repetitive dives. For example, ξ decreases with increased dive time so reducing the critical gradients, and increases with increasing surface intervals, restoring the gradient closer to the initial value.

In addition to the bubble growth or shrinkage resulting from gas diffusion across their surfaces, Wienke uses Equations of State (EOS), based on Boyle's Law, to describe the expansion or contraction of bubbles due to pressure changes during the dive. The rate of expansion or contraction is linked to the variable composition of the surfactants coating the bubbles. These surfactants may be either lipid (fatty) or aqueous (watery) and the bubble skins are assumed to be permeable under all ambient pressures.

Although different gas mixtures of nitrogen, oxygen and helium contain bubble distributions of differing sizes, the total limiting volume is the same.

To date, there has not been extensive formal field validation trials for the RGBM. However, it has been used for for many years for mixed gas and decompression diving, and a databank of dives has been created to record some of the experience with the RGBM in the field. By 2004, approximately 2300 dives were recorded in the databank with around 20 cases of DCI. Apparently, these cases occurred mainly after repetiive deep diving on nitrox, and reverse profiles.[9]

The RGBM has now been utilized in a variety of dive computers (e.g. Suunto, Mares, Dacor and others), tables (e.g. NAUI technical and recreational RGBM Tables), and decompression software (e.g. ABYSS and GAP) and its use continues to expand rapidly.

How do Bubble Models differ from Haldanian Models?

To adequately model the movement of gas within the body (gas kinetics), it is necessary to consider both dissolved gas, and gas in bubbles (free-phase gas). As discussed elsewhere in this book, the traditional Haldanian models rely on inert gas remaining dissolved in the blood and body tissues during decompression. The typical staged decompression profile produced by an Haldanian model utilizes relatively shallow stops in order to maximize the off-gassing gradient for the presumably dissolved inert gas. However, post-dive ultrasonic doppler monitoring of divers often indicates the presence of bubbles after such profiles. Once significant gas phase formation has occurred, further decompression calculations become far more difficult and this can sometimes greatly impact repetitive and multi-day diving.

Bubble models are specifically designed to cater for free-phase gas as well as dissolved gas. Using critical gradients (rather than maximum tensions as with Haldanian models) bubble models aim to minimize bubble growth by keeping the tension of inert gas within the bubbles equal to, or higher than, the tissue tension. In this way, inert gas will diffuse out from, rather than into, the bubbles, reducing the bubble size, rather than enabling them to grow. The most efficient elimination of free-phase gas is at greater ambient pressures as this is where the internal pressures of the bubbles are highest and, hence, the driving force of gas from the bubble is greatest.

The relative 'unsaturation' of the venous blood and tissues (see Chapter 4) provides a carrying capacity for excess inert gas during decompression. Also, since any bubbles formed are at ambient pressure (which is higher than the tissue or venous pressure), gas will tend to move from the bubbles into the venous blood, helping to resolve the bubbles.

Therefore, by utilizing a slow ascent rate and deeper decompression stops, bubble models aim to eliminate or minimize any differences in ambient pressure and total tissue tension (supersaturation) and thereby control the volume of free-phase gas within the body.

In general, bubble decompression models yield, slower ascent rates, deeper safety stops and more restrictive repetitive and multi-day diving, more consistent with current knowledge of safe diving practice. Bubble models tend to control bubble growth with deep stops, instead of treating bubbles in the shallow zone.

NAUI RGBM DIVE TABLES

In 2002, NAUI released some dive tables based on the Reduced Gradient Bubble Model.

The full set of 9 tables includes three air tables, three EAN32 and three EAN36 tables each covering the following altitude ranges:

- Sea-level to 2000 feet (610 metres)
- 2000 to 6000 feet (610-1829 metres)
- 6000 to 10000 feet (1829-3048 metres)

The tables are simple to use and require no calculations. They permit a series of up to three dives with minimum surface intervals of one hour. Repetitive dives must be no deeper than the previous dive(s). The maximum ascent rate is 30ft (9m) per minute and a safety stop at about 15ft /5m for 3 minutes. No more than 3 dives are to be made within a 12 hour period. After a 12 hour surface interval you begin again at Dive 1.

The Tables and associated rules for use are shown in Figures 21.1 and 21.2.

FIGURE 21.1

NAUI RGBM Dive Table – Air
Sea Level to 2000 feet / 610 metres.

Reduced Gradient Bubble Model (RGBM)
Dive Table - Air
Sea Level to 2,000 ft / 610 m

DIVE SAFETY THROUGH EDUCATION

DIVE ONE			DIVE TWO			DIVE THREE		
MAX DEPTHS		MDT	MAX DEPTHS		MDT	MAX DEPTHS		MDT
fsw	msw	minutes	fsw	msw	minutes	fsw	msw	minutes
130	40	10	80	24	30	30	9	150
120	36	13	75	23	30	30	9	150
110	33	16	70	21	40	30	9	150
100	30	20	65	20	40	30	9	150
90	27	25	60	18	55	30	9	150
80	24	30	55	17	55	30	9	150
70	21	40	50	15	80	30	9	150
60	18	55	45	14	80	30	9	150
50	15	80	40	12	110	30	9	150
40	12	110	35	11	110	30	9	150
30	9	150	30	9	150	30	9	150

This table is designed for scuba dives employing air.

Read the instructions on the back and seek proper training before using this table or compressed air. Even strict compliance with this table will not guarantee avoidance of decompression sickness.

USING THE RGBM TABLES

Example 1.

You wish to do three dives with surface intervals of 3 hours between dives. If the first dive is to 110ft (33m), what are the maximum allowable depths and durations of the repetitive dives?

Enter the section of the table for Dive 1 from the left at 100ft (30m) and move right to the MDT column to find the maximum dive time (MDT) for Dive 1. It is *20* minutes, which means that direct ascent to the safety stop must begin after no more than 20 minutes. Continue along this same row to the section for Dive 2 to get the maximum depth for Dive 2, which is 65ft (20m). The MDT at 65ft (20m) is *40* minutes. Continuing along this same you will see that the maximum depth for any third dive is 30ft (9m), for a maximum duration of 150 minutes.

FIGURE 21.2

RGBM Air Table – Rules for Table Use.

RGBM Air Tables

Sea Level to 2,000 ft / 610 m

Abbreviation Key

fsw = feet seawater   msw = meters seawater   MDT = Maximum Dive Time
SIT = Surface Interval Time   DCS = Decompression Sickness   fpm = feet per minute
                           mpm = meters per minute

Rules for Table Use

- Depth measuring devices may require correction for use at altitude and in fresh water to determine a diver's actual dive depths and ascent/descent rates.
- Find your first dive's maximum depth in fsw or msw in the left two columns (Dive One). Follow that row to the right to get your MDT for Dive One and continue to the next columns under Dive Two to determine permitted repetitive depth and MDT for your second dive. Continue to the next columns under Dive Three to determine repetitive depth and MDT for your third dive.
- A minimum SIT of 1:00 hour is required between dive one and dive two and dive three.
- If your actual dive depth is not listed, use the MDT for the next greater depth listed.
- Dive Two may be shallower, but cannot exceed depth and MDT to the immediate right and on the same row as Dive One. Dive Three may be shallower than the depth listed but may not exceed the MDT in column three.
- The maximum descent rate on all dives is 75 fpm (23 mpm).
- The maximum ascent rate is 30 fpm (9 mpm).
- All dives require a safety stop at about 15 fsw (5 msw) (+/- 3 feet or 1 meter) for 3 minutes.
- No more than three repetitive dives within a 12 hour period.
- After a single dive in an 18-hour period wait a minimum of 12 hours before flying or ascending to an altitude greater than 8,000 feet/2438 meters. After two dives wait 15 hours and after three dives wait 18 hours.
- Inverted depth profiles (a shallow dive followed by a deeper dive) and mandatory staged decompression dives are not permitted while using this table.
- If you accidentally exceed your MDT cease all diving activities for 24 hours. If exceeded by less than 5 minutes, conduct a decompression stop at about 15 fsw (5 msw) for 6 minutes; if exceeded by 5 to 10 minutes, stop at about 15 fsw (5 msw) for 9 minutes before surfacing.
- If symptoms of DCS manifest breathe oxygen and evacuate to the nearest recompression facility.
- Example 1: Dive 1 to 130 fsw (40 msw) for 10 minutes, followed by a 1:00 SIT: followed by Dive 2 to 80 fsw (24 msw) for 25 minutes; followed by a 1:00 SIT; followed by Dive 3 to 30 fsw (9 msw) for 150 minutes.
- Example 2: Dive 1 to 115 fsw (35 msw) for 10 minutes followed by a 1:30 minute SIT; followed by Dive 2 to 71 fsw (22 msw) for 25 minutes; followed by a 1:45 SIT; followed by Dive 3 to 25 fsw (8 msw) for 120 minutes.

Reprinted with permission NAUI Worldwide

Example 2.

You plan to conduct a series of three no-stop dives. The first dive is to a maximum depth of 120ft (36m), followed two hours later by a dive to a maximum depth of 70ft (21m). If you then wish to dive to 20ft (6m), what is the maximum no-stop time for each dive.

Enter the section of the table for Dive 1 from the left at 120ft (36m) and move right to the MDT column to find the MDT for Dive 1. It is *13* minutes. Then enter the section for Dive 2 at the maximum planned depth of 70ft (21m) and move to the right to find the MDT of *40* minutes. (Note that the maximum allowed depth for a second dive would be 75ft (23m).

The maximum allowed depth for a third dive is 30ft (9m) and the planned 20ft (6m) dive would have a maximum duration is 150 minutes.

Note that the ascent rate should not exceed 30ft (9m) per minute and a safety stop is required at the end of each dive.

REFERENCES

1. Yount DE, Hoffman DC. Decompression Theory: A dynamic critical volume hypothesis: In: Bachrach AJ and Matzen (eds). Underwater physiology VIII: Proceedings of the eighth symposium on underwater physiology. Undersea Medical Society, Bethesda, 1984:131-46.

2. Yount DE. Skins of varying permeability: A stabilization mechanism for gas cavitation nuclei. *J Acoust Soc Am* 1979; 91:49-360.

3. Yount DE, Kunkle TD, D'Arrigo JS et al. Stabilization of gas cavitation nuclei by surface active compounds. *Aviat Space Environ Med* 1977; 48:85-189.

4. Yount DE. Application of a bubble formation model to decompression sickness in rats and humans. *Aviat Space Environ Med* 1979; 50(1):44-50.

5. Yount DE. Application of bubble formation model to decompression sickness in fingerling salmon. *Undersea Biomed Res* 1981; 8(4):199-208.

6. Sands B. Radical Bends Treatment. *SCUBA Diver* 1986; Dec-Jan:22-5.

7. Yount DE, Hoffman DC. On the use of a bubble formation model to calculate diving tables. *Aviat Space Environ Med* 1986; 57:149-56.

8. Wienke BR. Basic Decompression Theory and Application. Flagstaff: Best Publishing Co.; 1991.

9. Weinke BR, O'Leary TR. RGBM Algorithm Overview: Concepts, bases, validation, testing and references. J. Comp. Phys. In press.

RECOMMENDED FURTHER READING

Wienke BR. Basic Decompression Theory and Application. Flagstaff: Best Publishing Co.; 1991.

Wienke BR. Online with the RGBM: A modern phase algorithm and diveware implementation. www.abysmal.com/web/library/articles

Some decompression dilemmas. www.abysmal.com/web/library/articles

Many thanks to Dr. Bruce Wienke for his editorial comments on this chapter.

© Max Gleeson

22

Decompression software

Until around the 1990s, if you wanted to go diving using mixed gases or high concentration mixtures of oxygen to accelerate your decompression, you needed to enlist the services of a decompression software designer to 'cut' you a set of tables for the proposed dive. The pioneer of this service was Dr. Bill Hamilton, who developed and refined decompression software that was often used for some of the earlier technical diving, especially in the USA. By the early 2000s, a plethora of decompression packages have emerged and make the process far easier for the aspiring technical diver. However, where in the past, the divers drew on the expertise of highly experienced decompression scientists, today's divers rely on a software programmer who may, or may not, have the depth of knowledge necessary to fully understand and /or appreciate many of the physiological and theoretical issues underpinning decompression.

Computer decompression software is based on decompression models. Therefore, to assess the usefulness of a particular program, one must consider a number of factors:

- Is the model used in the program appropriate for the planned profile (i.e. depth range, duration etc)?

- Has the model been correctly implemented by the programmer?

- Will the software generate profiles that permit known high risk exposures?

- What do the "conservatism" adjustments do and are they really making the dive more "conservative"?

- Does the program produce a workable run time?

- Does the program have a user-friendly interface?

- What sort of outputs (e.g. lost gas scenarios, deep, long etc) will it produce?

- Does the program throw up significant glitches and /or times that are clearly inappropriate?

In many ways, the first of these questions is the most difficult. All the readily available decompression software programs are based to a greater or lesser degree on the work of the late Prof. Albert Bühlmann, described in Chapters 17 and 24.

Bühlmann's model comprises two parts:

(1) the base model of gas movement through the tissue compartments, and

(2) the sets of "a" and "b" coefficient values that govern the rules of ascent.

The base component is the part that is common to all the models, including VPM (Varying Permeability Model) and RGBM (Reduced Gradient Bubble Model) (described in Chapter 21). It comprises 16 tissue compartments arranged in parallel, each assigned a half-time for the uptake and elimination of gas, which is modelled as a symmetrical exponential process. The partial pressures of the inert gases (usually helium and nitrogen) are added together and the helium uptake and elimination is assumed to occur at a rate 2.65 times that of nitrogen. Bühlmann's model has become the defacto standard for many reasons. Firstly, Bühlmann fully published his methodology, allowing and sometimes encouraging others to copy it. He also specifically produced a model for dive computer implementation (ZHL-16C). Finally, its widespread adoption in a range of dive computers has provided a level of confidence in the model, at least when applied to some recreational diving circumstances.

The Bühlmann model is an Haldanian model with ascent rules based on the idea of an allowed level of supersaturation in tissue compartments (i.e. M-values, explained in Chapters 4 and 13).

As discussed elsewhere in this book, two different approaches to gas uptake and elimination dominate decompression modelling. Currently, the most common are perfusion-based models, where the blood flow carrying the inert gas limits the gas kinetics. Diffusion-limited models (see Chapter 21), although more complex mathematically, also have their advocates. While it has been shown that these two models of gas exchange may approximate each other in shorter dives, shallower than about 60m (200ft)[1], for longer, deeper dives diffusion-based models are probably more appropriate.[2-7] Certainly, more recent studies of gas kinetics in sheep have indicated that the basic perfusion-based model does not adequately describe the gas kinetics and that some form of diffusion-perfusion model with gas exchange between arterioles and venules better describes the observed gas kinetics.[8,9]

While the derivation of Bühlmann's coefficients was based on dives including some to great depth, the actual testing of the derived tables was generally done to 40m or less. Recent work[10] has indicated that there may be a significant increase in risk in dives conducted deeper than 90m using this methodology. This is to some extent backed up by empirical observations of ichthyologists collecting specimens from depths in the 60-90m (200-300ft) range.[11]

Decompression programs presently available fall into three main groups:

- Basic Bühlmann models, usually ZHL-16 models.
- Modified Bühlmann models, e.g. Pro-Planner, GAP gradient factor model.
- "Bubble" models. E.g. VPM-B/E and RGBM*

A full critique of the strengths and weaknesses of each approach is beyond the scope of this chapter, however, we can observe the differences in the outputs of these models by comparing the schedules produced for a given input. In general, Neo-Haldanean type models such as *Proplanner* and *GAP* will produce deeper initial stops than the base Bühlmann model and as a consequence will produce a longer total run time. RGBM and VPM will also produce deeper initial stops but in the technical diving depth range also produce at shorter total decompression times. While this reduction in total decompression time may be reasonable, as RGBM and VPM have a greater proportion of the decompression deeper (a feature predicted by several newer models)[4,12,13], it is controversial as to whether either this approach or indeed the gradient factor approach with longer decompression times actually reduces decompression stress and DCS.[14-17]

---

* Some versions of RGBM are essentially a modified Bühlmann model with the gradients altered to produce an output which is more "like" that produced by the full RGBM program.

So, how do the outputs of these various programs compare?

For this analysis, we will look at three commercially available programs:

- *Proplanner*, Delta P Technology Limited U.K.
- *GAP* Gradient factor program, GAP-Software.
- *VPM-B*, HHS Software.

Proplanner is a ZHL-16 based program with proprietary modifications. These modifications include the insertion of empirical deep "micro-bubble" stops if this option is selected. *Proplanner* is currently DOS-based and is now somewhat less user-friendly than more recent Windows-based programs. Lost gas and various other scenarios must be run separately. It does, however, allow dive plans to correlate with the VR3 mixed gas dive computer. "Conservatism" can be added in two ways. The first is to add the so called "microbubble stops" (these are always on in the VR3) which add deep stops according to a proprietary empirical formula. The second is to add safety factors from 0 to 50%. This appears to reduce the maximum allowed supersaturation tensions both deep and in the shallows.

GAP from GAP-software, produces a program with both RGBM and the Gradient Factor (proportional M value reduction method). An older version of the Gradient factor program is available as freeware on the internet but is no longer supported. The Gradient Factor component utilizes the Bühlmann ZHL-16 programs (either B or C) and varies the Bühlmann allowed supersaturation gradients in accordance with the user's wishes. Typically, the deep gradients would be reduced to 25% of the Bühlmann value and the shallow gradients to 80%. This allows for complete control over the "conservatism". Usually the deeper and longer the dive the more the deep gradient is reduced. As previously mentioned, there

is only limited evidence to back up this approach. The corresponding RGBM profile is also shown for comparison and the user can select between them depending on which is considered better. RGBM "conservatism" can be selected from a series of virtual buttons ranging from "recreational" to "Extreme". This alters parameters such as the initial bubble nucleus size etc. Although these parameters are also directly user adjustable, such alterations should only be done by people very familiar with the Weinke model (if at all!). The program is Windows-based and, once the user is familiar with the interface, is easy to use. It produces reports including lost gas and deep/long scenarios, as well as a plethora of back-up tables.

VPM-B is the development of the Varying Permeability Model (described in Chapter 21). It utilizes the concept of keeping the evolved volume of gas below a critical amount by limiting supersaturation at depth. HHS's iteration of this model has probably the best user interface of any of the programs assessed here. One problem with the VPM algorithm is with the lost gas scenario. Since the program calculates the volume of gas evolved over the whole decompression, the deep stops it produces are based on the assumed gas selection. If the diver only discovers that the deco gas is not available when he is at the gas switch, the deeper stops done may not fit in with the new plan required.

Similarly to GAP, VPM offers "conservatism" adjustments. These range from "nominal" to "plus five". As with GAP RGBM, alterations of the conservatism feature alters some of the models initial parameters such as nuclei radius, critical radius and surface tension. A newer iteration, VPM-E has also addressed some of the criticisms that the shortened decompression profiles had surfacing inert gas tensions that were too high. It now produces longer run times for "expedition" type dives. However in the same iteration it allows for "accelerated" decompression with certain Helium-based mixes. How both approaches can be correct has been lost on this author!

Several comparative dives were done using the three programs and compared to the base Buhlmann model (GAP GF 90/90). Two of these are shown as Figures 22.1 and 22.2.

The bottom mix chosen was Tx15/65. Deco. gases of EAN36 and EAN 80 were used for the open-circuit dive.
The CCR dive was conducted using Tx15/65 throughout, with a constant PO_2 of 1.3.
The settings for the various programs, selected as 'typical' for technical divers were:
Bühlmann (using GAP - 90/90 gradient factors)
GAP - High 85: Low 20
Proplanner - 100% "microbubbles"
            20% safety factor
VPM - +Two
RGBM - Nominal

Figure 22.1

*Dive to 63m (206ft) for 25 minutes
using open circuit.*

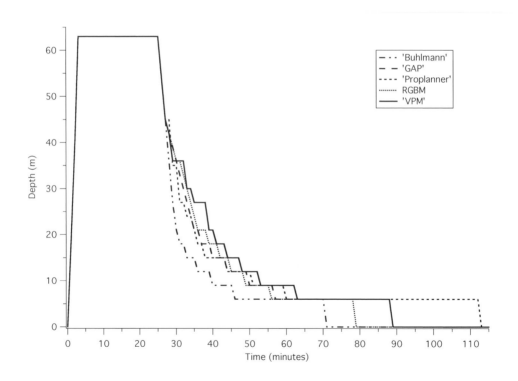

Figure 22.1

*Dive to 63m (206ft)for 25 minutes using
a closed-circuit rebreather.*

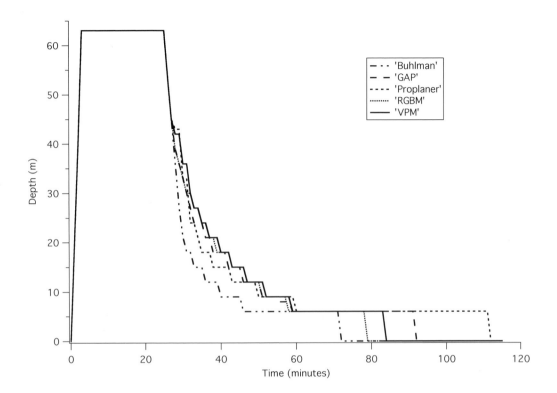

Conclusions

As can be seen, the two example profiles used produced very different results for overall decompression time using the same input, with overall decompression varying by almost 50%. While the reduction in deep supersaturation gradient has some theoretical basis and decompression based on this technique has been used successfully by many divers, it is still unvalidated and the level of DCS risk is unknown. Divers should evaluate the relevant peer reviewed literature (being very careful of unsubstantiated literature, such as much that is available on the internet) and make up their own minds as to the validity of the deep stop approach.

Unfortunately, none of the presently easily available decompression software programs have been validated in the range beyond 80m (264ft). From the recent literature it would appear that the use of the basic Bühlmann gas model may be inappropriate as depth exceeds 80m (264ft). Until either the present models undergo some formal validation in the deeper ranges, or new models incorporating more modern ideas of gas kinetics and bubble formation and interaction are implemented, technical divers utilizing commercially available decompression software should exercise caution when using these programs.

REFERENCES

1. Weinke BR. Equivalent multi-tissue and thermodynamic decompression algorithms. Int *J Biomed Comput* 1989; 24(4):227-45.

2. Hempleman HV (Ed). Investigation into the decompression tables. London: RNPRC; 1952.

3. Kidd DJ, Stubbs RA, Weaver RS. Comparative approaches to prophylactic decompression. In: 4th Symp Underwater Physiol. New York: Academic Press; 1972.

4. Hills BA, Decompression Sickness Vol 1 - The Biophysical Basis of Prevention and Treatment, Vol 1. New York: John Wiley & Sons; 1977:308.

5. Hills BA. A thermal analogue for the optimal decompression for divers: construction and use. *Phys Med Biol* 1967; 12(4):445-54.

6. Hempleman HV. Investigation into the decompression tables. Further basic facts on decompression sickness tables. London:RNPRC; 1957.

7. Hempleman HV. History and Evolution of Decompression procedures. In: Bennett PB, Elliott DH (eds). Physiology & Medicine of Diving, 3rd Edn. California: Best Publishing Co.; 1982:319-79.

8. Doolette DJ, Upton RN, Zheng D. Diffusion limited tissue equilibration and arteriovenous diffusion shunt describe skeletal muscle nitrous oxide kinetics at high and low blood flows in sheep. *Acta Physiol Scand* 2001; 172(3):167-77.

9. Doolette DJ, Upton RN, Grant C. Perfusion-diffusion compartment al models describe cerebral helium kinetics at high and low cerebral blood flows in sheep. *J Physiol* 2005; 563 (Pt 2):529-39.

10. Doolette D. Decompression practice and health outcome during a technical diving project. *SPUMS J* 2004. 34(4):189-95.

11. Pyle RL. Insights on Deep Bounce Dive Safety from the Technical diving Community. In: Lin Y (ed). Proceedings of the 16th Meeting of the United States-Japan Cooperative Programs on Natural Resources (UJNR), 1-3 Nov 2001, Honolulu; 2002:47-53.

12. Yount DE. Application of a bubble formation model to decompression sickness in rats and humans. *Aviat Space Environ Med* 1979; 50(1):44-50.

13. Wienke BR. Reduced gradient bubble model. *Int J Biomed Comput* 1990; 26(4):237-56.

14. Bennett PB et al. Theory and Development of Subsaturation Decompression Procedures for Depths in excess of 400ft. In: Underwater Physiology. Bethesda: FASEB; 1978.

15. Blatteau JE et al. Decompression profiles with deep stops: Comparative Doppler study with procedures of the French Navy. In EUBS, Proceedings of the 30th Annual Scientific meeting of the European Underwater Baromedical Society. Ajjaccio: EUBS; 2004.

16. Marroni A et al. A deep stop during decompression from 82fsw (25msw) significantly reduces bubbles and fas tissue gas tensions. *Undersea Hyperb Med* 2004; 31(2):233-43.

17. Cabarrou P, Mueller KG, Fust HD, Oser H, Krekeler H, Findeldey U. Development and testing of heliox dives in excess of 100 metres. In: Shilling CW, Beckett MX (eds). Underwater Physiology VI. Bethesda: FASEB; 1978.

*We are very grateful to **Dr. Andrew Fock** for providing this chapter. Thanks also to Dr. Bill Hamilton for his editorial comments.*

23

Multi-level diving

HISTORICAL BACKGROUND

Traditional decompression tables were designed for use by navy divers, whose diving is task-orientated, frequently requiring the divers to stay in one place and, consequently, at one depth for most of the dive. The diver generally goes to the maximum depth, spends the dive there and returns to the surface after completing any required decompression stops.

Recreational divers often dive quite differently to this. Sometimes our depth varies considerably during a dive and, at times, very little of the bottom time is spent at the actual maximum depth of the dive. Consequently, the practice of looking up the maximum depth for the total bottom time is often overly conservative.

For example, consider a dive where you go to 24m (80ft) for 5 minutes and then wish to spend the rest of the dive at 12m (40ft). The U.S. Navy Tables give a NDL of 40 minutes at 24m (80ft), so, using the tables by the rules, you must consider that the entire dive has been spent at 24m and begin to ascend to the surface after 40 minutes. No consideration is given to the fact that you have spent most of the dive far shallower than 24m.

In 1976, Dennis Graver first published a way of extrapolating the U.S. Navy Tables in order to account for the shallower sections of a *"Multi-level"* dive.[1]

A *"Multi-level"* dive is defined here as a dive where the diver spends significant bottom time shallower than the maximum depth and, so, extends the bottom time beyond the limits for a rectangular profile dive to the maximum depth.

THE REPETITIVE GROUP METHOD (GRAVER METHOD)

Many different dives will put you into the same Repetitive Group (RG). Using the U.S. Navy Tables you will be in group B after a dive to 24m (80ft) for 5 minutes; or to 18m (60ft) for 10 minutes; or 12m (40ft) for 15 minutes; and so on. Graver proposed that within a RG all dives are more or less equivalent with respect to the nitrogen content of the tissues. In other words, whether you dived to 24m (80ft) for 5 minutes to get into group B, or whether you dived to 12m (40ft) for 15 minutes, your nitrogen load will be about the same.*

If you surfaced after diving to 24m (80ft) for 5 minutes, you would surface in group B. If, instead of surfacing, you ascended to 12m (40ft), you would still be in group B and your previous 5 minutes at 24m (80ft) could be seen as equivalent to having already spent 15 minutes at the 12m (40ft) depth. In other words, the 15 minutes required to get into

---

* In reality this is not true as the distribution of the gas load between the various body tissues may be very different.

group B at 12m (40ft) can be taken as Residual Nitrogen Time at that depth. Since the NDL for 12m (40ft) is 200 minutes, theoretically, you could still spend a further 185 minutes at 12m (40ft) without needing to make a stop.

Similarly, if after the 5 minutes at 24m (80ft) you had ascended to 18m (60ft), instead of 12m (40ft), the 5 minutes at 24m could be seen as equivalent to 10 minutes at 18m - i.e. the time at 18m to go into group B. Since the NDL at 60ft is 60 minutes, you can, in theory, spend a further 60 -10 = 50 minutes at this depth before requiring a decompression stop.

This procedure assumes that the actual NDLs of the shallower sections are still applicable to this multi-level situation. In other words, after spending 5 minutes at 24m (80ft) and ascending to 18m (60ft), does the 60 minute NDL for 18m still apply?

To answer this, one has to go back to the mathematical model for the U.S. Navy Tables, and calculate the theoretical nitrogen pressure in the various half-time tissue compartments after each section of a multi-level dive. If, at any stage during a multi-level dive, the nitrogen pressure exceeds the critical value for that compartment, a decompression stop will be required. It can be shown that when the above multi-level method is used right to the NDLs, in some cases the critical pressure in a particular tissue, or multiple tissues, may be exceeded. This creates a much greater potential for decompression sickness (DCS). An example of this is shown in Table 23.1.

TABLE 23.1

Tissue nitrogen pressures (fsw) during a multi-level dive.

Depth/Time (fsw/min.)	Tissue Groups (Half-Time (Mo Value))					
	5(104)	10(88)	20(72)	40(58)	80(52)	120(51)
120/15	109.02	87.35	64.50	47.77	37.62	33.94
90/5	103.10	90.23	69.70	51.87	40.15	35.74
70/10	85.69	87.53	78.81	62.62	47.91	41.55
% of Max. Allowable Press. at surfacing	83%	100%	110%	108%	93%	82%

Reprinted from Huggins and Somers, 1981.

When 101 allowable (i.e. in theory, by this method) multi-level dives were analyzed using the U.S. Navy model and formulae, it was found that many of the dive profiles built up potentially dangerous nitrogen levels in the five faster tissue groups.[2] The reason for the violation is that the Repetitive Groups and Residual Nitrogen Times are based solely upon the gas pressure in the 120-minute tissue compartment, assuming that it has the highest nitrogen load during a surface interval. However, a surface interval of just under 10 minutes is necessary before this compartment's theoretical nitrogen level controls the decompression.

Before a 10-minute surface interval has elapsed, one or more of the other tissues will have a higher gas load and must be taken into consideration. A multi-level dive has no 10-minute surface interval between sections, and the Repetitive Group method does not take this problem into consideration. Therefore, the Repetitive Groups given are not always valid.

Graver realized this potential problem and made some recommendations in order to make the method a bit safer. However, despite Graver's recommendations, this method is not sound as it still pushes the diver too close to the limits. Huggins recommended further modifications to this Repetitive Group method.[2]

These were:

1. Use the following NDLs: 36m (120ft)/12, 21m (70ft)/40 and 18m (60ft)/50 instead of those previously suggested.
2. Take a 3m (10ft) stop for 5-15 minutes.
3. Keep at least one RG back from the limits on the table, especially females, older divers and less fit divers; and
4. Include ascent times to each higher level in the bottom time for the previous level.

Despite these recommendations, Huggins did not favor the method as he felt that these "safety factors" would not, or could not, be used consistently.

REPETITIVE GROUP - RESIDUAL NITROGEN METHOD

This method also utilizes the U.S. Navy Tables and treats the various levels of a multi-level dive as repetitive dives without any surface interval. It was first published by Bove in 1983.[3]

For example, consider a diver who spends 5 minutes at 24m (80ft) and then ascends to 12m (40ft). How long can they spend at 12m before a stop is required?

Using the tables as designed, the diver has around 35 minutes of bottom time still available. However, using the Repetitive Group-Residual Nitrogen method it can be extended, as follows:

If they had surfaced after 5 minutes at 24m (80ft), they would have had an RG of B. If, after a surface interval between 10 minutes and 2 hrs 10 min (i.e. RG is still B), the diver were to descend to 12m (40ft), they would have an RNT of 17 minutes and 183 minutes of bottom time available before a decompression stop was required.

The Repetitive Group-Residual Nitrogen method treats a multi-level dive as if the diver had surfaced between levels and then re-descended with the same RG. Various safety precautions were suggested for use with the method. These included restricting the dive to two levels only, staying shallower than 39m (130ft), reducing the NDLs and doing a safety stop, among others.

However, since there is no 10-minute surface interval between the different depth levels, this method suffers the same shortcomings as the Repetitive Group method. At times, the nitrogen pressures in the theoretical tissue compartments can become too high, exceeding the critical levels on which the U.S. Navy Tables are based and increasing the potential for DCS.

Other methods, based on the U.S. Navy Tables, to compute times for multi-level dives have emerged over the years. Many of these methods suffer from the same problem as those described above.

USING THE HUGGINS TABLES FOR MULTI-LEVEL DIVING

Rather than using U.S. Navy Tables as the basis of multi-level dive calculations, some divers adopted the more conservative "Huggins" tables.[4] These tables, described in more detail in Chapter 15, were built on the same model as the U.S. Navy Tables, with the same theoretical tissue compartments. However, Huggins reduced the maximum allowable tissue nitrogen levels to levels indicated by Doppler ultrasonic detection work to be less likely to produce bubbles and, hence, DCS. Also, by basing the RGs on all six tissue groups, rather than the single tissue used by the U.S. Navy, Huggins avoided the need for a 10-minute surface interval in order to allow the nitrogen levels in the faster compartments to fall below that of the 120-minute compartment. The shorter NDLs that resulted were more suitable for multi-level diving, and, in fact, for general recreational diving, whether multi-level or not.

If a diver used the Repetitive Group (Graver) method based on the Huggins tables, rather than on the U.S. Navy Tables, the new, lower critical nitrogen levels appeared not to be exceeded in any of the theoretical tissue types.[4] Multi-level divers who used the Huggins Tables greatly increased their bottom times (compared to standard single-level procedures), but build up lower (theoretical) body nitrogen levels than they would if they based their multi-level technique on U.S. Navy Tables.

The Huggins Tables are used in exactly the same way as the U.S. Navy Tables. They include a No-Decompression Table which gives RGs for various bottom times, a Surface Interval Credit Table and a Residual Nitrogen Table. However, *no testing was done to assess the safety of using the Huggins Tables for multi-level diving.*

NAUI TABLES

When NAUI developed its 1990 based on U.S. Navy Tables but with reduced NDLs, some researchers programmed a supercomputer to simulate all possible multi-level dives up to and including the standard U.S. Navy NDLs, using one-minute time intervals and 3m (10ft) depth increments. Approximately 16 million multi-level dives were analyzed. Dives for which the U.S. Navy M-values were not violated were

retained until the end of the multi-level calculations for further processing. Dives where any M-value was exceeded at any point were terminated. The researchers concluded that the maximum no-stop times that could be used in multi-level dive calculations that would not exceed the U.S. Navy M-values were very similar to the reduced NAUI NDLs.[5]

In other words, if the NAUI Tables were used for multi-level diving, in theory, the critical nitrogen tensions used for the U.S. Navy Tables would not be exceeded. This would certainly be safer than using the U.S. Navy Tables but not as conservative as using the Huggins Tables which also utilize reduced M-values.

USING THE DCIEM SPORT DIVING TABLES FOR MULTI-LEVEL DIVING[6]

The DCIEM multi-level diving procedures are based on the repetitive dive procedures used for surface intervals of less than 15 minutes. These procedures are known as the Step System. During a multi-level dive, the normal decompression process built into the ascent rate is interrupted. Additional precautions are included in the multi-level diving procedures to compensate for the interrupted decompression resulting from partial ascents.

Guidelines for Multi-level Dives

1. Conduct the **deepest part of the dive first.** Ascend to progressively shallower depths.

   Between each of the Steps in the dive profile, the minimum range of ascent is 20ft (6m). For example, if the maximum depth is 86ft (26m), Step 1 is rounded to 90ft (27m). Step 2 would have to be at 70ft (21m) or less. From depths exceeding 100ft (30m), the minimum range of ascent is 30ft (9m). No more than 4 Steps should be included in the dive profile.

2. **Stay within the No-Decompression Limits**

   If a No-D Limit is exceeded at any Step, terminate the dive and proceed to the Decompression Stops(s) specified in Table A.

3. **Finish in shallow water**. Immediately before surfacing, spend at least 5 minutes in the depth range between 20ft (6m) and 10ft (3m). Add this time to the total bottom time (EBT).

4. Allow for a minimum Surface Interval of at least one hour before the following dive.

First Dive - Multi-Level Procedure

Find the Repetitive Group (RG) for Step 1 according to the depth and actual bottom time (Table A).

Use the RG from Step 1 to determine an equivalent time for the same (or next higher) RG at Step 2. Add the planned actual bottom time at Step 2 to the equivalent time that corresponds to the RG. The total of the two times is the Effective Bottom Time (EBT). Find the RG for Step 2 according to the depth and EBT.

Use the RG from Step 2 to determine an equivalent time for the same RG at Step 3. Add the actual bottom time at Step 3 to the equivalent time. The total of the two times is the EBT. Find the RG for Step 3 according to the depth and EBT. Repeat this process for Step 4, if necessary.

Example: NO-D FIRST DIVE (3 STEP)

       Step 1: 90ft (27m) for 15 minutes
       Step 2: 60ft (18m) for 20 minutes
       Step 3: 30ft (9m) for 30 minutes

Step 1: 90ft (27m)   *- No-D Limit is 20min*
        actual bottom time = 15min,
        RG = C

Step 2: 60ft (18m) - *No-D Limit is 50min*
        equivalent time for RG "C" = 25min
        ADD actual bottom time = 20min
        EBT = 25 + 20 = 45 minutes, RG = F

Step 3: 30ft (9m) - *No-D Limit is 300min*
        equivalent time for RG "F" = 120min
        ADD actual bottom time = 20min
        EBT = 120 + 30 = 150min, RG = G

Second Dive Procedures

The Step System also allows the second dive to be a multi-level dive. The second dive should be shallower than the first dive. *A third dive may be conducted, but not as a multi-level dive.*

On a first dive, actual bottom time is used at Step 1 because the divers are free of residual nitrogen. On a second dive, the RG letter for Step 1 is based on Effective Bottom Time because of residual nitrogen remaining from the first dive.

For Step 1 of a second dive, the actual bottom time must not exceed the No-D Limit in Table C.

Example: NO-D REPETITIVE DIVE with RF of 1.4

       Step 1: 50ft (15m) for 35 minutes
       Step 2: 30ft (9m) for 25 minutes
       Step 3: 15ft (4.5m) for 10 minutes

Step 1: 50ft (15m) - *No-D Limit for RF 1.4 is 45 minutes* (Table C - actual bottom time not to exceed 45min)
        RNT = 75 (1ˢᵗ dive NDL)
             − 45 (rep. dive NDL) = 30min
        EBT = 30 (RNT) + 35 (ABT) = 65min,
        RG = G

The RG letter for Step 1 must be equal to or greater than the final RG from the first dive (in this case they are both G*)*. Otherwise, the final RG from the first dive is applied to Step 1. For example, if the RG for Step 1 is E, E would be raised to F.

Beyond Step 1, the procedures followed for repetitive dives are identical to those used for first dives.

Step 2: 30ft (9m) - *No-D Limit is 300 minutes*
        equivalent time for RG "G" = 150min
        ADD actual bottom time = 25min
        EBT = 150 + 25 = 175min, RG = H

Step 3: 15ft (4.5m) - *No-D Limit doesn't apply*
         equivalent time for RG "H" = 300min
         ADD actual bottom time = 10min
         EBT = 300 + 10 = 310min, RG = I

Example: NO-D REPETITIVE DIVE with RF 1.7

         Step 1: 80ft (24m) for 10min
         Step 2: 50ft (15m) for 20min
         Step 3: 30ft (9m) for 30min

Step 1: 80ft (24m) - *No-D Limit for RF 1.7 is*
         12 minutes (Table C - actual bottom
         time not to exceed 12min)
         RNT = 25 (1ˢᵗ dive NDL)
             – 12 (rep. dive NDL) = 13min
         EBT = 13 (RNT) + 10 (ABT) = 23min,
         RG = E (which must be equal to or
         higher than the final RF of the
         previous dive)

Step 2: 50ft (15m) - *No-D Limit is 75 minutes*
         equivalent time for RG "E" = 50min
         ADD actual bottom time = 20min
         EBT = 50 + 20 = 70 minutes, RG = G

Step 3: 30ft (9m) - *No-D Limit is 300min*
         equiv time for RG "G" = 150min
         ADD actual bottom time = 30min
         EBT = 150 + 30 = 180min,
         RG = H

Note:

The DCIEM Multi-Level procedure has not been extensively tested, but is more conservative and so likely to be safer than some of the other methods commonly practiced by recreational divers.

Example 1.

You are planning to dive to 100ft (30m) for 5 minutes before ascending to 66ft (20m) for 10 minutes. You will then ascend to 50ft (15m). If you used the DCIEM Multi-level Procedure, for how long could you remain at 50ft (15m) before a decompression stop is required?

Enter Table A (Table 18.1) at the 100ft (30m) row, and move along the row to find 5 minutes. The associated RG is A.

At 66ft (20m) an RG of A corresponds to a bottom time of 12 minutes, which is considered the time already spent at 66ft (20m). The EBT at 66ft (20m) is taken as 12 + 10 = 22 minutes, which gives a RG of D.

At 50ft (15m), an RG of D corresponds to 40 minutes, which is taken as the time already spent at 50ft (15m). Since the NDL for 50ft (15m) is 75 minutes, there is still 75 - 40 = 35 minutes of bottom time remaining.*

Example 2.

You are planning to dive to 120ft (36m) for 5 minutes before ascending to 90ft (27m) for 6 minutes. If you then wish to ascend to 40ft (12m), what is the No-D Limit at the 40ft (12m) level?

Enter Table A at 120ft (36m), and move along the row to find 5 minutes. The associated RG is A.

At 90ft (27m), a RG of A corresponds to a bottom time of 9 minutes, which is considered the time already spent at 90ft (27m). The EBT at 90ft (27m) is taken as 9 + 6 = 15 minutes, which gives a RG of C.

At 40ft (12m), a RG of C corresponds to 40 minutes, which is taken as the time already spent at 40ft (12m). Since the NDL for 40ft (12m) is 150 minutes, there is still 150 - 40 = *110* minutes of bottom time remaining.

THE BS-AC '88 TABLES MULTI-LEVEL PROCEDURE

The BS-AC has suggested a multi-level dive procedure based on the BS-AC '88 Tables.[7] It is essentially a Repetitive Group procedure and involves swapping from one table to another. The procedure is as follows:

---

* The PADI Wheel gives 42 minutes (35 minutes with the metric version). See Table 24.4 for comparative times on various dive computers for the same profile.

The first portion of the dive time is timed from leaving the surface to arriving at the second level. The second portion begins on arrival at the second level and ends on arrival at the third level, and so on. The final level used in a dive time calculation must be below 6m; you cannot include a 6m or 3m re-entry in a multi-level dive.

Ascent between the various levels is at a maximum rate of 15m/minute, and the ascent from 6m to the surface is at a rate of 6m/min.

On final surfacing, the usual Surfacing Code (SC) applies and is used for subsequent dive planning.

Divers are advised to go to the maximum depth at the start of the dive, to work progressively shallower throughout the dive and to avoid re-descent during the dive. However, if a diver does descend to a deeper level during the dive, and this level is more than 6m deeper than the previous maximum level, the diver is advised to move to the next higher table.[#] For example, if you are diving on Table A and have reached a maximum depth of 30m before ascending to 24m, and then you re-descend to 30m, you must assume that you began the dive on Table B and do the entire Multi-level calculation accordingly.

It is recommended that, if a Multi-level dive is contemplated, it is planned in advance on the surface, rather than underwater.

There has been no testing to determine the safety of applying the Multi-level dive procedure to the BS-AC '88 Tables.

Example 3.

You wish to conduct a single multi-level dive at sea-level. The first portion of the dive will be spent at 30m, and you will then ascend to 15m, arriving after 7 minutes of dive time has elapsed. After a further 10 minutes you intend to be at 9m. For how long can you remain at 9m before a decompression stop is required?

Enter Table A at the 30m row and look up 30m for 7 minutes. Moving down the column, the SC is *C*. Enter Table C at 15m and look up the 10 minutes of dive time for the second portion of the dive. Taking 11 minutes and moving down the column, the SC is *D*. Entering Table D at 9m, the available dive time is *29 minutes.* This means that you must arrive at 6m by the time the 29 minutes has expired and then take one minute to ascend from 6m to the surface.

Example 4.

You wish to conduct a single multi-level dive at sea-level using the BS-AC '88 Tables. You intend to dive to 21m before ascending to 15m, and arriving there after 13 minutes. You then plan to remain at 15m for 16 minutes before ascending directly to 9m. How long can you spend at 9m before requiring a stop?

Enter Table A at 21m and look up 13 minutes. Moving down the column, the SC is *C*. Enter Table C at 15m and look up the 16 minutes of dive time plus the extra time taken to ascend to the 9m level. Taking 17 minutes and moving down the column, the SC is *E*. Entering Table E at 9m, the available dive time is *9* minutes, at the end of which you must be at 6m to begin the final, slow ascent.

Example 5.

You have begun a single, sea-level dive to 11m. After 13 minutes at 11m you are forced to descend to 18m to retrieve a lost torch. You descend directly to 18m (arriving after 14 minutes of elapsed dive time) and by the time you find the torch and return to 11m, a further 6 minutes of dive time has elapsed. For how long can you remain at 11m before a stop is necessary?

This is to attempt to cater for the faster gas loading that may occur when bubbles, if present, are compressed during re-descent.

Since this dive involves a re-descent, you must begin the entire calculation on Table B, rather than Table A.

Looking up 12m for 14 minutes on Table B gives a SC of *C*. From Table C, 6 minutes at 18m yields a SC of *D*. From Table D, *8* minutes of dive time is still available, which includes the time taken to ascend from 11m to 6m.

THE PADI WHEEL

The "Wheel" has been designed specifically to cater for multi-level diving. The instruction booklet, accompanying the Wheel, contains a number of detailed examples on its use in multi-level dive situations, so further examples will not be presented here. Users of the Wheel are advised to read the instructions very carefully, and to ensure that they have mastered the Wheel before using it to calculate a multi-level dive.

The multi-level procedure using the Wheel is currently the only table-based multi-level procedure that has undergone any significant testing to assess its safety.[8,9]

DEEP TO SHALLOW?

Most multi-level dive procedures encourage a diver to ascend to progressively shallower depths during the dive and to spend some time in shallow water towards the end of the dive, rather than to ascend directly to the surface from depth. (This is sometimes referred to as a 'Forward Profile').

Bubbles will form if there is too much pressure change over too short a period during ascent. The greater the pressure reduction and the shorter the time of this pressure reduction, the greater the amount of resultant bubbles. In theory, working shallower during a dive reduces the relative pressure change at the end of the dive and so enables the tissues to eliminate their gas load in a more orderly manner.

Working deeper during a dive ('Reverse Dive Profile') may lead to greater inert gas loads in some tissues at the point of beginning to ascend and, possibly, a longer direct ascent, both of which are conducive to bubble formation.

In an attempt to find whether or not reverse profiles presented problems, a 1999 "Reverse Dive Profiles Workshop" was convened to determine whether or not there was an increased risk of DCS with reverse dive profiles. On the basis of the information presented, the Workshop concluded: "We find no reason for the diving communities to prohibit reverse dive profiles for no-decompression dives less than 130fsw (40msw) and depth differentials less than 40fsw (12msw)"[10]

So, despite the theoretical concerns, there was no data presented at that Workshop that proved that working deeper during a multi-level dive, or conducting repetitive dives to increasing depths, was inherently unsafe. One possible reason for the apparent divergence between theory (which in any case we know is in-exact) and practice, especially with multi-level dives, is the fact that most divers now do safety stops, or simply spend time in shallower water at the end of most dives and this may minimize potential issues that could be caused by the previous profile.

However, one recent report has been highly critical of the conclusions of the Workshop.[11] In addition, recent animal experiments appear to have demonstrated that some reverse profiles are dangerous (certainly to guinea pigs).[12,13] In these experiments, initially 11 guinea pigs were exposed without incident to a multi-level no-stop dive to a forward profile of 36m/24m/12m (120ft/80ft/40m). However, when the reverse profile was conducted on similar guinea pigs (with identical exposure times at the various depths), 6 of the 11 animals died from DCS. In a second series another group of 11 guinea pigs were exposed to a repetitive series of three no-stop dives to 30m (100ft), 20m (66ft) and 10m (33ft), again without incident. However, when a matched group of animals were exposed to the same dives in reverse order, one died from DCS. Extending the exposures to 36m, 24m and 12m (120ft, 80ft and 40ft) caused DCS in one animal in the 'Forward' group and 6 in the 'Reverse' group. The researchers found that the difference in DCS incidence between the 'Forward' and 'Reverse' profiles for repetitive dives was statistically significant (P=0.01) and concluded that, at least with the profiles chosen, it was less dangerous to perform the deeper dives first, than it was to perform them last.

These experiments do indicate that it may be dangerous in some circumstances to conduct reverse profile dives without compensating for this reversal by reducing the durations of exposure at the increasing depth levels. However, in reality, most modern computers and tables do include compensatory mechanisms, despite being largely unvalidated.

OFF-GASSING IN THE SHALLOWS

There is some experimental evidence that indicates that we may at times surface with less excess gas after ascending to and spending time in shallower water than we would have if we had not stopped in the shallows.[14]

A stop in relatively shallow water at the end of a dive may allow some of the excess nitrogen to diffuse out of the diver's body while still under pressure and before substantial bubble formation has occurred. Once sufficient bubbles have formed, the rate of nitrogen elimination is reduced as nitrogen diffuses into these bubbles and then takes longer to be eliminated from the body.

More recent studies have indicated that the addition of a deeper stop further reduces, and in many cases eliminates, Doppler detectable bubbles and so should further enhance inert gas elimination.[15]

Although we may surface with less excess gas after doing a safety stop than we would have if no stop was done, wherever possible, the time spent at the stop should be included if calculating the Repetitive Group from tables at the end of the dive. In this way any extra gas taken aboard by certain body tissues during the safety stop will be accounted for if a repetitive dive is planned.

IS MULTI-LEVEL DIVING SAFE?

It is difficult enough to test the large array of possible single-depth dive profiles, so it is impossible to validate the endless number of possible combinations of depth and time during various multi-level dives. Despite the proliferation of multi-level diving since the 1980s, there have been very few controlled trials to assess the safety of multi-level diving techniques.

The few tests that were done to test the validity of the multi-level program used by the "Edge" diving computer[16], and the tests conducted to assess the application of the PADI Wheel to multi-level diving[8,9] indicate that certain profiles are relatively safe.

DAN America's Project Dive Exploration data for 2002 contains details of more than 17,000 dives conducted that year. Of these, up to 75% of dives incorporated some multi-level component.[17] These data are largely taken from liveaboard dive vessels and resorts where multi-level diving may be more common. However, the reality is that most divers do now participate in multi-level diving, whether using dive computers, tables (or no guidance!) and there doesn't appear to be a proportionate increase in decompression illness.

Calculation errors can easily be made when tables are used for multi-level dive calculations. To minimize such errors, *the dive profile should be planned before entering the water.* By using a dive computer, a diver avoids the possibility of making these errors. However, the *dive computer must be reliable and conservative* in order to maximize the safety of the multi-level dive.

The following guidelines are suggested to minimize the risks involved with multi-level diving:

GUIDELINES FOR MULTI-LEVEL DIVING

- Use the DCIEM Tables, BS-AC '88 Tables, PADI Wheel or Huggins Tables, rather than a multi-level technique based directly on the U.S. Navy Tables. The Huggins and BS-AC '88 Tables appear to be more conservative than the others. The times allowed by the Wheel and the DCIEM Tables vary with respect to each other, depending on the dive.

  OR

  Use a reliable and *conservative* dive computer.

- If using tables, plan the dive profile before diving and then stick to the plan or dive more conservatively than the plan.

- Reduce the NDLs even more than usual to cater for any predisposing factors to decompression sickness that are relevant to you.

- If conducting reverse profiles, do so conservatively.

- Ascend slowly between levels and to the surface. An ascent rate of about 10m (33ft) per minute seems reasonable for depths shallower than about 24-30m (80-100ft).

- If using tables, include the time taken to ascend to a level in the "bottom" time of the previous level.

- Spend at least 3 minutes between 5-6m/15-20ft before surfacing, and include this time when calculating the RG after surfacing, where appropriate.

Table 23.2

Comparison of allowable times for a multi-level dive.

	Bottom Time Limits		
	Huggins	**PADI Wheel**	**DCIEM**
Step 1: *110ft (33m)* Actual bottom time = 10 min	15	16 (15)	12
Step 2: *70ft (21m)* Actual bottom time = 10 min	13	19 (16)	20
Step 3: *40ft (12m)*	0	72 (72)	90

Times in brackets are from the metric Wheel.
This profile cannot be conducted using the BS-AC 88 Tables.

Table 23.3

Comparison of allowable times for a pair of multi-level dives

	Bottom Time Limits		
	Huggins	**PADI Wheel**	**DCIEM**
DIVE 1			
Step 1: *120ft (36m)*	10	13 (13)	10
Actual bottom time = 5 min			
Step 2: *80ft (24m)*	17	20 (20)	15
Actual bottom time = 10 min			
Step 3: *40ft (12m)*	50	87 (91)	90
Actual bottom time = 50 min			
Surface Interval = 1^{1}/2 hr			
DIVE 2			
Step 1: *70ft (21m)*	14	24 (22)	16
Actual bottom time = 10 min			
Step 2: *50ft (15m)*	0	37 (31)	*

* A decompression stop would be required here. However, if Step 2 was at 40ft
(12m) or shallower, plenty of No-D bottom time would be available.

Times in brackets are from the metric Wheel.

This series of dives cannot be conducted using the BS-AC 88 Tables.

SUMMARY

- A "Multi-Level" dive is defined here as a dive where the diver spends significant bottom time shallower than the maximum depth and, so, extends the bottom time beyond the limits for a rectangular profile dive to the maximum depth.

- Various techniques have been introduced for planning multi-level dives. Some techniques, based on the Standard U.S. Navy Tables, create a higher gas load in the tissues than is allowed by the tables and may be more likely to cause DCS.

- Most multi-level techniques involve transferring a Repetitive Group between depths. However, this may not always be appropriate.

- Most multi-level diving techniques have not been validated. However, multi-level diving is now common practice and, when conducted in accordance with appropriate guidelines, appears to be relatively safe.

- A reliable, conservative dive computer or a table which has been designed, or appropriately adapted, to cater for multi-level diving should be used. (e.g. Huggins Tables, DCIEM Tables, PADI Wheel or BS-AC '88 Tables.)

- Predisposing factors to DCS must be accounted for, ascent should be slow, and a safety stop should be done.

- Total dive time should be used to determine the time allowed for any subsequent repetitive dive(s).

REFERENCES

1. Graver D. A Decompression Table Procedure for Multi-Level Diving. In: Fead L (ed). *Proceedings of the Eighth International Conference on Underwater Education.* California: NAUI; 1976.

2. Huggins KE, Somers LH. Mathematical Evaluation of Multi-Level Diving. Report No. MICHU-SG-81-207 Michigan Sea Grant Publications. Ann Arbor: University of Michigan; 1981.

3. Bove AA. RX for Divers. *Skin Diver* 1983; 33 (3):10.

4. Huggins KE. New No-Decompression Tables Based on No-Decompression Limits Determined by Ultrasonic Bubble Detection. Report No. MICHU-SG-81-205. Michigan Sea Grant Publications. Ann Arbor: University of Michigan; 1981

5. Wienke BR, Livingston JD, O'Leary TR. NAUI approach to reverse dive profiles. In:Lang MA and Lehner CE (eds). Proceedings of the Reverse Dive Profiles Workshop. October 29-30, 1999. Washington DC: Smithsonian Institution; 2000:247-57.

6. UDT Instructions for using the DCIEM Sport Diving Tables. Toronto: Universal Dive Techtronics, Inc.; 1996.

7. Busuttili M. The BS-AC '88 Decompression Tables - first review. *NDC Bulletin* 1989; 14:3-5.

8. Powell MR, Spencer MP, Rogers RE, Doppler Ultrasound Monitoring of Gas Phase Formation Following Decompression in Repetitive Dives. Santa Ana: Diving Science and Technology; 1988.

9. Rogers RE. Testing the Recreational Dive Planner. *SPUMS J* 1991; 21(3): 164-71.

10. Lang MA, Lehner CE (eds). Proceedings of the Reverse Dive Profiles Workshop. October 29-30, 1999. Washington DC: Smithsonian Institution; 2000.

11. McInnes S, Edmonds C, Bennett M. Reverse Dive Profiles: the Making of a myth. *SPUMS J* 2005; 35(3):139-43.

12. McInnes S, Edmonds C, Bennett M. The relative safety of forward and reverse multi-level dive profiles. *Undersea Hyperb Med* 2005; 22(supp): in press.

13. McInnes S, Edmonds C, Bennett M. The relative safety of forward and reverse repetitive dive profiles *Undersea Hyperb Med* 2005; 22(supp): in press.

14. Kindwall EP, Baz A, Lightfoot EN, Lanphier EH, Seireg A. Nitrogen Elimination in Man During Decompresion. *Undersea Biomed Res 1975*; 2 (4):285-97.

15. Marroni A, Bennett PB, Cronjé FJ et al. A deep stop during decompression from 82fsw (25m) significantly reduces bubbles and fast tissue gas tensions. *Undersea Hyperb Med* 2004; 31(2):233-43.

16. Huggins KE. Doppler Evaluation of Multi-Level Diving Profiles. Report No. MICHU-SG-84-300, Michigan Sea Grant Publications. Ann Arbor: University of Michigan; 1983.

17. Report on decompression Illness, dive fatalities and Project Dive Exploration. Durham, North Carolina: Divers Alert Network; 2004.

OTHER SOURCES

Bennett PB, Marroni A, Cronjé FJ. Deep Stops. *Alert Diver* 2004; May-June:38-43.

Dick APK, Vann RD, Mebane GY, Frezor MD. Decompression induced nitrogen elimination. *Undersea Biomed Res* 1984; 11(4):369-80.

Graver D. Using the U.S. Navy Dive Tables for Sport Diving. In: *Decompression In Depth*. California: PADI; 1979:13-21.

Huggins K. Multi-Level Diving, How Safe Is It? Bangasser S (ed). *Proceedings of International Conference on Underwater Education, I.Q. '85.* California: NAUI; 1985;176-88.

Huggins K. Tables, tables what's with all these tables? Bangasser S (ed). *Proceedings of International Conference on Underwater Education, I.Q. '85.* California: NAUI; 1985:189-204.

Huggins KE. Microprocessor Applications to Multi-Level Air Decompression Problems. Michigan Sea Grant College Program Report No. MICHU-SG-87-201 Michigan Sea Grant Publications. Ann Arbor: University of Michigan; 1987.

Thalmann ED, Butler F. A Procedure for Doing Multiple Level Dives on Air Using Repetitive Groups. Navy Experimental Diving Unit, Report No. 13-83. Bethesda: Department of the Navy; 1983.

Huggins K, Somers L. Mathematical Evaluation of Multi-Level Diving. Report No. MICHU-SG-81-207. Michigan: Michigan Sea Grant Publications; 1981.

Huggins K. Doppler Evaluation of Multi-Level Diving Profiles. Report No. MICHU-SG-84-300, Michigan: Michigan Sea Grant Publications; 1983.

Lang MA and Hamilton RW (eds). Proceedings of Dive Computer Workshop. University of Southern California Sea Grant Publication No. USCSG-TR-01-89. California: University of Southern California, 1989

Lang MA, Vann RD (eds). Proceedings of the Repetitive Diving Workshop. Washington, California: American Academy of Underwater Sciences; 1992.

The Wheel. Instructions for use and study guide. California: Diving Science and Technology Corp.; 2003.

RECOMMENDED FURTHER READING

Bennett PB, Marroni A, Cronjé FJ. Deep Stops. *Alert Diver* 2004; May-June: 38-43.

Lang MA, Lehner CE (eds). Proceedings of the Reverse Dive Profiles Workshop. October 29-30, 1999. Washington DC: Smithsonian Institution; 2000.

McInnes S, Edmonds C, Bennett M. Reverse Dive Profiles – The Making of a Myth. *SPUMS J*: in press.

Powell MR, Spencer MP, Rogers RE, Doppler Ultrasound Monitoring of Gas Phase Formation Following Decompression in Repetitive Dives. Santa Ana: Diving Science and Technology; 1988.

Many thanks to Gain Wong and Trevor Davies for checking various parts of this chapter.

© Michael Aw

24

Dive computers

HISTORICAL BACKGROUND

Since decompression sickness (DCS) in humans first reared its ugly head back in the mid-1800s, scientists and others have sought ways to better understand the mechanisms and to improve and simplify decompression calculations and procedures.

Haldane introduced his model and schedules at the beginning of this century and, since then, many decompression tables have been published. Although some of the more modern tables include multi-level methods to compensate for parts of a dive spent shallower than the maximum depth, most traditional tables require a diver to choose a no-decompression or decompression schedule based on the maximum depth and bottom time of a dive. The calculation assumes that the entire bottom time is spent at the maximum depth, and that the diver's body has absorbed the associated amount of nitrogen. However, in reality, most dives do not follow that pattern. A diver's depth normally varies throughout a dive and, often, very little of the bottom time is actually spent at the maximum depth. In this case, a diver's body should, theoretically, contain far less dissolved nitrogen than is assumed to be present when using the traditional, non-multi-level tables in the conventional manner. Some divers feel penalized for the time of the dive not spent at the maximum depth.

Obviously, the ideal situation is to have a device that tracks the exact dive profile and then calculates the decompression requirement according to the actual dive done. Such devices have emerged since the mid-1950s, some gaining notoriety.

Probably the best known of the very early decompression meters is the SOS decompression meter (Figure 24.1) which was designed in 1959 and emerged in the early 1960s. The meter represented a diver's body as one tissue. It contained a ceramic resistor through which gas was absorbed before passing into a constant volume chamber. Within the chamber was a bourdon tube which bent as the pressure changed, and the pressure level, which represented the amount of absorbed gas, was displayed on an attached gauge. On ascent, gas escaped back through the resistor and, eventually, when enough gas had escaped, the gauge indicated that a safe (supposedly) ascent was possible.

FIGURE 24.1

S.O.S. decompression meter.

A number of problems arose with the use of the SOS meter. Individual meters often varied greatly, and the no-decompression stop times for initial / single dives deeper than 18m (60ft) exceeded the U.S. Navy NDLs.[1] The meters gave inadequate decompression for repetitive dives when compared to the U.S. Navy tables and most other traditional tables. In 1971, the first six divers requiring treatment at the Royal Australian Navy School of Underwater Medicine chamber were divers who had ascended according to SOS decompression meters.[2]

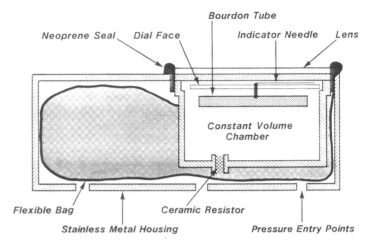

FIGURE 24.2

Schematic diagram of the S.O.S. decompression meter.

Reprinted from Huggins (1987)

The Defense and Civil Institute of Environmental Medicine (DCIEM) of Canada developed a decompression meter in 1962. It utilized four resistor-compartments to simulate nitrogen uptake and elimination in a diver. Initially, the compartments were set up in parallel so that each compartment was exposed to ambient pressure and so absorbed gas simultaneously. When tested, this configuration produced an unacceptable DCS incidence. The four units were then re-arranged in a series arrangement so that only the first was exposed to ambient pressure and gas passed from one compartment into the next. This configuration was tested on almost 4,000 test dives and produced a very low incidence of DCS.[2] The meter gave effective half-times from 5 to more than 300 minutes and it indicated current depth and safe ascent depth. The DCIEM unit never became available to recreational divers as it would have proved to be very expensive and would have required extensive, and costly, maintenance.

In 1975, Farallon released its Multi-Tissue Decomputer, which was designed to be a no-decompression stop meter. It consisted of four permeable membranes, two of which absorbed gas and two which released it. In 1976, the Royal Australian Navy tested two

meters and found them to give very divergent results. One became more conservative while the other became less so.[3] In addition, various mechanical problems eventuated. Tests done in the USA confirmed that the NDLs given by the meter often greatly exceed those of the U.S. Navy Tables[4] which, at that time, was believed in itself to be inherently dangerous.

Over the past 25 years or so, various multi-level table calculation methods emerged. Most of these methods require manipulations that are too complex for many divers, and require the dive plan to be known in advance and rigidly followed. Most techniques are largely unvalidated and their safety in certain situations is questionable. In addition, if time is spent at more than two or three levels, the calculations may become prohibitively complex. (see Chapter 23).

By the mid-1970s, with the advance in microprocessors (a chip which can contain a series of pre-programmed instructions), it became possible to construct a small computer capable of doing very complex multi-level calculations. Later technological innovations overcame some of the early technical restraints, and the diver now has access to the convenience of automatic, and generally more accurate, depth and time recording, together with accurately computed multi-level decompression schedules at affordable prices.

A microprocessor is capable of reading a pressure transducer (which converts pressure into electrical impulses) very rapidly and can apply nitrogen uptake and elimination algorithms (the mathematical equations which represent gas uptake and release) to this information every few seconds. These computers can, therefore, track a diver's exact profile and calculate decompression requirements according to it, rather than by the "rounded-up" profile which is used with traditional decompression tables.

Some of the early computers (e.g. Suunto SME-USN, Decobrain 1) had actual decompression tables programmed into their memory, and read the table to give the diver the appropriate decompression information. The tables programmed into these devices listed decompression information in discrete increments of depth (usually 3m(10ft)) and time (often 5-10 minutes), so they still did not give the exact (theoretical) decompression requirement for the actual dive done. The Decobrain 1 allowed table-like multi-level dive calculations but got confused easily.

To overcome this situation, current dive computers are programmed with the actual decompression model on which the table is based, rather than on the table itself. For example, if a computer is programmed with the model of the DCIEM Tables, it can simulate the loading and unloading of the four tissue compartments used in the DCIEM model and portray their theoretical nitrogen content at any particular depth and time during a dive or surface interval. In this manner, the exact decompression requirement given by the model can be calculated almost instantly.

FIGURE 24.3

The internal components of an Aladin Pro dive computer.

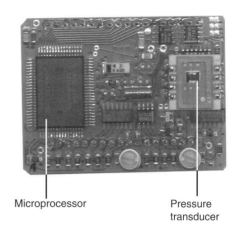

Microprocessor | Pressure transducer

The current generation of computers is essentially based on either modified U.S. Navy, Bühlmann or DCIEM models.

In 1983, there were two electronic dive computers available to recreational divers - the Decobrain, from Switzerland, and the Edge from the USA. By 2003, there were at least 75 different units available, based on approximately 15 different decompression algorithms.[5]

FIGURE 24.4

The Decobrain 2 (above) and Edge (below) computers.

Dive computers offer the diver a number of advantages over the tables. They eliminate the problem of divers making errors in their decompression calculations since the computers do the calculations automatically and accurately, in accordance to their model. By following the actual profile, rather than just the maximum depth, and by incorporating a number of tissue half-times rather than a single tissue half-time during a surface interval, the computers allow the diver much more bottom time on most dives, especially repetitive dives. They normally also measure depth and time very accurately, and many give the diver an indication of ascent rate which, in this author's view, is probably their greatest contribution to diver safety as it has helped to teach divers to ascend slowly, which in itself will reduce the likelihood of DCS.

Despite, and in some cases, because of some of these features, some diving scientists, doctors and educators still remain critical of these devices. It has been argued that divers will become too machine-dependent and would be at a loss, and in a potentially dangerous situation, if their computer failed while in use. However, it can be countered that modern dive computers are less likely to fail than divers are while reading the tables, and that there are some reasonable bail-out procedures in case of device failure. Probably the major fear of some of the computer critics is that many computers may still bring a diver too close to, or beyond, the limits of safe diving, especially during deep and/or multiple repetitive dives. [5, 6, 7, 8]

The safety of dive computers is discussed later in this chapter. However, it is important to understand from the outset that although the decompression models programmed into the model-based computers are designed to simulate nitrogen uptake and release in a diver's body, these are just models and cannot completely predict the gas flow in and out of our actual tissues. Our individual physiology is not always predictable as many factors influence the rate of gas uptake and

FIGURE 24.5

The evolution of the Uwatec 'Aladin' dive computers.

elimination and the possibility of consequent decompression illness. So, even though the computers follow their models exactly and the theoretical tissues programmed into the computer load and unload as expected, our bodies might not be behaving quite so predictably.

Why do computer times differ so much from those given by dive tables?

By shortening the initial NDLs and slowing down the ascent rate, dive computers attempt to minimize the bubble formation after the initial dive. This should enhance off-gassing, reduce residual nitrogen and thus enable longer no-decompression stop bottom times for repetitive dives. The Bühlmann Tables work on this premise. They utilize shorter initial NDLs than the U.S. Navy Tables, followed by a slow ascent, and this is why they sometimes allow longer no-decompression stop bottom times than are given by the U.S. Navy Tables for repetitive dives. However, using the Bühlmann Tables for repetitive dives is still more conservative than using many computers.

Because most tables are based on the off-gassing of a single, slow, tissue during the surface interval, they often have an inherent safety margin built into them. Repetitive Groups and Residual Nitrogen Times given in tables are designed to account for the highest gas loading that is theoretically possible, and are often based on a single tissue compartment only.* Since this tissue is a slow tissue, it off-gasses slowly on the surface. These tables (e.g. U.S. Navy Tables) assume that all of the tissue compartments are unloading at this rate and, so, may over-estimate the theoretical gas loads of the faster tissue compartments. This results in shorter repetitive dive times than would be allowed if the actual (theoretical) gas load in the faster compartments was considered. So, this crudeness of the table's calculations may lead to longer surface intervals than are required by the model, but introduces a margin of safety by assuming the diver has more residual nitrogen than the model dictates. However, many depth and time combinations may yield the same calculated Repetitive Group (see previous chapter), although, in reality, the nitrogen contents in the various body tissues are quite different.

Computers calculate repetitive dive times according to the exact (rather than the maximum possible) gas loading given by the model, taking into account all the tissues used in the model. This usually allows more dive time on repetitive dives than is allowed by tables, at the risk of being closer to the DCS threshold. However, in some situations the times can be similar. The deeper NDLs are determined by fast tissue compartments which absorb gas rapidly and which off-gas rapidly at the surface. Repetitive Groups are usually based on slower tissue compartments. If repetitive dive NDLs are compared in the depth range where the Repetitive Group tissue controls the NDL (i.e. shallow to moderate depths where slower tissues predominate the calculation), then the limits given by the tables and the computer should be close.

On some long dive sequences or in situations where repetitive dives are done over many consecutive days, the computers are sometimes slower to unload than tables as they are programmed with slower tissues than are used to determine the Repetitive Groups in most tables. This may occasionally lead to the situation where certain tables will allow you to begin a new day's diving without considering residual nitrogen from the previous day's (or night's) diving, whereas a computer may still carry over a penalty for certain shallower dives. However, if this occurs it will normally only apply to the first dive of the day, after which the advantages (or sometimes disadvantages depending on the outcome) of the computer models come into play and the computer then usually allow longer bottom times than most tables would allow for the following dives that day.

DIVE COMPUTER ALGORITHMS

As mentioned earlier, all decompression models include a series of mathematical equations that are designed to simulate inert gas kinetics within the body. Most of these models are based on Haldanian theory (see Chapter 13) utilizing a set of tissue compartments with varying half-times that act independently of each other (in parallel).

Many of the algorithms incorporated in dive computers are derived from the work of the late Professor Albert Bühlmann.[9] Derivatives of this (Haldanian) model are incorporated in the Uwatec series of computers, as well as many other brands.

The basic equations used in a Bühlmann model are shown below.[10] Many other major dive computers on the market use similar concepts and basic equations.

---

* This is not the case with the Bühlmann (1986) Tables which take into account gas loading in all of the theoretical tissue compartments.

1. *Calculating the partial pressure of nitrogen in the inspired gas:*

$$pN_2insp = (p_{amb} - 0.063\ bar) \times 0.79$$

where

pN_2insp = inspired nitrogen pressure
pamb   = ambient pressure
0.063   = the constant water vapour pressure in the lungs

2. *Calculating tissue nitrogen loading:*

$$pN_2 = pN_20 + (pN_2insp - pN_20) \times (1 - 2^{-\Delta/T})$$

where

pN_2 = partial pressure of nitrogen
pN_20 = initial partial pressure of nitrogen
T   = tissue compartment half-time
t   = time of exposure

Saturation is generally assumed to occur exponentially. In earlier models, desaturation was also assumed to occur exponentially and at the same rate. However, desaturation is now often treated as a modified exponential equation, with factors such as presumed or estimated bubble formation affecting and slowing down the rate of desaturation.

3. *Calculating the Tolerated Nitrogen Pressure / Ambient Pressure*

For each tissue compartment, it is assumed that there is a maximum nitrogen pressure that can be tolerated at a particular ambient pressure before bubble formation and / or decompression illness occurs. Tissue compartments with shorter half-times (presumed to represent body tissues with high blood supply such as blood and brain are set to be able to tolerate higher nitrogen pressures at a given depth (ambient pressure) than the "slower" tissue compartments.

$$Pamb_{tol} = (pN_2 - a) \times b$$

where

$Pamb_{tol}$ = minimum ambient pressure to which ascent can be made.
a and *b* are constants, verified through experimentation by Bühlmann.

Bühlmann conducted a variety of experiments including chamber trials with human volunteers. During these trials, certain mild symptoms of decompression illness were deemed acceptable and adjustments were not always done to try to eliminate these (Bühlmann AA, personal communication). However, with this model, alterations to the No-Decompression Limits and decompression requirements are easily made by adjusting the values of the constants *a* and/or *b* and this has been done by various dive computer programmers. In addition, user-selected "added safety" adjustments can readily be made by alterations to the constants.

As mentioned previously, early models of dive computers assumed that both gas uptake and elimination were exponential and occurred at identical rates. However, many current models are programmed to delay the predicted gas elimination rate to allow for the effects of bubble formation, constriction of blood vessels with cold, and various other factors that can affect the formation and movement of gas within our bodies (gas kinetics). In some units, external parameters such as temperature and gas consumption are integrated into the calculations.[11] Unfortunately, there is little data from which to construct appropriate gas kinetic equations.

COMPARING DIVE COMPUTERS

Current dive computers vary greatly in the no-stop times they allow and the decompression obligations indicated[5,8,12] and it is important that divers appreciate this difference so that they are more able to select the level of risk that they are willing to take. However, there is relatively little comparative data available by which to compare dive computers. A 2004 report that compared 15 dive computers over a series of exposures with known results on humans indicated that certain models may well need modification.[5] Another study provided further support for this view.[8] The latter study is described below:

One of each of a group of dive computers commonly used in the diving industry was selected and subjected to several series of pressure exposures in a small water-filled compression vessel. These pressure exposures ("dives") were designed to simulate as closely as possible actual depth-time diving profiles that do occur in the field, despite some being somewhat undesirable.

The dive computers tested were:

1. Suunto *Solution*.
2. Suunto *Vytec*.
3. Uwatec *Aladin Pro*.
4. Uwatec *Aladin Smart*.
5. Oceanic *Versa*.
6. Citizen *Cyber Aqualand*.
7. Cochrane *Commander*.

The Suunto Solution preceded the Suunto Vytec, and the Uwatec Aladin Pro preceded the Aladin Smart. The earlier models were tested as (i) they are still commonly used by divers; and (ii) to determine what differences in dive times and/or decompression requirements were generated by updated decompression algorithms incorporated in the newer models. All computers were set in the standard mode with no "safety" or altitude time reductions implemented.

The series of profiles tested were (times shown are bottom times):

1. *Repetitive series with reducing depths*
   36m / 10 minutes
   Surface interval 60 minutes
   30m / 18 minutes

2. *Repetitive series with increasing depths*
   27m / 18 minutes
   Surface interval 32 minutes
   30m / 16 minutes
   Surface interval 32 minutes
   36m / 10 minutes

FIGURE 24.6

Various dive computers ready for testing in a pressure vessel.

3. *Multi-level dive with reducing depth*
   30m / 5 minutes
   20m / 10 minutes
   15m / as indicated by dive computers

4. *Multi-level dive with increasing depth*
   15m / 15 minutes
   21m / 10 minutes
   27m / as indicated by dive computers

5. *Cyclic repetitive dive series**
   45m / 5 minutes
   Surface interval 60 minutes
   45m / 5 minutes
   Surface interval 60 minutes
   45m / 5 minutes

---

* The cyclic repetitive dive series (5) was chosen as it had been shown during in-water trials by the Royal Navy to be unsafe due to an unacceptable incidence of DCI.[13]

Computers were allowed sufficient time re-set between each series of profiles.

The No Stop times allowed and the decompression requirements indicated by the computers were then compared to those generated by the Canadian Forces (DCIEM) Tables[14]. The DCIEM tables were chosen for comparison as they are widely considered to be a benchmark for determining decompression risk.

The results are shown in Tables 24.1 to 24.6.

Note: The first number in the DCIEM column is the time given by the Tables. The number in brackets is the time given by the actual DCIEM model.

TABLE 24.1

Comparison of No-Decompression Limits.

Depth m / ft	Solution	Vytec	Alad Pro	Alad Smart	Versa	Coch. Cmder	Cyber Aqua	DCIEM	USN	B/mann
9 / 30	222	204	334	324	283	599	405	300	-	400
12 / 40	127	124	121	124	184	213	162	150	200	125
15 / 50	72	72	70	70	85	101	80	75	100	75
18 / 60	52	52	50	50	59	68	52	50	60	51
21 / 70	37	37	30	36	41	51	35	35	50	35
24 / 80	29	29	28	27	32	40	25	25	40	25
27 / 90	23	23	22	21	25	31	19	20	30	20
30 / 100	18	18	16	16	20	25	14	15	25	17
33 / 110	13	13	14	13	17	20	11	12	20	14
36 / 120	11	11	12	11	14	15	9	10	15	12
39 / 130	9	9	10	10	11	12	7	8	10	10
42 / 140	7	7	9	9	9	9	7	7	10	9

Note: These dive computer times are based on the metric models. Imperial models may vary for some depths.

TABLE 24.2

Repetitive dive with reducing depths.

	Solution	Vytec	Alad Pro	Alad Smart	Versa	Coch. Cmder	Cyber Aqua	DCIEM
Depth = **36m (120ft)** No Stop Time Allowed Bottom Time = 10 Ascent time = 3.5	10	10	11	11	13	15	11	10(10)
SI = 60								
Depth = **30m (100ft)** No Stop Time Allowed Bottom Time = 18	17	10	16	15	16	25	11	10(11)
Deco 6m (20ft)	0	0	0	0	0	0	0	3 (0)
Deco 3m (10ft)	1	13	1	1	0	0	7	9 (11)

All times in minutes unless otherwise indicated.

TABLE 24.3

Repetitive dive with increasing depths.

	Solution	Vytec	Alad Pro	Alad Smart	Versa	Coch. Cmder	Cyber Aqua	DCIEM
Depth = **27m (90ft)**								
No Stop Time Allowed	22	22	20	20	25	30	21	20(20)
Bottom Time = 18								
Ascent time = 3								
SI = 32								
Depth = **30m (100ft)**								
No Stop Time Allowed	12	10	10	12	11	21	9	9(9)
Bottom Time = 16								
Deco 6m (20ft)	0	0	0	0	0	0	0	3(0)
Deco 3m (10ft)	9	20	8	8	9	0	7	9(11)
SI = 32								
Depth = **36m (120ft)**								
No Stop Time Allowed	6	5	6	7	9	14	6	5(6)
Bottom Time = 10								
Deco 6m (20ft)	0	0	0	0	0	0	0	3 (0)
Deco 3m (10ft)	18	25	7	6	0	0	9	10(12)

All times in minutes unless otherwise indicated.

TABLE 24.4

Multi-level dive with reducing depths.

	Solution	Vytec	Alad Pro	Alad Smart	Versa	Coch. Cmder	Cyber Aqua	DCIEM
L1 Depth = **30m (100ft)**								
No Stop Time Allowed	18	16	16	16	20	25	16	15
Time at level 1 = 5								
Ascent to level 2 = 1								
L2 Depth = **20m (66ft)**								
No Stop Time Allowed	32	29	27	29	39	47	30	23
Time at level 2 = 10								
Ascent to level 3 = 0.5								
L3 Depth = **15m (50ft)**								
No Stop Time Allowed	44	40	37	41	61	75	52	35(29)

All times in minutes unless otherwise indicated.

TABLE 24.5

Multi-level dive with increasing depths.

	Solution	Vytec	Alad Pro	Alad Smart	Versa	Coch. Cmder	Cyber Aqua	DCIEM
L1 Depth = **15m (50ft)** *No Stop Time Allowed* Time at level 1 = 15 Descent to level 2 = 0.5	72	69	65	69	87	105	81	75
L2 Depth = **21m (70ft)** *No Stop Time Allowed* Time at level 2 = 10 Descent to level 3 = 0.5	27	24	25	25	31	43	26	23(15)
L3 Depth = **27m (90ft)** *No Stop Time Allowed*	10	7	6	8	11	18	7	0(0)

All times in minutes unless otherwise indicated.

TABLE 24.6

Cyclic bounce dives.

	Solution	Vytec	Alad Pro	Alad Smart	Versa	Coch. Cmder	Cyber Aqua	DCIEM
Depth = **45m (150ft)** *No Stop Time Allowed* Bottom Time = 5 Ascent time = 4.5	6	6	6	7	7	7	21	6(6)
SI = 60								
Depth = **45m (150ft)** *No Stop Time Allowed* Bottom Time = 5	6	4	6	7	5	7	6	5(6)
Deco 6m (20ft)	0	0	0	0	1	0	0	0(0)
Deco 3m (10ft)	0	3	0	0	10	0	0	0(0)
SI = 60								
Depth = **45m (150ft)** *No Stop Time Allowed* Bottom Time = 5	5	4	6	7	0	7	6	5(6)
Deco 6m (20ft)	0	0	0	0	3	0	0	0(0)
Deco 3m (10ft)	0	2	0	0	25	0	1	5(0)

All times in minutes unless otherwise indicated.

Observations:

- The *Vytec* yielded times similar to the DCIEM Tables more consistently than the other computers tested on these profiles.

- The *Vytec* was consistently more conservative than its predecessor, the *Solution*.

- The *Aladin Pro* and *Aladin Smart* generated similar No-Stop Times and decompression times on the profiles tested.

- The Cochrane *Commander* and Oceanic *Versa* were consistently less conservative than the other dive computers and the DCIEM tables, with the Commander being the least conservative. However, the exception was with the *Versa* on the series of deep, repetitive, "bounce" dives. In this case, it required decompression times well in excess of the DCIEM tables and the other dive computers. The decompression times indicated in these cases appear to be overly conservative, when compared to other decompression tables.

UNDERSTANDING THE DIFFERENCES BETWEEN COMPUTERS

Initial Dives

As can be seen from Table 24.1, most dive computers display similar No Decompression Limits (NDLs) for an initial, rectangular profile dive (except in the shallows). This is because the decompression models on which they are based generally perform in a similar fashion to the initial pressure exposure.

Repetitive Dives

Greater differences in decompression advice emerge with repetitive dives. In addition, further divergence may occur with situations such as a rapid ascent, increased breathing rate, cold water exposure and increasing depth of dive or repetitive dives as a result of programming features in the various models. The so-called "adaptive" dive computers are programmed to try to account for events that may increase inert gas load and/or bubble formation during the dive. However, although such events should reduce allowed no-stop dive time or increase decompression obligations and so inherently increase safety, there is unfortunately still relatively little data on which to base accurate computations.

Bubble formation is often handled by several methods, for example, entering data into a separate set of equations or by using conversion fractions (e.g. Reduced Gradient Bubble Model RGBM)[15] designed to determine the amount and effect of bubble formation, or by manipulating existing saturation-desaturation equations.

In addition to altering the constants, increasing the number and range of tissue compartments can also affect the decompression times, as well as the recommended interval to flying after diving, especially on repetitive dives. The longer half-times may come into play for multi-day repetitive diving as they allow for a presumed nitrogen load to be tracked for an extended period. The published tissue compartments and half-times for the computers tested are shown in Figure 24.7

In practice, the range and number of half times alone and the published initial dive NDLs may well paint a misleading picture of how a particular dive computer will perform in the field on real dives. Unfortunately, this is all most divers have to go on.

As seen in this experiment, the decompression advice displayed by different computers can and often does vary greatly, especially with repetitive dives. The decompression times indicated result from the combination of a variety of factors. These include the particular base decompression algorithm/model used, the amount and type of real dive data (if any) used to adjust the sensitivity of the base model, if and how adjustments are made to attempt to cater for bubble formation, and differences in measurement of the devices.

TABLE 24.7

Tissue compartments & half-times of computers tested.*

Computer	Tissues	Half Times (min)
Solution	9	2.5, 5, 10, 20, 40, 80, 120, 240, 480
Vytec	9	2.5, 5, 10, 20, 40, 80, 120, 240, 480
Aladin Pro	6	6, 14, 34, 64, 124, 320
Aladin Smart	8	5,10, 20, 40, 80, 160, 320, 640
Versa	12	5, 10, 20, 40, 80, 120, 160, 200, 320, 400, 480
Commander	16	0 - 1000
Cyber Aqua	4	approx. 21

* Taken from manufacturers' literature of provided directly by manufactuer.

ARE THE COMPUTERS SAFE?

Although dive computers are now a fact of life for divers, and table usage is becoming relatively uncommon, the safety of dive devices is still the subject of some debate. The main criticisms still focus on the following arguments:

1. The models on which the computers are based are not completely accurate. Dive computers will retain inaccuracies until the devices can directly measure an individual's actual tissue nitrogen levels and calculate safe decompression accordingly.

2. Any inherent safety margin of the tables, as well as the extra security gained by "rounding-off" the tables, is often lost in the computers, despite some increases in conservatism. This can give a diver more time, but will at times put them more at risk of decompression illness.

3. Although some of the models on which the tables are based have been well-tested for fixed-depth dives, there have been relatively few well-controlled and documented tests of the validity of the multi-level applications. For example, for each schedule, a minimum of 35 dives without DCS is needed before a DCS rate of less than 2% can be claimed with 95% confidence.[16] When one considers the seemingly infinite number of potential dive combinations, including multi-level and repetitive dives, it is obvious that sufficient controlled testing is impossible.

We do know that there have been many tens of millions of dives performed using computers, most without incident. With so many apparently safe dives carried out by computer-users, it might well appear that the computers are, indeed, safe devices. However, it is difficult to determine whether it is the computers themselves that are safe, or if the apparent safety lies in how divers are using them. Since most of the computer-assisted dives are undocumented, it is not known whether or not the divers dived to the limits given by their computers. **Unless the algorithms are tested to their limits, we cannot really know how safe the actual limits are.**

In an attempt to obtain relevant data, DAN has been involved in a very ambitious international project (Project Dive Exploration/Safe Dive) aimed at collecting and analyzing one million dives with known outcome (i.e. DCS or No DCS), downloaded from dive computers. The project is a long-term one that has already been running for 10 years. One of DAN's aims is to provide reliable feedback to dive computer and table designers and manufacturers to enable them to upgrade and improve their algorithms, based on the data collected.

Project Dive Exploration data for 1998 to 2002 indicated that from a sample of 6,611 divers, 77% reported using dive computers and only 2% used tables. Six percent of the divers reported following their dive guide and the method of determining decompression was not reported for the remaining 15%.[17] The majority of these reports have evolved through liveaboard dive operations and so may not be representative of all dive situations, such as the weekend diver. However, it is seems obvious that computer use is very widespread.

Dive accident reports can provide an overview of trends and possible problems, although without knowing the total population of divers involved, cannot provide a definitive comparison.

TABLE 24.8

DCS in Computer and Table Users 1997- 2002.

Year	1997	1998	1999	2000	2001	2002
Total DCS	452	422	389	603	414	348
% computer	60	61	62	73	67	72
% table	17	24	16	20	13	15

The above table, derived from DAN America accident reports for the years 1997 to 2002[17-22], shows that the percentage of divers treated for suspected DCS after using dive computers has increased to around 70%.

This high proportion of DCS associated with dive computers does not indicate that the devices are inherently unsafe. The trend no doubt largely reflects the increase in dive computer usage.

TABLE 24.9

Attributes of computer divers with DCS 1987-1997.[12]

Attribute	1997	1996	93-95	90-92	87-89
Within limits	93.7	92.1	92.5	**	**
Outside limits	6.3	7.9	16.1	40.9	39.4
Repetitive dive	81.4	84.5	80.7	69.0	63.7
Multi-level	79.9	75.6	76.1	78.8	71.4
> 24m (80ft)	77.7	73.2	78.3	73.1	86.5
Multi-day	54.3	57.0	52.1	48.6	53.2*
Decompression	20.4	18.5	21.6	24.5	32.7

** not recorded due to change in analysis method   * 1989 only

It is interesting to note that, for 1997, 93.7% of divers reported that they had suffered from DCS after having been diving within the limits of their computers (85.5% of tables users did likewise).[18] Although this trend has not been reported in later DAN America reports, it is a common occurrence and highlights the important fact that **diving within the limits of a dive computer will not eliminate the risk of DCS.**

Early data from dive computer usage indicated a relatively high incidence of DCS after dives involving mandatory stops. This incidence appears to have dropped over subsequent years, possibly as a result of the algorithms becoming more conservative and more accurate, and/or fewer divers are doing decompression stop dives using computers (which in our view seems unlikely).

Higher risk dive profiles for computer-users (and in most cases table-users) may include:

- deep dives; especially deep, repetitive dives
- decompression stop dives
- multi-day repetitive dives
- reverse profile multi-level dives unless an appropriate safety stop is made.

FIGURE 24.7

DCS Severity Ratio and computer usage 1987-2002[17-22, 24-27]

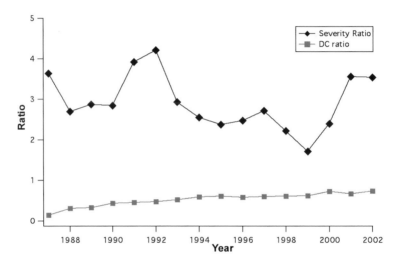

It has been sometimes been claimed that the severity of DCS has increased with the increasing use of dive computers. To investigate this claim, some researchers described what they termed the DCS Severity Ratio and, using DAN America data, plotted this ratio against the proportion of divers who were treated for DCI after using computers. The Severity Ratio was defined as the annual number of cases of DCS categorized as "Type 2" (neurological) per case of "Type 1" (musculoskeletal). The higher the ratio, the higher the proportion of DCS Type 2, which is generally regarded as more serious. [23]

Figure 24.7 has extended this concept over a longer period, 1987-2002, again using DAN America data.[17-22, 24-27] It is evident that the proportion of computer-users with DCS

has increased steadily, as discussed earlier. There is no clear trend in the severity of DCS, but it does not appear to have increased steadily with the increase in Computer Ratio.

This data must be interpreted cautiously, for several reasons, the main being the difficulty and, hence, variation in classification of DCS into the two categories used.

Currently most active divers use computers, therefore ongoing data will be more informative on the relative risks when using computers.

In summary, the accident data to date cannot be used to confirm whether or not dive computer use is associated with an increased risk of DCS. Increasing computer usage will inevitably lead to an increase in the percentage of computer-users represented in DCS statistics. However, it is obvious that divers can and do get DCS while using dive computers, although the likelihood will depend, to some extent, on how a diver uses their computer. Sometimes DCS results because the diver disobeys the advice given by the computer (or table). More often, however, divers have suffered from DCS after diving within the limits of the computer (or table), sometimes well within these limits.

Dive computers are aggressively marketed to divers and have been warmly embraced. The early marketing centred mainly on increasing dive time. Interestingly, some "advertorials" also suggested that computers were safer than tables - a rather precarious argument. However, greater maturity and the emergence of litigation involving dive computers have caused those who manufacture and market the devices to take greater care in how the units are promoted. Although one would imagine that consumers would not be so easily lulled into the belief that using a dive computer will eliminate the risk of DCS, this is not apparent as many divers still place too much reliance on the ability of their dive computer to predict the occurence of DCS.

To a large extent, the decompression illness rate in dive computer users will depend on how divers dive when they use their computers - on the type of dive profile, the rate of ascent and, importantly, on individual predisposing factors to DCS (present whether using computers or tables).

It appears that a diver who ascends slowly will have less chance of getting DCS, especially neurological DCS, than one who ascends more rapidly. These authors believe that a diver should ascend no faster than about 10m (33ft) per minute when shallower than about 24m (80ft). Most computers include an ascent rate indicator and/or alarm to tell a diver when they are exceeding the recommended ascent rate. The rate varies between computers and for different depth ranges, but it should roughly equate with the above recommendation and slower in shallower water. This function is an essential function of any dive computer.

If you exceed the recommended ascent rate at any stage during a dive, especially at, or near, the end of a dive, reduce your dive time substantially from that given by the computer for the rest of that dive, and for repetitive dives, and extend any stops.

We also recommend that, where possible, a diver goes to the maximum depth early in the dive and then progressively works shallower (see previous chapter).

Divers must be thoroughly educated in a computer's use so that they are familiar with the particular computer they are using, aware of the shortcomings of that computer and with the safe diving practices that should be adopted when using a computer.

Safe dive computer usage requires:

- A healthy distrust of the DC's limits.
- A diver educated in how to dive with the computer.
- A reliable, conservative computer.
- Adequate health and fitness for diving.
- Adherence to safe diving practices.
- A certain amount of good luck!
  (this is also true with tables)

GUIDELINES FOR USING DIVE COMPUTERS

- *Ascend slowly.* Never exceed the ascent rate recommended by the computer, and generally ascend at about 10m (33ft) per minute or slower when shallower than about 24m (80ft).

- *End the dive with a safety stop* of at least 5 minutes at 5-6m (15-20ft) and add a deeper stop on deeper dives. Avoid rectangular dive profiles.

- *Do not dive right to the limits given by the computers.* The limits may not be reliable, especially for repetitive dives. Computers, like dive tables, do not cater for individual susceptibility to DCS. These factors must be considered when deciding when to ascend to the safety or decompression stop and how much time to be spent at that stop. Reduce the limits progressively more for each dive in a series of repetitive dives. This is especially important when repetitive dives are conducted over multiple days.

- Also reduce the limits if multiple ascents are made within a dive or if you become cold, anxious or exert yourself during the dive.

- Be extra *conservative if doing reverse dive profiles.*

- Have a *back-up procedure* in the event of dive computer failure.

- If using a dive computer for multi-day, repetitive diving, it may be useful to *take a break after a few days* to allow your body to rid itself of some of the extra nitrogen load it has accumulated.

- Do not begin to use a dive computer if you have dived in the previous 24 hours without that computer.

- Ensure you are *well-hydrated* before and after diving.

- *Avoid altitude exposure and heavy exercise* too soon after diving

Dive computers are a wonderful invention and are increasingly replacing the use of dive tables. However, the algorithms still have shortcomings and need to be improved continually in order to maximize their safety. Divers must also be thoroughly educated in their use so that they are very familiar with the particular computer they are using, aware of the short-comings of that computer (and they all do have them!) and with the safe diving practices that should be adopted when using a computer.

REFERENCES

1. Quick D. Evaluation of the automatic decompression meter. RANSUM Report 2/74. Balmoral NSW: Royal Australian Navy School of Underwater Medicine; 1974.

2. Edmonds C. Bendomatic Decompression Meters. *SCUBA Diver* 1987; October: 22-7.

3. West D, Edmonds C. Evaluation of the Farallon Decompression Meter. RAN SUM Report 1/76. Balmoral NSW: Royal Australian Navy School of Underwater Medicine; 1976

4. Flynn E, Bayne C. Inert Gas Exchange: Experiments and Concepts. In: Diving Medical Officer Student Guide. Naval School of Diving and Salvage; 1978.

5. Huggins KE. Performance of dive computers exposed to profiles with known human subject results. *Undersea and Hyperb Med* 2004; 31(3):376.

SUMMARY

- Dive computers are designed to calculate the decompression requirement for the actual dive profile, rather than for the "rounded-off" profile which is used with tables.

- Current computers are programmed with an actual decompression model, rather than with tables.

- Computers eliminate errors in table calculations and, usually, provide much more bottom time than is given by the tables.

- Tables include inherent, or added, margins that provide a degree of safety if our body absorbs more nitrogen than predicted by the model. Computers do not include such margins as they follow the model exactly, although more conservatism has been added to later models. Some computers will allow adjustments to add a margin of safety.

- For single rectangular dives, the computers often give more conservative NDLs than the tables.

- On a multi-level dive, the computers will normally extend the allowable no-decompression stop bottom time far beyond that allowed by the tables, especially if the diver works shallower throughout the dive.

- Dive computers usually allow far more time for repetitive dives than is allowed by tables. This is an area of risk for both tables and computers; as is multi-day diving.

- The safety of dive computers has not been determined as too few validated tests have been done to determine the DCS risk associated with their use. However, this is generally also true for decompression tables!

- The computers rely on a slow ascent rate, and the times given are less valid if a diver has ascended faster than recommended.

- Computers can, and do, fail, and the diver must have an appropriate back-up procedure in the event of a computer failure during a dive.

6. Edmonds C. Misuse of algorithms in dive computers: The need for validation. In: Hamilton RW (ed). The effectiveness of dive computers in repetitive diving. UHMS Workshop 81(DC)6-1-94. Kensington, MD: Undersea and Hyperbaric Medical Soc.; 1995.

7. Hahn MH. Workman-Bühlmann algorithm for dive computers: A critical analysis. In: Hamilton RW (ed). The effectiveness of dive computers in repetitive diving. UHMS Workshop 81(DC)6-1-94. Kensington, MD: Undersea and Hyperbaric Medical Soc.; 1995.

8. Lippmann J, Wellard M. Comparing dive computers. *SPUMS J* 2004; 34:124-9.

9. Bühlmann AA. Decompression-Decompression Sickness. Berlin: Springer-Verlag; 1984.

10. Uwatec. Aladin Pro Manual. Hallwil; 1989.

11. Bühlmann AA. Behavior of dive computer algorithms in repetitive dives: Experience and needed modifications. In: Hamilton RW (ed). The

effectiveness of dive computers in repetitive diving. UHMS Workshop 81(DC)6-1-94. Kensington, MD: Undersea and Hyperbaric Medical Soc.; 1995

12. Hardy J. Review of current dive computers with critique and recommendations. In: Hamilton RW (ed). The effectiveness of dive computers in repetitive diving. UHMS Workshop 81(DC)6-1-94. Kensington, MD: Undersea and Hyperbaric Medical Soc.; 1995.

13. Leitch DR, Barnard EE. Observations on no-stop and repetitive air and oxynitrogen diving. *Undersea Biomed Res* 1982; 9(2):113-129.

14. Dept of National Defence - Canada. DCIEM Diving Manual. Richmond: Universal Dive Techtronics Inc; 1992.

15. Wienke BR. Basic decompression theory and application. Flagstaff: Best Publishing Company; 1991.

16. Shields T. Re-trial at sea of 70 and 80-meter 15 minute Trimix decompression schedules. AMTE(E) R82-409; 1982.

17. Report on decompression Illness, dive fatalities and Project Dive Exploration. Durham, North Carolina: Divers Alert Network; 2004.

18. Report on decompression Illness and dive fatalities. Durham, North Carolina: Divers Alert Network; 1999.

19. Report on decompression Illness and dive fatalities. Durham, North Carolina: Divers Alert Network; 2000.

20. Report on decompression Illness, dive fatalities and Project Dive Exploration. Durham, North Carolina: Divers Alert Network; 2001.

21. Report on decompression Illness, dive fatalities and Project Dive Exploration. Durham, North Carolina: Divers Alert Network; 2002.

22. Report on decompression Illness, dive fatalities and Project Dive Exploration. Durham, North Carolina: Divers Alert Network; 2003.

23. Mitchell S and Taylor L. DCI and dive computers. *Alert Diver SEAP*; July-Sept 2000:21-6.

24. Report on decompression Illness and dive fatalities. Durham, North Carolina: Divers Alert Network; 2000.

25. Report on decompression Illness and dive fatalities. Durham, North Carolina: Divers Alert Network; 1998.

26. Report on decompression Illness and dive fatalities. Durham, North Carolina: Divers Alert Network; 1997.

27. Report on diving accidents and fatalities. Durham, North Carolina: Divers Alert Network; 1996.

OTHER SOURCES

Bühlmann, AA. Personal communications.

Huggins K and Somers L. Mathematical Evaluation of Multi-Level Diving. Report No. MICHU-SG-81-207. Michigan, Michigan Sea Grant Publications; 1981.

Huggins K. Doppler Evaluation of Multi-Level Diving Profiles. Report No. MICHU-SG-84-300, Michigan, Michigan Sea Grant Publications; 1983.

Huggins K. Microprocessor Applications to Multi-Level Air Decompression Problems. Michigan Sea Grant College Program Report No. MICHU-SG-87-201, Michigan Sea Grant Publications. California, University of Michigan; 1987.

Lang MA, Hamilton RW (eds). Proceedings of Dive Computer Workshop. University of Southern California Sea Grant Publication No. USCSG-TR-01-89. California: University of Southern California; 1989.

Lang MA, Vann RD (eds). Proceedings of the Repetitive Diving Workshop. Washington, California, American Academy of Underwater Sciences; 1992.

Lang MA, Lehner CE (eds). Proceedings of the Reverse Dive Profile Workshop. Washington: Smithsonian Institution; 2000.

Lewis JE, Shreeves KW. Decompression Theory, Dive Tables and Dive Computers. Santa Ana: PADI; 1990.

Lippmann J. Dive computers and flying after a dive to 39m for 10 minutes. *SPUMS J* 1990; 20(1):6-7.

Thalmann ED. Phase II testing of decompression algorithms for use in the U.S. Navy underwater decompression computer. U.S. Navy Experimental Diving Unit Report 1-84; 1984.

Thalmann ED. Air N2O2 decompression computer algorithm development. U.S. Navy Experimental Diving Unit Report 8-85; 1986.

Wendling J, Schmutz J (eds). Safety Limits of Dive Computers. Dive Computer Workshop, Basel, 1992. Basel: Foundation for Hyperbaric Medicine; 1995.

RECOMMENDED FURTHER READING

Hamilton RW (ed). The effectiveness of dive computers in repetitive diving. UHMS Workshop 81(DC)6-1-94. Kensington, MD: Undersea and Hyperbaric Medical Soc.; 1995

Huggins K. Microprocessor Applications to Multi-Level Air Decompression Problems. Michigan Sea Grant College Program Report No. MICHU-SG-87-201, Michigan Sea Grant Publications. California, University of Michigan; 1987.

Lang MA and Hamilton RW (eds). Proceedings of Dive Computer Workshop. University of Southern California Sea Grant Publication No. USCSG-TR-01-89. California, University of Southern California; 1989.

Wendling J, Schmutz J (eds). Safety Limits of Dive Computers. Dive Computer Workshop, Basel, 1992. Basel: Foundation for Hyperbaric Medicine; 1995.

SECTION 3

Altitude & diving

© M. Leunig
Reprinted with permission

© David Bryant

Flying after diving

25

On completion of a compressed air dive our bodies inevitably contain residual dissolved nitrogen in an amount that is determined by factors such as the time and depths of the dives we have completed, and the ascent protocols used. In addition, it is likely that we will have formed at least some nitrogen bubbles in the blood and / or various body tissues. Over a period of time after the dive, the excess nitrogen is gradually eliminated and the bubbles gradually resolve. The accurate tracking of this process has proved to be an elusive goal, and this complicates two important issues: the calculation of safe no-decompression limits for repetitive dives, and the determination of a safe minimum interval prior to flying. It is the latter issue that we will tackle here.

If a diver whose blood and tissues are carrying a load of dissolved inert gas ascends to altitude, then as the ambient pressure falls, the blood and tissues may become supersatured and bubbles may form. In addition, if there are already inert gas bubbles present, any further supersaturation will promote its diffusion into the bubble, causing bubble growth. Bubbles will also grow in accordance with Boyle's law as ambient pressure falls. Such events can precipitate DCS, and this has been demonstrated many times in divers leaving dive sites by road over hills, and in divers returning home on airliners after diving holidays. Indeed, although something of a digression, it is worth noting that rapid ascent to extreme altitude in an unpressurized aircraft can precipitate DCS in aviators who left sea-level with no additional inert gas load at all.

The two common situations in which we encounter an ascent to altitude after diving are driving overland and flying. The prescription of safe parameters for driving and flying is a vexing issue, and one that is by no means fully resolved.

FLYING AFTER DIVING

Divers are traveling to dive more and more frequently. Although airliners are "pressurized", they are not pressurized to atmospheric pressure. Traveling in a passenger jet usually exposes the traveler to an equivalent altitude exposure of about 1,500-1,800m (5,000-6,000ft), but not more than 2,400m (8,000ft). Consequently, the possibility of inducing DCS by altitude exposure when flying home after a diving program has become an important issue.

How can this risk be minimized? If we think about it carefully, the parameters that we can regulate in order to minimize the risk of any ascent to altitude after diving are:

- The dive itself. The more conservative the dive(s), the less the residual nitrogen load, and the lower the risk of any ascent to altitude.

- The delay prior to ascending to altitude. The longer we wait prior to the altitude exposure, the greater the elimination of both residual nitrogen and bubbles, and the lower the risk.

- The altitude. The less altitude exposure, the lower the provocation for further bubble formation.

In practice, all of these parameters are manipulated to some degree. For example, it is fairly common practice to make the final dive(s) in a pre-travel diving sequence a little more conservative. However, it is the second strategy (imposing a delay) which receives the most attention. The problem though, is how to be sure we have waited long enough?

Various strategies have been tried over the years, and some of these are discussed below.

The D-Group Rule

This rule suggested that it should be safe to fly to 2,400m (8,000ft), as stated in the NOAA Diving Manual of the time, or to 3,000m (10,000ft) as stated by C.L. Smith in *Altitude Procedures for the Ocean Diver*, as long as one is in Repetitive Group D (or lower, i.e. A,B,C) of the U.S. Navy Tables.

This rule was applied in two ways. First, it implied that one could fly directly to 2,400m (8,000ft) immediately after dives to 12m (40ft) / 30 min, 18m (60ft) / 20 min, 24m (80ft) /15 min., 30m (100ft)/10 min., and so on, since the diver surfaced from these dives in group D. The other application was achieved using the Surface Interval Credit Table to find the proposed safe interval before flying to 2,400m (8,000ft) or, alternatively, 3,000m (10,000ft), following dives which result in a Repetitive Group greater than D. For example, after diving to 24m (80ft) for 25 minutes you are in Group F, but, after a surface interval of 1½ hours, you will be in Group D and, theoretically, should be safe to fly.

This rule has proven to be not conservative enough. One researcher gathered 47 cases where the diver had been in Group D, or lower, for between 7 to 40 hours before flying, did not show symptoms before flying, but had symptoms in the aircraft or shortly after landing.[1] A more recent study reported 5 cases of DCS in 49 participants who completed a single dive to 18m (60ft) for 55 minutes followed by ascent to 2,400m (8000ft) after meeting or exceeding the requirements of the group D rule.[2]

Edel's recommendations

Edel and co-workers,[3] contracted to NASA to establish guidelines for flying after diving, proposed the following procedure for flying to altitudes of 1,500-2,400m (5,000-8,000ft). Their recommendation was that a two hour surface interval be observed prior to flying in commercial aircraft, following dives made only within the No-Decompression Limits of the U.S. Navy Standard Air Decompression Tables, during the preceding 12 hours. Mild symptoms of decompression sickness were ignored in these experiments, and the recommendation did not apply to repetitive or decompression stop dives. It was suggested that, if decompression stop dives were made (or should have been made), then the diver should allow 24 hours between surfacing and flying.

The British adopted this system for use with their tables, and extended it to altitudes between 1,500-2,700m (5,000-9,000ft).

This system is in accordance with the theory and mathematics of the U.S. Navy Tables. However, its main failing is that it does not really take into account the length of the dive. It might be safe to fly two hours after some short no-decompression stop dives, since, after a short dive we unload excess gas fairly quickly. However, the two hour interval may be insufficient after longer dives. Indeed, this rule is almost certainly not conservative enough, and the same data presented by Vann and colleagues[2] in the discussion of the group D rule above is also relevant here. That is, there were 5 cases of DCS in of 49 participants who completed a single dive to 18m (60ft) for 55 min followed by ascent to 2,400m (8000ft) after meeting or exceeding the requirements of Edel's rule.

Other table-based recommendations

Various other recommendations emerged over the years which in a similar fashion to the D group rule. For example, the **BSAC '88** tables suggest that a diver who wishes to fly in a pressurized aircraft must wait until they have a Current Tissue Code of A or B (which equates to a surface interval of 0-4 hours after a sea level dive). In other circumstances, the Transfer Table is used to determine an appropriate Tissue Code to achieve before ascending to altitude is considered to be relatively safe. Intervals of up to 16 hours may be required before flying in an unpressurized aircraft (see Chapter 19).

The **DCIEM** Sport Diving Tables recommend that after a single no-decompression dive, you should allow enough surface interval time to elapse for your "Repetitive Factor" to diminish to *1.0* (this will take 9-18 hours, depending on the Repetitive Group after the final dive). After any other than a no-decompression first dive (i.e. after a repetitive dive or decompression stop dive) a minimum Surface Interval of *24 hours* is recommended before flying.

Other than the inherent lack of conservatism in the D-group rule and the BSAC '88 recommendations, the main problem shared by all of these table-based systems in the contemporary setting is that fewer and fewer divers are diving using tables any more. Recreational diving is increasingly performed using computers, and it is difficult or impossible to adapt these rules to the use of diving computers. Indeed, almost all of these computers have built-in flying after diving guide functions. The derivation of the flying after diving advice provided by the various diving computers is beyond the scope of this book, but we suspect that of all the data provided by a dive computer, the flying after diving recommendations are likely to be the most speculative. Some are based on the theoretical inert gas elimination from the tissue compartments utilized in the computer, while others are simply set to a 24 hour clock that counts back to zero. Many computers still allow flying after very short intervals, especially after single dives. As has been mentioned, the recent data from Vann and colleagues suggest that these recommendations are not conservative enough.[2] Indeed, we would recommend that **if the recommendations provided by your computer are less conservative than those promulgated by DAN (see below) then you should use the DAN guidelines by preference**.

The evolution of Diver's Alert Network advice

During most of the 1980s DAN recommended a 24 hour delay to flying after any diving. This paralleled the recommendations of the US Air force (which still recommends a delay of 24 hours). In 1989, the Undersea and Hyperbaric Medical Society (UHMS) conducted a workshop to address the issue.[1] This workshop endorsed the DAN recommendation, but suggested that for more trivial exposures a wait of 12 hours would be sufficient. The workshop defined a "more trivial exposure" as a total dive time (in the previous 48 hours) of less than 2 hours (and in the absence of decompression diving).

Recent work suggests that this rule functions reasonably well for single dives, but is probably not conservative enough for multiple dives which nevertheless come within the definition. For example, there were 2 cases of DCS out of 50 divers who completed dives to 18m (60ft) for 55 min, 18m for 20 min, and 18m for 20 min with one hour surface intervals between dives, and then followed this with a 2,400m (8000ft) altitude exposure some 14-15 hours after the last dive.[2] Interestingly, there were no cases of DCS in 51 trials of the same dive protocol when the divers waited 16-17 hours before altitude exposure (although the difference between these respective series, that is, between 2/50 and 0/51 is not statistically significant and may be due to random chance).

Despite the reduction in time before flying after 'trivial' diving exposures, the suggested wait of 24 hours after many repetitive and multiday exposures caused consternation in parts of the recreational dive community, who feared that enforced 24 hour pre-flight waits after diving in various resorts would harm their business by increasing the costs and reducing flexibility for traveling divers.

As a result of this concern, and in the absence of significant data to prove otherwise, in 1991 DAN revised its guidelines to recommend an interval of at least 12 hours after a single, no-stop dive, and longer than 12 hours after repetitive, decompression or multiday diving. [4]

As a result of the lack of appropriate data and the continued debate on the issue, DAN designed and conducted two studies involving exposing 'divers' to increased and then reduced ambient pressures in a chamber and monitoring and documenting the outcomes. In addition, DAN conducted a retrospective study using data reported by injured divers, and an investigation into divers who had either flown with symptoms of DCS, or had flown soon after recompression treatment.

Flying after diving trials

These trials, spearheaded by Dr. Dick Vann, were conducted at the hypo-hyberbaric facilities at Duke University, North Carolina. The trials ran from 1992 to 1999.* One to three dives were conducted in a single day with dry, resting subjects in a chamber to depths of 12, 18 or 30m (40, 60 or 100ft). These dives were followed by surface intervals ranging from 3-17 hours, prior to an exposure of 4 hours at an equivalent of 2,400m (8,000ft).

In all, 495 subjects had 802 exposures that resulted in 40 cases of DCS. As the surface interval increased, the incidence of DCS

---

* Subsequent trials have been completed and another continues at the time of writing.

reduced and there were no cases of DCS in the 52 trials with pre-flight surface intervals of 17 hours. Not surprising also, repetitive dives usually required longer surface intervals to achieve a low DCS incidence, than did single dives. [5]

On the basis of the above study, DAN has liaised with the diving community and developed the current guidelines for recreational divers: [6]

- For a single, no-decompression dive, a minimum pre-flight surface interval of 12 hours is suggested.

- For multiple dives per day, or multiple days of diving, a minimum pre-flight surface interval of 18 hours is suggested.

- For dives requiring decompression stops, there is little evidence on which to base a recommendation, but a pre-flight surface interval substantially longer than 18 hours appears prudent.

The above guidelines apply to air dives followed by flight to cabin altitudes of 600-2400m (2000-8000ft) without DCS symptoms.

Case-control study

In addition to the chamber trials, DAN researchers conducted a case-control study using 382 injured divers from the DAN dive injury database, with 245 injury-free divers as controls. This study compared relative risk between different surface intervals. As an example, it found that the relative risk of DCS after an 18m (60ft) dive followed by a 12 hour pre-flight interval was 2.5 times the risk than if the interval was extended to 24 hours.

Interestingly, 34% of the injured divers in the study had waited at least 24 hours before flying. [6]

So, although the chamber studies and subsequent recommendations indicated a pre-flight surface interval of 18 hours should suffice, this appears not to have been supported by the results of the case-controlled study. An important difference may be that the chamber trial were conducted on dry, resting subjects in a controlled environments, whereas the injury data was taken from actual divers in the field. Divers should be not interpret any such guidelines as meaning that one minute more than 12 hours (or 18 hours) is "safe". DAN's ambiguity on the issue is meant to reflect the lack of relevant data, and the imprecision in the little data that does exist. It is recommending as long a pre-flight surface interval as is practical. **These authors would advise at least 24 hours after the typical live-aboard diving trip.** However, even this is **no guarantee of safety**. Obviously, 48 hours would be even safer. We have seen DCS arise in divers who claim to have been symptom-free prior to flying some 36 to 48 hours after diving. Like most things in diving, leaving a generous pre-flight surface interval is an exercise in risk minimization rather than risk elimination. (For example, the U.S. Navy has a more flexible set of flying after diving guidelines that are based on DAN data. In some military situations, the extra risk may be warranted.)

TRAVEL BY ROAD AFTER DIVING

All roads (except perhaps in Holland) run above sea level to some degree, and this begs the fundamental question "what constitutes an altitude exposure?" There is no firm and clearly validated policy on this, but it is commonly held that if a road journey after diving does not exceed 300m (1,000ft) altitude then problems are very unlikely, even with relatively short delays between diving and driving. Like all "rules" in life, there are cases that provide the exception, but the "300m rule" has generally proven fairly robust. Clearly, common sense must prevail, and a diver would be foolish indeed to exit the water from a provocative dive and immediately drive straight to 300m (1,000ft). In practice, this would be very unlikely to occur.

Where roads exceed 300m (1,000ft) it is probably wise to impose some degree of delay between diving and making the journey. Unfortunately, there are no published guidelines to help with such decision-making. The flying after diving rules are almost certainly too conservative. In most cases, the natural delay involved in exiting the water, disassembling and packing equipment etc seems to be adequate to minimize risk. However, if there is an ascent to greater than 300m early in the road journey, or if the diving has been relatively provocative, then a sensible diver will impose a longer delay. Unfortunately, in the absence of any data that guides decision-making, it is impossible for us to provide any guidelines with an objective basis. Some dive operators have utilized the Group D rule in this context, and given the lower provocation of a modest road ascent compared to flying, this might be appropriate. The BSAC '88 Tables include procedures to assist with this issue, however, they are untested. Divers using computers will usually be unable to apply the Group D rule or other similar procedure. One strategy (also discussed in the next chapter on Diving at Altitude) that seems intuitively obvious, but which is invalid, is to plan your time and depth for a dive as though you are already at the altitude that will be reached during the drive. It has been reasoned that this will allow you to ascend to altitude immediately after the dive if you wish, and some have even advocated the use of this method for flying after diving. Unfortunately, although the dive will be somewhat more conservative than it otherwise would have been, it is still likely to result in some degree of bubble formation, and the behaviour of these bubbles during the subsequent ascent to altitude is highly unpredictable.

Sometimes it comes down to "giving it as much time as is practically available".

Flying with symptoms of decompression illness

Some divers have symptoms of DCS and still decide to fly. Sometimes this is because they fail to connect the symptoms to the dive, sometimes because they don't want to interrupt their travel plans. On other occasions they may be in a location without a chamber and want to get to treatment. Other divers board the plane without any noticeable problems but symptoms arise during or after the flight.

Symptoms can appear, or can worsen, at altitude through several proposed mechanisms. Reduction of the ambient pressure will expand existing bubbles and the lower partial pressure of oxygen in the cabin at altitude can cause or increase hypoxia in areas of marginal blood supply. In addition, the dehydration that can often be associated with a long flight thickens the blood and may affect circulation to compromised tissues.

DAN America data reports for 2000-04[8-12] provide details of a total of 2,438 DCI incidents. Of these, 10% of the divers reported having symptoms before flying, while 7.1% reported that symptoms had emerged during or after a flight. All of these cases (and additional earlier cases) were investigated on the basis of the severity of symptoms and the outcome after treatment.

It appears that flying with symptoms increased the severity of the symptoms and reduced the likelihood of complete relief after recompression and subsequent residual symptoms. It also appears that the shorter the surface interval before flying with symptoms, the greater the chance of residual problems.[13]

Additionally, recompression appeared to be equally successful with divers with symptoms who waited longer than 24 hours before flying and divers who did not fly at all before treatment. On the other hand, divers with symptoms who flew within 24 hours and then received treatment had a higher incidence of incomplete relief after treatment.

*The bottom line here appears to be that **you should avoid flying if you have symptoms of DCS after diving.*** However, if for some reason you have to fly, it is better to wait at least 24 hours before doing so, and then

seek assessment and treatment as soon as possible. If you have symptoms after diving, seek diving medical advice without delay and let them help you to decide what to do.

To summarize…

We can never be exactly sure when it becomes "safe to fly" after a dive as it will depend on the degree of inert gas loading, the degree of bubble formation, and for how long it persists. There is a gradual reduction of risk with time. It must now be apparent to you that, just as with decompression tables, where no table is completely safe for all divers all of the time, no guidelines for flying after diving can be guaranteed completely safe at all times. Flying shortly after a single, short dive might prove to be quite different to flying after a series of repetitive dives and some of the guidelines do not consider this. In addition, if we have formed "silent bubbles" during a dive, we may be "teetering on the edge of suffering DCS for many hours, or days, after the dive. Ascending to altitude will allow these bubbles to expand, possibly causing DCS. It appears that, at times, bubbles can take days, or even weeks, to resolve.

In the light of the sparse and conflicting evidence about flying after diving, some authorities, such as the US Air Force, suggest that **flying be avoided for at least 24 hours after diving.** This is a very sensible rule to follow, especially if repetitive dives have been done over a number of consecutive days, as is often done on diving holidays. Some people believe this rule to be too conservative, but a substantial and growing number of unfortunate divers have suffered DCS after flying earlier than this.

Flying after recompression treatment

In the USA, it is currently recommended that a diver who has received treatment for decompression illness should not fly for at least 3-7 days after the treatment, depending on residual symptoms, and, then, only with approval from the treating hyperbaric physician. In Australia, some experienced hyperbaric physicians currently recommend avoiding flying for at least 2 to 4 weeks after treatment since they believe bubbles may still be present for some weeks after treatment. Some data suggest that the approach taken by many units in the USA (wait about 3 days) may not be conservative enough, particularly if the diver still has symptoms on completion of hyperbaric treatment.[14] Once again, there is a distinct lack of data that helps us make rational recommendations, and many individual units tend to evolve policies that are based on their own experiences.

FLYING BEFORE DIVING

Tissues off-gas while flying and, depending on the duration of the flight, some tissues may take hours, or days, to return to their normal sea-level nitrogen levels.

Some divers believe that, if they fly to a sea level dive site and then dive before their tissue nitrogen levels have returned to normal, they will have less chance of getting DCS. Since they began the dive with lower nitrogen levels, the belief is that they should surface with lower nitrogen levels than a diver who had done the same dive, but who had not previously flown.

Theoretically, pre-dive nitrogen levels may be reduced if the flight was very long and the pre-dive interval very short. However, the diver's tissues might not respond as expected, and many other factors can affect the outcome. Flying has numerous physiological and psychological effects on us. We might arrive at our destination fatigued, dehydrated, disorientated, irritated and nervous. Certain biological reactions to the aircraft environment may also take their toll. Some of these factors can increase the likelihood of DCS.

Pre-dive flight should not be considered protective from DCS, and a diver should not dive until they feel physically and mentally recovered from flying.

SUMMARY

- DCS can be precipitated by ascending to altitude too soon after diving.

- A substantial number of divers have suffered DCS after flying many days after last diving.

- We can never be exactly sure when it becomes "safe to fly" after a dive as it will depend on the degree of bubble formation and for how long it persists. There is a gradual reduction of risk with time.

- Many of the available guidelines for flying after diving are not conservative enough. Some do not consider the length of the dive, or whether or not a repetitive dive(s) were done.

- A good policy is to wait at least 24 hours before flying after any dive.

- Avoid flying if you have symptoms of DCS. If flying cannot be avoided, wait at least 24 hours and arrange for a dive medical assessment soon after arriving at your destination.

- If possible symptoms of DCS emerge during or after a flight, arrange for a dive medical assessment as soon as possible.

- Do not dive if you are "jet-lagged". Wait until you feel well enough to dive safely.

REFERENCES

1. Sheffield P (ed). Proceedings of Flying After Diving Workshop. Bethesda: Undersea and Hyperbaric Medical Society; 1989.

2. Vann RD et al. A comparison of recent flying after diving experiments with published flying after diving guidelines. *Undersea Hyperb Med* 1996; 23(supp):A49

3. Edel P et al. Interval at sea level pressure required to prevent decompression sickness in humans who fly in commercial aircraft after diving. *Aerospace Med. 1969;* 40:1105-10.

4. Bennett PB. Flying after diving controversy. *Alert Diver* 1991; Sept/Oct:2.

5. Vann RD, Gerth, WA, Denoble PJ, Pieper CF, Thalmann ED. Experimental trials to assess the risks of decompression sickness in flying after diving. *Undersea Hyperb Med* 2004; 31(4):431-44.

6. Sheffield P, Vann R. DAN Flying After Diving Workshop Proceedings – May 2002. In: Vann R (ed). DAN Flying After Recreational Diving Workshop; 2004 May 2,2002. Durham NC: Divers Alert Network; 2004.

7. Flying after diving. *Alert Diver* 2005; Jul/Aug:38-41.

8. Report on decompression Illness, dive fatalities and Project Dive Exploration. Durham NC: Divers Alert Network; 2004.

9. Report on decompression Illness, dive fatalities and Project Dive Exploration. Durham NC: Divers Alert Network; 2003.

10. Report on decompression Illness, dive fatalities and Project Dive Exploration. Durham, NC: Divers Alert Network; 2002.

11. Report on decompression Illness, dive fatalities and Project Dive Exploration. Durham NC: Divers Alert Network; 2001.

12. Report on decompression Illness, dive fatalities and Project Dive Exploration. Durham NC: Divers Alert Network; 2000.

13. Freiberger J. Flying after multiday repetitive recreational diving. In: Sheffield P, Vann R (eds). DAN Flying After Recreational Diving Workshop; 2004 May 2,2002: Durham NC:Divers Alert Network; 2004:38-44.

14. Uguccioni DM et al. Commercial airflight after recompression therapy for decompression illness. *Undersea Hyperb Med 1999; 26(*supp):A100.

OTHER SOURCES

Freiberger JJ, Denoble PJ, Pieper CF, Uguccioni DM, Pollock NW, Vann RD. The relative risk of decompression sickness during and after air travel following diving. *Aviat Space and Environ Med* 2003; 73(10):980-4.

Pollock NW, Natoli MJ, Gerth W, Thalmann ED, Vann RD. Risk of decompression sickness during exposure to high cabin altitude after diving. *Aviat Space and Environ Med* 2003; 74(11):1163-68.

RECOMMENDED FURTHER READING

Flying after diving. *Alert Diver* 2005; Jul/Aug:38-41.

Many thanks to Dr. Richard Vann for reviewing this chapter.

26

Diving at altitude

More than 70 percent of the earth's surface is covered by water, most of this being our oceans and seas. Consequently, most diving is carried out in salt water and at sea level. As you know, there are many other bodies of water such as lakes, quarries, dams and rivers. Divers, strange, inquisitive creatures that we are, often wish to explore these places.

Many of these bodies of water are at altitudes higher than sea level, where the atmospheric pressure is reduced, and where the water is fresh, rather than salty. The lower density of the fresh water causes loss of buoyancy and affects depth gauge readings. The reduced atmospheric pressure also affects depth gauge readings and, in addition, will increase a diver's risk of decompression sickness (DCS) unless compensated for in decompression calculations. Physiological changes at high altitudes can also impair performance and predispose to certain other medical problems.

These changes, as well as possible differences in water temperature and visibility, will affect the manner in which we carry out such dives. Significant changes in diving practice and equipment usage are necessary in order to compensate for these differences. These adjustments will be discussed in detail in the following chapter.

A. Buoyancy Changes

As mentioned previously, fresh water (density = 1 kg/l or 62.366lb/ft²) is less dense than salt water (density = 1.025kg/l or 64.043lb/ft²) and, therefore, gives us less support. Because we lose buoyancy in fresh water, we must remove some of the weight from our weight-belt in order to re-establish neutral buoyancy in our diving gear. The actual amount of weight to be removed depends on the volume of the diver in their gear, and is usually about 2½ percent of their gross weight. In practice, most divers seem to remove about 1.5 to 4.5kg (3 to 10lbs) from their weight-belts.

An interesting phenomenon occurs at high altitudes. Wetsuits, which are impregnated with small air bubbles, begin to swell as the bubbles expand with the reduced atmospheric pressure. This expansion makes the suit bulkier and more buoyant. The phenomenon is relatively minor and usually only needs to be considered if a shallow dive is planned at a high altitude. As soon as moderate depth is reached, the water pressure will again compress the wetsuit and the added buoyancy will be lost. However, if not accounted for, it could become an issue when stops are planned at the end of the dive. A pre-dive buoyancy check is advisable. Non-neoprene drysuits are not affected.

Note:

In this chapter, units used in the decompression calculations are interchanged in accordance with the predominant units used in the various systems.

B. Changes to Depth Gauge Readings

All depth gauges used by divers determine depth by measuring pressure. These gauges will not function accurately in fresh water, unless calibrated for fresh water use. Many diving instruments are calibrated for fresh water and, therefore, indicate a depth that is slightly deeper than the actual depth when used in sea water. The accuracy depends on the salinity. In a gauge that is calibrated for sea water, the error due to fresh water alone is only about 3 percent, so, if we dive in fresh water at sea level, we are actually about 3 percent deeper than is indicated by our depth gauge.

Although this may at first appear to be a potentially serious issue, it usually does not present a problem. For most recreational diving the main purpose of the depth gauge is not to provide the actual depth, but to provide a measure of the pressure that our body is under so that the correct decompression schedule can be applied. If our depth gauge is calibrated for sea water and reads 10m (33ft) while we are diving in the ocean, then we are at an ambient pressure of about 2ATA, and our depth should actually be 10m (33ft). If the gauge reads 10m (33ft) while underwater in a mountain lake, our body is still under a pressure of approximately 2ATA, even though we are slightly deeper than 10m (33ft). To find a decompression schedule, we need to know the maximum pressure that we have been to, rather than the actual maximum depth. A well-calibrated, zero-adjust depth gauge should provide this information.

Many depth gauges will not function accurately at reduced atmospheric pressure. Some types of depth gauge give completely erroneous readings at any appreciable altitude above sea level. Most of the gauges are designed to read zero at 1ATA and will become increasingly inaccurate when atmospheric pressures fall

significantly below this. The higher the altitude, the greater the error in the depth gauge reading. Exceptions to this are gauges with a zero-adjustment mechanism, gauges which read the atmospheric pressure and compensate automatically, and capillary gauges.

Effects on Different Types of Depth Gauges

The non-zero-adjust diaphragm, open bourdon tube and closed bourdon tube gauges all indicate depths that are shallower than the actual depth, and the amount of inaccuracy will probably depend on the depth. They are designed to read zero at an ambient pressure of 1ATA. If the gauge has a pin preventing the needle moving past (i.e. shallower than) the zero mark, on the surface at altitude the needle will be pushed hard against the pin and will not leave the zero mark until the pressure has increased sufficiently on descent. Consequently, in the water, the gauge will give a reading that is shallower than the actual depth. If the gauge has no pin at zero, it will read less than zero on the surface at altitude, again reading too shallow underwater. The depth readings can be corrected by adding a depth corresponding to the difference between the atmospheric pressure at the altitude site, and 1ATA. An additional correction may be required to compensate for fresh water.

Some of the later diaphragm gauges include an adjustment screw, so that the gauge can be set to zero, hence, adjusted to the reduced atmospheric pressure before entering the water. These are the zero-adjust gauges. Bourdon tube gauges cannot be zero-adjusted. Adjusting the gauge to zero improves the accuracy of the reading but still may not provide true depth if the difference between fresh and salt water has not been accounted for. The gauge will show a depth which is about 3 percent shallower than the actual depth if it was calibrated for sea water.

Some dive computers will read the atmospheric pressure and automatically adjust for it. With others, an appropriate altitude range must be selected and activated on the device. Some computers will activate automatically at significant altitude. However, others need to be activated on the surface before the dive. Many dive computers are calibrated for fresh water and, therefore, once compensated for altitude, will read actual depth.

A simple procedure to determine actual depth from non-zero-adjust gauges is to first add 30cm per 300m (1ft per 1,000ft) of altitude, then add 3 percent of the gauge reading in order to account for the fresh water, if required. For zero-adjust gauges only the latter calculation may be necessary.[1,2] It is claimed that the average error of this procedure is less than 15cm (0.5ft) over a wide range of altitudes.[1]

Due to the reduced density in the air trapped within a capillary gauge, less water pressure is required at altitude, than at sea level, to compress the air to a given volume. As a result, the capillary gauge will always indicate a depth greater than the actual depth. In fact, a capillary gauge gives an equivalent sea level depth (i.e. the Theoretical Ocean Depth, discussed later in this chapter) that can be used for planning decompression. Unfortunately, it becomes difficult to read a capillary gauge accurately at depths greater than about 15m (50ft). If the true depth of the water is required, the simple procedure to determine the true depth from a capillary gauge (calibrated for sea water) is to subtract 3.5 percent of its reading per 300m (1,000ft) of elevation.[2] Evidently this works well at altitudes above 900m (3,000ft). At less than 300m (1,000ft) no correction is required.

If a capillary gauge is used to determine the depth of decompression stop(s) for a dive at altitude, the stop(s) will be slightly deeper than suggested, but this is safer than being shallower, as is likely with other gauges.

A depth gauge which is used for altitude diving must have the facility to be adjusted for the atmospheric pressure of the dive site.

If the actual depth of a dive in fresh water and/or at altitude is required, it can be determined by using a marked downline (i.e. straight, weighted line marked in 3m (10ft), or other, increments).

C. Changes to Decompression Procedures

When we ascend to altitude from sea level, our body tissues contain higher relative nitrogen pressures (tensions) than are present in normal atmospheric conditions. Nitrogen is off-gassed from the tissues until, eventually, the body nitrogen levels are in equilibrium with the new ambient nitrogen level. Although to complete acclimatization to an altitude can take several days, most of the excess nitrogen has left the body after a period of 12-24 hours. Some systems (e.g. U.S. Navy) consider that the diver has equilibrated with the new ambient pressure after a period of 12 hours.

Divers who reach a dive site at altitude quickly (by air) and dive immediately will have more excess nitrogen than those who have partly adapted during a slow transition to altitude, such as by road.

Most decompression systems are based on the concept that there is a critical ratio of nitrogen pressure in the body tissues to ambient pressure that can be tolerated without bubbles being formed.

i.e. If $\dfrac{\text{Tissue N}_2\ \text{Pressure}}{\text{Ambient Pressure}}$

exceeds a particular value bubbles will form. If the nitrogen pressure in the tissues increases too much, this ratio will increase beyond the critical level. Similarly, if the ambient pressure is reduced, the ratio will again increase and may exceed the critical level.

The decompression systems are designed so that a diver surfaces without this critical ratio being exceeded. Most tables apply to a diver who surfaces to the normal atmospheric pressure of 1ATA. However, when we ascend from a dive at altitude, we ascend to an atmospheric pressure which is less than 1ATA. If, while at altitude, we have dived near to the limits of the sea level table, the reduced ambient pressure may cause this critical ratio to be exceeded, excess bubbles may form, and DCS may result. Therefore, sea level tables cannot be safely used for diving at altitude without appropriate adjustments.

A number of special tables, or adjustments to standard tables, have emerged over the years, some of which will be discussed in the following section.

CROSS CORRECTIONS FOR DIVING AT ALTITUDE

This method, originally published in 1967, has been widely used in the USA and certain other countries in conjunction with the U.S. Navy Tables. The method involves determining a Theoretical Ocean Depth (TOD), often called the Equivalent (sea level) Depth, for a dive at altitude by multiplying the actual diving depth at altitude* by the ratio of atmospheric pressure at sea level to that at altitude. The Equivalent Depth and the actual bottom time are then used to enter the U.S. Navy Tables (or other compatible tables) to determine the diving schedule at altitude. The equivalent depth is usually expressed in feet (or metres) of sea water (fsw or msw).

The equation for determining the Equivalent Depth is:

$$\text{Equivalent (Ocean) Depth} = \frac{\text{Actual depth x Pressure at sea level}}{\text{Pressure at altitude}}$$

The ratio of (Pressure at sea level / Pressure at altitude) is sometimes referred to as the *Altitude Correction Factor*.

For example, at an altitude of 7,000ft (2,100m)[#], where the atmospheric pressure is about 0.77ATA (586.5mmHg), a dive to an actual (gauge) depth 30fsw (9msw) would have a TOD of:

$$ED = \frac{30 \times 760}{586.5} = 38.9\text{fsw (11.8msw)}$$

This theoretical depth is 8.9fsw deeper than the same depth at sea level. Thus, the correction says that for a 30fsw dive at 7,000 feet above sea level we would select a 40fsw (12msw) schedule from the U.S. Navy Standard Tables.

The depth of the corrected stop at altitude is calculated by multiplying the depth of the sea level equivalent stop by a ratio of atmospheric pressure at altitude to atmospheric pressure at sea level. (This ratio is the inverse of the Altitude Correction Factor so the stop depth will be shallower than at sea level).

$$\text{Altitude Stop Depth} = \text{Sea level stop depth} \times \frac{\text{Pressure at Altitude}}{\text{Pressure at sea level}}$$

For example, if a dive at an altitude of 5000ft (1500m) requires an equivalent sea level stop at 20fsw (6msw), the stop depth used at altitude is:

$$\text{Altitude stop depth (fsw)} = 20\text{fsw} \times \frac{842\text{mb}}{1013\text{mb}} = 16.6\text{fsw}$$

---

* The actual depth is taken as the depth shown on the gauge in feet of sea water (fsw) or metres of sea water (msw). As previously mentioned, this depth reading will not be accurate but is acceptable for these purposes.

The imperial-metric conversions given throughout this chapter have generally been rounded off.

If the diver has been at altitude for over 12-24 hours and all of his tissues are, therefore, essentially equilibrated at the new, reduced nitrogen pressure at the start of the dive, it can be shown mathematically that the calculated nitrogen tensions within the diver all lie within the "critical tissue pressures" of the U.S. Navy Tables. If the diver were to ascend instantaneously to altitude and then dive immediately, their nitrogen tension(s) may just exceed the critical value.[3] Since, in practice, this would be difficult to achieve, the Cross Corrections can be assumed to lie within the levels deemed acceptable by the U.S. Navy Tables and should provide the same degree of safety that the U.S. Navy Standard Tables provide at sea level. *Although these corrections have apparently been quite widely used with good results, they have never been experimentally validated.*

Using the Cross Altitude Correction Technique

Luckily, a diver who wishes to use altitude corrections in order to dive at altitude does not have to sit down and do the mathematical calculations. These calculations have already been done and the results are provided in Table 26.1. Table 26.1 has also been corrected for fresh water and accounts for rate of ascent.

We will now use this table to re-do the previous example of a dive to 30fsw (9msw) at an altitude of 7,000ft (2,100m).

Enter the top section of Table 26.1, from the left, at the planned dive depth of 30fsw and move right until intersection the column corresponding to an altitude of 7000ft. You get the number 40, which corresponds to a Theoretical Ocean Depth of 40fsw (rounded up from the 38.9fsw from before). The No Decompression Limit (NDL) for this 30fsw dive at altitude would be 200 minutes, which is the NDL for a 40fsw (12msw) dive at sea level.

The modified stop depths are found in the following manner:

Enter the "Water stops" section of Table 26.1, from the left, at the stop depth given by the U.S. Navy Standard Table. Move towards the right until intersecting the row corresponding to the required altitude. The resulting number gives the new (equivalent) stop depth.

Ascent Rate: The earlier versions of the correction tables included adjustments that progressively reduced the ascent rate at higher altitudes. However, these are no longer required due to the slower ascent rates routinely used in most diving these days.

Example 1.

Find the NDL for a dive to 60fsw (18msw) at an altitude of 8,000ft (2,400m) above sea level.

Enter the top section of Table 26.1, from the left, at 60fsw and move right until intersecting the 10,000ft column. You get 90fsw, which is the depth that you use to enter the U.S. Navy Tables. The NDL to be used will thus be *30 minutes*, which is the NDL for 90fsw (27msw).

Example 2.

Calculate the decompression required for a dive to 100fsw (30msw) for 20 minutes at an altitude of 5,000ft (1,500m).

Enter the top section of Table 26.1, from the left, at 100fsw and move right until reaching the 5,000ft column. The TOD is, therefore, 130fsw (39msw). Look up 130fsw (39msw) for a bottom time of 20 minutes in the U.S. Navy Tables. The decompression given is *4 minutes at 10fsw* (3msw).

Enter the lower part of Table 26.1, from the left, at 10fsw and move to the right until reaching the 5,000ft column. The modified stop depth is thus *8*fsw (2.4msw).

TABLE 26.1

Sea Level Equivalent Depth Table[3]

Actual Depth (fsw)	Altitude (feet)									
	1,000	2,000	3,000	4,000	5,000	6,000	7,000	8,000	9,000	10,000
10	10	15	15	15	15	15	15	15	15	15
15	15	20	20	20	20	20	20	25	25	25
20	20	25	25	25	25	25	30	30	30	30
25	25	30	30	30	35	35	35	35	35	40
30	30	35	35	35	40	40	40	50	50	50
35	35	40	40	50	50	50	50	50	50	60
40	40	50	50	50	50	50	60	60	60	60
45	45	50	60	60	60	60	60	70	70	70
50	50	60	60	60	70	70	70	70	70	80
55	55	60	70	70	70	70	80	80	80	80
60	60	70	70	70	80	80	80	90	90	90
65	65	70	80	80	80	90	90	90	100	100
70	70	80	80	90	90	90	100	100	100	110
75	75	90	90	90	100	100	100	110	110	110
80	80	90	90	100	100	100	110	110	120	120
85	85	100	100	100	110	110	120	120	120	130
90	90	100	110	110	110	120	120	130	130	140
95	95	110	110	110	120	120	130	130	140	140
100	100	110	120	120	130	130	130	140	140	150
105	105	120	120	130	130	140	140	150	150	160
110	110	120	130	130	140	140	150	150	160	160
115	115	130	130	140	140	150	150	160	170	170
120	120	130	140	140	150	150	160	170	170	180
125	125	140	140	150	160	160	170	170	180	190
130	130	140	150	160	160	170	170	180	190	190
135	135	150	160	160	170	170	180	190	190	200
140	140	160	160	170	170	180	190	190	200	210
145	145	160	170	170	180	190	190	200	210	
150	160	170	170	180	190	190	200	210		
155	170	170	180	180	190	200	210			
160	170	180	180	190	200	200				
165	180	180	190	200	200					
170	180	190	190	200						
175	190	190	200							
180	190	200	210							
185	200	200								
190	200									

Note: Numbers below this bar ⌐ are Exceptional Exposure Limits

Table Water Stops	Equivalent Stop Depths (fsw)									
10	10	9	9	9	8	8	8	7	7	7
20	19	19	18	17	17	16	15	15	14	14
30	29	28	27	26	25	24	23	22	21	21
40	39	37	36	35	33	32	31	30	29	28
50	48	47	45	43	42	40	39	37	36	34
60	58	56	54	52	50	48	46	45	43	41

Reprinted from the NOAA Diving Manual with permission from Best Publishing Company.

Repetitive Dives

The system can be extended to repetitive dives by using the Equivalent Depth of the repetitive dive to find the Residual Nitrogen Time before the dive, and subtracting this time from the NDL for the Equivalent Depth of the repetitive dive.

Example 3

Four hours after the dive in Example 2, the diver wishes to dive to a depth of 60fsw (18msw). Calculate the maximum allowable no-decompression stop bottom time for the second dive.

After the first dive the RG is H. Enter the U.S. Navy Surface Interval Credit Table at H and find the new RG after four hours surface interval. It is C. Use Table 26.1 to find the Equivalent Depth of the repetitive dive; it is 80fsw (24msw). Use the U.S. Navy Repetitive Dive Table to find the Residual Nitrogen Time (RNT) at the TOD of the repetitive dive. The RNT is 13 minutes.

Subtract this RNT from the NDL for the Equivalent Depth of the repetitive dive, which is 40 minutes. Therefore, the maximum bottom time is *27 minutes*.

Non-Acclimatized Divers

The above system applies to a diver who has equilibrated to the altitude of the dive site after spending 12 hours at that level. As previously mentioned, if a diver were to ascend quickly to altitude and dive immediately, their (theoretical) nitrogen levels may exceed those allowed by the U.S. Navy Tables. To overcome this problem a diver who is not equilibrated can select a Repetitive Group (RG) from Table 26.2. The RGs in Table 26.2 are identical to the RGs of the U.S. Navy Standard Air Table and can be used as such.

TABLE 26.2

Repetitive Groups Associated with Initial Ascent to Altitude.

Altitude		Repetitive Group
feet	metres	
1000	300	A
2000	600	B
3000	900	B
4000	1200	C
5000	1500	D
6000	1800	E
7000	2100	E
8000	2400	F
9000	2700	G
10000	3000	H

For example, a diver who has just arrived at 10,000ft (3,000m) and wishes to dive immediately can assume that they are in group H before the dive. If they wish to dive to a gauge depth 50fsw (15msw), they must first look up the Equivalent Depth from Table 26.1, which gives 80fsw.

The U.S. Navy Repetitive Dive Table must now be used to find the Residual Nitrogen Time for an RG of H at 80fsw (24msw), which is 38 minutes. The NDL for the dive is, therefore, 40 - 38 = 2 minutes. However, if the diver waits until acclimatized, the NDL would be 40 minutes.

Repetitive Dives at Different Altitudes

Example 4

After doing the dive in Example 1 for a bottom time of 30 minutes, the diver drives back to sea level and wishes to dive again. If the surface interval after the first dive has been five hours, find the maximum allowable no-decompression stop bottom time for a dive in the sea to 50fsw (15msw).

The RG after the first dive of 30 minutes at an Equivalent Depth of 90fsw (27msw), is H. After the surface interval the new RG is B. The RNT for the repetitive dive is thus 13 minutes and the required bottom time is *87 minutes*.

Example 5

After doing a sea level dive of 70fsw (21msw) for 20 minutes, a diver drives to a mountain lake at an altitude of 6,000ft (1,800m). Here, they wish to dive to a depth of 60fsw (18msw). The surface interval since the first dive has been three hours. What is the maximum allowable no-decompression stop bottom time for this dive at altitude?

In this situation, the initial sea level dive must be treated as if it had been done at an altitude of 6,000ft (1,800m). To find the RG after the first dive, first find the Equivalent Depth; which is 90fsw Use the U.S. Navy Tables to find the RG after a dive to 90fsw (27msw) for 20 minutes. It is F. The new RG after the surface interval will be C.

The Equivalent Depth of the repetitive dive is 80fsw (24msw). The RNT for the repetitive dive is, therefore, 13 minutes. Hence, the required bottom time is 40 - 13 = *27 minutes*.

PROCEDURES FOR USING THE DSAT / PADI RDP AT ALTITUDE

There are special rules and procedures that must be applied when using the DSAT/PADI Repetitive Dive Planner (Wheel or Table) at altitudes from 1,000ft (300m) to 10,000ft (3,000m). Two tables (shown together as Tables 26.3), derived from the original Cross Corrections, are used to find the Theoretical Ocean Depth and the depth of the safety / decompression stop. For extra safety, the depths were not converted to fresh water equivalents but the calculations were deliberately kept as for salt water, giving slightly deeper Equivalent Depths. Also, for the sake of conservatism, repetitive dive

restrictions were added, although they were not required by the model.

These rules, and associated examples, published in PADI's Altitude Diver Specialty Course Instructor Outline[5], are re-printed here with permission of PADI International Inc. *These procedures have not been validated by any extensive testing.* Nonetheless, it has been reported that the Cross Corrections have been used with the RDP for over 15 years without apparent problems.[6]

Using the Recreational Dive Planner at Altitude

1. RDP altitude range: The special procedures for using the RDP must be used when diving at or above 1000ft / 300m. The maximum altitude is 10,000ft / 3,000m.

2. Ascent procedures.

a. Ascend from all altitude dives at a rate not to exceed 30ft (9m) per minute.

b. A three-minute safety stop at the depth prescribed on the Theoretical Depth at Altitude Chart is required on all dives.

3. Repetitive Diving: Make no more than two dives per day when diving at altitude.

4. a. When arriving at an altitude dive site higher than where your travel originated from, you have *surfaced* from a greater pressure to a lower pressure. This means that the nitrogen pressure in your body is greater than the surrounding pressure, just like after surfacing from a dive. This *residual nitrogen* must be accounted for in planning an altitude dive just as you would in planning a repetitive dive.

b. You may allow a six-hour *surface interval* after arriving at altitude and make your first dive a *new dive*.

c. If you wish to dive in less than six hours, upon arrival at the altitude site, count two pressures groups for each 1,000ft (300m) of altitude to determine your beginning pressure group. You may allow

TABLE 26.3

Theoretical depth at Altitude (imperial).

Theoretical Depth at Altitude
IMPERIAL

Actual Depth	Theoretical Depth at Various Altitudes (in feet)									
	1000	2000	3000	4000	5000	6000	7000	8000	9000	10,000
0	0	0	0	0	0	0	0	0	0	0
10	10	11	11	12	12	12	13	13	14	15
20	21	21	22	23	24	25	26	27	28	29
30	31	32	33	35	36	37	39	40	42	44
40	41	43	45	46	48	50	52	54	56	58
50	52	54	56	58	60	62	65	67	70	73
60	62	64	67	69	72	75	78	81	84	87
70	72	75	78	81	84	87	91	94	98	102
80	83	86	89	92	96	100	103	108	112	116
90	93	97	100	104	108	112	116	121	126	131
100	103	107	111	116	120	124	129	134	140	
110	114	118	122	127	132	137				
120	124	129	134	139						
130	135	140								

© 1970 Skin Diver Magazine. Reprinted with permission.

SAFETY/EMERGENCY DECOMPRESSION STOP DEPTH

Stop	1000	2000	3000	4000	5000	6000	7000	8000	9000	10,000
	14	14	13	13	12	12	12	11	11	10

Reprinted with permission of PADI International.

a surface interval to reduce this pressure group. Round up fractions of 1,000ft (300m).

d.When diving above 8,000ft (2,400m), wait six hours.

Example:

A diver plans to dive 90 minutes after arriving at 5,000ft (1,500m). What would his Pressure Group be for planning the dive?

Answer: B. Count 10 pressure groups upon his arrival (two for each 1,000ft (300m) to get Pressure Group *J*. After 90-minute surface interval (Side Two of The Wheel, Table 2 on Table), Pressure Group J moves to Pressure Group *B*.

5.*Determining theoretical depths.*
   a. As mentioned earlier, the actual depth must be converted to a theoretical depth for use on the RDP.

b.Use the Theoretical Depth at Altitude Chart to make these conversions.

• Use the exact or next greater number

• Round altitudes up to the next 1,000ft/300m

• Round depths to the next greater depth.This can mean a depth is rounded when entering the Theoretical Depth at Altitude Chart, and then again when applying the theoretical depth to the RDP.

c.The Wheel, with its five-foot depth increments (2m on metric version), helps reduce unnecessary rounding in altitude diving. Its use for altitude diving is highly recommended.

*d.*Remember that capillary depth gauges will automatically read the theoretical depth, and no conversion is necessary.

*e.*The maximum depth for any dive is a theoretical depth of 130ft / 40m.

Example:

A diver at 3,300ft (1,000m) plans to dive to an actual depth of 47ft (14.3m). What depth will they use for dive planning on the RDP?

Answer: 60ft (18m). 3,300ft (1,000m) rounds to 4,000ft (1,200m) on the Theoretical Depth at Altitude Chart. 47ft (14.3m) rounds to 50ft / 16m. Find 50ft / 16m in the Actual Depth column of the Theoretical Depth at Altitude Chart and follow to the right until under the 4,000ft (1,200m) column. The theoretical depth is 58ft (18m). 58ft rounds to 60ft on the imperial RDP. (18m is found on the metric RDP).

Note: The required safety stop for this dive would be made at 13ft /4.5m) according to the Theoretical Depth at Altitude Chart.

6. *Special rules for acclimated divers.*

   *a.*After more than six hours at altitude, a diver's body nitrogen equilibrates (for practical purposes) with the surrounding altitude. Because of this lower body nitrogen level, less restrictive rules may be used when a diver already acclimated to altitude ascends to a higher altitude to dive.

   *b.*For the purposes of using the RDP, an *acclimated diver* is a diver who has spent six or more hours at an altitude between 4,000ft (1,200m) and 10,000ft (3,000m). Divers acclimated to less than 4,000ft (1,200m) follow procedures as if acclimated to sea level.

   *c.*For acclimated divers determining a pressure group upon arrival at an altitude higher than the acclimation altitude:

   Count four Pressure Groups for each 1,000ft (300m) of difference. Round up to nearest 1,000ft (300m) for acclimation altitude.

Example:

A diver is acclimated to 4,600ft (1,400m). What Pressure Group are they in upon arrival at a dive site at 5,763ft (1,757m).

Answer: H. 4,600ft (1,400m) rounds down to 4,000ft (1,200m); 5,763ft (1,757m) rounds up to 6,000ft (1,800m). This is a difference of 2,000ft (600m). Four Pressure Groups for each 1,000ft (300m) is 8 Pressure Groups, which is *H.*

d. acclimated divers may use the Pressure Group upon arrival provision for altitudes up to 10,000ft (3,000m).

e. Acclimated divers follow all other rules for altitude diving.

f. Acclimated divers may not mix altitudes by making a dive at one altitude and then making a repetitive dive at a higher altitude.

Example 1. (using imperial RDP)

A diver arrives at a lake at an altitude of 5,412ft. They plan to dive after 30 minutes to an actual depth of 38ft. What is the NDL?

Firstly 5,412ft must be rounded up to 6,000ft. Since the diver is not waiting for 6 hours before diving, he must add two Pressure Groups for every 1,000ft of altitude, which gives 12 Pressure Groups and puts him in Group L when arriving at altitude. After a surface interval of 30 minutes they are in Group G (according to Table 2 on The Table or Side 2 on the Wheel).

To find the Theoretical Depth at Altitude, enter Table 26.3, from the left, at 40ft and move along the row until intersecting the 6,000ft column. The TOD is 50ft. Then turn to the RDP (Table or Wheel) to find the NDL for a diver in Group G diving to 50ft. It is *54 minutes.*

Example 2. (using imperial RDP)

A diver wishes to make a 20-minute dive to 60ft at an altitude of 6,873ft. What is the minimum time they must wait before making this dive?

6,873ft rounds up to 7,000ft so they must count up 14 Pressure Groups and are in Group N on arrival at altitude. An actual depth of 60ft converts to a theoretical depth of 78ft (rounded to 80ft) when at an altitude of 6,873ft.

Using either Table 3 of The Table or Side 1 of The Wheel, it can be seen that the diver must be in Group C or above to make a 20-minute dive to 80ft. To move from Group N to Group C the diver must wait 1 hour 9 minutes.

Note:
It should take the diver 5 minutes to ascend from 60ft to the surface. This is made up of 2 minutes of ascent time (at 30ft/minute) plus the 3-minute safety stop.

The table below provides depth conversion information for use with metric RDPs. The rules given above also apply to the metric RDP.

TABLE 26.4

Theoretical Depth at Altitude (metric).

Theoretical Depth at Altitude

METRIC

Actual Depth	Theoretical Depth at Various Altitudes (in metres)									
	300	600	900	1200	1500	1800	2100	2400	2700	3000
10	10	11	11	12	12	12	13	13	14	14
12	12	13	13	14	14	15	15	16	17	17
14	15	15	16	16	17	17	18	19	19	20
16	17	17	18	18	19	20	21	21	22	23
18	19	19	20	21	22	22	23	24	25	26
20	21	21	22	23	24	25	26	27	28	29
22	23	24	25	25	26	27	28	29	31	32
24	25	26	27	28	29	30	31	32	33	35
26	27	28	29	30	31	32	34	35	36	38
28	29	30	31	32	34	35	36	38	39	40
30	31	32	33	35	36	37	39	40	42	
32	33	34	36	37	38	40	41			
34	35	37	38	39	41	42				
36	37	39	40	42						
38	39	41	42							
40	41									

Reprinted with permission of PADI International.

Example 3 (using metric RDP)

A diver arrives at a lake at an altitude of 1,600m and plans to dive after 30 minutes to an actual depth of 11m. What is his NDL?

First 1,600m must be rounded up to 1,800m. Since the diver is not waiting for 6 hours before diving, they must add two Pressure Groups for every 300m of altitude, which gives 12 Pressure Groups and puts them in Group L when arriving at altitude. After a surface interval of 30 minutes they are

Group G (according to Table 2 on The Table or Side 2 on the Wheel).

To find the Theoretical Depth at Altitude, enter Table 26.4 from the left, at 12m and move along the row until intersecting the 1,800m column. The TOD is 15m.
Turn to the RDP (Table or Wheel) to find the NDL for a diver in Group G diving to 15m. It is *47 minutes*.

Example 4 (using metric RDP)

A diver wishes to make a 20-minute dive to 18m at an altitude of 2,000m. What is the minimum time they must wait before making this dive?

2,000m rounds up to 2,100m, so they must count up 14 Pressure Groups and are in Group N on arrival at altitude.

An actual depth of 18m converts to a theoretical depth of 23m (rounded to 25m) when at an altitude of 2,000m.

Using either Table 3 of The Table or Side 1 of The Wheel, it can be seen that the diver must be in Group B or above to make a 20-minute dive to 18m. To move from Group N to Group B the diver must wait at *1 hour 31 minutes*.

Note:
It should take the diver 5 minutes to ascend from 18m to the surface. This is made up of 2 minutes of ascent time (at 9 m/minute) plus the 3-minute safety stop.

BSAC '88 TABLES

The BSAC '88 Tables, shown and described in Chapter 18, are produced for each of four different Altitude/Atmospheric Pressure Ranges. These are:

> *Level 1:* greater than 984 millibar
> *Level 2:* 899 - 984 millibar
> *Level 3:* 795 - 899 millibar
> *Level 4:* 701 – 795 millibar

In addition there is a Transfer Table to determine the Tissue Code when transferring between Altitude/Atmospheric

Pressure Levels and an Altitude/Atmospheric Pressure Chart to determine the correct Table Level to use.

Example 1.

Find the No-Stop Limit for a dive to 18m at an altitude of 2,400m above sea level (assuming that the diver has acclimatized). The atmospheric pressure at sea level is reported to be 995mb.

The first step is to determine the atmospheric pressure at sea level. This is quoted in weather forecasts or synoptic charts or can be read from a barometer. Once the atmospheric pressure at sea level is found, turn to the Altitude/Atmospheric Pressure Chart. Enter this chart from the bottom at the atmospheric pressure at sea level, and move upwards until intersecting the altitude of the planned dive site. For instance, at 3,000m, if the sea level pressure is less than 1,013mb you are out of the range of the tables and hence cannot use them. Similarly at 2,000m, if the sea level pressure is less than 1,013mb you are in Level 4, if it is greater than 1,013mb you are in Level 3.

In this case, you get *Level 4.* (In borderline cases it is prudent to take the more conservative situation, i.e. the higher level).

Turning to Level 4 Table A, enter at 18m in the depth column and move across to the right to the last no-stop time, which is the NDL and is *28* minutes.

Example 2.

Calculate the decompression required for a dive to 30m for 20 minutes at an altitude of 1,500m (again assuming that the diver has acclimatized). The atmospheric pressure at sea level is reported to be 1010mb.

First turn to the Altitude/Atmospheric Pressure Chart, enter from the bottom at 1,010mb and then move upwards to intersect with the row for 1,500m. In this case, you get Level 3. Turning to Level 3 Table A, enter at 30m in the depth column

© Dr. Jurg Wendling

© Mark Fyvie

and move across to the right to find 20 minutes or the next longer tabled time which, in this case, is 24 minutes. Move down this column to determine the required decompression which is a stop of *3 minutes at 6m* and the Surfacing Code will be G.

Example 3.

Four hours after the dive in Example 2, the diver wishes to dive to a depth of 18m. Calculate the maximum allowable No-Stop Time for the second dive at the same altitude.

Go to the Surface Interval Table Levels 2, 3 or 4 and enter from the left at the Surfacing Code from the previous dive - G. Move to the right until intersecting the section for a 4 hour surface interval. In this case, you are on the border of Codes C and D. A surface interval slightly greater than 4 hours will put you into D. (Otherwise it is more conservative to use C). If you take your new code as B, go to Level 3 Table B and enter from the left at the depth of the repetitive dive, 18m and move to the right to find the no-stop time which is *20 minutes*.

Example 4.

After doing the 18m dive in Example 1 but for a bottom time of 30 minutes (rather than the No-Stop Time of 28 minutes), the diver drives back to sea-level and wishes to dive again. If the surface interval after the first dive has been five hours, find the maximum allowable no-decompression stop bottom time for a dive in the sea to 15m. (The atmospheric pressure at sea level is greater than 984 mbar).

After the dive to 18m for 30 minutes at an altitude of 2,400m, a stop of 1 minute at 5m is required and the Surfacing Code is G.

Turn to the Transfer Table and enter from the left at the last Tissue Code of G. Select the row for level of the last dive (Level 4) and move right along this row until intersecting the column for the level of the next planned dive (Level 1). This gives a new Tissue Code of C. No credit is given for the transition between levels during the descent which assumed to be instantaneous. Go to the Surface Interval Table Level 1, enter at the Tissue Code of C, move right to find the Tissue Code after the 5 hour Surface Interval. It is B. Entering Level 1 Table B at 15m, the no-stop limit is shown as *48 minutes.*

Example 5.

After doing a sea-level dive of 21m for 20 minutes, a diver drives to a mountain lake at an altitude of 1,800m. Here, they wishe to dive to a depth of 18m. The surface interval since the first dive has been three hours. What is the maximum allowable No-Stop Time for this dive at altitude? (The atmospheric pressure at sea level is 1,000mb).

First, turn to the Altitude/Atmospheric Pressure Chart and check which Level is selected for a sea level dive with an atmospheric pressure of 1,000mb. In this case, it is Level 1 (However, had the atmospheric pressure been lower than 984mb we would have selected Level 2).

After the dive to 21m for 20 minutes the Surfacing Code is D. Again turn to the Altitude/Atmospheric Pressure Chart and enter from the bottom at 1,000mb and move upwards to intersect the row for 1,800m. In this case, you get Level 3. (For an atmospheric pressure lower than 990mbar you would select Level 4).

Using the Transfer Table, enter from the left at D(1). Moving right to the column for Level 3 you will see an "X", which means that it would be unsafe to ascend directly to this level. However, if the diver waited just over an hour at sea level before driving to altitude, her Tissue Code would reduce to C (Surface Interval Table Level 1) and, from the Transfer Table, C(1) would give a Tissue Code of F at Level 3. If we assume that two further hours of surface interval have elapsed at Level 3 (actually during the drive to altitude), then, from the Surface Interval Table Level

2, 3 and 4 the new Tissue Code before the next dive would be C. Entering Level 3 Table C, the maximum no-stop time at 18m is *9 minutes*.

THE BÜHLMANN ALTITUDE PROCEDURE

The Swiss, with their avid interest in diving in mountain lakes, have continuously researched the problems of altitude diving since at least the early 1970s. Their initial altitude tables, which were published in 1973[7], have undergone numerous revisions, all with quite intensive testing - currently far more testing than with any other altitude procedure. The resulting incidence of decompression illness (DCI) has apparently been low.

In order to allow greater safety, these tables assume that the diver has traveled to altitude very quickly and, consequently, has not yet adapted to the decreased atmospheric pressure. Adapting to altitude reduces the nitrogen tension in the tissues and, thus, provides additional safety.

The later widely published version of these tables, the Bühlmann (1986) Tables, includes three tables. The first is for dives between sea level and an altitude of 700m (2,300ft). The second is for use at altitudes between 701-2,500m. The third is for repetitive dives at all altitudes. These tables are shown, as discussed in Chapter 17.

The Bühlmann (1986) Tables were tested before being released. A total of 544 real dives were carried out at altitude, with no cases of decompression sickness resulting. 254 of the dives were carried out in Switzerland at altitudes between 1,000-2,600 metres. [8]

290 dives were done in Lake Titicaca, 3,800m above sea level. Most of the dives in Lake Titicaca were no-decompression stop dives, many of which were repetitive.[9]

The times given by these tables for no-stop dives at altitude are often in excess of those dictated by the Cross Corrections to the U.S. Navy Tables, and this has deterred some divers from using them. However, if the diver

Diving on ruins in Lake Titicaca. © Maj. Marc Moody

adheres to the recommended maximum ascent rate of 10m / 30ft per minute sufficient safety should be provided by these tables for most divers most of the time.

Using the Bühlmann (1986) Tables

Example 1.

Find the NDL for a dive to 18m (60ft) at an altitude of 2,400m (8,000ft).

Entering Table 17.7 (Page 235), from the left at 18m, the NDL is the bold figure at the top portion of the second column relating to the 18m depth increment. Hence, the NDL is *44 minutes.*

Example 2.

Calculate the decompression required for a dive to 30m (l00ft) for 20 minutes at an altitude of 1,500m (5,000 ft).

Enter Table 17.7 at the 30m section and find the exact, or next greater, bottom time in the second column. In this case, we can find the exact bottom time of 20 minutes. Moving right, the required decompression is seen to be *3 minutes at 2m* and the RG at the end of this dive is *E.*

Example 3.

Four hours after the dive in Example 2, the diver wishes to dive to a depth of 18m (60ft). Calculate the maximum allowable no-decompression stop bottom time for the second dive at the same altitude.

The RG at the end of the previous dive was E so enter the Repetitive Dive Table 0-2,500m (0-8,200ft) (i.e. Table 17.4 on page 233) from the left at E and move right to find the surface interval of 4 hours. It is in the "0" column which means that the following dive need not be treated as a repetitive dive.

Entering Table 17.7 from the left at 18m (60ft), the no-stop limit is written in bold in the BT column and is *51* minutes.

The Bühlmann decompression model and Tables are explained in detail in Chapter 17.

THE DCIEM PROCEDURE

The DCIEM Sport Diving Tables are designed for divers who work hard in cold water. The tables have been tested extensively using Doppler ultrasonic bubble detectors and have emerged from the testing with a very low bubbles and DCS incidence.

The DCIEM Sport Diving Tables include a table of depth corrections for diving at altitude, defined as diving at an altitude of 1,000ft (300m) or higher, above sea level.

For dives at altitudes of 1,000ft (300m) or greater, the depths of some of the decompression stops have been reduced in order to accommodate changes in atmospheric pressure.

They apply directly to divers who have spent at least 12 hours at that altitude and must be modified for non-acclimatized divers. This system works in a similar manner to the Cross Corrections to the U.S. Navy Tables, in that it provides an Effective Depth for the dive, and modified decompression stop depths.

Despite the similarities. this system is not compatible with the Cross system.

These depth corrections have not been experimentally validated by DCIEM but are more conservative than most other altitude procedures.

The DCIEM Sport Diving Tables are shown in full in Chapter 18. They will need to be referred to when completing the following exercises.

Table 26.5

Depth Corrections for Altitude Diving
(Table D)[10]

D: DEPTH CORRECTIONS

Actual Depth ↓ ↓		1000' ↳1999 300m ↳599		2000' ↳2999 600m ↳899		3000' ↳3999 900m ↳1199		4000' ↳4999 1200m ↳1499		5000' ↳5999 1500m ↳1799		6000' ↳6999 1800m ↳2099		7000' ↳7999 2100m ↳2399		8000' ↳10000 2400m ↳3000	
30'	9m	10	3	10	3	10	3	10	3	10	3	10	3	20	6	20	6
40'	12m	10	3	10	3	10	3	10	3	10	3	20	6	20	6	20	6
50'	15m	10	3	10	3	10	3	10	3	20	6	20	6	20	6	20	6
60'	18m	10	3	10	3	10	3	20	6	20	6	20	6	20	6	30	9
70'	21m	10	3	10	3	10	3	20	6	20	6	20	6	30	9	30	9
80'	24m	10	3	10	3	20	6	20	6	20	6	30	9	30	9	40	12
90'	27m	10	3	10	3	20	6	20	6	20	6	30	9	30	9	40	12
100'	30m	10	3	10	3	20	6	20	6	30	9	30	9	30	9	40	12
110'	33m	10	3	20	6	20	6	20	6	30	9	30	9	40	12		
120'	36m	10	3	20	6	20	6	30	9	30	9	30	9				
130'	39m	10	3	20	6	20	6										
140'	42m	10	3														

Add Depth Correction to Actual Depth of Altitude Dive

10'	3m	10	3.0	10	3.0	9	3.0	9	3.0	9	3.0	8	2.5	8	2.5	8	2.5
20'	6m	20	6.0	19	6.0	18	5.5	18	5.5	17	5.0	16	5.0	16	5.0	15	4.5

Actual Decompression Stop Depths (feet/*metres*) at Altitude

Published in Canada by Universal Dive Techtronics (UDT), Toronto & Vancouver

Reprinted with permission of DND, DRDC and UDT.

Note: Depth Corrections for depths from 150ft to 230ft (45m-69m) are provided in the DCIEM Diving Manual.[11]

1. Apply the following procedures only after you have acclimatized at the altitude of the dive for at least 12 hours:

   a. Establish the actual depth and the altitude;

   b. Find the depth correction by matching the actual depth with the altitude;

   c. Add the depth correction to the actual depth to determine the **Effective Depth** – the equivalent sea level depth for an Altitude Dive. Apply the Effective Depth to Table A (or to Table C for repetitive dives);

   d. If the dive exceeds the No-D Limit, decompress at the Actual Decompression Stop Depth given in Table D.

Example: Altitude is 6,000ft (1,800m)
Bottom Time is 35 minutes
Actual Depth = 60ft (18m)
    + Depth Correction = 20ft (6m)
Effective Depth   = 80ft (24m)
Stop Time is 10 min at 10ft (3m)
(Table A)
Actual Deco. Stop Depth is 8ft (2.5m)

2. If you must dive before 12 hours have elapsed, begin with the NEXT GREATER DEPTH instead of the actual depth. In the example given above, begin the procedure as if the actual depth were 70ft (21m). The Effective Depth would be 90ft (27m).

In this case, the decompression required and Actual Stop Depths would *be 5 minutes at 16ft (5m), and 10 minutes at 8ft (2.5m).*

See Note over page..

Note: The metric and imperial figures given for the Actual Stop Depths are not direct conversions. The metric table for Depth Correction was calculated separately. Because of the effect of "rounding" the numbers on the imperial table, the metric table equivalents may be slightly different from the imperial table.

Example 1.

Find the NDL for a dive to 60ft (18m) at an altitude of 8,000ft (2,400m) above sea level. (Assume that the diver has acclimatized to this altitude for at least 12 hours).

Enter Table D at the 60ft (18m) row and move across the row to intersect the 8,000-10,000ft (2,400-3,000m) column. 30(9) means that 30ft (9m) must be added to the depth of the dive.

Look up the NDL for 90ft (27m) in Table A. (on page 245) The No-D Limit is, thus, *20 minutes.*

Example 2.

Calculate the decompression required for a dive to 100ft (30m) for 20 minutes at an altitude of 5,000ft (1,500m). (Assume that the diver has acclimatized to this altitude for at least 12 hours).

Enter Table D at the 100ft (30m) row and move across the row to intersect the 5,000-5,999ft (1,500-1,799m column. 30(9) means that 30ft (9m) must be added to the depth of the dive.

Look up 130ft (39m) for 20 minutes in Table A. Taking the next longer tabled time of 21 minutes, the decompression shown is 10 minutes at 20ft (6m) and 10 minutes at 10ft (3m) with an RG of G. However, these stop depths will need to be corrected and the corrections are indicated at the bottom of Table D in the 5,000-5,999 column. The required stops are therefore *10 minutes at 17ft (5m) and 10 minutes at 9ft (3m).*

Example 3.

Four hours after the dive in Example 2, the diver wishes to dive to a depth of 60ft (18m). Calculate the maximum allowable no-decompression stop bottom time for the second dive at the same altitude.

The RG immediately after the first dive was G. Enter the DCIEM Surface Interval Table (page 246) from the left at G, and move right to the column containing 4 hours (4:00-5:59) to find the RF, which is 1.3.

Now the second dive is planned to 60ft (18m). However, at an altitude of 5,000ft (1,500m) this depth will need to be adjusted. Go to Table D, look up 60ft (18m) at 5,000-5,999 (1,500-1,799m) and it is indicated that 20ft (6m) needs to be added to the depth. This dive must then be treated as a dive to 80ft (24m).

From Table C, an RF of 1.3 at a depth of 80ft (24m) yields a No-D Limit of *16* minutes for this second dive.

Example 4.

After doing the dive in Example 1 for a bottom time of 20 minutes, the diver drives back to sea level and wishes to dive again. If the surface interval after the first dive has been five hours, find the maximum allowable no-decompression stop bottom time for a dive in the sea to 50ft (15m}.

The RG after the first no-stop dive was D. From Table B, the RF after a surface interval of 5 hours is 1.2.

Although this diver has not spent 12 hours at the new altitude, in this situation he can be treated as acclimatized *as he has descended to a lower altitude.*

Therefore, using the actual depth of 50ft (15m) for an RF of 1.2 in Table C, the No-D time is given as 5*5 minutes.*

Example 5.

After doing a sea level dive of 70ft (21m) for 20 minutes, a diver drives to a mountain lake at an altitude of 6,000ft (1,800m). Here, they wish to dive to a depth of 60ft (18m). The surface interval since the first dive has been three hours. What is the maximum allowable no-decompression stop bottom time for this dive at altitude?

The situation described in this example was not contemplated when the rules for using these tables at altitude were devised.[12] There is a considerable risk in ascending to altitude too soon after diving and in this situation, three hours surface interval may be clearly inadequate. Data from Japan on ascending to altitude after diving[13] and DAN's studies on flying after diving[14] indicate that a longer interval before ascent to altitude may be required in order to avoid DCS resulting from the first dive, much less than performing another dive at altitude. A surface interval of at least 12 hours is therefore advised.

However, one possible method that could be used to calculate the profiles in the example would be to assume that the initial dive was performed at 6,000ft (1,800m), rather than at sea level.

In this case, the first dive would be treated as a dive to 90ft (27m) instead of 70ft. and the RG after this 20-minute dive would be D. After a surface interval of 3 hours, the RF would be 1.2.

From Table D, a 60ft (18m) dive at 6,000ft is treated as a dive to 80ft (24m). However, the diver will not be acclimatized to the altitude of 6,000ft (1,800m) so the next tabled depth must be used and this dive is treated as a dive to 90ft (27m). Therefore, from Table A, the maximum No-D time is *20* minutes.

However, this procedure may in fact not be conservative enough. In this example, if the initial dive at 70ft (21m) had been calculated

at sea level (rather than at 6,000ft), the NST would have been the same as this. Hence it is probably safer to extend the surface interval to at least 12 hours.

Example 6.

What is the No-D Limit for a dive to 80ft (24m) at an altitude of 6,000ft (1,800m)?

Enter Table D at the 80ft (24m) row and move across the row to intersect the 6,000-6,999 (1,800-2,099) column. 30(9) means that 30ft (9m) must be added to the depth of the dive.

Look up the NDL for 110ft (33m) in Table A. The No-D Limit is, thus, *12* minutes.

Example 7.

Find the No-D Limit for a dive to 60ft (18m) at an altitude of 9,500ft (2,900m).

Enter Table D at the 60ft (18m) row and move across the row until intersecting the column corresponding to the required altitude, which is the 8,000-10,000ft (2,400-3,000m) column. The 30(9) means that we must add 30ft (9m) to the actual depth in order to find the Effective Depth. In this case the Effective Depth is 90ft (27m). Enter Table A at 90ft (27m) in order to determine the NDL of *20 minutes.*

USING EANx FOR DIVING AT ALTITUDE

There are several ways to calculate decompression schedules at altitude when using an EANx mix, rather than air.

The simplest method is to use a EANx / trimix dive computer that automatically adjusts for altitude. This avoids calculation errors but will not include some of the inherent rounding-up safety factors that are incorporated in some of the calculation methods. Hence, it is advisable to use a *conservative* dive computer, and, as always, not to push its limits.

The next simplest method is to use decompression software with altitude adjustments to generate dive schedules. There is a wide variety of such software readily available. The user simply enters the altitude (or atmospheric pressure at the desired altitude) and the schedule is generated. However, such software should be used with care, as discussed in Chapter 22.

Another method is to use published EANx Altitude Tables, such as those produced by IANTD.[15] Other methods include the EANx to Sea Level Equivalency Method and EANx Theoretical Ocean Depth Method.

The EANx to Sea Level Equivalency Method involves calculating the percentage of nitrogen that must be in a mix at a particular altitude to make it equivalent to air at sea level. Sea level air tables are then used to calculate decompression.

The EANx Theoretical Ocean Depth Method involves first calculating the equivalent air depth (EAD) of the mix using the usual methods for calculation of EAD. Then next step is to find the Theoretical Ocean Aid Depth (TOAD) which is then used to enter standard air tables.

The calculations involved in these latter methods carry a greater risk of error. IANTD provides certain tables to simplify this process.[15]

RGBM ALTITUDE TABLES

NAUI publishes and distributes two sets of altitude tables derived from Bruce Wienke's RGBM Model (Chapter 21). These no-stop tables, for altitudes of 2,000–6,000ft (610–829m) and 6,000-10,000ft (1,829-3,048m) are used similarly to the sea level tables described in Chapter 21.

Table 26.6

NAUI RGBM Table 2,000-6,000ft.

Reduced Gradient Bubble Model (RGBM)
Dive Table - Air
2,000 to 6,000 ft / 610 to 1829 m

DIVE SAFETY THROUGH EDUCATION

DIVE ONE			DIVE TWO		
MAX DEPTHS		MDT	MAX DEPTHS		MDT
fsw	msw	minutes	fsw	msw	minutes
110	33	9	70	21	28
100	30	13	65	20	28
90	27	17	60	18	38
80	24	22	55	17	38
70	21	28	50	15	54
60	18	38	45	14	54
50	15	54	40	12	85
40	12	85	35	11	85
30	9	125	30	9	125

This table is designed for scuba dives employing air.

Read the instructions on the back and seek proper training before using this table or compressed air. Even strict compliance with this table will not guarantee avoidance of decompression sickness.

Reprinted with permission NAUI Worldwide

Table 26.7

NAUI RGBM Table 6,000-10,000ft

Reduced Gradient Bubble Model (RGBM)

Dive Table - Air

6,000 to 10,000 ft / 1829 to 3048 m

DIVE SAFETY THROUGH EDUCATION

DIVE ONE			DIVE TWO		
MAX DEPTHS		MDT	MAX DEPTHS		MDT
fsw	msw	minutes	fsw	msw	minutes
90	27	11	60	18	28
80	24	15	55	17	28
70	21	21	50	15	40
60	18	28	45	14	40
50	15	40	40	12	64
40	12	64	35	11	64
30	9	103	30	9	103

This table is designed for scuba dives employing air.

Read the instructions on the back and seek proper training before using this table or compressed air. Even strict compliance with this table will not guarantee avoidance of decompression sickness.

ASCENDING TO A HIGHER ALTITUDE AFTER DIVING

Descending to a lower altitude after diving inherently reduces decompression stress due to the increasing ambient pressure. However, ascending to a higher altitude will increase the likelihood of DCS and must be accounted for. This sometimes occurs when a diver needs to drive over higher hills or mountains to return home after a dive.

The most conservative approach is to wait 12-24 hours, as with flying after diving.[14] However, this is not always practical.

An alternative is to calculate all dives as if they were conducted at the highest altitude that one would be exposed to. This will reduce the allowed dive times and increase the decompression obligations, so reducing decompression stress. However, this may not always be conservative enough as described above in Example 5 of the DCIEM Procedures.

OTHER CHANGES

Acute Mountain Sickness (AMS)

Acute mountain sickness (AMS) can occur after the relatively rapid ascent of unacclimatized persons to altitudes greater than about 2,500m (8,200ft).[16] The incidence and severity depend on the rate of ascent to altitude, the altitude itself, the length of stay at altitude (usually within 8-48 hours), level of exertion as well as individual physiological predispositions. Symptoms often begin with lightheadedness and a throbbing headache, and include fatigue, dizziness, loss of appetite, nausea, shortness of breath, sleeplessness and others.

Symptoms usually abate after a few days but occasionally can progress to life-threatening pulmonary oedema (fluid build-up in the lungs) and cerebral oedema (swelling of the brain). Oxygen can be beneficial in the management of victims of AMS but the most effective management option is to quickly bring the victim down to a significantly lower altitude.

Temperature

Most mountain lakes are substantially colder than the ocean, sometimes with temperatures as low as 4°C (37°F). So, when planning to dive at altitude, it is necessary to ensure that your exposure suit will be adequate. It is often preferable to wear a drysuit rather than a wetsuit.

If you are cold, you will not enjoy the dive as much and you will also be predisposed to DCS. In addition, some decompression systems require that certain safety factors be added to the schedules when the diver is cold. It is important to ensure that this is done. Such adjustments may include calculating the dive at the next greater TOD for the next greater tabled time, and/or increasing the Repetitive Group Letter by one increment when calculating a repetitive dive.

Although certain dive computers automatically adjust for colder water temperatures, this should not be relied upon and dive computer users should be increasingly conservative in colder water.

Mountain lakes are usually still, and in still waters one can often find levels of vastly different temperatures. These layers of varying temperature are called "thermoclines". A thermocline is related to seasonal changes, wind conditions, currents, depths and water density. Generally, the water is colder in the deeper layer, but this is not always the case. For example, during an expedition to Lake Titicaca, at an altitude of 3,812m (12,580ft), divers recorded the following temperatures during a dive[9]:

Air	18°C	(64°F)
5m (16.5ft)	8°C	(46°F)
10m (33ft)	12°C	(54°F)
25m (83ft)	14°C	(57°F)

The temperature change due to a thermocline can be quite dramatic and somewhat unpredictable.

Visibility

Still waters often contain a lot of silt. The silt settles if the water is undisturbed and often, under these conditions, visibility can be exceptional. If, however, the silt is disturbed, visibility may deteriorate dramatically. This presents an enormous problem to cave divers who must use guidelines in case silting occurs.

When diving in fresh water it is necessary to be aware of this potential problem and to take appropriate precautions, where necessary.

If a thermocline is present the visibility may change from one layer to the next. The surface layers are often less clear than the deeper and, generally, colder layers.

Hypoxia after Ascent from a Dive at Altitude

A diver surfacing from a dive at altitude is moving from a breathing gas which contains a high oxygen partial pressure, to an atmosphere in which the oxygen levels are lower than normal. As a result, it is possible that the diver may experience symptoms of hypoxia and breathing difficulties for a period after the dive. This could be accentuated in a diver who has been exerting themself.

In this situation, blackout after ascent could occur. A diver should anticipate this problem and minimize exertion after ascent.

Sun Protection

Ultra violet radiation is stronger at altitude due to the rarified air. Therefore it is important to use adequate sun protection to prevent sunburn.

First Aid Procedures and Supplies

Altitude dive sites are often remote and, in an emergency, there can be substantial delays for medical assistance. It is therefore essential to ensure that, when planning a dive at altitude, you have an appropriate Emergency Action Plan, as well as adequate and well-functioning first aid equipment. Among this equipment, it is essential to have a suitable oxygen unit with both demand and constant flow capability and sufficient oxygen supply to provide high concentration oxygen for the time it may take for medical aid to arrive. (Demand valve is often (but not always) more appropriate for managing a dive accident but a constant flow mask will be required in the event of AMS.) This planning should account for possible delays (in accordance with Murphy's Law!).

SUMMARY

- As fresh water is less dense than salt water we are less buoyant and, so, require less weight.

- Many depth gauges will not measure the depth accurately in fresh water as they are calibrated to measure the pressure change associated with depths of sea water.

- Many depth gauges will not account for the reduced atmospheric pressure at altitude. Altitude diving requires a well-calibrated, zero-adjustable depth gauge.

- Most mountain lakes are substantially colder than the ocean. Thermoclines often exist in these lakes.

- Still waters often contain a lot of silt. Visibility will diminish greatly if the silt is disturbed.

- Buoyancy changes occur due to fresh water and reduced ambient pressure and need to be accounted for.

- Acute Mountain Sickness can become a problem at altitudes in excess of 2,500m (8,200ft).

- When we ascend to altitude, nitrogen is off-gassed from our tissues until the nitrogen tension in the tissues is in equilibrium with the reduced nitrogen tension in the atmospheric air.

- It takes 12-24 hours before equilibrium is reached and we are acclimatized to the particular altitude.

- Most decompression tables are based on the diver surfacing to a pressure of 1ATA. At altitude, a diver surfaces to less than 1ATA, and this must be accounted for if the likelihood of DCS is to be minimized.

- Most tables require an additional depth correction to be added to the measured depth of the dive to account for the reduced atmospheric pressure.

REFERENCES

1. Smith C. Altitude Procedures for the Ocean Diver. California: NAUI; 1975.

2. Wienke BR. Diving Above Sea Level. Flagstaff Az: Best Publishing Co.; 1993.

3. Bassett B. And Yet Another approach to the Problems of Altitude Diving and Flying After Diving. In: Decompression in Depth. California: PADI;1979.

4. U.S. Navy Diving Manual. SS521-AG-PRO-010; 0910-LP-100-3199 Revision 4. Naval Sea Systems Command; 1999.

5. Altitude Diver Specialty Course Instructor Outline (Rev 10/01, Version 1.2). California: International PADI Inc.; 2001.

6. Richardson D. Personal communication.

7. Boni M, Schibli RA, Nussberger P, Bühlmann AA. Diving at diminished atmospheric pressure: air decompression tables for different altitudes. *Undersea Biomed Res* 1976; 3 (3):189-204.

8. Bühlmann AA. Diving At Altitude and Flying After Diving. UHMS Symposium, The Physiological Basis of Decompression. Duke University Medical Centre, Durham; 1987.

9. Moody M. Exercise Paddington Diamond. Viersen: U.K. Army Ordinance Services; 1988.

10. Nishi RY, Wong G. Instructions for using the DCIEM Sport Diving Tables. Toronto: UDT Inc.; 1996.

11. DCIEM Diving Manual. Part 1 Air Diving Tables and Procedures. Richmond, BC: Universal Dive Techtronics; 1992.

12. Nishi RY. Personal communication.

13. Yamani N, Mano Y, Shibayama M et al. Peculiar diving activity on sport divers who live in Kanto area: Decompression sickness occurred by driving to altitude after diving. Proceedings of 15th Meeting of United States-Japan Cooperative Program in Natural Resources (UJNR). Panel on Diving Physiology. Toyko: UJNR; 1999.

14. Vann RD, Gerth WA, Denoble PJ, Pieper CF, Thalmann ED. Experimental trials to assess the risks of decompression sickness in flying after diving. *Undersea Hyperb Med* 2004; 31(4):431-44.

15. Taylor GL. Student Manual and Workbook for Safer Altitude Diving. Vol 1: Air and Nitrox. Florida: International Association of Nitrox and Technical Divers Inc.; 1997.

16. Hackett PH, Roach RC. High-Altitude Medicine. In: Wilderness Medicine, 4th Edition. Auerbach PS (ed). Missouri: Mosby; 2001:2-43.

OTHER SOURCES

Bassett B. Decompression procedures for flying after diving, and diving at altitudes above sea level. Report No. SAM-TR-82-47, Brooks Air Force Base: United States Air Force School of Aerospace Medicine; 1982.

Bell RL, Thompson AC, Borowari RE. The Theoretical Structure and Testing of High Altitde Diving Tables. In: Decompression in Depth. California: PADI;1979.

Bühlmann AA. Decompression-Decompression Sickness. Heidelberg: Springer-Verlag; 1984.

Bühlmann AA. The Validity of a Multi-Tissue Model in Sport Diving Decompression. *Proceedings of the Diving Officers' Conference. London:* BS-AC; 1986.

Joiner JT (ed). NOAA Diving Manual. 4th Edn. Flagstaff: Best Publishing Company; 2001.

Smith C. Altitude Procedures for the Ocean Diver; NAUI, California, 1976

U.S. Navy Diving Manual. SS521-AG-PRO-010; 0910-LP-100-3199 Revision 4. Naval Sea Systems Command; 1999.

RECOMMENDED FURTHER READING

Hackett PH, Roach RC. High-Altitude Medicine. In: Wilderness Medicine, 4th Edition. Auerbach PS (ed). Missouri: Mosby; 2001:2-43.

Joiner JT (ed). NOAA Diving Manual. 4th Edn. Flagstaff: Best Publishing

Company; 2001.

U.S. Navy Diving Manual. SS521-AG-PRO-010; 0910-LP-100-3199 Revision 4. Naval Sea Systems Command; 1999.

Sincere thanks to Ron Nishi, Trevor Davies and Drew Richardson for reviewing various parts of this chapter.

Table 26.8

NDLs of Various Tables at Altitude.

Depth	Table	m 12	15	18	21	24	27	30	33	36	39
		ft 40	50	60	70	80	90	100	110	120	130
Sea level	*Table*										
	U.S. Navy	200	100	60	50	40	30	25	20	15	10
	BSAC 88	122	74	51	37	30	24	20	17	14	13
	Buhlmann	125	75	51	35	25	20	17	14	12	10
	DCIEM	150	75	50	35	25	20	15	12	10	8
	PADI	140	80	55	40	30	25	20	16	13	10
	Wienke	110	80	55	40	30	25	20	16	13	10
600m 2000ft	*Table*										
	U.S. Navy	100	60	50	40	30	25	20	15	10	10
	BSAC 88	92	55	37	27	22	18	15	12	10	10
	Buhlmann	125	75	51	35	25	20	17	14	12	10
	DCIEM	75	50	35	25	20	15	12	8	7	6
	PADI	80	55	40	30	25	20	16	13	10	8
	Wienke	85	54	38	28	22	17	13	9	-	-
1200m 4000ft	*Table*										
	U.S. Navy	100	60	50	40	30	25	20	15	10	10
	BSAC 88	77	46	31	23	19	15	12	10	8	8
	Buhlmann	99	62	44	30	22	18	15	12	10	9
	DCIEM	75	50	25	20	15	12	10	8	6	-
	PADI	80	55	40	30	25	20	16	13	10	8
	Wienke	85	54	38	28	22	17	13	9	-	-
1800m 6000ft	*Table*										
	U.S. Navy	100	50	40	30	25	20	10	10	5	5
	BSAC 88	77	46	31	23	19	15	12	10	8	8
	Buhlmann	99	62	44	30	22	18	15	12	10	9
	DCIEM	50	35	25	20	12	10	8	7	6	-
	PADI	80	40	30	25	20	13	10	8	-	-
	Wienke	64	40	28	21	15	11	-	-	-	-
2400m 8000ft	*Table*										
	U.S. Navy	60	50	40	25	20	15	10	5	5	5
	BSAC 88	68	41	28	21	17	14	11	9	8	-
	Buhlmann	99	62	44	30	22	18	15	12	10	9
	DCIEM	50	35	20	15	10	8	7	-	-	-
	PADI	55	40	25	20	16	10	8	-	-	-
	Wienke	64	40	28	21	15	11	-	-	-	-

© Keith Chesnut

SECTION 4

Technical & Occupational Diving

27

Introduction to technical diving

Perhaps the most significant trend in recreational diving practice to have emerged over the last decade is the growth in the use of so-called "technical diving" methods. These methods have been introduced mainly to facilitate one or both of two goals: to extend underwater duration, or to facilitate dives deeper than the conventional "recreational limit" of 40m, or 130ft, depending where in the world you dive. Many divers aspire to such goals, particularly the desire to explore deeper depths, and not surprisingly, there is rapidly growing interest in "technical diving". Perhaps the clearest confirmation of this came in 2001 when PADI introduced the DSAT Tec Diver Course in conjunction with its Diving Science and Technology (DSAT) subsidiary. Until then, and with the exception of a nitrox diver course, PADI had left the "technical" field to the smaller niche technical training agencies. This initiative indicates recognition that aspiring technical divers are a profitable market for training products. Almost certainly it heralds a new and larger generation of technical divers.

There has been much debate over which diving techniques should be referred to as "technical diving" and which should not. This is because techniques such as nitrox diving have now become so mainstream that some technical divers no longer consider they deserve the "technical" designation. We will avoid such semantic arguments, and for the purposes of this chapter, we will define technical diving in keeping with its goals as stated above. Thus diving practices utilized to extend duration and / or depth will be discussed. This embraces those frequently encountered diving techniques that *intentionally breach no-decompression limits ("decompression diving"), utilize gases other than air (including nitrox), or equipment other than single-cylinder open circuit scuba.*

This chapter is aimed mainly at providing some perspective on why these techniques are necessary. We will review the limitations on duration and depth imposed by scuba air diving, and in subsequent chapters we will review the technical diving methods that have evolved to help overcome those limitations. Unfortunately, technical diving is, well, technical. So there are frequent references to specialized issues such as gas laws and calculations used in the planning and execution of safe technical dives. This is unavoidable in even a moderately detailed review of the subject. However, it must be understood that while some techniques are quite thoroughly described, *these chapters are not intended to be a technical diving manual, nor a highly detailed educational resource for trained technical divers.*

Finally, it must be acknowledged that few human endeavours seem to generate more rancorous arguments about the best way of doing things than technical diving. Some of the vitriolic exchanges on internet technical diving forums can only be described as extraordinary. While many commentators place their egos before both common sense and the good of the sport, these authors want none of that. We applaud the achievements of other divers, and acknowledge everyone's right to an opinion on equipment configurations and practices. We are fully aware that our interpretations of some technical diving issues will not correspond exactly to the legitimate interpretations of others. That's life.

THE LIMITATIONS OF RECREATIONAL SCUBA AIR DIVING

Scuba air diving has limitations that have fueled the trend towards the development and use of technical diving methods. Most divers want to go deeper and stay longer, right? Anyone who has thought seriously about it will have come up against the limitations on the depth and duration of dives performed using standard scuba techniques. These limitations are briefly enumerated below before we consider the means used by technical divers to resolve them.

THE LIMITATIONS ON DURATION DURING RECREATIONAL SCUBA AIR DIVING

There are a number of factors that limit the amount of time that the scuba air diver can spend underwater.

Breathing gas supply

Perhaps the most intuitively obvious limitation on the duration of a scuba dive is the amount of breathing gas that can be carried. Conventional scuba diving is conducted with a single cylinder of air. More specific examples are discussed later, but typically these cylinders have internal volumes (usually referred to as "water capacity") of around 12 litres and they are filled to pressures around 200ATA. It's a big

assumption (because some divers are 'air pigs' whilst others appear not to require the stuff) but if we assume that a diver consumes about 20L of air per minute during "normal" finning at the surface, then the time the diver could spend finning at the surface while breathing from a 12L tank is obtained by multiplying the pressure when full by the internal volume to get the number of litres of air in the cylinder, and then dividing this by the air consumption rate (20lpm). Thus:

$$Duration = (200ATA \times 12L) \div 20lpm$$
$$= 120\ minutes$$

Of course, finning around at the surface is not the intended purpose of scuba equipment. So how does its use at depth influence the duration of the air supply? In calculating the approximate duration provided by the gas in the same cylinder at any given depth, the effects of increasing ambient pressure and Boyle's law must be taken into account. For example, a litre of air breathed at 50m (165ft) depth (where the ambient pressure is 6ATA) is 6 times as dense as when breathed at the surface. Put another way, after exhalation, that single litre of air will have expanded to 6 litres by the time it rises to the surface, and our 20lpm surface air consumption is therefore 20 x 6 = 120lpm at 50m (165ft). Thus, duration at 50m (165ft) is given by:

$$Duration = (200ATA \times 12L) \div (20lpm \times 6)$$
$$= 20\ minutes$$

This calculation assumes that we are happy to breathe the cylinder down until it is essentially empty. It is universally accepted in all forms of diving that this is unwise practice, and that a minimum "reserve" should remain in the cylinder on completion of the dive. In recreational diving, a reserve of 50ATA is frequently cited. Gas management planning in technical diving is discussed later, but for now let's assume that 50ATA is an appropriate reserve. We have to subtract this from our cylinder fill pressure when calculating duration.

Thus, our duration at 50m (165ft) allowing for a reserve of 50ATA is given by:

([200ATA – 50ATA] x 12) ÷ (20lpm x 6)
= 15 minutes

All of this can be summarized by the following equation:

EQUATION 1

Duration (minutes) =
$([P_{cyl} – P_{res}] \times WC) \div (SAC \times P_{amb})$

Where:
P_{cyl} = cylinder fill pressure in ATA
P_{res} = planned reserve pressure in ATA
P_{amb} = ambient pressure in ATA
WC = cylinder water capacity in L
SAC = surface air consumption in lpm

This formula has been used to calculate duration for dives over a range of depths in Table 27.1 (keeping the other relevant cylinder and air consumption parameters the same as for our 50m (165ft) dive in the earlier example). Note that durations are rounded down to the nearest whole minute.

Though obvious, it must be pointed out that while these figures are indicative of potential durations at depth, the gas supply must also last for the descent, ascent, and any decompression time required during the latter. It follows that *the actual duration available at depth using a typical single cylinder of air is much shorter than the times indicated*. Thus, it is clear that while the single cylinder configuration provides adequate duration for most shallow dives, as depth increases the gas supply provided by a typical single cylinder can become a critical limiting factor.

TABLE 27.1

Estimated duration for a single 12L water capacity cylinder filled to 200ATA, allowing a reserve of 50ATA, and assuming a surface air consumption of 20lpm.

Depth (m)	Duration (min)
Surface	90
10	45
20	30
30	22
40	18
50	15
60	12

No-decompression limits (NDLs)

The longer the dive, the greater the absorption of nitrogen into the body's tissues. As discussed previously, if there is sufficient nitrogen accumulation during the dive, then the diver will have to make obligatory "decompression stops" during the ascent. Conventional scuba diver training teaches "no- decompression diving" in which divers limit their underwater duration to avoid reaching so called "no decompression limits" and the need for obligatory decompression stops. These limits vary according to the dive table or computer used, but all become increasingly restrictive at deeper depths (see Table 27.2).

Cold

Depending on the water temperature, and the quality of the thermal protection employed, cold may become the limiting factor in the dive duration.

TABLE 27.2

No decompression limits (minutes) from 3 commonly used dive tables. Note, DCIEM refers to the Canadian Forces Tables, and RDP refers to the PADI Recreational Dive Planner.

Depth (m/ft)	US Navy	DCIEM	PADI RDP*
9/30	310	300	360
12/40	200	150	140
15/50	100	75	80
18/60	60	50	55
21/70	50	35	40
24/80	40	25	30
27/90	30	20	25
30/100	25	15	20
33/110	20	12	16
36/120	15	10	13
39/130	10	8	10

* These times are taken from the Imperial version of the RDP

THE LIMITATIONS ON DEPTH DURING RECREATIONAL SCUBA AIR DIVING

Recreational scuba diver training organizations have set a maximum recreational scuba depth limit of 40m / 130ft This depth is somewhat arbitrary, but a "limit" was undoubtedly necessary in recognition of the increasing influence of various factors that are more likely to complicate an air dive as depth increases.

Nitrogen narcosis

As previously discussed, the narcotic effect of the nitrogen in air becomes dangerously prominent at depths beyond 30 – 40m (100-132ft). Despite some divers' claims to the contrary, this occurs in everyone, albeit to variable degrees. It is progressive as depth increases. Notwithstanding fanciful stories of divers removing their regulators to kiss fish, narcosis has an insidious onset, and

may provoke accidents by causing divers to make mistakes. At extreme depths cognitive function can become dangerously impaired.

Oxygen toxicity

As previously discussed, as depth increases, the pressure of oxygen (PO_2) we are breathing increases. If this rises much above 1.4ATA, then there is a rapidly increasing risk of cerebral oxygen toxicity. Frequently, the first manifestation is unconsciousness and fitting; a decidedly unhelpful event when underwater at any depth. We can calculate the ambient pressure at which an air-breathing diver will be breathing 1.4ATA of oxygen by dividing 1.4 by the fraction of oxygen in air:

$$1.4 \div 0.21 = 6.7ATA$$

Since each 10 metres (33 feet) of seawater exerts 1ATA of pressure, 6.7ATA corresponds to:

(6.7 − 1ATA [for the atmosphere above the water]) x 10 = 57 metres (188ft) depth.

Thus, if the maximum desired PO_2 is 1.4ATA, then the "maximum operating depth" or "MOD" for air is 57m (188ft), and its use should be limited to depths less than this.

Work of breathing

At all depths, air must be supplied by the regulator at ambient pressure in order to facilitate breathing. Air supplied at greater pressure is denser by definition, and does not flow as freely through the tubes and orifices of the regulator, nor the lungs for that matter. It follows that the work required of the respiratory muscles in order to initiate and maintain normal air flow (the "work of breathing"), increases as depth increases. Since air is a "heavy" gas this can become very noticeable at extreme depth. Indeed, it would become exhausting to perform significant work at extreme depths breathing air.

Breathing gas supply

The breathing gas supply was discussed above as a limiting factor to duration underwater, and the effect of depth on duration of a fixed gas supply was also discussed. Referring back to that discussion, it is obvious that a gas supply of conventional size must limit depth because at extreme depths such a gas supply would be exhausted quickly.

Cold

As depth increases the water temperature often falls. This can occur quite precipitously if a thermocline is present.

No-decompression limits

The deeper the dive, the faster the diver absorbs nitrogen, and the faster they approach the no-decompression limit for the dive. Indeed, at depths approaching the recreational limit of 40m / 130ft where "no-decompression limits" are less than 10 minutes, so-called "no decompression diving" becomes highly impractical because of the very short bottom times available (see Table 27.2).

Individual technical diving techniques have evolved to address one or more of the above limitations. Some are primarily intended to enhance duration, while others are specifically targeted at extending the depth range. Frequently, several of the techniques discussed in the following chapters are combined to facilitate longer dives beyond the recreational depth range. Such dives would be dangerous at best, or simply impossible if performed using conventional single tank scuba air diving.

SUMMARY:

- Technical diving embraces diving techniques that intentionally breach no-decompression limits ("decompression diving"), utilize gases other than air (including nitrox), or equipment other than single-cylinder open circuit scuba.

- The limitations on underwater duration imposed by normal scuba diving include the size of the breathing gas supply, no decompression limits and cold.

- The limitations on depth imposed by normal scuba air diving include nitrogen narcosis, oxygen toxicity, the work of breathing, and no decompression limits.

- The technical diving methods described in subsequent chapters have largely been developed to overcome these limits.

© Simon Mitchell

28

Technical diving techniques 1 - Nitrox diving

Nitrox diving is probably the most widely utilized technical diving method. The term "nitrox" refers to mixtures of oxygen and nitrogen in which there is more oxygen than found in air. For this reason, nitrox is often referred to as "enriched air" or "enriched air – nitrox" (EANx). By convention, the mix is described by reference to its oxygen content. Thus, if a nitrox mix contains 36% oxygen, then it is referred to "nitrox 36" or "EANx36". Literal application of this nitrox classification system would designate air as "nitrox 21" but air is never referred to in this way. The rest of the mix must, by definition, consist of nitrogen, so a nitrox 36 mix must also contain 64% nitrogen. These percentages are frequently expressed as decimal fractions, especially in some of the calculations described below. Thus, the fraction of oxygen (FO_2) in nitrox 36 is 0.36, and the fraction of nitrogen (FN_2) is 0.64.

THE ADVANTAGES OF NITROX DIVING

Why might it be desirable to breathe a mix containing more oxygen and less nitrogen than air? There are several important reasons.

Reduced uptake of nitrogen

Since the amount of nitrogen taken up into the diver's blood and tissues during a dive is proportional to the inspired partial pressure of nitrogen, any reduction in the inspired fraction of nitrogen will reduce the amount of nitrogen absorbed. This can be illustrated by consideration of Table 28.1, which compares the approximate pressures of nitrogen breathed by an air diver and a diver using nitrox 40 over a range of depths.

A striking feature of these data is that the nitrox 40 diver is breathing the same pressure of nitrogen (2.4ATA) at 30m (100ft) as the air diver at 20m (66ft) (see shaded cells). It follows that the nitrox diver at 30m (100ft) will be absorbing the same amount of nitrogen as an air diver at 20m (66ft). Put another way, with respect to nitrogen absorption, the nitrox 40 diver at 30m (100ft) is at an "equivalent air depth" (EAD) of 20m (66ft). Calculation of the EAD for any combination of depth and nitrox mix is discussed later.

This reduction of nitrogen absorption during nitrox diving is an advantage that can be utilized in one of two ways.

Firstly, the nitrox diver can use the reduced absorption of nitrogen to increase allowable dive time. The equivalent air depth can be used in calculation of no-decompression limits (NDLs) (either using a dive table or nitrox dive computer), and since the EAD is always shallower than the actual depth, there will be an advantage in terms of allowable bottom time. In the example given in Table 28.1, the diver using nitrox 40 at 30m (100ft) has an EAD of 20m (66ft). Using the US Navy standard air tables (see Table

TABLE 28.1

*Inspired pressures of nitrogen at various depths
when breathing air and nitrox 40.*

Depth m (ft)	Ambient pressure (ATA)	PN_2 in air (ATA) ($FN_2 = 0.8$)	PN_2 in nitrox 40 (ATA) ($FN_2 = 0.6$)
Surface	1	0.8	0.6
10m (33ft)	2	1.6	1.2
20m (66ft)	3	*2.4*	1.8
30m (100ft)	4	3.2	*2.4*

Note 1: for simplicity, the % of nitrogen in air is rounded to 80% and the fraction of nitrogen (FN_2) in air therefore equals 0.8.

Note 2: For reasons that are described later, some technical diving agencies would consider the use of nitrox 40 at 30m (100ft) to be unwise. It is cited here as a convenient illustration of the potential effect of different on nitrox mixes on the PN_2 breathed at depth.

27.2), this diver is theoretically limited by a NDL of 50 minutes (the air diving NDL for 20m (66ft)) instead of 25 minutes (the air diving NDL for 30m (100ft))!

Alternatively, the nitrox diver can ignore this potential for increasing duration, and assume that he or she is using air for the purposes of bottom time calculation. In other words, the diver would use air diving NDLs. This has the advantage of widening the safety margin for avoiding DCS. In the example given in Table 28.1, if a nitrox 40 diver at 30m assumed they were using air and therefore used the air diving NDL for 30m (25 minutes), it would be equivalent to an air diver at 20m voluntarily using the NDL for 30m (thereby halving their allowable NDL from 50 to 25 minutes). Some occupational diving groups such as diving instructors or aquaculture workers, whose work involves reputed risk factors for DCS such as multiple ascents, have begun to utilize nitrox in this way.

Another oft-reported advantage for nitrox diving presumed to be associated with reduced nitrogen uptake is a reduced level of post dive fatigue. However, in the only

evaluation of this phenomenon in which fatigue was objectively measured and the divers were blinded to the gas they were breathing, no difference between nitrox and air diving was found.[1]

Accelerated elimination of nitrogen

In addition to reducing nitrogen uptake at depth, nitrox breathing will also hasten nitrogen elimination during decompression because a steeper gradient for nitrogen elimination between body tissues and the lungs is established. This phenomenon is particularly useful for reducing the length of stops during decompression diving, and we will return to this subject later.

Possible reduction in nitrogen narcosis

It is frequently argued that since the degree of nitrogen narcosis is directly proportional to the partial pressure of nitrogen breathed, then any reduction in the inspired fraction of nitrogen should reduce the narcotic effect. From Table 28.1 one might therefore predict that a nitrox 40 diver at 30m would be experiencing the same amount of narcosis as the air diver at 20m.

A counter argument frequently seen in internet debates on this issue holds that oxygen is just as narcotic as nitrogen and that replacing nitrogen with oxygen confers no benefit in this regard. We have reviewed the literature on this issue and find there are no definitive answers to the debate.[2] Indeed, there is evidence that supports both viewpoints to some extent.

First, it must be acknowledged that oxygen is more soluble in lipid and therefore has a higher theoretical narcotic potency than nitrogen at an equivalent partial pressure. However, it also must be noted that because oxygen is metabolized, its partial pressure in cells does not rise significantly when breathed within the pressure range that can be safely tolerated by humans (as used in diving). Thus, while oxygen is theoretically more narcotic than nitrogen, its partial pressure in tissues or cells may not rise sufficiently for this narcotic effect to be apparent, even when we substitute more oxygen for nitrogen in a nitrox mix.

Not surprisingly then, limited data demonstrate that for mixes containing only nitrogen and oxygen, decreasing the nitrogen to oxygen ratio (whilst remaining within a safe PO_2) does seem to decrease the narcotic effect and this supports the argument that nitrox mixes are worthwhile from this point of view. However, if nitrogen is held constant and the oxygen fraction of a mix is reduced by adding He (which is non-narcotic), then narcosis is also reduced. This infers that oxygen does have some narcotic effect, despite its metabolism in tissues.

In summary, nitrox should be <u>less</u> narcotic than air, but oxygen <u>does</u> have some narcotic effect. The nitrox - air difference may be too small to notice reliably.

THE DISADVANTAGES OF NITROX DIVING

Nitrox diving introduces a number of new, and in some cases costly items into the diver's repertoire of equipment, knowledge and skills. The use of nitrox undoubtedly raises the complexity of diving. While these issues are not strictly "disadvantages" in the true sense, they do impose the need for a more rigorous approach to the sport. Those who appreciate the simplicity of air diving could certainly interpret this as a "disadvantage". Some of the relevant issues are discussed below.

Oxygen cleanliness

Since oxygen promotes combustion, all materials that come into contact with oxygen-rich mixtures must be more rigorously cleaned to remove any flammable contaminants. This begins with the most fundamental aspect, the gas itself. In particular, the air that is added to oxygen in production of nitrox must be filtered to a higher standard of cleanliness than that normally used to fill scuba air cylinders. This means dedicated and more costly filtration systems. It is generally agreed that if mixes containing more than 40% oxygen are used, then all equipment including cylinders and regulators must be "oxygen clean" and dedicated for nitrox use only. Many believe that all cylinders for nitrox use must be dedicated and oxygen clean, no matter what mixes are used, because the most frequently utilized method of making nitrox involves bleeding pure oxygen into the cylinder to mix it with air (see below).

Oxygen cleanliness involves removing all silicone or hydrocarbon-based lubricants, particulate matter, and flammable material from the equipment. Special cleaning agents are used for this purpose. Oxygen compatible components (such as viton O-rings) and lubricants (such as Christo-lube® or Krytox®) are then utilized where necessary. Oxygen clean cylinders and regulators dedicated for nitrox use should be clearly labeled as such (see Figure 28.1).

FIGURE 28.1

Scuba cylinder designated for nitrox use showing clear anambiguous labeling.

Oxygen toxicity

Perhaps the most important "disadvantage" of nitrox is that the use of oxygen-rich mixes increases the potential for cerebral oxygen toxicity if appropriate techniques are not strictly adhered to. Oxygen toxicity has been discussed in more detail elsewhere but it is notable that unconsciousness and fitting, often without warning, may be the first manifestations. Such an event underwater is likely to be fatal.

The risk of cerebral oxygen toxicity is directly related to the PO_2 breathed by the diver and the duration over which an elevated PO_2 is breathed. A PO_2 of 1.4ATA is widely considered a safe limit for underwater use, though most agencies consider brief exposures to 1.6ATA in an "extreme exposure" to be tolerable. Much beyond this and the risk of toxicity begins to rise precipitously. This concept of a maximum tolerable PO_2 will arise time and again throughout any discussion of technical diving. Ensuring that the exposure to oxygen does not exceed the limits considered "safe" is the most important aspect of nitrox diving, and is considered in more detail below.

Cost

The process of establishing and maintaining oxygen cleanliness of equipment costs money, as does ownership of a separate set of equipment for nitrox use if this is considered necessary. In addition, nitrox is expensive to produce in comparison to merely filling cylinders with air. Not surprisingly, the cost of nitrox fills is usually at least twice that of normal air fills. The cost can be quite a lot higher for preparation of the very rich (high oxygen content) nitrox fills sometimes used by decompression divers (see later).

PLANNING A SAFE NITROX DIVE

Managing the PO_2

Clearly, one of the key aspects, if not THE key aspect, of nitrox diving is correct planning to ensure that a safe PO_2 is not exceeded. There are a number of important calculations pertaining to PO_2 that have to be mastered, and these are discussed below.

Let's begin with the most basic concept; the calculation of the PO_2 breathed during a dive using air, nitrox, or any other mix for that matter. This is determined by the ambient pressure at depth and the fraction of oxygen in the gas being breathed, thus:

EQUATION 2

PO_2 breathed at depth in ATA
$= FO_2 \times P_{amb}$

where:
FO_2 = fraction of oxygen in the mix
P_{amb} = the ambient pressure in ATA

Consider for example, an air dive to 30m (100ft). The PO_2 breathed by the diver at this depth will be:

0.21 (air is 21% oxygen) x
4ATA (ambient pressure at 30m)
= 0.84ATA

This is well below the widely accepted safe PO_2 of 1.4ATA.

Mindful of our example in Table 28.1 and the caution in Note 2 of the table's caption, we might be curious as to whether nitrox 40 should be used at the same depth? Using equation 2 we get:

0.40 (40% oxygen) x 4ATA = 1.6ATA.

As previously mentioned, a PO_2 of 1.6ATA is acceptable only for short exposures, and some would warn against exceeding 1.4ATA unless absolutely necessary. Certainly, it is clear that nitrox 40 should not be used any deeper than 30m (100ft). This highlights the importance of two very important dive planning calculations:

First, if you have a cylinder of nitrox, how do you go about calculating the ***maximum safe operating depth (MOD)*** to which you can take that mix? This is achieved using the formula:

EQUATION 3 (METRIC)

MOD (m) for a nitrox mix
= ([PO_{2max} ÷ FO_2] −1) x 10

EQUATION 3 (IMPERIAL)

MOD (ft) for a nitrox mix
= ([PO_{2max} ÷ FO_2] −1) x 33

where:

PO_{2max} = maximum tolerable PO_2 in ATA
FO_2 = the fraction of oxygen in the mix.

In our earlier discussion of oxygen toxicity, we informally introduced this concept to calculate a MOD for air (57m (188ft) if a maximum PO_2 of 1.4 is adopted). MODs for nitrox will obviously be *shallower* because nitrox contains more oxygen. Using our example of a nitrox 40 mix and adopting the usual maximum tolerable PO_2 of 1.4ATA, the MOD is calculated as follows:

MOD m = ([1.4ATA ÷ 0.4] − 1) x 10 = 25m

MOD ft = ([1.4ATA ÷ 0.4] − 1) x 33 = 83ft

Thus, the maximum depth to which a nitrox 40 mix should routinely be taken is 25m (83ft). This process of calculating a MOD for each breathing gas used underwater is one of the most important skills in technical diving gas management.

Second, if you know the depth you want to visit, how do you calculate the ***ideal fraction of oxygen*** in the nitrox mix you will use? The best mix is given by the formula:

EQUATION 4

Ideal fraction of oxygen in the mix

= PO_{2max} ÷ P_{amb}

where:

PO_{2max} = maximum tolerable PO_2 in ATA

P_{amb} = the ambient pressure in ATA

For example, if we plan a dive to 30m (100ft) with a maximum PO_2 of 1.4ATA, and want to use the ideal fraction of oxygen in the mix during our time at depth, we calculate that mix as follows:

Ideal fraction of oxygen in the mix
= 1.4ATA ÷ 4ATA
= 0.35

Thus, nitrox 35 is the ideal mix for this dive to minimize the risk of oxygen toxicity whilst also minimizing nitrogen absorption.

Managing the oxygen clock

We utilize the above calculations to ensure that the maximum safe PO_2 is not exceeded during diving. Unfortunately, avoiding a PO_2 in excess of the safe maximum is not quite all that is required in managing the risk of cerebral oxygen toxicity. Even the maximum "safe" PO_2 of 1.4ATA becomes less safe the longer you breathe it. Thus, in addition to avoiding exceeding a maximum PO_2, we must also watch the so-called "oxygen clock". The higher the PO_2 you are breathing, the shorter the safe time for which you can breathe it.

The time limits for single exposures and cumulative 24 hour exposures over a range PO_2s are given in Table 28.2.

The nitrox diver must keep track of their cumulative oxygen exposure throughout a day's diving in much the same way as residual nitrogen must also be tracked in dive planning. Thus, for each dive, the percentage of maximum oxygen exposure must be calculated using the formula:

EQUATION 5

% exposure
= (dive duration ÷ exposure limit) x 100

Note: Dive duration and exposure limit are in minutes.

For example, assume a diver uses nitrox 40 to dive to 20m for 55 minutes. We can deduce using *Equation 2* that the diver is breathing a PO_2 of 1.2ATA during the dive. This is below the 1.4ATA maximum safe limit, and from Table 27.2 we see that the maximum exposure duration for 1.2ATA is 210 minutes. The 55 minute dive duration is well within this limit. Using *Equation 5*, we calculate the % of maximum oxygen exposure accumulated during the dive as follows:

% exposure
= (55 min ÷ 210 min) x 100
= 27%

If the diver wishes to perform another dive on the same day, how is this initial exposure to 27% of the allowable oxygen exposure accounted for? A conservative approach to calculating the allowable exposure time for the next dive on that day would be to assume that 27% of the allowable time had already been used. Thus, if the same diver using nitrox 40 planned another dive to 20m (66ft) (where the PO_2 breathed would once again be 1.2 ATA) then he or she would have to deduct 27% of the usual allowable exposure time of 210 minutes. Thus, 27% of 210 is 57 minutes, and the new maximum allowable time is 210 – 57 = 153 minutes.

A less conservative approach acknowledges that the cumulative effect of oxygen exposure and the danger of subsequent toxicity falls with longer surface intervals between dives. Thus, like the fall of residual nitrogen between dives, the percentage of the accumulated percentage maximum oxygen exposure is also assumed to fall between dives. We say "assumed" because the data upon which these practices are based is somewhat sketchy and incomplete. Nevertheless, tables are available that allow the nitrox diver to reduce the accumulated % maximum oxygen exposure in accordance with the length of the surface interval. These are usually based on an exposure half-life of somewhere between 90 and 120 minutes. In other words, every 90 minutes the accumulated % maximum oxygen exposure is considered to fall by half. In our above example, the accumulated 27% of maximum exposure would fall to 14% after 90 minutes, and to 7% after 180 minutes.

TABLE 28.2		
NOAA exposure limits over a range of PO$_2$s		
PO$_2$ (ATA)	**Single exposure** (min)	**24 hour exposure** (min)
1.6	45	150
1.5	120	180
1.4	150	180
1.3	180	210
1.2	210	240
1.1	240	270
1.0	300	300
0.9	360	360
0.8	450	450
0.7	570	570
0.6	720	720

Managing decompression status

The concept of equivalent air depth (EAD) was introduced earlier. We deduced from Table 28.1 that it would be valid for the nitrox 40 diver at 30m (100ft) to use the air diving no decompression limit for 20m (66ft) given that the PN$_2$ breathed in both situations was the same. The EAD can be calculated for any depth and any nitrox mix using the following formula:

EQUATION 6 (METRIC)

EAD (m)

$$= ([FN_2 \times \{depth + 10\}] \div 0.79) - 10$$

EQUATION 6 (IMPERIAL)

EAD (m)

$$= ([FN_2 \times \{depth + 33\}] \div 0.79) - 33$$

where:
EAD = equivalent air depth in m / ft
FN$_2$ = fraction of nitrogen in the nitrox mix
depth = depth (m/ft) at which the nitrox is being used
0.79 = the fraction of nitrogen in air

Consider, for example, a nitrox 40 dive at 20m (66ft). The EAD is given by:

([0.6 x {20 + 10}] ÷ 0.79) – 10 = 13m
([0.6 x {66 + 33}] ÷ 0.79) – 33= 43ft

Therefore, for the purposes of calculating his or her no decompression limit (NDL), the diver using nitrox 40 at 20m (66ft) can assume they are diving at 13m (43ft) using air. Using the US Navy table (see Table 27.2), this means that instead of being limited by the normal air-diving NDL for 20 m (50 minutes), the diver using nitrox 40 has 100 minutes to spend at depth.

Dive management using nitrox dive tables and computers

A number of authorities have produced dive tables designed for specific nitrox mixes, and these remove the need for performing EAD calculations. The diver just goes to the dedicated table for the intended nitrox mix, and then uses the table in an identical fashion to air diving tables. (e.g. Table 28.3)

In addition, many companies now produce dedicated nitrox diving computers that automatically track decompression status, the PO_2, and the oxygen clock for the diver. Some of these computers will accommodate the use of only one preset nitrox mix during the dive, whereas others will allow a change of nitrox mix during the dive. The rationale for such mix changes is discussed further when decompression diving is considered.

MAKING NITROX

By far the most commonly used method for producing nitrox is simply to add oxygen then air in the correct proportions to an oxygen clean cylinder to produce the desired nitrox mix. Since the variable controlled by the mixer is the pressure of the gases added to the cylinder, this method is commonly referred to as "partial pressure blending". It

TABLE 28.3

NOAA Nitrox 32 Table.

Reprinted with permission of Best Publishing Co.

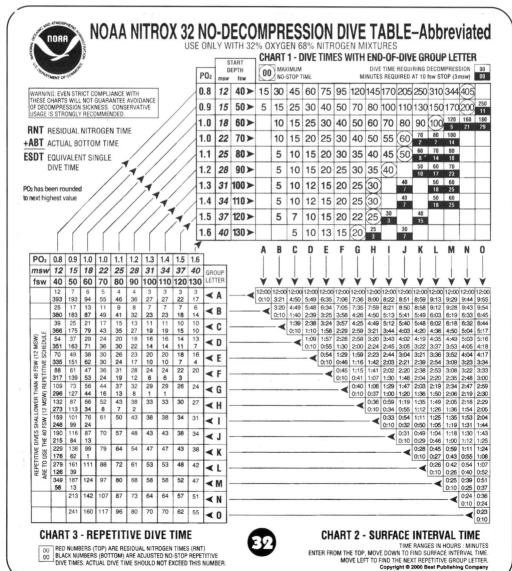

has the advantages of being relatively simple and of requiring minimal investment in specialized equipment. Indeed, it is commonly employed by technical divers who carry their own mixing panels or whips into the field. However, it has the disadvantage of involving decanting and handling of pure oxygen at high pressures with the frequently underestimated dangers inherent in this practice. Nevertheless, if performed carefully and accurately, partial pressure blending is a very useful and practical technique.

Tables are available which specify recipes for various nitrox mixes. The ingredients can also be relatively easily calculated. For example, if the mixer is starting with an empty cylinder, the pressure of oxygen that must be added to produce a mix of given composition is calculated as follows:

EQUATION 7

Pressure O$_2$
$$= (1 \div 0.79) \times T_p \times (T_{O2\%} - 0.21)$$

where:
Pressure O$_2$ = pressure of oxygen to be added in ATA
T_p = Target cylinder fill pressure in ATA
$T_{O2\%}$ = Target oxygen percentage in the mix expressed as a decimal fraction (e.g. 40% = 0.4)

For example, assume we wish to fill an empty cylinder with nitrox 40 to 200ATA. Using *Equation 7*, the pressure of oxygen we need to add to the cylinder is given by:

Pressure O$_2$
$$= (1 \div 0.79) \times 200 \times (0.4 - 0.21)$$
$$= 48ATA$$

Therefore, we would decant 48ATA of 100% oxygen into the cylinder, and then top it up to 200ATA with air. If done correctly, this will produce a nitrox 40 mix. It should be pointed out that this equation fails to take account of temperature changes in the decanted gases, and this can make a very big difference to the accuracy of the mix. Decanting into a cylinder causes adiabatic heating of the gas in the recipient cylinder. In accordance with Charles' Law the pressure will be higher on initial completion of filling than if the cylinder was allowed to cool to room temperature and the pressure measured again. It follows that gas additions should be performed very slowly and with the cylinder immersed in water, for the sake of both safety and causing minimal inaccuracy due to temperature-induced pressure change. The cylinder should be allowed to cool, pressure re-measured, and the oxygen topped up if necessary before addition of the air. This process should be repeated for the air addition.

More complex formulae are available which allow the blender to take into account any nitrox left in the cylinder from a previous dive. These calculations are beyond the scope of this book. Several other nitrox mixing techniques are utilized in the diving industry although these are invariably more complex and involve greater investment in costly equipment. Divers interested in any of this extra information, and in actually making nitrox by any method, should complete a gas blending course offered by several of the technical diving training agencies.

Nitrox analysis

In terms of critical nitrox diving skills, checking the oxygen content of a nitrox mix is second only to determining the ideal mix for a planned dive. A nitrox diver should NEVER enter the water without having independently established for him or herself the oxygen content of the nitrox mix they are using. The dive shop or supplier will measure and record the oxygen content of the mix when the diver's cylinder is filled, but if they are doing their job correctly, they will compel the diver to analyze the mix themselves and to log the results before taking the cylinder out of the shop.

Analysis for oxygen content is performed using devices with a galvanic cell as the central component. These cells produce an electrical current that is linearly proportional to the PO_2 in the gas to which they are exposed. The current is measured, electronically processed, and the result displayed as % oxygen content. The galvanic cells themselves cannot be turned off, and will last between 1 – 4 years. The devices are small and portable (see Figure 28.2), but not cheap, costing several hundreds of dollars. Replacement cells are also relatively expensive. It is not necessary for the nitrox diver to own an analyzer, since any shop supplying nitrox should have one available for the diver to check his or her mix. However, at least one personal analyzer is absolutely mandatory for any nitrox diver who blends his or her own mixes. Mathematics and meticulous mixing alone should never be relied upon to have produced the anticipated mix.

FIGURE 28.2

Oxygen analyzer showing connection to DIN fixed flow rate adapter. The adapter is attached to the cylinder to be analysed, and gas flows at a standardized rate to the analyzer.

The protocol used for oxygen analysis is important since variations in technique can produce different results. The correct method involves exposing the cell sensor to a measured and constant flow of nitrox using a flow rate adapter or similar as shown in Figure 28.2. A flow of 2 – 4lpm is recommended. The analyzer is exposed to air first and after approximately 2 minutes it is calibrated to read 20.9% (the exact fraction of oxygen in air). The analyzer is then exposed to the nitrox at exactly the same flow rate and for the same period of time, after which the reading is taken. Most protocols recommend then re-exposing the analyzer to air just to ensure that a reading of 20.9% is obtained again (thereby ensuring that the calibration did not "slip").

SUMMARY

Nitrox diving is a technique designed to reduce nitrogen absorption and therefore to extend allowable time underwater, rather than to extend depth. Indeed, as will have been appreciated from the discussion of oxygen toxicity, nitrox diving actually limits depth in comparison with air diving.

The use of nitrox is an important first step into the world of technical diving for several reasons. First, many of the related hazards (such as oxygen toxicity), and principles (such as maximum operating depths, the oxygen clock, and gas analysis) are highly relevant to other more advanced technical diving techniques. Second, many of these more advanced techniques incorporate the use of nitrox for various reasons, such as accelerated decompression during decompression diving (see below). Not surprisingly, a thorough grounding in the use of nitrox is vital for any aspiring technical diver.

- Nitrox diving refers to the use of nitrogen-oxygen mixtures that contain more oxygen than air.

- The advantages of nitrox diving include: reduced uptake of nitrogen and longer no decompression limits; accelerated elimination of nitrogen; and possibly a reduction in nitrogen narcosis.

- The disadvantages of nitrox diving include: an increased potential for oxygen toxicity and consequent limitation on depth; the need for oxygen cleanliness in equipment, increased costs.

- The most important safety consideration in nitrox diving is understanding how to calculate the maximum operating depth for nitrox mixes, and how to manage safe duration of oxygen exposures ("the oxygen clock").

- The most common means of making nitrox is "partial pressure blending" in which oxygen and air are mixed in appropriate proportions.

- Nitrox divers should own their own oxygen analyzer for checking the fraction of oxygen in their mix. This is mandatory if they blend their own nitrox.

REFERENCES

1. Harris RJ, Doolette DJ, Wilkinson DC, Williams DJ. Measurement of fatigue following 18msw dry chamber dives breathing air or enriched air nitrox. *Undersea Hyperb Med* 2003;30(4):285-91.

2. Bennett PB, Rostain JC. Inert gas narcosis. In: Brubakk AO, Neuman TS (Eds). Bennett and Elliott's Physiology and Medicine of Diving (5th ed). London: Harcourt Publishers; 2003: 300-22.

© Dr. Richard Harris

29

Technical diving techniques 2 - Configuration of equipment for longer dives

Both nitrox diving and the other technical diving methods that are yet to be discussed may involve much longer underwater durations than would be possible with the equipment configuration employed by most scuba divers. Therefore, before moving on to a discussion of other techniques, it is logical to briefly consider the changes in equipment configuration used by technical divers to extend their underwater duration.

EXTENDING GAS SUPPLY

The most obvious equipment requirement for longer duration diving is the prolongation of the diver's breathing gas supply. The most frequently encountered cylinders used in recreational diving are aluminium, and have a working pressure of 207ATA and water capacity of 11.2L. We can use *Equation 1* to show the duration of such a cylinder when used at 20m (66ft) (ambient pressure = 3ATA) during gentle swimming (assuming a SAC of 20lpm) and allowing for a 50ATA reserve.

Duration
= ([207ATA – 50ATA] x 11.2L)
÷ (20 lpm x 3ATA)
= 29 minutes

If we then refer to the example we worked when discussing *Equation 6*, we note that the no decompression limit for a diver using nitrox 40 at 20m (66ft) is 100 minutes. Thus, the use of nitrox 40 allows us a no decompression limit of 100 minutes, but the typical scuba tank allows us somewhat less than 30 minutes at that depth when the time required for ascent and descent is considered. This is quite a discrepancy. There seems little point in using a nitrox mix that allows three times the bottom time at our target depth than our nitrox supply would allow. How can we fix this problem? If we ignore the possibility of using rebreather technology (which is discussed later) then the obvious way of achieving this is to carry more gas using larger cylinders, more cylinders, or more large cylinders!

Cylinder size and pressure

There are a myriad of cylinders made from both aluminium and steel, with various water capacities and pressure ratings. Discussing the entire range is beyond the scope of this chapter. However, high capacity steel cylinders with a slightly higher pressure rating than the most frequently encountered aluminium recreational cylinders are popular with technical divers. Steel cylinders with a working pressure of 232ATA and water capacity of up to 18L are readily available. The compressed gas capacity of such cylinders is therefore 232ATA x 18L = 4176L. This compares with the aluminium cylinders described in the above paragraph (working pressure of 207ATA and water capacity of

11.2L) which hold 207ATA x 11.2L = 2318L of compressed gas. The combination of a higher working pressure and higher internal volume therefore vastly increases the compressed gas capacity of a cylinder. Using *Equation 1* and the same relevant parameters described in the above example, we can show that an 18L cylinder filled to 232ATA will provide a duration of 54 minutes at 20m (66ft). Thus;

Duration
= ([232ATA – 50ATA] x 18.0L)
*   ÷ (20lpm x 3ATA)*
= 54 minutes

This contrasts with the 29 minutes we calculated for the 11.2L aluminium cylinder earlier. It must be remembered that the larger high volume cylinders, particularly those made from steel, are negatively buoyant when full. An 18L steel cylinder exerts almost 6kg (13lbs) of negative buoyancy when full of air, and this would obviously double to 12kg (26lbs) if two were carried. Moreover, when empty, each 18L cylinder exerts only 1kg (2.2lbs) of negative buoyancy, and this potentially dramatic change must be considered when divers configure their weight. These buoyancy considerations have prompted some technical divers to discourage the use of steel cylinders, particularly as sling tanks (see below), but such a prohibition seems unnecessary provided adequate buoyancy control skills are exhibited.

It is appropriate while discussing cylinders to mention that the use of DIN ("Deutsche Industrie Norme") fittings is recommended for all regulator-to-cylinder couplings in technical diving. The difference between DIN couplings and the more familiar yoke clamp couplings that are commonly used in conventional recreational diving is illustrated in Figure 29.1. DIN couplings have a screw-in male fitting on the regulator that completely traps the O ring inside the female fitting on the tank valve. This makes it much less likely that a tank valve O ring will "blow" during the course of a dive if, for example,

the regulator first stage gets knocked. This is considered very important for all cylinders in technical dives that involve decompression, and especially where high-pressure cylinders are used.

FIGURE 29.1

The difference between DIN (left) and yoke (right) couplings (see text for explanation).

Twin sets

Technical divers frequently utilize two back mounted cylinders instead of the conventional single cylinder. Each cylinder has its own regulator and independent submersible pressure gauge, and used most commonly in technical diving, twin cylinders are "manifolded" (see Figure 29.2). This means that the two cylinders are linked by a manifold so that they potentially form one large common gas supply. There are 3 isolation valves in the system: a pillar valve on each cylinder and an isolation valve in the middle of the manifold. In this arrangement, turning off the pillar valve on one of the cylinders isolates the regulator on that side, not the gas in the cylinder. Thus, if the left hand pillar valve is turned off, the left hand regulator is isolated and cannot be used, but the right hand regulator still draws gas from both cylinders. If the manifold isolation valve is closed, then the system is effectively reduced to two separate scuba sets.

FIGURE 29.2

Diver wearing manifolded twinset.
Note the regulator on each cylinder valve, with the manifold and isolation valve between.

The reason for this arrangement is to maximize redundancy while coping with common scuba system failures. For example, if the left hand regulator free flows, then it can be isolated by closing the left hand pillar valve without limiting access to the gas contained in the left hand cylinder. More serious but much less common would be failure of a pillar valve O-ring or burst disk. If this were to happen then the affected cylinder can be isolated using the manifold isolation valve. If this were necessary, the diver is then limited to one cylinder and one regulator.

One of the regulator second stages in a manifolded twin set should have a long hose for the purpose of air sharing should this be needed. It has been a subject of great debate among divers, technical or otherwise, whether the air donor should donate the second stage which they are breathing from (in which case they should routinely breathe from the long hose), or whether they should retain their primary second stage and donate their secondary which is normally fixed in a convenient position on their equipment. In the latter scenario, the donor would breathe from their short hose second stage and fix the long hose second stage ready for donation. We will not address the complexities of this debate in this short summary.

Sling tanks

Twin sets effectively double the volume of gas that can be carried conveniently on the back. In some technical diving situations this still might not be sufficient, or alternatively, different gas mixtures might need to be carried to allow accelerated decompression (see decompression diving). With the capacity for carrying back mounted gas fully utilized, the next option is to use sling tanks.

Sling tanks are usually single scuba cylinders, each with its own independent regulator and submersible pressure gauge. The latter are usually held out of the way but ready for use by rubber straps (see Figure 29.3). They are usually attached to either or both sides of the diver using snap clips to D rings on the diver's harness or BCD (see Figure 29.4). Cylinders of any size can be used, depending on the diver's gas requirements and ability to cope with the extra equipment bulk.

FIGURE 29.3

An example of a typical sling tank for carrying extra gas (in this case nitrox).

FIGURE 29.4

Diver wearing sling tanks.

Perhaps the most important issue with respect to the use of sling tanks is clear labeling and consistent positioning, especially where they are used to carry different gases for different purposes. For example, a diver might conduct a prolonged decompression dive to 40m (132ft) using nitrox 28 in back mounted cylinders, but carrying a sling tank of nitrox 40 to be used during the ascent and stops between 30 and 6m (100 and 20ft), and a sling tank of nitrox 80 or pure oxygen to use for the shallow decompression stops. These changes to progressively higher oxygen mixes will accelerate decompression (see decompression diving below), but they also introduce a hazard. Consider for example, what might happen if the diver mistakenly began to breathe nitrox 80 instead of the nitrox 40 at 30m (100ft). *Equation 2* allows us to calculate the PO_2 the diver would be breathing:

PO_2 = 4ATA (ambient pressure at 30m /
100ft) x 0.8 (fraction of oxygen)
= 3.2ATA

This is a very high PO_2 and would be highly likely to induce a seizure if the mistake was not detected and rectified very quickly. Many technical divers have died as a result of mistakes like this. *Therefore, the nature of the gas contained in the tank and its MOD should be clearly displayed in the view of any accompanying divers.* Moreover, the diver (and his or her regular buddies) should adopt a policy of wearing similar gases on the same side consistently. For example, some divers always place the most oxygen rich mix on the left. It is also a good idea to colour code the sling tank second stages for the gas type in the tank.

Another hazard of carrying pressurized open circuit scuba systems that are not in constant use is that the regulator might free flow, perhaps without the diver being aware, thereby causing loss of some or all of the gas. For this reason, it is usually recommended that sling tank systems are turned on pre-dive, but then shut off at the tank valve until utilized.

EXTENDING THERMAL DURATION

There is little use in carrying sufficient gas for prolonged dives if thermal protection is inadequate to allow that gas supply to be fully exploited. While such issues are fairly obvious in temperate and many fresh water situations, cold can be a problem even in the tropics during deep dives when thermoclines may be encountered. The anticipated temperature and selection of appropriate thermal protection is an important aspect of technical dive planning.

Wetsuits may be adequate in some tropical situations, but drysuits coupled with an appropriate undergarment are frequently used for long technical dives. Gas for drysuit inflation must be drawn from one of the cylinders carried by the diver. If the dive involves the use of helium mixtures (see mixed gas diving) then a mix containing helium should not be used for drysuit inflation since helium readily conducts heat and will reduce the efficiency of the dry suit. Air is a reasonable choice, and some divers even carry a small cylinder of argon for dry suit inflation since argon has very good insulating properties. However, skin and core temperature measurements and diver opinion recorded in a blinded study of argon versus air as a dry suit inflation gas during cold water diving failed to demonstrate any advantage for argon.[1] Divers will have to form their own opinions on whether or not the theoretical advantages of argon are worth the extra trouble of carrying a special cylinder.

One problem of an extended period in a drysuit is urine. It is a well-known fact that despite the pathetic denials of many, all divers except the authors urinate in their wetsuits. A drysuit is another matter entirely. The reportedly pleasant suffusion of warmth as urine circulates around a wetsuit is unlikely to be as satisfying in a drysuit. Interestingly, most drysuit divers report that they are less likely to "need to go" than if they were wearing a wetsuit, and this makes some physiological sense. But given sufficient time, anyone's "capacity" is likely to be tested.

Solutions to this potentially unpleasant problem include the wearing of adult size absorbent nappies, or for males, the use of urine disposal devices. One version is best described as a condom connected by a tube to a collecting bag. These are often used for patients with mobility impairments and are available from most comprehensively stocked pharmacies. Alternatively, in some drysuits, the tube vents directly to the sea through a "pee valve" that can be opened and closed.

SUMMARY

- The extension of no decompression limits afforded by nitrox diving, and the extra duration required by decompression diving (see below) necessitate the carriage of a larger gas supply than provided by single cylinder scuba.

- This can be achieved by carrying larger cylinders, cylinders filled to a higher pressures, and multiple cylinders.

- The most common means of carrying multiple cylinders is the manifolded twin cylinder configuration, supplemented if necessary by extra cylinders carried as "sling tanks".

- Thermal protection must also be enhanced for longer dives in cool water, and this is best achieved by the use of a drysuit.

REFERENCE:

1. Risberg J, Hope A. Thermal insulation properties of argon used as a dry suit inflation gas. *Undersea and Hyperb Med* 2001;28(3):137-43.

© Dr. Richard Harris

30

Technical diving techniques 3 - Decompression diving

Training agencies in the recreational diving industry emphasize the difference between "decompression diving" (requiring decompression stops) and "no-decompression diving" (not requiring decompression stops). In reality, these terms are terrible misnomers since **all diving is decompression diving**. The ascent from a so-called "no-decompression" dive, although not requiring stops, is "decompression" by any other name, and unfortunately the "no-decompression" label tends to trivialize the importance of performing the ascent correctly. Make no mistake, "no-decompression" dives in the 20 – 36m (66-120ft) range that are not complicated by any obvious procedural problems have still produced serious cases of DCS. The correct ascent procedure from these dives is critically important. Having fired that salvo of pent up philosophical dogma, we acknowledge that the intention of the term "decompression diving" is to identify those dives whose time – depth envelope necessitates the performance of mandatory "decompression stops" during the ascent, and in the interests of consistency we'll stick with the terminology.

A quick look at Table 27.2 reveals that the maximum bottom time allowable at the deeper depths before decompression stops are mandatory becomes progressively shorter. Indeed, at depths below 40m / 130ft it becomes virtually impossible to perform dives that do not require stops. In addition,

even at the shallower depths, there are many reasons why an extended bottom time might be desirable, and this may require performing a "decompression dive".

Though self-apparent, it must be emphasized that the moment decompression stops become necessary, the option of ascending "directly" to the surface in a reasonably timely manner has been removed. It follows that the essence of decompression diving is the planning and safe execution of decompression stops. If these stops are not conducted properly, the risk of DCS rises in proportion to the degree of omitted decompression. In electing to perform decompression dives, the diver must therefore commit him or herself to a new level of meticulous planning and preparation to minimize the chances of complications.

PLANNING DECOMPRESSION DIVES

Performed properly, decompression dives are a complex business, and perhaps the best means of illustrating the important elements of the process is by example.

Lets assume we plan to dive to 45m (150ft) for 30 minutes using air throughout. Before any seasoned "tekkies" blow their hernia, we do unreservedly acknowledge that most modern technical divers would never conduct a decompression dive using air only. Instead, they would include changes to progressively richer nitrox mixes during the ascent to accelerate decompression. This practice will be discussed later. However, air decompression diving was prevalent in the not too distant past, and is still practiced by some. Moreover, for the purposes of illustrating some of the principles of decompression diving it is simpler to consider an air dive initially, and to return to gas switching for accelerated decompression later.

Planning the time and depth of stops

Even when we intend carrying a dive computer that will compute decompression stops in real time during the dive, we must plan the time, depth, and stop profile in advance. Once this is done, we can move on to plan the appropriate amount of air to carry and strategies for managing our air supply during the dive. Planning the profile usually begins with "looking up the dive" on a set of tables to establish the required stops. Table 30.1 shows the decompression requirements for our 45m (150ft) air dive

taken from the US Navy and DCIEM Air Diving Tables, and from a computer based decompression program called Proplanner® (Delta P Technology, UK) which is based on the Buhlmann decompression algorithms.

As you can see, there is a significant degree of variation in these decompression protocols. The US Navy is clearly less conservative than the other two. This does not indicate that it is inferior (or superior for that matter), but merely that its designers are prepared to tolerate a higher inherent risk of a diver developing DCS. A diver wishing to minimize their risk might choose one of the more conservative algorithms. In view of this variation between profiles, it is important that if a dive computer is going to be used to control the dive on the day, then the same tables on which the computer is based should be used for the pre-planning. For example, if you planned your required gas supply based on the US Navy Tables, and then controlled the actual dive using a computer based on Proplanner, you might find yourself running short of air during the ascent. For the purpose of this exercise, we will run with the Proplanner algorithm.

TABLE 30.1

Decompression stops prescribed by the US Navy and DCIEM tables, and Proplanner software for a 30 minute dive to 45m (150ft) using air throughout.

Stop depth *(m)*	USN	DCIEM	Proplanner*
28	Nil	Nil	1
20	Nil	Nil	1
12	Nil	6	3
9	Nil	7	6
6	8	9	15
3	24	35	30

For clarity, we present this example using metric stop depths only. There may be trivial variation in the algorithm for imperial depths.
* Proplanner Version 7.12C.
  Safety = 10%, microbubble = 20% (this setting was chosen, rather the bare algorithm with no conservatism added, as it is commonly used in the field.).

Checking the bottom gas

We have planned to use air throughout the dive. One of the first things the decompression diver must do is to ask "is my intended bottom gas appropriate?" It's the oxygen and nitrogen content that are important.

We must first check that the oxygen content will not be too high at our maximum depth. In other words, the MOD for air must be deeper than our intended depth. We have previously agreed that despite debate over the most appropriate limit, we will always try to avoid a PO_2 higher than 1.4ATA in order to prevent cerebral oxygen toxicity. With this in mind, we can use *Equation 3* to calculate the MOD for air as follows:

(1.4 [maximum PO₂] ÷ 0.21 [fraction of oxygen in air]) – 1) x 10 = 57m (188ft)

Our planned depth of 45m (150ft) is safely within the 57m (188ft) MOD for air.

In addition, we must also ensure that our total dose of oxygen does not exceed our maximum exposure limit. This would be very unlikely during air diving, but it is a good habit to become accustomed to. To do this we must first calculate the exact PO_2 we will be breathing at 45m (150ft). This is achieved using *Equation 2* as follows:

0.21 (fraction of oxygen in air)
x 5.5ATA (ambient pressure at 45m/150ft)
= 1.16ATA

If we now refer to Table 28.2, we see that the maximum exposure limit for a PO_2 of 1.2ATA (rounded up from 1.16) is 210 minutes. Our planned bottom time of 30 minutes is well within this maximum. Indeed, using equation 5, we can calculate our percentage of the maximum exposure limit as follows:

30 min (time breathing PO₂ 1.2ATA)
÷ 210 min (maximum limit) x 100
= 15%

Using air, we will contribute very little to our oxygen exposure during the ascent and decompression stops, and no further calculations are necessary. However, if we were changing to nitrox to accelerate our decompression during our stops (see later), then this would need to be taken into account.

We must also satisfy ourselves that we will not suffer intolerable narcosis on the proposed dive. For an air dive this is a fairly simple issue since air is the benchmark most divers are used to, and most experienced divers have a feel for their tolerance to narcosis at various depths while using it. There is great debate among technical diving agencies about an appropriate depth limit for air diving based on concerns about narcosis. Some suggest that 30m (100ft) is the maximum whilst others consider narcosis levels to be manageable while using air to depths around 45 – 50m (150-165ft). Almost everyone agrees that beyond 50m (165ft) it is most appropriate to use mixed gases (see later) to avoid excessive narcosis.

So, we have established that the exposures to both oxygen and nitrogen during our proposed air dive to 45m (150ft) for 30 minutes are acceptable, and we know what stops will be required during the ascent. Next comes the slightly more tricky business of calculating how much gas we should carry for the dive.

Planning gas supplies

Discovering that there is insufficient gas to complete decompression half way through the decompression is a decidedly unpleasant and dangerous experience, and one that is to be avoided at all costs. Planning is the key to avoiding such a situation. It must be pointed out that gas management planning strategies vary, and there are many combinations and permutations of dive scenarios that determine exactly which strategy will be adopted. The finer points of this process are best learned in a comprehensive technical diving course and by diving with experienced technical divers. However, one approach is detailed here to give the reader an appreciation of the factors involved, and some of the problems and pitfalls.

We already have most of the information required to plan our gas supply for our 45m (150ft) air dive, but there is one vital piece missing; our air consumption rate. Unfortunately, gas consumption underwater is so exquisitely sensitive to a variety of "unplannable" factors (mainly exercise levels) that it becomes highly debatable whether a formal measurement is of any more use than a rough estimate. Nevertheless, *some* basis for a plan is almost certainly better than *no* basis, and at early stage in their careers most technical divers therefore perform an experiment to estimate their gas consumption during normal underwater finning. Frequently, a similar experiment is performed during rest in order to simulate a decompression simulation. Let's take a little time out from our dive plan to describe how it is done.

Whilst diving, choose an area of still water and constant depth. Record the cylinder water capacity, exact cylinder pressure and the depth. Keeping depth constant, move around the bottom at normal dive speed for exactly 10 minutes and record the cylinder pressure again. Beware that there is a tendency to exaggerate speed during these experiments, which will result in overestimation of gas consumption. For consumption at rest, the experiment is the same except that the diver remains in the one spot for 10 minutes. Using the data gathered in this experiment, your air consumption can be calculated using *Equation 8*. Note that the equation converts air consumption at depth to an equivalent at the surface (surface air consumption or "SAC") since this is the form in which it is easiest to use in planning subsequent dives.

EQUATION 8

$$SAC = \frac{([P_{start} - P_{end}] \times WC) \div P_{amb}}{Duration}$$

where:
SAC = surface air consumption in lpm
P_{start} = cylinder pressure at start of 10 minutes in ATAs
P_{end} = cylinder pressure at end of 10 minutes in ATAs
WC = cylinder water capacity in litres
P_{amb} = ambient pressure in ATAs ([depth ÷ 10] + 1) for metric or ([depth ÷ 33] + 1) for imperial
Duration = duration of experiment in minutes

For example, assume we conduct a finning experiment at a depth of 10m (33ft) using a cylinder of 11.2L water capacity. The cylinder pressures are 180ATA at the start and 145ATA at the end. Using *Equation 8*, our surface air consumption is given by:

$$\frac{([180 - 145] \times 11.2) \div 2}{10} = 19.6lpm$$

We will round this figure to 20lpm, and we will also assume that we performed a resting experiment that showed our resting SAC to be 12lpm.

Be aware that hard finning, against a current for example, could easily cause our 20lpm SAC to balloon to twice as much or, considerably more.

So, lets go back to planning the air requirements for our 45m (150ft)/ 30 minute air dive using the Proplanner decompression algorithm, and SACs of 20lpm finning and 12lpm resting.

Unfortunately, it's a bit laborious and we must break the dive down into stages. If we start with the bottom time (which includes descent), we plan to spend 30 minutes at

45m (150ft). From our air consumption experiment we know that for each minute of normal finning at the surface we consume 20L of air, but we also know that at 45m (150ft) where the ambient pressure is 5.5ATA, the air supplied by the regulator will be 5.5 times as dense. Therefore, our SAC must be multiplied by 5.5 in order to calculate our actual gas consumption at 45m (150ft) Thus, 5.5 x 20 indicates a gas consumption of 110lpm, and for our 30 minutes period we will require 30 x 110 = 3300L. Most divers do not try to account for the slower gas consumption at shallower depths during the period of descent. Assuming the entire bottom time is actually spent on the bottom is the most conservative approach.

This calculation is summarized in equation 9 as follows:

EQUATION 9

Gas required for period at depth (L)
= Duration x SAC x P_{amb}

where:

Duration = length of period in minutes

SAC = surface air consumption rate in lpm

P_{amb} = ambient pressure in ATAs ([depth ÷ 10*] + 1)

* or 33 for imperial

Next there is the ascent and decompression stops. Our first stop (see Table 30.1) is at 28m, an ascent of 17m from the bottom at 45m (150ft). At an ascent rate of 9m (30ft) / min this initial ascent will take us 2 minutes. By convention (and to be conservative) the gas consumption for ascents between stops are usually calculated as though the ascent time was spent at the depth you just left. In other words, in this example we would consider ascent to the first stop to be another 2 minutes at 45m (150ft), and our air requirement for this ascent according to equation 9 is therefore 2 x 20 x 5.5 = 220L.

The first stop is at 28m for 1 minute. Now that we are established in what is hopefully a restful decompression routine, we will revert to using our resting SAC of 12lpm. We are at an ambient pressure of 3.8ATA and the duration of the stop is 1 minute. However, as previously, we must also add time for the next phase of our ascent (which we will treat as though we spent it at 28m). Where the ascent is 9m or less, adding 1 minute is standard. Our next stop is at 20m; an ascent of 8m. So we will add a minute to our time at 28m to account for this ascent. Using *Equation 9* our air requirement for this stop is therefore 2 x 12 x 3.8 = 92L.

It is convenient to construct a table for the performance of these calculations. Table 30.2 shows the required air supply calculations for the entire dive as prescribed by the decompression algorithm derived from Proplanner (see Table 30.1).

From Table 30.2 we can see that a total of 4742L of air will be required for our dive. However, a diver would be very unwise indeed to carry only the required amount of air, and a significant reserve must be built into our calculations. There are various regimens for determining reserve gas supplies, but one that widely pervades the technical diving world is the so-called "Rule of Thirds". This arose from cave diving, and dictates that the diver should use one third of the gas supply heading into the cave, one third coming out, leaving one third in reserve. It is less clearly applicable in decompression diving because the long slow ascent means that the dive is not symmetrical. Nevertheless, the notion that you should end your dive with a third of your gas in reserve has carried over into many technical diving activities. Applying the rule of thirds to our air dive means that we would want our planned air use of 4742L to constitute approximately 2/3 of our total air supply, which would therefore be about 1.5 x 4742 = 7113L.

TABLE 30.2

Calculation of air requirements for a 45m (150ft) dive for 30 minutes, decompressing according to a Proplanner algorithm (see Table 29.1) and assuming a SAC of 20lpm for quiet finning and 12lpm for resting during decompression. For clarity, we present this example using only metric depths.

Depth (m)	Duration (min)		Ascent time		Total duration		SAC (lpm)		P_{amb} (ATA)		Air required (L)
45	30	+	2	=	32	x	20	x	5.5	=	3520
28	1	+	1	=	2	x	12	x	3.8	=	92
20	1	+	1	=	2	x	12	x	3.0	=	72
12	3	+	1	=	4	x	12	x	2.2	=	106
9	6	+	1	=	7	x	12	x	1.9	=	160
6	15	+	1	=	16	x	12	x	1.6	=	308
3	30	+	1	=	31	x	12	x	1.3	=	484

Total duration of dive = **94**   Total air required = **4742**

To make the calculations relatively easy, and since a large safety margin is already built in, we'll round this down to 7000L. How should this 7000L of air be carried? The loss of the option to make a safe direct ascent to the surface during decompression diving means that every practical precaution must be taken to avoid having that situation forced upon us. The most important precautions in this regard focus on ensuring adequate gas supply (as we have calculated) and redundancy in critical equipment. For this reason, even if it were possible to carry 7000L of air in a single cylinder (which it is not), we would not plan to use a single cylinder on a decompression dive because of the inherent lack of redundancy in the event of regulator failure. A practical configuration for this dive would be a manifolded set of twin steel cylinders of 15L water capacity filled to 232ATA. This would provide just under 7000L of air (15 x 232 = 6960L to be precise), and the inherent redundancy in a manifolded twin system as described earlier. Again, this slight rounding down is very small in relation to the 1/3 safety margin we are building in.

A plan for managing our gas supply during the dive must be developed, and this must include determination of a gas pressure that, once reached, will mandate termination of bottom time, irrespective of whether the planned period at the bottom has been completed or not.

How do we estimate this pressure? Well, we want to ensure that we leave the bottom before we use more of our gas volume than budgeted for in our plan (Table 30.2). This volume can be calculated using *Equation 9*, and in the case of our air dive, this is done as follows:

30 min (duration) x 20lpm (SAC)
x 5.5ATA (P_{amb})
= 3300L

The corresponding cylinder pressure at which bottom time should be terminated can be calculated using *Equation 10*.

EQUATION **10**

Termination pressure
$= P_{cyl} - ([BG_{vol} \div TOT_{vol}] \times P_{cyl})$

where:

Termination pressure = minimum pressure
at which bottom time should be
terminated in ATAs

BG_{vol} = planned consumption of bottom gas
in litres

TOT_{vol} = total gas carried
(to allow 1/3 reserve) in litres

P_{cyl} = cylinder pressure when full in ATA

Assuming we opted for the cylinder configuration described above, we can therefore use *Equation 10* to calculate this pressure for our air dive as follows:

Termination pressure
= 232 − ([3300L ÷ 6960] x 232)
= 122ATA

In other words, we should monitor our underwater activities and location relative to the down line in order to arrive back at the line and leave the bottom by the time our pressure reaches 122ATA.

For completeness, buddies should be aware of each other's gas supplies and capabilities for mutual support in the event of one having a gas supply failure during the dive. In our example (see Table 30.2) we can see that the decompression after the full 30 minutes bottom time requires 1442L of air (if you try to add this up remember that 2 of the 32 minutes duration shown on the table at 45m (150ft) was actually spent making the first part of the ascent). Assuming that our buddy has the same gas consumption and equipment configuration, we can see that our plan to leave 1/3 of the total gas supply (1/3 x 6960 L =2320 L) remaining at the end of the dive means that either of us would have sufficient air to share to the surface from any point in the dive. The 2320L "reserve" we carry is greater than the 1442L required for another diver to make the ascent (provided their SAC is the same as ours). However, if we were more than a few minutes swim from the down line when the failure occurred, too much time and air may be lost trying to regain the down line and a very difficult air sharing ascent on a lift bag and reel (see later) might be necessary.

USING GAS SWITCHES TO ACCELERATE DECOMPRESSION

It must be reiterated that while our 45m (150ft) / 30 minute air dive provided an uncomplicated template for explaining various principles of decompression planning, few if any modern technical divers would actually conduct an air decompression dive. This is because one of the great and accessible advantages of learning to use nitrox is its application in accelerating decompression from dives like this. Breathing a mix with a higher oxygen content during decompression increases the gradient for diffusion of nitrogen out of tissues, into the blood, and to the lungs for elimination. The steeper this gradient, the more rapid the elimination of nitrogen, and the faster the decompression.

There are two examples that we should consider to illustrate these principles. First, lets see how much decompression would be required if we used air as the bottom gas as before, but changed to nitrox 80 (a frequently used decompression gas) during the decompression. Second, let's also perform the same dive using nitrox as the bottom gas in addition to using nitrox 80 during the decompression. For both examples, we need to calculate the depth at which it is safe to change to nitrox 80 during the decompression (assuming as before that we wish to avoid a PO_2 higher than 1.4ATA). We can use *Equation 3* to calculate the MOD for nitrox 80 as follows:

(1.4 [maximum PO_2] ÷ 0.80 [fraction of oxygen in Nx80]) − 1) x 10

= 7.5m (25ft)

Thus, it would be safe to change to nitrox 80 at the 6m (20ft) stop. We should mention for completeness that most technical divers would consider it reasonable to use nitrox 80 at 9m (30ft) (PO_2 = 1.52) for a short duration during the restful phase of a decompression, but for the purpose of our examples we will remain consistent with the "safe" PO_2 of 1.4.

For the second example, (using nitrox as the bottom gas), we need to calculate the ideal mix for a depth of 45m (150ft) so that the PO_2 does not exceed 1.4. We can use Equation 4 to calculate the fraction of oxygen in the ideal mix as follows:

1.4 (maximum PO_2) ÷ 5.5 (ambient pressure at target depth)

= 0.25

Thus, we can use nitrox 25 for this dive. Table 30.3 shows the decompression requirements for these two new scenarios calculated using Proplanner software. Our previous dive conducted on air throughout is included for comparison.

It is clear that the decompression is markedly shorter on both dives where nitrox is used. Use of the two nitrox mixes (regimen number 3) shaves almost half an hour off the decompression hang, and any decompression diver will attest to how such savings in time are appreciated. On longer deeper mixed gas dives (see later) the savings in time become even greater. Indeed, such dives would not be practical without several gas mix changes to accelerate decompression.

TABLE 30.3

Decompression from a 45m (150ft) dive for 30 minutes using 3 different gas regimens: 1 = air throughout (as previous); 2 = air to the 6m (20ft) stop, then changing to nitrox 80; 3 = nitrox 25 to the 6m (20ft) stop then changing to nitrox 80. Note that for the purposes of calculating total dive time, 8 minutes of travel time between stops has been added.
(Proplanner version 7.12C: safety factor 10%; microbubble factor 20%.)

Stop depth (m)	1. Air throughout		2. Air then Nx80		3. Nx25 then Nx80	
	Gas	Time	Gas	Time	Gas	Time
Bottom	Air	30	Air	30	Nx25	30
28	Air	1	Air	1	Nx25	1
20	Air	1	Air	1	Nx25	1
12	Air	3	Air	3	Nx25	1
9	Air	6	Air	6	Nx25	5
6	Air	15	Nx80	7	Nx80	6
3	Air	30	Nx80	14	Nx80	12
Travel		8		8		8
	Total =	94	Total =	70	Total =	64

Of course, the use of one or more progressively richer nitrox mixes for accelerated decompression introduces several new complexities to the dive.

In the planning stages, the accumulated oxygen dose arising from using enriched oxygen mixes during the decompression must be calculated to ensure that the accumulated exposure does not exceed the allowable maximum. For example, when planning the regimen 3 dive in Table 30.3, we would use *Equation 5* to calculate the % of maximum exposure accrued during the bottom time and each of decompression stops, and these percentages would be added together to give the total % of maximum exposure. The working is not shown here, but the total is approximately 35%, and this dive is therefore well within tolerance for oxygen exposure.

Gas supply calculations like those in Table 30.2 would be made for both gases to ensure that enough was carried to complete the dive and decompression, with a suitable reserve remaining. The bottom gas (nitrox 25) would be carried in a back mounted manifolded twin set, and the decompression gas would most likely be carried in a sling tank (see Figure 29.3) and clearly marked to avoid using the wrong gas at the wrong time.

Finally, we would like to reiterate our earlier observation that there are many opinions on such issues as choice of gases and decompression algorithms, gas planning, and other aspects of the diving we have described above. We emphasize that the dive planning steps we have outlined above are an example of process, not a statement of best practice. Technical diving novices training under various agencies may well be advised differently with regard to specifics, but the dive planning processes will be similar.

EQUIPMENT LOGISTICS

Moving away from our specific example above, it is appropriate to discuss aspects of equipment logistics for a "generic" decompression dive.

Equipment configuration

Various authorities have produced voluminous and frequently dogmatic accounts of the way equipment should be configured during decompression diving and technical diving in general. It is not uncommon to encounter sub-groups of divers who will simply not tolerate dissenting views on this issue. Such dogma is usually justified on the basis that commonality is an important issue for team function and safety, and this argument has merit. However, some divers take the equally legitimate view that individual variations based on personal needs and the type of diving being conducted are inevitable and need not detract from the successful operation of a dive team. It is a complex issue that is best discussed in detail with an experienced instructor.

We discussed the typical configuration of twin sets and sling tanks for carriage of bottom gas and decompression gases earlier. There are a few other generic points that can be made regarding equipment configuration for a decompression dive.

It is very important to establish a configuration that is as neat, tidy and orderly as possible. Decompression divers are frequently cluttered with all manner of equipment. There is a real risk of some items getting tangled with others, and of the diver behaving like a piece of mobile underwater "velcro" tape as exposed hoses and sundry items get caught on everything they swim past. This is a particular danger on wrecks. It follows that every attempt should be made to rationalize the items carried without compromising practical redundancy, and to streamline the equipment that is carried without compromising accessibility and utility. Almost every diver can tidy up their "hose runs" if they take a critical look at their present set up. Hoses that balloon out to the side are just asking to get hooked up!

In a related manner, great importance is placed on adjusting the trim of the equipment "package" so that the diver naturally adopts an orientation in the water that minimizes drag and the effort required to swim. In particular, considerable effort is put into configuring the weight distribution of the "backplate and wings" set up on which twin back mounted cylinders are typically carried. Detailed discussion of the pertinent issues are beyond the scope of this chapter, but these issues would constitute an important part of the guidance provided by a good technical diving instructor.

The importance of keeping the hands free during critical phases of the dive such as the descent and ascent cannot be overemphasized. Divers should not carry equipment like cameras in their hands during these periods because if there are any problems they may be very difficult to deal with one-handed. Quick release clips and other fastening devices are available for attaching extraneous equipment to harnesses.

Redundant equipment

There are several items of equipment other than the gas supply (discussed above) where redundancy is considered important.

The buoyancy control device (BCD) is an important example. In technical diving this is frequently not the typical jacket style BCD utilized in recreational diving, but more likely a "wing" style device which is incorporated into the cylinder harness system, but does not come over the shoulders. Decompression often involves carrying multiple cylinders of gas, particularly where there are gas changes during decompression. The weight of equipment in some cases is such that were the wing to fail, then the diver might struggle to leave the bottom, especially if not wearing a dry suit (which itself can be inflated). For this reason, many technical divers wear dual bladder wings with independent inflation systems. These are more expensive, but they only have to get you out of one tight situation to be more than worth the cost.

The size of individual wing bladder systems is also important given that a technical diver may carry a large twinset on the back and several large sling tanks on their sides. It would not be unusual for the negative buoyancy imposed when these systems are full to exceed 20kg (44lbs). This cannot be compensated merely by carrying less weight on the weight belt, because much of this negative buoyancy is lost when the tanks are "emptied" and the diver would be too "light" toward the end of the dive. The diver's BCD or wing must be able to hold sufficient volume to be able to compensate this extra weight at the beginning of the dive.

The diver should always have more than one means of monitoring their depth and time. Computers do fail occasionally, and if there are no alternative means of monitoring depth and time, the completion of an efficient decompression will be very difficult. Similarly, if using a computer to provide a decompression algorithm in real time, the diver should also carry some pre-written decompression tables (on a slate for example) for various likely combinations of time, depth and gas used. If the computer fails these can be used to control the ascent procedure.

Since loss of vision underwater is a potentially disastrous event especially on a decompression dive, some divers carry a redundant mask in a BCD pocket or around their neck (with the mask facing backwards). The latter position has the advantage that if the primary mask is lost, the spare can just be rotated to the front and cleared with a minimum of fuss. It may, however, tend to get in the way if carried around the neck. Some divers minimize the risk of losing their primary mask by wearing it with the strap underneath their hood.

Lines and buoys

A decompression dive should never ever take place in the absence of some sort of ascent line or reference. Ideally, there should be a buoyed line (often called a "down line") that passes as directly as possible down to the dive site. The divers will descend and ascend on this line. The buoy should be large enough to support several slightly negatively buoyant divers hanging on the line during decompression. Divers who make frequent decompression dives in areas where currents are strong often utilize a separate buoyed "decompression station" attached to the down line at about 12m (40ft). During ascent, they transfer onto the line leading to the decompression station, and then detach it from the anchored down line. Thus, the decompression station is now drifting free with the current and the divers do not have to hang on to a fixed down line as a current sweeps past. Sometimes the divers utilize horizontal decompression bars hanging at appropriate depths (e.g. 3, 6, and 9 metres/ 10, 20 and 30 feet) on a decompression station (see Figure 30.1). These are much easier to hang on to than a rope, and avoid the crowding problems that occur if several divers are trying to hang on a single rope at the same depth.

The practice of using the boat's anchor line as the descent / ascent / decompression line is strongly discouraged. In rough conditions the boat will whip its anchor line up and down in the water, often violently, and this makes safe decompression stops very difficult to conduct. In addition, if the boat is anchored with divers decompressing on the anchor line, then the options for responding to a situation such as one diver being swept away in a current, are very limited.

FIGURE 30.1

Two divers hanging comfortably side by side on a decompression station. Things would be much more difficult if they were trying to hang at the same depth on a single rope.

Miscellaneous equipment items for decompression diving

Decompression divers and technical divers in general are often innovative individuals and will develop or adapt various items of equipment for specific purposes. An aspiring technical diver will learn far more of these small but important "tricks of the trade" by spending time with experienced individuals than by reading superficial treatments of the subject in books! However, there are a few commonly used items that deserve mention.

1. **Reel and lift bag or diver surface marker buoy (DSMB).** Not all dives go according to plan, and an all too frequent complication of decompression dives is failure to make it back to the down line for the ascent. This forces the diver into making a highly dangerous ascent without a reference or support. To complete the required stops correctly would be technically very difficult. Moreover, if there is a current the diver may surface well away from the surface support and be very difficult to find. Consequently, a vital safety skill taught on decompression diving courses is the deployment of a lift bag or DSMB using line carried on a reel (see Figure 30.2), and then ascending suspended under the lift bag whilst slowly reeling in the line. This gives the diver both reference and support, and provides a surface marker that the boat can follow until the diver surfaces. It is recommended that divers write their name on the lift bag so that boat skippers know who it is they are following. This can be useful information in some circumstances. A lift bag or DSMB and reel should be considered compulsory items for decompression diving.

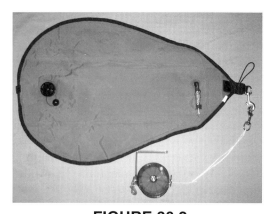

FIGURE 30.2
Lift bag (DSMB) and reel assembly.
(Note the combined overpressure release valve and manual dump valve near the top.)

2. **Strobe light.** A "common" cause of failure to make it back to the down line for the ascent is failure to find it. This is a likely scenario when a down line or anchor line falls close to, but not directly on a wreck, and divers have to swim beyond the range of visibility to the target. Moreover, sometimes a wreck might be visible from the down line because of its size, but the same might not be true in reverse. Divers can get lost on open bottom trying to regain the down line, with the unpleasant prospect of a difficult ascent. Strobe lights that can be activated and turned off underwater are very valuable under such circumstances. A strobe can be fixed on the down line 3 or 4 metres off the bottom, and this will invariably be visible for some distance after the down line disappears into the murk.

3. **Writing slates.** Slates have already been mentioned, but they should be emphasized again as an excellent means of accurate underwater communication. Many technical divers mount a curved slate on their arm using elastic rubber tubing which means they can write one handed underwater (they only have to hold the pencil, not the slate). Any strategy that frees a hand during decompression diving (which usually requires spending a lot of time using one hand to hang on to ropes) is very valuable.

4. Jon line. Another "hand-saving" innovation that becomes important during decompression is a simple device called a "Jon line". This consists of a short piece of rope, usually 1.5-2m (5-6ft) long, with a specially designed hook on one end that will clamp around the down line, and one or two quick release clips at the other end that will clip onto the D rings on the diver's harness shoulder straps (See Figure 30.3). At a prolonged decompression stop, and especially in a current, the diver can clip one end of the Jon line onto the down line and the other end onto his or her shoulder straps, and then hang free in the current. This is a very relaxing way to spend a deco stop, and *infinitely* preferable to hold the down line by hand.

5. Surface location devices. Since decompression diving frequently takes place in offshore settings, there is real potential for a diver to be lost on the surface with nowhere in swimming distance. It is vital that divers in such settings carry at least one visual surface location aid such as a safety sausage or flare. Air horns are also potentially useful, and there are now even personal EPIRBs (Emergency Position Indicating Radio Beacon), though technical divers should check their depth rating before subjecting these expensive devices to the crush test!

6. Shark pod. The dreaded danger of all decompression dives is to be forced to the surface by some unforeseen problem while there is still a large decompression obligation. Clearly, all the careful planning that goes into decompression diving is designed to prevent this from occurring. However, one potential complication that cannot be planned out of a dive is the appearance of a large shark that subsequently attempts to eat one or more of the divers. Such an event is rare, but there are well-documented cases of aggressive sharks disrupting decompression. There are not many options for fighting off shark attacks but

FIGURE 30.3

A "jon line" with a clip at one end to attach to the diver's harness, and a specially adapted rope hook at the other end to allow easy attachment and disengagement on the down line.

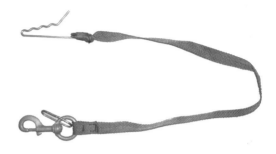

FIGURE 30.4

Divers on a decompression station with a shark pod suspended nearby (fore-ground).

one tool for repelling sharks is called a "shark pod" (see Figure 30.4). This is an electrical device that emits a strong electrical pulse that sharks find very unpleasant over several metres radius. These devices have successfully repelled inquisitive great whites, and there is no doubt that one feels significantly more secure decompressing in mid blue water out in the middle of nowhere when there is a shark pod ready to turn on and hanging nearby.

7. **Save a dive kit.** Decompression dives take too much time and effort to set up to allow them to be ruined by minor equipment failures. At least one diver in a group should carry a reasonably comprehensive kit of tools and spare parts so that retrievable failures are retrieved at the site without canceling the dive. Many items may be useful in such kits, but here are some ideas: several shifting spanners, large and small screw drivers (normal and Phillips heads), long nose pliers, short nose blunt pliers, circlip pliers, allen key set, O-ring pick, a range of O-rings including an O-ring kit for the regulators being used, cable ties of various sizes, electrical tape, silicone grease, oxygen compatible lubricant, a blower device that can attach to the BCD hose, spare regulator mouthpiece, swiss army knife.

Miscellaneous issues in decompression diving practice

We could occupy this entire book with a detailed discussion of issues relevant to the safe practical conduct of a decompression dive, but clearly this is impossible and once again, we refer interested divers to sources of proper decompression diving training. Nevertheless, there are a few key areas we consider worthy of highlighting that are discussed below, either because of their inherent importance, or because we frequently receive relevant questions.

Plan the dive and dive the plan

Gulp! What a cliché! But this axiom which is frequently quoted (but infrequently obeyed) in recreational diving is just <u>so</u> important in technical diving. We dedicated a lot of space to planning correct gases and gas management above, but there is no point (and considerable risk) in carefully planning the correct gases and decompression protocol for one depth and then going deeper; or determining the termination pressure for our bottom gas supply but then remaining at the bottom after we have reached that pressure. Sticking to the plan takes discipline and vigilance and if either of these break down, then the dive could be on the slippery slope towards disaster. Dive plans should be thoroughly understood by all participants (including those who remain on the boat (see below), and contingencies for adverse events should also be discussed and understood.

Pick your skipper carefully

In many decompression diving situations the knowledge and skills of the person looking after things on the boat topside is just as important as those of the divers themselves. Those in authority at the surface should be chosen carefully. A skipper or surface supervisor who is a technical diver themselves, and who has an intimate knowledge of the planned activities is far more likely to respond appropriately and take the correct options if things start to get out of shape. In serious deep decompression dives using mixed gas it is not unusual to use a dedicated surface supervisor, who is usually themselves an expert technical diver, to coordinate activities on the topside.

Carry your decompression gases everywhere

Of the many issues that we could highlight as important in conducting a decompression dive, we choose to focus on this one because it has been the root of a number of high profile, and in some cases fatal accidents. We refer to the practice of caching sling tanks containing decompression gases somewhere on the bottom so that the diver can swim around unencumbered by this extra weight. The obvious intention is to return to this cache prior to beginning the ascent to collect the sling tanks. The danger is also obvious. If for any reason the diver fails to recover those tanks, then a return to the surface with a critical burden of omitted decompression is inevitable. With few exceptions, the diver should retain all cylinders necessary for a safe decompression at all stages throughout the dive.

Take exceptional care when making gas switches during decompression

Switching to the wrong gas at the wrong stage of the dive can have disastrous consequences, and has been the cause of many accidents. In addition to clear the marking and consistent positioning of decompression gases previously mentioned, divers should develop a checking routine that will minimize the chances of a mistake. Some training agencies teach that gas switches should be witnessed by the diver's buddy who verifies that the correct switch is taking place.

SUMMARY

- Although all diving should be thought of as decompression diving, the definition is usually applied to those dives made in a time / depth envelope that requires mandatory decompression stops to be made during the ascent.

- There are many dive tables, computers, and software programs that can be used to plan a decompression dive (many of which are discussed elsewhere in this book). Some are obviously more conservative than others (that is, they prescribe longer decompression stops for an equivalent period at depth). There are little or no data describing the relative merits of these algorithms, and the user must choose a level of conservatism they are comfortable with.

- Gas supply planning is critically important in order to avoid omitted decompression. Divers should measure their surface air consumption equivalent during exercise and rest to aid in gas supply planning.

- Decompression diving is made more efficient by utilizing one or more different nitrox mixes to accelerate the decompression.

- Where nitrox is used, careful attention must be paid to calculating the MOD for each gas and tracking the oxygen exposure.

- Careful planning, and execution of the dive according to the plan are key components to decompression diving.

© Dr. Richard Harris

31

Technical diving techniques 4 -
Mixed gas diving

In the early part of this chapter, we discussed some of the factors that limit the duration and depth of conventional scuba air dives. Subsequently, we have discussed technical diving methods that extend our duration within the recreational diving depth range, and that permit us to dive at the extremes of that depth range. Specifically, we have seen how the use of nitrox lengthens the so called "no decompression limits" that control the time / depth envelopes of our dives, and we have briefly discussed some equipment configurations that allow us to carry sufficient gas to take advantage of that extra permitted time at depth. We have shown how decompression diving techniques allow us to enjoy useful bottom times at the extreme depths of the recreational air and nitrox diving range, and how the combination of decompression and nitrox diving techniques facilitates accelerated decompression from such dives.

However, we have yet to discuss how to overcome the barriers that impede dives to depths beyond the recreational air diving range. In particular, how can we avoid both the debilitating effects of nitrogen narcosis and the toxicity of the oxygen that would occur if we just took air deeper and deeper. The answer is that we must introduce a less narcotic gas into the mix to replace at least some of the nitrogen, and we must reduce the amount of oxygen in the mix below that found in air. Fundamentally, this is what "mixed gas diving" is all about.

INTRODUCING ANOTHER "DILUENT" OR "CARRIER GAS" TO REPLACE NITROGEN

In air or nitrox diving, the nitrogen acts as a "diluent" or "carrier" for the oxygen; reducing its concentration in our breathing gas and allowing us to proceed to greater depths than would be possible with pure oxygen because of concerns over oxygen toxicity. But as we have discussed, the nitrogen itself starts to cause problems when we go deeper. In particular, nitrogen narcosis can become very limiting. There are no fixed rules about exactly what depth the narcotic effect of the nitrogen in air becomes intolerable since different divers appear to be affected to different degrees. Some agencies take the view that dives beyond 30m (100ft) using air are hazardous and unnecessarily narcotic, whilst others will endorse the careful use of air as deep as 50m (165ft).

Wherever you draw your air diving limit, for deeper dives we need to substitute a less narcotic "diluent" gas into the mix. Mixed gas diving usually involves the introduction of helium into the breathing gas. Helium has some very relevant properties. First, it is much less narcotic than nitrogen. Indeed, it can be breathed at extreme depths with almost no narcotic effect at all. Second, it is very light, and is much easier to breathe than nitrogen at high pressures. The work of breathing is markedly reduced by helium at extreme depths.

Helium may be used to completely replace the nitrogen, leaving helium and oxygen only ("heliox"). Heliox is used most commonly by the military and commercial sectors because the complete absence of nitrogen narcosis means that delicate tasks (like defusing a mine) can be completed safely.

In deep recreational diving it is more common to replace only some of the nitrogen leaving a mix of helium, nitrogen, and oxygen; commonly known as *"trimix"*. There are three reasons for this. First, helium is very expensive (especially in countries outside the USA), and so using no more than necessary makes economic sense. Second, helium is a rapidly diffusing gas and we absorb it into our blood and tissues quickly. The corollary is also true (we outgas it quickly), and this will result in shorter decompressions from very long "saturation dives" where the rate of in-gassing is largely irrelevant because sufficient time is spent at depth for all tissues to be saturated with whatever inert gas is being breathed. However, for the type of short "bounce" dives performed by deep recreational divers, a pure helium-oxygen mix will usually result in a longer decompression requirement than a trimix with less helium and some nitrogen. The third reason for leaving some nitrogen in a deep recreational diving mix is described later (see "high pressure neurological syndrome").

REDUCING THE FRACTION OF OXYGEN BELOW THAT FOUND IN AIR

You might recall from our earlier discussion of oxygen toxicity that we showed the MOD for air to be 57m (188ft) (assuming we wish to avoid a PO_2 of more than 1.4ATA). It follows that to "safely" proceed to depths beyond 57m (188ft) we are required to reduce the fraction of oxygen in our

breathing mix below the 21% found in air. Thus, most trimix dives involve the use of so-called "hypoxic" mixes; in other words, mixes containing less oxygen than air. In this regard, it is worth noting that the minimum fraction of oxygen in a mix that can be breathed at the surface is around 16% (a PO_2 of 0.16ATA), and even this might make the diver feel slightly light-headed. Any less than this and the diver risks becoming unconscious.

PLANNING AN APPROPRIATE BOTTOM MIX

From the above it should be clear that trimix diving is a definite step in complexity above nitrox diving. In nitrox diving, it was vital to determine the ideal fraction of oxygen for the mix in relation to the planned depth of the dive in order to avoid oxygen toxicity. In trimix diving, not only do we have to take the fraction of oxygen into account, we also have to plan the nitrogen and helium content in order to avoid excessive narcosis.

How much oxygen?

Let's say we plan a dive to 90m (300ft) where the ambient pressure is 10ATA (1 for the atmosphere and 1 for each 10m (33ft) depth). How much oxygen should our "bottom gas" mixture contain? It is worth pointing out that we want to breathe as much oxygen as is safe, since more oxygen means less inert gas and less decompression. This being the case, we can use the same maths (*Equation 4*) as we used in calculating the oxygen content for nitrox mixes. Thus, assuming our maximum safe PO_2 is 1.4ATA as previously:

Ideal fraction of oxygen in the mix
= 1.4ATA ÷ 10ATA
= 0.14

Thus, we might plan to use a mix with 14% oxygen for breathing at 90m (297ft). You will recall that we cannot safely breathe such a lean oxygen mix at the surface, and so it will be necessary to start the first part of the descent on a richer mix (air for example). Once we are at a higher pressure it will be safe to change to the bottom mix and continue the descent. This point will obviously be reached at the depth where our bottom gas will be providing a PO_2 the same as we breathe at the surface on air (0.2ATA approximately). It can be calculated as using Equation 11.

Equation 11

Minimum safe depth (m) for hypoxic mix = ([0.2 ÷ FO_2] −1) x 10   (metric)

or

Minimum safe depth (ft) for hypoxic mix = ([0.2 ÷ FO_2] −1) x 33   (imperial)

where:
0.2 = minimum safe PO_2 in ATA
FO_2 = fraction of oxygen in the mix

For our 14% mix (FO_2 = 0.14) this gives:

Minimum safe depth for bottom mix
= ([0.2 ÷ 0.14] − 1) x 10
= 4.3m

or ([0.2 ÷ 0.14] − 1) x 33 = 14.2ft

Thus, we can safely change to our bottom mix once we reach 5m / 15ft (rounding deeper) during the descent.

How much nitrogen?

From the above discussion, you could deduce that in order to minimize cost and decompression requirements we would want to use the minimum amount of helium in the mix to reduce the amount of nitrogen narcosis to an acceptable level. Determination of an "acceptable level" of narcosis is a somewhat personal issue, and it might be influenced by the likely nature of the dive. We might be prepared to accept less narcosis if supervising inexperienced trimix trainees for example. However, most technical divers are prepared to accept a

level of narcosis equivalent to that they would experience when breathing air at 40m (132ft). A useful descriptive expression for this is to say that we are prepared to tolerate an "equivalent narcotic depth" (END) of 40m (132ft). Expressed more quantitatively, this is equivalent to breathing 3.95ATA of nitrogen (calculated by multiplying the fraction of nitrogen in air by the ambient pressure at 40m (132ft): 0.79 x 5ATA = 3.95ATA). Thus, whatever depth we are diving to using trimix, we are prepared to tolerate an END of 40m (132ft), or in other words, to be breathing 3.95ATA of nitrogen.

Continuing with our 90m (297ft) dive example, and assuming our END is to be 40m (132ft), we can calculate the ideal amount of nitrogen in the mix using the same maths as for *Equation 4*, but substituting the 1.4ATAs of oxygen with 3.95ATA of nitrogen. Thus, remembering that the ambient pressure at 90m (297ft) is 10ATA:

Ideal fraction of nitrogen in the mix
= 3.95ATA ÷ 10ATA
= 0.4

So, our bottom mix should contain 40% nitrogen.

A diver may desire a higher or lower END than 40m (132ft), and any target END can be entered into the following equation:

Equation 12

Metric
FN_2 = (((END ÷ 10) + 1) x 0.79) ÷ P_{amb}

Imperial
FN_2 = (((END ÷ 33) + 1) x 0.79) ÷ P_{amb}

where:
FN_2 = ideal fraction of nitrogen in the mix
END = equivalent narcotic depth (m or ft)
P_{amb} = ambient pressure at the target depth given by:
((actual depth m ÷ 10) + 1);
or in imperial ((actual depth ft ÷ 33 + 1)

We acknowledge the inherent assumption that narcosis is caused solely by nitrogen and that there is no contribution from oxygen. The related controversy was discussed earlier. It is possible that an hypoxic gas whose END is calculated in this way might be even less narcotic than predicted. If anything, this extra conservatism seems likely to be advantageous.

How much helium?

Having calculated the ideal fractions of oxygen and nitrogen for our bottom mix, it is now an easy matter to calculate the helium content. We simply subtract the fractions of oxygen and nitrogen from 1, and the remainder is the fraction of helium we require in our mix. Thus:

EQUATION 13

FHe in mix = 1 − FN$_2$ − FO$_2$

where:
FN$_2$ = ideal fraction of nitrogen in the mix
FO$_2$ = ideal fraction of oxygen in the mix

In our 90m (297ft) dive example, the fraction of helium in our mix would therefore be calculated as follows:

Fraction of helium required
= 1 − 0.4 − 0.14
= 0.46

Our mix would contain 14% oxygen, 46% helium and 40% nitrogen. By convention, this is referred to as trimix 14:46. The oxygen and helium percentages are specified in that order, and the percentage of nitrogen is left to inference.

Calculation of END

The above example illustrated how a trimix diver might calculate the ideal composition of bottom gas for a dive to a known depth.

Another commonly encountered scenario is that the diver will already have some trimix made up when a particular dive is proposed. In this setting, it is a case of checking to see if the gas you already have is suitable for the proposed dive. First, the diver must ensure that the MOD with respect to oxygen toxicity will not be exceeded. This is done as previously using *Equation 3*. Second, the diver must calculate the END for the mix when used at the proposed depth to ensure it does not exceed the tolerable limit. This can be done using the equivalent air depth (EAD) calculation (*Equation 6*) described in the nitrox diving section. In this sense, END and EAD are no different.

For example, a diver who has a supply of trimix 15:35 is offered a dive to 70m (231ft). Recall that the EAD formula is:

EAD =
((FN$_2$ x (depth + 10)) ÷ 0.79) − 10 *(metric)*
or
EAD =
((FN$_2$ x (depth+33)) ÷ 0.79)−33 *(imperial)*

Thus, the END using this mix at 70m (231ft) is given by:

END =
((0.5 x (70 + 10)) ÷ 0.79) − 10 = 40.6m
  or
END = ((0.5 x (231 + 33)) ÷ 0.79) − 33
    = 134ft

PLANNING AND EXECUTION OF MIXED GAS DIVES

Deep mixed gas dives rapidly accumulate a significant decompression obligation. Such dives must be approached with great care and due respect for the potentially disastrous consequences of unplanned premature ascent. Accidents that might result in only minor embarrassment in conventional air diving are likely to be fatal in deep mixed gas diving.

Other than the calculation of an ideal bottom mix (as above), the fundamental practices of mixed gas diving are not greatly different to those outlined for decompression diving using air or nitrox. Gas switches to mixes with less helium and progressively more oxygen in one form or another are almost invariably used during decompression in mixed gas diving. However, as with all of technical diving, there are varied opinions on how this is best done. Some favour staying on helium-based mixes for the entire ascent to the point where it is safe to breathe 100% oxygen. Others introduce progressively greater fractions of nitrogen, or use air itself as a decompression gas before changing to a very "rich" nitrox (e.g.

nitrox 80) or 100% oxygen at the very shallow stops. It is beyond the scope of this book to explore the arguments for and against these various strategies, and it is fair to say that the debates conducted elsewhere are laced with heavy doses of personal opinion (often dressed up as fact) and anecdote.

A very simple example of a possible dive profile using nitrox as a decompression gas is shown in Table 31.1. This shows a dive to 90m (297ft) for 15 minutes using the bottom mix derived in our calculations above (trimix 14:46) and planned using Proplanner software.

TABLE 31.1

Dive plan for 90m (297ft) for 15 minutes.
For clarity, we present this example using metric stop depths only.
There may be trivial variation in the algorithm for imperial depths.
(Proplanner version 7.12C: safety factor 0%; microbubble factor 20%).

Depth (m)	Stop time (min)	Gas
90	15 (bottom time)	Trimix 14:46
59	1	Trimix 14:46
43	1	Trimix 14:46
35	1	Nitrox 32
30	1	Nitrox 32
27	1	Nitrox 32
24	1	Nitrox 32
21	1	Nitrox 32
18	1	Nitrox 32
15	5	Nitrox 32
12	6	Nitrox 32
9	10	Nitrox 32
6	5	Nitrox 80
4.5	32	Nitrox 80
Total run time = approximately 90 minutes		

It must be pointed out that this is just one of many profiles that could be generated for this dive (even using the same gases) because the software provides several options for levels of conservatism and the imposition of deeper decompression stops. In addition, decompression could be accelerated by introduction of a richer nitrox mix at a shallower depth. Not surprisingly, trimix divers will spend much time in the planning stages working out which combinations of gases give them the most efficient (but hopefully safe) decompression. In some very deep dives the first switch may even be to another trimix with more oxygen, more nitrogen, and less helium; then to air; and then to progressively richer nitrox mixes. However, it must be remembered that all of these gases have to be carried in the correct quantities. The example in Table 31.1 was restricted to 3 gases because 3 gases are relatively easy to carry (1 gas back-mounted and 2 gases in sling tanks). For all of these gas switches, careful attention must be paid to the MOD for each gas, the volume that must be carried to complete the required stops, and the effect of the gas's use on the "oxygen clock" as described in the earlier section on decompression diving.

MAKING TRIMIX

Air, helium and oxygen are blended together to make trimix, although for some hypoxic mixes it is only necessary to use air and helium. A partial pressure blending technique is used as was described for making nitrox. If the blender is starting with an empty cylinder, then the "ingredients" for the mix can be calculated using the following formulae.

EQUATION 14

Pressure He = T_P x $T_{He\%}$

where:
Pressure He = pressure of helium to be added in ATA
T_P = Target cylinder fill pressure in ATA
$T_{He\%}$ = Target helium percentage in the mix expressed as a decimal fraction (e.g. 40% = 0.4)

EQUATION 15

Pressure Air = (T_P x $T_{N2\%}$) ÷ 0.79

where:
Pressure Air
     = pressure of air to be added in ATA
T_P = Target cylinder fill pressure in ATA
$T_{N2\%}$ = Target nitrogen percentage in the mix expressed as a decimal fraction (e.g. 40% = 0.4)
0.79 = fraction of nitrogen in air

EQUATION 16

**Pressure O_2
= T_P x ($T_{O2\%}$ - ((0.21 ÷ 0.79) x $T_{N2\%}$))**

where:
Pressure O_2 = pressure of oxygen to be added in ATA
T_P = Target cylinder fill pressure in ATA
$T_{O2\%}$ = Target oxygen percentage in the mix expressed as a decimal fraction (e.g. 14% = 0.14)
$T_{N2\%}$ = Target nitrogen percentage in the mix expressed as a decimal fraction (e.g. 40% = 0.4)
0.79 = fraction of nitrogen in air

The latter calculation for oxygen can be verified by subtracting the required pressures of helium and air calculated in *Equations 14 and 15* from the target cylinder fill pressure. The result should be the same as the required pressure of oxygen given by *Equation 16*. More complex formulae are available for calculating the required ingredients for a mix when there is residual mix of known composition remaining in the cylinder.

The oxygen content of finished mixes must <u>always</u> be checked using a dedicated analyzer using the methods previously described. Helium analyzers are available, and while the use of such a device to check mixing accuracy is desirable, they are expensive and often not used.

As previously mentioned during our discussions of nitrox blending, great care and proper training are essential for accurate gas blending and safe decanting of high pressure pure oxygen. **All divers blending their own trimix should undergo dedicated gas blender training** before blending any gas for in water use.

THE HIGH PRESSURE NEUROLOGICAL SYNDROME (HPNS)

One diving medical problem of unique relevance to deep mixed gas diving is the high-pressure neurological syndrome (HPNS). This is a mysterious condition that has the potential to produce a variety of symptoms that include tremor, nausea, disorientation and other neurological problems. Like nitrogen narcosis its onset is very depth dependent and is rarely seen during dives shallower than 150m (495ft) (so its not something many of us have to worry about!). Moreover, like nitrogen narcosis, there is a marked inter-individual variation in susceptibility to its effects.

The cause is still not completely understood, but it may relate to a combined effect of pressure and the gas being breathed on the cell membranes of our nervous system. Paradoxically, we breathe helium in order to avoid nitrogen narcosis, yet breathing pure helium-oxygen mixtures is strongly associated with the HPNS. In another

paradox, adding a little nitrogen to the mix often ameliorates the effects, and this constitutes the third reason (alluded to earlier) for leaving some nitrogen in gas mixes for deep diving.

Divers required to work at extreme depths do exhibit a degree of adaptation to the symptoms over the course of the dive, although this is not invariable. Slow compressions have been found to facilitate this adaptation though these would not be feasible in extreme technical bounce dives. Like nitrogen narcosis, there do not appear to be any after effects from the HPNS, although transient alterations in behaviour persisting for a time after a dive have been reported.

SUMMARY

- Mixed gases are usually used to facilitate deeper diving than is practical using air. Mixed gases usually contain less nitrogen and less oxygen than air.

- Helium is used as an alternative diluent for oxygen because it is effectively non-narcotic. It is also a lighter gas and easier to breathe at greater depths.

- Most mixed gas dives are performed using one or more mixes of oxygen, helium and nitrogen ("trimix") tailored to the intended depth(s). Some nitrogen is left in the mix because this has economic advantages, and for most typical technical dives there are usually decompression advantages. In very deep dives, a small amount of nitrogen in the mix may help ameliorate the effects of the high pressure neurological syndrome (HPNS).

- Trimix recipes must be formulated with careful attention to the MOD (oxygen content) and END (nitrogen content).

- Divers making their own trimix must complete gas blending training.

32

Technical diving techniques 5 - Rebreather diving

While it is true that all of the technical diving techniques discussed to this point do contribute to an extension of duration or depth in some way, none have addressed the fundamental issue that limits duration on dives in which a self contained breathing apparatus is used; the inherent inefficiency of open circuit systems that vent exhaled gas to the water.

As we discussed at the very beginning of this chapter, on deep dives the effects of Boyle's law result in very high gas consumption. We showed that a surface gas consumption of 20lpm becomes 120lpm at 50m (165ft). All this gas is lost just so the diver can extract somewhere in the vicinity of 300 to 1500ml (0.3 to 1.5 litres) of oxygen per minute (depending on how hard they are working) from the gas breathed. Let's emphasize that: 120lpm of gas breathed just to extract 0.3 – 1.5lpm of oxygen! Thus, open circuit scuba is a very inefficient system, particularly when expensive gas mixes containing helium are being used at deeper depths. This is where rebreathers have a distinct advantage. They recycle the breathing gas so that much less gas is used, and the cost of expensive gases like helium is vastly reduced.

REBREATHER BASICS:

A simple analogy to explain the concept of a rebreather is to think of breathing in and out of a plastic bag via two pieces of plastic tubing. Now put a one-way valve allowing flow in opposite directions in each of the tubes, so that one tube allows you only to inhale from the bag and the other allows you only to exhale into it, thus forming a "loop". You can breathe in and out of the bag ("counterlung") without losing any of the gas and you now have a "rebreather"!

However, as you breathe, the levels of exhaled CO_2 in the loop will increase, and the level of oxygen will correspondingly decrease. This is what one of the authors (SJM) failed to appreciate during his first "rebreather" dives undertaken by clamping a hot water bottle over his mouth and nose with his head underwater in the bath at about age 7. His brother used to delight in how disoriented he was after prolonged episodes of this, and he clearly didn't understand the physiology. What he needed, and all proper rebreathers have, is a CO_2 absorbent 'scrubber' to remove the CO_2 before the gas is rebreathed, and a gas addition system to top up the oxygen in the loop as it is consumed. This *breathing loop* with a *"counterlung"*, CO_2 *scrubber,* and *gas addition system* are the fundamental constituents of all rebreather systems. The stylized layout common to all rebreathers is shown in Figure 32.1.

Essentially, it is the type of gas addition system by which rebreathers are classified, but before we go on to consider these, it is logical to briefly discuss those generic components that form the loop in all rebreathers.

FIGURE 32.1

Stylised rebreather layout.

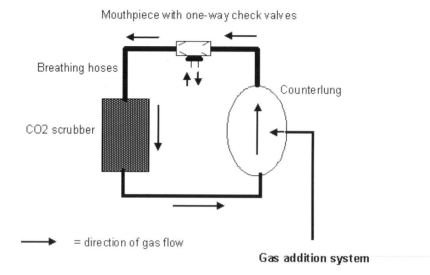

GENERIC COMPONENTS OF ALL REBREATHER SYSTEMS

From Figure 32.1 we can see that the breathing hoses, CO_2 scrubber and counterlung are common components in all rebreathers.

Breathing hoses

The rebreather breathing hoses appear, on the face of it, to be a relatively simple component: usually two corrugated rubber hoses (one for inhalation and one for exhalation) with a mouthpiece in the middle. However, appropriate use and care of the hoses is vital for several reasons. First, the mouthpiece contains one-way check valves to ensure that flow through the loop is only in one direction. If these were malfunctioning it could result in highly dangerous rebreathing of unscrubbed and poorly oxygenated gas. Second, the hoses represent arguably the most vulnerable component of an otherwise well protected loop system. A rupture or disconnect of the hoses would result in an unrecoverable flood of the loop, and the diver would have to "bail-

out" onto another gas supply (assuming that one is carried!). Finally, and in relation to this second point, the mouthpiece has a valve system that must be closed to prevent flooding of the loop when the mouthpiece is removed in the water. The diver cannot simply remove and replace the mouthpiece underwater as they can when using open circuit scuba.

An increasingly popular modification to rebreather breathing hoses is the incorporation of an open circuit regulator in the mouthpiece, with a switching system that allows an instant transfer to open circuit breathing without the need to remove the rebreather mouthpiece in making the transfer. This invariably makes the mouthpiece more cumbersome, and necessitates both the running of a low pressure gas supply hose alongside the rebreather hoses, and the carrying of an appropriate cylinder of open circuit bailout gas from which to run the low pressure supply. However, this extra complexity and cost) seem justified. There are an increasing number of reports of rebreather divers developing CO_2 toxicity (see later) and failing to make the transfer to open circuit bailout even though open circuit systems were carried for that purpose. Invariably these divers will remark on the fact that the CO_2 made them so short of breath that they could not bring themselves to take the rebreather mouthpiece out for fear of drowning. With an integrated rebreather / open circuit mouthpiece the transfer can be made with the mere "flick of a switch".

CO_2 scrubber

The scrubbing of CO_2 from rebreather systems is almost an entire science in itself, and we can only scratch the surface of this complex subject here. The scrubber assembly consists of a canister with one or more inlet and outlet holes to allow gas flow through the medium contained within. There are many designs and characteristic flow paths referred to by such terms as "axial" and "radial", but at the end of the day, they are all designed to efficiently expose the gas to the scrubber material by ensuring that gas flow is evenly distributed around that material and by minimizing so-called "channeling" which would result in poor contact between gas and scrubber material.

Several compounds are used as scrubber material. The most common is soda lime, a mixture of sodium hydroxide and calcium hydroxide. Lithium hydroxide is a more expensive alternative. These compounds react with the CO_2 in the exhaled gas to remove the former.

For sodium hydroxide / calcium hydroxide compounds, the relevant reactions are as follows:

$$CO_2 + 2NaOH \rightarrow Na_2CO_3 + H_2O + heat$$

Then:

$$Na_2CO_3 + Ca(OH)_2 \rightarrow 2NaOH + CaCO_3$$

Thus, you can see that the sodium hydroxide is the compound that actually reacts with the CO_2. The calcium hydroxide is used to regenerate the sodium hydroxide, being converted to calcium carbonate in the process. This continues until all the calcium hydroxide is consumed. You can also see that the reaction liberates heat and water, and the consequent warming and humidification of the breathing gas is one clear advantage of diving a rebreather in temperate water (but it's maybe not so great in very warm tropical water). Not surprisingly, a given amount of absorbent can only remove a finite amount of CO_2, so a newly charged scrubber canister has a "duration" that is measured in hours.

This duration is influenced by a variety of factors, not the least of which is the amount of scrubber material contained in the canister. This varies considerably between rebreathers. In addition, the reaction is inhibited at cold temperature, and scrubber duration is reduced when diving in very cold water. Duration is also reduced if the diver is indulging in a pattern of hard underwater work and is therefore producing more CO_2.

Safe scrubber duration has been a hotly debated and contentious issue. There is frequently a disparity between the scrubber durations recommended by the manufacturers of rebreathers and scrubber materials, and the durations reported by many technical divers. For example, assuming a diver swimming at 0.8 knots, the US Navy recommends a duration of 5 hours (under ideal conditions) for the comparatively large scrubber in the Mk16 rebreather, yet recreational technical divers using this device commonly use the scrubber for 10 hours or more.

It is important to distinguish the predicted duration of a scrubber (which could be called its "static capacity") from its "dynamic efficiency". Dynamic efficiency or capacity is the scrubber's moment to moment ability to remove a CO_2 load presented to it. For example, we might start a dive with brand new soda lime in our scrubber, yet even in the first 5 minutes of diving when there is still a huge amount of duration left, there could be some CO_2 "break through" into the inhalation hoses if the scrubber's dynamic capacity is overwhelmed.

Factors that can reduce dynamic capacity include decreased temperature, increased depth, partial flooding, partial expiry of scrubber material and improper packing of the scrubber.

The effect of temperature is easily explained on the basis that the reaction between CO_2 and the scrubber material is slower at low temperatures.

The effect of extreme depth is interesting. All other factors being equal, we still produce the same number of CO_2 molecules irrespective of the depth we are at. However, the deeper we go, the greater the pressure (and number of molecules) of other gas in the rebreather loop. One theory holds that in this setting there may be a lower chance of contact or interaction between the relatively sparse CO_2 molecules and the scrubber material because of "crowding" from other gas molecules.

The effect of partial flooding of the scrubber with wetting of the material is almost certainly to impair contact between the scrubber material and CO_2 molecules. This may reduce dynamic capacity, though there is surprisingly little data available to confirm this suspicion. As a slight digression, we should mention that flooding of the loop with significant amounts of water resulting in free water in the scrubber will most likely make the rebreather unusable, and the mixture of scrubber material with water has frequently been referred to in the rebreather literature as a "caustic cocktail". Migration of mixture products up the inhalation limb of the loop may cause lung injury if these products are inhaled. The potential for such events forms one of many strong arguments for rebreather divers to carry some form of bailout gas supply sufficient to get them to the surface should the rebreather fail.

The effect of partial expiry of scrubber material is reasonably obvious. If some of the scrubber material has already absorbed as much CO_2 as it can, then there are less actively absorbing particles of material available. The longer the scrubber is used, the more relevant this becomes. This effectively means that the scrubber has progressively less active absorbing surface area available, and the probability of dynamic capacity being exceeded rises with time.

The effect of improper packing is an uneven distribution of scrubber material resulting in so-called "channeling" since gas flow will tend to favour the path of least resistance. This is most likely if the scrubber is packed too loosely, resulting in a gravity-dependent shift in material during the dive. CO_2 is less likely to be completely removed if larger volumes of gas are flowing rapidly through a less resistant small area of scrubber.

Obviously, dynamic capacity is more likely to be overwhelmed if CO_2 is presented to the scrubber at a greater rate, especially since an increased rate of CO_2 delivery is usually accompanied by a much greater flow rate of gas through the scrubber thereby reducing the "dwell time" during which the CO_2 from each breath is in contact with the scrubber material.

Just to top all this off, it is likely that given equivalent amounts of scrubber material, the design and flow characteristics of a scrubber canister potentially influence both its static and dynamic capacity, and particularly the latter. Indeed, advocacy for one rebreather over another is frequently focused on design issues. Unfortunately, this is yet another area in the field that this somewhat "dogma rich and data poor". Many manufacturers and military groups claim to have data defining the efficiency of their design, but these data are rarely released for consideration by the diving public.

The reason for this considerable focus on design and efficiency issues in rebreather scrubbers is that their failure can have catastrophic consequences. If CO_2 levels in the inhaled gas are allowed to rise, then the diver may suffer CO_2 toxicity and its unpleasant and dangerous symptoms such as headache, shortness of breath, disorientation, impaired cognition, and ultimately, unconsciousness.

With this in mind, it is notable that until recently there was no incorporation of any CO_2 or scrubber monitoring technology into rebreathers. Indeed, at the time of writing there is still no rebreather (including the most sophisticated electronic closed circuit devices) that incorporates any form of actual PCO_2 monitoring in the loop, though this may change over the next few years. Some units incorporate "temperature stick" devices in the scrubber. These devices track the active front of maximal chemical interaction between CO_2 and scrubber material by measuring the temperature across a single track through the scrubber material stack. The scrubber material tends to expire first where the exhaled gas enters the canister, and then progressively through the stack towards the gas exit portal(s). As this occurs, the temperature front moves in the same direction. At some point determined by the manufacturer, the device will indicate that expiry has reached a threshold where replacement is necessary. The merit of these devices has been the subject of considerable debate which is beyond the scope of this book. However, is seems reasonable to point out that while temperature sticks give some indication of remaining static capacity, they may give no warning if dynamic capacity is exceeded and if CO_2 is being rebreathed. In the opinion of these authors, this significantly limits their utility in rebreather diving. Indeed, it could even be argued that they may impute a false sense of security. On the other hand, if diver is fully cognizant of the issues discussed here then intelligent and potentially useful interpretation of their output is possible.

Counterlung

The counterlung is essentially a bag that provides capacitance to the loop so that the diver can freely inhale and exhale without any ingress or egress of gas from outside the loop. As you might expect, there must be an over-pressure relief valve that will vent when excess gas flows into the counterlung, and when gas expands during ascent. It's a fairly simple principle, but like most things in diving, there are various subtle design points that are considered important. For example: the volume of the counterlung must be such that a heavily built hard working diver will still be able inhale and exhale freely without "bottoming" the bag; and the loop should be designed so that any moisture that gathers in the counterlung cannot freely access the CO_2 scrubber canister.

The counterlung is positioned differently in various rebreathers. These positions can be broadly classified as: on the back, on the chest, and over the shoulder. In the latter case the counterlung is actually incorporated within the BCD / harness assembly. These various positions affect the breathing characteristics of the rebreather according to the counterlung's position relative to the lungs. In the horizontally swimming diver with the counterlung on the back, the counterlung is actually at a slightly lower pressure than the lungs thus making exhalation easy but inhalation slightly more difficult. The opposite is true for the counterlung located on the chest; and for the shoulder mounted counterlung there should be little difference between exhalation and inhalation resistance. These characteristics will change as the diver changes their orientation in the water.

SPECIFIC REBREATHER TYPES

Although there are subtle variations, two broad categories of rebreather are frequently used in recreational rebreather diving: semi-closed circuit and closed circuit rebreathers. There are a number of differences between these classes of devices, but as suggested previously, it is the gas addition system that is the definitive feature. The key aim of the gas addition systems in both types of rebreathers is to ensure that the oxygen levels in the loop never become dangerously high or dangerously low. They achieve this in quite different ways.

Semi-closed circuit rebreathers (SCRs)

Semi-closed circuit rebreathers (SCRs) are the simpler of the two types of devices, but in many respects, the principles of their operation are harder to explain.

These rebreathers use a relatively simple gas addition system that feeds oxygen-rich gas into the loop at a fixed rate. The rate of gas addition is calculated to be more than enough to maintain an appropriate fraction of oxygen (FO_2) in the loop at the level of work anticipated.

It is fair to say that the vast majority of applications for SCRs are in the recreational depth range where nitrox mixtures are used as the fresh gas. Thus, the rebreather constantly injects nitrox into the loop at a fixed rate calculated to maintain the fraction of oxygen at an appropriate level. Most SCRs also have a valve that bleeds nitrox into the counterlung to maintain its volume when it is compressed during descent.

These design features are summarized in Figure 32.2.

FIGURE 32.2

Stylised SCR layout.

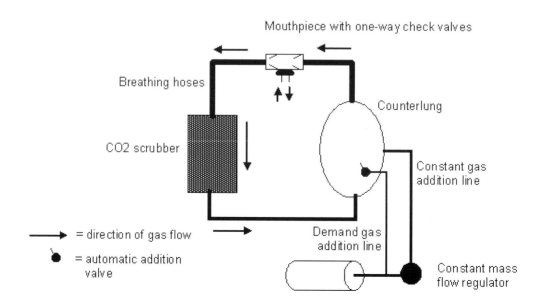

Like any other nitrox dive, the decision over which nitrox mix should be used is usually based on the planned maximum depth and the maximum PO_2 considered tolerable. As you might anticipate, the diver will be breathing somewhat less than the fraction of oxygen in the chosen nitrox mix after it has been injected into the SCR and mixed with the other gas already in the loop. Nevertheless, by convention, the choice of nitrox mix and the depth limitation for the dive are based on normal nitrox diving principals so that there is no chance of encountering a dangerously high PO_2 even if the diver was to breathe directly from his or her gas supply cylinder. Thus, for example, if we plan an SCR dive to 20m (66ft) with a maximum tolerable PO_2 of 1.4ATA, we can use *Equation 4* to calculate the ideal nitrox mix as follows:

Ideal FO_2
= 1.4ATA (maximum PO_2) ÷
  3ATA (ambient pressure)
= 0.46

Thus, so long as the nitrox mix used does not exceed 46% oxygen, then there is no chance of exceeding a PO_2 of 1.4 on a 20m (66ft) dive.

The next issue that logically arises is the rate at which the nitrox should be injected into the loop. This is a somewhat murky and confused aspect of SCR operation. Here's why - During a dive, the factors that will influence the oxygen level in the SCR loop are: the rate at which oxygen is consumed by the diver (which is determined by work rate); the rate of injection of nitrox, and the fraction of oxygen in the nitrox mix. The latter two factors are objective and easily measured, but the work rate of the diver is not. How on earth does the diver know what his or her work rate (and oxygen consumption) will be during the dive? The answer is that they simply don't know, and assumptions must be made. This is where things can get tricky. If the work rate is underestimated then the flow of nitrox into the loop might be insufficient to maintain the

PO_2 at a safe level. If the work rate is overestimated then the flow of nitrox may be excessive and the duration of the gas supply unnecessarily short.

In short then, the rate at which nitrox must be injected into the SCR loop hinges on the diver's work rate and consequent oxygen consumption (which we must estimate in advance). In practice, although somewhat complicated formulae are available for the purpose, the task of calculating nitrox flow rates is usually undertaken by the SCR manufacturers who provide preset rates for various nitrox mixes. In the case of the widely used *Drager Dolphin* SCRs, the flow rates have been calculated conservatively so that even at an extreme oxygen consumption of 2.5lpm, the FO_2 in the loop will not fall below 0.17 (17%) (just above the minimum required to maintain consciousness at the surface!). As you might imagine, the higher the fraction of oxygen in the nitrox, the lower the flow rate required and the longer the duration of the nitrox supply. However, the trade off when using very oxygen-rich mixes is a shallower maximum depth.

Even though the rates at which nitrox is injected into the SCR loop are calculated conservatively to maintain safe levels at high workloads, we still cannot escape the fact that variations in the rate of oxygen consumption are not matched by changes in the flow rate of nitrox into the SCR loop. Thus, the FO_2 actually breathed by the diver (the percentage of oxygen in the loop) will change as workload and oxygen consumption changes throughout the dive. Rebreather manufacturers usually calculate the expected oxygen percentages in the loop for a variety of nitrox mixes at assumed levels of oxygen consumption and provide these data in their user manuals. For example, Table 32.1 shows the loop FO_2 / oxygen percentage at various levels of oxygen consumption when 40% nitrox is injected into the Drager Dolphin SCR at the manufacturer's preset rate of 10.4lpm.

TABLE 32.1

Loop FO$_2$ and % at various levels of oxygen consumption using nitrox 40 at the manufacturer's preset flow rate in the Drager Dolphin SCR.

Diver O$_2$ consumption *(lpm)*	Loop FO$_2$	Loop O$_2$ %
0.3	0.38	38
1.0	0.329	32.9
1.5	0.288	28.8
2.5	0.186	18.6

Thus, assuming we employed a Drager Dolphin for our SCR dive to 20m (66ft) using nitrox 40, the actual oxygen percentage we will breathe could range anywhere from 38% to 18% depending on our exercise rate and oxygen consumption. This potential for variation presents us with obvious problems when we are trying to calculate our no decompression limits using tables or computers. Unless you are equipped with a computer that interfaces with an oxygen sensor in your SCR loop, there is little choice other than to make an assumption about the prevailing nitrox mix in the loop throughout the majority of the dive. Opinions and practices do vary, but for an "average" dive, it is considered reasonable to assume an oxygen consumption rate of either 1.0 or 1.5lpm depending on whether the level of exertion expected is mild or moderate. From Table 32.1 we can see that these assumptions imply we will be breathing nitrox 32 or nitrox 28 respectively. To calculate our no decompression limits we can then program our assumed nitrox mix (either nitrox 32 or 28) into a dedicated nitrox dive computer, use it with a dedicated nitrox dive table, or use it to calculate an EAD (*Equation 6*) for use with an air diving table.

One last slightly confusing issue that needs clarification is the nature of the "constant mass flow" regulators that are used to deliver the nitrox to the SCR loop. You may recall from previous comments that open circuit scuba makes inefficient use of our gas supply because as depth increases increasingly larger volumes of gas must be used to ventilate the diver's lungs. For example, on open circuit scuba a 1L breath of air exhaled at 20m (66ft) where the pressure is 3ATA will expand to 3L by the time it reaches the surface, and yet the amount of oxygen the diver will have extracted from that air will be no different to what he or she was extracting at the surface (assuming workload has not changed). This latter point is very important. Put another way, provided the workload does not change, the number of molecules of oxygen metabolized by the diver per minute remains constant irrespective of depth. It follows that the number of oxygen molecules injected per minute into the SCR loop does not need to change with depth. The constant mass flow regulator on the SCR ensures that this is so. We set a flow rate in terms of volume per minute at the surface, and the constant mass flow regulator ensures that the same number of molecules of gas are injected to the loop each minute no matter what depth we are at. You will recall that the flow rate for nitrox 40 in the Drager Dolphin SCR was preset to 10.4lpm at the surface. Unlike a normal regulator that would deliver 3 times that volume at 20m / 66ft (3ATA), the constant mass flow regulator merely delivers the same number of molecules of gas. Put another way, if you collected the regulator's gas output over 1 minute at 20m (66ft) and took it to the surface, you would still only have 10.4L of gas.

This critical function is central to the efficient use of gas by SCRs. Since the surface equivalent flow rate does not change as depth increases, it is fairly easy to calculate your expected duration, and it is equally easy to see that durations are prolonged compared with open circuit scuba. For example, consider that we carry nitrox 40 for a SCR dive at 20m (66ft) in a 5L cylinder pressurized to 200ATA (total of 1000L of gas). Since our preset flow rate is 10.4lpm it is obvious that our 1000L of nitrox will last well over 1 hour. This is very efficient use of gas.

Despite the unavoidably convoluted explanation of these various issues, the actual use of an SCR is relatively uncomplicated. As we have discussed, the key steps in planning an SCR dive are:

1. calculating the most appropriate nitrox mix for the depth being dived;
2. setting the SCR constant mass flow regulator to deliver a flow rate appropriate for that mix (usually pre-set by the manufacturer);
3. calculating (or using a dive computer to derive) decompression status after estimating the nitrox mix in the loop (based on data like that in Table 32.1).

The advantages of diving an SCR over normal scuba air diving include those outlined earlier for nitrox diving. In addition, for the reasons outlined above, SCRs provide longer durations with smaller gas supplies. Despite the complexity of the underlying principles, their operation is relatively simple and foolproof. Another frequently cited advantage of rebreathers is less bubbling, a feature appreciated by many photographers. However, since the SCR diver does not metabolize the nitrogen component of the nitrox that is constantly flowing into the loop, the excess gas must be periodically vented to prevent over-inflation of the counterlung. It follows that SCRs do produce some bubbles, but not nearly as many as during open circuit scuba diving. The requirement to periodically vent some gas is the feature that gives rise to the name "semi-closed circuit" rebreather.

There are few disadvantages for SCRs over open circuit scuba other than the cost and the higher level of maintenance required. However, there are a number of perceived disadvantages when SCRs are compared to the more expensive and complicated closed circuit rebreathers (CCRs) (see below). First, the frequent uncertainty over the exact oxygen content in the loop concerns many SCR divers, whereas oxygen content in the CCR loop is closely monitored and regulated (see below). In addition, SCRs used in their standard nitrox diving mode restrict the safe depth range commensurate with the oxygen content of the nitrox mix used, whereas CCRs potentially facilitate very deep diving. Finally, as you will see, CCRs make even more efficient use of small gas supplies. Unfortunately, CCRs cost a lot of money to purchase and maintain when compared to SCRs.

Closed-circuit rebreathers (CCRs)

If a diver uses mixed gas (heliox or trimix) to advance into deeper, extended duration dives, then carriage of the required gas volume may impose some limitations, and the bill for that expensive helium you are going to blow out into the water will hurt. Although CCRs are not just for deep diving, there is no doubt they provide huge advantages in this endeavour by conserving expensive gas. The same deep dive can be carried out on a CCR with a fraction of the gas supply that would be used on an open circuit dive.

The reader is reminded that the basic rebreather loop (Figure 32.1) is much the same in a CCR as any other rebreather. It is the gas addition system that is unique. Indeed, the gas addition system in a CCR is a big step ahead of the SCR in its sophistication and gas efficiency. Remember, in a SCR the oxygen was added to the loop at a constant rate in premixed nitrox. In CCRs there are independent cylinders of two gases: pure oxygen, and a *diluent gas* (named so because it is used to dilute the oxygen in the loop) (see Figures 32.3 and 32.4). Oxygen and the diluent are added to the breathing loop *separately* to form an appropriate mix. The means by which this mix is made will be described in a moment, but first let's pause to consider the gases in the two cylinders. The oxygen is easy. It is always just pure oxygen. The choice of diluent takes a little more explaining.

FIGURE 32.3

Stylised CCR layout.

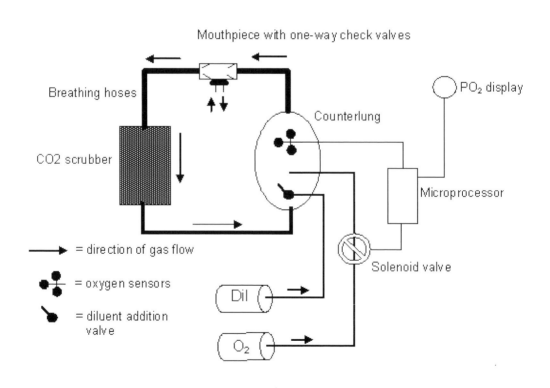

FIGURE 32.4

US Navy Mark 16 CCR. Note the two spherical gas cylinders: the left cylinder contains diluent gas and the right contains oxygen. They are mixed in the large combined counter-lung and CO_2 scrubber assembly sitting above the cylinders. Mixing is controlled by a microprocessor that is found in the small black cylindrical pod between the cylinders.

Diluent gas

The diluent gas is chosen according to the nature of the dive. If a dive within the normal recreational diving range (< 40m / 130ft) is planned, then it is very common to use plain old air as the diluent. In this setting, the rebreather blends air and oxygen in the loop to make nitrox. If a deep dive is contemplated, air is no longer a suitable diluent for the same reasons it is not suitable for deep diving on open circuit. In this case the diver will fill the diluent cylinder with either heliox or trimix, and the rebreather will blend it with oxygen to produce an appropriate mixed gas. The choice between these gases is based on the same principles applied with using them on open circuit. Military divers often choose heliox (no nitrogen) because no narcosis can be tolerated when defusing a mine! Technical divers usually choose trimix. In CCR diving this is mainly because of the shorter decompressions that usually result, rather than any concerns over consumption and cost of helium.

Some are probably wondering why there any need to have oxygen in the diluent at all given that the CCR is going to automatically blend oxygen with the diluent in the loop. Technically speaking, there is no reason to have oxygen in the diluent. You could dive a CCR with pure helium, or a mixture of nitrogen and helium in the diluent cylinder. However, some CCRs provide an open circuit connection to their diluent cylinder so that the diver can breathe directly from it in the event of a total rebreather failure. Clearly, this would be of little use if it contained no oxygen at all. There are several other "failure mode" drills that CCR divers are taught in their training that would not be possible if the diluent contained no oxygen. Thus, the presence of some oxygen in the diluent cylinder is a safety feature rather than a necessity.

The CCR diver does need to be careful about the fraction of oxygen in the diluent mix, especially for deep dives. Remember, the diluent is there to dilute the oxygen so that the PO_2 can remain within safe limits at the planned depth. It will be no use if the diluent itself contains sufficient oxygen that the PO_2 will exceed our maximum safe limit at that depth. For example, if a dive is planned to 90m (297ft) and we wish to avoid a PO_2 of more than 1.4ATA, we can use *Equation 4* to calculate the maximum fraction of oxygen in our diluent mix:

Max. fraction of oxygen
= 1.4 (maximum PO_2) ÷
*   10 (ambient pressure)*
= 0.14

Thus, if we used a diluent containing 14% oxygen, we would reach our maximum PO_2 on arrival at the target depth without the rebreather having to add any oxygen. In practice, most CCR users would employ a diluent with slightly less oxygen, rather than use one that will generate a maximum PO_2 at the target depth. For a 90m (297ft) dive a diluent with 10% oxygen would be fairly common. This gives a little leeway in case the diver had to venture deeper than the planned depth.

Gas addition system

The key feature of CCR operation is a gas addition system that blends the diluent and oxygen to maintain a constant pressure of oxygen (PO_2) in the loop. The expression "constant PO_2" is used a little reservedly because it is not quite constant during all phases of the dive; especially the descent (see below). However, for the most part, the CCR maintains the PO_2 in the loop at a constant "set point" that is selected by the diver. In most CCRs the blend is achieved by mechanical addition of diluent in response to changes in the volume of the counterlung, and microprocessor or manually controlled addition of oxygen in response to the actual PO_2 in the loop. If this all sounds a bit technical, bear with us and all will be explained.

In all CCRs diluent is introduced into the loop when the counterlung volume falls. The most obvious and important requirement for diluent addition is during the descent when the counterlung is compressed and gas must be added to restore its volume. Some CCRs have an automatic diluent addition valve, and in some the diver must manually operate the valve when he or she feels the counterlung "bottoming out" during inhalation.

In broad terms, oxygen addition can be handled in two ways: either by an electronically operated and essentially automated system, or by the diver themselves, that is, manually. Since the most prevalent CCRs are of the former design, we will focus our commentary on the operation of these devices, and mention the manual ones later.

In "electronic CCRs" oxygen is added through an electronically operated solenoid valve when the PO_2 in the loop falls below the set point selected by the diver. There are oxygen sensors of the same type used in oxygen analyzers in the loop. Typically 3 sensors are used, with an electronic algorithm that averages the readings from all 3 (unless one deviates by more than a certain threshold, in which case it is ignored). When addition of diluent or consumption of oxygen causes the averaged PO_2 reading to fall below the set point, the solenoid valve opens intermittently, letting oxygen into the loop until the PO_2 set point is restored. All CCRs have at least one display that allows the user to read the actual PO_2 in the loop. Usually these displays will allow the user to read each oxygen sensor individually. In addition, all CCRs have a visual and/or audible alarm system which will warn the user if the loop PO_2 is too low or too high. The layout of the gas addition system in electronic CCRs that facilitates these functions is shown in Figure 32.3.

A hypothetical dive

Let's try to pull this together in a practical example to illustrate the function of an electronic CCR. For simplicity, we'll consider a dive in which a CCR is being taken to 30m (100ft) using air as the diluent. In keeping with the previous examples, we will assume that the diver has elected to use a PO_2 set point of 1.4ATA.

The descent is a tricky part of any CCR dive because the PO_2 in the loop will rise as the gas inside it is compressed, even in the absence of any oxygen addition. For this reason, (and depending on the set point and dive plan) the dive rarely begins with the PO_2 at the set point. In our example (set point of 1.4ATA), this would be impossible because even with 100% oxygen in the loop the PO_2 would only be 1ATA at the surface! You can imagine what would happen to the PO_2 as we initiated our descent with 100% oxygen in the loop; as the ambient pressure increased it would rapidly reach toxic levels.

CCR dives therefore begin with a modest, safe PO_2 in the loop (such as 0.5 – 0.7ATA), and this is judged so that by the time the target depth is reached the PO_2 will be nearing the desired set point. Some electronic rebreathers allow the changing of set points during the dive. In this case a low set point would be selected at the surface and during the first part of the descent so that oxygen levels would not rise too quickly. The higher final set point would be selected at or near the bottom. The management of PO_2 during descents does vary between rebreathers and so it is difficult to give a universal protocol for our hypothetical dive. However, as an example, one of the authors (SJM) using a US Navy Mark 15.5 electronic CCR would start the descent with a PO_2 of approximately 0.5ATA and switch the rebreather on with a set point of 1.4ATA after the first 10m (33ft). Due to oxygen being metabolized during the descent, and since oxygen delivery by the solenoid is intentionally slow, this might actually result in a PO_2 of slightly less than 1.4ATA on arrival at 30m (100ft), but this would be quickly corrected by the automatic oxygen addition system.

Descent is also characterized by compression of the counterlung by the increasing pressure of the surrounding water. This loss of volume must be compensated by the addition of gas as mentioned above or we will not be able to breathe. For obvious reasons, we cannot use oxygen for this purpose, so "diluent" (air in this case) is added, either manually by the diver as he feels the counterlung emptying with each breath, or automatically via an automatic diluent addition valve that is tripped by low counterlung volume. In accordance with its name, the "diluent" dilutes the oxygen and so decreases the PO_2. This, of course, will be detected by the oxygen sensor system, and will trigger the addition of more oxygen.

Events during the period at depth are much easier to follow. If the PO_2 in the loop is not quite at our set point of 1.4ATA on arrival at 30m (100ft) then the solenoid valve will open to allow oxygen in to the loop. If the PO_2 is in excess of the set point 1.4ATA (a situation we would want to avoid) then the rebreather will do nothing; allowing the PO_2 to gradually fall to the set point as we as consume oxygen from the loop. In this situation, if we wanted to bring the PO_2 back down quickly, we could manually add diluent until the PO_2 read out showed it to be back at set point.

During our bottom time, when oxygen consumption causes the PO_2 to fall below our set point of 1.4ATA, the solenoid valve will open allowing oxygen into the loop to maintain a "constant PO_2". This addition of pure oxygen only in response to its removal by metabolism is a major difference from SCRs which add nitrox at a fixed rate calculated to almost invariably exceed the metabolic needs for oxygen. It means that CCRs are very frugal with gas, especially if the diver is not working hard, and that they truly make no bubbles until the diver begins to ascend (see below).

During ascent the gas in the counterlung expands and some is vented as necessary through an overpressure relief valve or exhaled through the nose by the diver. In this sense CCRs are not truly "closed". In addition, the minute a diver begins ascent, the PO_2 in the loop will begin to fall as the ambient pressure falls. Once again this will cause the solenoid valve to be activated to maintain the PO_2. Provided the ascent is conducted at a normal rate the oxygen addition via the solenoid valve should be able to keep pace with the falling PO_2 to maintain the set point of 1.4ATA.

Mention must be made here of the line of "manual" CCRs such as the "KISS" rebreather that are growing in popularity. They differ from the electronic devices described above in that the diver him or herself acts as the "oxygen controller". There is a constant mass flow valve that continuously adds oxygen to the loop at a rate (about 700ml per minute) designed to be just less than needed by a gently swimming diver. This means that if the diver forgets to manually add oxygen, the PO_2 it will not plummet quickly. Moreover, this continuous rate should be sufficient to maintain oxygenation if the diver were to become unconscious. The idea is that the diver supplements this continuous oxygen feed to maintain their desired set point by manual addition (a push button valve), prompted by monitoring the read out from 3 oxygen sensors. These CCRs are simpler, cheaper and perhaps less prone to failure than electronic devices. Perhaps the main disadvantage is that the accuracy of the constant PO_2 is highly dependent on the vigilance of the operator.

The constant PO_2 advantage

The maintenance of a "constant PO_2" is a huge advantage because it ensures that the diver is breathing the ideal gas mix at every depth they visit. Consider our 30m (100ft) dive. If we performed this dive using open circuit nitrox we would use *Equation 4* to calculate the ideal (maximum) fraction of

oxygen in our nitrox mix. Assuming we use 1.4ATA as our maximum PO_2, then the calculation is as follows:

Ideal fraction of oxygen
= 1.4 ÷ 4ATA (ambient pressure
*   at 30m / 100ft)*
= 0.35

Thus, we would use nitrox 35 for this dive.

At the risk of stating the obvious, this means we would be breathing nitrox 35 at 30m (100ft), and at 20, 10, and 5m (66, 33, 16.5ft) during the ascent. In other words, the mix does not change. The same is essentially true for an SCR which, provided the work rate does not change, will provide a constant nitrox mix throughout the dive. Things are completely different for CCRs which maintain a constant PO_2. Using a variant of equation 4, we can calculate the fraction of oxygen in the loop at different depths when a constant PO_2 of 1.4ATA is maintained for our 30m (100ft) dive. At 30m (100ft) the fraction of oxygen in the loop will be 0.35 as for the nitrox dive. But consider what happens as the PO_2 is kept constant as we move to a shallower depth. At 20m (66ft) the fraction of oxygen in the loop is given by:

Fraction of oxygen in the loop
= 1.4 (PO2) ÷ 3ATA (ambient pressure)
= 0.47

Thus, at 20m (66ft) the CCR diver is breathing nitrox 47. If the same calculation is made for 10m (33ft) the CCR diver is shown to be breathing nitrox 70. At 5m (16.5ft) the CCR diver is breathing almost pure oxygen! Thus, a major advantage of the CCR is that whereas an open circuit nitrox or SCR diver can only be breathing the ideal mix at the deepest planned depth, the CCR diver is breathing the ideal mix (in terms of minimizing nitrogen absorption or retention) throughout the dive. CCRs therefore not only provide prolonged underwater duration and extend the depth range (provided the correct diluent is used), they also minimize the decompression obligation by maximizing oxygen breathing and minimizing inert gas absorption. This advantage does come at the cost of having to watch the oxygen clock (see earlier) very carefully. Not surprisingly, CCRs are widely regarded as the ultimate deep diving tool.

Tracking decompression status

The use of a constant PO_2 rebreather requires special algorithms for calculating decompression obligations. Standard nitrox or mixed gas dive tables and computers are not designed for use during constant PO_2 diving. There are some constant PO_2 military tables but by far the most prevalent approach to dive planning by CCR divers is to use one of several purpose designed constant PO_2 decompression algorithms that can be run on a PC. The user is required to enter the depth, planned bottom time, the diluent and the PO_2 (and other optional settings that alter conservatism and other parameters). The program then provides a decompression algorithm for the dive.

Decompression tables calculated using constant PO_2 algorithms are fine for square profile dives, but as with dive tables used for conventional diving, if a multilevel dive is being conducted it becomes more difficult to track decompression status. This task is considerably simplified by the use of a dive computer, but currently the Delta P Technology VR3 (operating a Bühlmann-based algorithm *Proplanner*) is the only widely available dive computer programmed with constant PO_2 algorithms. No doubt this field will expand and other models will become available.

Availability of CCRs

This issue is not discussed in detail because the information may become dated very quickly. However, it is fair to say that at the time of publication by far the most prevalent CCR in recreational technical diving is the *Buddy Inspiration* manufactured by AP

valves in the U.K. These are well made devices that are marketed at a reasonable price by comparison with some of the others that are available. An increasing number of others are becoming available. The *PRISM Topaz* manufactured by PRISM in the U.S.A. is understood to be available by order. A new and very impressive arrival in 2005, the *Ouroboros* manufactured by Delta P Technologies in the U.K., is arguably the most advanced recreational CCR currently available, and its price reflects this. The *KISS* line of manual CCRs is becoming increasingly popular and is readily available.

Second hand CCRs, including examples from lines that are no longer manufactured, are available from time to time. The *Cis-Lunar* rebreather which was the flagship of the recreational CCR range in the late 1990s has recently gone out of production, but examples of this device will continue to be used for some time. There are also a number of ex US Military rebreathers in the *Mark 15* and 15.5 family used by recreational technical divers (see Figure 32.5). These are popular with serious technical divers because of their large CO_2 scrubber capacity and proven depth capability, but they are hard to obtain. Apart from the size of his or her bank balance, perhaps the most important considerations for the prospective CCR diver in choosing a device is the availability of technical support and parts, and the availability of instructors who are truly expert in the use of the intended rebreather.

FIGURE 32.5

A diver wearing a US Navy Mk 15.5 CCR.
Note the large sling tanks of bailout gas.

REBREATHER PROBLEMS

Rebreathers, and particularly CCRs are complex devices and their use introduces a number of hazards that are either absent or less likely to arise in the use of open circuit scuba equipment. Most prominent among these hazards is the development of PO_2s in the loop that are either too high or too low. Either can be disastrous. A high PO_2 can induce a seizure without warning while a low PO_2 can result in unconsciousness, also without warning.

There are numerous ways either state can be induced. A comprehensive discussion of the failure modes of rebreathers is beyond the scope of this chapter, but it is worthwhile to consider the following examples.

In an SCR hypoxia could arise because the wrong gas (air for example) is mistakenly pumped into the loop supply cylinder. It could also in occur because the diver works too hard for a long period, or works hard just before an ascent. For the latter reason, SCR divers are advised to manually flush the loop with fresh gas just before making an ascent. An excessively high PO_2 could occur, as with any other nitrox dive, if the diver ventured too deep for the nitrox mix being used.

In a CCR, hypoxia could arise because the diver exhausts the oxygen supply, forgets to turn the rebreather on, makes an ascent at sufficient speed that the solenoid valve cannot add oxygen quickly enough to maintain the PO_2, or because of a solenoid failure or electronics failure. An excessively high PO_2 could occur if an oxygen rich mix was mistakenly added to the diluent cylinder, the solenoid or manual oxygen injection valves jammed open, or if the diver made a rapid descent when diving at an established high PO_2 set point (such as 1.4ATA). It should be noted that none of the currently available CCRs automatically add diluent to lower the PO_2 if it rises above the set point during a descent.

Both types of rebreather are prone to scrubber failure if the scrubber material is used for too long, the scrubber is incorrectly packed, or if the scrubber's dynamic capacity is exceeded thus allowing "break through" (see earlier). Both types are also prone to catastrophic loop floods, for example, induced by ripping of one of the breathing hoses. If the loop floods, the rebreather is completely unusable.

Perhaps not surprisingly, there is emerging evidence for a disturbingly high fatality rate in the use of electronic CCRs by recreational technical divers (it may approach 0.5% over a 5 year period). The reasons for this are unknown. Mechanical problems or failures with the devices themselves are rarely identified, and user errors are much more frequently cited. It must also be conceded that, especially with respect to CCRs, the devices facilitate a level of complex diving that was hitherto out of the range of most. Some of the deep long dives being conducted with these devices are inherently risky in their own right, irrespective of the breathing system used.

In recognition of these various problems (and there are many more), most technical divers using rebreathers for deep diving carry open circuit bail out gas supplies so that if the rebreather fails for any reason the diver can surface safely on open circuit. Whilst the necessity to carry this open circuit bailout gas negates some of the advantages of the rebreather, the risk of not doing so is widely considered to be too high.

© Dr. Richard Harris

SUMMARY

- Rebreathers address the fundamentally inefficient use of gas when using open circuit scuba equipment, by recycling exhaled gas instead of releasing it into the water.

- All rebreathers incorporate a rebreathing loop, a CO_2 scrubbing system, and a gas addition system.

- The loop consists of inhalation and exhalation hoses with check valves to ensure unidirectional flow, and a counterlung which the diver breathes in and out of. Counterlungs may be positioned on the back, over the shoulder or on the front of the diver.

- CO_2 scrubbers vary in size, design and efficiency. The scrubber material has a limited duration of use and must be replaced after this period. Scrubber efficiency is potentially reduced by cold temperatures, increased depth, incorrect packing procedures, partial flooding of the scrubber, and very high flow rates of gas through the scrubber.

- Most rebreathers utilized by technical divers can be classified as either semi-closed (SCRs), or closed circuit rebreathers (CCRs).

- SCRs utilize a constant mass flow regulator to ensure that there is a constant flow of an appropriate oxygen-containing gas (usually nitrox) flowing into the loop throughout the dive. Flow is calculated to ensure the loop oxygen levels remain appropriate over a range of activity (from rest to exercise).

- CCRs usually utilize an electronic oxygen measurement system to trigger addition of small amounts of pure oxygen to the loop only when it is required to maintain a predetermined "set point". In this way, closed circuit devices are even more efficient than semi-closed devices. A separate cylinder of diluent gas provides volume to the loop when required.

- In CCR diving, the choice of diluent gas revolves around the type of dive being undertaken. For deep dives, helium-containing diluents are used.

- The CCR system of maintaining a constant PO_2 means that the gas mix in the loop changes throughout the dive to ensure the diver is breathing close to an optimal mix from a decompression point of view.

- Rebreather diving introduces many new concepts and practical skills, and there are periods (particularly descent and ascent) where the use of these devices introduces a significantly greater degree of task loading.

- Thorough and expert training is <u>absolutely essential</u> prior to the use of any rebreather device.

RECOMMENDED READING

Mount T. Technical Diver Encyclopedia. USA: IANTD; 1998.

Gentile G. The Technical Diving Handbook. Philadelphia: Gary Gentile Productions; 1998.

33

Decompression emergencies

Since technical diving techniques are generally utilized to facilitate diving beyond the usual depth and time limits of conventional air diving, it is hardly surprising that the consequences of an adverse event are potentially more serious. The risk of omitting decompression stops if something goes wrong, and the occurrence of decompression sickness are particular worries for technical divers. Not surprisingly, the issues of how to manage omitted decompression and DCS are frequently discussed.

OMITTED DECOMPRESSION

Diving and hyperbaric physicians are frequently asked about the optimum course of action should a diver surface having omitted a decompression obligation. Omitted decompression events are not infrequent, even in recreational scuba. As technical diving becomes more widespread, more divers can be expected to find themselves in a situation where a response to omitted decompression will be necessary.

Before proceeding, there are two very important points that should be emphasized. Firstly, the term "decompression" should not be considered relevant only to "decompression diving". Even in recreational "no decompression" dives, the normal slow ascent is a form of decompression, and a rapid ascent from a dive that has not accrued a requirement for decompression stops can therefore be considered omitted decompression, albeit of a milder less provocative type. Secondly, there is no standard textbook advice for these situations, and no universally accepted right or wrong response.

The four possible responses to omitted decompression, and their relevant advantages and disadvantages are discussed below.

Option 1:

Do nothing, but monitor the diver for symptoms of DCS.

Clearly, if decompression is omitted the risk of DCS is greater than if it had been completed, and the worse the omission, the more likely the development of DCS. However, just because decompression has been omitted, it is not inevitable that the diver will suffer DCS. Indeed, if the omission is relatively minor, the risk may be small. Thus, one plausible option is for the diver to rest and monitor themselves carefully for the development of any symptoms. Strenuous activity after a dive has been shown to precipitate DCS, so the diver should not do any hard physical work or exercise such as pulling up a heavy anchor or lifting heavy equipment. In this, and all other options, the diver should not dive again for at least 24 hours. If the diver develops symptoms, proactive first aid as described in Chapter 5 becomes imperative.

The advantages of the "do nothing" approach are that it is simple, requires no resources, time or effort, and the chances are that many divers in this situation will not develop symptoms of DCS (depending on the degree of omitted decompression). The disadvantages are that nothing is actively being done to decrease risk and it follows that of all the options discussed here, this is the one most likely to result in symptoms. This option is most likely to be utilized following a rapid ascent in a so-called "no-decompression" dive, or following a "decompression dive" in which only a few minutes of decompression have been omitted. It should not be chosen following significant omission of decompression.

Option 2:

Re-enter the water with a fresh supply of air (or nitrox) and complete an omitted decompression procedure.

Many diving tables or decompression planning algorithms have an associated procedure that can be followed in the event of an omitted decompression provided there are no symptoms of DCS, there is sufficient air (or nitrox) to complete the omitted decompression procedure, and the procedure can be initiated quickly. Most published protocols involve going deeper than the first omitted stop, and conducting a series of stops over a longer period than the original omitted decompression. For example, the US Navy recommends the following: repeat all stops below 12m (40ft), then go to 12m (40ft) for $1/3$ of the 3m (10ft) stop time; 9m (30ft) for of the 3m (10ft) stop time; 6m (20ft) for $1/2$ of the 3m (10ft) stop time; and 3m (10ft) for 1 $1/2$ the 3m (10ft) stop time. This needs to be initiated quickly and the US Navy recommends no more than 5 minutes from surfacing. If this option is taken, the diver must always be escorted during the omitted decompression procedure.

The advantages of this procedure are that if it is instituted early (especially within 5 minutes) it can be effective, and it is an active intervention that is likely to reduce the risk of DCS. However, the disadvantages are that it requires both knowledge of the correct protocols, and the time and resources to set up a proper decompression line (if there is not already one in place). There is also the potential for hypothermia and the development of symptoms of DCS whilst the diver is underwater.

With respect to this option, re-entering the water breathing air is widely discouraged **if symptoms of DCS have already appeared.** The conventional wisdom is that in-water recompression on air should not be used as a treatment for DCS. The reasons for this are two-fold. Re-entering the water after symptoms have developed has frequently proved ineffectual (unless oxygen is also administered; see Option 4) and delays the correct treatment and management. Symptoms may resolve initially under pressure but rarely is the relief sustained after the inevitable decompression. Also there is a real risk that symptoms can worsen and the diver can rapidly deteriorate underwater, putting them in considerable potential danger.

Option 3:

Breathe 100% oxygen at the surface.

This option involves administering 100% oxygen upon exiting the water, even if no symptoms of DCS have developed. The diver is kept at rest and monitored for manifestations of DCS. If the diver does become symptomatic, the full first aid for DCS is then implemented.

The advantages of this are that it is relatively easy to do and it is almost certainly beneficial if done for at least 30-60 minutes. It also means that if symptoms do develop, the diver is not placed in extra danger by being underwater. The disadvantages are that using the oxygen for this diver depletes the supply, which, if further diving is conducted by others, could be needed for another if an emergency were to arise later. There may also be technical limitations in the equipment making it difficult to deliver 100% O_2 to both divers in a buddy pair, unless sufficient and suitable oxygen equipment and supply are available.

Option 4

Breathe 100% oxygen underwater.

Breathing 100% oxygen underwater has the potential to be a highly effective means of preventing emergence of DCS after a significant omitted decompression. However, this strategy requires proper training and equipment, and is most often invoked by technical divers for emergency in-water oxygen recompression of a diver who has actually developed DCS (see In-water recompression). It is unlikely to be a valid option for recreational (non-technical) divers who have omitted decompression because they are unlikely to have the knowledge or equipment to do it "safely". The major risk is oxygen toxicity manifest as a seizure. If this occurred and unless the diver was wearing a full-face mask, it would be very likely to result in drowning. The advantage of this technique is that it has the potential to be very successful in preventing DCS. The disadvantage is that it is equipment and expertise intensive, and carries the danger of oxygen toxicity.

Which option is recommended?

As stated earlier, there is no textbook answer to this question. To some extent the response depends upon the degree of omitted decompression. If it were very minor (for example, one or two minutes decompression omitted), we would lean towards Options 1 or 2. If there was a significant omission of decompression, we would certainly favour the more active interventions such as breathing 100% 0_2 at

the surface, or possibly immediate in-water recompression with air or nitrox provided the diver was asymptomatic. If properly equipped, appropriate expertise was available and the sea and weather conditions were suitable, we would have little hesitation instituting in-water oxygen breathing after a significant omitted decompression, even for a diver with certain symptoms (see below). However, the need for proper training, equipment and appropriate conditions is emphasized.

Whatever option is taken the diver should rest and not dive for at least 24 hours after completion of the procedure. If symptoms develop, DCS first aid must be administered and contact made with medical personnel via the appropriate diving emergency hotline with evacuation following soon after.

IN-WATER RECOMPRESSION

When DCS occurs in any diving setting whether it be recreational, technical or commercial, it is important that the correct first aid measures are put in place. These were discussed in Chapter 5, along with a review of definitive management using recompression and hyperbaric oxygen delivered in a recompression chamber.

A related issue that is commonly raised in discussions of DCS management, particularly among technical divers is whether or not it is advisable to recompress a victim of DCS in the water at the dive site before (or instead of) evacuation to a recompression chamber. The ensuing debate remains one of the most controversial issues in diving medicine. Antagonists (who are usually conservative diving physicians) argue that recompression breathing air is ineffective and may make matters worse, and that recreational divers have neither the expertise nor the equipment to run a safe in-water recompression on oxygen. The most dogmatic opinions suggest that divers with symptoms should not re-enter the water under any circumstances, and that the only safe course of action is to evacuate the diver to the nearest recompression chamber.

This notion is frequently challenged. Clearly, in some remote locations the prolonged nature of evacuation may allow the disease to progress significantly and perhaps irreversibly before treatment. In addition, claims of in-water recompression on air being "inevitably" unsuccessful are probably exaggerated. Finally, in this age of technical diving more groups *are* equipped for, and capable of, conducting in-water recompression on oxygen.

As always in diving medicine, the major impediment to resolving this argument is the lack of any data generated in properly designed trials. This is hardly surprising. It would be very difficult to get scientific ethics committee approval to conduct a comparative human trial of various interventions administered at different intervals after development of serious symptoms. However, there are one or two "facts", and an abundance of anecdote upon which we can form the basis of an opinion.

First, there is one key point upon which most diving physicians and commentators would agree: the window of opportunity for reliably effective intervention in rapidly progressive spinal DCS (manifest as sensory changes and weakness in the limbs) is often very short. It is almost certainly measured in minutes rather than hours. Our usual claim that "the shorter the delay the better the outcome" implies an inverse linear relationship between delay and outcome, and this may be too simplistic. For example, it seems probable that a vastly superior outcome is associated with treatment within 15 minutes compared to an hour, but there may be much less difference in outcome between recompression started at 2 hours as compared to 4 hours. While there have been conspicuous exceptions, there are many cases of devastating spinal DCS that do not respond to definitive recompression

when the delay to treatment starts to drag out beyond an hour or so (although this "critical time threshold" is not clearly established). Indeed, once the disease progression is well established, we sometimes see further deterioration during recompression! Not surprisingly, there is an increasing body of opinion that it is not merely a case of treatment "sooner rather than later", but rather of treatment "very soon or you may be wasting your time".

Second, there are now many reports of individuals who have experienced complete resolution of rapidly progressive symptoms of spinal DCS when in-water recompression is initiated within minutes of symptom onset. On some occasions, the recompression has involved the use of air rather than oxygen. There is one well-documented and famous case of two Hawaiian divers who simultaneously became very sick after identical deep air dives. One diver refused to be evacuated and insisted on returning to the water to effect as much in-water recompression as the air in two scuba tanks would allow, while the other was evacuated to a recompression chamber several hours away. The diver who recompressed himself in-water was found swimming around on the surface several hours later, apparently cured. The other diver died during evacuation in the helicopter.

We have to be very careful interpreting the significance of such stories. Despite their identical dives, these divers may have been suffering disease of quite different severity. Moreover, it is the stories with a happy ending that tend to get widely reported, and tales of disasters or poor outcomes during in-water recompression probably do not get aired as widely. Nevertheless, there is much anecdotal support for the practice, especially when it is properly conducted using oxygen.

This combination of a poor prognosis for full recovery in delayed treatment of serious spinal DCS (even when the delay is relatively short), and apparent success in the use of in-water techniques forms a potent argument for the use of such techniques when they are employed by divers with some experience in the use of the equipment and gases that will maximize the changes of a good outcome. Technical divers fit this description perfectly. At a personal level, the authors would have no hesitation in recompressing themselves in the water in response to early symptoms of spinal DCS if definitive treatment was not readily available, and provided the protocols described below could be followed.

Injured divers suitable for in-water recompression

In-water recompression is recommended for treatment of certain early symptoms of serious DCS. In particular, it is recommended when there are early and progressive symptoms of spinal involvement, such as weakness or numbness in the arms or legs. It is less certain whether the inherent risks are justified in the treatment of milder symptoms such as musculoskeletal pain only. This is a value judgement, and no definitive opinion can be expressed. *Injured divers for whom IWR is contemplated should be conscious and not in obvious danger of becoming unconscious.* They must have adequate thermal protection. In this regard, on technical diving operations where IWR is planned as a contingency it is wise if divers remain in their wet or drysuits for at least 30 minutes after the dive (the period of maximal risk for development of serious symptoms). Getting a deteriorating diver back into a wet or drysuit might be difficult and time consuming.

Equipment for in-water recompression

The following items of equipment must be available for IWR:

1. *An oxygen supply that is adequate for the duration of the recompression protocol* (see below). Oxygen could be delivered via an open circuit scuba-type system, a regulator and whip connected to a surface supply of oxygen, or a rebreather.

2. Whatever the nature of the oxygen supply, it should be administered through a *full-face mask system*, or a mouthpiece that is held in place by a sealing retainer system.

3. *A weighted descent line long enough to cope with the protocol used.* Ideally, the "line" should have a decompression bar arrangement (see Figure 30.1) at the shallower depths to make long stays more comfortable.

4. *A means to attach the diver to the descent line or decompression bars.* A "jon line" (see Figure 30.3) would be appropriate.

Protocol for in-water recompression

Action must be taken as soon as the diver reports symptoms. The diver should be given 100% oxygen while the situation is evaluated. Assuming that the necessary equipment is available, other issues that should be considered in deciding whether to proceed with IWR include the nature of the symptoms, the time to the nearest definitive recompression facility, the surface conditions, and the time of day (the various protocols require at least 2 to 3 hours in the water). Once the decision to proceed is made, the recompression must be initiated as quickly as possible.

A variety of IWR protocols have been proposed. None are supported over and above the others by any outcome data. The most commonly cited protocol in Australia is that described by Dr. Carl Edmonds. This involves breathing oxygen at 9m (30ft) for 30 minutes in less serious cases, or 60 to 90 minutes in progressively more serious cases. After a maximum of 90 minutes, ascent is commenced at the very slow rate of 1 metre every 12 minutes. It will be immediately obvious that such an exposure breaks the usual "oxygen clock" rules, and there is a concomitantly increased risk of oxygen seizure. This is why it is considered very unwise to perform oxygen IWR without a full-face mask that will protect the victim's airway in the event of a seizure. On arrival at the surface, the injured diver should continue to be given oxygen using a one hour on (oxygen) - one hour off (breathing air) regimen. Contact should be made with a diving physician during administration of the protocol and it will often be necessary to evacuate the diver to a recompression chamber on completion.

Those wishing to learn more about IWR and the various protocols are referred to the Undersea and Hyperbaric Medical Society Workshop Report on this subject (see "Recommended Reading" at the end of this chapter).

> *It should be borne in mind at all times that oxygen IWR is a controversial technique and carries with it the risk of in-water oxygen seizure, failure (to cure the symptoms), and even deterioration in the diver's condition despite the treatment. Divers utilize the technique at their own risk. Similarly, notwithstanding anecdotal support for its use, IWR using air is highly controversial and cannot be recommended.*

SUMMARY

- Technical diving, and decompression diving in particular, raises the likelihood of divers encountering diving emergencies in the field. The appropriate response to omitted decompression and DCI are frequent topics of discussion.

- Options for an omitted decompression situation include: doing nothing and observing the diver; re-entering the water to complete an omitted decompression procedure; breathing 100% oxygen at the surface; and breathing 100% oxygen underwater. All have their advantages and disadvantages.

- In-water recompression is an option for early presenting cases of DCI, especially where it is likely there will be a significant delay in obtaining definitive treatment in a recompression chamber.

- In water recompression should only be undertaken for cooperative fully conscious divers, and where the team is <u>suitably equipped</u> to conduct the procedure. This includes capability for "safely" administering 100% oxygen underwater.

RECOMMENDED FURTHER READING

Edmonds C, Lowry C, Pennefather J, Walker R. Diving and Subaquatic Medicine (4th Edn). London: Arnold; 2002:161-4.

Mount T. Technical Diver Encyclopedia. USA: IANTD; 1998.

Gentile G. The Technical Diving Handbook. Philadelphia: Gary Gentile Productions; 1998.

Kay E, Spencer MP (eds). In-Water Recompression. Proceedings of the Forty-Eighth Workshop of the Undersea and Hyperbaric Medical Society. Kensington MD: Undersea and Hyperbaric Medical Society; 1999.

34

Occupational ("Commercial") Diving

Many of us who become passionate divers are attracted by the notion of somehow making diving a career. There are many options for the budding "career diver", including diving instruction, dive guiding, scientific diving, underwater photography, construction diving, military diving, sea-harvesting, aquaculture, and diving medicine. In this chapter, we will briefly describe the nature of the work undertaken by these various groups, the training involved, and the likely avenues of employment.

Before tackling these various sub-categories of diving career, we should like to emphasize the fact that we prefer the term "occupational diving" to "commercial diving" since it is a more precise and meaningful definition. Occupational diving embraces all divers who make all or part of their living from some form of diving activity. You do not have to work on a North Sea oil rig to be classed as an occupational diver.

DIVING INSTRUCTION AND DIVE GUIDING

Diving Instructors and Dive Guides (commonly referred to as Divemasters) are perhaps the largest group of occupational divers on a global scale. Certainly, this is one of the most accessible occupational diving fields to the general diving population.

The work

Divemasters are certified to supervise recreational diving activity. Most commonly this involves supervising dive trips on dive charter boats. The divemaster is expected to obtain information about the participating divers' training and experience, ensure they are paired with a suitable buddy, provide them with a briefing about the dive site and important local diving practices, and to supervise the conduct of the divers as they prepare for the dive, leave the boat, and return to the boat. Frequently divemasters will also escort divers during the dive. Divemasters are certified to assist instructors during the training of divers through the various levels of attainment. All of these roles carry a high level of responsibility and must be taken on with the utmost diligence.

Instructors are certified to train novice divers, and to bring trained divers through the various levels of certification. The bread and butter work for a dive instructor is the open water diver course which typically involves a number of classroom and confined water sessions followed by at least 4 open water dives. These courses can be immensely satisfying but very labour intensive and are sometimes energy-sapping affairs if the students have any academic or practical difficulties.

Diving instructors are expected to be active in teaching the range of "continuing education" courses, such as Advanced Diver, Rescue Diver, and even Divemaster courses. Once again, these courses are quite time-intensive lasting from 2-3 days for an Advanced course, to more than a week for a Divemaster course. Because of the higher level of knowledge imparted, they can be quite academically challenging courses for the instructor to teach.

Depending on the ratings they hold, instructors may be expected to teach so-called "specialty courses" such as boat diver, underwater photographer, underwater naturalist, among others. These courses are typically short and practical in orientation. Instructors in some locations also spend a lot of time conducting so-called "resort dives". These dives involve providing novices with a short introduction to key aspects of diving theory and practice, and a dive in a tightly-controlled open water environment in which one instructor usually only looks after one or two students. It is an experience designed to whet the student's appetite for further training.

In the modern context, instructors may expected to have a wide range of other relevant diving industry skills such as boat handling, compressor operation, and sales skills. The latter is considered very important by many industry employers, and instructors pay is sometimes linked to equipment sales volumes.

The training

The readily available hierarchy of training offered by most training agencies makes it relatively easy, some believe too easy, for a motivated diver to progress to divemaster and then instructor relatively quickly. Typically, the diver completes an open water course, an advanced diver course, a rescue diver course, and a divemaster course with a few short "specialty courses" along the way, before enrolling in what is often referred to as an Instructor Development Course or IDC. This is usually 1 to 2 weeks long, and most would agree, a reasonably challenging experience. The focus is mainly on grooming the candidates for effective teaching, and there are numerous assessments of their teaching ability which many find moderately intimidating at first. The IDC is followed by an Instructor Examination or IE, which is conducted by an independent assessor appointed by the training organization. This is usually a two-day affair and involves assessment of theoretical knowledge, knowledge of the training agency's standards and procedures, and teaching ability in the classroom, pool, and open water. Most candidates who make it to the IE are successful. Most contemporary employers require instructors and divemasters to have current first aid and oxygen administration qualifications.

Of course, the candidate must accumulate a suitable degree of experience as a diver and divemaster as they progress along the path we have described above, and herein lies one of the most controversial issues in diving today. Without going too deeply into the specifics, it is possible for an instructor to go through the entire program in 3 to 6 months, and to emerge as a fully qualified dive instructor with around 100 dives under their belt, most of them obtained under training of one sort or another. Some believe that this is too little experience of "real" diving, and that the graduates lack both the credibility and the "real world exposure" to operate safely and effectively in the dive industry. These authors have some sympathy toward this view, though this comment must be balanced by the fact that the end users of diving instructor's services (the dive shop owners) are not exactly throwing their hands up in horror over the incompetence of the staff on offer. Indeed, operators whose opinions are well trusted by the authors, have observed that some graduates of these relatively fast-track programs are the best instructors they have seen.

Comments

Diving instruction can be a vastly rewarding job. Diving instructors frequently take novice divers who are nervous and whose self esteem is at risk, and introduce them to this wondrous activity that allays their fears, reinforces their self esteem, and provides them with a lot of fun in the process. A lot of powerful affirmation goes on in a typical dive course, for both the instructor and student. These elements potentially make diving instruction highly enjoyable professionally and socially.

However, these comments have to be balanced by a few negatives. It is tiring work that requires a lot of energy from the instructor to keep the trainees enthusiastic through the highs and lows of a course. At times it can be very frustrating, especially if the instructor is unlucky enough to have a class with generally poor skill levels. Some instructors (and divemasters) are required to dive too consistently without adequate rest periods and are, therefore, more at risk of getting decompression illness. On top of all of this, instructors are not usually particularly well paid, especially considering the amount of responsibility they take on. In the latter regard, there are significant public and professional liability issues. Diving instructors can be, and are sued for alleged negligence. Many cases are successfully defended, and there is insurance for those that are not, but whether the negligence is real or imagined, this is not a pleasant experience for anyone. Finally, a real danger of an active career in diving instruction is that the diving instructor loses their passion for their own recreational diving.

With the above in mind, it is not surprising that many divers have utilized instructional qualifications to travel, and to embark on a fun and adventurous occupational activity for a finite period before moving on to some other employment. Not many instructors continue to teach as their primary source of income for their entire working lives.

SCIENTIFIC DIVING

Scientific divers are a much smaller group who usually get involved in diving as a part of their employment in a biological, environmental or archeological sciences field. For example, a marine biology graduate employed by a marine laboratory may be required to dive as part of their work, but they are not employed primarily as a diver. This would be the typical scenario for most scientific divers. Some of the biggest employers may utilize career scientific divers, but most would fall into the "biologist first, diver second" category.

The work

Scientific diving embraces a myriad of potential activities specific to the projects being undertaken. Most scientific divers in the biological sciences would be required to perform tasks such as: swimming a transect line or utilizing a marked quadrant to count species of interest in a standardized fashion; taking serial photographs of specific objects or areas; making behavioural observations; performing fresh water drift dives to count fish, and many others. Divers in the environmental sciences might be required to take core samples from the sea floor, and obtain samples of organic and inorganic material for laboratory analysis. Archeological divers might be involved in the painstaking surveying and mapping of sites of interest. It is emphasized once again, however, that most divers in these fields would spend majority of their time engaged in some related but non-diving activity.

The training

Since most institutions have their own particular tasks and requirements, many run tailored scientific diving courses "in house" or "on the job". Many accept recreational diving qualifications (plus a suitable degree of experience) as the entry level for further training as a scientific diver. Some institutional courses have achieved accreditation under schemes such as the

Australian Diver Accreditation Scheme (ADAS) (see Construction Diving below). Information about the specifics of scientific diver training would need to be obtained from the particular institute a diver was interested in working for.

Comments

Scientific diving is an interesting and adventurous sideline to employment in certain jobs in the biological and environmental sciences. Unlike construction diving, scientific diving frequently takes place in pleasant environments and the diving could be classified as "serious but interesting and fun". Unfortunately, there are virtually no jobs in which you do nothing but scientific diving, and the best way into this field is through training in a scientific discipline that will necessitate diving as part of the job. Equally unfortunately, such jobs are few and far between in the modern setting, and even a PhD in marine biology is no guarantee of the desired position.

UNDERWATER PHOTOGRAPHY

Almost not worth mentioning, but wouldn't we all like to make our living taking photos underwater? There are very, very few divers who truly make their living taking underwater photos. Those that do are self-selected geniuses in the field like David Doubilet whose work cannot be replicated by many. Unfortunately, although you can take courses and workshops in underwater photography, these simply do not prepare you with the skills to do it full time and make a living out of it. The "way in" initially is to develop a natural talent and exhibit it in photographic competitions. Once you are producing consistently good results, the internet and various photo libraries present good opportunities for selling your photos.

MILITARY DIVING

Most navies operate diving teams of one sort or another, and in many larger armed forces the army (particularly special forces) often run diving teams as well. We will focus on naval divers and the models we are drawing from are mainly Australasian, though most of the following comments are applicable to military divers anywhere.

The work

Military divers might be expected to engage in a wide range of activities which include ship's husbandry, attack swimming, mine countermeasures, search and recovery, submarine rescue, remote operated vehicle (ROV) operations and explosive ordinance disposal.

Ship's husbandry involves tasks like hull inspections, cleaning of sonar transponders and other miscellaneous tasks. It is frequently conducted using normal scuba equipment.

Attack swimming is usually conducted for the purpose of sabotage (such as putting mines on ships) or as a means of arriving somewhere on shore undetected. Attack divers usually use closed-circuit oxygen rebreathers because they are small, light, have a long duration, and make no bubbles. Attack operations are frequently conducted at night and require well-honed navigational and diving skills. In particular, the use of closed-circuit oxygen rebreathers is a potentially hazardous task because if depth is not accurately maintained, there is a real risk of oxygen toxicity. These operations are invariably very physically demanding.

Mine countermeasures involves a highly specialized set of skills, both in the technical aspects of neutralizing mines, and with respect to the diving itself. Modern mines often sit very deep, and divers may have to dive to depths up to 90m (300ft) in completing their tasks. Mixed gas rebreathers are sometimes used for this type of work.

Search and rescue work is extraordinarily varied, ranging as it can from removing the occupants of a sunken car in a 5m pond, to diving on a sunken submarine in 110m (360ft) (as the Norwegians did with the Kursk). Shallow work is often conducted using standard scuba equipment, while the deeper work is undertaken using mixed gas rebreathers or surface supply mixed gas equipment.

The training

Most navies operate several tiers of diving involvement. Frequently, it is possible to become involved in diving on a part time basis. For example, in Australia and New Zealand, sailors from other naval branches (such as seamen and cooks) can train as "ship's divers" whilst remaining in their original branches. These divers are trained for scuba air only, and would be used for basic diving tasks that might arise in the normal course of operating a ship. They do not participate in the more specialized work of navy divers described above. Different militaries have different policies on recruitment into the full time diving branch. Some will recruit trainees specifically to join as divers, while others require that you join initially in another branch and change to the diving branch later, usually after training as a "ship's diver".

Whatever the method of recruitment, the training as a full time navy diver is intentionally designed to be physically and psychologically arduous, as is the training for any "special forces" branch. Unless you are superbly fit and mentally strong, basically you can forget it. There is a copious quantity of ritualized embuggerance designed to weed out those who cannot cope when the going gets tough. Courses usually last many months and contain periods when the living conditions will be hard, and sleep deprivation will be the norm. Equally though, successful trainees will learn to dive using a wide variety of highly specialized diving equipment, and even the most florid sense of adventure will be satisfied. A strong sense of camaraderie and teamwork is encouraged, and there is a profound sense of satisfaction in surviving the ordeal.

Comments

Military diving is not for everyone. It is high on adventure and challenge, but (very) low on pleasure diving and appreciation of the ocean's wonders. The training is extremely hard. Some characters who thought they were very tough have been seen to drop out of these courses. Indeed, of those who present themselves for selection, very few actually make it. It should be borne in mind at all times that you are volunteering yourself for training in some very dangerous activities. Moreover, although it may appear to be stating the obvious, various military diving activities may ultimately be conducted in hostile environments in which others are trying to kill you with bullets, explosives, nets and sonar. It is important to have a clear perspective on this. The best place to gather more accurate information on diving in the particular service that interests you is through the local recruiting office.

CONSTRUCTION DIVING

Construction diving is something of a default bin for all the activities that don't fit into the various other categories. Not all of it involves "construction" as such, but there will usually be some sort of "constructive" purpose to the dive. Construction diving covers a wide range of activities from simple to complex, and a range of technologies from basic to advanced. For example, cleaning a hull on a boat, changing a bolt on a wharf pile, and locking out of a bell during a saturation dive on an oil rig are all examples of construction dives, albeit at different points on the continuum of complexity.

The work

As implied above, construction diving work is highly varied in terms of its nature and complexity. Since most readers will not find the concept of using scuba equipment to clean the hull of a boat particularly foreign or interesting, we will focus on the more advanced end of the scale, in particular, offshore construction work.

The offshore oil and gas industry has been one of the biggest employers of divers over the last few decades. There are many potential construction and maintenance tasks necessary in the operation of offshore drilling and pumping platforms. Some can be dealt with by conducting "bounce" dives in which the diver descends, does the job, and then decompresses. However, these tasks are frequently complex, time consuming and on-going, and the technique of saturation diving has been developed to cope with this in the most efficient way. In saturation diving, the divers actually live under pressure for days or weeks inside a habitat. The advantage of this is that once their body tissues are saturated with inert gas (see Chapters 3 and 4) no more can be absorbed and staying under pressure for longer periods of time incurs no further decompression penalty. Under these circumstances, the divers can make multiple excursions or "lock-outs" from the bell habitat and perform underwater work with little or no regard to dive times or decompression requirements. Instead, duration is limited mainly by fatigue and cold. Obviously, because the divers are saturated with inert gas at what is sometimes quite a considerable depth, their ultimate decompression from the dive will take a long time (days), but this is still a much more efficient (and safer) method of diving than trying to achieve the same output using a multiple bounce dive technique.

Saturation divers are usually utilizing mixed gases, and their diving equipment almost invariably involves the use of helmets with umbilicals that carry communications wires as well as the gas supply. These divers are required to have a range of special skills such as underwater welding and cutting. Living in "sat" is not the most pleasant experience a diver is likely to have. While most of the habitats are made as comfortable as possible, privacy is at a premium, and you are stuck with others not of your choosing in a moderately stressful environment for long periods at a time. This is not an ideal formula for social harmony, and "sat" divers must be adaptable easy-going individuals who can readily cope with the idiosyncrasies of others.

The training

In Australasia, the best construction diver training is provided by those schools accredited under the Australian Diver Accreditiation Scheme (ADAS). This scheme provides benchmarks for competency of divers at various levels, and most importantly, is recognized by the United Kingdom Health and Safety Executive (HSE). Recognition of training by the HSE is vital to offshore employment prospects because many of the international companies that employ divers require this.

There are 4 levels of training (Parts 1 – 4) under the ADAS scheme. Each part takes about a month to complete. Part 1 (equivalent to the HSE Part 4!) covers no-decompression scuba air diving to 30m (100ft). The use of small hand held tools and inspection techniques are also covered. Part 2 (=HSE Part 3) covers surface supply diving on air to 30m (100ft), and the extra skills covered include cutting and welding, the use of pneumatic and hydraulic tools, photography and videography, and use of explosives. Part 3 (=HSE Part 2) covers surface supply diving on air to 50m (165ft) and introduces the use of wet bells and hot water suits. There is also training in the use of hyperbaric chambers for decompression, and in particular, the surface decompression on oxygen (SurDO$_2$) technique. This involves the divers completing part of their decompression in the water, followed by surfacing and rapid transfer to a recompression chamber to complete the rest of their decompression dry and breathing pure oxygen. Finally, the Part 4 (equivalent to the HSE Part 1) covers bell diving, saturation diving and use of mixed gases, but this training is not currently available in Australia or New Zealand.

Training as a construction diver is not cheap and costs several thousands of dollars.

Comments

There are many construction divers who have based their entire career on diving, and this is certainly still possible. It is a demanding career, and means a lot of time away from home. It is also moderately hazardous, although the industry seems reasonably well regulated at present. There has been a trend away from the use of divers (particularly saturation divers) and toward increasing utilization of remote operated vehicles (ROVs) or divers in one-atmosphere suits in many construction settings. This has reduced the availability of jobs in the offshore industry, and the trend may gather further momentum.

SEA HARVESTING AND AQUACULTURE

A number of divers are employed in the sea harvesting and aquaculture industries. Sea harvesting divers are usually self-employed, and either own quota allowing them to take species such as abalone, or contract themselves out to others who do. Aquaculture divers usually work in salmon, tuna or mussel farms and are employed by the farm owners.

The work

Sea harvesting work is frequently seasonal and usually arduous. Divers often spend long periods in the water and payment is usually linked to productivity. Aquaculture diving takes many forms. However, a good example is the work on salmon farms which involves daily dives into the holding nets to remove dead fish and to clean and make repairs to the nets. Such work frequently takes place in temperate water and is physical in nature. Both the sea harvesting and aquaculture industries have long records of unusual practices, poor training, and poor safety when it comes to diving. While this remains true for some quarters of the sea harvesting industry, most aquaculture operations have vastly improved their practices in recent years.

The training

Sea harvesting and aquaculture operations would seek to employ only pre-trained and experienced divers. Although there has been a tendency to settle for recreational diving qualifications in the past, most aquaculture operations in Australasia would now be seeking divers with ADAS accredited qualifications (or equivalent in other countries).

CAREERS IN DIVING MEDICINE

Given our role as commentators on diving medical issues, divers often ask us how they can make a career out of the physiological or medical aspects of diving. Perhaps surprisingly, it is not an uncommon aspiration. While all divers share a love of diving itself, some enthusiastically embrace particular aspects of diving science. Many find the physiology and medicine of diving to be a particularly fascinating aspect of the sport; one that is interesting both academically and practically. After all, our expectation of being able to properly manage a diving medical emergency imbues a little of the diving physician into each of us.

Through various means, a number of divers have managed to turn their interest in diving physiology and medicine into a career. Such a quest has certainly dictated the course of the authors' professional lives. Some of the relevant options are outlined below.

1. Train as a doctor

Perhaps the most obvious route into a diving medicine career is as a doctor. The major obstacle in this path is obtaining your medical degree. In the US, Japan, and most European countries this is an MD (Doctor of Medicine). In the Commonwealth countries it is often called an "MB ChB" or "MB BS" which in both cases stands for Bachelor of Medicine and Bachelor of Surgery. The terminology is irrelevant since the courses in most western countries are essentially equivalent.

Training as a medical doctor involves 6 or 7 years at university. The first 3 years is usually occupied completing an undergraduate degree in relevant biomedical sciences. The next 3 or 4 years is spent learning real medicine. Much of this time is spent on the wards in hospitals. It is a humbling experience. It seems that for every fact you learn, there are dozens more that you would like to commit to memory but can't. You seem to spend a lot of time learning what you don't know! Personally, I do not think medicine is a conceptually difficult course compared, for example, to physics or higher mathematics. However, nothing matches medicine for the sheer bulk of material you are expected to commit to memory and regurgitate word-perfect on command. You need an organized mind and a good study habit. Notwithstanding all of this, medicine is great fun to learn, and an immensely satisfying career.

It may surprise you to know that there are few undergraduate medical courses anywhere in the world that give diving medicine more than a passing mention. Most doctors emerge from medical school understanding less about diving medicine than the average Rescue Diver. This begs the question: Where does the world get its diving medicine experts? From all sorts of medical disciplines is the not-very-specific answer.

The few doctors who leave medical school and go straight into training solely as a diving physician usually do so through the military. This is the path taken by one of the authors (SJM), and it has the advantage of giving the physician exposure to a wide range of diving activities, including submarine medicine, as well as training in the treatment of diving related diseases. Many well-known diving medicine authorities such as Des Gorman, Carl Edmonds, Ed Thalmann and James Francis spent time in the military to acquire such experience. It must be conceded that the military is not the only way in which a doctor can get "hands on" experience in a range of non-recreational diving activities. A few, such as David Elliott and Robert Wong obtained much of their practical experience of diving operations through a long association with commercial diving. Others, such as Caroline Fife, through salvage and archaeological diving.

Very few doctors take a "pure diving medicine" approach to their career. The majority who involve themselves in diving medicine have usually trained in some other medical discipline before developing diving medicine as a "sideline" to their principal specialty. Such doctors may be anesthesiologists, emergency physicians, surgeons or other specialists working in hospitals that have a recompression chamber. Their diving interest leads them to participate in the activities of that chamber. In many respects this is the "safest" path to take since skills in another specialty gives the doctor more career "flexibility". There are very few jobs available for doctors trained in diving medicine alone.

It is noteworthy that diving physicians almost always become involved in the related field of "hyperbaric medicine". Hyperbaric medicine involves the administration of hyperbaric oxygen to patients with medical problems not related to diving. There are about ten non-diving ailments such as foot ulcers in diabetics in which hyperbaric oxygen is of benefit. Not surprisingly, many modern "diving physicians" are expert in both diving and hyperbaric medicine. A recent and significant development has been the introduction of board certification (specialist) examinations in diving and hyperbaric medicine through the American Board of Preventative Medicine, and certification in the field through the Australian and New Zealand College of Anaesthetists. This has established diving and hyperbaric medicine as a well-defined medical field in its own right, and in addition, the examination curriculum provides structure for training in the discipline that was previously lacking.

2. Train as a Nurse

Diving and hyperbaric medicine units must have appropriately trained nursing staff. Diving and hyperbaric nurses begin their careers by completing normal nursing training. In the modern context, this usually entails a 3 year university or technical institute course which encompasses both academic and practical work. Once graduated as a Registered Nurse, then further training as a "hyperbaric nurse" can be undertaken. Most diving and hyperbaric facilities run their own in-house training programs, but the curricula will invariably comply with requirements laid down by an appropriate expert body, such as the Barometric Nurses Association (BNA) in the USA or the Hyperbaric Technicians and Nurses Association (HTNA) in Australia.

Diving and Hyperbaric nurses have a "hands-on" role in the unit. Most treatments of divers with decompression illness are conducted in so-called multiplace recompression chambers that can accommodate at least several occupants at once. In this setting the patient is always accompanied by a hyperbaric nurse during treatment. These nurses may face the challenge of an unconscious mechanically-ventilated patient in a hyperbaric environment, and so their training and experience is critical. In addition, in hyperbaric units that treat problem wounds, the vitally important task of wound care is usually delegated to expert nurses. The hyperbaric nurse with good wound care knowledge and skills is worth their weight in gold. Many hyperbaric nurses, such a

Christy Pirone from Australia and Valerie Larson-Lohr from the USA, have made spectacular contributions to the development of the diving and hyperbaric medicine field as a whole.

3. Train as a Hyperbaric Technician

Multiplace diving and hyperbaric medicine facilities are technically complex with their compressors, gas storage systems, fire control systems, environmental monitoring and control systems, and many other components. In addition, someone has to "drive" the hyperbaric chamber while the patient(s) and nurse(s) are inside. The maintenance of these systems and "driving" the chamber according to the "prescription" ordered by the doctor is the responsibility of the Certified Hyperbaric Technician (CHT). Many CHTs come from military diving or engineering backgrounds during which they were exposed to hyperbaric chamber operation. Once again, some units train CHTs in house according to requirements specified by expert organizations such as the HTNA.

As with nursing, there is no limit to the recognition and potential that can be achieved as a CHT. Perhaps the most spectacular example of this is Dick Clarke, Director of the Richland Hospital Hyperbaric Unit in Columbia, South Carolina, USA. Dick, formerly a diver in the Royal Navy, has progressed as a CHT to administration of a very prestigious hyperbaric medicine unit, and to running some ground breaking research programs. So thorough and expert is his commentary on complex medical matters that one can easily form the impression that he is a senior and experienced doctor in the field.

4. Train as a Diving Medical Technician

The term "Diving Medical Technician" (DMT) is one most commonly associated with the offshore commercial diving industry. Diving Medical Technicians combine at least some of the skills of both the hyperbaric nurse and technician. They are usually trained in advanced first aid with particular emphasis on treatment of diving diseases, and in some aspects of recompression chamber operation. Their role is management of an unexpected emergency in the offshore diving setting. The DMT must have a broad range of skills to cope with the many types of emergency that may arise. These skills are acquired on courses, usually of several weeks duration, such as that conducted at the Royal Adelaide Hospital in Adelaide, Australia. Participants spend time in the classroom, in the hyperbaric unit learning chamber operation, and in the hospital emergency room learning advanced first aid techniques. Most DMTs are actually commercial divers. Their additional DMT training allows them to instantly adapt to an emergency situation arising in whatever part of the diving operation they happen to be involved in.

5. Get involved in research and education

An often overlooked avenue for development of a diving medicine career is the field of research and education. A higher research-degree program such as that for a PhD can be designed to address an issue in diving and hyperbaric medicine. Unfortunately, there are a limited number of opportunities to continue diving medicine research as a career, with funding for research being the main constraint. Nevertheless, some "non-medical" scientists have built very impressive careers in diving medicine based on research in the field. Possibly, the most outstanding example of this is Peter Bennett PhD DSc, Past President of International DAN and co-editor of the "bible" in the field: "The Physiology and Medicine of Diving". There are other motivated academics with relevant degrees such as Jolie Bookspan PhD, Dick Vann PhD, and Donna Uguccioni MS in the USA, and David Dootlette and one of he authors (JL) from Australia who have forged related careers for themselves; partly in diving research and partly in diver education. Some, such as Lynn Taylor PhD in New

Zealand, enjoy "part time" roles as diving medicine educators while maintaining careers in other areas; a little like diving doctors who have another speciality as their primary career activity.

Breaking into this type of work is the most difficult part. The Divers Alert Network (DAN) is probably the biggest single employer of "academic diving medicine and safety educators" in the USA, and interested divers should perhaps contact one of their staff for advice on career development. A number of diving scientists are employed by the US Military.

It is clear from the above that there are at least several options for a career in diving medicine. However, because of the slightly unusual nature of the field, the diver who wishes to take his or her interest in diving medicine to career level has to be motivated and prepared to "ferret out" potential avenues for training and employment. Unfortunately we cannot simply arrive at a university and instruct them to train us for a career in diving medicine according to some pre-arranged script. Like diving itself, establishing the path to such a career is an adventure with some obstacles that will need to be overcome. Many have done it.

APPENDICES

1. U.S. Navy Air Diving Tables.

2. DCIEM Air Diving Tables.

3. Bühlmann High Altitude Tables.

APPENDIX 1

U.S. Navy Air Diving Tables.[1]

1. U.S. Navy Diving Manual. SS521-AG-PRO-010; 0910-LP-100-3199 Revision 4. Naval Sea Systems Command; 1999.

Table 9-8. *U.S. Navy Standard Air Decompression Table.*

Depth feet/meters	Bottom time (min)	Time first stop (min:sec)	50 15.2	40 12.1	30 9.1	20 6.0	10 3.0	Total decompression time (min:sec)	Repetitive group
40 12.1	200						0	1:20	*
	210	1:00					2	3:20	N
	230	1:00					7	8:20	N
	250	1:00					11	12:20	O
	270	1:00					15	16:20	O
	300	1:00					19	20:20	Z
	Exceptional Exposure								
	360	1:00					23	24:20	**
	480	1:00					41	42:20	**
	720	1:00					69	70:20	**
50 15.2	100						0	1:40	*
	110	1:20					3	4:40	L
	120	1:20					5	6:40	M
	140	1:20					10	11:40	M
	160	1:20					21	22:40	N
	180	1:20					29	30:40	O
	200	1:20					35	36:40	O
	220	1:20					40	41:40	Z
	240	1:20					47	48:40	Z
60 18.2	60						0	2:00	*
	70	1:40					2	4:00	K
	80	1:40					7	9:00	L
	100	1:40					14	16:00	M
	120	1:40					26	28:00	N
	140	1:40					39	41:00	O
	160	1:40					48	50:00	Z
	180	1:40					56	58:00	Z
	200	1:20				1	69	72:00	Z
	Exceptional Exposure								
	240	1:20				2	79	83:00	**
	360	1:20				20	119	141:00	**
	480	1:20				44	148	194:00	**
	720	1:20				78	187	267:00	**
70 21.3	50						0	2:20	*
	60	2:00					8	10:20	K
	70	2:00					14	16:20	L
	80	2:00					18	20:20	M
	90	2:00					23	25:20	N
	100	2:00					33	35:20	N
	110	1:40				2	41	45:20	O
	120	1:40				4	47	53:20	O
	130	1:40				6	52	60:20	O
	140	1:40				8	56	66:20	Z
	150	1:40				9	61	72:20	Z
	160	1:40				13	72	87:20	Z
	170	1:40				19	79	100:20	Z

* See No Decompression Table for repetitive groups
** Repetitive dives may not follow exceptional exposure dives

Table 9-8. U.S. Navy Standard Air Decompression Table (Continued).

Depth feet/meters	Bottom time (min)	Time first stop (min:sec)	Decompression stops (feet/meters) 50 15.2	40 12.1	30 9.1	20 6.0	10 3.0	Total decompression time (min:sec)	Repetitive group
80 **24.3**	40						0	2:40	*
	50	2:20					10	12:40	K
	60	2:20					17	19:40	L
	70	2:20					23	25:40	M
	80	2:00				2	31	35:40	N
	90	2:00				7	39	48:40	N
	100	2:00				11	46	59:40	O
	110	2:00				13	53	68:40	O
	120	2:00				17	56	75:40	Z
	130	2:00				19	63	83:40	Z
	140	2:00				26	69	97:40	Z
	150	2:00				32	77	111:40	Z
	Exceptional Exposure								
	180	2:00				35	85	122:40	**
	240	1:40			6	52	120	180:40	**
	360	1:40			29	90	160	281:40	**
	480	1:40			59	107	187	355:40	**
	720	1:20		17	108	142	187	456:40	**
90 **28.7**	30						0	3:00	*
	40	2:40					7	10:00	J
	50	2:40					18	21:00	L
	60	2:40					25	28:00	M
	70	2:20				7	30	40:00	N
	80	2:20				13	40	56:00	N
	90	2:20				18	48	69:00	O
	100	2:20				21	54	78:00	Z
	110	2:20				24	61	88:00	Z
	120	2:20				32	68	103:00	Z
	130	2:00			5	36	74	118:00	Z
100 **30.4**	25						0	3:20	*
	30	3:00					3	6:20	I
	40	3:00					15	18:20	K
	50	2:40				2	24	29:20	L
	60	2:40				9	28	40:20	N
	70	2:40				17	39	59:20	O
	80	2:40				23	48	74:20	O
	90	2:20			3	23	57	86:20	Z
	100	2:20			7	23	66	99:20	Z
	110	2:20			10	34	72	119:20	Z
	120	2:20			12	41	78	134:20	Z
	Exceptional Exposure								
	180	2:00		1	29	53	118	204:20	**
	240	2:00		14	42	84	142	285:20	**
	360	1:40	2	42	73	111	187	418:20	**
	480	1:40	21	61	91	142	187	505:20	**
	720	1:40	55	106	122	142	187	615:20	**

* See No Decompression Table for repetitive groups
** Repetitive dives may not follow exceptional exposure dives

Table 9-8. *U.S. Navy Standard Air Decompression Table (Continued).*

Depth feet/meters

110
33.1

Bottom time (min)	Time first stop (min:sec)	Decompression stops (feet/meters) 50 15.2	40 12.1	30 9.1	20 6.0	10 3.0	Total decompression time (min:sec)	Repetitive group
20						0	3:40	*
25	3:20					3	6:40	H
30	3:20					7	10:40	J
40	3:00				2	21	26:40	L
50	3:00				8	26	37:40	M
60	3:00				18	36	57:40	N
70	2:40			1	23	48	75:40	O
80	2:40			7	23	57	90:40	Z
90	2:40			12	30	64	109:40	Z
100	2:40			15	37	72	127:40	Z

Depth feet/meters

120
36.5

Bottom time (min)	Time first stop (min:sec)	Decompression stops (feet/meters) 70 21.3	60 18.2	50 15.2	40 12.1	30 9.1	20 6.0	10 3.0	Total decompression time (min:sec)	Repetitive group
15								0	4:00	*
20	3:40							2	6:00	H
25	3:40							6	10:00	I
30	3:40							14	18:00	J
40	3:20						5	25	34:00	L
50	3:20						15	31	50:00	N
60	3:00					2	22	45	73:00	O
70	3:00					9	23	55	91:00	O
80	3:00					15	27	63	109:00	Z
90	3:00					19	37	74	134:00	Z
100	3:00					23	45	80	152:00	Z
Exceptional Exposure										
120	2:40				10	19	47	98	178:00	**
180	2:20			5	27	37	76	137	286:00	**
240	2:20			23	35	60	97	179	398:00	**
360	2:00		18	45	64	93	142	187	553:00	**
480	1:40	3	41	64	93	122	142	187	656:00	**
720	1:40	32	74	100	114	122	142	187	775:00	**

Depth feet/meters

130
39.6

10								0	4:20	*
15	4:00							1	5:20	F
20	4:00							4	8:20	H
25	4:00							10	14:20	J
30	3:40						3	18	25:20	M
40	3:40						10	25	39:20	N
50	3:20					3	21	37	65:20	O
60	3:20					9	23	52	88:20	Z
70	3:20					16	24	61	105:20	Z
80	3:00				3	19	35	72	133:20	Z
90	3:00				8	19	45	80	156:20	Z

* See No Decompression Table for repetitive groups
** Repetitive dives may not follow exceptional exposure dives

Table 9-8. *U.S. Navy Standard Air Decompression Table (Continued).*

Depth feet/meters	Bottom time (min)	Time first stop (min:sec)	Decompression stops (feet/meters) 90 27.4	80 24.3	70 21.3	60 18.2	50 15.2	40 12.1	30 9.1	20 6.0	10 3.0	Total decompression time (min:sec)	Repetitive group
140	10											0	4:40	*
42.6	15	4:20										2	6:40	G
	20	4:20										6	10:40	I
	25	4:00									2	14	20:40	J
	30	4:00									5	21	30:40	K
	40	3:40								2	16	26	48:40	N
	50	3:40								6	24	44	78:40	O
	60	3:40								16	23	56	99:40	Z
	70	3:20							4	19	32	68	127:40	Z
	80	3:20							10	23	41	79	157:40	Z

Exceptional Exposure

Depth feet/meters	Bottom time (min)	Time first stop (min:sec)	90	80	70	60	50	40	30	20	10	Total decompression time (min:sec)	Repetitive group
	90	3:00					2	14	18	42	88	168:40	**
	120	3:00					12	14	36	56	120	242:40	**
	180	2:40				10	26	32	54	94	168	388:40	**
	240	2:20			8	28	34	50	78	124	187	513:40	**
	360	2:00		9	32	42	64	84	122	142	187	686:40	**
	480	2:00		31	44	59	100	114	122	142	187	803:40	**
	720	1:40	16	56	88	97	100	114	122	142	187	926:40	**
150	5										0	5:00	C
45.7	10	4:40									1	6:00	E
	15	4:40									3	8:00	G
	20	4:20								2	7	14:00	H
	25	4:20								4	17	26:00	K
	30	4:20								8	24	37:00	L
	40	4:00							5	19	33	62:00	N
	50	4:00							12	23	51	91:00	O
	60	3:40						3	19	26	62	115:00	Z
	70	3:40						11	19	39	75	149:00	Z
	80	3:20					1	17	19	50	84	176:00	Z
160	5										0	5:20	D
48.7	10	5:00									1	6:20	F
	15	4:40								1	4	10:20	H
	20	4:40								3	11	19:20	J
	25	4:40								7	20	32:20	K
	30	4:20							2	11	25	43:20	M
	40	4:20							7	23	39	74:20	N
	50	4:00						2	16	23	55	101:20	Z
	60	4:00						9	19	33	69	135:20	Z

Exceptional Exposure

Depth feet/meters	Bottom time (min)	Time first stop (min:sec)	90	80	70	60	50	40	30	20	10	Total decompression time (min:sec)	Repetitive group
	70	3:40					1	17	22	44	80	169:20	**

* See No Decompression Table for repetitive groups
** Repetitive dives may not follow exceptional exposure dives

Table 9-8. U.S. Navy Standard Air Decompression Table (Continued).

Depth feet/meters	Bottom time (min)	Time first stop (min:sec)	110 33.5	100 30.4	90 27.4	80 24.3	70 21.3	60 18.2	50 15.2	40 12.1	30 9.1	20 6.0	10 3.0	Total decompression time (min:sec)	Repetitive group
170 **51.8**	5												0	5:40	D
	10	5:20											2	7:40	F
	15	5:00										2	5	12:40	H
	20	5:00										4	15	24:40	J
	25	4:40									2	7	23	37:40	L
	30	4:40									4	13	26	48:40	M
	40	4:20								1	10	23	45	84:40	O
	50	4:20								5	18	23	61	112:40	Z
	60	4:00							2	15	22	37	74	155:40	Z
Exceptional Exposure	70	4:00						8	17	19	51	86		186:40	**
	90	3:40					12	12	14	34	52	120		249:40	**
	120	3:00				2	10	12	18	32	42	82	156	359:40	**
	180	2:40			4	10	22	28	34	50	78	120	187	538:40	**
	240	2:40			18	24	30	42	50	70	116	142	187	684:40	**
	360	2:20		22	34	40	52	60	98	114	122	142	187	876:40	**
	480	2:00	14	40	42	56	91	97	100	114	122	142	187	1010:40	**
180 **54.8**	5												0	6:00	D
	10	5:40											3	9:00	F
	15	5:20										3	6	15:00	I
	20	5:00									1	5	17	29:00	J
	25	5:00									3	10	24	43:00	L
	30	5:00									6	17	27	56:00	N
	40	4:40								3	14	23	50	96:00	O
	50	4:20							2	9	19	30	65	131:00	Z
	60	4:20							5	16	19	44	81	171:00	Z
190 **57.9**	5	5:40											0	6:20	D
	10	5:40										1	3	10:20	G
	15	5:40										6	7	17:20	I
	20	5:20									2	6	20	34:20	K
	25	:5:20									5	11	25	47:20	M
	30	5:00								1	8	19	32	66:20	N
	40	5:00								8	14	23	55	106:20	O
Exceptional Exposure	50	4:40							4	13	22	33	72	150:20	**
	60	4:40							10	17	19	50	84	186:20	**

*   See No Decompression Table for repetitive groups
** Repetitive dives may not follow exceptional exposure dives

Table 9-8. U.S. Navy Standard Air Decompression Table (Continued).

Depth feet/meters	Bottom time (min)	Time first stop (min:sec)	130 39.6	120 36.5	110 33.5	100 30.4	90 27.4	80 24.3	70 21.3	60 18.2	50 15.2	40 12.1	30 9.1	20 6.0	10 3.0	Total decompression time (min:sec)
200 **60.9**	Exceptional Exposure															
	5	6:20													1	7:40
	10	6:00												1	4	11:40
	15	5:40											1	4	10	21:40
	20	5:40											3	7	27	43:40
	25	5:40											7	14	25	52:40
	30	5:20										2	9	22	37	76:40
	40	5:00									2	8	17	23	59	115:40
	50	5:00									6	16	22	39	75	164:40
	60	4:40								2	13	17	24	51	89	202:40
	90	3:40					1	10	10	12	12	30	38	74	134	327:40
	120	3:20				6	10	10	10	24	28	40	64	98	180	476:40
	180	2:40		1	10	10	18	24	24	42	48	70	106	142	187	688:40
	240	2:40		6	20	24	24	36	42	54	68	114	122	142	187	845:40
	360	2:20	12	22	36	40	44	56	82	98	100	114	122	142	187	1061:40
210 **64.0**	Exceptional Exposure															
	5	6:40													1	8:00
	10	6:20												2	4	13:00
	15	6:00											1	5	13	26:00
	20	6:00											4	10	23	44:00
	25	5:40										2	7	17	27	60:00
	30	5:40										4	9	24	41	85:00
	40	5:20									4	9	19	26	63	128:00
	50	5:20								1	9	17	19	45	80	178:00
220 **67.0**	Exceptional Exposure															
	5	7:00													1	8:20
	10	6:40												2	5	14:20
	15	6:20											2	5	16	30:20
	20	6:00										1	3	11	24	46:20
	25	6:00										3	8	19	33	70:20
	30	5:40									1	7	10	23	47	95:20
	40	5:40									6	12	22	29	68	144:20
	50	5:20								3	12	17	18	51	86	194:20
230 **70.1**	Exceptional Exposure															
	5	7:20													2	9:40
	10	6:20											1	2	6	16:40
	15	6:20											3	6	18	34:40
	20	6:20										2	5	12	26	52:40
	25	6:20										4	8	22	37	78:40
	30	6:00									2	8	12	23	51	103:40
	40	5:40								1	7	15	22	34	74	160:40
	50	5:40								5	14	16	24	51	89	206:40

Table 9-8. U.S. Navy Standard Air Decompression Table (Continued).

Depth 240 feet / 73.1 meters — Decompression stops (feet/meters)

Exceptional Exposure

Bottom time (min)	Time first stop (min:sec)	130 / 39.6	120 / 36.5	110 / 33.5	100 / 30.4	90 / 27.4	80 / 24.3	70 / 21.3	60 / 18.2	50 / 15.2	40 / 12.1	30 / 9.1	20 / 6.0	10 / 3.0	Total decompression time (min:sec)
5	7:40													2	10:00
10	7:00											1	3	6	18:00
15	7:00											4	6	21	39:00
20	6:40										3	6	15	25	57:00
25	6:20									1	4	9	24	40	86:00
30	6:20									4	8	15	22	56	113:00
40	6:00								3	7	17	22	39	75	171:00
50	5:40							1	8	15	16	29	51	94	222:00

Depth 250 feet / 76.2 meters — Decompression stops (feet/meters)

Exceptional Exposure

Bottom time (min)	Time first stop (min:sec)	200 / 60.9	190 / 57.9	180 / 54.8	170 / 51.8	160 / 48.7	150 / 45.7	140 / 42.6	130 / 39.6	120 / 36.5	110 / 33.5	100 / 30.4	90 / 27.4	80 / 24.3	70 / 21.3	60 / 18.2	50 / 15.2	40 / 12.1	30 / 9.1	20 / 6.0	10 / 3.0	Total decompression time (min:sec)
5	7:40																			1	2	11:20
10	7:20																		1	4	7	20:20
15	7:00																	1	4	7	22	42:20
20	7:00																	4	7	17	27	63:20
25	6:40																2	7	10	24	45	96:20
30	6:40																6	7	17	23	59	120:20
40	6:20															5	9	17	19	45	79	182:20
60	5:20												4	10	10	10	12	22	36	64	164	302:20
90	4:20									8	10	10	10	10	10	28	28	44	68	98	186	518:20
120	3:40							5	10	10	10	10	16	24	24	36	48	64	94	142	187	688:20
180	3:00				4	8	8	10	22	24	24	32	42	44	60	84	114	122	142	187		935:20
240	3:00				9	14	21	22	22	40	40	42	56	76	98	100	114	114	122	142	187	1113:20

Depth 260 feet / 79.2 meters

Exceptional Exposure

Bottom time (min)	Time first stop (min:sec)	200 / 60.9	190 / 57.9	180 / 54.8	170 / 51.8	160 / 48.7	150 / 45.7	140 / 42.6	130 / 39.6	120 / 36.5	110 / 33.5	100 / 30.4	90 / 27.4	80 / 24.3	70 / 21.3	60 / 18.2	50 / 15.2	40 / 12.1	30 / 9.1	20 / 6.0	10 / 3.0	Total decompression time (min:sec)
5	8:00																			1	2	11:40
10	7:40																		2	4	9	23:40
15	7:20																	2	4	10	22	46:40
20	7:00																1	4	7	20	31	71:40
25	7:00																3	8	11	23	50	103:40
30	6:40															2	6	8	19	26	61	130:40
40	6:20														1	6	11	16	19	49	84	194:40

Depth 270 feet / 82.3 meters

Exceptional Exposure

Bottom time (min)	Time first stop (min:sec)	200 / 60.9	190 / 57.9	180 / 54.8	170 / 51.8	160 / 48.7	150 / 45.7	140 / 42.6	130 / 39.6	120 / 36.5	110 / 33.5	100 / 30.4	90 / 27.4	80 / 24.3	70 / 21.3	60 / 18.2	50 / 15.2	40 / 12.1	30 / 9.1	20 / 6.0	10 / 3.0	Total decompression time (min:sec)
5	8:20																			1	3	13:00
10	8:00																		2	5	11	27:00
15	7:40																	3	4	11	24	51:00
20	7:20																2	3	9	21	35	79:00
25	7:00															2	3	8	13	23	53	111:00
30	7:00															3	6	12	22	27	64	143:00
40	6:40														5	6	11	17	22	51	88	209:00

Table 9-8. *U.S. Navy Standard Air Decompression Table (Continued).*

Depth feet/meters	Bottom time (min)	Time first stop (min:sec)	200 / 60.9	190 / 57.9	180 / 54.8	170 / 51.8	160 / 48.7	150 / 45.7	140 / 42.6	130 / 39.6	120 / 36.5	110 / 33.5	100 / 30.4	90 / 27.4	80 / 24.3	70 / 21.3	60 / 18.2	50 / 15.2	40 / 12.1	30 / 9.1	20 / 6.0	10 / 3.0	Total decompression time (min:sec)
280 **85.3** Exceptional Exposure																							
	5	8:40																			2	2	13:20
	10	8:00																	1	2	5	13	30:20
	15	7:40																1	3	4	11	26	54:20
	20	7:40																3	4	8	23	39	86:20
	25	7:20															2	5	7	16	23	56	118:20
	30	7:00														1	3	7	13	22	30	70	155:20
	40	6:40													1	6	6	13	17	27	51	93	223:20
290 **88.4** Exceptional Exposure																							
	5	9:00																			2	3	14:40
	10	8:20																	1	3	5	16	34:40
	15	8:00																1	3	6	12	26	57:40
	20	8:00																3	7	9	23	43	94:40
	25	7:40															3	5	8	17	23	60	125:40
	30	7:20														1	5	6	16	22	36	72	167:40
	40	7:00													3	5	7	15	16	32	51	95	233:40
300 **91.4** Exceptional Exposure																							
	5	9:20																			3	3	16:00
	10	8:40																	1	3	6	17	37:00
	15	8:20																2	3	6	15	26	62:00
	20	8:00															2	3	7	10	23	47	102:00
	25	7:40														1	3	6	8	19	26	61	134:00
	30	7:40														2	5	7	17	22	39	75	177:00
	40	7:20													4	6	9	15	17	34	51	90	'236:00
	60	6:00									4	10	10	10	10	10	14	28	32	50	90	187	465:00
	90	4:40					'3	8	8	10	10	10	10	16	24	24	34	48	64	90	142	187	698:00
	120	4:00			4	8	8	8	8	10	14	24	24	24	34	42	58	66	102	122	142	187	895:00
	180	3:30	6	8	8	8	14	20	21	21	28	40	40	48	56	82	98	100	114	122	142	187	1173:00

APPENDIX 2

DCIEM Air Diving Tables.[1]

The Department of National Defence (Canada), Defence and Civil Institute of Environmental Medicine (DCIEM), and

1. DCIEM Diving Manual. Part 1 Air Diving Tables and Procedures. Richmond BC: Universal Dive Techtronics; 1992.

TABLE 1: STANDARD AIR DECOMPRESSION (FEET)

Depth (fsw)	Bottom Time (min)	Stop Times (min) at Different Depths (fsw)								Decom. Time (min)	Repet. Group
		80	70	60	50	40	30	20	10		
20	30	-	-	-	-	-	-	-	-	1	A
	60	-	-	-	-	-	-	-	-	1	B
	90	-	-	-	-	-	-	-	-	1	C
	120	-	-	-	-	-	-	-	-	1	D
	150	-	-	-	-	-	-	-	-	1	E
	180	-	-	-	-	-	-	-	-	1	F
	240	-	-	-	-	-	-	-	-	1	G
	300	-	-	-	-	-	-	-	-	1	H
	360	-	-	-	-	-	-	-	-	1	I
	420	-	-	-	-	-	-	-	-	1	J
	480	-	-	-	-	-	-	-	-	1	K
	600	-	-	-	-	-	-	-	-	1	L
	720	-	-	-	-	-	-	-	-	1	M
30	30	-	-	-	-	-	-	-	-	1	A
	60	-	-	-	-	-	-	-	-	1	C
	90	-	-	-	-	-	-	-	-	1	D
	120	-	-	-	-	-	-	-	-	1	F
	150	-	-	-	-	-	-	-	-	1	G
	180	-	-	-	-	-	-	-	-	1	H
	210	-	-	-	-	-	-	-	-	1	J
	240	-	-	-	-	-	-	-	-	1	K
	270	-	-	-	-	-	-	-	-	1	L
	300	-	-	-	-	-	-	-	-	1	M
	330	-	-	-	-	-	-	-	3	3	N
	360	-	-	-	-	-	-	-	5	5	O
	390	-	-	-	-	-	-	-	7	7	
	400	-	-	-	-	-	-	-	10	10	
	420	-	-	-	-	-	-	-	14	14	
	450	-	-	-	-	-	-	-	19	19	
	480	-	-	-	-	-	-	-	23	23	

TABLE 1: STANDARD AIR DECOMPRESSION (FEET)

Depth (fsw)	Bottom Time (min)	Stop Times (min) at Different Depths (fsw)								Decom. Time (min)	Repet. Group
		80	70	60	50	40	30	20	10		
40	20	-	-	-	-	-	-	-	-	1	A
	30	-	-	-	-	-	-	-	-	1	B
	60	-	-	-	-	-	-	-	-	1	D
	90	-	-	-	-	-	-	-	-	1	G
	120	-	-	-	-	-	-	-	-	1	H
	150	-	-	-	-	-	-	-	-	1	J
	160	-	-	-	-	-	-	-	3	3	K
	170	-	-	-	-	-	-	-	5	5	L
	180	-	-	-	-	-	-	-	8	8	M
	190	-	-	-	-	-	-	-	10	10	
	200	-	-	-	-	-	-	-	14	14	
	210	-	-	-	-	-	-	-	18	18	
	240	-	-	-	-	-	-	-	28	28	
	270	-	-	-	-	-	-	-	38	38	
	300	-	-	-	-	-	-	-	48	48	
	330	-	-	-	-	-	-	-	57	57	
	360	-	-	-	-	-	-	-	66	66	
50	10	-	-	-	-	-	-	-	-	1	A
	20	-	-	-	-	-	-	-	-	1	B
	30	-	-	-	-	-	-	-	-	1	C
	40	-	-	-	-	-	-	-	-	1	D
	50	-	-	-	-	-	-	-	-	1	E
	60	-	-	-	-	-	-	-	-	1	F
	75	-	-	-	-	-	-	-	-	1	G
	100	-	-	-	-	-	-	-	6	6	I
	120	-	-	-	-	-	-	-	12	12	K
	130	-	-	-	-	-	-	-	18	18	L
	140	-	-	-	-	-	-	-	24	24	M
	150	-	-	-	-	-	-	-	29	29	
	160	-	-	-	-	-	-	-	33	33	
	170	-	-	-	-	-	-	-	38	38	
	180	-	-	-	-	-	-	-	43	43	
	200	-	-	-	-	-	-	-	53	53	
	220	-	-	-	-	-	-	-	63	63	
	240	-	-	-	-	-	-	-	74	74	
	260	-	-	-	-	-	-	-	86	86	
	280	-	-	-	-	-	-	-	97	97	

Depth (fsw)	Bottom Time (min)	80	70	60	50	40	30	20	10	Decom. Time (min)	Repet. Group
		Stop Times (min) at Different Depths (fsw)									
60	10	-	-	-	-	-	-	-	-	1	A
	20	-	-	-	-	-	-	-	-	1	B
	30	-	-	-	-	-	-	-	-	1	D
	40	-	-	-	-	-	-	-	-	1	E
	50	-	-	-	-	-	-	-	-	1	F
	60	-	-	-	-	-	-	-	5	5	G
	80	-	-	-	-	-	-	-	10	10	I
	90	-	-	-	-	-	-	-	19	19	J
	100	-	-	-	-	-	-	-	26	26	K
	110	-	-	-	-	-	-	-	32	32	L
	120	-	-	-	-	-	-	2	37	39	M
	130	-	-	-	-	-	-	2	43	45	
	140	-	-	-	-	-	-	3	49	52	
	150	-	-	-	-	-	-	3	55	58	
	160	-	-	-	-	-	-	4	62	66	
	170	-	-	-	-	-	-	4	70	74	
	180	-	-	-	-	-	-	5	77	82	
	190	-	-	-	-	-	-	5	85	90	
	200	-	-	-	-	-	-	11	90	101	
	210	-	-	-	-	-	-	15	96	111	
	220	-	-	-	-	-	-	19	102	121	
	230	-	-	-	-	-	-	23	108	131	
	240	-	-	-	-	-	-	27	114	141	

Depth (fsw)	Bottom Time (min)	80	70	60	50	40	30	20	10	Decom. Time (min)	Repet. Group
		Stop Times (min) at Different Depths (fsw)									
70	10	-	-	-	-	-	-	-	-	1	A
	20	-	-	-	-	-	-	-	-	1	C
	25	-	-	-	-	-	-	-	-	1	D
	35	-	-	-	-	-	-	-	-	1	E
	40	-	-	-	-	-	-	-	5	5	F
	50	-	-	-	-	-	-	-	10	10	G
	60	-	-	-	-	-	-	2	11	13	H
	70	-	-	-	-	-	-	3	19	22	J
	80	-	-	-	-	-	-	4	27	31	K
	90	-	-	-	-	-	-	5	34	39	M
	100	-	-	-	-	-	-	6	41	47	N
	110	-	-	-	-	-	-	7	48	55	
	120	-	-	-	-	-	-	8	56	64	
	130	-	-	-	-	-	-	9	65	74	
	140	-	-	-	-	-	-	11	74	85	
	150	-	-	-	-	-	-	17	81	98	
	160	-	-	-	-	-	-	22	89	111	
	170	-	-	-	-	-	-	27	98	125	
	180	-	-	-	-	-	-	31	107	138	
	190	-	-	-	-	-	-	36	115	151	
	200	-	-	-	-	-	2	39	123	164	

Depth (fsw)	Bottom Time (min)	Stop Times (min) at Different Depths (fsw)								Decom. Time (min)	Repet. Group
		80	70	60	50	40	30	20	10		
80	10	-	-	-	-	-	-	-	-	2	A
	15	-	-	-	-	-	-	-	-	2	C
	20	-	-	-	-	-	-	-	-	2	D
	25	-	-	-	-	-	-	-	-	2	E
	30	-	-	-	-	-	-	-	6	6	F
	40	-	-	-	-	-	-	2	10	12	G
	50	-	-	-	-	-	-	4	12	16	H
	55	-	-	-	-	-	-	5	17	22	I
	60	-	-	-	-	-	-	6	22	28	J
	65	-	-	-	-	-	-	7	27	34	J
	70	-	-	-	-	-	-	8	31	39	K
	75	-	-	-	-	-	-	9	35	44	L
	80	-	-	-	-	-	-	9	40	49	M
	85	-	-	-	-	-	-	10	44	54	
	90	-	-	-	-	-	-	11	48	59	
	95	-	-	-	-	-	-	11	53	64	
	100	-	-	-	-	-	2	10	58	70	
	110	-	-	-	-	-	3	14	66	83	
	120	-	-	-	-	-	3	20	76	99	
	130	-	-	-	-	-	4	24	87	115	
	140	-	-	-	-	-	5	29	98	132	
	150	-	-	-	-	-	5	35	109	149	
	160	-	-	-	-	-	6	40	120	166	

Depth (fsw)	Bottom Time (min)	Stop Times (min) at Different Depths (fsw)								Decom. Time (min)	Repet. Group
		80	70	60	50	40	30	20	10		
90	5	-	-	-	-	-	-	-	-	2	A
	10	-	-	-	-	-	-	-	-	2	B
	15	-	-	-	-	-	-	-	-	2	C
	20	-	-	-	-	-	-	-	-	2	D
	25	-	-	-	-	-	-	-	8	8	E
	30	-	-	-	-	-	-	3	9	12	F
	40	-	-	-	-	-	-	6	11	17	H
	45	-	-	-	-	-	-	7	16	23	I
	50	-	-	-	-	-	-	9	21	30	J
	55	-	-	-	-	-	-	10	27	37	K
	60	-	-	-	-	-	2	9	32	43	L
	65	-	-	-	-	-	3	9	37	49	
	70	-	-	-	-	-	4	9	42	55	
	75	-	-	-	-	-	4	10	47	61	
	80	-	-	-	-	-	5	10	53	68	
	85	-	-	-	-	-	5	11	59	75	
	90	-	-	-	-	-	6	15	62	83	
	95	-	-	-	-	-	6	18	68	92	
	100	-	-	-	-	-	7	21	73	101	
	110	-	-	-	-	-	8	26	87	121	
	120	-	-	-	-	-	8	33	101	142	

Depth (fsw)	Bottom Time (min)	Stop Times (min) at Different Depths (fsw)								Decom. Time (min)	Repet. Group
		80	70	60	50	40	30	20	10		
100	5	-	-	-	-	-	-	-	-	2	A
	10	-	-	-	-	-	-	-	-	2	B
	15	-	-	-	-	-	-	-	-	2	D
	20	-	-	-	-	-	-	-	8	8	E
	25	-	-	-	-	-	-	3	10	13	F
	30	-	-	-	-	-	-	6	10	16	G
	35	-	-	-	-	-	-	8	11	19	H
	40	-	-	-	-	-	-	9	18	27	I
	45	-	-	-	-	-	3	8	25	36	J
	50	-	-	-	-	-	4	9	30	43	K
	55	-	-	-	-	-	5	9	37	51	L
	60	-	-	-	-	-	6	9	43	58	
	65	-	-	-	-	-	7	10	48	65	
	70	-	-	-	-	-	8	10	55	73	
	75	-	-	-	-	-	8	15	59	82	
	80	-	-	-	-	-	9	18	65	92	
	85	-	-	-	-	2	8	22	71	103	
	90	-	-	-	-	2	8	25	79	114	
	95	-	-	-	-	3	8	29	87	127	
	100	-	-	-	-	3	9	32	95	139	
	105	-	-	-	-	4	8	36	104	152	
	110	-	-	-	-	4	9	39	112	164	

Depth (fsw)	Bottom Time (min)	Stop Times (min) at Different Depths (fsw)								Decom. Time (min)	Repet. Group
		80	70	60	50	40	30	20	10		
110	5	-	-	-	-	-	-	-	-	2	A
	10	-	-	-	-	-	-	-	-	2	B
	12	-	-	-	-	-	-	-	-	2	C
	15	-	-	-	-	-	-	-	5	5	D
	20	-	-	-	-	-	-	3	9	12	F
	25	-	-	-	-	-	-	6	10	16	G
	30	-	-	-	-	-	-	9	11	20	H
	35	-	-	-	-	-	4	7	19	30	I
	40	-	-	-	-	-	5	8	26	39	J
	45	-	-	-	-	-	6	9	33	48	K
	50	-	-	-	-	-	8	9	39	56	M
	55	-	-	-	-	-	9	9	46	64	N
	60	-	-	-	-	3	7	11	53	74	
	65	-	-	-	-	3	8	16	58	85	
	70	-	-	-	-	4	8	20	64	96	
	75	-	-	-	-	5	8	23	73	109	
	80	-	-	-	-	5	8	28	81	122	
	85	-	-	-	-	6	8	32	91	137	
	90	-	-	-	-	6	9	35	101	151	
	95	-	-	-	-	7	9	40	111	167	
	100	-	-	-	-	7	10	44	120	181	
	105	-	-	-	-	8	13	46	129	196	
	110	-	-	-	-	8	16	50	136	210	

Depth (fsw)	Bottom Time (min)	Stop Times (min) at Different Depths (fsw)								Decom. Time (min)	Repet. Group
		80	70	60	50	40	30	20	10		
120	5	-	-	-	-	-	-	-	-	2	A
	10	-	-	-	-	-	-	-	-	2	C
	15	-	-	-	-	-	-	-	10	10	E
	20	-	-	-	-	-	-	5	10	15	F
	25	-	-	-	-	-	-	9	11	20	G
	30	-	-	-	-	-	5	7	17	29	I
	35	-	-	-	-	-	6	9	25	40	J
	40	-	-	-	-	-	8	9	33	50	K
	45	-	-	-	-	3	7	9	41	60	M
	50	-	-	-	-	4	7	10	49	70	N
	55	-	-	-	-	5	7	15	54	81	
	60	-	-	-	-	6	8	19	61	94	
	65	-	-	-	-	7	8	23	70	108	
	70	-	-	-	-	7	9	27	80	123	
	75	-	-	-	2	6	9	32	91	140	
	80	-	-	-	3	6	9	37	103	158	
	85	-	-	-	3	7	10	41	114	175	
	90	-	-	-	3	7	14	44	124	192	
	95	-	-	-	4	7	16	49	134	210	
	100	-	-	-	4	7	20	53	142	226	

TABLE 1: STANDARD AIR DECOMPRESSION (FEET)

Depth (fsw)	Bottom Time (min)	80	70	60	50	40	30	20	10	Decom. Time (min)	Repet. Group
		\multicolumn{8}{c}{Stop Times (min) at Different Depths (fsw)}		
130	5	-	-	-	-	-	-	-	-	2	A
	8	-	-	-	-	-	-	-	-	2	B
	10	-	-	-	-	-	-	-	5	5	C
	15	-	-	-	-	-	-	4	9	13	E
	20	-	-	-	-	-	-	8	10	18	G
	25	-	-	-	-	-	5	7	12	24	H
	30	-	-	-	-	-	7	8	23	38	J
	35	-	-	-	-	3	6	9	32	50	K
	40	-	-	-	-	5	6	10	40	61	M
	45	-	-	-	-	6	7	10	50	73	N
	50	-	-	-	-	7	8	16	55	86	
	55	-	-	-	2	6	8	21	64	101	
	60	-	-	-	3	6	8	26	75	118	
	65	-	-	-	4	6	9	31	86	136	
	70	-	-	-	5	6	9	36	100	156	
	75	-	-	-	5	7	11	40	113	176	
	80	-	-	-	6	7	15	44	125	197	
	85	-	-	-	6	7	18	49	135	215	
	90	-	-	-	7	7	22	54	144	234	
140	7	-	-	-	-	-	-	-	-	2	B
	10	-	-	-	-	-	-	-	7	7	D
	15	-	-	-	-	-	-	6	9	15	F
	20	-	-	-	-	-	4	7	11	22	G
	25	-	-	-	-	-	7	8	19	34	I
	30	-	-	-	-	4	6	9	29	48	K
	35	-	-	-	-	6	6	10	39	61	L
	40	-	-	-	-	7	7	10	49	73	N
	45	-	-	-	3	6	7	17	56	89	O
	50	-	-	-	4	6	8	22	65	105	
	55	-	-	-	5	6	9	27	78	125	
	60	-	-	-	6	6	9	33	91	145	
	65	-	-	-	7	6	11	38	106	168	
	70	-	-	2	5	7	15	42	120	191	
	75	-	-	3	5	8	18	47	133	214	
	80	-	-	3	6	8	21	54	143	235	
	85	-	-	4	6	8	25	61	151	255	
	90	-	-	4	6	8	30	68	157	273	

TABLE 1: STANDARD AIR DECOMPRESSION (FEET)

Depth (fsw)	Bottom Time (min)	Stop Times (min) at Different Depths (fsw)								Decom. Time (min)	Repet. Group
		80	70	60	50	40	30	20	10		
150	6	-	-	-	-	-	-	-	-	3	B
	10	-	-	-	-	-	-	-	9	9	D
	15	-	-	-	-	-	-	8	10	18	F
	20	-	-	-	-	-	6	8	11	25	H
	25	-	-	-	-	4	6	8	25	43	J
	30	-	-	-	-	6	7	9	35	57	K
	35	-	-	-	3	5	7	10	46	71	M
	40	-	-	-	4	6	8	16	54	88	O
	45	-	-	-	6	6	8	22	65	107	
	50	-	-	-	7	6	9	28	78	128	
	55	-	-	3	5	6	10	34	94	152	
	60	-	-	4	5	7	13	39	110	178	
	65	-	-	4	6	7	17	44	125	203	
	70	-	-	5	6	7	21	50	139	228	
	75	-	-	6	5	8	25	58	148	250	
	80	-	-	6	6	8	29	67	155	271	
160	6	-	-	-	-	-	-	-	-	3	B
	10	-	-	-	-	-	-	3	9	12	D
	15	-	-	-	-	-	4	7	10	21	G
	20	-	-	-	-	3	5	8	16	32	H
	25	-	-	-	-	6	6	9	30	51	K
	30	-	-	-	4	5	6	10	42	67	M
	35	-	-	-	5	6	7	14	52	84	N
	40	-	-	-	7	6	8	21	62	104	
	45	-	-	3	5	6	9	28	76	127	
	50	-	-	4	5	7	9	35	93	153	
	55	-	-	5	6	7	14	39	112	183	
	60	-	-	6	6	7	18	45	129	211	
	65	-	3	4	6	8	22	53	142	238	
	70	-	3	5	6	8	27	62	152	263	

TABLE 1: STANDARD AIR DECOMPRESSION (FEET)

Depth (fsw)	Bottom Time (min)	Stop Times (min) at Different Depths (fsw)								Decom. Time (min)	Repet. Group
		80	70	60	50	40	30	20	10		
170	5	-	-	-	-	-	-	-	-	3	B
	10	-	-	-	-	-	-	5	9	14	D
	15	-	-	-	-	-	6	7	10	23	G
	20	-	-	-	-	5	6	8	22	41	I
	25	-	-	-	3	5	6	10	35	59	K
	30	-	-	-	6	5	7	11	48	77	M
	35	-	-	3	4	6	8	19	58	98	O
	40	-	-	4	5	6	9	26	72	122	
	45	-	-	6	5	6	10	34	91	152	
	50	-	3	4	5	7	14	39	111	183	
	55	-	3	5	5	8	19	45	129	214	
	60	-	4	5	6	8	23	54	144	244	
	65	-	5	5	6	8	29	64	154	271	
	70	-	5	5	7	12	31	76	160	296	
180	5	-	-	-	-	-	-	-	-	3	B
	10	-	-	-	-	-	-	7	9	16	E
	15	-	-	-	-	-	8	7	11	26	H
	20	-	-	-	-	7	6	8	27	48	J
	25	-	-	-	5	5	7	10	40	67	M
	30	-	-	3	5	5	8	15	53	89	O
	35	-	-	5	5	6	8	24	66	114	
	40	-	3	4	5	6	9	32	85	144	
	45	-	4	4	5	7	14	38	107	179	
	50	-	5	4	6	7	19	45	127	213	
	55	-	5	5	6	8	24	53	144	245	
	60	3	3	5	7	9	29	65	155	276	

TABLE 1: STANDARD AIR DECOMPRESSION (FEET)

Depth (fsw)	Bottom Time (min)	Stop Times (min) at Different Depths (fsw)										Decom. Time (min)
		100	90	80	70	60	50	40	30	20	10	
190	5	-	-	-	-	-	-	-	-	-	-	3
	10	-	-	-	-	-	-	-	-	8	10	18
	15	-	-	-	-	-	-	4	5	8	13	30
	20	-	-	-	-	-	4	5	6	9	31	55
	25	-	-	-	-	3	4	5	7	11	46	76
	30	-	-	-	-	5	5	5	8	20	58	101
	35	-	-	-	3	4	5	6	9	29	76	132
	40	-	-	-	5	4	5	7	12	36	100	169
	45	-	-	-	6	4	6	7	18	43	123	207
	50	-	-	3	4	4	6	8	24	52	141	242
	55	-	-	4	4	5	6	10	28	65	154	276
200	5	-	-	-	-	-	-	-	-	-	4	4
	10	-	-	-	-	-	-	-	4	6	10	20
	15	-	-	-	-	-	-	6	5	8	18	37
	20	-	-	-	-	-	6	4	7	9	36	62
	25	-	-	-	-	5	4	5	8	14	51	87
	30	-	-	-	3	4	5	6	8	24	67	117
	35	-	-	-	5	4	5	7	9	34	89	153
	40	-	-	3	3	5	5	8	16	40	115	195
	45	-	-	4	4	4	6	8	22	49	137	234
	50	-	-	5	4	5	6	10	27	62	153	272
210	5	-	-	-	-	-	-	-	-	-	6	6
	10	-	-	-	-	-	-	-	5	7	10	22
	15	-	-	-	-	-	-	7	6	8	22	43
	20	-	-	-	-	4	3	5	7	10	40	69
	25	-	-	-	-	6	5	5	8	18	55	97
	30	-	-	-	5	4	5	6	9	29	76	134
	35	-	-	3	4	4	5	7	14	36	103	176
	40	-	-	5	3	5	6	8	19	46	130	222
	45	-	-	6	4	4	7	8	27	57	149	262
	50	-	3	4	4	5	7	13	31	74	160	301

TABLE 1: STANDARD AIR DECOMPRESSION (FEET)

Depth (fsw)	Bottom Time (min)	Stop Times (min) at Different Depths (fsw)										Decom. Time (min)
		100	90	80	70	60	50	40	30	20	10	
220	5	-	-	-	-	-	-	-	-	-	7	7
	10	-	-	-	-	-	-	-	7	7	10	24
	15	-	-	-	-	-	5	4	6	8	27	50
	20	-	-	-	-	5	4	5	7	10	46	77
	25	-	-	-	4	4	4	6	9	22	61	110
	30	-	-	3	4	4	5	7	9	33	87	152
	35	-	-	5	3	5	5	8	17	40	117	200
	40	-	3	3	4	5	6	8	24	52	142	247
	45		4	3	4	6	6	12	29	68	157	289
230	5	-	-	-	-	-	-	-	-	-	8	8
	10	-	-	-	-	-	-	-	8	7	11	26
	15	-	-	-	-	-	6	4	7	9	30	56
	20	-	-	-	-	6	4	6	7	14	48	85
	25	-	-	-	6	4	4	7	8	26	69	124
	30	-	-	5	3	4	6	7	12	36	100	173
	35	-	4	3	3	5	6	8	20	46	131	226
	40	-	5	3	4	5	6	10	27	61	151	272
240	5	-	-	-	-	-	-	-	-	-	9	9
	10	-	-	-	-	-	-	5	5	7	11	28
	15	-	-	-	-	-	7	5	6	9	34	61
	20	-	-	-	5	3	4	6	8	17	53	96
	25	-	-	4	3	4	5	7	9	29	78	139
	30	-	4	2	4	4	6	7	16	39	113	195
	35	-	5	3	4	5	6	8	24	52	142	249
	40	4	2	4	4	5	7	13	30	71	159	299

TABLE 1: STANDARD AIR DECOMPRESSION (METRES)

Depth (msw)	Bottom Time (min)	Stop Times (min) at Different Depths (msw)								Decom. Time (min)	Repet. Group
		24	21	18	15	12	9	6	3		
6	30	-	-	-	-	-	-	-	-	1	A
	60	-	-	-	-	-	-	-	-	1	B
	90	-	-	-	-	-	-	-	-	1	C
	120	-	-	-	-	-	-	-	-	1	D
	150	-	-	-	-	-	-	-	-	1	E
	180	-	-	-	-	-	-	-	-	1	F
	240	-	-	-	-	-	-	-	-	1	G
	300	-	-	-	-	-	-	-	-	1	H
	360	-	-	-	-	-	-	-	-	1	I
	420	-	-	-	-	-	-	-	-	1	J
	480	-	-	-	-	-	-	-	-	1	K
	600	-	-	-	-	-	-	-	-	1	L
	720	-	-	-	-	-	-	-	-	1	M
9	30	-	-	-	-	-	-	-	-	1	A
	60	-	-	-	-	-	-	-	-	1	C
	90	-	-	-	-	-	-	-	-	1	D
	120	-	-	-	-	-	-	-	-	1	F
	150	-	-	-	-	-	-	-	-	1	G
	180	-	-	-	-	-	-	-	-	1	H
	210	-	-	-	-	-	-	-	-	1	J
	240	-	-	-	-	-	-	-	-	1	K
	270	-	-	-	-	-	-	-	-	1	L
	300	-	-	-	-	-	-	-	-	1	M
	330	-	-	-	-	-	-	-	3	3	N
	360	-	-	-	-	-	-	-	5	5	O
	400	-	-	-	-	-	-	-	7	7	
	420	-	-	-	-	-	-	-	10	10	
	450	-	-	-	-	-	-	-	15	15	
	480	-	-	-	-	-	-	-	20	20	

TABLE 1: STANDARD AIR DECOMPRESSION (METRES)

Depth (msw)	Bottom Time (min)	24	21	18	15	12	9	6	3	Decom. Time (min)	Repet. Group
		Stop Times (min) at Different Depths (msw)									
12	20	-	-	-	-	-	-	-	-	1	A
	30	-	-	-	-	-	-	-	-	1	B
	60	-	-	-	-	-	-	-	-	1	D
	90	-	-	-	-	-	-	-	-	1	G
	120	-	-	-	-	-	-	-	-	1	H
	150	-	-	-	-	-	-	-	-	1	J
	180	-	-	-	-	-	-	-	5	5	M
	200	-	-	-	-	-	-	-	10	10	
	210	-	-	-	-	-	-	-	15	15	·
	220	-	-	-	-	-	-	-	19	19	
	240	-	-	-	-	-	-	-	26	26	
	270	-	-	-	-	-	-	-	35	35	
	300	-	-	-	-	-	-	-	44	44	
	330	-	-	-	-	-	-	-	53	53	
	360	-	-	-	-	-	-	-	62	62	
15	10	-	-	-	-	-	-	-	-	1	A
	20	-	-	-	-	-	-	-	-	1	B
	30	-	-	-	-	-	-	-	-	1	C
	40	-	-	-	-	-	-	-	-	1	D
	50	-	-	-	-	-	-	-	-	1	E
	60	-	-	-	-	-	-	-	-	1	F
	75	-	-	-	-	-	-	-	-	1	G
	100	-	-	-	-	-	-	-	5	5	I
	120	-	-	-	-	-	-	-	10	10	K
	125	-	-	-	-	-	-	-	13	13	K
	130	-	-	-	-	-	-	-	16	16	L
	140	-	-	-	-	-	-	-	21	21	M
	150	-	-	-	-	-	-	-	26	26	
	160	-	-	-	-	-	-	-	31	31	
	170	-	-	-	-	-	-	-	35	35	
	180	-	-	-	-	-	-	-	40	40	
	200	-	-	-	-	-	-	-	50	50	
	220	-	-	-	-	-	-	-	59	59	
	240	-	-	-	-	-	-	-	70	70	
	260	-	-	-	-	-	-	-	81	81	
	280	-	-	-	-	-	-	-	91	91	

Depth (msw)	Bottom Time (min)	Stop Times (min) at Different Depths (msw)								Decom. Time (min)	Repet. Group
		24	21	18	15	12	9	6	3		
18	10	-	-	-	-	-	-	-	-	1	A
	20	-	-	-	-	-	-	-	-	1	B
	30	-	-	-	-	-	-	-	-	1	D
	40	-	-	-	-	-	-	-	-	1	E
	50	-	-	-	-	-	-	-	-	1	F
	60	-	-	-	-	-	-	-	5	5	G
	80	-	-	-	-	-	-	-	10	10	I
	90	-	-	-	-	-	-	-	16	16	J
	100	-	-	-	-	-	-	-	24	24	K
	110	-	-	-	-	-	-	-	30	30	L
	120	-	-	-	-	-	-	-	36	36	M
	130	-	-	-	-	-	-	2	40	42	
	140	-	-	-	-	-	-	2	46	48	
	150	-	-	-	-	-	-	3	52	55	
	160	-	-	-	-	-	-	3	59	62	
	170	-	-	-	-	-	-	4	65	69	
	180	-	-	-	-	-	-	4	73	77	
	190	-	-	-	-	-	-	5	80	85	
	200	-	-	-	-	-	-	7	87	94	
	210	-	-	-	-	-	-	13	91	104	
	220	-	-	-	-	-	-	17	97	114	
	230	-	-	-	-	-	-	21	103	124	
	240	-	-	-	-	-	-	24	109	133	

Depth (msw)	Bottom Time (min)	Stop Times (min) at Different Depths (msw)								Decom. Time (min)	Repet. Group
		24	21	18	15	12	9	6	3		
21	10	-	-	-	-	-	-	-	-	1	A
	20	-	-	-	-	-	-	-	-	1	C
	25	-	-	-	-	-	-	-	-	1	D
	30	-	-	-	-	-	-	-	-	1	D
	35	-	-	-	-	-	-	-	-	1	E
	40	-	-	-	-	-	-	-	5	5	F
	50	-	-	-	-	-	-	-	10	10	G
	60	-	-	-	-	-	-	-	12	12	H
	70	-	-	-	-	-	-	3	17	20	J
	80	-	-	-	-	-	-	4	25	29	K
	90	-	-	-	-	-	-	5	32	37	M
	100	-	-	-	-	-	-	6	39	45	N
	110	-	-	-	-	-	-	7	46	53	
	120	-	-	-	-	-	-	7	54	61	
	130	-	-	-	-	-	-	8	62	70	
	140	-	-	-	-	-	-	9	71	80	
	150	-	-	-	-	-	-	15	77	92	
	160	-	-	-	-	-	-	20	85	105	
	170	-	-	-	-	-	-	25	93	118	
	180	-	-	-	-	-	-	29	101	130	
	190	-	-	-	-	-	-	34	109	143	
	200	-	-	-	-	-	-	38	117	155	

Depth (msw)	Bottom Time (min)	Stop Times (min) at Different Depths (msw)								Decom. Time (min)	Repet. Group
		24	21	18	15	12	9	6	3		
24	10	-	-	-	-	-	-	-	-	2	A
	15	-	-	-	-	-	-	-	-	2	C
	20	-	-	-	-	-	-	-	-	2	D
	25	-	-	-	-	-	-	-	-	2	E
	30	-	-	-	-	-	-	-	5	5	F
	40	-	-	-	-	-	-	-	11	11	G
	50	-	-	-	-	-	-	4	11	15	H
	55	-	-	-	-	-	-	5	15	20	I
	60	-	-	-	-	-	-	6	21	27	J
	65	-	-	-	-	-	-	7	25	32	J
	70	-	-	-	-	-	-	7	30	37	K
	75	-	-	-	-	-	-	8	34	42	L
	80	-	-	-	-	-	-	9	37	46	M
	85	-	-	-	-	-	-	9	42	51	
	90	-	-	-	-	-	-	10	46	56	
	95	-	-	-	-	-	-	11	50	61	
	100	-	-	-	-	-	-	11	55	66	
	110	-	-	-	-	-	2	12	64	78	
	120	-	-	-	-	-	3	18	72	93	
	130	-	-	-	-	-	4	23	82	109	
	140	-	-	-	-	-	4	28	93	125	
	150	-	-	-	-	-	5	33	104	142	
	160	-	-	-	-	-	5	39	114	158	

Depth (msw)	Bottom Time (min)	Stop Times (min) at Different Depths (msw)								Decom. Time (min)	Repet. Group
		24	21	18	15	12	9	6	3		
27	5	-	-	-	-	-	-	-	-	2	A
	10	-	-	-	-	-	-	-	-	2	B
	15	-	-	-	-	-	-	-	-	2	C
	20	-	-	-	-	-	-	-	-	2	D
	25	-	-	-	-	-	-	-	7	7	E
	30	-	-	-	-	-	-	2	9	11	F
	40	-	-	-	-	-	-	6	10	16	H
	45	-	-	-	-	-	-	7	14	21	I
	50	-	-	-	-	-	-	8	20	28	J
	55	-	-	-	-	-	-	9	26	35	K
	60	-	-	-	-	-	2	8	31	41	L
	65	-	-	-	-	-	3	8	36	47	
	70	-	-	-	-	-	3	9	40	52	
	75	-	-	-	-	-	4	9	46	59	
	80	-	-	-	-	-	4	10	51	65	
	85	-	-	-	-	-	5	10	56	71	
	90	-	-	-	-	-	5	14	60	79	
	95	-	-	-	-	-	6	17	64	87	
	100	-	-	-	-	-	6	20	70	96	
	110	-	-	-	-	-	7	26	82	115	
	120	-	-	-	-	-	8	31	95	134	

Depth (msw)	Bottom Time (min)	Stop Times (min) at Different Depths (msw)								Decom. Time (min)	Repet. Group
		24	21	18	15	12	9	6	3		
30	5	-	-	-	-	-	-	-	-	2	A
	10	-	-	-	-	-	-	-	-	2	B
	15	-	-	-	-	-	-	-	-	2	D
	20	-	-	-	-	-	-	-	8	8	E
	25	-	-	-	-	-	-	3	9	12	F
	30	-	-	-	-	-	-	5	10	15	G
	35	-	-	-	-	-	-	7	11	18	H
	40	-	-	-	-	-	-	9	16	25	I
	45	-	-	-	-	-	3	8	23	34	J
	50	-	-	-	-	-	4	8	29	41	K
	55	-	-	-	-	-	5	9	34	48	L
	60	-	-	-	-	-	6	9	40	55	
	65	-	-	-	-	-	6	10	46	62	
	70	-	-	-	-	-	7	10	52	69	
	75	-	-	-	-	-	8	14	56	78	
	80	-	-	-	-	-	8	18	61	87	
	85	-	-	-	-	-	9	21	67	97	
	90	-	-	-	-	2	8	24	75	109	
	95	-	-	-	-	3	8	27	82	120	
	100	-	-	-	-	3	8	31	90	132	
	105	-	-	-	-	3	9	34	98	144	
	110	-	-	-	-	4	8	38	106	156	

Depth (msw)	Bottom Time (min)	Stop Times (min) at Different Depths (msw)								Decom. Time (min)	Repet. Group
		24	21	18	15	12	9	6	3		
33	5	-	-	-	-	-	-	-	-	2	A
	10	-	-	-	-	-	-	-	-	2	B
	12	-	-	-	-	-	-	-	-	2	C
	15	-	-	-	-	-	-	-	5	5	D
	20	-	-	-	-	-	-	3	9	12	F
	25	-	-	-	-	-	-	6	10	16	G
	30	-	-	-	-	-	-	9	10	19	H
	35	-	-	-	-	-	3	8	16	27	I
	40	-	-	-	-	-	5	8	24	37	J
	45	-	-	-	-	-	6	9	31	46	K
	50	-	-	-	-	-	7	9	38	54	M
	55	-	-	-	-	-	8	10	44	62	N
	60	-	-	-	-	2	7	10	51	70	
	65	-	-	-	-	3	7	15	55	80	
	70	-	-	-	-	4	7	19	62	92	
	75	-	-	-	-	4	8	23	68	103	
	80	-	-	-	-	5	8	26	77	116	
	85	-	-	-	-	5	9	30	86	130	
	90	-	-	-	-	6	9	34	95	144	
	95	-	-	-	-	6	9	38	105	158	
	100	-	-	-	-	7	9	42	114	172	
	105	-	-	-	-	7	12	45	123	187	
	110	-	-	-	-	8	15	48	130	201	

TABLE 1: STANDARD AIR DECOMPRESSION (METRES)

Depth (msw)	Bottom Time (min)	Stop Times (min) at Different Depths (msw)								Decom. Time (min)	Repet. Group
		24	21	18	15	12	9	6	3		
36	5	-	-	-	-	-	-	-	-	2	A
	10	-	-	-	-	-	-	-	-	2	C
	15	-	-	-	-	-	-	-	10	10	E
	20	-	-	-	-	-	-	5	10	15	F
	25	-	-	-	-	-	-	9	10	19	G
	30	-	-	-	-	-	4	8	14	26	I
	35	-	-	-	-	-	6	8	24	38	J
	40	-	-	-	-	-	8	8	32	48	K
	45	-	-	-	-	3	6	10	38	57	M
	50	-	-	-	-	4	7	10	46	67	N
	55	-	-	-	-	5	7	13	53	78	
	60	-	-	-	-	6	7	18	59	90	
	65	-	-	-	-	6	8	22	66	102	
	70	-	-	-	-	7	8	27	75	117	
	75	-	-	-	-	8	8	31	86	133	
	80	-	-	-	2	6	9	35	97	149	
	85	-	-	-	3	6	10	40	107	166	
	90	-	-	-	3	7	13	42	118	183	
	95	-	-	-	4	6	16	46	128	200	
	100	-	-	-	4	7	19	50	136	216	

TABLE 1: STANDARD AIR DECOMPRESSION (METRES)

Depth (msw)	Bottom Time (min)	Stop Times (min) at Different Depths (msw)								Decom. Time (min)	Repet. Group
		24	21	18	15	12	9	6	3		
39	5	-	-	-	-	-	-	-	-	2	A
	8	-	-	-	-	-	-	-	-	2	B
	10	-	-	-	-	-	-	-	5	5	C
	15	-	-	-	-	-	-	4	8	12	E
	20	-	-	-	-	-	-	8	10	18	G
	25	-	-	-	-	-	5	7	11	23	H
	30	-	-	-	-	-	7	8	22	37	J
	35	-	-	-	-	3	6	9	30	48	K
	40	-	-	-	-	4	7	9	39	59	M
	45	-	-	-	-	6	7	10	47	70	N
	50	-	-	-	-	7	7	15	53	82	
	55	-	-	-	2	6	8	20	61	97	
	60	-	-	-	3	6	8	25	70	112	
	65	-	-	-	4	6	8	30	82	130	
	70	-	-	-	4	7	9	34	94	148	
	75	-	-	-	5	6	11	39	106	167	
	80	-	-	-	5	7	14	42	118	186	
	85	-	-	-	6	7	17	47	129	206	
	90	-	-	-	6	8	20	52	138	224	
42	7	-	-	-	-	-	-	-	-	2	B
	10	-	-	-	-	-	-	-	7	7	D
	15	-	-	-	-	-	-	6	9	15	F
	20	-	-	-	-	-	4	7	10	21	G
	25	-	-	-	-	-	7	8	17	32	I
	30	-	-	-	-	4	6	8	28	46	K
	35	-	-	-	-	5	7	9	37	58	L
	40	-	-	-	-	7	7	10	46	70	N
	45	-	-	-	3	5	8	16	53	85	O
	50	-	-	-	4	6	8	21	62	101	
	55	-	-	-	5	6	8	27	73	119	
	60	-	-	-	6	6	9	32	86	139	
	65	-	-	-	6	7	10	37	99	159	
	70	-	-	-	7	7	14	40	114	182	
	75	-	-	3	5	7	18	45	126	204	
	80	-	-	3	6	7	21	51	137	225	
	85	-	-	4	5	8	25	57	146	245	
	90	-	-	4	6	8	28	65	152	263	

TABLE 1: STANDARD AIR DECOMPRESSION (METRES)

Depth (msw)	Bottom Time (min)	Stop Times (min) at Different Depths (msw)								Decom. Time (min)	Repet. Group
		24	21	18	15	12	9	6	3		
45	7	-	-	-	-	-	-	-	-	3	B
	10	-	-	-	-	-	-	-	9	9	D
	15	-	-	-	-	-	-	8	9	17	F
	20	-	-	-	-	-	6	7	11	24	H
	25	-	-	-	-	4	5	8	23	40	J
	30	-	-	-	-	6	6	9	34	55	K
	35	-	-	-	3	5	7	10	44	69	M
	40	-	-	-	4	6	7	15	52	84	O
	45	-	-	-	5	6	8	21	61	101	
	50	-	-	-	6	7	8	27	73	121	
	55	-	-	3	5	6	9	33	88	144	
	60	-	-	3	5	7	12	38	103	168	
	65	-	-	4	5	8	16	42	119	194	
	70	-	-	5	5	8	20	48	132	218	
	75	-	-	5	6	8	24	55	142	240	
	80	-	-	6	6	8	28	63	150	261	
48	6	-	-	-	-	-	-	-	-	3	B
	10	-	-	-	-	-	-	-	11	11	D
	15	-	-	-	-	-	4	6	10	20	G
	20	-	-	-	-	-	8	8	14	30	H
	25	-	-	-	-	6	6	8	29	49	K
	30	-	-	-	3	5	7	9	40	64	M
	35	-	-	-	5	5	8	13	49	80	N
	40	-	-	-	6	6	8	20	59	99	
	45	-	-	3	5	6	9	26	72	121	
	50	-	-	4	5	7	9	33	88	146	
	55	-	-	5	5	7	13	38	105	173	
	60	-	-	6	5	8	17	43	122	201	
	65	-	-	7	5	8	22	50	135	227	
	70	-	3	4	6	8	26	58	146	251	

TABLE 1: STANDARD AIR DECOMPRESSION (METRES)

Depth (msw)	Bottom Time (min)	Stop Times (min) at Different Depths (msw)								Decom. Time (min)	Repet. Group
		24	21	18	15	12	9	6	3		
51	6	-	-	-	-	-	-	-	-	3	B
	10	-	-	-	-	-	-	5	8	13	D
	15	-	-	-	-	-	5	7	10	22	G
	20	-	-	-	-	5	5	8	20	38	I
	25	-	-	-	3	5	6	9	33	56	K
	30	-	-	-	5	5	7	10	46	73	M
	35	-	-	3	4	6	8	18	55	94	O
	40	-	-	4	5	6	8	26	68	117	
	45	-	-	5	5	7	9	32	85	143	
	50	-	-	6	6	7	13	37	105	174	
	55	-	3	4	6	7	18	44	122	204	
	60	-	4	4	6	8	23	51	137	233	
	65	-	5	4	6	9	27	61	148	260	
	70	-	5	5	6	12	30	72	155	285	
54	5	-	-	-	-	-	-	-	-	3	B
	10	-	-	-	-	-	-	6	9	15	E
	15	-	-	-	-	-	7	7	11	25	H
	20	-	-	-	-	6	6	8	25	45	J
	25	-	-	-	5	5	7	9	39	65	M
	30	-	-	3	4	6	7	15	50	85	O
	35	-	-	5	4	6	8	23	62	108	
	40	-	-	6	5	7	9	30	80	137	
	45	-	4	4	5	7	13	36	101	170	
	50	-	4	5	5	8	18	42	121	203	
	55	-	5	5	6	8	23	51	137	235	
	60	-	6	5	6	9	28	61	149	264	

TABLE 1: STANDARD AIR DECOMPRESSION (METRES)

Depth (msw)	Bottom Time (min)	Stop Times (min) at Different Depths (msw)										Decom. Time (min)
		30	27	24	21	18	15	12	9	6	3	
57	5	-	-	-	-	-	-	-	-	-	-	3
	10	-	-	-	-	-	-	-	-	8	9	17
	15	-	-	-	-	-	-	4	5	7	11	27
	20	-	-	-	-	-	4	4	6	9	29	52
	25	-	-	-	-	-	7	5	7	10	44	73
	30	-	-	-	-	5	4	6	8	19	55	97
	35	-	-	-	3	4	5	6	9	27	72	126
	40	-	-	-	4	4	5	7	11	35	93	159
	45	-	-	-	5	5	5	8	17	41	116	197
	50	-	-	3	3	5	6	8	22	50	135	232
	55	-	-	4	3	5	7	9	27	61	149	265
60	5	-	-	-	-	-	-	-	-	-	-	4
	10	-	-	-	-	-	-	-	-	10	9	19
	15	-	-	-	-	-	-	5	6	8	16	35
	20	-	-	-	-	-	5	5	6	10	33	59
	25	-	-	-	-	5	4	5	7	14	48	83
	30	-	-	-	3	4	4	6	9	23	62	111
	35	-	-	-	5	4	5	6	10	32	84	146
	40	-	-	-	6	4	6	7	15	38	109	185
	45	-	-	4	3	5	6	8	21	47	131	225
	50	-	-	5	4	4	7	9	27	58	147	261
63	5	-	-	-	-	-	-	-	-	-	5	5
	10	-	-	-	-	-	-	-	5	6	10	21
	15	-	-	-	-	-	-	7	6	8	20	41
	20	-	-	-	-	-	7	5	7	9	39	67
	25	-	-	-	-	6	4	6	8	17	52	93
	30	-	-	-	5	4	4	7	8	28	71	127
	35	-	-	3	3	4	6	7	12	35	97	167
	40	-	-	4	4	4	6	8	19	43	123	211
	45	-	-	5	4	5	6	9	25	54	142	250
	50	-	3	3	4	6	6	13	29	70	154	288

TABLE 1: STANDARD AIR DECOMPRESSION (METRES)

Depth (msw)	Bottom Time (min)	Stop Times (min) at Different Depths (msw)										Decom. Time (min)
		30	27	24	21	18	15	12	9	6	3	
66	5	-	-	-	-	-	-	-	-	-	7	7
	10	-	-	-	-	-	-	-	7	6	10	23
	15	-	-	-	-	-	4	5	5	9	24	47
	20	-	-	-	-	5	4	5	7	10	43	74
	25	-	-	-	4	4	4	6	8	21	58	105
	30	-	-	3	3	4	5	7	9	32	81	144
	35	-	-	5	3	4	6	7	16	39	110	190
	40	-	3	3	4	4	7	8	23	49	135	236
	45	-	4	3	4	5	7	11	28	65	151	278
69	5	-	-	-	-	-	-	-	-	-	8	8
	10	-	-	-	-	-	-	-	8	7	10	25
	15	-	-	-	-	-	6	4	6	9	28	53
	20	-	-	-	-	6	4	6	7	12	47	82
	25	-	-	-	6	3	5	6	9	24	65	118
	30	-	-	5	3	4	5	7	12	35	93	164
	35	-	3	3	4	4	6	8	19	44	123	214
	40	-	5	3	4	5	6	9	27	57	146	262
72	5	-	-	-	-	-	-	-	-	-	9	9
	10	-	-	-	-	-	-	4	5	7	11	27
	15	-	-	-	-	-	7	5	6	9	32	59
	20	-	-	-	4	4	4	5	8	16	50	91
	25	-	-	4	3	4	5	6	9	28	73	132
	30	-	-	6	3	5	5	8	15	37	106	185
	35	-	5	3	4	4	6	9	23	49	135	238
	40	3	3	3	4	6	6	13	28	67	153	286

APPENDIX 3

Bühlmann High Altitude Tables.

BÜHLMANN HIGH ALTITUDE TABLE

(2501-4500M above sea level)

NO-DECOMPRESSION LIMITS. AIR DIVING DECOMPRESSION TABLE

2501 - 4500 m above sea level   (24 hrs at altitude)

Depth m	BT min	9	6	4	2	RG
9	204				1	G
12	88				1	G
	100				5	G
	110				9	G
	120				13	G
15	50				1	E
	60				2	F
	70				8	G
	80				14	G
	90				20	G
18	32				1	D
	40				3	F
	50				7	F
	60			1	13	G
	70			3	17	G
21	22				1	D
	30				3	E
	35				6	F
	40			1	7	F
	45			3	10	F
	50			4	13	G
	55			6	15	G
	60			8	18	G
24	16				1	D
	25				4	E
	30			1	6	F
	35			3	8	F
	40			5	12	F
	45		1	6	15	F
	50		3	7	18	G

Depth m	BT min	9	6	4	2	RG
27	14				1	D
	20				4	E
	25			2	6	E
	30			5	7	F
	35		2	5	12	F
	40		4	6	15	G
30	11				1	D
	15				3	D
	20			2	5	E
	25		1	4	7	F
	30		3	5	11	F
	35	1	4	7	15	G
33	9				1	D
	12				2	D
	15			1	4	E
	18			3	5	F
	21		1	4	6	F
	24		3	5	7	F
	27	1	3	6	11	G
36	8				1	D
	12			1	3	D
	15			3	4	E
	18		1	4	6	F
	21		3	5	7	F
	24	1	4	6	11	F
	27	3	4	7	14	G
39	7				1	D
	12			2	4	E
	15		1	4	5	E
	18	1	2	5	6	F
	21	2	3	6	10	F
	24	3	5	6	14	G

© A.A.Buehlmann, University of Zurich, Switzerland 1987

```
        NO-DECOMPRESSION LIMITS. AIR DIVING DECOMPRESSION TABLE

            2501 - 4500 m above sea level    (24 hrs at altitude)
```

Depth m	BT min	\multicolumn{5}{c}{Stops}					RG
		12	9	6	4	2	
42	7					1	D
	9				1	3	E
	12			1	3	4	E
	15		1	2	4	6	F
	18		2	3	5	9	F
	21		4	4	6	13	F
	24	1	5	5	8	16	G
45	6					1	C
	9				2	3	E
	12			2	3	5	F
	15		2	3	4	7	F
	18		3	4	6	11	F
	21	1	5	5	7	15	G
48	6					1	C
	9			1	2	4	E
	12		1	2	4	6	F
	15		3	3	5	9	F
	18	1	4	5	6	14	G
51	5					1	C
	9			2	2	5	E
	12		2	3	4	6	F
	15	1	3	4	6	11	F
	18	2	5	5	7	16	G
54	6				1	2	E
	9		1	2	3	5	F
	12		3	3	5	7	F
	15	2	4	5	6	13	G

© A.A.Buehlmann, University of Zurich, Switzerland 1987

REPETITIVE DIVE TIME-TABLE   0 - 4500 m above sea level

Surface Interval Times   "0" ✈

						A	2	2
RG at start of				B	20	2	2
surface interval			C	10	25	3	3
		D	10	15	30	3	3
	E	10	15	25	45	4	3
F	20	30	45	75	90	8	4
G	25	45	60	75	100	130	12	5
G	F	E	D	C	B	A	hrs	hrs

RG at end of surface interval

Example:
Previous dive: 24 m, 35 min =
Repetitive Group **(RG) = F**
- after 45 min at surface: **RG = C**
- after 90 min at surface: **RG = A**
  (intermediate time: use next
  shorter interval time)
- after 4 hrs: flying is permitted
- after 8 hrs: **RG = "0"**, no more
  Residual Nitrogen Time **(RNT)**

RG for No-Decompression Dives and RNT for Repetitive Dives

Repetitive dive depth m (intermediate depths: use next **shallower** depth)

RG	9	12	15	18	21	24	27	30	33	36	39	42	45	48	51	54	57
A	25	19	16	14	12	11	10	9	8	7	7	6	6	6	5	5	5
B	37	25	20	17	15	13	12	11	10	9	8	7	7	6	5	5	5
C	55	37	29	25	22	20	18	16	14	12	11	10	9	8	7	7	6
D	81	57	41	33	28	24	21	19	17	15	14	13	11	10	9	9	8
E	105	82	59	44	37	30	26	23	21	19	17	16	14	13	12	11	10
F	130	111	88	68	53	42	35	30	27	24	21	19	17	16	15	14	13

Example: RG = C at end of surface interval. Planned depth of repetitive dive =
27 m. **RNT = 18 min**, to be added to Bottom Time (BT) of repetitive dive.

INDEX